TREASURY OF THEMES
AND ILLUSTRATIONS

R. C. REIN'S

Treasury of Themes and Illustrations

**Thousands of Bible References
Quotations and Illustrations
Topically Arranged
for the Christian Communicator**

Cover design by Lorraine Franke

NORTHWESTERN PUBLISHING HOUSE
Milwaukee, Wisconsin

Library of Congress Catalog Card Number 81-86245
Northwestern Publishing House
3624 W. North Ave., Milwaukee WI 53208-0902
©1983 by Northwestern Publishing House. All rights reserved.
Published 1983
Printed in the United States of America
ISBN 0-8100-0152-7

CONTENTS

PREFACE

While this book contains many subjects of interest to all Christian readers, it is intended especially for Christian pastors and teachers.

Two important questions that Christian pastors and teachers ask when preparing their assignments are: What does the Bible say? And how can I apply its truths in my preaching and teaching? The answer to both of these questions requires diligent study and research. This book of references is not intended to be a substitute for such work, for nothing should take the place of personal Bible study, nor can anything else supply the joy and conviction that comes from personal discovery of Bible truths. Rather than to supplant, the purpose of these outlines and resources is to supplement such private study.

However, there are times when, because of their involvement with many other duties, pastors and teachers cannot do as much outside reading as they would like. The search for suitable illustrations of Bible truths is especially time consuming and often proves futile and frustrating. It is especially this need that the materials in this book are intended to fill. The abundance of hymn selections and poetry may also serve a personal devotional purpose.

Of the more than one hundred different subjects treated, seventy-five have been outlined and have been associated with illustrations and other resource helps. As the title suggests, this book combines and associates Bible truths with illustrations from life.

Jesus Christ and his redemptive work form a large portion of the material and are treated in sequence, ranging from his birth to his second coming. These outlines are listed under the heading JESUS CHRIST. Additional material dealing with this central truth of the Scriptures includes outlines and resources on such subjects as conversion, faith, justification, redemption, repentance, sin, and sacrifice.

All of the material is presented from an approach and conviction which regards the Bible as the divinely inspired Word of God and the supreme authority in all matters of faith and life.

The "General Index" at the close of the book gives a complete overview of the subjects treated and is intended as a ready help. A separate page entitled "Index for the Church Year," lists numbers in the outlines and resources that deal with festivals and observances which occur from the beginning of the Church year to its close.

Much of the material in this book was gathered over a period of fifty years in the writer's work as a parish pastor and district executive. Unfortunately, in this accumulation, the sources were sometimes lost or unavailable. Wherever possible, credit has been given.

7

Those who use this book will have favorite illustrations and other resource material in their files which they may wish to add to the subjects treated. A convenient cross-reference may be created by assigning numbers to your files as are found in this book and by indicating such associations with a corresponding note in the margin of this book.

While this *Treasury of Themes and Illustrations* will be of special aid to pastors and teachers who are beginning their ministry, the need for such helps increases as one's own resources are depleted with the passing years. The Bible-based, Christ-centered, and life-related materials offered in this book were assimilated with the above objectives in mind and for the purpose of assisting in making known to others the message of God's Word.

"God's Word is our great heritage
And shall be ours forever;
To spread its light from age to age
Shall be our chief endeavor.
Through life it guides our way,
In death it is our stay.
Lord grant, while worlds endure,
We keep its teachings pure
Throughout all generations."
(Nikolai F. S. Grundtwig)

R. C. Rein

AFFLICTION 1-36

(ref.: Cross, the Christian 262-272; Providence, Divine 1195-1221)

General Considerations

1 Sin is the source of all evil. Without it there would be no suffering in the world: Gn 2:16,17; Ro 5:12; 6:23; Ga 6:7. But there are times when an individual, or nation, may suffer because of some particular sin: Lv 26:14f; Jdg 2:11-15; Ezr 9:10-15; Ps 106:36-46; Jr 2:19; Ac 12:21-23 *ref.13.*

2 In addition to enduring afflictions which befall all mankind, Christian people must also suffer for the sake of Christ and his gospel: Mt 16:24; Jn 15:18f; Ac 14:22; 2 Tm 3:12; 1 Pe 2:21; 4:12-16.

False Views Concerning Suffering

3 Man's life in this world is governed by fate; he is the helpless victim of circumstances in which he lives: cf. 1 Cor 15:32.

4 Every particular suffering is the consequence of a particular sin: cf. Job 4:7,8; Lk 13:1-4; Jn 9:2,3; cp. Ac 28:1-5.

5 Those who seem to prosper in this world stand in special favor with God, while those who suffer affliction and want are the objects of God's special wrath: cf. Ps 37; 73; 94; Hab 1:3.

Correct Views Concerning Suffering

6 With reference to unbelievers, God's purpose is to show

That he hates and punishes sin: Ex 20:5,6; Ps 7:11; Pr 1:24-33; Ro 1:18; Eph 5:6;

That in his love he seeks to turn them from their evil ways and lead them to repentance: Ps 94:12; Pr 3:11,12; Ro 2:3-6; 2 Pe 3:9; *ref. 17.*

7 With reference to believers —

Although God's people, too, must live in a world that has been corrupted through sin, the afflictions that befall them are not punishments for their sins, for their sins have already been atoned for through Christ's sacrifice: Ro 8:1,33,34; Eph 1:7; 1 Jn 1:7;

Holy Scriptures reveal many purposes for which God afflicts those who are his children by faith in Jesus Christ, e.g.,

To show that he deals with them as a loving father deals with his erring child; he corrects them to prevent them from perishing with the evil world: Dt 8:5; Ps 119:67,71,75,76; Jr 2:19; 1 Cor 11:32; He 12:5-11; *ref. 14-17;*

To purify and strengthen their faith: Job 23:10; Ps 66:10; Is 48:10; 1 Pe 1:6,7; Re 2:10; *ref. 18-23;*

To make them more fruitful in good works: Jn 15:1,2,8; He 12:11; *ref. 32;*

9

To draw them closer to himself: Ps 78:34,35; Is 26:16; Ho 5:15; *ref. 21*;

To make them more considerate of the afflictions of others: 2 Cor 1:4-7; cp. Is 58:10,11; Ro 12:15; 1 Cor 12:26,27; Ga 6:2; He 13:3; *ref. 24*;

To further the gospel: Php 1:12-18;

To serve God's glory by making his work in them manifest to them and to others: Jn 9:3,35-38; 11:40-42,45; 2 Cor 12:7-10; cp. Lk 18:35-43; Jn 12:9-11; 2 Cor 4:10; Php 1:12-14;

To create in them a longing desire for deliverance from the bondage of corruption caused by sin and to point them to their final redemption: Ro 8:18,22,23; 2 Cor 4:17,18; 5:2; Php 1:23; Col 3:1-3;

That they might finally be partakers of his holiness, He 12:10, and attain to the fullness of eternal life in heaven, which is their inheritance as his children by faith in Jesus Christ: Mt 25:34; Ro 8:15-17; 1 Pe 1:7-9;

8 God's purposes in afflicting Christian people are not always evident: Is 10:15; 45:9; 55:8,9; Jn 13:7; Ro 11:33 — and some of these may never be fully understood in this life: 1 Cor 13:12. But his ways are always right: Dt. 32:4; Ps 18:30; 119:137; 145:17; Mk 7:37; Re 15:3, and he assures us that in everything he works for the good of those who love him: Jr 29:11; Ro 8:28; cp. Gn 50:20; *ref. 25-31*.

Christian Attitude Toward Affliction

9 Humble resignation to the will of God: Ps 143:10; Mt 6:10; 26:39; *ref. 33,34*;

10 Unwavering trust in God's promises: Job 13:15; 23:10; Ps 37:5; 56:3; 57:1; Is 12:2; 26:4; 54:7,8,10; *ref. 35*;

11 Patient waiting for the accomplishment of God's purposes: Ps 25:5; 37:7; 40:1; 130:6; Hab 2:1-3; Lk 21:19; Ro 5:3-5; 12:12; He 10:36; 11:22-24; 12:1; Jas 1:3,4; 5:7,8;

12 Firm reliance in Christ's help: Jn 16:23; He 2:18; 4:15,16; 12:2; *ref. 36*.

Resources

13 Why must I suffer? Why did this happen to me? Why are my prayers not answered? Why does God allow such calamities as wars, earthquakes, fires, floods, and famines to occur? Why does he permit evil to triumph in the world? Does he not realize what is going on?

These and similar anxious thoughts and perplexing problems have troubled the children of God in every age. Job, the proverbial crossbearer, was a striking example: Job 3:1f; 6:1,2; 7:19-21; 10:1f. Others, like him, have cried out: "How long will you forget me, O Lord? for ever? how long will you hide your face from me?" see Ps 6:3; 10:1; 13:1; 35:17; 79:5; 89:46; 90:13; 94:3; Hab 1:2.

Although the full answer to such troublesome questions may never be known, Holy Scriptures do give a soul-satisfying explanation. And that answer convinces us that "behind the dim unknown God stands within the shadow keeping watch above his own." It tells us that "in everything God works for good with those who love him," Ro 8:28. It speaks comfort to our troubled soul and says:

> God liveth still!
> Soul, despair not, fear no ill!
> God is good; from his compassion
>   earthly help and comfort flow;
> Strong is his right hand to fashion
>   All things well for man below;
> Trial, oft the most distressing,
>   In the end has proved a blessing.
> Wherefore, then, my soul despair?
> God still lives, who heareth prayer.
> — J. F. Zihn

ref. 1-8.

† † †

14 While a loving father chastens his son for the child's good, he sometimes makes a mistake because his knowledge is not perfect. But despite these mistakes, the son honors and respects his father, especially in later life, because he recognizes that the loving purpose of the chastening was to turn him from his evil way, or to teach and train him to be obedient, reverent, honest, considerate of others, and the like. How much more willingly should not we submit to the chastening of our heavenly Father who never makes a mistake, whose very essence is love, and who chastens us for our eternal good! *ref. 7.*

† † †

15 Though necessity is forced upon him, a loving father takes no pleasure in chastening his son. No sooner has he chastened his son when he again embraces him in love. In like manner, God does not delight in chastening his children. "Though he cause grief," says the prophet Jeremiah, "yet will he have compassion according to the multitude of his mercies. For he does not afflict willingly nor grieve the children of men," Lm 3:32,33; see also Jr 29:11; 1 Cor 10:13; *ref. 9.*

16
> All his strokes and scourges truly
>   for the moment grievous prove,
> And yet, when I weigh them duly,
>   Are but tokens of his love.
> — Paul Gerhardt

ref. 9

17 On a ranch in one of our western States a sheepherder deliberately broke the leg of one of his sheep. When asked why he had done this, he replied: "This sheep would not stay with the flock. It often wandered far away and paid no attention to my call. So I broke its leg to prevent it from getting lost or being destroyed by a beast of prey. Now this sheep stays close to my side and promptly responds to my call." *ref. 7.*

11

† † †

18 If you ask, "How will I know when God's purpose has been accomplished in my affliction?" then ask the refiner, "How do you know when the metal is done?" He will tell you, "When I can see my face in it." God's loving purpose will be accomplished when you see your face in his refining fire of affliction. Then will we also be ready to say in the words of the psalmist: "I know, O Lord, that thy judgments are right, and that thou in faithfulness hast afflicted me. Let, I pray thee, thy merciful kindness be for my comfort, according to thy word unto thy servant," Ps 119:75,76; *ref. 7*.

19
In the furnace God may prove thee
  Thence to bring thee forth more bright,
But can never cease to love thee;
  God is with thee,
God, thine everlasting Light.
— Thomas Kelly
ref.7

20
When through fiery trials thy pathway shall lie,
My grace, all-sufficient, shall be thy supply.
The flames shall not hurt thee; I only design
Thy dross to consume and thy gold to refine.

When thro' the deep waters I call thee to go,
The rivers of sorrow shall not overflow;
For I will be with thee thy troubles to bless
And sanctify to thee thy deepest distress.
— G. Keith (?)
ref. 7

† † †

21 God sometimes puts us on our back in order that we may look up; *ref. 7*.

† † †

22 As the beauty of the stars is revealed by the darkness of the night, so the dark hour of affliction reveals to us the goodness and mercy of our God; *ref. 7*.

† † †

23 During World War I, when it was no longer possible to import the singing canaries from the Harz Mountains in Germany, a dealer in New York devised a plan for training American canaries to sing the songs of the Harz Mountain canaries by listening to a recording of their songs. At first the plan proved unsuccessful. But then the dealer discovered that by covering the cages of the canaries with thick cloth so that all the light was shut out, the birds quickly learned their song; *ref. 7,8*.

— selected

† † †

24 When Dr. Moon, of Brighton, England, was stricken with blindness at the height of his career, his first reaction was one of resentment and rebellion against God. But later he asked himself if there might be some way in which he could help the blind to read the Word of God. And God provided a way. While Dr. Moon's eyes were still sightless he developed the Moon system of the alphabet and ever since thousands of blind people throughout the world have been enabled to read the Bible; *ref. 7.*

— selected

† † †

25 The mind of a child often finds it impossible to grasp the reasoning of the parent who chastens him. How much less can our finite mind understand the reasoning of our infinite and all-knowing Father in heaven, who says: "My thoughts are not your thoughts, neither are your ways my ways.... For as the heavens are higher than the earth, so are my ways higher than your ways, and my thoughts than your thoughts," Is 55:8,9.

> Can a child presume to choose
> Where or how to live?
> Can a father's love refuse
> All the best to give?
> — Lawrence Tuttiett

"If you then, being evil," says Christ, "know how to give good gifts to your children, how much more shall your Father which is in heaven give good things to them that ask him?" Mt 7:11; *ref. 8.*

† † †

26
> God moves in a mysterious way
> His wonders to perform;
> He plants his footsteps in the sea
> And rides upon the storm.
>
> Deep in unfathomable mines
> Of never failing skill
> He treasures up his bright designs
> And works his sov'reign will.
> — William Cowper

ref. 8,10

† † †

27
> My life is but a weaving
> Between my Lord and me;
> I cannot choose the colors
> Nor all the pattern see.
> Oftimes he weaveth sorrow,
> And I in foolish pride
> Forget he sees the upper
> And I the under side.

13

Not till the loom is silent
And the shuttles cease to fly,
Shall God unroll the canvass
And explain the reason why
The dark threads are as needful
In the weaver's skillful hand
As the threads of gold and silver
In the pattern he has planned.

— Anon

ref. 8

† † †

28 Martin Luther once compared God's ways to a Hebrew book which must be read backward. Often when we patiently wait to the end, when God's purpose has been accomplished, we can retrace his ways and understand why he dealt with us in the manner he did; *ref. 8.*

† † †

29
His ways are love — though they transcend
Our feeblest range of sight,
They wind through darkness to their end
In everlasting light.

— Anon

ref. 8

† † †

30 The statement that "in all things God works for the good of those who love him," Ro 8:28, is all-inclusive. In the overruling providence of God, sorrow as well as joy, adversity as well as prosperity, sickness as well as health, and even death as well as life, work together for good. Even death cannot sever us from Christ, for, "If we live, we live to the Lord, and if we die, we die to the Lord; so then, whether we live or whether we die, we are the Lord's," Ro 14:8; *ref. 8,10.*

† † †

31
Sometime when all life's lessons have been learned
And sun and stars forevermore have set,
The things which our weak judgment here has spurned,
The things o'er which we grieved with lashes wet,
Will flash before us out of life's dark night
As stars shine most in deeper tints of blue;
And we shall see how all God's plans were right
And how what seemed reproof was love most true.

But not today. Then be content, poor heart;
God's plans like lilies pure and white unfold.
We must not tear the close-shut leaves apart —
Time will reveal the calyces of gold.

14

And if through patient toil we reach the land
  Where tired feet, with sandals loose, may rest —
Where we shall clearly know and understand —
  I know that we will say that "God knows best."
                              — Mary Riley Smith
ref. 8

† † †

32 It is said that small stones in a cultivated field increase the crop yield by attracting moisture and radiating heat. It is a mistake, therefore, to remove them. So, too, our afflictions are intended to cause us to bring forth more fruit to the glory of God, and therefore we should not ask to be relieved of them: Jn 15:2,8; 2 Cor 12:8,9; *ref. 7.*

† † †

33
Thy way, not mine, O Lord,
  However dark it be.
Lead me by Thine own hand;
  Choose thou the path for me.
I dare not choose my lot;
  I would not if I might.
Choose thou for me, my God;
  So shall I walk aright.
                              — Horatius Bonar
ref. 9,10

† † †

34
Thy ways, O Lord, with wise design
  Are framed upon thy throne above,
And ev'ry dark and bending line
  Meets in the center of thy love.
                              — Ambrose Serle
ref. 8

† † †

35
When winds are raging o'er the upper ocean
  And billows wild contend with angry roar,
'Tis said, far down beneath the wild commotion
That peaceful stillness reigneth evermore.

Far, far beneath the noise of tempest dieth,
  And silver waves chime ever peacefully,
And no rude storm, how fierce soe'er it flieth,
  Disturbs the Sabbath of that deeper sea.
                              — Harriet Beecher Stowe
ref. 10,11

† † †

15

36 The beautiful hymn, *What a Friend We Have in Jesus,* was written by Joseph Scriven in a time of great stress and deep sorrow. On the day before his intended wedding, his bride to be met with a boating accident and was drowned. Shocked by the tragic news of her death, and almost driven to the point of despair, Joseph Scriven recalled how he and his bride to be had agreed that they would take all of their troubles to the Lord in prayer. Then he knelt in prayer for three hours and asked God to strengthen his faith. The Lord answered his prayer by comforting his troubled heart with heavenly peace. A short time later Scriven's mother had to pass through the deep waters of tribulation. For her comfort, and from his own experience, he wrote this hymn:

> What a Friend we have in Jesus,
>> All our sins and griefs to bear!
> What a privilege to carry
>> Ev'rything to God in prayer!
> Oh, what peace we often forfeit,
>> Oh, what needless pain we bear,
> All because we do not carry
>> Ev'rything to God in prayer!
>
> Have we trials and temptations?
>> Is there trouble anywhere?
> We should never be discouraged,
>> Take it to the Lord in prayer.
> Can we find a Friend so faithful
>> Who will all our sorrows share?
> Jesus knows our ev'ry weakness —
>> Take it to the Lord in prayer!
>
> Are we weak and heavy laden,
>> Cumbered with a load of care?
> Precious Savior, still our Refuge —
>> Take it to the Lord in prayer.
> Do thy friends despise, forsake thee?
>> Take it to the Lord in prayer;
> In his arms he'll take and shield thee,
>> Thou wilt find a solace there.
> *ref. 12*

(ref.: Young People 1649-1666)

37 A time of physical infirmity: Ps 71:9,18; Ec 12:1-7; *ref. 42, 297.*

38 To be regarded with respect and honor: Lv 19:32; Job 32:6; Pr 16:31; 20:29; 23:22; 1 Tm 5:1,2; *ref. 43.*

39 God's special promises to the aged: Ps 37:25; 92:12-15; 103:5; Is 40:29-31; 46:4; cp. Dt 34:7; Jos 14:10,11; Lk 2:36,37; *ref. 44.*

40 Christ, the living hope of the aged: Gn 49:18; Lk 2:25-32,36-38; 2 Cor 5:1-4; Php 1:21-23; 3:12-14; 2 Tm 4:6-8,18; He 11:13-16; *ref. 45,46.*

41 Biblical examples of honoring the aged: Gn 47:1-7; 1 Sm 3:1f; 1 Kgs 2:19; Jn 19:25-27; of dishonoring the aged: Job 19:18; 30:12; 2 Kgs 2:23,24; Is 3:5; cp. Ro 1:30; 2 Tm 3:1,2; *ref. 1089,1488.*

Resources

42
God keep my heart attuned to laughter
When youth is done;
When all the days are gray days, coming after
The warmth, the sun.
Ah! keep me then from bitterness, from grieving,
When life seems cold;
God keep me always loving and believing
As I grow old.
— Anon
ref. 37

43 Far from being a time of inactivity, old age is often a time of great productivity. Thus, e.g.,

Galileo, the astronomer, was 73 years of age when he made some of his most important discoveries;

The great Italian composer Verdi wrote his wonderful opera *Othello* at 74 and *Falstaff* at 80;

The Venetian master Titian painted his canvass *Battle of Le Panto* at the age of 98;

The poet Goethe finished *Faust* when he was 82;

Elihu Root revamped the World Court at 84;

Edison built chemical plants after he was 67;

The poet Tennyson wrote his poem "Crossing the Bar" when he was 83;

Winston Churchill was past 70 when he was guiding the fate of England in the bitterest years of her existence, as was also General MacArthur when he served as supreme commander of the occupation in Japan; *ref. 38.*

† † †

44
E'en down to old age all my people shall prove
My sov'reign, eternal, unchangeable love;
And when hoary hairs their temples adorn,
Like lambs they shall still in my bosom be borne.

The soul that on Jesus hath leaned for repose
I will not, I will not, desert to its foes;
That soul, though all hell should endeavor to shake,
I'll never, no never, no never, forsake!
— O. Keith (?)

ref. 39,40

45 "I am on the bright side of seventy," said an aged man of God; "the brighter side, because nearer to everlasting glory."

— selected

As the winter strips the leaves from around us, so that we may see the distant regions they formerly concealed, so old age takes away our enjoyments only to enlarge the prospect of the coming eternity.

Jean Richter

The depraved and sinful heart does not of itself grow better, but goes on from bad to worse. But the heart renewed by divine grace, grows steadily in the divine likeness; its path is that of the just, that shineth more and more to the perfect day.

— Bulwer-Lytton

As the grave grows nearer my theology is growing strangely simple, and it begins and ends with Christ as the only Savior of the lost.

— H. B. Whipple

Ref. 40

† † †

46
Grow old along with me!
The best is yet to be,
The last of life, for which the first was made.
Our times are in his hand,
Who saith, "A whole I planned,
Youth shows but half; trust God;
See all, nor be afraid."
— Rabbi Ben Ezra

Ref. 39,40

ANGELS, THE HOLY 47-68

(ref.: Satan and the Evil Angels 1309-1321)

Their Origin

47 They are a part of God's creation, but there is no specific biblical reference as to when they came into being: Gn 1:31; 2:1,2; Col 1:16. There is an inference in Job 38:4-7 that they were made on the first day of creation, at the very beginning. Unlike the evil angels, they did not forfeit their first estate by sinning against God, and because of this steadfastness God has confirmed them in their bliss: Mt 18:10; 1 Tm 5:21; *Ref. 60.*

Their Nature

48 They are described as being

Spirits: Ps 104:4; He 1:7,14;

Holy: Mt 25:31;

Wise: 2 Sm 14:20;

Mighty: Ps 103:20, 2 Th 1:7;

Able to move swiftly: Dn 9:21;

Innumerable: Ps 68:17; Dn 7:10; Mt 26:53; Lk 2:13; He 12:22; Re 5:11;

Immortal: Mt 22:30; Lk 15:10; 20:36; *Ref. 61,66.*

Their Names

49 Various names and titles are ascribed to them, including,

Archangel: 1 Th 4:16; Jd 9;

Cherubim: Gn 3:24; Ex 37:7-9; 1 Kgs 6:23-28; Ps 99:1;

Seraphim: Is 6:1,2;

Sons of God: Job 38:4-7;

Morning stars: Job 38:4-7;

Watchers and holy ones: Dn 4:13;

Heavenly host: Lk 2:13;

Individual names: Gabriel: Dn 8:16; 9:21; Lk 1:19,26; Michael: Dn 10:13; 12:1; Jd 9; *Ref. 59,62,65.*

Their Ranks

50 There are Bible references which seem to indicate various ranks and orders among the angels with regard to their various offices and services: Is 6:2,3; Ro 8:38; Eph 1:21; 3:10; Col 1:16; 2:10; 1 Th 4:16; He 9:5; 1 Pe 3:22; 2 Pe 2:10,11; Jd 9.

Their Work

51 They worship God: Ps 148:1,2; Is 6:3; Lk 2:13,14; He 1:6; Re 5:11,12; 7:11; 11:15; *ref. 66.*

52 They carry out God's commands and serve as God's messengers: Ps 103:20,21; Mt 6:10; Lk 11:2, e.g.,

When Abraham was about to offer his son Isaac: Gn 22:11,12;

Announcing the birth of John the Baptist to Zacharias: Lk 1:11-20;

Announcing the conception of Christ to the Virgin Mary: Lk 1:26-38;

Announcing the birth of Christ to the shepherds: Lk 2:9-14;

Announcing Christ's resurrection from the dead: Mt 28:1-7; Mk 16:5-7;

Announcing Christ's second return to his disciples: Ac 1:10,11;

Directing Philip to the Ethiopian Eunuch: Ac 8:26;

Instructing Cornelius to send for the Apostle Peter: Ac 10:3-6; *Ref. 63,64.*

53 They serve God's people by guarding them against danger and delivering them in time of trouble: Ps 34:7; 91:10-12; He 1:14, e.g., they

Warned and protected Lot and his family against the destruction of Sodom and Gomorrah: Gn 19:1,12,13;

Guarded the Israelites against Pharaoh: Ex 14:19; 23:20;

Provided food for Elijah when he fled from Ahab and Jezebel: 1 Kgs 19:5-8;

Protected Elijah against the Syrians: 2 Kgs 6:17;

Delivered Hezekiah and Jerusalem from the hands of the Syrians: 2 Kgs 19:35;

Delivered Daniel's three friends from the fiery furnace: Dn 3:24-28;

Delivered Daniel from the lion's den: Dn 6:21,22;

Delivered the Apostle Peter from prison: Ac 5:19; 12:5-11; *ref. 62-64,67.*

54 They ministered to Christ: Mt 4:11; 26:53; Mk 1:13; Lk 22:43; cp. Mt 2:13,19,20.

55 They rejoice at the extension of Christ's kingdom: Lk 15:7,10; Eph 3:9-11; 1 Pe 1:12; Re 7:11; 14:6,7; 19:6,7.

56 They carry the souls of believers to heaven: Lk 16:22; cp. 2 Kgs 2:11.

57 They will be Christ's assistants on the day of the final judgment: Mt 13:49; 24:31; 25:31; Mk 13:27; Lk 9:26; 12:9; 1 Cor 15:51,52; 1 Th 4:16; 2 Th 1:7-10; Jd 14:15; *ref. 1603.*

They Serve As Our Example

58 From them we should learn

To worship God and to acknowledge Christ as Lord of all: Ps 9:11; 67:3; 104:33; He 13:15; 1 Pe 2:9;

To do God's will on earth as gladly as they do his will in heaven: Mt 6:10; 22:37-40; 28:19,20; Jn 13:34; 14:15,21; 15:10,14; 1 Jn 3:23,24;

To minister to the needs of our fellowmen: Is 58:7; Mt 25:35-40; Ro 12:13; 15:1; Ga 6:10; He 13:2,3,16; Jas 1:27.

> To comfort and to bless,
> To find a balm for woe,
> To tend the lone and fatherless,
> Is angels' work below.
> — William Walsham How

ref. 68

59 The term "angel," *angelos* in Greek, is an official title denoting a messenger. The Hebrew term is *malach,* from the root which signifies "to send." This general term is also applied in Scriptures to men who discharge the office of an ambassador, e.g., Gn 32:3; Lk 7:24; Jas 2:25, and to ministers of the gospel: Re 1:20; 2:1,8,12,18; 3:1,7,14; *ref. 49.*

† † †

60 It is possible to be saved without knowing anything about angels. But it is an entirely different matter to deny the existence of angels, as did the Sadducees — that is, to deny a doctrine which is clearly taught in the Bible from Genesis to Revelation: Ac 23:8; cp. Lk 20: 27-38; *ref. 47.*

† † †

61 The angels are spirits, invisible, personal, conscious and intelligent beings endowed with mind and will, but not composed of body and soul as human beings are: Lk 24:39; cp. Eph 6:12. To deny their existence because one cannot see them is as wise as to deny the existence of the wind, or of electricity, or of gravity, because they cannot be seen.

While God is also a Spirit, Jn 4:24, angels differ from the nature of God in other ways that distinguish the creature from the Creator. God is an infinite Spirit; angels are finite in the sense that they are dependent upon God. There are also other attributes of God which angels do not share: *ref. 48,404.*

† † †

62 While all of the angels are spoken of as ministering to God's people, (He 1:14), it is inferred in Gn 48:16; Mt 18:10, and in Ac 12:15 that every Christian has his own guardian angel; *ref. 49.*

† † †

63
How oft do they their silver bowers leave
   To come to succor us that succor want!
How oft do they with golden pinions cleave,
   The flitting skies like flying pursuivant
Against foul fiends to aid us militant!
   They for us fight, they watch and duly ward
And their bright squadrons round about us plant;
   And all for love and nothing for reward;
O, why should heavenly God to men have such regard?
                                        — Edmund Spencer
ref. 52,53

† † †

21

64 Although angels do not have bodies, they sometimes appeared in the form and appearance of men to make themselves manifest, e.g., when appearing to Abraham, Gn 18:1,2f; to Lot, Gn 19:1-3; to Jacob, Gn 32:1,2; to Balaam, Nu 22:31; to Gideon, Jdg 6:11; to Manoah, Jdg 13:3; to Zacharias, Lk 1:11; to the Virgin Mary, Lk 1:26-28; to the shepherds, Lk 2:10,11; to the women at the empty tomb of the risen Savior, Lk 24:4-7; to the disciples on the Mount of Ascension, Ac 1:10,11; *ref. 48,52.*

† † †

65 The expression "the Angel of the Lord" — see, e.g., Gn 16:7; 21:17; 22:11; 31:11; Ex 3:2; 14:19; 23:20-23; 32:34; Nu 22:23 — refers to Christ who appeared to the patriarchs in human form and thus gave them, as it were, a preview of his future incarnation. Note also the reference to Christ in Mal 3:1, where he is spoken of as "the messenger [angel] of the covenant"; *ref. 49.*

† † †

66 The angels are a part of the Church Triumphant, even as are the souls of the saints which have been translated from this world to heaven: Eph 3:14,15.

> The saints on earth and those above
> But one communion make;
> Joined to their Lord in bonds of love,
> All of his grace partake.
>
> One family, we dwell in him,
> One Church above, beneath;
> Tho' now divided by the stream,
> The narrow stream, of death.
> — Isaac Watts

ref. 48

† † †

67
> Though destruction walk around us,
> Though the arrows past us fly,
> Angel guards from thee surround us;
> We are safe if thou art nigh.
> — James Edmeston

ref. 53

† † †

68
> May we thy precepts, Lord, fulfill
> And do on earth our Father's will
> As angels do above;

Still walk in Christ, the living Way,
With all thy children and obey
The law of Christian love.

— Edward Osler

ref. 58

BAPTISM, SACRAMENT OF 69-90

(ref.: Lord's Supper 941-962)

Its Essence

69 It is a sacred act ordained by God in which, in the name of the Father and of the Son and of the Holy Ghost, water is applied to a living person by sprinkling, pouring, or immersion: Mt 28:19; *ref. 76-79, 85.*

70 It was instituted by Christ and is meant for "all nations": Mt 28:18-20;

71 Since the fall of Adam and Eve all mankind is spiritually dead in trespasses and sins and in need of a spiritual rebirth: Jn 3:3-6; Eph 2:1.

72 Little children are included in Christ's command to make disciples of all nations by baptizing them:

Children are shapen in iniquity and conceived in sin: Ps 51:5; they are sinful flesh born of sinful flesh: Jn 3:6; the imagination of their heart is evil from youth: Gn 8:21; they, as well as adults, are the objects of Christ's redeeming love: Mk 10:13-16; cp. Mt 18:1-6,14;

In the New Testament baptism is the rite of initiation into God's family. Compare the rite of circumcision in the Old Testament, which occurred on the eighth day after the birth of a male child: see Col 2:11-13. Baptism is to be administered to all members of the household: Ac 10:33,47,48; 16:15,33; 18:8; 1 Cor 1:16; see also Ac 2:38,39; *ref. 80-83,90.*

73 Its power is derived from Christ's command and from his word used in connection with the water when baptism is administered: Mt 28:18,19; Eph 5:25,26; see also Jn 6:63; 15:3; Ro 1:16; He 4:12; Jas 1:21; 1 Pe 1:23; *ref. 84.*

Its Benefits, or Blessings

74 It bestows the blessings of forgiveness of sins, life, and salvation to all who believe the words and promises of Christ: Mk 16:16; Ac 2:38; 22:16; 1 Cor 6:11; Tt 3:5-7; 1 Pe 3:21;

By it believers enter into the kingdom of God: Jn 3:5; they become a new creation in Christ: 2 Cor 5:17; Ga 3:27; they receive the gift of the Holy Spirit: Ac 2:38; Tt 3:5; they are spiritually reborn and made the children of God and heirs of eternal life: Ro 8:14-17; Ga 3:26,27; they are implanted in Christ's body, the church: 1 Cor 12:13; Eph 5:26,27.

Its Relation to Christian Life

75 In baptism the believer puts on Christ, so that all the benefits of Christ's redemptive work become his own: Ga 3:27;

In baptism the believer is buried with Christ into death, so that the body of sin might be destroyed; and, as Christ was raised from the dead by the glory of God the Father, so the baptized believer rises with him to newness of life: Ro 6:3-6f; see also 1 Cor 6:9-11; Eph 4:22-24f; Col 2:11-13; 3:1-10f; 1 Pe 3:21; *ref. 86,87;*

In baptism the believer is made a member of the communion of saints, that is, Christ's church, and is joined with them in the unity of the Holy Spirit: Eph 4:3-6; see also 1 Cor 10:17; 12:13;

In baptism God established his everlasting covenant with believers which encourages them to good works, comforts them in every affliction, and assures them of the hope of eternal life: 1 Cor 6:11; Col 2:12; Tt 3:5-7; cp. Is 54:10; Ro 8:14-17; *ref. 88-90.*

Resources

76 The word "sacrament" does not occur in the Scriptures. It is a word derived from Latin, and used of a thing dedicated, or solemnly separated. The early church fathers, among them Ambrose and Augustine, adopted the word into ecclesiastical language and used it to represent "a holy thing, a secret, an inscrutable mystery." Jerome employed it as such in his Latin Bible, e.g., Dn 2:18; 1 Cor 4:1; 1 Tm 3:16.

When used as a reference to the rites which have the command of God, and to which the promise of grace has been added, we may define a sacrament as "a sacred act (a) instituted by God, (b) in which there are certain visible means (water, bread, wine) connected with his word, and (c) by which God offers, gives, and seals unto us the forgiveness of sins which Christ has earned for us."

In this definition we have features which distinguish baptism and the Lord's Supper from all other rites, customs and ceremonies — features which cause them to stand forth in a class by themselves, as unique institutions.

In addition to baptism and the Lord's Supper, the Roman Catholic Church asserts that there are five more sacraments, viz., confirmation, penance, extreme unction, ordination, and matrimony. However, none of these latter five qualify under the above definition: *ref. 69,70,85.*

† † †

77 The definition given for baptism in *ref. 69* notes that "water is applied to a living person," to avoid the erroneous impression that baptism may also be applied for the dead. The biblical way of salvation rules out any kind of vicarious baptism, salvation being by *personal* faith and *personal* baptism: Mt 28:19,20; Mk 16:15,16; Ac 2:38; 16:31 22:16; Ro 1:16,17; cp. Ac 8:36-38. Moreover, He 9:27 denies the possibility of conversion after death. Therefore 1 Cor 15:29 cannot be quoted in favor of vicarious baptism. The Greek preposition *hyper* here may mean "over" or "with reference to" (instead of "for") the baptism of Christians who had since died. Their baptism, Paul is simply asserting rhetorically, was part and parcel of their hope of the resurrection of the body to eternal life; *ref. 69.*

† † †

78 Both baptism and the Lord's Supper are holy sacraments. But there is also a difference between the two:

Baptism is called the sacrament of initiation; the Lord's Supper, the sacrament of confirmation (the reception of baptism precedes the use of the Lord's Supper);

Baptism is to be administred only once in an individual's lifetime; the Lord's Supper is to be administered frequently: Ac 2:42; 1 Cor 11:24,26; Lk 22:19;

Baptism has as its purpose the generation of faith in infants or the confirmation of faith in adults; the Lord's Supper has as its purpose the strengthening and preservation of a mature faith, capable of self-examination.

While a person can be saved without being baptized (e.g., a deathbed conversion), it is, as Augustine noted, not the failure to be baptized but the refusal, or contempt, of baptism that damns: Mk 16:16; cp. Lk 7:29,30; *ref. 69,85,88.*

† † †

79 The word "baptize" means to apply water, but it does not specify the way in which the water is to be applied. The Greek term *baptizein* signified not merely immersion, but also washing, sprinkling, pouring — in fact, *any* ceremonial application of water, as the following passages indicate: "washing": Mk 7:3,4; Lk 11:38; Ac 22:16; cp. Eph 5:25,26; "pouring": cp. Mt 3:11 with Ac 2:1-4,17; "sprinkling": cp. He 9:10 with Ex 24:8 and Nu 19:13,19; "immersion": Ro 6:3,4.

Christ's baptismal command means to apply *water,* which allows for no substitute. The water may be river, lake, well, running or standing water. The amount of water that is used is insignificant, since the purpose of baptism is not to cleanse the body, but to cleanse from sin and to save the soul: 1 Pe 3:21; see also Ex 24:8 and cp. He 11:28; 12:24; 1 Pe 1:2; *ref. 69,70.*

† † †

80 The usual objection against infant baptism is that "they can't believe." But it is also true that "adults can't believe." Saving faith is not a work on the part of man, but a divine gift which is bestowed solely by the work of the Holy Spirit: Eph 2:8,9; 1 Cor 12:3; Php 2:13. Man by birth and nature is "dead in trespasses and sins," Eph 2:1. As he contributed nothing to his physical birth so he can contribute nothing to the miracle of his spiritual rebirth, which is wrought in him by the Holy Spirit: Jn 3:3-6; 1 Cor 2:14; Tt 3:5-7. Christ declared that little children do believe: Mt 18:6; see also Mt 21:15,16; Mk 10:13-16; Lk 1:15,44.

The Holy Spirit through baptism works regeneration and conversion; in the case of those in whom saving faith has already been wrought, the Holy Spirit through baptism seals and strengthens their faith. Accordingly, little children are first to be baptized and then instructed, while older persons, who can intelligently comprehend the gospel and express themselves, are first to be instructed and then baptized; *ref. 70,81,82,90.*

81   The Savior kindly calls
        Our children to his breast;
      He folds them in his gracious arms,
        Himself declares them blest.

      "Let them approach," he cries,
        Nor scorn their humble claim;
      The heirs of heav'n are such as these,
        For such as these I came."

      With joy we bring them, Lord,
        Devoting them to thee,
      Imploring that, as we are thine,
        Thine may our offspring be.
            — Philip Doddridge
    ref. 70,81,82,90

82 A little Chinese boy, the youngest of three children, asked his father to allow him to be baptized. The father told him that he was too young, that he might fall away from Christ if he made his confession when he was still a little boy. The child thought for a moment, and then replied: "Has not Jesus promised to carry lambs in his arms? I am only a little boy, so it will be easier for Jesus to carry me." The strong faith of the child won over the father. He was taken to the service and was baptized with his brother and sister; *ref. 70,81,82,90.*

† † †

A Sponsor's Prayer

83 Lord Jesus, Lover of children and Savior of my soul, bless me and the little one whom I shall sponsor at baptism today. Make me worthy of this high trust and confidence. Praise be to your holy name that you have instituted the blessed sacrament of holy baptism also for the forgiveness of the sins of children and that through the washing of regeneration you claim them as your own and heirs of everlasting life. Today you privilege me to bring this child to you. Stir my soul to a realization of the great obligations of this hour. Make of me a good and faithful sponsor. Teach me frequently and fervently to pray for my godchild. Enable me at all times to give my godchild the inspiration of a godly example. If the privileged burden should fall upon me, through the death or negligence of the parents, to rear this child in the nurture and admonition of the Lord, then grant me grace and guidance in this noble task, knowing that the child is yours and that the task is yours and mine. Grant me the joy one day of hearing this little one personally confess you before men and then be admitted into communicant member-

ship with your holy church. Hear me, I pray thee, for the sake of your holy
name. Amen.

— selected

ref. 70

† † †

84 A striking analogy of baptism is found in the cleansing of Naaman, the
Syrian, from his leprosy, 2 Kgs 5:1-14:

Naaman was afflicted with a deadly disease and could not cure himself.
The leprosy of sin is a deadly and damning disease from which man
cannot free himself: Ps 49:7,8; Jr 2:22;

Naaman was invited to go to the prophet of God and be healed. Sinners are
invited to be baptized and cleansed: Ac 2:38; 22:16;

Naaman regarded Elisha's directive to dip in the Jordan River for cleansing as a foolish request. Man considers the command to be cleansed from
his sins by the water of baptism as foolishness: cp. Jn 3:4; 1 Cor 1:18; 2:14;

Naaman's cleansing was not effected simply by the water of the Jordan
River but by the cleansing power of God's command spoken by the
prophet. The effectiveness of the water of baptism receives its power from
the almighty power of Christ's command and from Christ's words connected with the water: Mt 28:18-20; Eph 5:25-27;

Naaman's "flesh came again like unto the flesh of a little child, and he
was clean," v.14. Baptism is "the washing of regeneration, and renewing
of the Holy Ghost," Tt 3:5; by its power man becomes a new creation in
Christ and walks in newness of life: Ro 6:3-6ff; 2 Cor 5:17; *ref. 73.*

† † †

85 When the word is added to the element it becomes a sacrament.

— Augustine

ref. 69,70

† † †

86 In daily repentance the Christian appropriates the forgiveness of sins
and the strength needed to lead a godly life granted him in baptism. His
Christian life, as Luther said, "is nothing else than a daily baptism, once
begun and ever to be continued"; *ref. 75.*

† † †

87 While baptism is to be received but once, Holy Scriptures prevail upon all
baptized believers to remind themselves of their baptism continually and to
use it for their comfort and for their growth in sanctification: Ro 6:3ff; Col
2:11,12; *ref. 75.*

† † †

88 As in the case of the sacrament of the Lord's Supper, so also in the
sacrament of holy baptism, God adds the visible element to the word to make

27

the offer and the bestowal all the more compelling to the individual recipient.

God takes the individual aside to assure him most intimately and personally that Christ's merits were won for him and intended for him.

Moreover, baptism serves as a *seal,* just as circumcision served as a seal in the Old Testament, Ro 4:11. The person who receives the promise has that promise *sealed,* made absolutely sure and certain; *ref. 75.*

† † †

We may fail God, but God will never fail us. We may sin, but God's covenant, which he established with us in holy baptism, will never be broken on his part. Like the prodigal son, we may be assured that God will receive and pardon all who turn to him in repentance: Is 54:10; Lk 15:18-24; 2 Cor 1:20; *ref. 75.*

† † †

89 In speaking of the significance of baptizing with water, Martin Luther wrote: "It signifies that the Old Adam in us should, by daily contrition and repentance, be drowned and die with all sins and evil lusts and, again, a new man should daily come forth and arise, who shall live before God in righteousness and purety forever"; see Ro 6:4; *ref. 75.*

† † †

90
> Said a precious little laddie,
> To his father one bright day,
> "Can you tell me more of Jesus?
> Did he wash my sins away?"
>
> O, my son, but you're so little,
> Wait until you older grow,
> Bigger folks 'tis true, do need him,
> But little folks are safe, you know.
>
> Said the father to his laddie,
> As a storm was coming on,
> "Are the sheep all safely sheltered,
> Safe within the fold, my son?"
>
> "All the big ones are, my father
> But the lambs, I let them go,
> For I didn't think it mattered,
> Little ones are safe, you know.

— Anon

ref. 70,81,82,90

BIBLE, THE HOLY 91-141

(ref.: Law and Gospel 884-891)

91 The Book: Ps 40:7; He 10:7; the Book of the Lord: Is 34:16; the Book of the Law: Dt 31:26; Jos 1:8; Ga 3:10;

The Law of Moses, the Prophets, and the Psalms: Mt 5:17; Lk 24:44;

The Word of God: Lk 11:28; 1 Th 2:13; the Word of Christ: Col 3:16; the Word of Life: Ac 5:20; Ph 2:16; the Word of Truth: 2 Tm 2:15; Jas 1:18;

Scriptures: Mt 22:29; Jn 5:39; 2 Tm 3:16; Holy Scriptures: Ro 1:2; 2 Tm 3:15;

The Oracles of God: Ac 7:38; Ro 3:2; He 5:12; 1 Pe 4:11.

Descriptions

92 Food: Ps 119:103; Jr 15:16; 1 Pe 2:2;

Seed: Lk 8:11; incorruptible seed, 1 Pe 1:23;

Hammer: Jr 23:29;

Sword: He 4:12; Sword of the Spirit, Eph 6:17;

Lamp and Light: Ps 119:105; Fire: Jr 5:14; 23:29;

Truth: Jn 17:17; Jas 1:18;

The Power of God: Ro 1:16; cp. Jn 6:63; 1 Pe 1:23.

The Way the Bible Was Written

93 It was written by men as God's instruments; these men were called prophets, evangelists and apostles; They were men of various stations in life, e.g., David (King); Amos (Shepherd); Matthew (Tax-collector); Luke (Physician); Paul (Tentmaker); Peter, James and John (Fishermen).

94 It was verbally inspired by the Holy Ghost; the Holy Spirit breathed into the hearts of the writers and instructed them as to what they were to write: 2 Sm 23:2; Mt 22:43; Jn 16:13; 1 Cor 2:13; 2 Tm 3:16; He 3:7; 10:15; 2 Pe 1:21; the Holy Spirit gave them the very words they wrote: Jn 10:34-36; 1 Cor 2:13; Ga 3:16; *ref. 104-109,112,114,115.*

The Bible Is the Written Word of God

95 The witness of the Old Testament:

The expression "thus saith the Lord," or its equivalent, is used by the holy writers more than 2500 times, e.g., Is 1:24; Jr 5:14; 23:32; Eze 13:6; Am 1:3,9,11,13;

The holy writers claim to have been inspired, e.g., Ex 34:27; 2 Sm 23:1-3; Is 8:1,5,11; 34:16; 59:21; Jr 1:9; 36:1,2; Eze 1:3; Ac 1:16; 1 Cor 2:13;

Christ frequently quotes from the Old Testament and refers to it as the Word of God, e.g., Mt 4:4,7,10; 5:17,18; 22:29-32, 42-44; 26:54; Mk 7:10; 10:19; Lk 4:16-21; 16:31; 18:31; 24:27,44-46; Jn 5:39,46,47; 7:22,23; 10:34-36;

The New Testament writers repeatedly refer to the Old Testament as the Word of God, e.g., Mt 1:22,23; 2:4-6,17,23; 8:17; 12:17; 21:4,5; 24:15; 27:9,35; Lk 1:67-70; Ac 1:16,20; 2:16-21; 4:25; 10:43; 24:14; 28:25-27; Ro 1:1,2; 2 Tm 3:15,16; He 1:1; 3:7; 4:7; 2 Pe 1:19-21.

96 The witness of the New Testament:

Christ promised that his words would endure forever: Mt 24:35; Lk 21:33; and that the truth which he proclaimed can be known: Jn 8:31,32. He commanded his disciples to preach his gospel in all the world and to teach the things he commanded: Mt 28:18-20; Mk 16:15; Lk 24:45-48; Ac 1:8. He sent them the Holy Spirit to guide them in all truth: Jn 14:26; 16:13; Ac 2:1f; and declared that men should believe in him through the apostles' word: Jn 17:20; cp. Col 3:16;

The writers of the New Testament testified that they did not write their own words but the words which the Holy Spirit inspired them to write: 1 Cor 2:12,13; 14:37; 1 Th 2:13; 1 Pe 1:10-12; 2 Pe 3:2; 1 Jn 1:1,3,4;

The witness of the New Testament Christian Church which is built on the words of the apostles as well as on the words of the prophets: Jn 17:20; Eph 2:20; Cp. 2 Pe 3:2,16.

97 The convincing testimony of the Holy Spirit: Jn 3:3; 7:17; 1 Cor 2:4,5,10-14; 1 Th 2:13; 1 Jn 5:9,10; *ref. 114.*

98 Additional testimony:

The perfect unity in the message of the various writers who lived over a span of 1600 years; *ref. 114,115.*

The testimony of the scriptural prophecies that have been fulfilled and are being fulfilled: 1 Kgs 8:56; Is 40:8; 42:9; 45:21; 46:9-11; Eze 12:25; Mt 5:18; 24:35; Lk 17:22-30; 21:5-33; Ac 3:18; 20:29,30; 1 Tm 4:1-3; 2 Tm 3:1-5; 4:3,4; 2 Pe 3:3-10; *ref. 114,115,120,141.*

The fulfillment of many Old Testament prophecies in the person and work of Jesus Christ; *ref. 578ff.*

The Bible's triumph over persistent attacks: Ps 119:89; cp. Mt 24:35; Lk 21:33; 1 Pe 1:24,25; *ref. 116-120,141.*

The transforming power of the Bible in the lives of men and nations: 2 Cor 5:17; cp. e.g., Mk 5:1-8,15; Ro 1:16; 1 Tm 1:12-15; *ref. 121,134.*

The Makeup of the Bible

99 The Old Testament:

From Genesis to Malachi, 39 books, beginning with the five books of Moses, written c. 1500 B.C., and covering the years before the coming of Christ;

Historical and doctrinal books: Genesis to Esther;

Poetical books: Job to Song of Solomon;

Prophetical books: Isaiah to Malachi.

Note: Historical and prophetical books also include much poetry, and the poetical books also include history and prophecy. Strictly speaking, therefore, it is not entirely accurate to classify either the Old or the New Testament books in a manner like the above.

100 The New Testament:

From Matthew to Revelation, 27 books, covering approximaely 100 years;

Historical books: Matthew to Acts;

Doctrinal books: all the books of the New Testament, but especially the Epistles, from Romans to Jude.

Prophetical book: The Revelation of St. John; *ref. 110,111.*

101   The Purpose of the Bible

To reveal Jesus Christ as the heaven-sent Savior to a sinlost world: Lk 2:10,11; 19:10; 24:17,44-46; Jn 3:16,17; 5:39; 14:6; 17:3; 20:31; Ac 4:12; 10:43; Ro 1:16; 10:14; 16:25,26; 1 Cor 15:3,4; 1 Tm 1:15; Jas 1:21; 1 Jn 5:11-13,20; *ref. 112;*

To guide us in all matters pertaining to doctrine and life: Ps 36:9; Is 8:20; Lk 16:29-31; Jn 8:31,32; 17:17; Ro 16:17; 1 Tm 6:3-5; 2 Tm 3:16,17; 1 Pe 4:11; *ref. 113.*

102   The Completeness of the Bible

It is not intended as a textbook in history, science, etc., but when it speaks on these subjects such statements, like all others, are unerring truth: Dt 32:4; 2 Sm 7:28; Ps 33:4; 108:4; 119:160; 146:6; Pr 30:5; Jn 7:28; 8:31,32; 10:35; 17:17; Eph 5:9; Col 1:5; Jas 1:18; 1 Pe 1:25;

It is not a complete revelation of all divine things: Ro 11:33,34; 1 Cor 2:9; 13:12; 1 Jn 3:2; but it does teach all that is necessary for our eternal salvation: Jn 5:39; 8:31,32; 17:20; 2 Tm 3:15;

No one is to add to it or to take away from it: Dt 4:2; 12:32; Jos 23:6; Pr 30:5,6; Is 8:20; Mt 5:17-19; Lk 16:29-31; 1 Tm 6:3,4; He 1:1,2; Re 22:18,19.

103   Personal Attitude in Using the Bible

We are to find Christ in it: Lk 24:27,44-47; Jn 1:41,45; 5:39; 20:30,31; Ac 10:43; 2 Tm 3:15; *ref. 112;*

We are to order our lives according to its teachings: Ps 119:9,11,105,130; Is 8:20; Mt 7:21; Ro 15:4; 1 Cor 10:11; Col 3:16; 2 Tm 3:16,17; Jas 1:22-25; 2 Pe 1:19; *ref. 138;*

We are to regard it with reverence as the Word of God: Dt 6:6,7; Ps 119:47,72,103; Is 66:2; 1 Th 2:13; and humbly to subject our reason to its divine authority: Mt 11:25; Lk 10:16; 2 Cor 10:5; Jas 4:6; *ref. 122-125;*

We are to hear it gladly when it is preached and taught: Mt 13:23; Lk 10:39; 11:28; Ac 2:42; 11:17; 1 Th 2:13; He 10:25;

We are to read, study and meditate upon it: Dt 17:19; Ps 119:97; Jos 1:8; Is 34:16; Lk 2:19,51; Jn 5:39; Ac 17:11; 1 Pe 2:2; *ref. 126-137,140;*

We are to teach it to our children: Gn 18:19; Dt 4:9,10; 6:6-9; 11:18-21; Jos 8:35; 24:15; 2 Chr 17:9; Ps 78:1-7; Mt 28:20; *ref. 321-324.*

We are to help spread its saving message to all mankind: Mt 24:14; 28:18-20; Mk 13:10; 16:15; Lk 24:47,48; Ac 1:8; 8:4; Php 2:15,16, and to pray that it may have free course and be glorified in all the world: Eph 6:19; 1 Th 5:25; 2 Th 3:1; *ref. 139,1020-1081.*

Resources

104 Inspiration is the miraculous process by which the Holy Spirit guided the holy men to speak the things he desired them to speak, and to write the things he desired them to write in the precise manner and in the very words in which he desired these words to be spoken or written, while at the same time using the study, research, personal experience and the various styles of the writers for this purpose: 1 Cor 2:13. Thus the Holy Scriptures, while written by men, are God-inspired, or God-breathed: 2 Tm 3:16; 1 Th 2:13. As such these Scriptures are God's Word and their message never changes. Through them God continues to speak to all men of all ages to the end of time: Ps 119:89; Mt 24:35; Lk 21:33; Jn 10:35; 17:17; 1 Pe 1:25; *ref. 94-98.*

† † †

105 The Bible *is* the Word of God. It does not merely "contain" the Word of God, as though it were merely a history of God's revelation or a compilation of God's acts as recorded by men and thus subject to error or admissible of human additions. Nor does the Bible first "become" the Word of God for a person when by some "encounter" he is brought in touch with that Word. On the contrary, the Bible is the Word of God objectively, even apart from any contact with it: Mt 10:14,15; 11:20-24; Lk 11:29-32; Jn 12:47,48.

To hold that the Bible merely "contains" the Word of God leads to endless confusion and unbridled license which lets every person judge for himself which parts are and which parts are not the Word of God: Jdg 17:6; 21:25; *ref. 94-98.*

106 The fact that the original monographs of the holy writers are lost and that there are variant readings in the manuscripts that we possess does not refute the doctrine of inspiration. The differences in the various manuscripts, many of which can be attributed to the errors of copyists, are trivial and unessential. They do not affect the teachings of the Bible any more than a copying mistake would invalidate the Constitution of the United States.

Professor Moses Stuart, one of the ablest scholars of modern times, said: "Out of some 800,000 readings of the Bible that have been collected, about 795,000 are about of as much importance as the question in English orthography is whether the word 'honor,' or 'savior' should be spelled with a 'u' or without it." He notes that there exist only ten or twelve verses in which the variant readings have any significance at all. In some instances these variants consist but in the difference of a single word, or sometimes even of a single letter, and in no case do they affect any Scripture doctrine; *ref. 94-98.*

107 To hold the view that we do not have a reliable Bible poses the alternatives of saying either that God was unable to communicate his word to us clearly, or that he did not want to do so. Both of these alternatives are blasphemous; *ref. 94-98.*

† † †

108 As to variations in quotations, J. M. Gray wrote: "The same Spirit who spoke through the Old Testament also spoke through the evangelists and apostles. (1 Pe 1:10-12). Part of the testimony of the Spirit is the citation and explanation of Old Testament passages. When an author quotes himself he may quote as he pleases, and give a different turn to an expression here and there as changed conditions of affairs render it necessary or desirable"; *ref. 94-98.*

† † †

109 Either the writers of the Bible spoke the truth and were supernaturally empowered by the Holy Spirit to write God's own words, or they were dishonest. In other words, either the Bible is what it claims to be, a Book of God's own words and therefore infallible and inerrant, or it is beneath our recognition and not to be classed with ordinarily dependable literature.
— Sunday School Times

ref. 94-98

† † †

110 The sixty-six books of the Bible are grouped together according to their respective classifications and do not always follow a historical sequence. Thus, to illustrate, the Book of Job, which historically is one of the oldest books written, is not placed at the beginning of the Old Testament but is listed with the group of poetical books. So, too, the books of the prophets (Isaiah-Malachi) are grouped together as a unit, although some of their messages were delivered at various times during the reigns of the kings of Israel spoken of in First and Second Kings, and First and Second Chronicles, while others were delivered during the exile in Babylon (Jeremiah, Ezekiel, Daniel), and still others following that exile (Haggai, Zechariah, Malachi).

In the New Testament the accounts of the four Gospels are followed historically by the Book of Acts. The Epistles, however, do not follow a historical sequence but are grouped according to their writers; *ref. 99,100.*

† † †

111
> Thy Word is like a garden, Lord,
>   With flowers bright and fair;
> And every one who seeks may pluck
>   A lovely cluster there.
>
> Thy Word is like a deep, deep mine
>   And jewels rich and rare
> Are hidden in its mighty depths
>   For every searcher there.

— Gospel Herald

ref. 101

† † †

112 In the discharge of my duties for forty years as professor of Sanskrit in the University of Oxford, I have devoted as much time as any man living to

33

the study of the sacred books of the East, and I have found the one key-note, the one diapason, so to speak, of all these so-called sacred books, whether it be the Veda of the Brahmans, the Puranas of Siva and Vishnu, the Koran of the Mohammedans, the Zend-Avesta of the Parsees, the Tripitaka of the Buddhists — *the one refrain through all* — *salvation by works.* They all say that salvation must be purchased, must be bought with a price, and that the sole price, the sole purchase-money, must be our works and deservings. Our own Bible, our sacred book of the East, is from beginning to end a protest against this doctrine. Good works are, indeed, enjoined upon us, in that sacred book of the East, far more strongly than in any other sacred book of the East; but, they are only the outcome of a grateful heart — they are only a thank-offering, the fruits of our faith. They are never the ransom-money of the true disciple of Christ. Let us not shut our eyes to what is excellent and true and of good report in these sacred books, but let us teach Hindus, Buddhists, Mohammedans, that there is only one sacred book of the East that can be their mainstay in that awful hour when they pass all alone into the unseen world. It is the sacred book which contains that faithful saying, worthy to be received of all men, women, and children, and not merely of us Christians — that Christ Jesus came into the world to save sinners.

— Max Mueller

ref. 94-98,101,103

† † †

113

> How precious is the Book Divine,
>   By inspiration giv'n!
> Bright as a lamp its doctrines shine
>   To guide our souls to heav'n.
>
> Its light, descending from above
>   Our gloomy world to cheer,
> Displays a Savior's boundless love
>   And brings his glories near.
>
> It shows to man his wand'ring ways
>   And where his feet have trod,
> And brings to view the matchless grace
>   Of a forgiving God.
>
> This lamp through all the tedious night
>   Of life shall guide our way
> Till we behold the clearer light
>   Of an eternal day.

— John Fawcett

ref. 100,101

† † †

114 The heavenliness of the matter, the efficacy of the doctrine, the majesty of the style, the consent of all the parts, the scope of the whole (which is to give all glory to God), the full discovery it makes of the only way of man's

salvation, the many other incomparable excellencies, and the entire perfection thereof, are arguments whereby it doth abundantly evidence itself to be the Word of God; yet, notwithstanding our full persuasion and assurance thereof, is from the inward work of the Holy Spirit, bearing witness by and with the Word in our hearts.
— Presbyterian Confession of Faith

ref. 94-98

† † †

115
Whence but from heaven could men unskill'd in arts,
In several ages born, in several parts,
Weave such agreeing truths? or how, or why
Should all conspire to cheat us with a lie?
Unasked their pains, ungrateful their advice,
Starving their gain, and martyrdom their price.
— Dryden

ref. 94-98

† † †

116 The infidel Voltaire boasted: "In twenty years Christianity will be no more. My single hand shall destroy the edifice it took twelve apostles to rear." Some years later, after his death, his very printing press was used in the printing of the New Testament; *ref. 98.*

† † †

117 A strange thing happened during the Crimean war at Sevastopol, the Russian city on the Black Sea. A shell burst in the hillside outside of the city and opened a spring. A fountain bubbled forth where the shot had fallen, and during the remaining siege the thirsty troops who were stationed nearby came and drank from its pure and cold water. Intended as a messenger of death from the enemy, the missile became a bearer of mercy to the parched and weary soldiers. So, too, in the very midst of the attacks upon the Bible, God opens new fountains of its truth to supply the wants of his people, and the curse of the enemy becomes a blessing to his foe; *ref. 98.*

† † †

118 Defend the Bible? I would just as soon attempt to defend a lion. I say, let it loose; it will defend itself;
— Spurgeon

ref. 98

† † †

119
By powers of empire banned and burned,
By pagan pride rejected, spurned,
The Word still stands, the Christian's trust,
While haughty empires lie in dust.

35

Abiding, steadfast, firm, and sure,
The teachings of the Word endure;
Blest he who trusts this steadfast Word,
His anchor holds in Christ, the Lord.
                    — Emanuel Cronenwett
ref. 98

† † †

120 The Bible has been the object of many vicious attacks. Infidel philoso-phers, atheistic scientists, skeptic astronomers, doubting archeologists, and agnostic explorers, inspired by satanic ingenuity and skill, have marshalled their forces against the written Word of God. Despotism has thundered forth its edicts against it. The enemies of truth and righteousness have cursed it. But despite all persecution, suppression, and destruction, "the Word of the Lord endures forever," 1 Pe 1:25.

Wide as the world is thy command,
  Vast as eternity thy love;
Firm as a rock thy truth must stand
  When rolling years shall cease to move.
                    — Isaac Watts
ref. 98

† † †

121 Charles Darwin made two trips around the world. On his first trip he came to an island inhabited by cannibals. His crew was afraid to land. Twenty years later he came to the same island again, and now he found the children going to school, the women were clothed, and the men were work-ing. What accounted for the change? A missionary had been there with the gospel; *ref. 98*.

† † †

122 A New York enthusiast had a good collection of etchings. One, which hung over his desk, was of the leaning tower of Pisa. For quite some time he noticed that it persisted in hanging crooked despite the fact that he straight-ened it every morning. At last he spoke to his maid and asked her if she was responsible for its lopsided condition. "Why, yes," she said, "I have to hang it crooked to make the tower hang straight!" — Even so, some find it necessary to twist the Scriptures in order to justify their own actions and try to make their lives appear right.
                    — Hallock

ref. 103

† † †

123 I read the Word of God without prepossession or bias, and come to it with a resolution to take my sense from it, and not with a design to bring to it the sense of my system.

— John Locke, Philosopher

ref. 103

† † †

124 Take all the Bible on reason that you can, and the balance by faith, and you will live and die a better man.

— Abraham Lincoln

ref. 103

† † †

125 Mark Twain is reported to have said: "Many people are troubled about the Scriptures which are mysterious and hard to understand. I am most troubled about those which I can understand"; *ref. 103.*

† † †

126

Though the cover is worn,
And the pages are torn,
And though places bear traces of tears,
Yet more precious than gold
Is the Book, worn and old,
That can shatter and scatter my fears.

When I prayerfully look
In the precious old Book,
Many pleasures and treasures I see;
Many tokens of love
From the Father above
Who is nearest and dearest to me.

This old Book is my guide;
'Tis a friend by my side,
It will lighten and brighten my way;
And each promise, I find,
Soothes and gladdens the mind
As I read it and heed it today.

To this Book I will cling,
Of its worth I will sing,
Though great losses and crosses be mine;
For I cannot despair,
Though surrounded by care
While possessing this blessing divine.

— Edmund Pillifaut, in
Bible Society Record (10/1927)

ref. 103

† † †

127 I myself am an enemy of my books, and I often wish that they might perish, for I am afraid lest they hinder the reader from reading for himself, the Bible, which is the fountain and source of all wisdom.

— Martin Luther

ref. 103

† † †

128 The first and almost the only book deserving of universal attention is the Bible. I speak as a man of the world to men of the world, and I say to you, "Search the Scriptures!" ... The earlier my children begin to read it, the more confident will be my hope that they will prove useful citizens of their country and respectable members of society.

— John Quincy Adams

ref. 103

† † †

129 God in his mercy has shown me that this Word is an inexhaustible storehouse from which he dispenses rich stores of precious truths to his servants as he pleases and as they are ready to receive them.

— Dr. Howard Kelly,
Johns Hopkins University

ref. 103

130 The Bible is a book in comparison with which all others in my eyes are of minor importance and which in all my perplexities and distresses has never failed to give me light and strength.

— Robert E. Lee

ref. 103

† † †

131 No one is truly educated who is ignorant of the Bible, and no one is really ignorant who knows the Bible.

— Wm. Lyon Phelps

ref. 102

† † †

132 Hold fast to the Bible as the sheet-anchor of your liberties; write its precepts on your hearts and practice them in your lives. To the influence of this Book we are indebted for the progress of our civilizaiton, and to this we must look as our guide in the future.

— Ulysses S. Grant

ref. 103

† † †

133 It is impossible to rightly govern the world without God and the Bible.

— George Washington

ref. 103

† † †

134 If we abide by the principles taught in the Bible, our country will go on prospering and to prosper; but if we and our posterity neglect its instruction and authority, no man can tell how sudden a catastrophe can overwhelm us and bury all of our glory in profound obscurity.
— Daniel Webster

ref. 103

† † †

135 The Bible is no mere book, but a living creature, with a power that conquers all that oppose it.
— Napoleon

ref. 103

† † †

136 I have known ninety-five of the world's great men in my time, and of them eighty-seven were followers of the Bible.
— William E. Gladstone

ref. 103

† † †

137 All I taught of art, everything I have written, whatever greatness has been in any thought of mine, whatever I have done in my life, has simply been due to the fact that, when I was a child, my mother daily read with me a part of the Bible, and daily made me learn a part of it by heart.
— John Ruskin

ref. 103

† † †

138 The translation of the Bible into life is still the best translation; *ref. 103*.

† † †

139
O Word of God incarnate,
  O Wisdom from on high,
O Truth unchanged, unchanging,
  O Light of our dark sky —
We praise thee for the radiance
  That from the hallowed page,
A lantern to our footsteps,
  Shines on from age to age.
— William W. How

ref. 103

† † †

140   It is one thing to read the Bible through,
Another thing to read to learn and do.
Some read it with design to learn to read,
But to the subject pay but little heed.
Some read it as their duty once a week,
But no instruction from their Bible seek;
While others read it with but little care,
With no regard to how they read, nor where.
Some read it as a history, to know
How people lived three thousand years ago.
Some read it to bring themselves into repute,
By showing others how they can dispute;
While others read because their neighbors do,
To see how long 'twill take to read it through.
Some read it for the wonders that are there —
How David killed a lion and a bear;
While others read it with uncommon care,
Hoping to find some contradictions there.
Some read it as though it did not speak to them,
But to the people at Jerusalem.
One reads it as a book of mysteries,
And won't believe the very thing he sees.
One reads with father's specs upon his head,
And sees the thing just as his father said.
Some read to prove a pre-adopted creed —
Hence understand but little that they read;
For every passage in the book they bend
To make it suit that all-important end!
Some people read, as I have often thought,
To teach the book instead of being taught.
And some there are that read it out of spite —
I fear there are but few who read it right.
So many people in these latter days,
Have read the Bible in so many ways
That few can tell which system is the best,
For every party contradicts the rest!
But read it prayerfully, and you will see,
Although men contradict, God's words agree.
For what the early Bible prophets wrote,
We find that Christ and his apostles quote;
So trust no creed that trembles to recall
What has been penned by one and verified by all.
— Anon

ref. 103

† † †

40

141   Last eve I paused beside a blacksmith's door,
And heard the anvil sing the vesper chime;
Then, looking in, I saw upon the floor
Old hammers, worn with beating years of time.

"How many anvils have you had," said I,
"To wear and batter all those hammers so?"
"Just one," he said, then, with a twinkling eye,
"The anvil wears the hammer out, you know."

And so, I thought, the anvil of God's Word
For ages skeptic blows have beat upon;
Yet, though the noise of falling blows was heard,
The anvil is unharmed — the hammers gone.
                — Dr. John Clifford
ref. 103

† † †

CHILDREN 142-158

(ref.: Education, Christian 315-358; Home 534-556; Young People 1649-1666)

142   General References

They are a gift from God: Gn 33:5; 48:9; Jos 24:3; 1 Sm 1:5,6,27; Ps 113:9; 127:3; Is 8:18; *ref. 146;*

They bring joy to parents: Ps 127:4,5; 128:3; Pr 15:20; 17:6; 23:25; Lk 1:57,58;

Each one is precious in God's eyes: Mt 18:10-14;

They can believe: Mt 18:6, and praise God: Ps 8:2; 148:12,13; Mt 21:15,16; *ref. 149,155;*

They can be effective missionaries: 2 Kgs 5:1-3f; Mt 21:15,16; *ref. 155;*

They learn by example as well as by precept, for good or for ill: *ref. 150,151,321;*

They were present with their parents at worship services: 2 Chr 20:13; Ezr 8:21; Ne 12:43; Mt 21:15,16; *ref. 153,157,158.*

143   God's Command to Children

To honor and obey their parents: Ex 20:12; Dt 5:16; Pr 30:17; Mt 15:4; Eph 6:2; Col 3:20; *ref. 1466,1467,1488;*

To serve their parents: 1 Tm 5:4; *ref. 147,148,151;*

To honor the aged: Lv 19:32; Pr 23:22; 1 Pe 5:5; Examples: Joseph, Gn 46:29; 47:11,12; Solomon, 1 Kgs 2:19; Elisha, 2 Kgs 2:12; Jesus, Lk 2:51;

To serve God in early youth Ps 148:12,13; Ec 12:1f; *ref. 147-158.*

144   Christ's Regard For Children

He loves them and wants to bless them: Mt 18:10-14; 19:13-15; Mk 10:14; *ref. 154,157;*

He took time to observe them at play: Mt 11:16,17;

He referred to them as examples of true greatness: Mt 18:1-6;

He defended them: Mt 21:15,16;

He warned against offending them: Mt 18:6;

He died also for their sins: 2 Cor 5:15; 1 Tm 2:6;

He spoke of them as his lambs and wants them to be taught his Word: Jn 21:15-17; Ac 20:28; cp. Is 40:11; Mt 28:19,20; *ref. 80-83,90,147,149,154.*

Duties Toward Children

Duties of parents: *ref. 321.*

Duties of the church: *ref. 325,326.*

145 Biblical Examples

Examples of pious children: Abel, Gn 4:4; 1 Jn 3:12; Joseph, Gn 39:9; Jephthah's daughter, Jdg 11:36; Samuel, 1 Sm 2:18,26; 3:1; Josiah, 2 Chr 34:1-3; John the Baptist, Lk 1:80; Timothy, 2 Tm 1:5; 3:15; Jesus, Lk 2:49,52.

Examples of wicked children: Cain, Gn 4:8; 1 Jn 3:12; Esau, Gn 25:33,34; sons of Eli, 1 Sm 2:12; sons of Samuel, 1 Sm 8:3; Absalom, 2 Sm 15:1-6ff; children of Bethel, 2 Kgs 2:23,24; daughter of Herodias, Mt 14:6-8.

Resources

146 In ancient Greece children that were born with defects were put to death. Pagan Rome was no better. If the father approved of the child, the child was spared; if not, the child was destroyed. Today we boast that we are more civilized. But many are guilty of the same vile sin, and it is only that they commit it in a different form. Instead of waiting to dispose of the child after it has been born they take steps to prevent its birth. They want to enjoy the privileges of married life but do not want to assume the obligations of parenthood. They commit murder in order to set at naught one of the chief purposes for which God instituted the sacred ordinance of marriage: Gn 1:28; cp. Ps 127:3-5; Ps 128:1-6 *ref. 142.*

† † †

147 "Tell me," said a mother to the pastor, "when shall I begin the religious instruction and training of my child?" "How old is your child?" asked the pastor. When the mother said, "He's five years old now," the pastor replied: "Hurry home as fast as you can. You've already lost the five best years!" *ref. 142.*

148 "Are you doing any literary work?" asked a friend of a Christian mother. "Yes," she replied, "I am writing two books." "What are their titles?" asked the friend. "John and Mary," answered the mother. "You see," she continued, "my business is to write upon the hearts and minds of my children the lessons they must learn to fit them for this life and for the life to come"; *ref. 142.*

† † †

149 The hearts of little children, though not sinless, are still free from many vicious habits and soul-destroying characteristics, and therefore they are more qualified to worship God than many adults whose hearts have been hardened by age-old sins. Children often see when their elders are blind; they sing when others are silent; they often receive blessings which others lose. The Bible speaks of a strong faith as a childlike faith, and Christ declared that the greatest virtue that one can possess is that of a spirit of meekness and humility such as is found in little children: Mt 18:1ff; *ref. 144.*

150 We teach by what we say and do or fail to say and do, as well as by the attitudes which we display, whether favorable or unfavorable, e.g., by our presence or absence when worship services are held, by our attention or lack of it when God's word is preached and taught, by our devotion or lack of it when singing the Lord's praises: Ps 122:1; Ec 5:1; Col 3:16,17; He 10:23-25.

We also teach by precept and example, by our attitude and conduct, in our relations with our fellowmen, e.g., when we speak or fail to speak to them of our faith; when we admonish and exhort them, or fail to do so; when we come to their assistance in time of need and pray for them, or fail to do so: Mt 18:15; 25:35ff; Mk 5:19,20; 2 Cor 3:2; Php 2:15,16; Jas 5:16; 1 Pe 2:9-12.

The Good Samaritan, spoken of in Christ's parable, taught an object lesson when he helped the wounded traveler. But the priest and the Levite also taught an object lesson when they saw a need and passed by on the other side: Lk 10:30f; cp. Ga 6:10; 1 Jn 3:17,18; 4:20,21; *ref. 142.*

† † †

151 Proverbs 22:6 instructs: "Train up a child in the way he *should* go," not in the way he *would* go. By birth and nature the child knows only the wrong way. If he is to know the right way he must be taught and trained. The failure on the part of many parents to recognize this truth constitutes one of the greatest of all tragedies.

152 The folly of letting children "decide for themselves" is exemplified in an incident related to the poet Coleridge. After listening to the arguments of a visitor who favored the view of letting children choose for themselves, the poet asked his visitor if he would like to see his garden and then led him to a plot that was overgrown with weeds. "Why, this is no garden," said the visitor. "True," replied the poet, "but it is still in this condition because it has not yet come to the age of discretion and choice. You see," he added, "I thought it unfair to prejudice the soil toward roses and strawberries"; *ref. 143.*

† † †

153 Dr. Albert Schweitzer once said: "From the services in which I joined as a child, I have taken into life a feeling for what is solemn, and a need for quiet and self-recollection, without which I cannot realize the meaning of life. I cannot therefore support the opinion of those who would not let children take part in services regularly until they to some extent understand. The important thing is not that they should understand everything, but that they shall feel something of what is serious and solemn. The fact that the child sees his elders full of devotion and has to feel something of their devotion himself — that is what gives the service its meaning for him"; *ref. 142,143.*

† † †

154

Gracious Savior, gentle Shepherd,
　Children all are dear to thee;
Gathered with thine arms and carried,
　In thy bosom may they be;
Sweetly, fondly, safely, tended,
　From all want and danger free.

Tender Shepherd, never leave them,
　Never let them go astray;
By thy warning love directed,
　May they walk the narrow way!
Thus direct them, thus defend them,
　Lest they fall an easy prey.

Cleanse their hearts from sinful folly
　In the stream thy love supplied,
Mingled stream of blood and water
　Flowing from thy wounded side;
And to heav'nly pastures lead them,
　Where thine own still waters glide.

Let thy holy Word instruct them;
　Fill their minds with heavenly light;
Let thy powerful grace constrain them
　To approve whate'er is right;
Let them feel thy yoke is easy,
　Let them prove thy burden light.

Taught to lisp thy holy praises
　Which on earth thy children sing,
Both with lips and hearts, unfeigned,
　Glad thank-offerings may they bring;
Then with all the saints in glory
　Join to praise their Lord and King.

— Jane E. Leeson

ref. 144

† † †

155 (While children are greatly influenced by their parents, the reverse is also often true.) An unbeliever one day was troubled in his mind as he sat in his quiet room on a Sunday morning alone. His little girl, the only near relative he had, had gone to Sunday School. He had often told her that there is no God, and to impress this upon her he had posted cards on the wall with the inscription: "God is nowhere." Yet his skepticism gave him no real satisfaction.

On this Sunday, as soon as his daughter had returned home and begun to speak of the heavenly Father and his great love in Christ Jesus, about whom the lesson had turned, he pointed to one of the cards and said: "Read that!" She was yet too young to read fluently, and so she spelled out his words very laboriously: "G-o-d-i-s-n-o-w-h-e-r-e." "That's it," she said, "God is now here! Daddy, isn't that true?"

The heart of the man, who had turned against God when his beloved wife was taken from him, was greatly touched by this reply of his darling daughter, and he answered slowly: "Yes, my dear; that is true. God is now here!" He burst into tears and, sobbing, drew his daughter to his heart. His infidelity had been overcome by the sweet faith of the little child.

— Selected

Ps. 8:2; *ref. 142*

† † †

156 Missionary Taylor told of a young convert who once said to him that he would wait until he learned more about Christ before making a public confession, to which he replied: "Do you expect a candle first to become useful when it is half burnt down?" "No," said the convert, "but as soon as I light it." "Very well," said the missionary, "go and do thou likewise!" Very soon after that the young man won fifty converts for Christ through his testimony; *ref. 143*.

† † †

157
Hosanna, loud hosanna,
   The little children sang;
Thro' pillard court and Temple
   The lovely anthem rang.
To Jesus, who had blessed them,
   Close folded to his breast,
The children sang their praises,
   The simplest and the best.

"Hosanna in the highest!"
   That ancient song we sing,
For Christ is our Redeemer,
   The Lord of heav'n our King.
Oh, may we ever praise him
   With heart and life and voice
And in his blissful presence
   Eternally rejoice!

— Jeannette Thredfall

ref. 142,143

† † †

45

158   Shepherd of tender youth,
Guiding in love and truth
   Thro'devious ways;
Christ, our triumphant King,
We come thy name to sing
And here our children bring
   To join thy praise.
                — Clement of Alexandria

ref. 142

CHURCH, THE CHRISTIAN 159-200

(ref.: Discipleship, Christian 300-314)

Various Names for the Church

159 Assembly of saints: Ps 89:7; 111:1; He 12:23.

Body of Christ: Ro 12:4,5; Eph 1:23; 4:12,15; 5:23.

Bride of Christ: Re 19:7; 21:2; 22:17.

Christ's Church: Mt 16:18; the Church: Mt 18:17.

Family in heaven and earth: Eph 3:15

Church of the living God: 1 Tm 3:15; Church of God: 1 Cor 1:2.

Flock of God: Is 40:11; Mt 26:31; Lk 12:32; Ac 20:28.

God's building: 1 Cor 3:9.

God's husbandry: 1 Cor 3:9.

His people: Ps 100:3; Zch 9:16.

House of God: 1 Tm 3:15; He 10:21; Household of God: Eph 2:19.

Israel of God: Ga 6:16.

Temple of God: 1 Cor 3:16; 2 Cor 6:16; Eph 2:20-22.

Temple of Holy Spirit: 1 Cor 6:19.

Sheep of his pasture: Ps 100:3.

Spiritual house: 1 Pe 2:5

ref. 164

Nature of the Church

160 It is divinely instituted: 1 Tm 3:15; Christ is its Head, Foundation, and Cornerstone: Mt 16:16-18; 1 Cor 3:11; Eph 1:3-5,22,23; 4:15; 5:23; Col 1:24; and it is built upon the divinely inspired teachings of the apostles and prophets: Eph 2:20; cp. Jn 17:20; *ref. 165,168,169.*

All believers in Christ throughout the world are members of it: Ro 12:4,5; 1 Cor 10:17; 12:12,13; Ga 3:26-28; 1 Pe 2:5; Re 5:9,10; *ref. 167,176.*

It is one, undivided church: Ac 4:32; Ro 12:5; 1 Cor 10:17; 12:12,13; Ga 3:28; Eph 4:4-6; *ref. 167.*

It is eternal: Ps 46:4,5; 125:1,2; Mt 16:18; Lk 1:33; 2 Pe 1:11; *ref. 166.*

The Marks of the Church

161 It is invisible in the sense that only God knows who the true believers are: Lk 17:20,21; Jn 10:14; 1 Cor 8:3; 2 Tm 2:19; cp. 1 Kgs 19:8-18;

It is visible in the sense that it is found where the gospel is preached and the holy sacraments are administered according to Christ's institution: Mt 28:19,20; Mk 16:15,16; Lk 11:28; 22:19,20; Jn 3:5; Ac 2:41,42; 1 Cor 1:2; Ga 1:2; Eph 1:1; Php 1:1; Col 1:2; 1 Th 1:1; cp. Is 55:10,11; *ref. 169.*

The Work of the Church

162 To teach all nations all that Christ, the Lord of the church, has commanded: Mt 28:18-20; *ref. 315-358;*

To preach Christ's gospel in all the world: Mk 16:15; and to administer the holy sacraments: Mt 28:19; Mk 16:16; Lk 22:19; Jn 3:5; Ac 2:38; 10:48; 1 Cor 10:16,17; 11:26 *ref. 169;*

To exercise the Office of the Keys: Mt 18:15-20; Jn 20:21-23; 1 Cor 5:1-5; 2 Cor 13:2; Tt 3:10;

To do mission work: Mt 28:18,19; Mk 16:15; Lk 24:46-48; Ac 1:8; *ref. 169,1020-1081.*

To be active in works of faith and labors of love: Ac 6:1-7; 11:27-30; Ga 5:6; 6:10; He 13:16; 1 Jn 3:14-18; *ref. 163.*

Responsibilities of Church Membership

163 To attend worship services regularly: Lk 10:16; 11:28; Jn 8:47; He 10:25; cp. Ps 26:6-8; 27:4; 84;1,2; 122:1; to partake of the Lord's Supper frequently: Lk 22:19,20; Ac 2:42; 1 Cor 11:26; to be a doer of the word and not a hearer only: Jas 1:21-25; cp Mt 7:21; Lk 8:4-15; Jn 13:17; *ref. 170-175, 177-184;*

To grow in grace and Christian knowledge: Eph 1:15-23; 3:14-19; 4:14-16; Col 1:9-11; 1 Pe 2:2; 2 Pe 3:18;

To use the talents God has entrusted for service in Christ's kingdom: Mt 25:14-30; Lk 19:12f; Ro 12:3-8; 1 Cor 12:4-30; 1 Pe 4:10,11; *ref. 183-187,1368;*

To witness for Christ by word and deed: Mt 5:13-16; Mk 5:19,20; Ac 1:8; 4:20; 2 Cor 3:2,3; Php 2:15,16; 1 Pe 2:9-12; *ref. 181, Mission Work 1020-1081;*

To be active in works of faith and labors of love: Mt 25:34-40; Ga 5:6; 6:10; He 13:16; 1 Jn 3:14-18. *ref. 183-200, 974-975;*

To support the ministry of the word through prayers and offerings: 1 Cor 9:14; Ga 6:6; Eph 6:19; 1 Th 5:25; 2 Th 3:1,2; 1 Tm 5:18; *ref. 173,176,198,200.*

164 The derivation of the word "church" is not certain. It is, perhaps, derived from the Greek *kyriake,* which means belonging to the Lord (*kurios*), or the Lord's house. The word used most frequently in the original Greek to designate the church is *ekklesia,* an assembly called out by some legitimate authority. The word is used this way more than a hundred times in the New Testament, e.g., Mt 16:18; 18:17; Ac 9:14; 1 Cor 10:32; Eph 1:22; 5:25-27. Derived form a root which means to call (*ekkalein*), the word "church" thus designates those who have been called together by Christ, or the whole company of God's elect.

In a wider sense the word "church" is also used to designate a church building, a congregation, a denomination, or a religious establishment; *ref. 159.*

† † †

165
>   The church's one Foundation
>   Is Jesus Christ, her Lord;
>   She is his new creation
>   By water and the word.
>   From heav'n he came and sought her
>   To be his holy Bride;
>   With his own blood he bought her,
>   And for her life he died.
>   — Samuel J. Stone

ref. 160

† † †

166 During World War II, in the city of Worms, the bronze statues of Martin Luther and his fellow reformers defied the bombings, strafings and artillery fire in 1945 much as the original Luther defied the imperial order to recant in 1521. The Luther monument escaped damage, although explosives dug craters only a short distance from its base.

So, too, the very gates of hell cannot prevail against the church. Built upon Christ as its foundation, the church cannot perish.

>   Crowns and thrones may perish,
>   Kingdoms rise and wane,
>   But the church of Jesus
>   Constant will remain.
>   Gates of hell can never
>   'Gainst that church prevail;
>   We have Christ's own promise,
>   And that cannot fail.
>   — Sabine Baring-Gould

ref. 160

† † †

167   Blest be the tie that binds
        Our hearts in Christian love;
     The fellowship of kindred minds
        Is like to that above.

     Before our Father's throne
        We pour our ardent prayers;
     Our fears, our hopes, our aims are one,
        Our comforts and our cares.

                           — John Fawcett

ref. 160

† † †

168 When the cornerstone of a certain church was laid it bore the inscription, "We Preach Christ Crucified." But in the course of time creeping ivy covered a portion of the cornerstone and now one could read only the first two words of the inscription, "We Preach." Meanwhile the message that was formerly proclaimed in the church had also changed. The philosophy of "demythologizing" the Scriptures had crept into the church and had produced its effects. The virgin birth of Christ, his miracles, his substitutionary death and his resurrection were no longer proclaimed. The church still preached, but it no longer preached "Christ Crucified," and therefore its message was as helpless to save sin-burdened souls "as a ragged doll would be able to assuage the tears of a grief-stricken mother mourning the loss of her only child"; *ref. 161,162.*

† † †

169   The Church is a vessel
        Sent out on the seas,
     Her banner uplifted,
        Her sails to the breeze;

     Her port every nation,
        The waste and the wild,
     The moor and the pampas,
        The heathen enisled;

     Her cargo the gospel,
        Her tidings of joy;
     Her crew the disciples
        In loving employ;

     Her Captain and Pilot,
        So mighty to save,
     Is Lord of the tempest,
        The wind, and the wave.

                         — W. M. Czamanske

ref. 160,162

† † †

170 A vacant congregation once wrote to Spurgeon's Divinity School and asked for a minister that would fill the church. The Doctor replied by stating that they made them only big enough to fill the pulpit, and that the congregation had to fill the church; *ref. 163.*

† † †

171 A lady phoned the pastor shortly before the church service was to begin and inquired: "Do you expect the president to be in church this morning?" The pastor's reply was: "Madam, I do not know whether or not the President of the United States will be in church this morning, but I do know that God will be there, and that should be sufficient reason for you to attend"; *ref. 163.*

† † †

172 Going to church is like going shopping. You generally get what you go for, no more and no less. You may go into a store where the shelves are loaded with hundreds of thousands of dollars' worth of goods and buy only a paper of pins. So you may go into God's storehouse of grace and take nothing away but the impression that the leading soloist has made on you. But even poor preaching and meager services furnish rich rewards to the soul that is really hungry and thirsty after righteousness.

— selected

ref. 163

† † †

173

Prayer Before Church

Lord Jesus, bless the pastor's word
And bless my hearing, too,
That after all is said and heard,
I may believe and do. Amen.

— Anon

174

Thy presence, gracious God, afford,
Prepare us to receive thy word;
Now let thy voice engage our ear,
And faith be mixed with what we hear.

Distracting thoughts and cares remove,
And fix our hearts and hopes above;
With food divine may we be fed,
And satisfied with living bread.

— J. Fawcett

ref. 163

† † †

175 In an Order dated May 2nd, 1778, at Valley Forge, George Washington wrote: "The Commander-in-Chief directs that divine service be performed every Sunday at eleven o'clock in each brigade which has a chaplain. Those brigades which have none will attend the place of worship nearest to them. It is expected that officers of all ranks will, by their attendance, set an example to their men. While we are on duty performing the duty of good soldiers we certainly ought not to be inattentive to the highest duties of religion. To the distinguished characteristics of a patriot it should be our highest glory to add the more distinguished characteristics of a Christian"; *ref. 163.*

† † †

176 God make the door of this church wide enough to receive all who need human love, fellowship and fatherly care; and narrow enough to shut out all envy, pride, and hate; make the threshold smooth so as to be no stumbling-block to children, to the weak or straying feet, but rugged and strong enough to turn back the tempter's power. God, make the doorway of this church to many souls the gateway of thy eternal kingdom.

— Anon

ref. 162

† † †

177 A beggar met a kind man on the highway. Seeing the beggar's need, the good man, having $7 in his pocket, proceeded to give him $6. Then the beggar knocked the merciful man down and stole the seventh dollar. He was a miserable wretch. But tell me, how base is the man to whom the Lord gives six days of the week but who proceeds to take the Lord's day also for his own selfish purpose!

— selected

178 A minister was conversing with a man who professed conversion. "Have you united with a church?" he asked him. "No, the dying thief never united with a church and he went to heaven," was the answer.

"Have you ever been at the Lord's Table?" "No, the dying thief never did either, and he was accepted."

"Have you ever given to missions?" "No, the dying thief did not, and he was not judged for it."

"Well, my friend," said the minister, "the difference between you two seems to be that he was a dying thief and you are a living one."

— C. H. Kilmer

ref. 163

179 A pastor went to the home of one of his parishioners whose absence from church services he had keenly felt. Without speaking a word the pastor went to the fireplace, took the pair of tongs, and lifted a live coal out of the fire. Both men watched as the flame died and the glowing coal became a dead, black cinder. "You won't have to say a word," said the member to the pastor, "I'll be back in my place next Sunday."

— selected

51

180 A stranger passing some mines in Pennsylvania asked a little boy why the field was so full of mules. The boy replied: "These mules are worked in the mine during the week and are brought up into the light on Sunday to keep them from going blind." As a Christian I, too, need to come up on Sunday, after the worries, struggles, and hardships of the week, to let the light of God's Word shine into my heart, lest I become spiritually blind.

— selected

181 A little girl had been pleading with her father to come to church with her. After a long argument the father finally said: "You and your mother go your way and I will go mine." "But, Daddy," said the little girl, "which way are you going?" This was a question that the father had not expected, and he didn't know the answer.

182 To say, "I don't need the church," is mere bravado. I needed it when my father died; I needed it when we were married and when our babies were taken from us, and I shall need it again, sooner or later, and need it badly. I am in good health now, and I could, I suppose, get along very nicely without a clergyman or choir or even prayer. But what sort of man is he who scorns and neglects and despises his best friend until his hour of tribulation?

— Edgar A. Guest

ref. 163

† † †

183 An aged lady, as she left the church one Sunday morning, was met by a young man on the street who asked: "Is the sermon done already?" "No," she replied, "It isn't done; it's only preached. I'm going out to do it now."

184 It is also a solemn thing to *hear* the Word preached. Take heed, therefore, how you hear, Lk 8:18. A lady who was present . . . where the celebrated E. Erskine was assisting was much impressed by the sermon. She went the next Sabbath to his own place of worship to hear him; but to her surprise, she felt none of those strong impressions she experienced in hearing him before. Wondering at this, she called on Mr. Erskine, and, stating the cause, asked what he thought might be the reason for such a difference in her feelings. He replied: "Madam, the reason is this: last Sunday you went to hear Jesus Christ; today you came to hear Ebenezer Erskine."

— Parren

ref. 163

† † †

185 The church is made up entirely of willing workers. There are those who are willing to work; and there are those who are willing to let them.

186   If all the others CAME like you
            Would there seldom be a vacant pew?
            Or would the opposite be true,
            If all the others came like you?

If all the others GAVE like you,
Then how much giving would your church do?
Would the bills be paid as they fell due,
If all the others gave like you?

If all the others WORKED like you,
Then how much service would your church do?
Would the Master's plans be carried through,
If all the others worked like you?

— Anon

ref. 163

† † †

187 Last Sunday I voted to close the church: not intentionally, not maliciously, perhaps, but carelessly, thoughtlessly, lazily, indifferently, I voted. I voted to close its doors that its witness and its testimony might be stopped. I voted to close the open Bible on its pulpit.... I voted for every missionary of the church to be called home, every native worker supported by the church to stop preaching, every hospital, every school, every dispensary in its foreign mission fields to close. And I voted that its colleges and seminaries close their doors and no longer bother to train its youth for Christian service. I voted for every home missionary project to be abandoned, every influence for good and right and for truth in our community to be curtailed and finally stopped. I voted for the darkness of superstition, the degrading influence of sin, the blight of ignorance and the curse of selfish greed once again to settle their damning load on the shoulders of an already overburdened world.

I voted all this, I say, and more, too . . . things that all human intellect cannot grasp and the human mind cannot find words to express. Carelessly, thoughtlessly, lazily, indifferently, I voted.

For, you see, I could have gone and I should have gone, but I didn't. I stayed away from church last Sunday.

— adapted from *Exchange*

ref. 163

† † †

188 "Is it a strong congregation?"

"Yes," was the reply.

"How many members are there?"

"Thirty."

"Thirty! Are they so wealthy?"

"No, many of them are poor."

"How, then, can you say it is a strong church?"

"Because they are earnest, devoted, at peace, loving each other, following the Word of God in all things, instant in prayer, and striving together to do the Lord's work. Such a congregation is strong, whether composed of thirty or three hundred members."

— *The Lutheran Annual*

189 A church is not measured in greatness by the beauty of its architecture or the ability of its ministry, but by the people who truly live and faithfully serve that for which it stands.

— John Bunyan

ref. 163

† † †

190
A good thing to remember,
And a better thing to do,
Is to work with the construction gang
And not with the wrecking crew.

— Anon

191
I watched them tear a building down,
A gang of men in a busy town.
With a ho-heave-ho and lusty yell
They swung a beam, and a building fell.
I asked the foreman: "Are these men skilled
As the men you'd hire if you had to build?"
He gave a laugh and said: "No, indeed!
Just common labor is all I need.
I can easily wreck in a day or two
What builders have taken a year to do."
And I thought to myself as I went away,
Which of these roles have I tried to play?
Am I a builder who works with care,
Giving the best and doing my share?
Am I shaping my deeds by a well-made plan,
Patiently doing the best I can?
Or am I a wrecker who walks the town
Content with the labor of tearing down?

— Anon

192 Two laborers were trying to place a stone in position on the foundation wall of a new building. A crowd was standing around looking on, and each one offered his criticism and counsel freely and loudly, but did not so much as lift a finger to help.

"That reminds me of church work," said a passerby to his friend.

"Why?"

"Because two men are doing the work, and twenty are doing the talking."

— W. G. Polack

ref. 163

† † †

193 There are thousands of stars which the eye of man has never seen, but which year by year help to light up the starry sky to enhance its glory.

When the Queen Mary and the Queen Elizabeth sail out of a harbor to the open seas, much of the work of moving them is done by little tugboats that

54

accompany the ships before and behind, pushing, pulling, puffing, panting, and guiding them safely on their way. While the great ships catch the eyes of the observing crowds, only scanty attention is given to the little tugs that do all the work.

What if *your* name is unpraised and *your* labor is unsung? If only you are faithful in using your talents which the Lord has given you, *he* will remember and reward. Serve the *Lord* with gladness where you are, where God has placed you to serve him in his kingdom.

— selected

194 A famous but highly temperamental soprano soloist was rehearsing to sing. Toscanini, the conductor, gave her the same instructions he gave to the other members of his orchestra. But that proved too much for the vanity of the singer, and she angrily remonstrated: "But, sir, I am the star of this performance."

Toscanini answered quietly: "Madam, in this performance there are no stars." Then he continued his instruction. He knew that unless the soloist, members of the chorus and the orchestra were willing to work together in perfect harmony, there would be no performance worth hearing.

Unity of thought and action are essential to success. Nowhere is this more true than in Christ's work. Good leadership is indeed necessary, but if everyone desires to have solo parts and be the star, there is bound to be failure.

— *Choice Gleanings Calendar*

ref. 160,163

† † †

195 Not doing more than the average is what keeps the average down.

196 As in machinery, it is not motion but friction that wrecks the church.

197
It is easier to preach than to practice,
It is easier to say than to do;
Most sermons are heard by the many
But taken to heart by the few.

It is easier to cheer than to battle,
It is easier to stay than to go;
To drift you but lay down the oars,
To go up the stream you must row.

— Anon

198
More tithes and fewer drives;
More action and less faction;
More workers and fewer shirkers;
More backers and fewer slackers;
More praying and less straying.

— Anon

199 Some churches are so cold that one would believe the members are God's frozen people instead of his chosen people.

55

200 An artist was asked to paint a picture of a decaying church. To the astonishment of many, instead of putting on the canvass an old, tottering ruin, the artist painted a stately edifice of modern grandeur. Through the open portals could be seen the richly carved pulpit, the magnificent organ, and the beautiful stained glass windows. Within the grand entrance was an offering plate of elaborate design for the offerings to missions. A cobweb was over the receptacle for foreign missions!

— Gospel Herald

ref. 163

CHURCH AND STATE 201-204

(ref.: Government, Civil 435-460; Kingdom of Christ 650-663)

Their Respective Spheres

201 The work of the state and of the church neither include nor exclude each other. They are, side by side, in different domains; the state caring primarily for the bodily welfare of man, and the church caring primarily for man's spiritual wellbeing. Both are divinely sanctioned, for both are ordinances of God. In their respective spheres both demand our support: Mt 22:21.

Their Different Functions

202 The state is visible; the church is invisible: Lk 17:20;

The state is temporal; the church is eternal: Lk 1:33;

The state is secular; the church is spiritual: Jn 18:36,37;

The state is ruled by men; the church is ruled by Christ: Mt 23:8,10; Eph 1:22,23; 2:20-22;

The state seeks the bodily welfare of men; the church seeks the spiritual welfare of men: Ac 26:18; Eph 4:11-16; Col 1:12-14;

The state uses physical force as a means of executing its business; the church uses the spiritual weapons of God's Word to accomplish its purpose: Mt 26:52,53; 2 Cor 10:4; Eph 6:17; He 4:12,13; Zch 4:6;

The state is guided by natural law and the dictates of reason and conscience in its rule; the church is guided by the moral law of God and the gospel of Christ: Ps 119:9,105; Is 8:20; Mt 28:20; 1 Pe 4:11;

People are members of the state by birth; people become members of the church by spiritual regeneration: Jn 3:5; Ga 3:26.

Mutual Respect and Support

203 The state should respect the church as a moral influence for good; the church should respect the state as God's minister for the protection and preservation of peace and order which enables it to carry on its work: Ro 13:1-7; 1 Tm 2:1-3; Tt 3:1; 1 Pe 2:13,14;

The state must not interfere with the work of the church; the church must not interfere with the work of the state: Mt 22:21; Lk 12:14; Ac 18:12-16; 23:29; 25:11,17-21.

Resources

204 The state must not enact laws favoring any one religion, nor use its powers to force people to worship (cf. the First Amendment of the Constitution of the U.S.).

The church must not strive for temporal power or use its influence to compel the state to enact civil legislation or use its political power to compel its members to perform religious duties (e.g., Sabbath laws; enforced religion in public schools; sending an ambassador to the Vatican, etc.); *ref. 201-203.*

CONFESSION 205-209

(ref.: Faith 359; Repentance 1253f)

The Necessity of Confession

205 On the necessity of confession see Lv 26:40-45; 2 Chr 7:14; Ps 32:3-5; 51:1-12; Pr 28:13; 1 Jn 1:8,9; *ref. 208,209.*

The Nature of Confession

206 All sins, known and unknown, are to be confessed to God: Ps 19:12; Jr 2:22; 16:17; 23:24; Mt 6:12; Lk 15:18-21;

Sins against our fellowmen are to be confessed to them, as well as to God: Mt 5:23,24; 18:15; Jas 5:16; *ref. 208.*

Examples of Confession

207 Achan: Jos 7:20; Saul: 1 Sm 15:24; David: 2 Sm 12:13; 24:10; Ps 32:5; 41:4; 51:3,4; Job: Job 7:20; Peter: Lk 5:8; the prodigal son: Lk 15:18; the malefactor: Lk 23:41; see also Lv 16:20-22; *ref. 208,209.*

Resources

208 One of the hardest things in life is to confess to a wrong and to ask for forgiveness. Because of the perverseness of his nature, which he inherited from his parents Adam and Eve, man seeks to hide his sin or, failing in that, tries to shift the blame for it upon someone else, Gn 3:6-13. But the Scriptures declare: "He that covereth his sins shall not prosper; but whoso confesseth and forsaketh them shall have mercy," Pr 28:13.

A certain prince once visited a prison with the intention of freeing one of the prisoners. He spoke to each prisoner in turn, asking each one why he was being punished. One after the other the prisoners offered excuses for their crime. At length, however, the prince came to one who frankly confessed his guilt and admitted that he was receiving his just punishment. The prince released that man.

It is thus, says St. John, that God deals with us: "If we say that we have no sin, we deceive ourselves, and the truth is not in us. If we confess our sins, he is faithful and just to forgive us our sins, and to cleanse us from all unrighteousness. If we say that we have not sinned, we make him a liar, and his Word is not in us," 1 Jn 1:8-10; *ref. 205-207.*

† † †

209 Luke 15 records Christ's parables of the Lost Sheep, the Lost Coin, and the Lost Son. The chapter begins with the words, "Now the tax collectors and 'sinners' were all gathering around to hear him [Christ]. But the Pharisees and the teachers of the law muttered, 'This man welcomes sinners and eats with them.' "

Speaking on this text, a pastor once pointed out how these words stress two important truths. They tell us, first, that *only Jesus receives sinners;* he alone is their Friend and Savior, and there is none other to whom they can turn for forgiveness and help. But secondly, these words also tell us that *Jesus receives only sinners,* only such who acknowledge their guilt and seek his forgiveness. "It is not the healthy," he said, "who need a doctor, but the sick. I have not come to call the righteous, but sinners," Mk 2:17.

> Jesus sinners doth receive;
>   Oh, may all this saying ponder
> Who in sin's delusions live
>   And from God and heaven wander!
> Here is hope for all who grieve —
>   Jesus sinners doth receive.
>   — Erdmann Neumeister

ref. 205,206

CONSCIENCE 210-224

(ref.: Law of God 865-896; Ten Commandments 1460-1502)

Bible References

210 The Old Testament: The word "conscience" does not occur in the Old Testament. However, the functions of conscience are referred to in a number of ways, e.g.:

Following their transgression of God's command, Adam and Eve were afraid and tried to hide themselves: Gn 3:10;

After Cain had killed his brother Abel he was filled with remorse: Gn 4:13;

Jacob's sons were troubled by an evil conscience for having sold their brother Joseph into slavery: Gn 42:21f;

David's conscience bothered him day and night because of his sin against Bathsheba and Uriah: 2 Sm 12:13; Ps 32:3-5; 38:1-10; 40:12; 51:1-4.

211 The New Testament: In the New Testament the word "conscience" occurs thirty times, with various shades of meaning: Jn 8:9; Ac 23:1; 24:16; Ro 2:15; 9:1; 13:5; 1 Cor 8:7,10,12; 10:25,27-29; 2 Cor 1:12; 4:2; 5:11;1 Tm 1:5,19; 3:9; 4:2; 2 Tm 1:3; Tt 1:15; He 9:9,14; 10:2,22; 13:18; 1 Pe 2:19; 3:16,21; *ref. 213.*

Various Descriptions

212 A *good* and *enlightened,* or a *clear* conscience: one that is guided by the Word of God and in agreement with the moral law of God as revealed in Holy Scriptures: Ps 12:6; 19:7-11; 36:9; 119:105,130; Pr 6:23; 30:5; Ac 23:1; 24:16; 1 Tm 1:5,19; 3:9; 2 Tm 1:3; He 13:18; 1 Pe 3:16,21; 2 Pe 1:19. Such a conscience is one that has been cleansed by the atoning blood of Christ: He 9:13,14; 1 Pe 2:19; 3:21; 1 Jn 1:7; *ref. 214-219.*

An *accusing* and *evil* conscience: one whose voice testifies loud and clear and unmistakably: Jn 8:9; He 10:22; *ref. 221,222.*

An *erring* conscience: one that does not conform to the will of God laid down in the rule of his law: Ro 14:5; 1 Cor 8:7; *ref. 223.*

A *weak* conscience: one whose voice has been suppressed so that it registers only faintly if at all: 1 Cor 8:7,10,12;

A *doubting* conscience: one which cannot come to a definite conclusion in some undertaking or act: Ro 14:23;

A *seared* or *dead* conscience: one that has been suppressed and silenced so repeatedly that it has become insensitive: 1 Tm 4:2; Tt 1:15.

Resources

213 Conscience is a precious gift of God with which all men are endowed from birth. Like the intellectual ability to perceive, to think, to reason, to learn, and to remember, and like the physical ability to see, to hear, to speak, and to feel, so conscience is a wonderful faculty of the soul, the inner voice, which makes a person conscious of God who revealed himself in the moral law as being holy and as demanding holiness of all men.

Man's understanding of what is right and wrong is based on his knowledge of the moral law of God written in his heart: Ro 1:19,20; 2:14,15. Acting as a monitor, conscience urges man to do what he believes to be morally right and to avoid doing what he believes to be morally wrong. It is like an alarm clock. Failure to heed the voice of conscience results in silencing, and eventually hardening, it to a point where it ceases to function.

However, man's conscience is not always an unerring guide. As a part of his total being, man's conscience too has been corrupted by sin: Gn 8:21; Ps 51:5; Eph 2:1-3. As a consequence, the law of God written in his heart has been largely obscured, and his knowledge of what is right and wrong is incomplete and in need of instruction by God's Word: Ro 7:7; cp Mt 5:28; 1 Jn 3:15. Nevertheless, the natural knowledge of the law of God and the voice of conscience serve a good and vital purpose. The law of God serves as a curb which checks, at least in a measure, the course outbursts of sin. And the voice of conscience, even though subject to human weakness, testifies against man and prevents him, at least in a measure, from carrying out all the rash desires that lurk in his sinful heart, or it may help to prevent him from repeating his sinful acts: Gn 4:6,7; Jr 17:9; Mt 15:19; Ro 3:10-18; ref. 210-212.

† † †

214 Only those whose hearts have been purified and cleansed by the precious blood of Christ are conscious of the fact that God requires us to conform our whole life to his will as it is revealed in the Bible. Only Christians strive "to have always a conscience void of offence toward God, and toward men": see Ac 24:16; 1 Tm 1:5.

215
> Order my footsteps by thy word
> And make my heart sincere;
> Let sin have no dominion, Lord,
> But keep my conscience clear.
>
> — Isaac Watts

ref. 212

† † †

216 So long as the conscience of man is not directed by the Word of God it remains an evil conscience; the sinner owes a continual debt that he cannot pay: He 10:1-3. It is only through faith in Jesus Christ and his atoning sacrifice that the evil conscience of man becomes a good conscience, for in Christ the debt is paid: 1 Pe 2:19; 3:21.

217
> In vain we call old notions fudge
> And bend our conscience to our dealing.
> The Ten Commandments will not budge
> And stealing will be stealing.
>
> — Motto of American Copyright League

ref. 212

† † †

218 Labor to keep in your breast that little spark of celestial fire, called conscience.

— George Washington

219 I desire to conduct the affairs of this administration that if at the end, when I come to lay down the reins of power, I have lost every other friend on earth, I shall have at least one friend left, and that friend shall be down inside me.

ref. 212

— Abraham Lincoln

† † †

220 When at the Diet of Worms, Martin Luther was asked to recant, he replied, "My conscience is bound in God's Word. I cannot and will not recant anything. Here I stand, I cannot do otherwise. God help me! Amen"; *ref. 212*.

† † †

221 Many a criminal, accused and stricken by an evil conscience, has been led to confess his crime. Conscience is man's constant companion from which he cannot run away. A person may indeed commit a sin and succeed in concealing it from men. But it is impossible to hide an evil conscience from the eyes of the omniscient God who searches the heart, who understands our thoughts afar off, and who knows our every way and every word we speak: Ps 44:21; 139:1-12; Jr 17:10.

222 A man who went to steal corn from his neighbor's field took his little boy with him to keep a lookout and to warn him in case anyone came along. Before he began to pluck the corn he looked around and seeing no one he began to fill his bag with corn. Just then his son cried out: "Father, there is one way you haven't looked yet!" The father, supposing that someone was coming, asked his son which way he meant, and the son replied: "You forgot to look up!" Conscience-stricken, the father took the boy by the hand and hurried home without the corn.

ref. 211,212

— Walter B. Knight

† † †

223 Even the conscience of Christian people sometimes errs because they are not perfect and because their knowledge of God's will as revealed in his Word is deficient. A case in point is the "conscientious objector" who misunderstands the commandment, "Thou shall not commit murder!" Ex 20:13, to mean that even the established government does not have the right to wage a just war or to exact the supreme penalty of life in the case of a capital crime: cp Ezr 7:26; Pr 24:21; Mt 22:21; Jn 19:11; Ro 13:1-7; Tt 3:1; 1 Pe 2:13,14,17.

Meanwhile, however, as Martin Luther so aptly said, it is unsafe and dishonest to act contrary to one's conscience: cp Ac 4:19,20; 5:29.

224   Give me a healthy frame,
And may I have within
A conscience free from blame,
A soul unhurt by sin.
                                    — Johann Herrmann
ref. 212

CONVERSION 225-241

(ref.: Holy Spirit 506-533)

What It Is

225 In the narrower sense, conversion is the work of God by which man is *brought* from his natural state of sin, wrath, and spiritual death into a state of spiritual life, faith, and grace: Eph 2:1-9; Col 1:13,14;

In the wider sense, it is the entire process by which man is transformed into a new creature in Christ and *continues* in a state of faith and spiritual life. Thus it includes within its scope the fruits of saving faith: 2 Cor 5:17; Eph 2:8-10;

Other expressions in Scripture for conversion are "new birth," or being "born again": Jn 1:13; 3:3,5; 1 Pe 1:23; 1 Jn 2:29; 3:9; 4:7; "washing of regeneration and renewing of the Holy Ghost," Tt 3:5; and being "begotten" by the Word of truth: Jas 1:18; 1 Pe 1:3; 1 Jn 5:1; *ref. 230-232.*

Why It Is Necessary

226 By birth and nature all mankind are conceived and born in sin: Ps 51:5; sinful flesh born of sinful flesh: Jn 3:6; Ro 3:23, 5:12; inclined only toward that which is evil in the sight of God: Gn 8:21; Ro 8:7; under the wrath of God, the bondage of Satan, and the slavery of sin: Ro 1:18; Eph 2:1-3; 4:18; 1 Jn 5:19;

Left to themselves, all mankind would be helplessly, hopelessly and eternally lost: Ps 49:7,8; Is 64:6; Jr 2:22; Ro 3:20; *ref. 230,231.*

When It takes Place

227 Conversion takes place when, by the power of the Holy Spirit working through the law and the gospel, a person is brought to the knowledge of his sin and comes to faith in Christ as his Savior from sin. The Bible speaks of this as a *turning* of the heart of man from sin to grace: Ps 51:13; Ac 2:37,38; 3:19; 9:35; 11:21; 14:15; 26:18; Jas 5:19,20; 1 Pe 2:25; *ref. 232-236.*

How It Is Accomplished

228 Not by man's effort: Jn 6:44; Ro 3:24,25; 8:7; 1 Cor 1:23; 2:14; Eph 2:1,8,9; Php 2:13; 2 Tm 1:9; Tt 3:5-7;

But by the Holy Spirit working through the means of grace (the gospel in word and sacrament): Jn 1:13; 3:5; 6:63; 15:3; Ro 1:17; 1 Cor 4:15; 6:11; 12:3; Ga 1:15; 2:16; 1 Th 2:13; 2 Th 2:14; Jas 1:18; 1 Pe 1:23; *ref. 237,239,241.*

Its Results for Us

229 We have been released from our sins, delivered from Satan's kingdom of darkness and translated into the kingdom of God, called the children of God and heirs of heaven and eternal life: Jn 3:5,6; Ro 8:16,17,30; Ga 3:26; Col 1:12-14; Tt 3:5-7;

We are led by the Holy Spirit: Ro 8:14-17; Ga 5:22-26; Eph 5:8,9;

We serve Christ in newness of life: Lk 1:74,75; Ro 6:4-13; 2 Cor 5:17; Ga 2:20; Eph 2:10; 4:21-24f; Php 1:21;

We look forward in hope to eternal glory: Ro 8:18-23; 2 Cor 4:17,18; 1 Pe 1:3-9; *ref. 233-237,240,241.*

Resources

230 The biblical teaching of conversion is of paramount importance because it shows how the salvation which was won by Christ becomes the possession of the individual sinner for his eternal salvation; *ref. 226.*

231
> All our knowledge, sense, and sight
> Lie in deepest darkness shrouded
> Till thy Spirit breaks our night
> With the beams of truth unclouded.
> — Tobias Clausnitzer

ref. 225

† † †

232 Conversion takes place when the Holy Spirit works repentance and faith in the heart of the sinner. Some Christians are able to recall the exact time of their conversion: the conversion of Saul: Ac 9:3f; of Cornelius and his household: Ac 10:44-48; of the jailor at Philippi and his household: Ac 16:30-33; of Lydia and her household: Ac 16:14,15. For others, the working of spiritual knowledge and faith is like the seed that springs up, "he knoweth not how," Mk 4:27. For many the spiritual rebirth was effected in infancy, through holy baptism: cp Jn 3:5; Ac 2:38,39; Tt 3:5-7; 1 Pe 3:21. It is not essential that we should know the exact time of our conversion, but it is necessary to know that we have been converted, and this we know in the fact that we believe the promises of God; *ref. 227.*

† † †

233 St. Augustine is known as one of the great fathers of the early church. Prior to his conversion to Christ, at the age of thirty-two, his life had been stained by many heinous sins. His pious mother, Monica, had often prayed for him and had tried to lead him to Christ, but to no avail. Like Felix, the governor of whom we read in Acts 24, Augustine thought that the matter of his soul's salvation could be put off until some later time. "Lord, make me a Christian," he said, "but not yet!"

One day while walking in a garden, Augustine heard a child's voice from a neighboring house repeating in Latin the simple words: "*Tolle! Lege!*" (Take up and read!). He quickly picked up a copy of St. Paul's letter to the Romans, which he had been reading previously, opened it to chapter 13 and read, Let us walk honestly, as in the day; not in rioting and drunkenness, not in chambering and wantonness, not in strife and envying. But put on the Lord Jesus Christ, and make no provision to fulfill the desires of the flesh! After reading these words he went to his home, told his mother of his experience and of his intention to become a Christian.

Later Augustine referred to the incident of his conversion and wrote in his *Confessions*: "I grasped the book, opened it, and in silence read that paragraph on which my eyes first fell — 'Not in rioting and drunkenness, not in chambering and wantonness, not in strife and envying. But put on the Lord Jesus Christ, and make no provision to fulfill the desires of the flesh!' No further would I read, nor did I need; for instantly, as the sentence ended — by a light, as it were, of serenity which infused my heart — all the gloom of doubt vanished away"; *ref. 227,229.*

† † †

234 Martin Luther's experience was very much like that of the Apostle Paul. Like Paul, Luther sought his righteousness by the works of the law (cp. Php 3:4-14). As a pious monk, Luther was most zealous in performing every work to which the church had directed him, such as fasting, praying, meditating, beating his body, making pilgrimages, and the like. The church of his day had falsely taught him that when the "gospel" speaks of righteousness of God, it means the righteousness which God demands from us, whereas in truth it means the righteousness which Christ has procured for us by his atoning death on the cross. By the grace of God, Luther made that wonderful discovery while studying those words as they are quoted in the context of Paul's Letter to the Romans, "the just shall live by faith" (Ro 1:17). And when he made that discovery, he joyfully exclaimed, "All the Scriptures now appeared to me in a different light. Now I felt myself reborn. This message became for me the gate that leads to Paradise!"

Now, with a clear understanding of Paul's inspired words, Luther wrote, "You, O Lord Jesus, are my righteousness, and I am your sin; you have taken what was mine, and have given me what was yours!" *ref. 227, 229.*

† † †

235 On the day of his conversion, John Bunyan wrote: "I was so taken with the love and mercy of God that I knew not how to contain myself till I got home. I thought I could have spoken of his love to the very crows that sat upon the ploughed lands before me"; *ref. 229.*

† † †

236 John Newton, who wrote the hymn "How Sweet the Name of Jesus Sounds," confessed, "I was once a wild thing on the coast of Africa, but the

Lord caught me and tamed me; and now people come to see me like the lions in the Tower. Doubt if the Lord can convert a heathen? Look at me!" *ref. 227,229.*

† † †

237

Lord, 'tis not that I did choose thee;
  That, I know, could never be;
For this heart would still refuse thee
  Had thy grace not chosen me.

Thou hast from the sin that stained me
  Washed and cleansed and set me free,
And unto this end ordained me,
  That I ever live to thee.

'Twas thy grace in Christ that called me,
  Taught my darkened heart and mind;
Else this world had yet enthralled me,
  To thy heav'nly glories blind.

Now my heart owns none above thee;
  For thy grace alone I thirst,
Knowing well that, if I love thee,
  Thou, O Lord, didst love me first.

— Josiah Conder

ref. 228

† † †

238 A young preacher went to Spurgeon to ask why he did not have conversions in his ministry.

"You do not expect to make a convert after every sermon, do you?" Spurgeon asked.

The young preacher replied, "Oh, no, of course I do not expect them after every sermon."

"That is just the reason why you do not get them after every sermon," was Spurgeon's reply.

— The Missionary Worker

ref. 227

† † †

239 The manner of conversion remains a mystery to the mind of natural man: 1 Cor 1:18; 2:14. When Nicodemus asked how it would be possible for a person to be born again, Christ answered: "Do not marvel that I told you, you must be born again. The wind blows wherever it pleases. You hear its sound, but you cannot tell where it comes from or where it is going. So it is with everyone born of the Spirit," Jn 3:7,8.

When Nicodemus still tried to reason this matter out in his mind, and asked:

65

"How can these things be?" Christ replied: "If I have told you earthly things and you do not believe them, how will you believe if I tell you about heavenly things?"

One might ask similar questions, like these: If you cannot understand how a seed that is sown in the ground dies and produces a new plant, how do you hope to understand how a person who is dead in trespasses and sins can be spiritually reborn? If you cannot understand the marvel of human birth, how can you understand the mystery of the incarnation of the Son of God? If you cannot understand such a common thing as energy that is stored up in countless atoms so small that they cannot be seen and which is stored up everywhere, how can you hope to understand the concept of God who is invisible, eternal, omnipotent, and present everywhere? If you cannot understand countless mysteries in creation, how do you hope to understand the mysterious essence and work of the Creator? cp Ro 11:33-36; 1 Tm 1:17; 6:16; 1 Jn 4:12; Is 55:8,9; *ref. 227.*

240 Back in the third century Cyprian the Bishop of Carthage wrote to his friend Donatus: "It is a bad world, Donatus, an incredibly bad world. But I have discovered, in the midst of it, a quiet and holy people who have learned a great secret. They have found a joy which is a thousand times better than any of the pleasures of our sinful life. They are despised and persecuted, but they care not. They are masters of their souls. These people, Donatus, are Christians — and I am one of them."

— Sunday School Times
ref. 229

† † †

241   How can I thank thee, Lord
           For all thy lovingkindness,
        That thou hast patiently
           Borne with me in my blindness?
        When dead in many sins
           And trespasses I lay
        I kindled, holy God,
           Thine anger ev'ry day.

        It is thy work alone
           That I am now converted;
        O'er Satan's work in me
           Thou hast thy pow'r asserted,
        Thy mercy and thy grace
           That rise afresh each morn
        Have turned my stoney heart
           Into a heart newborn.

        Grant that thy Spirit's help
           To me be always given
        Lest I shoud fall again
           And lose the way to heaven;

66

That he may give me strength
In mine infirmity
And e'er renew my heart
To serve thee willingly.
— David Denicke
ref. 227,229

CREATION 242-261

(ref.: Providence, Divine 1195-1221)

The Creation of the World Was an Act of God

242 Before the creation of the world only God was there: Gn 1:1f; Ps 90:1,2; Col 1:17; He 1:10-12;

In the beginning God created heaven and earth and all things visible and invisible: Gn 1:1f; 2:7; Ex 20:11; Ps 89:11; 146:6; Ac 4:24; 14:15; 17:24; Ro 1:20; Col 1:16,17; He 3:4; *ref. 245-251.*

God created all things by his Word: Gn 1:3f; Ps 33:6,9; Jn 1:1-3; He 11:3;

Creation was an act of the Triune God: Gn 1:2; Job 26:13; Ps 33:6; 104:30; Jn 1:1-3; 1 Cor 8:6; Eph 3:9; Col 1:16,17; He 1:1-3;

The creation revealed God's goodness: Ps 136:1f; his power: Ps 115:3, and his wisdom: Ps 19:1; 104:24; 136:5; Jr 10:12; *ref. 252-257,259-261.*

Man is the Crown of God's Creation

243 God created man and woman and gave them dominion over all of his creatures: Gn 1:26-28;

God formed man out of the dust of the earth and breathed into him the breath of life: Gn 2:7,21-23; see also Ps 139:14;

God created man in his own image: Gn 1:26,27; man was made like God in this, that man was without sin and desired to do God's will: Eph 4:24; Col 3:10.

The Purpose of Creation

244 To serve for the glory and praise of God: Ps 19:1; 26:7; 97:6; 103:22; 136:1f; 139:14; 145:10; 148-150;

To serve for the welfare of man: Gn 1:28; Ps 65:9; 92:4; 104:24; 111:2; 115:16; Eccl 3:11; Mt 5:45; 6:26-30; Ac 14:17; 1 Tm 6:17; *ref. 252-256.*

Resources

245 Henry Ward Beecher, a famous minister, had in his study a beautiful globe which pictured the stars in the heavens. One day when Robert Ingersoll, who was an unbeliever, visited the minister, he saw the globe. "This is a wonderful piece of work," he said, "who made it?" Mr. Beecher, pretending to be surprised, answered: "Who made it? Why, nobody made it. It just happened."

This famous minister wanted to impress upon the unbeliever that it is foolish to suppose that things just originate themselves. The beautiful globe in his study did not come into being by itself. Some master builder had made it. What was true of that tiny model is also true of the world itself, as the Scriptures declare when they say: "Every house is built by someone, but God is the builder of everything," He 3:4.

† † †

246 There is no possibility of "spontaneous generation," that is, of life originating by itself. Life only comes from life. This simple but important truth is recognized, for example, when surgical instruments in a hospital are placed into a sterilized container to prevent any contact with life-bearing germs.

Moreover, each form of life reproduces only its own form of life: Gn 1:11. Therefore failure to acknowledge God as the Creator poses the impossible task of explaining the origin of the myriads of complex forms of life in the world, each of which reproduces only itself; *ref. 242,243.*

† † †

247 Professor Edwin Conklin, the great Princeton University biologist said: "The probability of life originating from accident is comparable to the probability of the Unabridged Dictionary resulting from an explosion in a printing factory."

248 "It is to me unthinkable that a real atheist should exist at all. Every man who is sufficiently in his senses to recognize his own ability and comprehend the problem of existence must also recognize the existence of Something, a Power, a Being, in whom and because of whom he himself lives. It is God that gives meaning to the mystery of life."

— Prof. R. A. Millikan, Nobel Prize Winner

249 "Posterity will one day laugh at the foolishness of the modern materialistic philosopher. The more I study nature, the more I stand amazed at the works of the Creator. I pray while I am engaged in my work in the laboratory. Happy is the man who has a God in his heart to whom obedience is rendered."

— Louis Pasteur

250 A young high school teacher of science did not conceal from his class that he was an agnostic, if not an atheist. He told the students: "Unless you shake off the old-fashioned views and accept the new, the world will leave you behind. Putting your faith in God may be all right, but you cannot stop there. Take rain-making! What did our fathers get for all their faith? The dust bowl! Now all we do is to send up a plane, drop some chemicals on a cloud, and it rains. No question about that, is there?" To the teacher's surprise a drawling farm boy remarked: "Sure there's a question. Who supplies the cloud?"

— Power

ref. 242,243

† † †

251 There are times when an atheist's faith fails him. While Bishop Dubbe, of the German Evangelical Church, was on a passage across the Atlantic, he endured shipwreck. As the vessel was sinking, a blatant infidel who had several times made light of the good bishop's religious belief, began to cry, "Lord, have mercy upon us!" "Don't say that," said the bishop, who was standing at his side, "you have no faith in prayer." "O bishop," said the frightened skeptic, "there is a vast difference between being on dry land and on the deck of a sinking ship!"

— James Mooers

ref. 242,243

† † †

252
> There's not a plant nor flower below
>   But makes thy glories known;
> And clouds arise and tempests blow
>   By order from thy throne.

— Isaac Watts

ref. 242

† † †

253 In his explanation of the First Article of the *Apostles' Creed,* Martin Luther summarized the work of creation in the words:

"I believe that God has made me with all creatures, giving me my body and soul, eyes, ears, and all my members, my reason and all my faculties; and that he still preserves me; therefore richly and daily providing clothing and shoes, meat and drink, house and home, wife and children, land, cattle, and all my goods, and all that I need to keep my body and life; defending me against all danger, and guarding and protecting me from all evil; and all this purely out of fatherly, divine goodness and mercy, without any merit or worthiness in me; for all of which it is my duty to thank and praise, to serve and obey him. This is most certainly true"; *ref. 242-244.*

† † †

254
> There's not a tint that paints the rose
>   Or decks the lily fair,
> Or streaks the humblest flow'r that blows,
>   But God has placed it there.
> There's not of grass a single blade
>   Or leaf of loviest green,
> Where heavenly skill is not displayed
>   And heavenly wisdom seen.

69

There's not a star whose twinkling light
   Shines on the distant earth,
And cheers the silent gloom of night,
   But God has given it birth.

There's not a place on earth's vast round,
   In ocean deep or air,
Where skill and wisdom are not found:
   For God is everywhere.

Around, within, below, above,
   His providence extends;
He everywhere displays his love,
   And power with mercy blends.
              — James Cowden Wallace

255 A professor once said: "I know just exactly the composition of this seed." He was professor of biology and held in his hand a little brown seed, which he showed to his friends. "This seed," he said, "has in it nitrogen, hydrogen, and carbon. I know the exact proportions; I understand perfectly how it is put together and how it works. But still that seed puzzles me; there is something about it which I cannot comprehend. I can make a seed that will look exactly like it. But if I plant that seed, it will come to naught; its elements will be absorbed by the soil. It will perish, decay, be no more. Yet if I plant the seed which God has made, it will become a plant and bear fruit, because it contains the mysterious principle which we call the life's principle. God has made the seed a living thing, which I cannot do, which science cannot do."

256
        O Lord my God, when I in awesome wonder
           Consider all the worlds thy hands have made,
        I see the stars, I hear the rolling thunder,
           Thy pow'r thro'out the universe displayed.
        Then sings my soul, my Saviour God, to thee;
           How great thou art, how great thou art!
                      — Stuart K. Hine

ref. 242-244

257 A professor of astronomy had the following to say about a few stars: "Polaris, the familiar north star, is one of the nearest to the earth, and yet the light from it is seventy years in reaching the earth, while the sun, at a distance of ninety-three million miles, sends its light to us in eight and one-half minutes. If the north star were the same distance, its light would appear one hundred times as bright as the sun. Marvelous as this is, the light of Deneb is eighteen times brighter than that of Polaris; Antares, twenty times; Rigel, forty, and Canopus, one hundred!

"Halley's comet, which was visible the last time in 1910, makes a circuit of ten billion miles once every seventy-five years, approximately, going at the rate of an average speed a trifle less than four and a half miles a second.

"The mind is deeply dazed when contemplating such wonders of the universe. And yet there is something more wonderful than any or all of these combined. Reflect upon these words in the eighth psalm: "When I consider thy heavens, the work of thy fingers, the moon and the stars which thou hast ordained; what is man that thou art mindful of him? and the son of man, that thou visitest him? For thou hast made him a little lower than the angels and hast crowned him with glory and honor.' "

— selected

258   Praise to the Lord, the Almighty, the King of creation!
O my soul, praise him, for he is thy Health and Salvation!
Join the full throng;
Wake, harp and psalter and song;
Sound forth in glad adoration!

— Joachim Neander

259 "To us, as we look at the stars on a winter night, they seem close together; but in reality they are so far apart that human arithmetic can hardly count the distance. The most distant stars of the Milky Way are calculated to be one hundred thousand trillions of miles distant from the earth. The successful measurement of the great star Betelgeuse, makes our vast sun look like a mere dot. Our sun is 860,400 miles in diameter; but it would take 27,000,000 of our suns to make one star like Betelgeuse, whose diameter is 350,000,000 miles.

"We boast of our airplanes, although almost every day we read of one crashing, with the immediate annihilation of all who sailed in it; but what shall we say of these great engines of the Creator? An airplane traveling at the rate of 100 miles per hour would require 1,000 years to circumnavigate a star like Betelgeuse, and that without stopping a second for birth and death of successive generations of pilots.

"When we have facts and figures like these pronounced to us, and then remember that we are dealing only with that universe which is visible to man's eye, or within the range of man's vision augmented by the most powerful lens, our mind begins to reel, and we request the astronomer to roll up his chart and put a cap over his telescope and let our amazed and staggering intellects rest."

— Clarence E. Macartney

260 "How do you know whether there is a God?" was once asked of a Bedouin; and he replied, "How do I know whether a camel or a man passed by my tent last night? By their footprints in the sand." — "The heavens declare the glory of God." (Ps 19:1).

— *Christian Digest*

261   The heav'ns declare thy glory, Lord;
In ev'ry star thy wisdom shines;
But when our eyes behold thy word,
We read thy name in fairer lines.

The rolling sun, the changing light,
   And nights and days, thy pow'r confess,
But the blest volume thou hast writ
   Reveals thy justice and thy grace.

Sun, moon, and stars convey thy praise
   'Round the whole earth, and never stand:
So when thy truth began its race,
   It touch'd and glanc'd on ev'ry land.

Nor shall thy spreading gospel rest
   Till thro' the world thy truth has run;
Till Christ has all the nations bless'd
   That see the light or feel the sun.
                              — Isaac Watts
ref. 242-244

CROSS, THE CHRISTIAN 262-272

(ref.: Affliction 1-36)

False Views

262 It is a false view to identify the "cross" with every form of suffering that befalls mankind whether they are Christians or not, e.g., suffering hunger, thirst, loss of property, sickness, and death.

It is likewise a false view to identify as a "cross" the suffering that Christian people sometimes bring upon themselves through their own sinful folly: cp 1 Pe 2:20; 4:12-16; *ref. 1-36.*

Correct View

263 By the Christian cross is meant the sufferings that Christian people are called upon to endure in the world for Christ's sake and for the sake of his gospel, such as self-denial, the pain and shame of ridicule, persecution, and, if need be, death: Mt 10:38; 16:24; 24:9; Mk 8:34; 10:21; Lk 9:23; 14:27; Jn 15:18-21; 16:1-4; Ac 14:22; 2 Tm 3:12; 1 Pe 2:21; *ref. 264-272.*

While Christ's cross alone atones for sin, his followers are called upon to bear the Christian cross so that they might be conformed to his image: Ro 8:29; 2 Cor 4:10,11; Ga 2:20; 5:24. As the cross was the way to glory for Christ, Php 2:8-11, so it is for his followers the way that leads to the crown of life: Mt 5:11,12; Ro 8:18; 2 Cor 4:16-18; 2 Tm 4:6-8,18; Re 2:10. For as the Christian cross conforms them to the likeness of Christ's death, so it also makes them partakers of his resurrection and of his life: Ro 6:3,4; 8:17; 2 Cor 1:7; 4:11; Php 3:10; Col 3:3,4; 2 Tm 2:12; 1 Pe 4:12-14; Re 7:14-17; *ref. 266,268,270-272.*

---

264 Every Christian is called upon to bear his, or her, own cross. — A man who once complained that his cross was too heavy to bear had a dream. He dreamed that he was in a large room in which there were many crosses. He was told that, since he believed his cross was too heavy, he could lay it down and choose another cross which might suit him better. He gladly laid down his cross and began his search for a lighter one. Several crosses that he found were much smaller than the one he had, but he soon discovered that they were too heavy for his shoulders. Finally, after looking over all the crosses, he found one that seemed to fit his strength exactly. However, when he examined it more closely he found that it was the same cross which, on entering the room, he had laid down: cp. 1 Cor 10:13; *ref. 263.*

† † †

265 Martin Luther designed a coat of arms in 1530. It pictures a black cross on a red heart, imposed on a white rose in a blue field, surrounded by a golden ring. The meaning is that

> A Christian heart discerns a rose
> Beneath the cross with all its woes.

266
> Shun not suffering, shame and loss,
> Learn of him to bear the cross.
> — J. Montgomery

ref. 263

† † †

267 In his *Imitation of Christ,* Thomas A Kempis wrote: "Jesus has many lovers of his kingdom, but few bearers of his cross. All are disposed to rejoice with him, but few to suffer for his sake. Many follow him to the breaking of bread, but few to the drinking of his bitter cup"; *ref. 263.*

† † †

268 Years ago a missionary told how on religious festival days in Mexico peddlers would go about the streets selling crucifixes and miniature crosses. As they passed back and forth on the city streets they called out: "Cheap cross! Cheap cross! Who will buy a cheap cross!" The Cross that our Lord and Savior Jesus Christ bore for us was not a cheap or a light cross. It was weighted with the sins of the world, and that terrible weight bowed him to the ground: Is 53:6; Jn 1:29. Nor is it a cheap or light cross that we are to bear as his followers, for it means losing our life for his sake: Mt 16:24,25.

269
Come, follow me, the Savior spake,
    All in my way abiding;
Deny yourselves, the world forsake,
    Obey my call and guiding.
Oh, bear the cross, whate'er betide,
    Take my example for your guide.

Then let us follow Christ, our Lord,
    And take the cross appointed
And, firmly clinging to his Word,
    In suffering be undaunted.
For who bears not the battle's strain
    The crown of life shall not obtain.
— Johann Scheffler
ref. 263

† † †

270 The carpenters who belonged to the early guilds chose as their motto the words of Christ, "I am the Door," Jn 10:9. In keeping with that motto they decided to make all doors so that the space between the two smaller upper panels and the two larger lower panels would form a cross. This custom has come down to our time; *ref. 263*.

† † †

271
Jesus, I my cross have taken,
    All to leave and follow thee;
Destitute; despised, forsaken,
    Thou from hence my all shalt be.
Perish ev'ry fond ambition,
    All I've sought or hoped or known;
Yet how rich is my condition!
God and heav'n are still mine own.
— Henry Francis Lyte

272
The consecrated cross I'll bear
    Till death shall set me free,
And then go home, my crown to wear,
    For there's a crown for me.
— Thomas Shepherd
ref. 263

(ref.: Resurrection of the body 1263-1275)

273 Death entered the world as a consequence of sin: Gn 2:16,17; Ro 6:23; Jas 1:15; and it comes to all mankind because all have sinned: Ro 3:23; 5:12; He 9:27; *ref. 281,282.*

274 Christ destroyed the power of death: 1 Cor 15:54-57; 2 Tm 1:10; He 2:14,15: Re 1:18; *ref. 283-291,294-296,753,768,774.*

275 Christ's victory over death becomes our victory through faith in him: Jn 5:24; 11:25,26; Ro 6:23; 1 Cor 15:57; but temporal death leads to eternal death for all who reject Christ in unbelief: Eze 18:4,20; Mt 25:41,46; Lk 16:22-24; Jn 3:18,36; 2 Th 1:7-10; He 9:27; 10:26-31; 2 Pe 2:9; 1 Jn 5:11,12; Jude 14,15; *ref. 283-291.*

276 The certainty of death, as well as the uncertainty as to when it will come to us, should cause us to:

Make proper preparations for it: 2 Kgs 20:1; Ps 39:4; 90:12; or for the Lord's return during our lifetime: Mt 24:44; Mk 13:32-37; *ref. 286,293, 298,299,505, 604,1616,1617,1620,1624;*

277 Recognize that the time allotted to us is short at best: Job 14:1,2; Ps 90:9,10; 102:11; 103:15,16; Jas 4:14; 1 Pe 1:24; and that it is a time of grace to seek the things that belong to our peace with God: Ec 12:1f; Is 55:6,7; Mt 23:37,38; Lk 19:42; 2 Cor 6:2.

278 Make the fullest possible use of our time: Ec 9:10; Jn 9:4; Eph 5:16; Col 4:5; especially in living our life to the praise and glory of God: Mt 5:16; Php 2:15,16; 1 Pe 2:9-12; *ref. 1322-1342;*

279 Set our affections on things above, as pilgrims passing through this world on their way to heaven: 1 Chr 29:15; Mt 6:19-21; Php 3:20; Col 3:1-3; He 11:13-16; *ref. 286;*

280 Pray God to grant us a blessed death: Nu 23:10; Ps 116:15; Lk 2:29,30; 2 Tm 4:6-8,18; *ref. 295,296.*

---

281 It is related of Xerxes that, when about to cross from Asia over to Europe, he ordered a review to be held of all his forces on the shores of the Hellespont. A magnificent throne was erected upon a lofty peak. Seated on this pinnacle of gold he gazed upon his men on ship and shore. No sight could have been more dazzling. The hillsides were white with tents, the sea with sails. Banners glittering with gold and silver floated in the sunlight. But in the midst of such transcending glory and deepest homage, where many nobles were urging to kiss the hem of his garment and worship him as a god, the mighty Xerxes wept!

Amazed at such an act, expressive of feelings so contrary to those in which they were indulging, they reverently inquired as to the cause of his tears.

"Alas," said Xerxes, "of all this vast multitude not one will be left on earth a hundred years hence!"

— selected

282
        Remember friend
          As you pass by
        As you are now
          So once was I.
        As I am now, you
          Soon will be,
        Prepare for death
          And follow me.

— tombstone in
Tekamah Cemetery, Nebraska

ref. 273

† † †

283 What is our death but a night's sleep? For as through sleep all the weariness and faintness pass away and cease, and the powers of the spirit come back again, so that in the morning we rise, fresh and strong and joyous, so at the Last Day we shall rise again as if we had only slept a night, and shall be fresh and strong.

— Luther

284 A sunset in one land is a sunrise in another. Death is only life's beginning in another realm.

285
        He is not dead; he only sleeps,
          Safe in the arms of him who keeps
        His lambs secure from earth's alarm,
          From grief and sin and foes that harm.

        He is not dead; though tears may flow,
          Faith whispers: "It is better so."
        With joy we'll meet on that fair shore,
          Where God's own children weep no more.

— Anon

ref. 275

† † †

286 Dwight L. Moody had a friend who lost five children by scarlet fever. The grief-stricken parents sought relief in traveling. In Palestine they saw a shepherd at a river bank call his sheep to cross the stream. But the frightened creatures stood shivering on the brink of the water. Finally he took two lambs in his arms, stepped into the stream and crossed it. Immediately the older sheep plunged in after him, and soon the entire flock was safe on the other bank, ready to find fresh, green pastures. That was a lesson for the bereaved father and mother. They realized that the Good Shepherd had taken their five children across the stream of death into the happiness of heaven so that in God's good time the parents could follow them into the celestial fold.

— selected

287 A little girl was walking through the cemetery. It was almost dark, and someone asked her whether she was not afraid. "Oh, no," she said, "I only cross the cemetery to get home."

288 When I go down to the grave, I must say like so many others, "I have finished my day's work." But I cannot say, "I have finished my life." My day's work will begin the next morning. The tomb is not a blind alley. It is a thoroughfare. It closes in the twilight to open in the dawn.

— Victor Hugo

ref. 275,278-280

289 Savonarola, a reformer of the church, was burnt at Florence on 23 May 1498. When the Roman bishop pronounced the words, "I separate thee from the church," the martyr calmly replied: "From the church militant, but not from the church triumphant."

290 A Christian physician died and was mourned by his widow. But she conquered her grief with her Christian faith and trust. Over his office door she hung a little card which he customarily placed there when he was called out on business. The card read, "Gone for a little while; will be back soon."

291
> Only a little while,
>   A moment it may be,
> Ere I shall see him face to face,
>   Who died, who lives for me.
> Only a little while,
>   The wilderness to roam,
> And then the Father's home above
>   My dwelling-place, my home.

— Anon

ref. 275,279

† † †

292 Shortly before his death Augustine asked one of his disciples to print on the wall of his room the words, "Blessed is he whose transgressions are forgiven, whose sins are covered. Blessed is the man whose sin the Lord does not count against him and in whose spirit is no deceit," Ps 32:1,2. Then, gazing on these words, he died; *ref. 280*.

† † †

293 When the executioner asked Sir Walter Raleigh whether his head was layed aright on the block, Raleigh replied, "It matters little how the head lies, provided the heart is right"; *ref. 276*.

† † †

77

294 Death is not the end; it is only a beginning. Death is not the master of the house; he is only the porter at the King's lodge, appointed to open the gate and let the King's guests into the realm of eternal day. And so shall we ever be with the Lord.

The range of our threescore years and ten is not a landlocked lake enclosed within the shorelines of seventy years. It is an arm of the sea. And so we must build for those larger waters. We are immortal! How, then, shall we live today in prospect of eternal tomorrow?

— J. W. Jowett

ref. 275,279

† † †

295 John Pierpont Morgan, the millionaire, wrote in his will: "I commit my soul into the hands of my Savior, in full confidence that having redeemed it and washed it in his most precious blood, he will present it faultless before the throne of my Heavenly Father, and I entreat my children to maintain and defend at all hazards and at any cost of personal sacrifice the blessed doctrine of the complete atonement for sin through the blood of Jesus Christ, once offered, and through that alone."

296 On her death-bed, Queen Victoria called for the hymn:

"Rock of Ages, cleft for me,
Let me hide myself in thee."

297 When John Quincy Adams was eighty years of age a friend said to him: "Well, how is John Quincy Adams?"

"Thank you," he said, "John Quincy Adams is quite well. But the house where he lives is becoming dilapidated. It is tottering. Time and the seasons have nearly destroyed it, and it is becoming quite uninhabitable. I shall have to move soon. But John Quincy Adams is quite well, thank you."

— *The Gospel Herald*

ref. 279,280

† † †

298 A nurse whose services were in great demand was asked to care for a certain patient. Before giving her consent she asked the friend of the patient who approached her with the request, "Is your friend a Christian?"

"Yes," said the friend of the patient, "he is a Christian in the highest sense of the term, a man who lives in the fear of God. But I should like to know your reason for such an inquiry."

"Sir," answered the nurse, "I was the nurse that attended Voltaire in his last illness, and, for all the wealth of Europe, I would never see another infidel die"; *ref. 276.*

299 Thomas Paine, the noted American infidel, said, "I would give worlds if *The Age of Reason* [which he wrote] had never been published. O Lord, help me! O God, what have I done to suffer so much? But there is no God! But if there should be, what will be come of me hereafter? Stay with me, for God's

78

sake! Send even a child to stay with me, for it is Hell to be alone. If ever the Devil had an agent, I have been that one"; *ref. 276.*

DISCIPLESHIP, CHRISTIAN 300-314

(ref.: Faith 359-383; Service, Christian 1322-1342)

The Meaning of Christian Discipleship

300 Knowing Jesus Christ as the Son of God and accepting him in faith as one's Savior from sin: Mt 16:16; Jn 3:16; 6:69; 11:27; 14:6; 17:3; Ac 4:12; *ref. 359,361;*

Acknowledging Christ's words as the words of God and accepting his teaching as infallible truth: Jn 5:24; 6:68,69; 8:31,32; 14:10; 17:8; *ref. 361-363;*

Learning of Christ and striving to do his will: Mt 7:24f; 11:29; 12:50; 28:20; Jn 13:17; 14:23; 15:10,14; Eph 4:14-16; 2 Pe 3:18; *ref. 307-309;*

Patterning one's life after that of Christ and following his example: Mt 11:29; Mk 10:42-45; Jn 13:15; Php 2:5f; 1 Pe 2:21; *ref. 304,305,311.*

The Obligations and Duties of Christian Discipleship

301 Obligations:

Denying oneself by placing one's life and all that it offers in the service of Christ: Mk 8:34,35; Lk 5:27,28; 9:57-62; 14:26,33; 1 Cor 6:19,20; 2 Cor 5:15; Ga 2:20; Php 1:21; 3:7-11; *ref, 306,309.*

Bearing the Christian cross by willingly suffering for Christ's sake and for the sake of his gospel: Mt 10:16-22; Lk 9:23; Jn 15:20,21; 16:2,3; Ac 4:18-20; 5:41; 14:22; Ro 8:17,35,36; 2 Cor 4:10; Php 3:10; 2 Tm 3:12; 1 Pe 2:21; 4:13; *ref. 262-272,306,307.*

302 Duties:

Bearing personal witness for Christ by word: Mt 4:19; 10:32; Mk 5:19; Jn 1:42,45; 4:28-30; 1 Cor 9:22; glorifying God through a Christian life: Mt 5:16; Jn 15:8,16; Ro 12:1,2; 1 Cor 6:10; 10:31; 2 Cor 3:2,3; 5:15; Php 2:15,16; 1 Pe 2:9-12; and uniting with like-minded Christians in proclaiming the gospel in all the world: Mt 28:18-20; Mk 16:15; Lk 24:47; Jn 20:21; Ac 1:8; *ref. 307, 314;* see Mission Work 1020-1081.

Supporting the cause of Christ's kingdom through the use of God-given talents: Mt 25:14f; Ro 12:6-8; 1 Cor 12:7f; 1 Pe 4:10; by prayers: Mt 9:38; Ro 15:30; Eph 6:19; 1 Th 5:25; 2 Th 3:1; and by offerings: Ac 11:29; 1 Cor 9:14; 16:2; 2 Cor 9:7f; *ref. 1368,1369.*

Being active in works of love Mt 25:35-40; Jn 13:35; 15:12; Ac 11:29; Ga 5:6; 6:9,10; He 13:16; 1 Jn 3:14; *ref. 312,313*

The Rewards of Christian Discipleship

303 Blessings in this life — peace with God: Jn 14:27; Ro 5:1; Php 4:7; the abiding presence of Christ and of the Holy Spirit: Mt 28:20; Jn 14:16,17; the assurance of Christ's intercession and constant love: Ro 8:31-39; He 4:15,16;

1 Jn 2:1,2; and God's promise to supply every needful blessing: Ro 8:32; Php 4:19.

Blessings in the world to come — the inheritance of eternal life in heaven: Mt 5:11,12; 10:32; 25:34; Lk 18:28-30; Jn 5:24; 10:27-30; 14:2,3; 17:24; 2 Tm 2:11,12; 4:8,18; Jas 1:12; 1 Pe 1:3-9; 1 Jn 3:2; Re 2:10.

Resources

304 The Bible ascribes various titles to Christians. They are called children of God, Ga 3:26; sons of God, 1 Jn 3:1; blessed of the Father, Mt 25:34; heirs of God, Ro 8:17; believers, Ac 5:14; saints, Eph 2:19; the elect, Mt 24:22; the salt of the earth and the light of the world, Mt 5:13,16; a chosen generation, a royal priesthood, a holy nation, a special people, 1 Pe 2:9. But the designation used most frequently is the title "disciple." This word, which occurs more than 250 times in the New Testament, denotes a believer, a learner, a follower of Christ.

The word "disciple" is also used with reference to the followers of John the Baptist, the followers of the Pharisees, and the followers of Moses: Mt 9:14; 22:15,16; Jn 9:28. When used with reference to Christ the word is sometimes used to designate the twelve apostles: Mt 10:1-4; Lk 18:31. Often it is used of all believers: Mt 16:24; Lk 6:13; 7:11; 19:37; Jn 8:31; 13:35; 15:8; and sometimes it is used of those who merely followed Christ out of curiosity or for other reasons: Jn 6:66; 12:42,43; 19:38,39; *ref. 300.*

305 Christ frequently used the title "disciple" when speaking of his followers. It is unfortunate, therefore, that this word has fallen into disuse among us, and sadder still that the phrase "disciple of Christ" has been supplanted by such a common phrase as "member of the church." The two expressions can mean something quite different. Being a "member of the church" may mean nothing more than having one's name on the church's membership roll and supporting the *church* as an organization, while being a "disciple of Christ," in the biblical meaning of that word means something far more.

While membership in the church ought to be synonymous with being a disciple of Christ, it is not so in the case of those who are members of the church in name only. One can go through the outward mechanics of joining the church without sincerely assuming the obligations of Christian discipleship. One can pledge loyalty to the *church* without believing in Christ, the Head of the Church. One can say "Lord, Lord," and still not do the will of the Father in heaven: Mt 7:21. One can assemble in God's house with God's people and draw nigh unto God with the mouth and honor him with the lips while the heart is far removed from him: Mt 15:8. One can have a form of godliness and yet deny its power: 2 Tm 3:5. One can profess to know God and yet in works deny him: Tt 1:16. One can have his name on the church records without having it written in heaven: Lk 10:20. But only they are truly disciples who have been spiritually reborn and made new creatures in Christ, that is, who believe in him: Jn 3:5; 2 Cor 5:17; *ref. 300.*

306 The obligations of being a disciple of Christ are no different today from what they have been in the past. And they are as hard as ever. Christ cautions those who would follow him to sit down first and to count the cost: Lk 14:25-33.

The same tests, the same requirements, and the same difficulties that confronted Christ's disciples of old still face us today: Lk 9:57-62; *ref. 301,302.*

† † †

307 When Christ chose his first disciples he did so for the purpose of having them assist him in his work: Mt 4:19. His personal ministry on earth was to last for only three years. After his redemptive work was finished others would extend the kingdom of grace that he had established. In preparation for this work Christ carefully instructed his disciples, especially the chosen twelve, and from time to time gave them opportunities for putting their learning into practice: Mt 10:5f; Mk 6:7-13; Lk 9:1f; 10:1f.

The duties of Christian discipleship have not changed. The work in Christ's kingdom goes on from one generation to the next; *ref. 300-302.*

† † †

308 Christian discipleship does not imply perfection. Because of their sinful flesh, Christian people are still guilty of sinning: Ro 7:14-25; Ga 5:17. They make mistakes, just as did the disciples in the days of Christ: Mt 15:23; 18:1; 20:20f; 26:6f,40,51,56; Mk 10:13; Lk 9:54f; Ga 2:11f. As disciples, they are always pupils at the feet of the Master; Christ continues to teach, and they continue to learn. But recognizing their deficiencies, they constantly seek to improve as they strive for perfection: Php 3:12-14; *ref. 300.*

† † †

309 Today, as on the memorable occasions when he first gave the command, "Follow Me!" the Savior again and again repeats his call to discipleship: Mt 4:19-22; Lk 5:27,28; Jn 21:22. It is a call to those who have not known him before but who need him above all else. It is a call to those who, like Peter, have until now followed him only afar off; a call to those who, like Nicodemus and Joseph of Arimathea, have been his disciples only in secret; a call to those who, like the multitude in his day, have been following him only out of curiosity; a call to those who have been his followers in name only, because they have hoped to find some personal advantage in it; a call to those who, like Judas, have been disloyal to him. It is a call to every man woman, and child, to repent, to follow him, to take up their cross, and to lose their life in this world for his sake that they might find eternal life in heaven.

Jesus, I would follow thee,
One of thy disciples be;
Guide my whole life by thy Word,
Live each lesson I have heard.
Make my noblest wish to be
Constantly to follow thee.

Jesus, I would follow thee,
One of thy disciples be;
Bear the cross, myself deny
That I unto sin may die.
May thy love my spirit fill
Ceaselessly to do thy will.

Jesus, I would follow thee,
One of thy disciples be;
Suffer persecution, shame,
Die to glorify thy name,
And at last, from sin set free,
Evermore to live with thee.

— R. C. Rein

ref. 301-303

† † †

310 During the persecution of Christians under the Roman emperor Diocletian many faithful confessors of Jesus Christ were cruelly put to death. The calm fortitude, even joy, with which these martyrs went to their death amazed a young Roman soldier named Adrianus. He inquired of one what might be the reason for such joyfulness in the face of a cruel death. He was told, "We are looking for the blessed treasures of heaven, which eye has not seen, nor ear heard, neither is man's heart able to consider the things which God has prepared for those who love him" (cp 1 Cor 2:9,10). This made such a deep impression upon the Roman soldier that he embraced Christianity and himself later died a martyr, happy in the faith that there was also for him a crown of life; *ref. 303.*

† † †

311 The famous painter Doré once lost his passport while traveling through a foreign country. When the official demanded it, he said: "I am sorry to say that I lost my passport. I can only tell you that I am Doré, the artist."

"Ah!" said the officer sneeringly, "we'll see very quickly whether you are Doré," and, handing him a pencil and paper, he said: "Prove it, if you are."

Taking the pencil the artist with a few strokes sketched a group of peasants, who happened to be standing by, with such inimitable skill that the officer said: "Yes, no doubt of it, you must be Doré": cp 2 Cor 3:2,3; *ref. 300.*

† † †

312 A chinaman, of whom it was known that he had never heard the gospel preached, came to a mission compound and expressed the desire to join the Christian congregation. When he was asked why he wished to take that step without first learning of the teachings of the Christian religion, he replied: "But I have *seen* the gospel." The Christian missionaries in his land were living letters of Christ. By their exemplary lives and self-sacrificing service they had so impessed this man with the power of the Christian religion that he desired to investigate and embrace it; *ref. 302.*

313 Francis of Assisi, a famous preacher of the Middle Ages, once invited a young monk to travel with him to a town where he was to preach. They walked through the town, talking as they went, and then returned. The young man asked when they were going to preach. Francis said, "My son, we have been preaching. We were preaching while we were walking. We have been seen and looked at; our behavior has been remarked upon; we have delivered our morning sermon." Then he added: "You see, my son, it is of no use that we walk anywhere to preach, unless we preach as we walk"; *ref. 302.*

† † †

314 The venerable Polycarp, bishop of Smyrna, had sat at the feet of the Apostle John. At the time of the Easter festival in the year 155 he was arrested by heathen soldiers. At the threat of death he was ordered to curse Christ. This was his noble answer: "Six and eighty years have I served him, and he has done me nothing but good. How could I curse him, my Lord and my Savior?" He was burned to death because he refused to renounce his faith; but being faithful unto death, he gained the imperishable crown of glory; *ref. 302.*

(ref.: Children 142-158; Home 534-556; Teachers, Teaching 1434-1459; Young People 1649-1666)

A Definition

315 Its essence:

It involves all of the teaching and training efforts on the part of the Christian home and the Christian church to impart beliefs and practices that center in Jesus Christ, "in whom are hidden all the treasures of wisdom and knowledge," Col 2:3; Eph 3:19; *ref. 330-339.*

316 Its object:

Its object is the conversion and spiritual growth and perfection of souls, that man might have a knowledge and understanding of God, of himself, and of the universe in which he lives; a proper appreciation of his relationship to God and to his fellowmen; and a correct knowledge of the gospel, so that he, living to the praise of his Creator and Redeemer, may enter eternal life: Ps 111:10; 119:9,105; Jn 17:3; 1 Cor 10:31; Php 3:8-11; 2 Tm 3:15-17; 1 Pe 2:2; 2 Pe 3:18; *ref. 330-339.*

317 Its means:

It is accomplished through the use of the Word of God (and the holy sacraments of baptism and the Lord's Supper, which receive their power through that Word), by means of which the Holy Spirit performs his gracious work of regeneration and sanctification into the heart of man: Lk 22:19,20; Jn 3:5; 6:63; Ro 10:17; Eph 5:26; Jas 1:18; 1 Pe 1:22,23; *ref. 330-339,358.*

The Need For Christian Education

318 Because of sin man forfeited the eternal life for which God had created him: Gn 3:22-24; Is 59:2; Ro 3:23; 5:12. That eternal life can be restored only through Jesus Christ whom Holy Scriptures reveal as the heaven-sent Savior of the world: Jn 1:4; 3:16; 5:24; 10:10; 14:6; 17:3; Ac 4:12; Ro 5:21; 6:23; 1 Tm 1:15; 2 Tm 1:9,10; 1 Jn 5:11,12,20; *ref. 330,332-334.*

319 By birth and nature man is spiritually corrupt, dead in trespasses and sins, an enemy of God, inclined only toward evil, and ignorant of his true origin, purpose, and destiny: Gn 8:21; Ps 51:5; Ec 7:20; Is 64:6; Mt 15:19; Ac 17:23; Ro 3:23; 8:7; 10:3; 1 Cor 2:14; Eph 2:1; 4:18; he is in need of a spiritual rebirth which can be effected only by the power of the Holy Spirit working through the Word of God: Jn 3:5; 6:63; 1 Cor 2:14; 12:3; Jas 1:18; 1 Pe 2:23; *ref. 317,330,332,334,358.*

320 God's Word is the only source for man's spiritual rebirth and the only source for his spiritual growth: Jn 15:3-5; Eph 1:17-23; 3:16-19; 4:14,15; Col 1:9-11; He 5:12-14; 1 Pe 2:2; 2 Pe 1:5-8; 3:18; *ref. 317,330,332,334,358.*

A Duty of the Christian Home

321 God has established the home as a teaching agency. Parents are the child's first and most influential teachers. They teach both by precept and by example for good or for ill, both by what they do and by what they fail to do. Examples of good home influence: Samuel, 1 Sm 1:26-28; 2:26; Solomon,

1 Chr 28:9; 29:19; Jehoshaphat, 2 Chr 17:3; Uzziah, 2 Chr 26:4; John the Baptist, Lk 1:5,6,80; Timothy, 2 Tm 1:5; 3:15. Examples of evil influence: Adonijah, 1 Kgs 1:6; Ahaziah, 2 Chr 22:2-4; the rebellious Israelites, Jr 9:13,14; the daughter of Herodias, Mt 14:8; *ref. 340-349.*

322 God has imposed upon parents not only the duty to provide for their physical needs, 1 Tm 5:8, but also the responsibility.:

Love their children: Tt 2:4;

Pray for them: Gn 17:18; 1 Sm 1:11,28; 1 Chr 29:19; Job 1:5; Mt 15:22; 17:15; Jn 4:46,47;

Teach them his Word, tell of his wonderful works, and train them to walk in his ways: Gn 18:19; Dt 4:9; 6:6-9; 11:18-21; 31:13; 32:46; Ps 78:1-8; Pr 22:6; Is 38:19; Ro 15:4; 1 Cor 10:11; Eph 6:4; 2 Tm 1:5; 3:15;

Correct them when needed: Dt 8:5; Pr 3:12; 13:24; 19:18; 23:13,14; 29:15; Eph 6:4;

Bring them to Christ: Mt 19:13,14; Mk 10:13,14; and to worship services: 2 Chr 20:13; Ezr 8:21; Ne 12:43; Mt 21:15,16; *ref. 340-349.*

323 Parental instruction and training is to begin in earliest infancy: Jdg 13:8; 1 Sm 1:24-28; Ps 148:12,13; Ec 12:1; Is 28:9; Lk 2:21-24; *ref. 340-349.*

324 The home offers numerous opportunities for Christian instruction and training, e.g.,

Assembling at the family altar for daily study of God's Word and prayer: Gn 18:19; Jos 24:15; 2 Tm 1:5; 3:15;

Practicing Christian teachings, e.g., by demonstrating compassion, forgiveness, love, obedience, reverence, service, sacrifice, trust, etc.;

Observing special joyful occasions — e.g., birth, baptism, confirmation day, graduation, wedding, and the like, as well as events such as those involving misfortune, sickness and death — with reference to God's Word; *ref. 340-349.*

A Duty of the Christian Church

325 Christ has commanded the church to preach and to teach his Word: Mt 28:18-20; Mk 16:15; cp. Jn 21:15-17; Ac 5:42; 11:26; 13:1; 15:35; 18:11,25: 20:28; 28:31; 1 Cor 12:28; Eph 4:11; 2 Tm 2:2; He 13:7,17; 1 Pe 5:2; *ref. 350.*

326 The church's teaching task is not to supplant, but to supplement, the task of the home by giving help and guidance, reinforcing the instruction given by parents, and supplying the teaching and training that the home does not provide. The ideal is a close cooperation between the church and the home as partners; *ref. 350,357.*

The church's duties involve the responsibility to provide:

Bible-based directives from the pulpit on Christian instruction and training;

Adequate facilities in which to teach;

Well-trained teachers, teacher meetings, library;

Teaching agencies for preschool and elementary-age children, for youths, and for adults, e.g., Sunday school, weekday classes; vacation Bible school; seasonal educational and training opportunities for youths and adults which enable them to grow in grace and in their knowledge of Christ: cp Eph 4:11-13; 1 Pe 2:2; 2 Pe 3:18;

Bible-based, Christ-centered, and life-related lessons, audiovisual aids, equipment and supplies;

Close cooperation with the home through parent-teacher meetings, counseling services, clinics and seminars;

Education and training in mission outreach (teaching to reach, reaching to teach);

Encouragement to young men and women to prepare for professional church work;

Necessary finances and effective supervision in directing and promoting the congregation's program of Christian education.

Benefits of a Christian Education

327 For the home:
It satisfies the foremost needs of parents and children, the needs of their immortal souls: Mk 8:36,37; Lk 10:42; 2 Tm 3:15-17; and assures them of the Lord's blessing: Gn 18:19; Ps 127:1; 128:1-6; *ref. 356.*

It enables parents and children to teach each other and to learn from one another: Eph 4:14-16; Col 3:16; 1 Th 3:12;

It affords opportunities to parents and children to put Christian principles into practice: Eph 5:22-28; 6:1-4; Col 3:18-21; 2 Tm 1:5; 1 Pe 3:7-9; cp 1 Sm 2:26; Lk 2:40,52.

328 For the church:
It produces well-indoctrinated and spiritually strong members: 1 Cor 12:4-7; 2 Cor 9:10; Eph 3:14-21; 4:11-16; Col 1:9-14; 1 Th 3:12; 2 Th 1:3; 1 Pe 2:2; 2 Pe 1:5-8; 3:18;

It supplies willing workers: Ac 18:24-28; Ro 16:1f; Eph 4:16; Php 4:13; 1 Th 2:14.

329 For the nation:
It prepares citizens who honor, respect, and obey their government, who pray for all in authority and seek the welfare of the community, nation, and world: Jr 29:7; Mt 22:21; Ro 13:1-7; 1 Tm 2:1-4; Tt 3:1; 1 Pe 2:13-17;

It results in God's blessing: Dt 28:1f; Ps 33:12; 66:7; 72:17; Pr 11:11; 14:34; Is 26:1-4; *ref. 351-356,438.*

Resources

330 Holy Scriptures declare: "The fear of the Lord is the beginning of wisdom; all who follow his precepts have a good understanding," Ps 111:10; cp Pr 1:7; 8:13; 9:10.

The source of all true knowledge, the foundation on which all true education rests, is the loving reverence for God which stands in awe of his holiness, marvels at his wonderful works, praises him for his goodness and mercy, and willingly obeys his commandments. Far beyond the knowledge of material things, true wisdom implies the knowledge of salvation from sin and its dreadful, deadly, and damning consequences through Jesus Christ, the Savior of the world.

Only when man's life is guided by a reverent desire to please God with whom he has become reconciled through the atoning sacrifice and death of Christ — only when man is motivated by love and thankfulness to serve his Maker and Redeemer can it be said that he is truly educated. This is the knowledge that gives a proper appreciation and a right judgment of the true values of life; this is life eternal: Jn 17:3; 1 Tm 4:8; Php 3:8; *ref. 315-320.*

† † †

331 Fine school buildings, competent teachers and institutions are not enough. Christian education is the only hope of the nation. It is the very soul of education. And education, like the human being, once it has lost its soul, has nothing left that is worth having. . . . Statutes and crusades for more machinery to force morality will never create righteousness. That must come form the heart and the enlightened mind.

— Chicago Tribune, March 28, 1923

ref. 318-320.

† † †

332 The words "knowledge" and "wisdom" are sometimes used interchangeably. More accurately, however, "knowledge" embraces all that has been perceived or grasped by the mind, while "wisdom" involves the application of what has been learned by exercising discretion and judgment. Combining the two, man develops a philosophy, or system of principles, for the conduct of life.

In 1 Cor 1:18-25 the holy writer declares that all the knowledge and wisdom of the world could not discover a way in which sinful man could become reconciled with a holy and righteous God, and then it points out that in the wisdom of God this was accomplished by the atoning death of Jesus Christ. This wisdom of God, which is foolishness to the mind of natural man, is the power of God unto salvation to everyone who believes; and it can be known only to those to whom the Holy Spirit reveals it: 1 Cor 2:6-14; Eph 2:1; 4:18.

Thus the true treasures of wisdom and knowledge are hid in Jesus Christ: Col 2:3; Eph 3:19. He stands in the center of all history, for he is the Creator and Ruler of all history. All history will end in him: Jn 1:1-3; 1 Cor 8:6; Col 1:16,17; He 1:2,3; 1 Jn 1:1-3. This is a mystery so profound that only God can reveal it, but a truth so essential that without the knowledge of it all the accummulated philosophy of the ages is utter foolishness; cp Ro 1:18-22; 1 Cor 1:20,21.

333   Wisdom's highest, noblest treasure,
                Jesus, lies concealed in thee;
            Grant that this may still the measure
                Of my will and actions be.
            The gain of this one thing all loss can requite
            And teach me in all things to find true delight.
            Oh, if I of Christ have this knowledge divine,
            The fullness of heavenly wisdom is mine.
                            — Johann H. Schroeder

334 Man's greatest need is to know the love of Christ, which "surpasses knowledge," Eph 3:19. For the possession of it St. Paul was ready to suffer the loss of all things: Php 3:8; cp. Mt 13:45,46. The surpassing worth of it implies an understanding of Christ's person and work. It means not only to know, but also, by the power of the Holy Spirit, to acknowledge Jesus Christ as the incarnate Son of God and one's own heaven-sent Savior from sin: Ro 4:24-5:1; 2 Cor 5:21; Php 3:9. It means to recognize that the true end of life is to know the life that never ends, the eternal life that is found only in Jesus Christ and which he alone can give: Jn 1:4; 3:16; 5:24; 6:47; 10:10; 14:6; 17:3; Php 3:10,11; 1 Jn 5:11,12,20; *ref. 315-320.*

† † †

335 The purpose of education is to impart knowledge that may be used. But knowledge acquired may be used for evil purposes as well as for good. Some of the worst crimes are those committed by master minds. Instead of turning the fruits of knowledge into helpful channels for the glory of God and the benefit of humanity, men often employ them for selfish and sinful purposes and for the destruction of that which is good. True education, therefore, embraces not only knowledge but also wisdom which involves the discretionary power to choose and to judge rightly; cp Pr 4:7; 8:10; *ref. 316.*

† † †

336 Often the most highly educated people are the most unhappy in their personal, family and social life. This is so because secular knowledge cannot satisfy man's inner need, the need of his immortal soul. It affects the outward life but neglects the heart. It cannot quiet an accusing conscience terrified by sin. It cannot heal a broken heart. It cannot comfort a sorrowing soul. It cannot give information concerning the life to come nor make preparations for it; *ref. 318-320.*

† † †

337 To accomplish its purpose Christian education must reach not only the intellect but also the emotions and will, and then be translated into action (head-heart-hands). Its concern is that the learner not only knows, but that he also does the Lord's will, Mt 28:20. Knowledge must be accompanied by attitude, and attitude must express itself in conduct. "If you know these things," says Christ, "happy are you if you do them," Jn 13:17. Again he declared, "Not everyone who says to me, Lord, Lord, will enter the kingdom of heaven, but he who does the will of my Father in heaven," Mt 7:21; see also v 24-27; Ec 5:1; Eze 33:32; Lk 11:28; Jas 1:22-25; *ref. 315-317.*

† † †

338 A little girl about to enter kindergarten lost her birth-certificate which she was to present at the time of her enrollment. Approaching the teacher with tears in her eyes she sobbed, "I've lost my excuse for being born!" — It is important to acquire all the knowledge that you can. But unless you have discovered the surpassing knowledge of Jesus Christ you have "lost your excuse for being born." For only when you have found the eternal life that is in Christ have you discovered the purpose for which God created you, that you might live in eternal fellowship with him: cp. Mk 8:36,37; *ref. 316.*

† † †

339 The pious Israelites made phylacteries, or strips of parchment, on which passages from the law of God were written. They enclosed these in small boxes which they bound to their forehead and left wrist and wore at the time of prayer. Similar strips with Scripture passages were enclosed in a reed or colander and placed on the door-posts in the home see Dt 6:6-9, 11:18-20; cp. Mt 23:5. The purpose was that both they and their children might always and everywhere have the commandments of the Lord in view and in mind, so as to observe them constantly; *ref. 315-320.*

† † †

340

A careful man I ought to be;
   A little fellow follows me;
I do not dare to go astray
   For fear he'll go the selfsame way.

I cannot once escape his eyes,
   Whate'er he sees me do, he tries;
Like me, he says, he's going to be,
   The little chap who follows me.

He thinks that I am good and fine,
   Believes in every word of mine.
The base in me he must not see,
   The little chap who follows me.

I must remember as I go,
   Through summer's fun and winter's snow,
I'm building for the years to be
   The little chap who follows me.

— Anon

ref. 321-324

† † †

89

341 "Pick a safe trail, Daddy, I'm coming too." It was the voice of a child calling to his father who had gone into a rugged mountainous region in search of a lost sheep. The father had instructed the child to remain behind, but before he had gone far the child called to him: "Pick a safe trail, Daddy, I'm coming too." — Whether parents are conscious of the fact or not, they are picking a trail for their children by their attitudes and conduct, by their likes and dislikes, by their loyalties and prejudices, by their hate and fear, by their love and trust; *ref. 321-324.*

† † †

342 Manoah and his wife inquired regarding the Lord's will concerning their child even before the child was born: Jdg 13:12; see also Lk 1:66; *ref. 321-324.*

† † †

343 Martin Luther said, "No greater harm can come to Christendom than that of neglecting our children."

344 One of the greatest evils of our day is that of over-permissiveness which parents allow their children in the name of freedom, over-permissiveness which not only permits but even encourages children to do what they please, for fear that if they are restrained they will be inhibited and develop an "inferiority complex." Parents who make no demands and set no rules for conduct are not helping but hindering the mental, moral and spiritual growth of their children. Much of the rebellion among children and young people is not against over-strictness, but against over-permissiveness. Children look to their parents for instruction and guidance, and they expect parents to discipline them when correction is needed. If such guidance is not given, children conclude that their parents do not care enough about them to enforce even the simplest rules that are necessary for their proper growth into true manhood and womanhood, and as a result they often do drastic things to command attention. Nowhere is this more evident than in the area of sexual freedom and its evil results.

345 Another tragic mistake that many parents make is that of foolishly supposing that they have discharged their parental responsibilities when they have given their children everything that money can buy. Then, when their son or daughter ends up as a delinquent these parents frantically look around for someone to blame. They gave their children everything that money could buy, but failed to give them love, the one essential that money cannot buy. Many delinquent youths today are young people who came from prosperous homes and who are literally fed up with the materialism of our age because they have experienced that "man does not live by bread alone," and that "a man's life does not consist in the abundance of things which he possesses," Mt 4:4; Lk 12:15.

346 Another type of delinquent parents are the phony parents who set up standards for their children to live by but who themselves do not live according to those standards. Children and young people are quick to sense the hypocrisy of parents who demand a price of good conduct in them which they themselves are not willing to pay.

347 Luther Burbank, the great botanist, once said: "If we had paid no more attention to our plants than we have to our children, we would now be living in a jungle of weeds"; *ref. 321-326.*

† † †

348 The church that is not concerned about the Christian instruction and training of its children and youth need not worry about its future — it has no future.

349 When a mother with a child in her arms was asked by a friend who greatly admired her child: "Would you consider giving your child to me?" she promptly replied, "I should say not." But then, knowing of the friend's love for her child, she added, "You may hold him a little while." — The church cannot and surely does not wish to take children from their parents. But it does ask for the privilege of holding their children for a little while in worship services and Sunday School; *ref. 321-326.*

† † †

350 Contrasting the huge expenditures that the state made for weapons of war with the paltry sum that it expended for education, Martin Luther wrote in his *Letter to the Nobility*: "If we must annually spend large sums on muskets, roads, bridges, dams, and the like, in order that the city may have temporal peace and comfort, why should we not apply as much to our poor, neglected youth, in order that they may have a skillful schoolmaster or two?"

351 Of all the dispositions that lead to political prosperity, religion and morality are indispensable supports. . . . Reason and experience both forbid us to expect that national morality can prevail in exclusion of religious principles.

— George Washington

352 What makes men good Christians makes them good citizens.

— Daniel Webster

353 The strength of our country is the strength of its religious convictions.

— Calvin Coolidge

354 No nation can prosper, no nation can survive if it ever forgets Almighty God.

— Warren C. Harding

355 A State Supreme Court judge said that during the twenty-three years in which he served on the bench, 4000 boys under the age of 21 were convicted of crime before him, and that only three of those 4000 had received a religious training.

— Judge Lewis L. Fawcett,
New York State Supreme Court

ref. 321-326,329

† † †

91

356 A father, finding that his young son had nothing to do, tore a page out of the magazine that he himself was reading. The page contained a map of the world. After cutting up the page into a number of sections, the father handed it to the boy and asked him to piece it together again. Within a few minutes the boy finished the job and brought the completed map back. Astonished, the father asked: "How did you manage to do it so quickly?" "Well, Daddy," said the lad," on the back of the map was a picture of a boy. I knew that if I could build the boy right, the world would come out right too." — If we build our children right, then the church, the home, the nation and the world will come out all right, too; *ref. 321-329.*

† † †

357   Home Visitation Program
V — italizes the work of the congregation
I — ncreases enrollment
S — ecures home cooperation
I — nspires regular attendance
T — ies the home closer to the church
A — ffords soul-winning opportunity
T — ypifies the loving concern of Christ
I — nsures growth in grace
O — pens the doors of homes to Christ
N — urtures friendliness and good will.
— selected

ref. 326

† † †

358 There is no conflict between Christianity and true science. There are truths which man can discover without divine revelation, and we cannot but marvel at many discoveries that science has made and which have brought blessings to mankind.

But there is a vast difference between science and *philosophy*. Science deals with facts, while philosophy deals with man-made theories and hypotheses. True science deals with the material universe, with things that can be tested and proved. Man-made philosophy, on the other hand, goes far beyond this and presumes to have answers for questions relating to the spiritual realm and the unseen world. It is against this latter philosophy, which some falsely call science, that the Scriptures warn: Col 2:1-10; 1 Tm 6:20.

But science is not a substitute for Christianity. Science can, indeed, make discoveries and can harness the forces of nature to a point. But it cannot guide man's behavior in controlling the forces he has harnessed. Man is responsible for the proper use of these powers. Science is only a tool, and the manner in which man uses this tool depends upon his understanding of the purpose of life which Christianity alone can give. Far from supplying a cure-all to the world's problems, the kind of science that relies on man-made philosophy has often failed and has within it the potential of leading mankind to the brink of ruin.

Only in a Christian home and school is a child able to learn the proper relationship between God's Word, science and philosophy; *ref. 316,318-320.*

FAITH, SAVING 359-383

(ref.: Hope 557-564; Trust 1532-1552)

Definition

359 Saving faith is the work of God whereby the sinner apprehends the salvation won for him by Christ and which is offered to him through the gospel, not because of any merit or worthiness in him but solely as God's free gift of grace: Jn 6:28,29; Ro 1:16,17; 3:25,28; 4:3; 5:1; 6:23; 11:6; Ga 2:16; Eph 2:8,9; Php 3:9; 2 Tm 1:9; Tt 3:5-7. Saving faith is bound up with repentance (changing one's mind): Mt 3:2; 4:17; Mk 1:15; Ac 2:38,39; 3:19; *ref. 368,370-372.*

360 Scriptures speak of saving faith as

Believing in Jesus Christ: Jn 3:15,16; 6:35,40; 11:25; 20:31; Ac 10:43; 13:39; 16:30,31; Ro 10:9,10;

Hearing and believing Christ's word: Jn 5:24; 8:31,32; 10:27,28; 15:3; 2 Jn 9;

Coming to Christ: Mt 11:28,29; Lk 14:17;

Winning Christ: Php 3:7-9;

Receiving Christ: Mt 10:40; Jn 1:12; Col 2:6;

Following Christ: Mt 4:19; 16:24; Lk 5:27,28; Jn 8:12; 10:27.

The Essence of Saving Faith

To have saving faith does not mean merely to recognize the existence of Christ and the power of God: Jas 2:19; cp. Mt 8:28,29; Mk 1:23-25; 3:11; Lk 4:41; Ac 19:15. Rather, it embraces

361 A *knowledge and understanding* of God and of his son, Jesus Christ, whom he sent as the Savior of the world: Jn 17:3; Php 3:8-11; 1 Tm 2:4-6; 1 Jn 4:7-16; 5:20. The mind of natural man is not capable of such knowledge but is opposed to it and considers it foolishness: Ro 3:10-12; 8:7; 10:14; 1 Cor 1:23; 2:14; 2 Cor 4:3,4; Eph 4:18. It is the work of God revealed by the Holy Spirit through the gospel: Lk 1:76-79; Jn 6:28,29; Ro 1:16,17; 10:17; 1 Cor 1:24,25; 2:4-13; 2 Cor 4:6; 2 Tm 3:15; 1 Pe 1:10-12; *ref. 370,371,374-376,378,379.*

362 A *willing assent* which joyfully accepts what God graciously offers and obeys such invitations as "Repent and believe the Gospel!" Mk 1:15; "Come, for all things are now ready!" Lk 14:17; "Follow Me!" Lk 5:27,28; "Be reconciled to God!" 2 Cor 5:19; cp. Ac 8:5-8,36-39; 16:30-34; Ro 5:11. It is a transformation wrought by the Holy Spirit, who overcomes man's natural resistance and unwillingness: 1 Cor 6:9-11; Eph 2:1-9; Col 2:13; *ref. 370.*

363 A *confident trust* in God's power and grace and the certainty of the fulfillment of his promises through Christ, especially the assurance that all believers are the children of God and heirs of eternal life: Job 13:15; 19:25; Jn 17:8; Ro 4:18-22; 5:1,2; 8:32-39; 2 Cor 1:20; Php 4:13; Col 1:5,23; 2:2; 1 Th 1:5;

1 Tm 4:10; 2 Tm 1:12; 4:7,8,18; Tt 1:2; 3:7; He 6:18,19; 10:22; 11:1-40; 13:5,6; 1 Pe 1:3-9; 2 Pe 1:2-4; 1 Jn 5:14. This confidence is wrought by the Holy Spirit: Ro 8:16,17,24-29; Ga 4:6; 1 Jn 3:24; 4:13; *ref. 367-371,377,378,380,381,383.*

The Fruits of Saving Faith

364 A spiritual rebirth: Jn 3:3-6; 5:24; 2 Cor 5:17; Eph 2:1-9; Tt 3:5; 1 Pe 1:3,23; 1 Jn 5:1; *ref. 367.*

A new relationship with God: Jn 1:12,13; Ro 8:14-17; Ga 2:20; 3:26,27; 4:4-7; Eph 2:19-22; Col 1:12-14; Tt 3:5-7; 1 Jn 3:1,2; Re 1:5,6; and a new relationship with one's fellowmen: Jn 13:35; 15:12; 1 Th 3:12; 1 Pe 1:22; 1 Jn 2:9,10; 3:11,14,23,24; 4:7,20,21; *ref. 370;*

A new spiritual life which proves its presence by works of faith and labors of love: Mt 5:16; 25:34-36; Ro 6; 8:1-13; Ga 5:6,22-26; Eph 2:10; 4:13,17-32; 5:1-11; Col 3:1-10; Tt 2:11-14; 1 Pe 2:9-12;

A joyful hope of eternal life in the world to come: Ro 5:2; 8:22-25; 12:12; 15:13; 1 Cor 15:19,20; Eph 1:18; Col 1:5,23,27; 1 Th 4:13-18; 5:8; 2 Th 2:16,17; Tt 1:2; 2:13; He 6:18,19; 1 Pe 1:3-5; 1 Jn 3:1,2; *ref. 368,380.*

Faith and Christian Life

365 Believers are exhorted to:

Walk by faith and not by sight: Mt 14:29-31; Jn 20:24-29; 2 Cor 4:17,18; 5:7; He 11:13; 1 Pe 1:8; and not doubt: Mt 6:30; 11:3; 21:21; Mk 11:23; Lk 1:20; 12:29; Ro 14:23; 1 Tm 2:8; Jas 1:5,6; *ref. 371,372,275;*

Guard against unbelief: Mk 4:40; 16:14; Lk 24:25,26; Ro 4:20; Ga 1:6; 4:9; 1 Tm 1:19,20; 4:1; 2 Tm 3:8; 4:10; He 3:12; 4:11; 6:4-6; 2 Pe 2:20; 3:17; Jude 5; Re 2:4; *ref. 378,383;*

Be established in faith: Eph 4:14,15; Col 1:23; 2:7; continually trust in the Lord: Ps 37:3,5; 42:11; 62:8; 115:9-11; Pr 3:5; Is 26:4; Jr 17:7; 2 Cor 5:7; 1 Tm 4:10, and hold fast to their faith, especially when it is being tested: Job 13:15; Mk 7:24-30; Ac 14:22; Ro 4:20; 5:3-5; 1 Cor 10:13; 1 Th 3:2-4; 2 Tm 3:12-14; He 11:8-10,17-19; 12:6-10; Jas 1:2,3,12; 1 Pe 1:5-7; 2:20,21; 4:12-16; Re 2:10; *ref. 369;*

Grow in faith: Lk 17:5; 2 Cor 10:15; Eph 1:15-23; *ref. 367;*

Let Christ dwell in their hearts by faith: Ga 2:20; Eph 3:17;

Offer their prayers in faith: Mt 21:22; He 11:6; Jas 1:5,6; 1 Jn 5:14,15; *ref. 374,1150,1161,1164,1169,1181;*

Show the fruits of faith in their lives: Ro 1:8; 16:19; Ga 5:6; Col 1:3-14; 1 Th 1:3-10; Jas 2:17,18; cp Mt 7:21-23; 25:34-40; *ref. 373;*

Fight the good fight of faith and resist the devil by faith: Eph 6:16; 1 Th 5:8; 1 Tm 6:12; 1 Pe 5:8,9; *ref. 382;*

Contend for the faith: Jude 3; *ref. 382;*

Preserve the unity of faith: Eph 4:1-6; Php 1:27;

Testify to their faith: Ac 4:20; 24:15,16; 26:22,23; Jas 2:15-17; 1 Pe 3:15.

Examples of Strong and Weak Faith

366 Examples of strong faith:

Abel, Enoch, Noah, Abraham and Sarah, Isaac, Jacob, Joseph, Moses, Rahab, Gideon, Barak, Samson, Jephthah, David, Samuel and the prophets: He 11:4-39;

Job: 19:25-27;

Joseph: Mt 1:24;

The leper: Mt 8:2;

The centurion: Mt 8:10;

The ruler: Mt 9:18;

The afflicted woman: Mt 9:20f

The blind man: Mt 9:28;

Many that were deceased: Mt 14:35,36;

The Syrophenician woman: Mt 15:28;

The nobleman: Jn 4:46-52;

Paul: Ac 27:25; Ro 8:35f; Php 4:13; 2 Tm 1:11,12; 4:7,8,18.

Examples of weak faith:

Zacharias: Lk 1:18-20;

Christ's disciples:　Mt 6:30; 8:26; 14:31; 16:8; Mk 16:14; Lk 24:11,25.

Resources

367
　　Oh, for a faith that will not shrink
　　　Tho' pressed by many a foe;
　　That will not tremble on the brink
　　　Of poverty or woe;

　　That will not murmur nor complain
　　　Beneath the chast'ning rod,
　　But in the hour of grief or pain
　　　Can lean upon its God;

　　A faith that shines more bright and clear
　　　When tempests rage without;
　　That, when in danger, knows no fear,
　　　In darkness feels no doubt;

　　That bears unmoved the world's dread frown
　　　Nor heeds its scornful smile;
　　That sin's wild ocean cannot drown
　　　Nor Satan's arts beguile;

　　A faith that keeps the narrow way
　　　Till life's last spark is fled
　　And with a pure and heavenly ray
　　　Lights up the dying bed.

Lord, give us such a faith as this;
And then, what'er may come,
We'll taste e'en now the hallowed bliss
Of an eternal home.
— William H. Bathurst
ref. 365

† † †

368 When Dr. John Paton, a missionary in the New Hebrides, began trans-lating the Gospel of John into the language of the natives he could not find a word in their language for "believe." And so he set his manuscript aside.

One day a native, who had been working hard, came into Dr. Paton's office and, sitting in one chair and putting his feet upon another, he used a native word which meant "I am resting my whole weight on these two chairs." Hearing this, Dr. Paton said, "I have found my word for 'believe.' " He then proceeded to translate the Gospel of John, using for the English word "believe," the word of the natives which meant "I am resting my whole weight upon"; *ref. 359,363,364.*

369 Faith does not rely upon material things, but upon God and upon his mighty power.

When Alexander von Humboldt, the German traveler and naturalist, experi-enced his first earthquake, the house he was in began to crack and fall about him. Hastily he sought refuge in another house, but found that it, too, was in ruin. Lifting his eyes to the hills, he saw that they were staggering like drunken men. Looking to the sea he saw the bare keel of a ship in the mud, for the waters had fled. The ground under his feet trembled; there was no place of security anywhere. In his despair, however, he looked up and there, above the ruins about him he saw that the heavens were unmoved.
— selected
ref. 363

370 Justifying faith is faith in the promises of God. . . . To believe in Christ means to believe what the Bible says about him. In that sense, saving faith is nothing else but agreement with statements of the Bible.
— Siegbert W. Becker
ref. 361-364

† † †

371 Dr. McCormick, in "The Heart of Prayer," tells of a good woman whose daughter had died after a painful illness. She came to her minister and said, "I fear I have lost my faith in prayer. I used to believe that anything I asked for in the name of Christ, I would receive. When my child was sick, I besought God in an agony of desire for her recovery. I believed that God would answer my prayer. When she died I was stunned, not merely because of my grief, but because it seemed to me that God had failed me. I still pray, but the old faith in prayer is gone."

This good woman was the victim of wrong teaching. She had, in a word, been led to substitute faith in prayer for faith in God. If our faith in prayer is uppermost, then any disappointment will share that faith. But if faith in God is the great fact of life, then no matter what may be the outcome of our petitions we will still trust.

— *The Presbyterian*

ref. 363,365

† † †

372
My faith looks up to thee,
Thou Lamb of Calvary,
 Savior divine.
Now hear me while I pray;
Take all my guilt away;
Oh, let me from this day
 Be wholly thine!

— Ray Palmer

ref. 359,365

† † †

373 Faith is a living, busy, active, efficacious thing, so that it is impossible for it not incessantly to do good works. It does not ask whether good works are to be done, but before the question is asked it has already done them.

— Martin Luther

ref. 365

† † †

374 An aged widow in Scotland had to make her livelihood by carrying butter and eggs to the market every morning. Her path lay over a great mountain. It was a hard climb for the old lady, and she often thought how pleasant it would be if the mountain were not there. One Sunday she listened with rapt attention to the minister's sermon in which he said that if we had faith we could move mountains. That night she prayed that God would move the mountain that was causing her so much trouble. Very early the following morning she arose, drew back the curtain to see if the mountain was still there. "Ah," she said, "I knew you would be there!" *ref. 361,365.*

† † †

375 A mother and her four-year-old daughter were preparing to retire for the night. The child was afraid of the dark, and the mother, on this occasion alone with the child, felt fear also. When the light was out, the child caught a glimpse of the moon outside the window. "Mother," she asked, "is the moon God's light?" "Yes," said the mother. the next question was, "Will God put out his light and go to sleep?" The mother replied, "No, my child. God never goes to sleep." Then out of a simplicity of a child's faith, she said that which

gave reassurance to the fear-filled mother, "Well, as long as God is awake, I am not afraid."

— Sunday School Times

ref. 363,365

† † †

376 Faith does not reply on one's senses, but on God's promises, and it trusts God's Word, whether felt or not: Jn 20:29. Martin Luther expressed it as follows:

> For feelings come and feelings go,
>   And feelings are deceiving;
> My warrant is the Word of God,
>   Naught else is worth believing.
>
> Though all my heart should feel condemned
>   For want of some sweet token,
> There is One greater than my heart
>   Whose word cannot be broken.
>
> I'll trust in God's unchanging Word
>   Till soul and body sever;
> For, though all things shall pass away,
>   His Word shall stand forever.

ref. 361

† † †

377 The drummer boy in Napoleon's army was asked in a certain battle to beat a retreat. He replied to his superior: "Sir, I do not know how! But I can beat a charge that will make the dead fall into line. I beat it for many a victory in the past. May I beat it here?" Consent was given. The charge was beaten. Victory was gained.

"Everyone born of God has overcome the world. This is the victory that has overcome the world, even our faith," 1 Jn 5:4; ref. 363.

† † †

378

> Dark are the skies of the faithless,
>   Bitter their hours of grief,
> Heavy the blow that is struck by woe
>   To the children of unbelief;
> Having no God to turn to,
>   Having no Savior to trust,
> They're tossed about by the winds of doubt
>   As helpless as grains of dust.

— Anon

ref. 361,365

† † †

379 Sometimes we hear one say: "As long as I am sincere, I'll come out all right in the end." Is that true? Read the following:

In a hospital in the State of New York carbon dioxide instead of oxygen was administered to a patient, and death resulted immediately. Upon examination it was found that the tank had been mislabeled before it reached the hospital. Surely, no one wanted the tragedy to happen. The manufacturer was sincere, the surgeon was sincere, the anesthetist was sincere, and certainly hospital authorities and the patient were sincere. Yet, all were sincerely mistaken about the "oxygen." Not sincerity alone, but certainty, is needed; *ref. 361.*

† † †

380
> Faith, mighty faith the promise sees
>   And rests on that alone;
> Laughs at impossibilities,
>   And says it shall be done.

— Wesley

ref. 363,364

381 In the battle of Alma, when one of the regiments was being beaten back by the Russians, the ensign in front stood his ground as the troops retreated. The captain shouted to him to bring back the colors. But the reply of the ensign was: "Bring up the men to the colors!" *ref. 363.*

† † †

382
> Faith of our fathers, living faith,
>   In spite of dungeons, fire, and sword!
> It cannot die because its springs
>   Flow from the ever-living Word.
> Faith of our fathers, living faith!
> Lord, keep us in this faith till death!
>
> Faith of our fathers, holy faith,
>   Thrice hallowed by the Savior's cross,
> To which we lift our trusting eyes
>   And count for it all things but loss.
> Faith of our fathers, holy faith!
> Lord, keep us in this faith till death!

— F. W. Faber

383
> Doubt sees the obstacles;
>   Faith sees the way.
> Doubt sees the darkest night;
>   Faith sees the day.
> Doubt dreads to take the step,
>   Faith soars on high.
> Doubt questions, "Who believes?"
>   Faith answers, "I."

— Anon

ref. 365

99

Its Privilege

384 Christian freedom means the freedom of believers in Christ from the curse of the law: Jn 8:34-36; Ro 6:14; 8:2; 10:4; Ga 3:13; 4:4-7; 5:1; and from the Levitical ceremonies of the Old Testament: Ac 15:10; 1 Cor 8:8; Ga 3:24,25; 4:9-11; Col 2:16,17,23; He 9:10, *ref. 386,387,391.*

Its Restrictions

385 While Christian liberty includes the liberty to choose in matters that are neither commanded nor forbidden by the Word of God, Ro 14:13,14, it is not something absolute, for there are circumstances when the exercise of it becomes sinful, e.g.,

When it is used as an excuse for loose living: 1 Cor 8:9; 10:23; Ga 5:13; 1 Pe 2:16;

When it is used presumptuously to judge the actions of others: Mt 15:9; 23:13f; Ro 14:1-6;

When the use of it causes an offense to a weak brother: Mt 18:6; Ro 14:13-23; 1 Cor 6:12,13; 8:9-13; 10:23-33. Our conduct toward our brother should rather be one of love and consideration for his convictions: Jn 13:34; 15:12; Ro 15:1-3; 1 Cor 9:22; 10:33; Ga 5:13; 1 Jn 4:20,21; *ref. 386,389,390,392-394.*

Resources

386 Christian freedom is a precious and priceless privilege. But it also bears the responsibility of regarding the freedom of one's fellowman as well as one's own.

Martin Luther put it aptly when he said, "The Christian is a free man; he is the lord over all things and subject to no man," and then added, "The Christian is a servant of all things, and subject to all men."

In his relationship to God, the Christian is indeed free to do anything that God has not forbidden. However, in his relationship to his fellowmen the law of Christian love demands that the Christian avoid doing anything that would offend a fellow Christian who is weak in faith and spiritual understanding. Likewise, a Christian should take care not to give offense to the unbelieving world: 1 Cor 10:23,32,33; *ref. 384,385.*

† † †

387
Teach me, my God and King,
In all things thee to see,
And what I do in anything
To do it as to thee.

— Moule

ref. 585

† † †

388 Included among the things that God has neither commanded nor forbidden for the Christian are, e.g., the observance of certain days and the eating of certain meats: Ro 14:1-6; 1 Cor 10:23-33; Ga 4:9-11; Col 2:16,17; moderate drinking of wine, fasting during Lent, the use of instrumental music in worship, the use of certain forms for worship and the like. Matters of this nature are known as "adiaphora," that is, matters that are morally indifferent, or neutral; *ref. 384.*

† † †

389 It is not the use, but the abuse, of a thing that makes it sinful: 1 Cor 7:31. Thus, for example, it is not wrong in itself to drink wine, but it is wrong to drink wine to excess. It is not wrong to eat, but it is wrong to become gluttonous. It is not wrong to play cards, but it is wrong to waste on card-playing many precious hours that should be spent more profitably elsewhere. It is not wrong to spend money for hobbies and recreation, but it is wrong when this is not done in moderation and in keeping with obligations such as providing properly for one's family or giving worthy support for the work of the church; *ref. 385.*

† † †

390 Civil liberty, like Christian freedom is a precious, priceless privilege. To possess and to retain it, people are ready to fight, to suffer, and if necessary to die. Like Patrick Henry they cry out: "Give me liberty, or give me death!"

But while civil liberty includes many privileges, such as the freedom to think, to speak, and to go where one pleases, it also involves definite responsibilities. Its privileges cease when they interfere with the privileges of someone else. It cannot demand its rights when the granting of those rights endanger the safety and life of others. Thus, to quote a familiar example, freedom of speech does not grant the individual the right to shout "Fire!" in a crowded theatre; *ref. 384,385.*

† † †

391 In one of his letters John Adams wrote, "Posterity! You will never know how much it cost the present generation to preserve your freedom! I hope you will make a good use of it. If you do not, I shall repent in heaven that I ever took half the pains to preserve it."

If it were possible, how many similar words would one hear coming from the graves in countless battle fields!

392 The following words are inscribed on the Plymouth Rock monument: This spot marks the final resting place of the Pilgrims of the Mayflower. In weariness and hunger and in cold, fighting the wilderness and burying their dead in common graves that the Indians should not know how many had perished, they here laid the foundations of a state in which all men for countless ages should have liberty to worship God in their own way. All you who pass by and see this stone remember, and dedicate yourselves anew to the resolution that you will not rest until this lofty ideal shall have been realized throughout the earth.

393 I have sworn upon the altar of God, eternal hostility against every form of tyranny over the mind of man.

— Thomas Jefferson

† † †

394 Is life so dear, or peace so sweet, as to be purchased at the price of chains and slavery? Forbid it, Almighty God! I know not what course others may take, but as for me, give me liberty, or give me death.

— Patrick Henry

ref. 384

GOD 395-415

(ref.: Holy Spirit 506-533; Jesus Christ 578f)

The Existence of God

395 *Natural knowledge:* The true nature of God cannot be perceived by human reason: Jn 1:18; 5:37; 1 Tm 6:16; still man knows from natural knowledge, that God exists:

The existence of the world testifies to God's power, wisdom, goodness and love: Ps 19:1; 145:9,15,16; Ac 14:15-17; 17:26-28; Ro 1:20,21,25; He 3:4;

396 The voice of man's conscience testifies to the Law of God written in his heart: Ro 2:14,15; *ref. 210.*

397 *Revealed knowledge:* Man's natural knowledge has been corrupted through sin: Ro 1:21; 1 Cor 2:14; therefore God's true nature can be known only through the revelation that he has given of himself:

398 In Holy Scriptures: Dt 4:32-35; 29:29; Is 42:8; 43:10,11; 44:6; 1 Cor 2:10-13; 2 Tm 3:16; 2 Pe 1:21; *ref. 101.*

399 In the person and work of his Son Jesus Christ: Mt 11:27; 17:5; Jn 1:14, 18; 12:49; 14:6,9,10; 15:15; 17:3; Col 2:9; 1 Tm 3:16; He 1:1,2; 1 Jn 5:20; *ref. 409,414.*

The Essence of God

400 Both the Old and the New Testaments declare the unity of God's essence. They teach:

That God is one (monotheism): Dt 6:4; 1 Cor 8:4-6; 1 Tm 2:5; that there is only one true God: Dt 4:35; 32:39; 2 Sm 7:22; Ps 86:10; Is 43:10; 44:6; 45:22; and that the gods of the heathen are nothing: Lv 19:4; 26:1; Ps 115:3,4; Jr 2:11; 10:5,14,15; Ac 14:15; 1 Cor 8:4;

401 That any worship outside of and apart from, or any worship in addition to, the worship of the one true God is idolatry: Ex 20:3-6; Is 42:8; Mt 4:10; and that the sacrifices of the heathen are offered not to God but to devils: Ac 14:15; 1 Cor 10:20; *ref. 408,1460.*

402 Both the Old and the New Testaments declare that the only true God is the Triune God:

There are three distinct persons, Father, Son and Holy Ghost, in one divine being, or essence (the Holy Trinity): Gn 1:1,2 (*Elohim*, is the majestic plural form of the Hebrew word for God. We translate it in the singular, as "God"); Nu 6:24-26; Ps 2:7; 45:6,7; 110:1; Is 6:3; 48:16; 63:8-10; Mt 3:16,17; 28:19; Jn 14:15,16,26; 15:26; 2 Cor 13:14; Ga 4:6; Eph 3:14-16; 1 Jn 5:7; *ref. 411,412.*

403 The Father has begotten the Son from eternity; the Son is begotten from the Father from eternity: Ps 2:7; Jn 1:18; the Holy Ghost from eternity proceeds from the Father and the Son: Jn 15:26; *ref. 406.*

The Attributes of God

404 Holy Scriptures teach that "God is a spirit," Jn 4:24, and that he is
Eternal: Dt 33:27; Ps 90:1,2; Is 57:15; Lm 5:19; Re 1:8;
Unchangeable: Ps 102:27; Mal 3:6;
Omnipotent: Gn 17:1; 18:14; Ps 115:3; 135:6; Mt 19:26; Lk 1:37;
Omniscient: Job 34:21; Ps 139:1-4; 147:5; Jn 21:17; He 4:13; 1 Jn 3:20;
Omnipresent: 1 Kgs 8:27; Ps 139:8-10; Jr 23:23,24;
Holy: Ex 15:11; Lv 19:2; Ps 99:9; Is 6:3;
Just: Dt 32:4; Ps 92:15; Ro 2:2;
Faithful: Dt 7:9; 1 Kgs 8:56; Ps 36:5; 1 Cor 1:9; 2 Tm 2:13; Tt 1:2;
Benevolent (good): Ps 34:8; 136:1; 145:9; Mt 5:45;
Merciful: Ps 136:1; 145:9; Lk 1:78,79; Tt 3:4,5;
Longsuffering: Ex 34:6,7; 1 Pe 3:20; 2 Pe 3:9;
Gracious: Ex 34:6,7; Tt 2:11;
Love: 1 Jn 4:8,16.

Names Ascribed to God

405 General references:
Almighty God: Gn 17:1; Ex 6:3;
Creator: Is 40:28;
Eternal God: Dt 33:27;
God of gods: Dt 10:17;
Holy One: Is 40:25; Holy One of Israel: Ps 71:22; Is 43:3;
I AM: Ex 3:14; Jehovah: Ex 6:3; Ps 83:18;
Lord: Ex 3:4,7; Is 50:10; Lord of Hosts: 1 Sm 1:11; Is 6:3; Mal 1:11;
Lord of lords: Dt 10:17; Lord of Sabaoth: Jas 5:4;
Most High: Dt 32:8; Dn 4:17;
Redeemer: Is 41:14;
Savior: Is 43:3.

406 Special references to
God the Father: Ps 89:26; Is 63:16; Jr 31:9; Mal 2:10; Mt 3:17; 6:9; 11:27; 17:5; 18:35; Jn 3:35; 5:17,20,21,26,37; 6:46; 8:16,18; 10:29,30,38; 12:49; 14:2,11,24; 15:1; 16:27; 17:1f; Eph 4:6; Jas 1:17; 1 Pe 1:17;

God the Son: *ref. Jesus Christ, divine names 615f*;
God the Holy Ghost: *ref. Holy Spirit, divine names 510f.*

Resources

407 When Mark Twain was touring Europe, he received an invitation to visit the Kaiser. "Why, papa," exclaimed his little daughter, when she heard of it, "If this keeps up, there won't be anybody left for you to get acquainted with but God."

† † †

408 The people of Israel had forsaken God for Ashtoreth, Chemosh, and Milcom. We call that idolatry . . . and we still practice it.

A famous Chinese gentleman stood in the new York Stock Exchange not so long ago, after having visited our half-empty churches. He was so impressed with the furor and intensity of the Exchange that he cried, "Ah, this is their REAL religion! This is what they care about!" Well, is it?

Wouldn't you say that we are worshiping Mars, the god of war, as much as we worship Jesus Christ? Every able-bodied boy in the country may be forced to give two years of his life to the art of war; how many give two years to Jesus Christ?

Others worship Bacchus; they live to have a good time. Others worship the god of the machine, or the god of the cash register, or the god of athletics, or. . . . How many more can you supply?

— Frank S. Mead in
Tarbell's Teachers' Guide, 1954

ref. 401

† † †

409 Daniel Webster was once asked at a dinner party, "What is the greatest idea that ever entered your mind?" After a pause, he answered, "The greatest idea that ever entered my mind is the idea of personal responsibility to a personal God"; *ref. 397,399.*

† † †

410 The richest man in the world, Croesus, once asked the wisest man in the world, Thales, "What is God?" The philosopher asked for a day in which to deliberate, and then for another, and then for another, and another, and another — and at length confessed that he was not able to answer, that the longer he deliberated, the more difficult it was for him to frame an answer.

The fiery Tertulian, the early Church Father, eagerly seized upon this incident and said it was an example of the world's ignorance of God outside of Christ. "There," he exclaimed, "is the wisest man in the world, and he

cannot tell you who God is. But the most ignorant mechanic among the Christians knows God, and is able to make him known unto others."
— Clarence E. Macartney

ref. 397-399

411 It is said of St. Augustine that he was once in great distress of mind how he might comprehend and describe the article concerning the Trinity. While he was engaged deeply with his thoughts, he tells that he dreamed he was walking along the seashore. There he saw a little child who had dug a hole in the sand, and was busily engaged in dipping the ocean water into the hole with a shell.

"What are you doing?" asked the church father.

"With this pail," said the child, "I'm going to empty the water of the ocean and pour it into this hole."

"You will never be able to do that," said Augustine.

"True," said the child, "but it is just as foolish for you to try to empty the mysteries of the infinite Triune God with the little dipper of your mind."

412   Holy Father, holy Son,
                    Holy Spirit, three we name thee;
                 Though in essence only one,
                    Undivided God we claim thee
                 And, adoring, bend the knee
                    While we own the mystery.
                                         — Anon
          ref. 402,403

† † †

413 A farmer once came to Dr. Luther and said that he could not understand the Creed when it speaks of God Almighty. "Neither can I nor all the doctors," said the Reformer, "but only believe it in all simplicity and take that God Almighty for your Lord, and he will take care of you and all you have, and bring you safely through all your troubles"; *ref. 404.*

† † †

414 A Roman emperor, after a successful military campaign, was returning to Rome in triumph, as was the custom of those days. Kings were chained to his chariot wheels as trophies of his triumph. He did not enter through the gates of the city, because that was too common; everybody did that. He ordered a breach in the walls to be made for him and thus made his entry. Great throngs filled the city streets to welcome the mighty hero.

While passing through one of the crowded thoroughfares, a little girl, wild with joy, dashed toward the chariot. The police stopped her and said, "That is the chariot of the emperor and you must not try to reach him." But the little one replied, "He may be your emperor, but he is my father." And in a moment she was not only in the chariot, but also in her father's arms.
                                         — selected
ref. 397-399

105

415 To the artist he is the One Altogether Lovely.
To the architect he is the Chief Cornerstone.
To the astronomer he is the Sun of Righteousness.
To the baker he is the Living Bread.
To the banker he is the Hidden Treasure.
To the biologist he is the Life.
To the builder he is the Sure Foundation.
To the Carpenter he is the Door.
To the doctor he is the Great Physician.
To the educator he is the Great Teacher.
To the engineer he is the New and Living Way.
To the farmer he is the Sower, and the Lord of the Harvest.
To the florist he is the Rose of Sharon and the Lily of the Valley.
To the geologist he is the Rock of Ages.
To the horticulturist he is the True Vine.
To the judge he is the Righteous Judge, the Judge of all men.
To the juror he is the Faithful and True Witness.
To the jeweler he is the Pearl of Great Price.
To the lawyer he is the Counselor, the Lawgiver, the Advocate.
To the newspaperman he is the Tidings of Great Joy.
To the oculist he is the Light of the Eyes.
To the philanthropist he is the Giver.
To the preacher he is the Word of God.
To the sculptor he is the Living Stone.
To the servant he is the Master.
To the student he is the Incarnate Truth.
To the statesman he is the Desire of all Nations.
To the theologian he is the Author and Finisher of our faith.
To the toiler he is the Giver of Rest.

— selected

GOOD WORKS 416-434

(ref.: Grace 461-478; Justification 850-864; Service 1322-1342)

The Nature of Good Works

416 They do not obtain justification before God: Is 64:6; Ro 3:20-26; 4:1-5,16; 11:6; Ga 2:16; 3:5-11; 5:4,5; Eph 2:8,9; 2 Tm 1:9; Tt 3:5-7; *ref. 427-431;*

417 They are the result of a living faith in Jesus Christ: Jn 15:3-8,16; 2 Cor 5:17; Ga 5:6; Jas 2:14-18; *ref. 427-431;*

418 They are the fruits of the Holy Spirit: Ga 5:22,23; Eph 2:10; 5:9; Php 1:11; *ref. 427-432.*

The Purpose of Good Works

419 They are performed to the glory of God: Mt 5:16; Jn 15:8; Ro 7:4; 1 Cor 10:31; Php 1:11; Col 3:17; 1 Pe 2:9;

420 They are performed for the benefit of others: Mt 25:35-40; Ga 5:13; 6:10; 1 Tm 6:18; He 13:16; and they lead others to glorify God: Mt 5:16; 2 Cor 9:12-14; 1 Pe 2:11,12; *ref. 432.*

Exhortations To Do Good Works

421 Christian people are exhorted to abound in good works: Jn 15:3-8; 2 Cor 9:8; Php 1:11; Col 1:10; 3:12-14; Tt 2:14; 3:1,8,14; He 13:20,21; and to provoke one another to love and good works: Tt 3:8; He 10:24; *ref. 432;*

422 Christian ministers are exhorted to be a pattern of good works: 1 Tm 4:12; Tt 2:7.

Rewards for Good Works

423 Even though the so-called "good works" of unbelievers are performed from wrong motives, God in his righteousness and goodness rewards them in this life: Mt 6:1-5; Jn 5:44; 12:43; *ref. 433,434;*

424 Even though it is God who performs the good works through Christian people, he graciously rewards these works as though his people performed them: Is 26:12; Php 1:6; 2:13; He 6:9-11; Jas 1:25; Re 14:13; cp. Lk 17:10; *ref. 433,434.*

Examples of Doing Good Works

425 Christ: Mk 7:37; Lk 19:37; Jn 5:36; 9:4; 10:32; Ac 10:38;

426 Believers: Mary of Bethany: Mt 26:7-10; Dorcas: Ac 9:36; the Thessalonians: 1 Th 1:3; see also Mt 25:34-40; Lk 10:30-37; *ref. 432.*

Resources

427
By grace! None dare lay claim to merit;
Our works and conduct have no worth.
God in his love sent our Redeemer,
Christ Jesus, to this sinful earth;

His death did for our sins atone,
And we are saved by grace alone.
                              — Christian L. Scheidt
ref. 416

† † †

428 Good works are anything that Christians think, say, or do in faith, according to the Ten Commandments, for the glory of God and the benefit of their fellowmen; *ref. 417,418.*

† † †

429 Christian people are not saved because they do good works, they do good works because they have been saved; *ref. 416-418.*

† † †

430   'Tis not by works of righteousness
                        Which our own hands have done,
                        But we are saved by God's free grace
                        Abounding thro' his Son.
                              — Isaac Watts
        ref. 416-418

† † †

431 It is essential that we ever affirm the doctrine of justification by grace, for Christ's sake, through faith, because: a) it is the chief doctrine of the Christian religion: Ac 4:12; 10:43; b) it distinguishes the Christian religion from false religions, all of which teach salvation by works: Ga 5:4,5; c) it gives enduring comfort to penitent sinners: Mt 9:2; Ac 16:30,31,34; d) it gives all glory to God: Re 1:5,6; *ref. 416-418.*

† † †

432 Faith is not man's opinion and dream, . . . but it is a divine work in us that changes and begets us anew of God: Jn 1:13. It mortifies the old Adam, transforms us into entirely different men in heart, mind, will, sense and powers, and brings with it the Holy Ghost. Oh, this faith is a living, busy, active, efficacious thing, so that it is impossible for it not incessantly to do good works. It does not ask whether good works are to be done, but before the question is asked it has already done them. But he who does not do these works is a faithless man, who is always groping and looking for faith and good works and knows neither what faith or good works are, though he prate in many words concerning faith and good works.
                              — Martin Luther
ref. 416-420

† † †

433 Rewards in the kingdom of God are rewards of grace, not of merit. God owes us nothing, we owe him everything. Even when we do all things that he has commanded us — and our conscience tells us that we never do that — we must still confess that we are unprofitable servants, for we have done only "that which was our duty to do," Lk 17:9,10. But despite the fact that we have in no wise deserved it, God is pleased, for Christ's sake, graciously to reward our labors for him and to crown them with priceless blessings in time and eternity: Mt 5:11,12; 19:27-29; 25:34; Ro 8:18; *ref. 423-424.*

† † †

434 Far from doing Christ a favor when we serve him, he does us the highest honor by allowing us to serve him. The immeasurable debt of love and service that we owe him cannot begin to compare to the matchless love he showed for us when he gave his life for the incalculable debt of our sins. As we contemplate his wondrous love for us, our redeemed and ransomed hearts respond:

> Were the whole realm of nature mine,
> That were a tribute far too small;
> Love so amazing, so divine,
> Demands my soul, my life, my all.
> — Isaac Watts

ref. 423,424

GOVERNMENT, CIVIL 435-460

(ref.: Church and State 201-204)

The Nature of Government

435 It is a divine institution to promote peace and order, so far as this is possible, in a world of sin and unrighteousness: Pr 8:15; Ro 13:1-7; 1 Tm 2:1-3; Tt 3:1; 1 Pe 2:13,14; see also Dn 2:21; 4:17,25; 5:21; Mt 22:21; Jn 19:10,11; *ref. 440,441.*

The Duties of Government

436 Its duties are to promote the general welfare of its people by protecting the rights of individuals and groups and by defending the State against dangers from within and without. To this end it exercises legislative, judicial and executive power: Ac 25:11; Ro 13:4-7; 1 Tm 2:1,2; *ref. 439,441, 442,449,451,457,458.*

The Duties of Citizens

437 They are under obligations to
Honor all governmental persons as God's representatives: Ro 13:5-7; Tt 3:1; 1 Pe 2:13,14; *ref. 440,443,445;*

Speak well of those in authority: Ex 22:28; Ezr 7:26; Ac 23:5; *ref. 446;*

Obey those who have been placed in authority: Ro 13:5; Tt 3:1; 1 Pe 2:13,14; except where such obedience would require disobedience to God: Ac 4:19; 5:29; *ref. 449,457;*

Cheerfully pay taxes: Mt 22:21; Ro 13:6;

Seek the welfare of the government by voting intelligently and by offering the use of their talents in public service: see Jr 29:4-7; *ref. 448,456,457,460;*

Pray for all in authority: Ps 127:1; Ezr 6:10; 1 Tm 2:1-3; *ref. 444,447,450, 453,459.*

The Christian and His Government

438 The Christian holds two citizenships, one in the nation in which he dwells, the other in the kingdom of God in which he was made a member by faith in Jesus Christ and into which he entered through holy baptism: Jn 3:6; Col 1:12-14; Php 3:20; *ref. 448,460;*

The Christian renders his duties to his government not only for fear of punishment but for conscience' sake, because he recognizes that his government is God's representative: Ro 13:5,6; *ref. 440,441;*

The Christian is the ideal citizen, for only one who is motivated by the love of Christ can be truly motivated to love and serve his fellowmen: Ga 2:20; 1 Jn 4:19-21. The Christian's chief concern, therefore, is not for political change but for a spiritual renewal that makes men new creatures in Christ: 2 Cor 5:17.

---

439 In carrying out its legislative, judicial and executive functions government must follow the natural law as it is still inscribed in the heart of natural man, as well as the dictates of reason, experience and common sense. At times this may involve legislation that does not reflect the high standards of the moral law of God. Thus, in the Commonwealth of Israel, because of the hardness of their hearts, Moses permitted divorce, which was not sanctioned by the moral law of God: Mt 19:7-9.

† † †

440 Even where government officials are disreputable persons, we are to honor and obey them for the sake of their office as God's ministers. Even when impractical laws are passed which are not to our liking we are to obey them while they are in force. Meanwhile we are permitted to use all legal ways and means to have such laws abrogated and to strive for substituting better legislation. Because government is a divine institution, to obey or to disobey is a conscience matter, a moral obligation, an issue which involves the question of right and wrong in the eyes of God. To fail in this respect is to sin against God's Law. Holy Scriptures therefore declare: "They that resist shall receive to themselves damnation," Ro 13:2; *ref. 435*.

† † †

441 Civil government is an outgrowth of family government and an extension of the rule of parents in the home: see Gn 18:19; Dt 6:1ff. The manner in which God dealt with men directly and prescribed laws for them developed into other forms of government. As time passed, the theocratic form of government in Israel was supplanted by the rule of the judges, and that, in turn, was changed into the rule of kings which had long before been in vogue among the heathen nations.

While civil government as such is of divine origin, God has not prescribed the particular form that it must take; *ref. 435*.

† † †

442

What makes a nation great?

Not serried ranks with flags unfurled,
Nor armored ships that gird the world,
Nor hoarded wealth nor busy mills,
Nor cattle on a thousand hills,
Not sages wise, nor schools nor laws,
Not boasted deed in freedom's cause —
All these may be, and yet the state
In the eye of God be far from great.

That land is great which knows the Lord,
Whose songs are guided by his Word;
Where justice rules 'twixt man and man,
Where love controls in art and plan;
Where, breathing in his native air,
Each soul finds joy in praise and prayer —
Thus may our country, good and great,
Be God's delight — man's best estate.
                                    — Alexander Blackburn
     ref. 436-439

† † †

443 I recognize the sublime truth announced in the Holy Scriptures and proven by all history — that those nations only are blest whose God is the Lord; see Ps 33:12; *ref. 435,437.*

                                    — Abraham Lincoln

† † †

444 Almighty God, we make our earnest prayer that thou wilt keep the United States in thy holy protection, and that thou wilt most graciously be pleased to dispose us all to do justice, to love mercy, and to demean ourselves with that charity, humility, and pacific temper of mind which were the characteristics of the Divine Author of our blessed religion, and without an humble imitation of whose example in these things we can never hope to be a happy nation. Grant our supplications, we beseech thee, through Jesus Christ our Lord.   Amen.

                              — George Washington, written at
                              Newburgh, June 8, 1783, and sent
                                 to the governors of all the States

† † †

445 God wills that we honor the government as his minister, through which he bestows valuable blessings upon us. . . . If you knew that someone had saved your child's life you would be heartily thankful to him. Why are you not thankful to your government which daily protects you, your wife, and children from murder? For if the government did not check the wicked people, when would we be safe? Therefore when you look upon your wife and children, you should bear in mind: these are God's gifts, which I may keep by means of the government. And as you love your children, so you should love your country.

                                    — Martin Luther
     ref. 437

† † †

446 During the crucial days of the Civil War a delegation visited the President and criticized him in no uncertain terms for the lack of satisfactory progress in the war. Mr. Lincoln listened patiently and then gave his striking reply:

"Suppose, gentlemen," said the President, "all the property that you were worth was in gold, and you put it in the hands of Blondin to carry across the Niagara River on a rope. Would you shake the cable and keep shouting at him, 'Blondin, stand up a little straighter . . . go a little faster . . . lean a little more to the north or to the south?' No, you would hold your breath as well as your tongue, and keep your hands off until he was safely over. The government is carrying an immense weight, . . . untold treasures are in their hands; they are doing the best they can. Don't badger them; keep silence, and we will carry you safely across."

— selected

ref. 437

† † †

447
God bless our native land!
　Firm may she ever stand
　　Thro' storm and night!
When the wild tempests rave,
　Ruler of wind and wave,
　Do thou our country save
　　By thy great might.

For her our prayer shall rise
　To God above the skies;
　　On him we wait.

Thou who art ever nigh,
　Guarding with watchful eye,
　To thee aloud we cry,
　　God save the State.

— Charles T. Brooks

ref. 437

† † †

448 Our nation cannot survive materially unless it is redeemed spiritually. It can be saved only by becoming permeated with the spirit of Christ and being made free and happy by the practices which spring out of the spirit. Only thus can discontent be driven out and all the shadows lifted from the road ahead.

— Woodrow Wilson

† † †

449 History fails to record a single precedent in which nations subject to moral decay have not passed into political and economic decline. There has been either a spiritual awakening to overcome the moral lapse, or a progressive deterioration leading to ultimate national disaster.

— General Douglas MacArthur

ref. 435-438

† † †

450

My Flag! my Flag! my dear old Flag!
My Country's and my own!
For liberty and justice stands,
Protects my church and home.
All other flags are naught to me,
To them I'll not be true.
My Flag, my Flag, shall always be
The Red, the White, and Blue.

My Flag! my Flag! my dear old Flag!
My father's and my own!
May God uphold it evermore
Against insidious foes!
May every one of you with me
Each day this vow renew:
My Flag, my Flag, shall always be
The Red, the White, the Blue!

— J. H. Hartenberger

ref. 437

† † †

451 The words carved in stone at the base of the Statue of Liberty were written by a Jewish refugee from Europe:

Give me your Tired, your Poor,
Your Huddled Masses Yearning to
    Breathe Free,
The Wretched Refuse of Your Teeming
    Shore.
Send These, the Homeless, Tempest-
    tossed to me.
I Lift My Lamp Beside the Golden Door.

ref. 436

† † †

452 One day when the Civil War was raging at its worst, a minister said to President Lincoln: "I surely hope the Lord is on our side." To which Lincoln replied, "I am not at all concerned about that, for I know that the Lord is always on the side of the right; but it is my constant anxiety and prayer that I and this nation be on the Lord's side."

— Baptist Standard

ref. 436

† † †

453   Almighty God, who hast given us
            this good land for our heritage;
We humbly beseech thee that we may always
            prove ourselves a people mindful
of thy favor and glad to do thy will.
            Bless our land with honorable industry,
sound learning, and pure manners.
            Save us from violence, discord and confusion;
from pride and arrogancy, and from every evil way.
            Defend our liberties and fashion into one
united people the multitudes brought hither
            out of many kindreds and tongues.
Endue with the spirit of wisdom those whom
            in thy Name we entrust the authority of
                government,
that there may be justice and peace at home,
            and that, through obedience to thy law, we may
show forth thy praise among the nations of the earth.
            In the time of prosperity, fill our hearts
with thankfulness, and in the day of trouble,
            suffer not our trust in thee to fail;
all this we ask
through Jesus Christ our Lord.
                 — Rev. George Lyman Locke
ref. 437

† † †

454 The greatest wealth of a city does not consist in great treasures, firm walls, beautiful houses, and abundant munitions of war. Indeed, where all these are found and reckless fools come into power, the city sustains the greatest injury. But the highest welfare and safety and power of a city consists in able, wise, learned, upright, cultivated citizens, who can preserve, secure, and utilize every treasure and advantage.
                 — Martin Luther
ref. 436-438

† † †

455   The Building of the Ship
        Thou, too, sail on, O ship of State!
        Sail on, O Union, strong and great!
        Humanity with all its fears,
        With all the hopes of future years,
        Is hanging breathless on thy fate!
        We know what Master laid thy keel,
        What Workmen wrought thy ribs of steel,

Who made each mast, and sail, and rope,
What anvils rang, what hammers beat,
In what a forge and what a heat
Were shaped the anchors of thy hope!
Fear not each sudden sound and shock,
'Tis of the wave and not the rock;
'Tis but the flapping of the sail,
And not a rent made by the gale!
In spite of rock and tempest's roar,
In spite of false lights on the shore,
Sail on, nor fear to breast the sea!
Our hearts, our hopes, are all with thee,
Our hearts, our hopes, our prayers, our tears,
Our faith triumphant o'er our fears,
Are all with thee — are all with thee!
— Henry Wadsworth Longfellow
ref. 437,438

† † †

456 The only thing necessary for the triumph of evil is that good men do nothing.

— Edmund Burke

ref. 437,438

† † †

457 On April 3, 1918, the House of Representatives adopted the following words of William Tyler Page as the American Creed:

"I believe in the United States of America as a government of the people, by the people, for the people; whose just powers are derived from the consent of the governed; a democracy in a republic; a sovereign nation of many sovereign states; a perfect union, one and inseparable; established upon those principles of freedom, equality, justice, and humanity for which American patriots sacrificed their lives and fortunes. I therefore believe it is my duty to my country to love it, to support its constitution, to obey its laws, to respect its flag, and to defend it against all enemies"; *ref. 437,438.*

† † †

458 The flag with its red from heaven's morning glow, its white from heaven's fleecy chariots, and blue from its azure dome, pleading for love, purity, and loyalty.

— Anon

ref. 436

† † †

459 God bless our service men!
Guard and watch over them
Where'er they go;
Let thine eternal Word,
Thy Spirit's mighty sword,
Sustain them all, O Lord,
And strength bestow.

We pray thee Lord of hosts,
For those who guard our coasts,
Thy strength provide;
Let thy protecting hand
Guard those who now may stand
In many a far-off land,
Be thou their Guide.

From peril, Lord, keep free
All those upon the sea
Who on thee call;
Restrain the lurking foe,
Who seeks their overthrow,
Protect them as they go,
Lord, spare them all!

Lord, hear our fervent prayer
For those who fly by air,
Thy help afford;
Guide thou their distant flight,
Keep them by day and night,
Uphold them by thy might,
Spare them, O Lord! Amen.

— Anon

ref. 437

† † †

460 Before electric lights came into use the streets were lighted with gas lamps, each of which in turn was lit by a lamplighter. When darkness fell one could not see the lamplighter in person, but one could observe where he had been by seeing the lamps he had lighted.

So, too, one can observe the influence of Christian people by the lamps they have lighted in this world of darkness. Christians are not of the world, but they are in the world where Christ exerts his almighty power through them in the social structure. As citizens in a kingdom of this world as well as citizens in Christ's kingdom of grace, they exert their influence and seek the welfare of the state as well as that of the church: Mt 5:14-16; 2 Cor 3:2,3; Php 2:15,16; 1 Pe 2:9-12; *ref. 437,438.*

GRACE 461-478

(ref.: Faith 359-383; Justification 850-864; Redemption 1223-1252)

A Definition

461 The word "grace" is used in Holy Scriptures in various ways:

With reference to God's attitude of kindness, love, and mercy toward all of his creatures: Ps 33:5; 136:1f; 145:8,9; Mt 5:45; Ro 10:12;

462 With reference to God's loving and forgiving attitude toward sinners, not because of any merit or worthiness in them, but solely and alone because this grace has been acquired for them by Christ's redemptive work in their behalf: Ro 3:24; 2 Cor 5:19; Eph 2:8,9; 2 Tm 1:9; Tt 2:11; 1 Jn 2:2. This truth, which is a mystery to the mind of natural man, Eph 6:19, is revealed in the gospel — which is called "the gospel of the grace of God," Ac 20:24; "the gospel of Christ," 1 Cor 9:12; Php 1:27; and "the revelation of the mystery which was kept secret since the world began," Ro 16:25; *ref. 469-475,478.*

463 With reference to "enabling grace," to indicate the good works which God by reason of his grace through Christ performs in all believers: Ro 15:15; 1 Cor 1:4,5; 3:10; 15:10; 2 Cor 1:12; 9:8; Php 4:13; 1 Tm 1:12; 1 Pe 4:10,11; 5:5. This grace is never the cause of salvation but the result of man's being saved. Good works are not done to obtain salvation or to merit grace, but are always only thank-offerings for the grace of salvation, which has already been received by faith: Ga 2:16; Eph 2:8-10; *ref. 470,477.*

How It Is Obtained

464 God's saving grace through Christ is meant for all mankind: Lk 2:10,11; Jn 3:16; Ro 3:23,24; 2 Cor 5:19; 1 Tm 2:3-6; Tt 2:11; 1 Jn 2:2; *ref. 469.*

465 It is offered in the gospel, in word and in the sacraments of baptism and the Lord's Supper: Is 55:1; Mt 26:26-28; 28:19; Mk 16:15,16; Jn 3:3,5; 5:24; 6:63; 15:3; Ac 2:37,38; 22:16; Ro 1:16,17; 10:17; 2 Cor 5:18-20; Ga 3:27; Tt 3:5-7; Jas 1:21; 1 Pe 1:10-12,23; 3:21; Re 3:20; 22:17; *ref. 469,471,478.*

467 Man can resist God's grace and reject it in unbelief: Mt 7:26,27; 23:37; Lk 14:17,18; 19:42; Ac 7:51; 13:45,46; 17:32; 2 Cor 6:1; Ga 2:21; He 4:2. Holy Scriptures therefore repeatedly warn against rejecting salvation: Jn 8:24; 2 Cor 6:1,2; 1 Tm 1:18-20; He 3:12,15-19; 4:13; 2 Pe 3:17; Jude 5; *ref. 476.*

468 Grace once obtained, can be lost, but it can be found again in true repentance: Is 1:18-20; 55:7; Joel 2:13; Mic 7:18; Lk 15:11-24; He 6:4-6; 10:26-29; 2 Pe 2:20-22; Re 2:4,5; *ref. 470,475.*

Resources

469 The word "grace" is used in daily conversation as a word to describe qualities like beauty, charm, movement and expression. Or it may be used to denote a period of time granted beyond a set date for the performance of an act or the payment of an obligation. We also speak of a person as being in good or bad graces when he is in favor of disfavor with someone else.

But when the Bible speaks of "the grace of God," as it often does, the expression stands in a class by itself and refers to the kindness, love, mercy and good will that God showed by sending his Son Jesus Christ into the world to be our Savior from sin, Tt 2:11. The Bible also refers to it as "the grace of our Lord Jesus Christ," 2 Cor 8:7, because it is in him and through him alone that God bestows this grace: Jn 1:17; Ro 6:23; Ga 6:18.

Because this grace of God in and through Jesus Christ is all-sufficient to cleanse every sin, Ro 5:20, and because God's wondrous love in Christ is unchanging and never-failing, Ro 8:35-39, Christian people are encouraged to approach the "throne of grace" in heaven, where they can find mercy and help in time of need: He 4:16; *ref. 462,465.*

† † †

470 The Apostle Paul, who wrote "by the grace of God I am what I am," 1 Cor 15:10, could never forget the wondrous way in which God revealed his grace to him: see Ac 9:1-9. Overwhelmed by God's mercy and love, he regarded himself as the chief of sinners, 1 Tm 1:12-15, as one born out of due time, 1 Cor 15:8-10, and the least of all saints, Eph 3:7,8. God's grace, manifested so mightily in Paul, became his all-consuming passion in his life and work: see Php 3:7,8f.

Every Christian must confess that it was the same grace of God which saved him. For even as God is the Source of all of our material blessings, so it is by his grace alone that we are saved: Eph 2:1-9; Ro 3:23,24; 4:16; 11:6. Moreover, it is this grace of God alone that daily forgives our sins and removes our transgressions from us: see Ps 103:10-12. And it is this wondrous grace alone that enables us to "foil the Tempter's power" and which, when we fall, assures us that

> Though great our sins and sore our woes,
> His grace much more aboundeth;
> His helping love no limit knows,
> Our utmost need it soundeth.
> — Martin Luther

ref. 462,463

† † †

471
> By grace! This ground of faith is certain;
> So long as God is true, it stands.
> What saints have penned by inspiration,
> What in his Word our God commands.
> What our whole faith must rest upon,
> Is grace alone, grace in his Son.
> — Christian L. Scheidt

ref. 462,463

† † †

472 "Would you be my loyal subject if I should exercise grace instead of justice and forgive your crime!" said Queen Elizabeth to her would-be assassin. "That, madam, would be no grace at all, to found your grace on the condition of my merit." "Then I pardon you unconditionally," said the Queen. "That," replied the proud French woman as she clasped the Queen's feet, "that is queenly grace, and now I am your slave for life."

— Gospel Herald

ref. 462

† † †

473 The evangelist Spurgeon told of an old man, a coachman, who once carried him in his cab. As the famous preacher entered the vehicle he dropped a remark concerning the coachman's age, and then added, "Well, I hope that you have seen to it that yours will be a pleasant lot, when this life comes to an end."

"Yes, sir," answered the old man, "I think I have; for as far as I know, I have never been drunk in my life, I have never used a profane word, and, then I also go to church now and then."

He seemed to be quite satisfied with himself and was greatly surprised when Spurgeon expressed his grave doubts as to his going to heaven, if he should die in such a self-righteous state of mind.

This self-confidence is very common among persons that call themselves Christians; even though they may not always express it in the words of the old cab driver, it is always the same idea: that they will get to heaven because of the good they have done, or the evil they have left undone.

— selected

ref. 462

† † †

474 A man can no more take a supply of grace for the future than he can eat enough today to last him for the next six months, or take sufficient air into his lungs to sustain life for a week to come. We must draw upon God's boundless stores for grace from day to day, as we need it.

— D. L. Moody

ref. 463

† † †

475 John Newton in his earlier years was an infidel and a seller of slaves in Africa. But by the grace of God he was led to faith in Christ. In his joy and amazement at God's grace he subsequently wrote the beautiful hymn:

Amazing grace! how sweet the sound,
That saved a wretch like me!
I once was lost, but now am found,
Was blind, but now I see.

'Twas grace that taught my heart to fear,
  And grace my fears relieved;
How precious did that grace appear
  The hour I first believed!

Through many dangers, toils and snares,
  I have already come;
'Tis grace hath brought me safe thus far,
  And grace will lead me home.
ref. 462,463

† † †

476 All men by birth and nature resist the grace of God, Ro 8:7. Obduracy, hardening of the heart, is a protracted resistance which takes place after man repeatedly, willfully and stubbornly resists God's Word and will and stubbornly rejects God's salvation in Christ: Mt 11:20-26; 13:14,15; 23:37,38; Jn 12:40; Ac 7:51; Ro 11:9. It is only after man has thus repeatedly hardened his heart that God then, as a just consequence, withdraws his saving grace from him. This was demonstrated in the case of the Egyptian Pharaoh who rejected the signs he received from Moses. In Ex 4:21 the Lord told Moses the final outcome: "I will harden his heart." During the five plagues Pharaoh hardens his heart progressively; then after the sixth God's hardening sets in: Ex 9:12. After the seventh it is again Pharaoh who hardens himself, Ex 9:35; then it is God who finally hardens, and there is no turning back: Ex 10:20,27; 11:10; 14:4,5; *ref. 467.*

† † †

477   When he leads through some valley of trouble,
  His omnipotent hand we can trace;
For the trials and sorrows he sends us
  Are part of his lessons in grace.
                                        — Anon
ref. 463

† † †

478 A certain person, seeking a drink of water, was bewildered as he approached a fountain which bore the inscription: "Stoop and drink!" After looking in vain for a button to push or a handle to turn he walked away still thirsty. Had he followed the directions, his thirst would have been assuaged, for the flow of the fountain was controlled by an electric eye. To receive water from it one had to stoop, just as the directions indicated.

God's grace in Christ is offered freely. All that anyone must do to receive it is to believe, to stoop and drink, as the poet paraphrased it in the words:

I heard the voice of Jesus say,
  "Behold, I freely give
The living water; thirsty one,
  Stoop down and drink and live."

121

I came to Jesus and I drank
Of that life-giving stream.
My thirst was quenched, my soul revived,
And now I live in him.

— Horatius Bonar

ref. 462,464-466

HEAVEN 479-492

(ref.: Hell 493-505)

The Reality of Heaven and Its Occupants

479 The Bible speaks of heaven as a place which was created by God, although it does not state definitely where heaven is located: Gn 1:1; Jn 14:2; Re 10:6; *ref. 487-489.*

480 It is the abode of God, although God is at the same time present everywhere: Dt 26:15; 1 Kgs 8:27,30; Is 66:1; Jr 23:24; Ps 139:7-11; Mt 5:34; 6:9; Ac 17:28. The same is also said of Christ and of the Holy Spirit: Ps 139:7,8; Mt 28:18,20; Mk 16:19; Jn 1:1f; 6:38; Ac 1:9f; Php 1:23; *ref. 487-489.*

481 It is also the abode of the holy angels, who constantly behold the face of God, sing his praises, and carry out his commands: Ps 103:20,21; Is 6:1-3; Mt 18:10; 24:36; *ref. 487-489.*

482 It is also the dwelling place of the souls of the departed in Christ: Lk 16:22; 23:43; Re 7:9; cp. Mt 17:1-3; 22:29-32; *ref. 487-489.*

The Nature of Heaven

483 It is a place of

Incomparable beauty: Re 21:27; 22:15; cp. 1 Cor 6:9,10; Eph 5:5;

Fulness of joy: Ps 16:11; 17:15; Mt 18:10; *see also* 1 Cor 13:12; Php 1:23; 1 Pe 1:3-5;

Perfect rest: He 4:9,10; Re 14:13;

Indescribable bliss: 1 Cor 2:9; 2 Cor 12:4;

Absence of all suffering: Re 7:16,17; 21:4;

Everlasting blessedness: Lk 16:9; 2 Cor 4:17,18; 5:1, where the redeemed forever sing the praises of God and Christ: Re 5:11,12; *ref. 490-492.*

The Future State of Believers in Heaven

484 The resurrected bodies of the believers, wondrously glorified, will be reunited with their immortal souls: Php 3:21; 1 Cor 15:42f;

Believers will recognize their loved ones who have fallen asleep in the Lord: 1 Th 4:13-18; cp Mt 17:3,4;

The divine image of holiness and perfection, lost through sin, will be fully restored: Ps 17:15; 1 Cor 13:9-12; He 12:23; 1 Jn 3:2;

There will be degrees of glory in accordance with the works of faith and labors of love performed on earth: Dn 12:3f; Mt 16:27; 19:28; 1 Cor 3:8; 2 Cor 9:6; *ref. 488,490,492.*

How To Get to Heaven

485 The only way to heaven and eternal life is through Jesus Christ the heaven-sent Savior of the world: Jn 3:16,36; 5:24; 10:9; 14:6; 17:3; Ac 4:12; 1 Pe 1:3-5; 1 Jn 5:11,12; *ref. 492;*

486 To get to heaven is the ultimate object of our Christian hope and striving: Lk 13:24; Php 2:12; 3:13-21; He 3:12-4:11; 2 Pe 3:10-14; cp Lk 2:28-32; *ref. 490,492.*

Resources

487 People in all ages and in all nations have held a belief in some form of man's existence after death in a spirit world. Included in the natural knowledge which God implanted in man from the time of creation is the conviction of a final judgment in which the rights of this life will be rewarded and the wrongs of this life will be punished, in which the secrets of men's hearts will be revealed and all hidden things of darkness will be brought to light: Ec 12:14; Lk 12:2; 1 Cor 4:5. But this knowledge and conviction, like all other knowledge that God implanted in man's heart, has become blurred and corrupted through sin so that, at best, man's knowledge of a future life is darkened: 1 Cor 2:14; Eph 4:18.

The only reliable knowledge that we can have of the future life is not derived from reason, nor from nature, but solely and alone from the revelation which God has given concerning it in his holy Word: cp. 2 Pe 1:19; *ref. 479-484.*

† † †

488 The word "heaven," and the adjective "heavenly," are customarily associated with something that is supremely good and earnestly to be desired. Even among uncultured and uncivilized tribes and nations the idea of a heaven forms the central thought of religious belief. But their conception of heaven is a product of their imagination and assumes characteristics corresponding to their national traits. Thus, for example, North American Indians, who found their greatest delight in hunting, commonly referred to heaven as a "happy hunting ground." Norsemen held that the souls of the heroes who were slain in battle were forthwith carried by the handmaidens of Odin to Valhalla, the palace of Odin, in which dwell the souls of the heroes slain in battle. The heaven of Mohanmedans offers wine, women and the gratification of lust; *ref. 479-482.*

† † †

489 The Bible uses various expressions to describe heaven. Thus, for example, heaven is spoken of as

The Garden of Eden: Gn 2:8; 3:23; Is 51:3; Eze 36:35;

Paradise: Gn 2:8f; Lk 23:43; 2 Cor 12:4; Re 2:7;

A kingdom: Mt 25:34; Lk 12:32; 2 Tm 4:18;

God's Throne: Mt 5:34; 23:22; Ac 7:49; Is 6:1;
An unfading inheritance: 1 Pe 1:4;
A rest for the people of God: He 4:9;
Abraham's bosom: Lk 16:22;
A marriage supper: Re 19:9;
A tree of life: Re 2:7; 22:14; cp. Gn 2:9; 3:24;
The Father's house: Jn 14:2;
The New Jerusalem: He 11:10,16; 13:14; Re 21:2,10; 22:1f; *ref. 483.*

† † †

490

I'm but a stranger here,
  Heav'n is my home;
Earth is a desert drear,
  Heav'n is my home.
Danger and sorrow stand
Round me on ev'ry hand;
Heav'n is my fatherland,
  Heav'n is my home.

There at my Savior's side
  Heav'n is my home;
I shall be glorified,
  Heav'n is my home.
There are the good and blest,
Those I love most and best;
And there I, too, shall rest,
  Heav'n is my home.
— T. R. Taylor
ref. 484,486

† † †

491 A little girl was walking with her father one night under the starry sky. Looking up, she said, "Father, I have been thinking that if the wrong side of Heaven is so beautiful, what will the right side be?"
— Christian Endeavor World
ref. 479-484

† † †

492

Jerusalem the golden,
  With milk and honey blest,
Beneath thy contemplation
  Sink heart and voice opprest.
I know not, oh, I know not,
  What joys await us there,
What radiancy of glory,
  What bliss beyond compare.

O sweet and blessed country,
    The home of God's elect!
O sweet and blessed country
    That eager hearts expect!
Jesus, in mercy brings us
    To that dear land of rest,
Who art, with God the Father
    And Spirit, ever blest.
— Bernard of Morlas

ref. 485,486

HELL 493-505

(ref.: Heaven: 479-492; Satan and the evil angels 1309-1321)

The Reality of Hell and Its Occupants

493 The Bible teaches the existence of hell as well as the existence of heaven: Dn 12:2; Mt 7:13,14; 25:46; Jn 5:28,29; 2 Th 1:7-10; *ref. 499-503.*

494 Hell is the abode prepared by God for the devil and his evil angels: Mt 25:41; 2 Pe 2:4; Jd 6; *ref. 503.*

495 Hell is the destiny of all the wicked who depart this life without faith in the Savior, Jesus Christ: Mt 23:33; 25:41,46; Mk 3:29; 16:16; Jn 3:18,36; 2 Th 1:7-9; He 10:28-31; 1 Jn 5:11,12; *ref. 502,503.*

The Nature of Hell

496 A place of torment: Mt 8:12; 10:28; 25:46; Mk 9:43,44; Lk 16:23,24; *ref. 499;*

Outer darkness and separation from God: Mt 8:12; 22:13; 2 Th 1:7-9; 2 Pe 2:4,17; Jd 6; *ref. 499;*

An unending punishment: Mt 25:46; Mk 3:29; Lk 3:17; 2 Th 1:9; Re 14:11; 20:10; *ref. 499;*

Degrees of punishment: Mt 11:21,24; 23:14; Lk 12:47ff; Ro 2:5,6; 2 Cor 5:10; *ref. 499.*

How To Escape The Punishment of Hell

497 By faith alone in Jesus Christ, the Savior of the world: Mt 3:2; 4:17; Mk 16:16; Jn 3:16,18,36; 5:24; 6:40; 10:9; 14:6; 17:3; Ac 2:38,39; 3:19; 4:12; 16:31; Ro 8:1; He 2:3; 1 Jn 5:11,12; for Christ has conquered Satan and the forces of hell for all of lost mankind: Mt 4:1-11; 16:18; Jn 12:31; 14:30; Col 2:15; He 2:14,15; 1 Pe 3:18,19; 1 Jn 3:8; Re 20:10; *ref. 504,505.*

498 By constantly seeking the things that belong to our peace with God: Is 55:6,7; Mt 6:19-21; Mk 8:34-38; Lk 19:42; Ro 13:11-14; 2 Cor 6:2; Tt 2:11-14; 1 Jn 2:15-17; cp Lk 12:16-21; *ref. 504, 505.*

Resources

499 The Bible uses a number of different words when speaking of hell and its eternal punishment, e.g.,

Sheol: The etymology of this Hebrew word is obscure. In the KJV the word is translated "grave" 39 times; "pit" 3 times; "hell" 30 times, and "deep" one time. In each instance the immediate and the remote context must determine its meaning, e.g.,

"Grave" is the resting place of man's mortal remains: Job 17:16; Is 38:10;

"Realm of the dead" is the place into which all enter who depart this life, the righteous as well as the wicked: Gn 37:35; Job 7:9; 14:13; Ps 31:17; 89:48;

"Hell" is the place where the judgment of God overtakes the evildoers: Nu 16:30,33; Dt 32:22; Ps 49:14,15; Pr 5:5.

Hades: a Hebrew and Greek term which, like *sheol* denotes the unseen world of the dead: Ac 2:27,31; Re 20:13,14. However, in Mt 11:23, Lk 16:23, and other passages, it denotes the place of torment to which the unbelievers will be condemned.

Gehenna: a Hebrew and Greek word for abode of the wicked after death: Mt 5:22,29; 10:28; Mk 9:43,45; Lk 12:5; Jas 3:6. Originally it was the name given to a deep, narrow glen southwest of Jerusalem which was so called from the cries of little children who were thrown into the fiery arms of Moloch: 2 Chr 28:3; 33:6; 2 Kgs 23:10; Jr 2:23; 7:31,32; 31:40.

Abyssos: a Hebrew and Greek word derived from an adjective meaning bottomless, unbounded. It is used in Scriptures to denote

The deep: Gn 1:2;

The depth of the sea as a symbol of great distress and anguish of soul: Ps 71:20;

The abode of the dead, the grave: Ro 10:7;

Hell, as the abode of the evil spirits presided over by Apollyon, the destroyer, Satan: Re 9:1,11.

Tartaros: a Greek word not found in the Bible, but occurring in a verb meaning to hold captive in Tartaros. Tartaros is the name for a dark subterranean region regarded by the ancient Greeks as the abode where the wicked suffer punishment for their evil deeds; it answers to the Gehenna of the New Testament, which is a designation of hell: 2 Pe 2:4; *ref. 493-496.*

† † †

500 As to the geographical location of hell, or whether its flames are material or immaterial, let us not speculate on what God has not revealed. Rather, let us follow the advice of St. Augustine and consider instead how we may escape the torments of hell; *ref. 496.*

† † †

501 To one who claimed to have got rid of hell, Voltaire replied: "I congratulate you, for I have not been able to do that myself." Someone has said that if there were no hell we should have to invent one. However that may be, if there were no word that carried with it the implication of our word "hell," we should be compelled to coin some word which would fit the facts of the heart; for without such a word as "hell," one of the deepest, strongest sentiments and convictions of the heart would have no equivalent in expression. Words are only pictures, or symbols, of reality.

— Clarence E. Macartney

ref. 493-495

† † †

502 Those who hold the erroneous view that the wicked will be annihilated must interpret all passages referring to hell and eternal punishment, eternal damnation, and eternal destruction as signifying that the wicked will cease to exist. But this would result in a false construction on the texts in which these terms occur. For example, we read in Matthew 8:12, "The children of the kingdom shall be cast out into outer darkness; there shall be weeping and gnashing of teeth." After a person is annihilated, how can he weep and gnash his teeth? Again, we read in Matthew 11:23f, "It will be more tolerable for the land of Sodom in the day of judgment than for Capernaum." But how could this be if the inhabitants of both cities are annihilated? Compare also such passages as Mt 25:46; Mk 3:28,29; Jn 3:36; Ro 2:7-9; 2 Cor 4:18; 1 Pe 1:23f and similar passages where the temporal and the eternal are contrasted. To deny the one would be to deny the other also; *ref. 493-495*.

† † †

503 "One of the objections raised to the doctrine of eternal punishment is that it is inconsistent with the love of God to condemn men to unending perdition. It must be remembered, however, that while God is love, his love is only one of his attributes. Justice is also one of his attributes. Since God is a perfect being, we find in him the perfect and harmonious expression of all his attributes. It is significant, too, that the most solemn and explicit declarations of eternal punishment recorded in Scripture were spoken by the forgiving and compassionate Savior: Mt 25:41; Mk 9:43,44; *ref. 493-495*.

† † †

504 George Whitefield, while preaching once on the text, "The door was shut," had two flippant young men in his congregation. One was heard to say to the other in mirth, "What if the door be shut? Another will open!" Mr. Whitefield said later in the sermon, "It is possible that there may be someone here who is careless and trifling, and says: 'What matter if the door be shut? Another will open!'" The two young men looked at each other in alarm. Mr. Whitefield proceeded: "Yes, another door will open. It will be the door to the bottomless pit, the door to hell!"

— *Sunday School Times*

ref. 497,498

127

505 A certain king once presented his court jester with a staff, saying, "Keep this staff, fool, and if ever you find someone who is a greater fool than you are, give it to him." Sometime later the king became deathly ill. The court jester came to visit him and was told that his lord must soon leave him. "And where will you go?" asked the jester. "To another world," replied the king. "When will you return again, after a month?" "No," said the king. "When will you return," asked the jester. And the king replied, "Never!" "Never," said the jester, and then asked, "What preparations have you made for your subsistence in this new place where you are going?" "None," said the king. "None?" asked the jester, "Is it possible that you have made no preparations? You are leaving forever, and you have not been the least concerned as to what will become of you in yonder world? Here, here, take the staff that you gave me, for I have never been guilty of such folly"; *ref. 497,498.*

HOLY SPIRIT 506-533

(ref.: God 395-415; Pentecost)

General References to the Holy Spirit

506 In the Old Testament: Gn 1:2; 6:3; 2 Sm 23:2; 2 Chr 24:20; Job 26:13; Ps 33:6; 51:10-12; 139:7; Is 32:15; 44:3; 59:21; 63:10; Eze 36:27; Jl 2:28,29; Mic 3:8; Zch 4:6; 12:10; *ref. 514.*

Prophetic References to the Holy Spirit

507 In connection with Christ's work: Is 11:1,2; 42:1-4; 61:1-3; Mt 1:20,21; 3:11; Lk 1:35; Jn 1:32,33; *ref. 524.*

Prophetic References to Pentecost

508 The festival of the Holy Spirit: Jl 2:28,29; Zch 12:10; Is 32:15; 44:3; Mt 3:11; Lk 24:49; Jn 7:37-39; 14:16,17,26; 15:26; 16:7f; Ac 1:4,5,8; 2:1-5,16-21; *ref. 524,528.*

The Person of the Holy Spirit

509 Holy Scriptures speak of the Holy Spirit as being true God, together with the Father and the Son, one of the three Persons of the Holy Trinity: 2 Sm 23:1,2; Mt 3:16,17; 28:19; Jn 3:32-34; 14:26; 15:26; 2 Cor 13:14; 1 Pe 1:2; 1 Jn 5:7; see also Is 48:12,13,16; 61:1; 63:8-10; *ref. 521,524.*

510 His divine names:

God: Ac 5:3,4;

Holy Ghost: Jn 14:26; 20:22; Ac 1:8; 2:38;

Holy Spirit: Ps 51:11; Lk 11:13; Eph 1:13;

Spirit of God: Gn 1:2; Ro 8:9; 1 Cor 2:10,11; 3:16;

Spirit of the Lord: Is 61:1; 2 Cor 3:17;

Holy Spirit of God: Eph 4:30;

Eternal Spirit: He 9:14;

Spirit of Holiness: Ro 1:4;

The Spirit of Truth who proceeds from the Father: Jn 14:16,17,26; 15:26;

Spirit of wisdom and revelation: Eph 1:17;

Spirit of life: Ro 8:2;

Spirit of glory and of God: 1 Pe 4:14.

511 His divine attributes:

Eternality: He 9:14;

Omniscience: Is 40:13; 1 Cor 2:10,11;

Omnipresence: Ps 139:7-10;

Omnipotence: 1 Cor 12:4-11;

Truthfulness: Jn 14:16,17; 15:26.

512 His divine works:

He is the Giver of life who participated in creating the world and man: Gn 1:2,26; 2:7; Job 26:13; 33:4; Ps 33:6; 104:29,30; Is 42:5;

He inspired the prophets, evangelists and apostles to write the very words of the Scriptures: 2 Sm 23:2; 2 Chr 24:20; Mic 3:8; Mt 22:42-45; Ac 1:16; 28:25-27; 1 Cor 2:10-13; 2 Tm 3:16; He 3:7; 10:15,16; 1 Pe 1:10,11; 2 Pe 1:21; Re 14:13; *ref. 94,524*;

He was instrumental in the conception and birth of Jesus of the Virgin Mary: Mt 1:20,21; Lk 1:35;

He anointed Jesus at the time of his baptism, inaugurated him into his public ministry and empowered him for his work: Mt 3:16; 4:1; 12:28; Lk 4:17-21; 11:20; Jn 1:32-34; Ac 10:38; Ro 8:11; He 9:14; cp Is 11:2,3; 42:1-4; 61:1,2;

He performs the work of regeneration: Jn 3:5-8; Tt 3:5-7; *ref. 517-519,523-528,530*; see also *Conversion 225,241*;

He dispenses spiritual gifts to the church: 1 Cor 12:4-11; *ref. 517, 520-523,528-530,532,533*;

He receives honor, glory and worship equal to that of the Father and the Son: Is 6:3; Jn 16:13-15; cp Mt 10:20 with Ga 4:6; 2 Cor 13:14; 1 Pe 4:14; *ref. 521.*

The Work of the Holy Spirit: Sanctification

513 Sanctification in the narrow sense refers to conversion, or regeneration (the new birth). Through the means of grace (word and sacraments) the Holy Spirit calls men, quickens them from spiritual death to spiritual life by convicting them of their sins, by creating saving faith in Christ as their Redeemer from sin, and by making them new creatures in Christ: Jn 1:12,13; 3:3-6; 6:63; 15:3; 16:8-12; 17:17; Ac 2:37,38; 16:14; 26:18; Ro 1:16; 8:1,2,14; 10:17; 1 Cor 2:14; 4:15; 12:3; 2 Cor 5:17; Eph 2:1,5,8; 5:26; 1 Th 1:5; 2:13,14; Tt 3:5-7; He 10:14-17; Jas 1:18,21; 1 Pe 1:23; Re 22:17; cp also Is 55:1; Lk 14:17; *ref. 517-519.*

514 Sanctification in the wider sense refers to all that the Holy Spirit does for believers in Christ by illuminating them with his gifts, renewing them in the image of God, and finally perfecting them in glory. To accomplish this purpose he

Makes the heart of believers his temple and the Christian Church his dwelling place: Jn 14:17; Ro 8:9; 1 Cor 3:16; 6:11,19; Eph 2:22; 2 Tm 1:14; *ref. 521,522;*

Unites all believers in Christ: Ro 12:5; Eph 2:13-22; 4:3-6; 1 Cor 12:13; and directs the work of the Christian Church: Jn 20:21-23; Ac 1:8; 2:41,47; 8:28f,39; 10:19,20; 13:2,4; 16:6,7; 20:28; *ref. 523;*

Bestows his gifts to believers for their spiritual growth and for the edification and furtherance of the Christian Church: Lk 11:13; Jn 20:21-23; 1 Cor 12:4-13; 14:4,5; Eph 4:12,16; cp Gn 41:38; Ex 28:3; 31:3; 35:30-35; Nu 11:17,25; Jdg 3:10; 6:34; 11:29; 13:25; 14:6,19; 15:14; 1 Sm 10:9,10; 16:13,14; Dn 4:8; 5:11-14;

Teaches believers: Lk 12:11,12; Jn 14:26; 15:26; 16:14,15; 1 Cor 2:13; and guides them in all truth: Jn 16:12,13; 1 Cor 2:9-14; 1 Jn 2:27;

Glorifies Christ and transforms believers into Christ's image: Jn 16:14; Ro 5:5; 8:29; 2 Cor 3:18; 4:10,11;

Renews and purifies believers and enables them to strive against their flesh: Ro 8:1,2,8-13; 1 Cor 6:11; 2 Cor 4:16; Ga 5:17,18; Eph 3:16; 4:22-24; 5:25-27; Tt 3:5-7; He 9:13,14; 1 Pe 1:22;

Produces in believers the fruits of Christian faith: Ro 6:20-23; 14:17; Ga 5:22,23; Eph 2:10; 5:8,9; Php 2:13; cp Jn 15:1-8; *ref 520-523;*

Gives believers the courage to witness for Christ and speaks through them: Mt 10:16-20; Ac 1:8; 2:4; 4:8f; 7:55; 13:9f;

Through the testimony of believers convicts the world of sin, of righteousness, and of judgment: Jn 16:7-11;

Strengthens believers in the assurance that they are the children of God: Ro 8:16,17,23; Ga 3:26,27; 4:6; 1 Jn 3:24; 4:13;

Teaches believers to pray: Ro 8:15,26,27;

Comforts believers in their sorrow: Jn 14:16; 16:6,7; Ac 9:31; and sustains their hope: Ro 5:1-5; 8:24-27; 15:13; 2 Cor 4:16-18; 1 Pe 1:3-5;

Keeps believers in the saving faith and leads them to eternal glory: Ro 8:28-30; 2 Cor 1:22; Php 1:6; Tt 3:5-7; 1 Pe 1:2,5. His presence and work are the pledge of their final redemption: Ro 8:16,17,23; 2 Cor 1:22; 3:18; 5:1-5; Eph 1:13,14; 4:30; 1 Pe 1:9; 2 Pe 1:3,4; 1 Jn 2:25; *ref. 523.*

The Fruits of the Spirit

515 See list in Ga 5:22,23;

Love to God and fellowmen: 1 Jn 4:19-21; cp 1 Cor 13;

Joy in salvation: Lk 2:10,11; Ac 8:8,39; 16:25-34; Ro 5:11; 8:15-17,35-39; Php 4:4-6;

Peace that flows from sins forgiven: Is 59:2; Lk 2:14,27-32; Jn 14:27; Php 4:7; He 13:20,21; *ref. 1134-1146;*

Longsuffering, or patience, to defer anger and to bear injuries in the face of provocations and ill-treatment, after the example of Christ: 1 Pe 2:19-25;

Gentleness and goodness; kindness in rendering service to others and goodness in bestowing help to those in need, after the example of Christ: Ac 10:38; cp Mt 25:35-46;

Faith, meekness, and temperance; faithfulness, justice and honesty in what we profess and promise to others; meekness and gentleness in esteeming others greater than one's self: cp Mk 10:42-45; temperance, self-control and mastery over appetites, tempers and passions: cp Col 3:5-8; 1 Pe 4:3-5; *ref. 525,533.*

The Believer's Relation to the Holy Spirit

516 They owe their conversion and all of their spiritual gifts to the work of the Holy Spirit: Jn 1:12,13; 3:3-5; 1 Cor 2:14; 3:16; 6:19; 12:1-13; 2 Cor 4:6; Ga 5:22,23; Eph 2:1-10; Php 2:13; 2 Th 2:13,14; 2 Tm 1:9; Tt 3:5-7; Jas 1:18; 1 Pe 1:23; 2:9; *ref. 517-519,523-528,530;*

They are admonished to walk in the Spirit and not to fulfill the lusts of the flesh: Ro 8:1-13; 12:2; cp Ro 6; Ga 5:16-18,25; 6:8; Eph 4:1; 5:1-11; Php 1:9-11; *ref. 531,532;*

They are urged to maintain the unity of the Spirit: Ro 15:5,6; 1 Cor 1:10; Eph 4:3; Php 1:27;

They are exhorted to be filled with the Spirit: Ro 8:14; Eph 5:18; to pray for cleansing and for the presence and help of the Spirit in their lives: Ps 51:1-12; Lk 11:13; *ref. 521,522,525,530;*

They are warned not to grieve nor to quench the Holy Spirit: Eph 4:30; 1 Th 5:19; He 10:26-29; cp Gn 6:3; 2 Sm 23:2,3; 2 Chr 24:20; Is 63:10; Ac 7:51.

Resources

517 The Holy Spirit performs his work of regeneration and sanctification in the hearts of men through the Word of God and the holy sacraments, baptism and the Lord's Supper, which receive their power through this Word. Word and sacraments are "means of grace" because they are the means, or channels, through which the Holy Spirit offers, conveys and seals the grace of God which Christ merited for us.

Christ's Word, which includes all the words of the Holy Scriptures, is God's Word: Jn 14:24; 1 Cor 2:13; 2 Tm 3:16. These are not ordinary words, but living words; their almighty power is demonstrated, for example, in the fact that the heavens were made "by the word of the Lord": Ps 33:6; cp Jn 1:1-4; and in the fact that all things in heaven and earth are upheld "by the Word of his power": He 1:3; cp Col 1:16,17.

Christ spoke of this word as "Spirit and life," Jn 6:63; and he told his disciples that it was through his word that they were cleansed, Jn 15:3. St. Paul called this word "the Word of Life," Php 2:16; "the power of God unto salvation to everyone that believes," Ro 1:16; and "the Sword of the Spirit,"

131

Eph 6:17; see also He 4:12,13. St. Peter referred to it as an "incorruptible Seed" by which men are spiritually reborn, and as a Word that "lives and abides forever": 1 Pe 1:23,25. St. James called it "the Word of Truth" which is able to save a man's soul: Jas 1:18,21; cp also Jr 23:29; Ac 2:37.

The Word of God includes both law and gospel. Through the word of the law the Holy Spirit shows man his sins and the wrath of God: Ro 3:20; 4:15; 7:7,13; Ga 3:10; through the word of the gospel he reveals Jesus Christ, the Savior, and the grace of God: Lk 2:10,11; Jn 3:16; Ac 16:31; Ro 1:16; 2 Th 2:14. Both law and gospel are necessary, for unless man is brought to the realization of his sins he cannot see the need for a Savior: Ac 2:37-39; 16:31,32; Ga 3:24-27; Eph 2:1-9; *ref. 884-891.*

† † †

518
Holy Ghost, with light divine
Shine upon this heart of mine;
Chase the shades of night away,
Turn the darkness into day.

Let me see my Savior's face,
Let me all his beauties trace;
Show those glorious truths to me
Which are only known to thee.

Holy Ghost, with pow'r divine
Cleanse this guilty heart of mine;
In thy mercy pity me,
From sin's bondage set me free.

See, to thee I yield my heart,
Shed thy life through every part;
A pure temple I would be
Wholly dedicate to thee.

— Andrew Reed

ref. 514,516

† † †

519 The words through which the Holy Spirit performs his gracious work in the hearts of men are the words that we have in the Scriptures. The Holy Spirit inspired holy men of God to write them: 1 Cor 2:13; 2 Tm 3:16. Here lies the source of spiritual power. Alas, that so many know nothing of it! — It took the world thousands of years to discover atomic energy, although it was always there. Today there are still millions who have not discovered the almighty power of God's Word, though it is within easy reach of everyone; *ref. 512-514,527.*

† † †

520 A phenomenal amount of potential electric power is stored up in the water of Niagara River as it flows over Niagara Falls. By mutual agreement the governments of Canada and the United States have limited the amount

132

of that water that can be diverted for this purpose. But even this limited amount produces a vast amount of electricity for lighting homes and cities, and for industrial purposes. — Stored up in the hearts of Christian people is the unlimited power of the gospel. It is the word of the Triune God, who is able to do exceeding abundantly above all that we can ask or think: Eph 3:20; cp Ac 1:8; 4:33; 6:8; 19:11,12; Php 4:13; 1 Th 1:5. What miracles would happen in the work of the Christian church if we truly were to realize that no limitations have been placed on the use of that power! *ref. 514-516.*

† † †

521 Scriptures speak of the indwelling of the Triune God in the hearts of believers: Jn 14:16,17,20; 17:23; 1 Cor 6:19; Ga 2:20; Eph 3:17-19. This mystery is revealed only in part: see Jn 3:8. Not only does it mean that the will of believers conforms with the will of God, that there is mutual love between them, but also that the Triune God himself indeed dwells in their hearts. This is a most comforting truth, for we know that where God is present he is also accomplishing his good and gracious will and that the Holy Spirit who began his good work in us will also perform it until the day of Jesus Christ: Php 1:6; *ref. 513,514.*

† † †

522 Speaking of the indwelling Christ, A. J. Gordon wrote: "Imagine one without genius and devoid of the artist's training, sitting down before Raphael's famous picture of the Transfiguration and attempting to reproduce it. How crude and mechanical and lifeless his work would be! But if such a thing were possible that the spirit of Raphael should enter into the man and obtain mastery of his mind and eye and hand, it would be entirely possible that he should paint this masterpiece; for it would simply be Raphael reproducing Raphael. And this in a mystery is what is true of the disciple filled with the Holy Spirit. Christ by the Spirit dwells within him as a divine life, and Christ is able to image forth Christ from the interior life of the outward example"; *ref. 513,514.*

† † †

523 In his explanation of the Third Article of the *Apostles' Creed,* Martin Luther summarized the work of the Holy Spirit as follows: "I believe that I cannot by my own reason or strength believe in Jesus Christ, my Lord, or come to him; but the Holy Ghost has called me by the gospel, enlightened me with his gifts, sanctified and kept me in the true faith; even as he calls, gathers, enlightens, and sanctifies the whole Christian church on earth, and keeps it with Jesus Christ in the one true faith; in which Christian church he daily and richly forgives all sins to me and all believers, and will at the last day raise up me and all the dead, and give unto me and all believers in Christ eternal life. This is most certainly true"; *ref. 513,514.*

524 The Nicene Creed expresses the faith of the Christian church in the Holy Ghost and his work in the words: "... And I believe in the Holy Ghost, the Lord and Giver of Life, who proceedeth from the Father and the Son, who with the Father and the Son together is worshiped and glorified, who spake by the prophets"; *ref. 509,514.*

525   O Holy Spirit, enter in
And in our hearts thy work begin,
Thy temple deign to make us;
Sun of the soul, thou Light Divine,
Around and in us brightly shine,
To joy and gladness wake us
That we, In thee,
Truly living, To thee giving
Prayer unceasing,
May in love be still increasing.

Thou Fountain, whence all wisdom flows
Which God on pious hearts bestows,
Grant us thy consolation
That in our pure faith's unity
We faithful witnesses may be
Of grace that brings salvation.
Hear us, Cheer us
By thy teaching; Let our preaching
And our labor
Praise thee, Lord, and serve our neighbor.
       — Michael Schirmer
ref. 515,516

† † †

526 Without the gracious work of the Holy Spirit, man would not and could not know Jesus Christ as his Savior: 1 Cor 2:11-14; 12:3. All the blessings of Christ's redemptive work would be like a buried treasure, the existence of which would not be known, much less found; *ref. 513,514.*

† † †

527 Christ compared the work of the Holy Spirit to the mysterious work of the wind, whose origin and manner is unknown to men, but the reality of which is undeniable: Jn 3:8; cp. Ac 2:1,2ff.

Where does the wind come from, and where does it go? How does it start, and how does it stop? These are simple questions, but all of our sophisticated meteorological knowledge cannot supply the answer. Yet no one questions the reality of the wind, for one can hear its roar, feel its breeze, measure its velocity, and see its results in the bending of trees or in the destruction that it sometimes causes.

So, says Christ, "is everyone that is born of the Spirit." One cannot see the Spirit, for he is invisible, like the wind. But one cannot question the Holy Spirit's work, for where his regenerating power has been in operation man becomes a new creation and his life is ruled by another power; *ref. 513,514.*

528 The *Festival of Pentecost,* followed by Christmas and Easter, is the third major festival of the Church year. It traces its origin back to Old Testament times when it was celebrated at the completion of the grain harvest: Ex 34:22,23; 2 Chr 8:12,13; 1 Kgs 9:25. It fell on the fiftieth day after the waving of the sheaf of new grain, which gave rise to the name Pentecost, or fiftieth day, Ac 2:1.

It was also called the Feast of Harvest, or Day of Firstfruits, because the firstfruits of the wheat harvest were then presented as a thank-offering to the Lord: Ex 23:16; 34:22; Nu 28:26.

The most notable Pentecost was the one which occurred on the fiftieth day after the resurrection of Christ, Ac 2:1ff. On that day the Holy Spirit was poured out on the disciples in fulfillment of Christ's promise: Lk 24:49; Ac 1:8; and they were given the miraculous gift to speak in many different languages and to declare the wonderful truths of Christ's gospel to the multitudes who had come to Jerusalem from many different lands to observe this Festival of Pentecost.

Pentecost is commonly regarded as the birthday of the Christian church in its outward, visible form. For, as a result of the wonderful work of the Holy Spirit through the word of the gospel preached by the disciples, three thousand souls were added to the church on that day, Ac 2:41. These converts to Christ were the *firstfruits* of the great spiritual harvest that the Holy Spirit has gathered into the Christian church ever since through the gospel of Christ.

As we commemorate this festival we recall with grateful hearts that it was by the power of this same Holy Spirit that we were brought into the church: 2 Th 2:13,14; *ref. 508.*

† † †

529 In the great naval battle of Salamis, in which the Persian fleet was utterly routed, Themistocles, the heroic commander of the Greeks, tarried on shore until nine in the morning. His delay caused great impatience among the patriots and some accused him of cowardice and even of treason. But the experienced Greek leader was aware that at nine o'clock in the morning the land breeze would spring up and fill the sails of the vessels and send them to sea where the Persian fleet was waiting for them. By doing so he released the rowers to be warriors.

Believers in their work for Christ must rely on the strength of the Holy Spirit and not try to accomplish things by their own help. "Wait for the gift my Father promised, which you have heard me speak about," Ac 1:4.

— *The Illustrator*

ref. 516

† † †

135

530 A church was having its first service following the installation of a new organ. No sooner had the service begun when the electric current failed through some imperfection in the installation. An electrician was hastily summoned and he discovered the trouble almost immediately. Scribbling a few words on paper the electrician asked the usher to deliver it to the pastor. Reading the note, the pastor read: "After the prayer the power will be on."

Christian prayer brings the power of God down from above. It was so for the disciples at that first Pentecost: Ac 1:8; 2:1f. It is so for us today. Much prayer, much power, little prayer, little power; no prayer, no power.

— selected

ref. 516

† † †

531 The Christian's life is a constant struggle of the flesh against the spirit: Ga 5:17; cp Ro 7:14-25.

A heathen convert to Christianity once came to the missionary and said, "When I was a heathen I had only one heart, a black one; but now that I am a Christian I have two hearts, a black one and a white one, and these two hearts constantly oppose each other. The black heart always desires the things that the devil wills, and the white heart always desires the things that God wills." With tears in his eyes, the convert then asked the missionary why this was so.

"Return in peace," said the missionary, "and do not be troubled any longer. The very fact that you have two hearts shows that you are a Christian, for the heathen have but one heart, a black one. Continue in your spiritual warfare, but always see to it that your white heart wins the victory. Then all will be well, and you will receive the crown of life. And, when at last you enter heaven, your black heart will have disappeared altogether"; *ref. 516*.

† † †

532 It is the amazingly wonderful spiritual strength which the Holy Spirit supplies that enables us to discharge our Christian duties, that gives us power to overcome the devil, the world, and our own sinful flesh, that gives us courage in danger, patience in trial, joy in sorrow, peace in time of trouble, and hope in the midst of despair. "Not by might nor by power, but by my Spirit, says the Lord Almighty," Zch 4:6. It is that Source of spiritual strength that enables us to say with the apostle Paul: "I can do everything through him who gives me strength," Php 4:13; cp also Ex 15:2; Ps 73:25,26; Is 45:24.

533
Renew me, O eternal Light,
And let my heart and soul be bright,
Illumined with the light of grace
That issues from thy holy face.

Destroy in me the lust of sin,
  From all impureness make me clean,
Oh, grant me pow'r and strength, my God,
  To strive against my flesh and blood!

Create in me a new heart, Lord,
  That gladly I obey thy word
And naught but what thou wilt, desire;
  With such new life my soul inspire.

Grant that I only thee may love
  And seek those things which are above
Till I behold thee face to face,
  O Light eternal, through thy grace.
                  — Johann F. Ruopp

ref. 516

HOME 534-556

(ref.: Children 142-158; Education, Christian 315-358)

An Institution Established by God

534 God is the source of the home: Gen 2:8.

Its sanctity is to be respected: Ex 20:17; Dt. 5:21; Mic 2:2;

It is a place to provide for family need: Pr 31:10-31;

It is to be governed by Christ's teachings: Mt 7:24-27; Ps 127:1;

It is a reflection of heaven: Jn 14:1-3; 2 Cor 5:1; Re 22:14; *ref. 540-545.*

A School for Christian Instruction and Training

535 See items under Education, Christian, *ref. 321-324.*

Virtues That Build and Strengthen Home Life

536 Faithfulness in marriage: Mt 19:4-6; Eph 5:22-29; 1 Pe 3:7;

Love: Ro 12:10; 13:10; 1 Cor 13:4-7; 1 Pe 4:8;

Kindness, forbearance and forgiveness: Mk 11:25; Eph 4:32; 5:21; Col 3:13;

Contentment: Pr 15:16; Mt 6:25-34; 1 Tm 6:6-9; He 13:5;

Diligence: Pr 6:6-11; 10:4; 13:4; 31:27; Ro 12:11; 1 Tm 5:8; *ref. 534, 547-552,556.*

Evils That Disrupt and Destroy Home Life

537 Unfaithfulness in marriage: Ex 20:14; Mt 19:5-8; 1 Cor 6:9; 7:15; Eph 5:3-7;

Jealousy: Gn 37:4,11; Nu 12:1,2;

Greed: Pr 15:27; Lk 12:13-21; 1 Tm 6:6-10; 1 Jn 2:15-17;

Malice and strife: Pr 15:18; 18:19; 21:9,19; Ga 5:14,15;

Slothfulness: Pr 19:15; 24;3f; Ec 10:18; 1 Tm 5:8; *ref. 539,546,548,553-555.*

Examples of Pious Homes

538 Elkanah and Hannah: 1 Sm 1:1-3;
Zacharias and Elizabeth: Lk 1:5,6;
Joseph and Mary: Lk 1:27; 2:22,41;
Mary and Martha: Lk 10:38-42;
Lois and Eunice: 2 Tm 1:5; 3:15.

Examples of Unhappy Homes

539 Abraham and Sarah: Gn 21:9-11;
Isaac and Rebekah: Gn 26;34,35; 27:41,46;
Jacob and Rachel; Gn 37:4,11,18-20;
Manoah and his wife: Jdg 14:1-3;
Herod and Herodias: Mt 14:3-11.

Resources

540 Christ is the Head of this house, the unseen Guest at every meal, the silent Listener to every conversation.

541

Oh, blest the house, whate'er befall,
    Where Jesus Christ is all in all;
Yea, if he were not dwelling there,
    How dark and poor and void it were!

Oh, blest that house where faith you find
    And all within have set their mind
To trust their God and serve him still
    And do in all his holy will!

Oh, blest the parents who give heed
    Unto their children's foremost need
And weary not of care or cost!
    May none to them and heav'n be lost!

Blest such a house, it prospers well,
    In peace and joy the parents dwell,
And in their children's lot is shown
    How richly God can bless his own.

Then here will I and mine today
    A solemn covenant make and say:
Though all the world forsake thy word,
    I and my house will serve the Lord.
           — Christoph C. L. von Pfeil

ref. 534,536,538

† † †

542 Why is the Christian home such a fine and precious thing? Because it is the garden of the Lord, a nursery for human lives to grow in. Its seclusion, its shelter, its wise and careful culture are invaluable to growing souls, and nothing can make up for the lack of them. The home is the God-appointed educator of mankind. We have a multitude of institutions we call schools, but the real schools, where lessons of life are learned, are the homes of America.

— *Baltimore Sun*

543 When David Lloyd George, former Prime Minister of Great Britain, visited America he said: "I would so much like to see your homes. That is where a nation's true greatness lies." The following morning a newspaper reported the headline: "Nation's greatness dies in home, visiting Britain says." — The headline should have read *"lies* in home," but *"dies"* is also correct, for a nation's greatness either lies, or it dies, in the home; *ref. 534-539.*

† † †

544 What place on earth so nearly resembles heaven as a home like this, where, superadded to the love of its members to each other, is mutual love to the blessed God; where attention is paid not only to the physical and mental duties, but also the higher duties of religion; where there is not only a family circle and table, but also a family altar; where attention is paid not only to books in general, but where the family Bible is loved and honored as the Word of God; where not only earthly music is heard, but heavenly hymns are sung, whose sweet notes angels bend to hear and which float to heaven like incense from golden altars; where unions are formed not for this world only, but unions which shall be perpetuated in heaven forever — golden links, which even death's rude hand can never sever but for a moment, to be reunited eternally in the home of the blest.

— George C. Baldwin, D.D.

545
What tender cords my heart entwine,
What fondest memories combine
To turn my thoughts, where'er I roam,
Back to my childhood's happy home!

I see its sheltered, vine-clad walls,
Where roses climb and fragrance falls,
Where echoes of my mother's prayer
Still linger in the evening air.

Within those walls, from early youth,
I learned to know the Word of Truth;
And that first choice, the better part,
Is still the joy of all my heart.

And there I vowed that all my days
I would be worthy of her praise
Who pledged me by the Savior's love
To meet her in the home above.

— W. M. Czamanske

ref. 534-536,538

139

546 When home ties are loosened, when men and women cease to regard a worthy family life with all its duties fully performed and all its responsibilities lived up to, as the life best worth living, then evil days for the commonwealth are at hand.

— Theodore Roosevelt

ref. 537,539

† † †

547 Many years ago an English magazine put on a contest to define the word "home." Among the many definitions submitted the five following were selected as worthy of special attention:

Home is a world of strife shut out and a world of love shut in.

Home is the place where the great are small and the small are great.

Home is the place where we grumble the most and are treated the best.

Home is the only place where the faults and failings of humanity are covered with the mantle of charity.

Home is the father's kingdom, the mother's world, the children's paradise.

ref. 534-536,538

† † †

548 The family is a fundamental organization of human society. Church and state are dependent upon the family for their existence and for whatever makes them beneficial in the world. It was in the family that the church was organized and human government was instituted. There marriage was divinely solemnized. Without family virtues the church could not exist and society would soon relapse into anarchy and barbarism. Good people are therefore alarmed at any sign of the decay in family religion.

— selected

ref. 534-539

† † †

549 "The influence of a religious home almost always exerts itself in some way for good in after-years. The most wayward children can never quite forget the old Christian home, wherein a praying father and mother have asked God's blessings upon their lives. Such prayer lingers long in the memory and ever serves as a beacon-light to guide the wanderer home. Ours is therefore an earnest plea for more religion in the homes and for more real, true Christian homes in the community"; cp Lk 15:17-19.

— Anon

ref. 534-536,538

† † †

550 If there is righteousness in the heart, there is beauty in the character. If there is beauty in the character, there will be harmony in the home. If there is harmony in the home, there will be order in the nation. When there is order in the nation, there will be peace in the world.

— Chinese proverb

ref. 536

† † †

551 How we thrill when we hear the word "Home!" There is something in us that responds to that famous song by John Howard Payne. Payne was born in New York City in 1791, and his experience of home life was very brief. At the age of thirteen he went to work and his father's failure in business made it necessary for him to earn more money. He went on the stage and then crossed to London, where he had success. Finally, he became American Consul at Tunis, in Africa, where he died and where he was buried. The thing by which he is remembered today is not the fact that he was an actor, nor the fact that he was a consul, but the fact that he wrote the simple words:

> 'Mid pleasures and palaces, though we may roam,
> Be it ever so humble, there's no place like HOME!

It was because of that song that Americans went to Africa and brought back his body, and buried it in Washington. As that body was taken down Pennsylvania Avenue, it was preceded by the Marine Band, and followed by the President and Vice President of the United States, and the Supreme Court adjourned and many of the nation's greatest assembled to do him honor. Why? What battle had he fought? None. What book had he written? None. What invention had he brought forth? None. What monument had he carved? None. He had simply written a little song about "Home," and in that lyric Payne had struck a chord that immortalized his name.

— selected

ref. 534-536,538

† † †

552 The picture of the family circle, the father, mother and children sitting together reading the Bible, is a scene of inspiring beauty. There the word of God is at work — molding character, lighting the path of good, inspiring deeds of service. Religion has a vital meaning, touching every aspect of life. God is there in the home, working through purposeful lives to create his kingdom.

— J. Edgar Hoover

553 I believe that a prime factor in the disregard of youth for law lies in an equal or greater disregard for law and order on the part of the adults of our generation.... Seek to evade it though you may, seek to apologize, nevertheless upon the shoulders of grownup America rests the burden of this condition. When the youngster begins to show disrespect for law and order, you can be sure that he learned something of that attitude at home or because those in the home failed to keep him in the right company and isolated from bad examples.

— J. Edgar Hoover

554 If there is to be any hope for the future of America then we as a nation must return to God and the practice of daily and family prayer. Can we have peace without morality? Can we build homes without God? Can we have worthy parents who do not know and practice his teachings? Our nation is sorely in need of a return to the days when God was a part of each household, when families arose in the morning with a prayer on their lips and ended the day by gathering together to place themselves in his care. A godless home is a breeding ground for moral decay and crime.

— J. Edgar Hoover

555 There is a legend which tells of a castle on the Rhine that was never completed. During the day the workmen strove to build it. But at night evil spirits came and destroyed their work. — The process of Christian instruction and training is never completed. Even when the home and the church are doing their best to provide it, they must constantly be aware of the fact that there are many evil influences from without that seek to vitiate their efforts; *ref. 534-539.*

† † †

556

Bless this house, O Lord, we pray,
  Make it safe by night and day;
Bless these walls, so firm and stout,
  Keeping want and trouble out;
Bless the roof and chimneys tall,
  Let thy peace lie over all;
Bless this door, that it may prove
  Ever open to joy and love.

Bless these windows shining bright,
  Letting in God's heav'nly light,
Bless the hearth a blazing there,
  With smoke ascending like a prayer.

Bless the folk who dwell within,
  Keep them pure and free from sin,
Bless us all that we may be
  Fit, O Lord, to dwell with thee.

— Helen Paylor

ref. 534-536,538

HOPE, THE CHRISTIAN'S 557-564

(ref.: Faith, 359-383; Trust 1532-1552)

The Nature of Christian Hope

557 It looks into the future and grasps that which is real, yet invisible: He 11:1,13;

It trusts in something one cannot see or perceive, simply because God has promised it: Ro 8:24,25; He 11:11; cp. Jn 20:29;

It relies on God's Word when all visible evidence appears to contradict all reasonable expectations, and thus it "hopes against hope": Ps 42:11; 119:74,81,114,147; 130:5; Ro 4:18; *ref. 561,562.*

Examples: Abraham: Ro 4:18-22; He 11:8-10,17-19; Sarah: He 11:11,12; the heroes of faith mentioned in He 11:1-40; the centurion: Mt 8:5-10; Martha of Bethany: Jn 11:21,22.

The Basis of Christian Hope

558 It is founded on the truth of the gospel, Col 1:5,23, and is grounded on the certain fact of Christ's resurrection which makes it a "living hope": 1 Pe 1:3f; cp Ro 5:10; 8:31-39;

It is based on the fact that, as God's covenant in the Old Testament was based on the hope that his promises of the coming Christ would be fulfilled, so God again will fulfill all his promises in the Christ who has come: Ro 15:4; 2 Cor 1:20; 2 Tm 1:12; 4:18; He 10:23; 13:5; 1 Pe 1:3-9.

The Result of Christian Hope

560 It gives believers an anchor for their soul: He 6:18,19; *ref. 563,564;*

It causes them to rejoice always: Ro 5:1-5; 12:12; 15:4; Php 4:4; 1 Pe 1:8; *ref. 561;*

It inspires them to live a Christian life: 2 Cor 7:1; 2 Th 2:16,17; Tt 2:11-14; 2 Pe 3:11,12; 1 Jn 3:3; *ref. 561,562.*

Resources

561 Alpine travelers tell of a little flower, called Soldanella, which forces its way through the deep snow of the Alps and hangs its tiny bell-shaped blossom over the icy cleft. — So also Christian hope helps believers to force their way above the sorrow and cares of this life, and above the wintry snow of trouble and bereavement, up towards the heaven where Christ has promised us a home, where we shall be like him and see him as he is; *ref. 557,560.*

† † †

562
Haste, then, on from grace to glory,
Armed by faith and winged by prayer;
Heaven's eternal day's before thee,
God's own hand shall guide thee there.

Soon shall close the earthly mission,
Swift shall pass thy pilgrim days,
Hope soon change to glad fruition,
Faith to sight, and prayer to praise.

— Henry Francis Lyte

ref. 557,558,560

† † †

563 No one who knows what can happen at sea would go to sea in a vessel that carried no anchor, even though it were the greatest and the most modern liner afloat, for circumstances might arise when the hope of the ship and all her company would depend, not on the captain or the crew, the engines, the compass, or the steering gear, but on the anchor. When all else has failed there is hope in the anchor.

— Clarence E. Macartney

564
My hope is built on nothing less
Than Jesus' blood and righteousness;
I dare not trust the sweetest frame,
But wholly lean on Jesus' name.
On Christ, the solid Rock, I stand;
All other ground is sinking sand.

When darkness veils his lovely face,
I rest on his unchanging grace;
In ev'ry high and stormy gale,
My anchor holds within the veil.
On Christ, the solid Rock, I stand;
All other ground is sinking sand.

— Lazarus Spengler

ref. 557-560

Warning Against Hypocrisy

565 Warnings are recorded in Ps 50:7-23; Is 1:1-16; 9:17; 29:15; Mt 15:8,9; 23:13-33; Lk 12:1,2; *ref. 569,570.*

Various Forms of Hypocrisy

566 Having a form of godliness but denying the power thereof: 2 Tm 3:5; professing to know God, but denying him in works: Tt 1:16; honoring God with the lips while the heart is far removed from him: Is 29:13; Mt 15:7,8; cp Is 1:11-16; Appearing righteous from without but being full of iniquity within: Mt 23:25-33; *ref. 572;*

Giving the appearance of piety for the purpose of obtaining the good will and praises of men: 2 Kgs 10:16; Mt 6:1-8,16; 23:5-7; Lk 18:11,12; 2 Cor 5:12; Ga 2:11-14; *ref. 571,572;*

Saying one thing but meaning something else: Pr 23:7; 26:25,26; Mt 22:16f; 23:3; Lk 6:46; 12:1; 1 Tm 4:2; Jas 2:15,16; cp Mt 7:21-23; *ref. 573;*

Being concerned about trifles but ignoring essential things: Mt 23:16,17, 23,24; cp Ga 4:10,11; *ref. 574;*

Finding the minutest fault in others while blinded to far greater personal faults: Mt 7:3-5; 23:24; Lk 13:15,16; Jn 7:23; Ro 2:1,21; *ref. 572.*

Punishment For Hypocrisy

567 God's wrath: Job 15:34,35; 36:13; Is 10:6; 29:15; Jr 42:20-22;

Eternal damnation: Is 33:14; Mt 23:29-33; 24:51.

Examples of Hypocrisy

568 Cain: Gn 4:3f;

Absalom: 2 Sm 15:1-6;

The Jews: Jr 3:10,20;

The Scribes and Pharisees: Mt 23:1-7,13-33;

Judas: Mt 26:49; Jn 12:6;

The Herodians: Mk 12:13-15;

Ananias and Sapphira: Ac 5:1-8;

Simon: Ac 8:13ff;

Peter: Ga 2:11-14;

False prophets: Jr 14:14; Mt 7:15; 24:11.

Resources

569 Honesty is not only the deepest policy, but the highest wisdom; since, however difficult it may be for integrity to get on, it is a thousand times more difficult for knavery to get off; and no error is more fatal than that of those who think that Virtue has no other reward because they have heard that she is her own. I hope I shall always possess firmness and virtue enough to maintain what I consider the most enviable of all titles, the character of an "honest man."

— George Washington

† † †

570   Dare to be honest, good, and sincere;
Dare to be upright, and you never need fear.
Dare to be brave in the cause of the right,
Dare with the enemy ever to fight.
Dare to be loving and patient each day;
Dare to speak the truth, whatever you say.
Dare to be gentle and orderly, too;
Dare to shun evil, whatever you do.
Dare to speak kindly, and ever be true;
Dare to do right, and you'll find your way through.

— *Gospel Herald*

ref. 565,566

† † †

571 A famous painter once exhibited a picture in London of a friar in his robes. Looking at the picture from a distance, the friar seemed to be in an attitude of prayer, his head bowed over a book, his hands clasped upon his breast, his eyes cast down in humble adoration. On a nearer view the book turned out to be a punch-bowl, into which the friar was squeezing a lemon. "A hypocrite is one who neither is what he seems nor seems what he is."

— Ida L. Moulton

ref. 566

† † †

572 Hypocrisy at its worst was exemplified by the members of the Jewish Council. Their trial of Christ was a hollow mockery, since they had already determined beforehand that he must die: Jn 11:47-53.

But their hypocrisy was also evidenced in many other ways. They were scrupulous about keeping the traditions of the elders, but heedlessly transgressed the commandments of God: Mt 15:1-9; Mk 7:1-13. They sounded a trumpet before them when giving alms, that they might have glory of men: Mt 6:2; they loved to pray standing in the synagogue or on street corners where they might be seen by men: Mt 6:16; they pulled an ox or an ass from a pit on the Sabbath day, but held it to be unlawful to heal a sick person on that day: Lk 14:3-5. At the time of Christ's trial they refused to enter the judgment hall of Pilate, a Gentile, lest they should be defiled, but at the same time their hearts were filled with murderous hatred toward Christ: Jn 18:28. They claimed to be the children of God, but constantly plotted how they might kill Christ, the Son of God: Lk 22:2.

573 That expediency is but another form of hypocrisy is seen in the action of Caiaphas, the high priest. When the Jewish Council was at a loss to know how to deal with Christ, he said: "You know nothing at all! You do not realize that it is better for you that one man die for the people than that the whole nation perish," Jn 11:49,50. Unwittingly, these words were a prophecy: v. 51,52; but their intent in the mind of Caiaphas was that it would be in his interest, in the interest of the Council and in the interest of the Jewish nation that Jesus should be sacrificed for their personal, earthly advantage.

Expediency, like every other form of hypocrisy, breeds conceit, selfishness, greed, spiritual blindness and treachery which will stoop to any means to gain a desired end. Hundreds of thousands are sacrificed on the field of battle if it is deemed expedient for the interests of those in power. Millions can quickly be unemployed if it is deemed expedient for those at the head of capital or at the head of labor. Other people's lives and fortunes are as nothing if they stand in the way of the place and prerogatives of certain individuals; *ref. 566*

† † †

574 Another brand of hypocrisy is that of empty formalism. Its dangers become a reality when the observance of religious rituals, customs and traditions becomes an end in itself rather than an aid in worshiping Christ and glorifying God: see Ps 50:7-14; Is 1:10-17; Mt 7:21; *ref. 566.*

† † †

575 A man once said: "I handled a strange hundred-dollar bill the other day. It had done a heap of good. It had paid a widow's rent and bought food for hungry children. It had squared up three or four small accounts; made a church treasurer happy when he found it in the collection plate; made the custodian happier when his back salary had been paid with it. After a time it came back to the bank, but only to be rejected.

"What's wrong?" asked the depositor who had brought it in.

"Counterfeit," said the teller, his suspicions confirmed.

All the good deeds of the counterfeit bill did not enable it to pass at the bank, where it really counted, when its *real* character was discovered.

Sham-Christians may succeed in concealing their hypocrisy from men for a time, but their wickedness cannot escape the all-seeing eye of God: Is 29:15; Jr 17:10; 23:24; Mt 22:18; 24:51; *ref. 566.*

576 "Did you ever hear of a counterfeit hundred-dollar bill?"

"Yes."

"Why was it counterfeited?"

"Because the genuine bill was worth counterfeiting."

"Did you ever see a scrap of brown paper counterfeited?"

"No."

"Why not?"

"Because it was not worth counterfeiting."

"Did you ever see a counterfeit Christian?"

"Yes."

"Why was he counterfeited?"

"I suppose, because a Christian is worth counterfeiting."

"Did you ever see a counterfeit infidel?"

"No."

"Why not?"

— selected

ref. 566

† † †

577
Therefore thou alone, my Savior,
    Shalt be All in All to me;
Search my heart and my behavior,
    Root out all hypocrisy.
Restrain me from wand'ring on pathways unholy
And through all life's pilgrimage keep my heart
    lowly.

— Johann H. Schroeder

ref. 565

JESUS CHRIST, BIRTH OF (Christmas) 578-611

Prophecies Relating to His Birth and Their Fulfillment

578 The first prophecy was given to Adam and Eve in Eden, Gn 3:15, and repeated to the patriarchs: Gn 12:3; 26:4; 28:14; cp Ga 3:16; 4:4;

Some revealed the place of his birth: Mic 5:2; cp Mt 2:4-6; Is 9:1,2; cp Mt 4:14-16;

Some spoke of his virgin birth: Is 7:14; cp Mt 1:18-23; Lk 1:34, 35;

Some announced the preparation for his coming: Is 40:3-5; Mal 3:1-Mt 3:3; Lk 1:13-17,76-79;

Some announced his flight into Egypt in infancy: Ho 11:1; cp Mt 2:14,15; *Ref. 582-588.*

Events Associated With His Birth

579 The account of his birth: Mt 1:18-25; Lk 2:1-10;

The visit of the wise men from the East: Mt 2:1-12;

The flight into Egypt: Mt 2:13-23; *ref. 589-591.*

The Purpose of His Coming Into the World

580 To fulfill the law of God for lost mankind and thus to deliver us from the curse of that law: Mt 3:15; 5:17; Ro 10:4; Ga 3:13; 4:4,5;

To suffer and to die in our stead and thus to free us from the power and dominion of

Sin: Is 53:4-8; Mt 1:21; 20:28; Lk 2:10,11; 19:10; Jn 1:29; Ro 5:8; 1 Cor 15:3,4; 2 Cor 5:19,21; 1 Tm 1:15; 1 Pe 1:18,19; 2:24; 1 Jn 1:7; 2:2; 3:5; 4:10,14; Re 1:5;

Death: 1 Cor 15:55-57; 2 Tm 1:10; He 2:14,15; Re 1:18;

Satan and hell: Lk 1:74; Jn 12:31; Col 2:15; He 2:14,15; 1 Jn 3:8;

To open the door to heaven and eternal life to all believers: Jn 3:14-16; 5:24; 10:10; 14:6; 17:3; 1 Jn 5:11,12;

To establish his church for the proclamation of his gospel in all the world: Mt 3:1-5; 4:17; 28:18-20; Mk 16:15; Lk 24:46-48; Ac 1:8; cp Is 9:6,7; Lk 1:32,33; see also *Mission Work 1020-1081; ref. 588; 592-600; 1223-1252.*

His Birth in the Human Heart

581 He comes through the gospel in word and sacrament: *ref. baptism 69-90; Lord's Supper 941-962;*

He finds entrance into the human heart through repentance and faith; *ref. 601-611,1253-1262.*

Resources

582 Prior to his conversion to Christianity, Justin Martyr searched in vain for the truth in the philosophies of his day. One day he met a Christian who pointed out to him how the prophets of old had foretold the coming of Christ and how their prophecies were fulfilled. Thereupon Justin Martyr made a study of the Old Testament prophecies and discovered that they were indeed fulfilled in the person and work of Jesus Christ. Through this study the Holy Spirit convinced him that the Bible was indeed the Word of God. He then devoted his life to the spread and vindication of Christianity until the day he suffered martyrdom at Rome under Marcus Aurelius in the year 166 A.D. Referring to those prophecies, he said: "To describe a thing that should come to pass long before it is in being, and to bring it to pass, this or nothing is the work of God"; cp Is 19:12; 45:20-22; *ref. 578,579.*

† † †

583　　　　　　Lo, what the Word in times of old
　　　　　　　　Of future days and deeds foretold
　　　　　　　　Is all fulfilled while ages roll,
　　　　　　　　As traced on the prophetic scroll.
　　　　　　　　　　　　　　— Emanuel Cronewett
　　　　　　ref. 578,579

† † †

584 It has been correctly said that the New Testament is contained in the Old Testament and that the Old Testament is revealed in the New Testament. This is particularly evident in the Messianic prophecies, which run like a golden thread through the Old Testament and then find their fulfillment in the person and work of Jesus Christ. The Old Testament points

149

forward to Christ, and the New Testament points back to him. Thus Christ and his cross form the heart and center of all Holy Scriptures: Lk 24:44-47; Jn 1:41,45; 5:39,46,47; Ac 10:43. This is symbolized in a beautiful way in the sign language used by the deaf who refer to the Bible as the "Jesus Book." (The sign is made by alternately using the tip of the middle finger of each hand to point to the center of the palm of each hand, thus symbolizing the nails driven through Christ's hands. The palms of the hand are then placed together facing each other and are then opened as one opens a book.) *ref. 578,579.*

† † †

585 The saints of old lived in the dark age of prophecy. We live in the glorious light of the New Testament age which has witnessed the fulfillment of that which the Scriptures of old foretold concerning Christ. We have stood at the manger and beheld his wondrous birth. We have witnessed his mighty miracles. We have heard his victorious cry from the cross declaring the completion of his redemptive work. We have gazed into the empty tomb which proclaimed his triumphant resurrection. We have seen his majectic ascension into heaven as the Conqueror over sin, death, Satan and hell. We have experienced the transforming power of his love in our lives and have observed its saving power in the lives of others. We have seen his kingdom established in all the world.

To us, therefore, his words apply in an even greater measure than when he first spoke them to his disciples: "Blessed are the eyes that see what you see. For I tell you that many prophets and kings wanted to see what you see but did not see it, and to hear what you hear but did not hear it," Lk 10:23,24; *ref. 578,579.*

† † †

586 The time for Christ's coming was most opportune. More than a century before his birth, the Scriptures of the Old Testament had been translated into the Greek language, known as the Septuagint (*LXX*). The Greek language was now understood and used by a large part of the world. Thus God had prepared the way for proclaiming the Christmas tidings of great joy to all people.

The precise time of Christ's coming was most opportune for yet another reason. Socially, politically and morally the world of that day had degenerated to the point where even heathen philosophers acknowledged that it was beyond repair. Idolatry was rampant. Morality had degenerated into shameless violence and luxury. The sanctity of marriage was no longer recognized and sexual sins were commonplace. Judgment was perverted and might was right. Spiritual darkness covered the earth: see Is 60:2. Like the world about it, the worship of the true God had degenerated into mere formalism. God's laws had been set aside, and those who were supposed to be the religious leaders of the people were teaching for doctrines the commandments of men. Only a small remnant of the faithful remained: cp Mk 7:5-13; Lk 19:45,46; *ref. 578,579.*

150

† † †

587 There is a legend that at the birth of Christ everything stood still, that night-birds flying in the air were motionless, that the shepherd reaching his crook toward the sheep held it still, that people eating a meal held their hand midway between the dish and the mouth, and that everyone awake had a sudden inclination to be still.

Historically this legend is far from the truth, for there was almost nothing that the world thought less about, and paid less attention to, than the Babe that was born in the manger. And yet in a deeper sense the fiction was fact. The world did stop still at the birth of Christ and began its thoughts and acts anew from the impulse of his life and love. And whatever it has of goodness or greatness today it has derived from him.

— W. G. Polack

ref. 578,579

† † †

588

O little town of Bethlehem,
How still we see thee lie!
Above thy deep and dreamless sleep
The silent stars go by;
Yet in thy darkness shineth
The everlasting Light;
The hopes and fears of all the years
Are met in thee tonight.

— Phillips Brooks

ref. 578,580

† † †

589   How The Nations of The World Say "Merry Christmas"

Africa — Usoro Moakara
Bohemia — Vesele Vanoce
China — Tin Hao Nian
Croatia — Sretan Bozic
Denmark — Glaedelig Jul
France — Bon Noel
Germany — Froehliche Weinachten
Greece — Kala Christougenna
Hungary — Boldog Karacsonyi
       Unnepeket
Holland — Vrolijke Kertstmis

Italy — Felice Natale
Japan — Kinga Shinnen
Mexico — Feliz Navidad
Norway — Gledelig Jul
Poland — Wesolych Swiat
Portugal — Boas Festas
Rumania — Graciun Felicitatiune
Spain — Felices Pascuas
Sweden — Glad Julen
Turkey — Ichok Yilara

ref. 580

† † †

590 A significant event associated with the birth of Christ was the visit of the Wise Men from the East: Mt 2:1-12. The herald angel had declared that the Christmas tidings of great joy were meant for all people: Lk 2:10,11. The

151

magi from the East were the firstfruits of the great harvest of Gentiles who, in the course of time, would be drawn to Christ and rejoice in him: Is 60:1-6; Lk 2:28-32; Ro 15:8-12. On January 6th the Christian church commemorates their visit as the Festival of Epiphany, which is often referred to as the "Christmas of the Gentiles."

The Sundays following January 6th are designated on the calendar of the Church year as the "Sundays after Epiphany." The word Epiphany is derived from the Greek and literally means a shining forth, or manifestation. Applied to Christ it refers to the manner in which he revealed himself as the Son of God and Savior of the world.

The fact that the Child born in Bethlehem was a true man required no proof. But the fact that he is the Son of God, God made manifest in the flesh, in whom all the fulness of the Godhead dwells bodily, needed demonstrating: Col 2:9; 1 Tm 3:16. Epiphany supplied that need. The glory which was revealed to the shepherds and to the Wise Men at the time of his birth was manifested again and again, e.g., at his baptism: Mt 3:13-17; in his person and work: Mt 8:27; 13:54; 15:31; Mk 2:12; 7:37; Jn 2:11; Ac 2:22; in his teaching: Mt 7:28,29; Lk 2:46,47; 4:22,36; Jn 6:68,69; 7:46; in his transfiguration: Lk 9:28-36; in his death: Mt 27:54; and in his resurrection: Ro 1:4. See also Jn 1:14; 20:30,31; 1 Jn 1:1-3.

Epiphany also refers to the manifestation of Jesus as the Savior of the world: 1 Jn 4:14. Its message is therefore meant for all ages. As God led the Wise Men from the East to Bethlehem by a star, so he now leads men to him through his Word: Jn 5:39; Ac 10:43; 2 Pe 1:19.

Epiphany also points to the future, to the end of time, when Christ will appear again visibly and in all of his glory, when every eye will see him, when every knee will have to bow before him, and when every tongue will have to confess that he is Lord, to the glory of God the Father: Mt 25:31; Lk 21:27; Php 2:10,11; Re 1:7.

> As with gladness men of old
> Did the guiding star behold;
> As with joy they hailed its light,
> Leading onward, beaming bright,
> So, most gracious Lord, may we
> Evermore be led by thee!
>
> — William D. Dix

> Grant us grace to see thee, Lord,
> Mirrored in thy holy Word;
> May we imitate thee now
> And be pure as pure art thou
> That we like to thee may be
> At thy great Epiphany
> And may praise thee, ever blest,
> God in man made manifest.
>
> — Christopher Wordsworth

591 The Wise Men from the East rejoiced with exceeding joy when they saw the star that heralded the coming of Christ: Mt 2:2,9,10.

The star is a symbol of joy. How anxiously people wait for the morning star when they spend a fear-filled night on a storm-tossed sea, or when lost in woods or mountain, or when suffering on a bed of pain! Ps 130:5-8; Ac 27:20. For they know that when the morning star appears the night is almost over and the day is near.

Such was the joy of God's people of old when, through the tender mercies of God, the Dayspring from on High appeared and gave light to those who sat in darkness and in the shadow of death, to guide their feet in the way of peace: Mt 4:12-17; Lk 1:78,79; 2:29,30. Such is also the joy of sinners today when Christ, the Daystar rises in their hearts to dispel the darkness of sin and unbelief: Ac 8: 5-8; 26:18; Col 1:12-14. And such will also be the joy of all believers when at the close of this world's dark night, the Morningstar returns and "the night of weeping shall be the morn of song"; Lk 21:28; Ro 8:18; Re 22:16.

> Oh, come, thou Dayspring from on high,
> And cheer us by the drawing nigh;
> Disperse the gloomy clouds of night
> And death's dark shadows put to flight.
> Rejoice! Rejoice! Emmanuel
> Shall come to thee, O Israel.
> — Latin author unknown
> Tr., John M. Neale

ref. 579

† † †

592 A professor in psychology once gave a word-suggestion to his class of forty students attending one of our great universities. He asked them to write after the word "Christmas" the first word that flashed across their mind regarding that festive day. When the papers were returned, such words were given as "tree," "holly," "mistletoe," "gifts," "turkey," "holiday," "carols," "Santa Claus" — but not one of the forty students had written "the birth of the Savior."

> — Sunday School Times

ref. 581

† † †

593
> Christmas means
> Hearts warmed by the
> Realization that,
> In spite of our
> Sin, God loved us so
> That he gave his Son.

*M*ay we respond
*A*t this Christmas
*S*eason with our love and worship.

— Anon

ref. 580

† † †

594 In one of our midwestern cities it was customary around Christmas time to place a manger scene in the city's central park. Someone always supplied a blanket to keep the Baby Jesus warm in the crib. But one night the Baby Jesus was missing. Someone had taken the life-size figurine which symbolized the essence of Christmas. In reporting this the daily newspaper said that the City Council expressed the hope that the figurine would be returned before Christmas and that someone would supply a blanket, and added, "It would be difficult to find a replacement!"

† † †

595 A little girl who had never attended Sunday school or received any religious training in her home, was sick in the hospital. At Christmas, the nativity story was read in the children's ward. The little girl was enchanted. After the service she turned to her grim-looking nurse and said: "Have you ever heard that story before?" "Oh, yes, answered the nurse, many times." "Well," said the little girl, "you certainly don't look like it!"

If we have heard the story of Christ and his love it ought to make a difference in our lives. If God has come down to us and spoken to us and put his hand upon us, then we are changed. If, through the grace of Christ, we are given a new name, we ought to have a new look, a Christian look.

— selected

† † †

596   Let us all with gladsome voice
   Praise the God of heaven,
Who, to bid our hearts rejoice,
   His own Son has given.

— Anon

ref. 580

† † †

597 What is there about the birth of Jesus Christ that fills the hearts of old and young with joy? What is it, after nearly 2000 years, that sets the world ablaze with Christmas festivities? The answer is found in the fact that all mankind is lost in sin and in need of a Savior, that on that first Christmas the heaven-sent Savior of the world was born, and that these tidings of great joy are meant for all mankind in all ages: Lk 2:10,11; See also Is 52:7-10; Ac 4:12; 13:47,48.

Since all he comes to ransom,
   By all be he adored,
The infant born in Bethl'em,
   The Savior and the Lord.
Repeat the hymn again:
"To God on high be glory
And peace on earth to men."

— St. Germanus

ref. 580

† † †

598 O children, do you see him black or fair,
This Babe to whom you raise your prayer?
Do you see him yellow with almond eye,
The Baby Jesus praised on high?
O children of all lands, you see,
God made his Son to look like thee.

— Anon

599 Lord Jesus, you were born of a Hebrew mother. You rejoiced in the faith exhibited by a Syrian woman and a Roman soldier. You welcomed Greeks who sought you out. You let an African help carry your cross; help us to bring together people of all races and nations as co-inheritors of your kingdom.

— Herman Dietzfelbinger,
Lutheran Bishop, Munich

600 That the joyful tidings of Christmas are meant for "all people" is symbolized by the fact that Christ's birthplace was at the crossroads of the world's continents, Asia, Africa and Europe. The Babe of Bethlehem is God's priceless gift to the whole world: Lk 2:10,11; Jn 3:16; 1 Jn 4:14; and it is God's earnest desire that all nations should hear this good news: Mt 28:19; Lk 24:47; Ac 10:35; 1 Tm 2:3,4; 2 Pe 3:9.

We celebrate Christmas today because others in the past brought the good news to us. Like the shepherds of Bethlehem, it is now our obligation and privilege to make known abroad the things which were told us concerning this Child: Lk 2:17; 2:38; Jn 1:40,41,45; 4:29; *ref. 580,581,1020-1081.*

† † †

601 So this is now the mark by which we shall all certainly know whether the birth of the Lord Jesus Christ is effective in us: if we take upon ourselves the need of our neighbor; *ref. 581.*

— Martin Luther

† † †

602
　　　Though Christ a thousand times
　　　　in Bethlehem be born,
　　　If he is not born in thee,
　　　　thy soul is all forlorn.

— Anon

ref. 581

† † †

603 The mission of John the Baptist was to prepare the way for the coming of Christ: Is 40:1-5; Mt 3:1-3. His message, "Repent, for the kingdom of heaven is at hand," is the same message that Christ proclaimed when he began his public ministry: Mt 3:2; 4:17.

With the coming of Christ, the kingdom of God was now to be ushered in. But it was not the kind of a kingdom that many supposed it would be; not a kingdom of this world, but the kingdom of heaven: Jn 18:36,37. It was not a kingdom of might supported by physical power, but a kingdom of righteousness, truth, and grace, supported by the word of the gospel; not a kingdom ruled by men, but God's rule in the hearts of men which would be revealed in Jesus Christ; *ref. 581,650f, 1253-1262.*

† † †

604
　　　When keeping Jesus' birthday
　　　'Tis common now to bring
　　　A lot of gifts to others
　　　And not give him a thing.

— Anon

605 Ronnie could hardly wait for the sharing period at kindergarten. He had brought his much-prized manger scene to show to others. As he put each piece in its place, he would comment: "This is a wise man." "This is a shepherd." But the children kept asking, "Where is the Baby Jesus?" He set the last piece in place. It was a sheep. Tearfully, he said to the teacher, "I've lost the Baby Jesus."

We have been preparing for Christmas. We have shopped for gifts, decorated the house, and sent cards. The rush, the crowds, and the many duties have taken from some of us the last resource of energy and patience.

How tragic it is for us if we discover at the close of our preparations for Christmas that we, too, have lost Christ from the scene! Christmas is the anniversary of the birth of Jesus Christ. In our hearts and homes are we making him the center of our celebration?

— *The Upper Room*

606 A mother was putting her little girl to bed. It was time to say her prayers. Childlike, the girl lisped the first four petitions of the Lord's Prayer. She was not quite sure of the fifth, and so in her innocence she prayed, "And forgive us our Christmases!"

Millions of Americans will have need to pray that prayer on Decmeber 26th. If ever there is a season being desecrated by the great masses of our population, it is the season which the Christian church has set aside to celebrate the birth of Jesus Christ, the Son of God.

— selected

ref. 580,581

† † †

607
    Make you straight what long was crooked
      Make the rougher places plain;
    Let your hearts be true and humble
      As befits his holy reign.

— Johann Olearius

    Then cleansed be ev'ry Christian breast
      And furnished for so great a Guest.
    Yea, let us each our hearts prepare
      For Christ to come and enter there.

— Charles Coffin

608 A beautiful painting by Holman Hunt portrays Christ knocking at the door. When Mr. Hunt was asked why there was no handle on the door, he replied: "That door is the door of the human heart. It can be opened only from the inside."

Christ died for all: 2 Cor 5:15; and he earnestly desires the salvation of all men: 1 Tm 2:4; 2 Pe 3:9. But he will not force his way into our lives. Yet, it is he alone who can open the door of our heart: see Ac 16:14. The very words with which he calls to us and invites us to let him in are the words of eternal life: Jn 6:63,68; 15:3; Ro 1:16; He 4:12,13; Jas 1:18,21; 1 Pe 1:23. His very call is the means by which he enters our heart and himself opens the door for us Php 2:13.

609 A little boy standing next to his father and looking at the picture of Christ standing at the door, asked, "Daddy, did he get in?" *ref. 581.*

† † †

610 In Isaiah 40:1,2 the Lord foretold the end of the captivity of his people in the land of Babylon. To impress upon the Israelites the preparations that would be needed for the return to their homeland, the Lord instructed Isaiah to write: "A voice of one calling: 'In the desert prepare the way for the Lord; make straight in the wilderness a highway for our God. Every valley shall be raised up every mountain and hill made low; the rough ground shall become level, the rugged places a plain. And the glory of the Lord will be revealed, and all mankind together will see it. For the mouth of the Lord has spoken it,' " v. 3-5.

While it was literally true that there was a great stretch of desert between Babylon where they were held in captivity and their homeland in Palestine, so that a road had to be prepared for their return, the greater significance of the prophet's words was that men would have to prepare a way in their hearts to receive the promised Redeemer. It was with reference to this that John the Baptist, the forerunner of Christ, quoted these words from Isaiah

157

when he came preaching in the wilderness of Judea and saying: "Repent, for the kingdom of heaven is near," Mt 3:2.

The sinful heart of man is like a wilderness in which pride and prejudice, selfishness and self-righteousness, and every form of evil dwells: Jr 17:9; Mt 15:19. These obstacles which separate man from God must be removed to prepare the way of the Lord: Is 59:1.

Through the preaching of the law "mountains and hills are made low," the proud and self-righteous who exalt themselves are humbled. And through the preaching of the gospel the "valleys are raised up," those who groan under the heavy burden of their sins are lifted up and comforted by the assurance of forgiveness: Mt 11:28; Lk 18:9-14. As a result, "the crooked is made straight and the rough places plain": converted sinners become new creatures in Christ — no longer yielding their members as servants to sin but as servants of righteousness unto holiness: Lk 1:74,75; Ro 6; 13:11-14; 2 Cor 5:15-17.

611
Once he came in blessing,
    All our ills redressing;
Came in likeness lowly,
    Son of God most holy;
Bore the cross to save us,
    Hope and freedom gave us.

Still he comes within us,
    Still his voice would win us
From the sins that hurt us;
    Would to Truth convert us
From our foolish errors
    Ere he comes in terrors.

                       — Johann Roh

ref. 581

JESUS CHRIST, PERSON OF 612-639

God and Man in One Person

612 His human nature: He is truly a man

Though he was conceived by the Holy Ghost, he was born a human child of a human mother: Is 7:14; 9:6; Mt 1:21; Lk 1:31,35; Jn 1:14;

He is expressly called Man, or the Son of Man: Mt 8:20,27; 11:19; 16:13; 24:27; Mk 2:7,10; 8:38; 10:45; Lk 19:10; Jn 1:51; 5:27; 19:5; 1 Tm 2:5;

He possessed a true physical body and grew physically: Lk 2:7,40,42; 3:23; 24:39; Jn 19:38-42;

He hungered and thirsted, ate and drank: Mt 4:2; 11:19; Lk 24:42,43; Jn 4:7; 19:28; experienced weariness, sorrow and pain, and all the sufferings that befall mankind: Mt 8:16,17; 26:37,38; Jn 4:6; He 2:18; 4:15; he slept: Lk 8:23; Mk 4:38; he wept: Lk 19:41; Jn 11:35; He 5:7; he died: Lk 23:46; he was buried: Jn 19:38-42; *ref. 623.*

613 He differs from all mankind in that he is without sin:

The testimony of Scriptures: Is 53:9; 2 Cor 5:21; He 4:15; 7:26; 1 Pe 2:22,23; 1 Jn 3:5;

The testimony of God the Father: Mt 3:17; 17:5; 2 Pe 1:16-18;

The testimony of his disciples, who acknowledged him as the Son of God, the promised Messiah and Savior of the world: Mt 16:16; Jn 1:45,49; 6:68,69; 11:27; 20:28,31; 1 Jn 1:1-3;

The testimony of his enemies: Judas, Mt 27:4; Pilate: Mt 27:24; Lk 23:4; Jn 18:38; 19:4,6; Pilate's wife: Mt 27:19; Herod: Lk 23:15; the penitent malefactor: Lk 23:41; the centurion and some of his soldiers: Mt 27:54; Mk 15:39; Lk 23:47; see also Jn 8:46;

The testimony of devils: Mt 8:29; Mk 1:24; 3:11; Lk 4:41; *ref. 624-626,632.*

614 His divine nature:

The testimony of God the Father: Mt 3:17; 17:5; Jn 12:28; Ac 2:22;

The testimony of Christ himself: Lk 22:70,71; Jn 5:17-47; 8:14f,58; 9:35-38; 10:30,36,38; 12:45; 14:7-10; 16:15;

The testimony of John the Baptist: Mt 3:11; Jn 1:15,23,27,29-34;

The testimony of Scriptures: Mk 1:1; Lk 24:27,44-46; Jn 1:1-3,14; 3:18; 5:39,46; Ro 1:4; 9:5; 1 Cor 15:3,4; Col 1:15-19; 2:9; 1 Tm 3:16; He 1:3; 1 Jn 4:15; 5:20;

The testimony of his disciples: Mt 14:33; 16:16; Mk 15:39; Jn 1:34,49; 4:29; 6:68,69; 11:27; 20:28; Ac 8:37; 9:20;

The testimony of angels: Lk 1:35; 2:9-14; 24:3-7; Ac 1:10,11; He 1:6; Re 5:11,12;

The (unwanted) testimony of devils: Mt 8:29; Lk 4:41.

615 Divine names ascribed to him:

Alpha and Omega: Re 1:8; 22:13;
Blessed and only Potentate: 1 Tm 6:15;
Christ of God: Lk 9:20;
Eternal Life: 1 Jn 5:20;
Eternal Word: Jn 1:1-3,14; Word of Life: 1 Jn 1:1;

Everlasting Father: Is 9:6;
Express Image of God: 2 Cor 4:4; Col 1:15-18; He 1:3;
God: Is 9:6; Jn 20:28; Ro 9:5; true God: 1 Jn 5:20;
Holy One: Ac 3:14; 4:27;
Immanuel: Is 7:14; Mt 1:23;
King of Kings and Lord of Lords: Ac 10:36; 1 Tm 6:15; Re 1:5; 19:16;
Lamb of God: Jn 1:29; Re 13:8;
Lord of All: Ac 10:36;
Lord of Glory: 1 Cor 2:8;
Lord of Righteousness: Jr 23:6; cp Ro 10:4; 1 Cor 1:30; Php 3:9;
Messiah: Jn 1:41; 4:25;
Prince of Life: Ac 3:15;
Prince of Peace: Is 9:6;
Resurrection and the Life: Jn 11:25;
Savior of the World: Jn 3:16,17; Lk 2:10,11; 1 Jn 4:14;
Son of God: Mt 16:16; 26:63,64; Lk 4:41; Jn 3:16,18; Jn 6:69; 11:27; 20:31; He 10:29; 1 Jn 4:15; 5:11,12;
Son of the Highest: Lk 1:32; *ref. 627-631.*

616 Divine attributes ascribed to him:

Equality with the Father: Jn 5:23; 10:30; 14:8-11; Col 2:9;
Eternality (changelessness): Mic 5:2; Jn 1:1; 8:58; 17:5,24; Col 1:15-18; He 13:8;
Omniscience: Mt 21:2f; 26:21f,31-34; Lk 5:4-6; 18:31-33; Jn 1:48; 2:25; 21:6,7;
Omnipresence: Mt 18:20; 28:20; Ac 18:9,10; Col 2:3; He 13:6;
Omnipotence: Mt 9:6; 28:18; Lk 8:25; Jn 1:3; 10:18; 17:2; Ro 1:4; 1 Cor 8:6; Eph 1:20-23; 3:9; Col 1:16; He 1:1-3; *ref. 617,627-631.*

617 Divine works ascribed to him:

Creation of world: Jn 1:1-3; 1 Cor 8:6; Eph 3:9; Col 1:16,17; He 1:2;
Preservation of the world: Col 1:17; He 1:3;
Final judgment of the world: Mt 25:31f; Jn 5:22,27; Ac 10:42; 17:31; Ro 2:16; 14:10; 2 Tm 4:1;
The power to forgive sins: Mk 2:3-12;
His miracles: Ac 2:22, e.g., he healed the sick: Mt 4:23,24; 9:35; cast out devils: Mk 1:25,26; Ac 10:38; cleansed lepers: Mt 8:3; Lk 17:11-19; opened the eyes of the blind: Mt 9:27-30; Jn 9:1-7; made the deaf to hear and the dumb to speak: Mk 9:25,26; Lk 11:14; and the lame to walk: Mt 21:14; changed water into wine: Jn 2:9; fed the multitudes in a miraculous manner: Mt 14:15-21; 15:32-38; stilled the tempest: Mt 8:23-27; 14:25-33; walked on the sea: Jn 6:19; raised the dead: Mk 5:35-43; Lk 7:11-17; Jn 11:38-44; raised himself from the dead: Lk 18:33; Jn 2:19; 10:17,18; Ro 1:4; 1 Cor 15:3,4; 15:54-57; *ref. 627-631.*

618 Divine glory ascribed to him: Mt 14:33; 28:19; Jn 5:23; 12:13; 17:5,24; Php 2:10,11; He 1:6; Re 5:12,13.

619 The mysterious union of his divine and human natures: Lk 1:35; Jn 1:14; Col 2:9; 1 Tm 3:16; cp Ac 20:28; 1 Jn 1:7; *ref. 630,631.*

620 Seven Outstanding Traits that Characterize Christ

Sinlessness: *ref. 613;*

Obedience and faithfulness: Mt 3:15; 26:39; Lk 2:49,51; Jn 4:34; 6:38; 9:4; 14:31; 15:10; 17:4; Ro 5:19; Php 2:8; He 3:1,2; 12:2;

Love: Jn 13:1; 15:9,12,13; Ro 8:35-39; 2 Cor 5:14; Ga 2:20; Eph 3:19; 1 Jn 3:16;

Compassion: Mt 9:36; 14:14; 15:32; 20:34; 23:37; Mk 1:41; Lk 7:13; 19:41,42; Jn 11:35;

Meekness: Is 53:7; Mt 11:29; 20:28; 21:4,5; Jn 13:4,5; 2 Cor 8:9; 10:1; Php 2:5-8; 1 Pe 2:23;

Patience in suffering: Mt 27:13,14; Mk 15:3; Ro 15:5; He 12:2; 1 Pe 2:23; Is 53:7;

His life of prayer: Mk 1:35; 6:46; Lk 5:16; 6:12; 9:28; 22:31,32; 23:34; Jn 17:1-26.

The Two States in His Life and Work

621 His state of humiliation, Php 2:5-8, consisted in

His lowly birth: Lk 2:7;

His life of poverty and humble service: Mt 8:20; 11:29; 20:28; Lk 22:27; Jn 13:4,5; 2 Cor 8:9; cp Is 53:2;

His rejection by those he came to save: Is 53:3; Mt 8:34; 23:37; Lk 4:28,29; 23:18; Jn 1:11; 8:40,59;

The mockery and suffering he endured at the hands of sinful men: Mt 2:13; 27:29,30; Mk 15:16-20; Lk 22:63; 23:11,36,39; Jn 19:1-3; He 12:3; cp Ps 22:6-8,14-16;

His shameful death by crucifixion: Lk 22:37; 23:33; Ac 8:33; Ga 3:13; Php 2:8; *ref. 633-639.*

622 His state of exaltation, Php 2:9-11, consisted in

His victorious descent into hell: Eph 4:8; Col 2:15; 1 Pe 3:18,19; *ref. 795,796;*

His triumphant resurrection from the dead: Mt 28:1f; Mk 16:1f; Lk 24:1ff; Jn 20:1f; Ro 1:4; *ref. 796-807;*

His majestic ascension into heaven and his exaltation to God's right hand of power: Mt 28:18; Mk 16:19; Lk 24:50,51; Ac 1:9; Eph 1:20-23; 4:10; 1 Pe 3:22; *ref. 808-826;*

His rule as Lord over all and as Head of his Church: Mk 16:19,20; Ac 1:3-9; 2:34-36; Ro 8:34; 1 Cor 15:25; Eph 1:19-22; 4:10-12; cp Ps 2:6-12; 110:1; Is 9:6; Dn 7:14; *ref. 650-663;*

His return to glory as Judge of the living and the dead: Mt 25:31f; Ac 1:11; 10:42; 17:31; Ro 14:9; 2 Cor 5:10; Php 2:9-11; 2 Th 1:7-10; Jude 14,15; *ref. 827-849; 1600-1620.*

Resources

623 Here is a man who was born in an obscure village, the child of a peasant woman. He grew up in another obscure village. He worked in a carpenter shop until he was thirty, and then for three years he was an itinerant preacher.

He never owned a home. He never wrote a book. He never had a family. He never went to college. . . . He never traveled two hundred miles from the place where he was born. He never did one of the things that usually accompany greatness.

While still a young man, the tide of popular opinion turned against him. His friends ran away. One of them denied him. He was turned over to his enemies. He went through the mockery of a trial. He was nailed to a cross between two thieves. While he was dying his executioners gambled for the only piece of property he had on earth. When he was dead he was taken down and laid in a borrowed grave, through the pity of a friend.

Close to twenty centuries have come and gone, and today he is the centerpiece of the human race. I am far within the mark when I say that all the armies that ever marched, all the navies that were ever built, all the parliaments that ever sat, all the kings that ever reigned . . . all of them, put together, have not affected the life, or death, of man as powerfully as that ONE SOLITARY LIFE.

— Anon

ref.612,613.

† † †

624   Beautiful Savior,
King of Creation,
Son of God and Son of Man!
Truly I'd love thee,
Truly I'd serve thee,
Light of my soul, my Joy, my Crown.

Fair are the meadows,
Fair are the woodlands,
Robed in flow'rs of blooming spring;
Jesus is fairer,
Jesus is purer;
He makes our sorr'wing spirit sing.

Fair is the sunshine,
Fair is the moonlight,
Bright the sparkling stars on high;
Jesus shines brighter,
Jesus shines purer,
Than all the angels in the sky.

Beautiful Savior,
Lord of the nations,
Son of God and Son of Man!

Glory and honor,
Praise, adoration,
Now and forevermore be thine!

— Anon, 1677
ref. 613-619

† † †

625 Socrates taught forty years, Plato for fifty, Aristotle for forty, and Jesus for only three years; yet those three years accomplished infinitely more than the combined one hundred and thirty years of the teaching of Socrates, Plato and Aristotle, three of the greatest men of all antiquity; *ref. 613-619*.

† † †

626 Jesus painted no picture; yet the paintings of Raphael, Michelangelo and Leonardo da Vinci recieved their inspiration from him.

Jesus wrote no poetry; but Dante, Milton and scores of the world's greatest poets received their inspiration from him.

Jesus composed no music; still Hadyn, Handel, Beethoven, Bach and Mendelssohn reached their highest perfection of melody in the hymns, symphonies and oratorios written in his praise.

Thus every sphere of human greatness has been incomparably enriched by the humble carpenter of Nazareth.

But his unique contribution to the race of men is the salvation of the soul. Philosophy could not accomplish that — nor art — nor literature — nor music. Only Jesus can break the power of sin; only he can speak "power into the strengthless soul and life into the dead."

The world admires Christ afar off. Some adopt him as their example, and try to pattern their lives after his, but only a relatively few acknowledge him to be their Savior, though his prime function is to save sinners.

— selected
ref. 613-619

† † †

627
Veiled in flesh the Godhead see,
Hail th' incarnate Deity!
Pleased as Man with man to dwell;
Jesus, our Immanuel.

— Charles Wesley
ref. 614-619

† † †

628 What do you think of Christ, whose Son is he? Whom do you say that he is?

A man saw a big stone lying in a shallow brook. He took it home to keep his door ajar. Years later a geologist came to the man's home, saw the stone and

163

pronounced it the biggest lump of gold ever found east of the Rockies.

Many people looked upon Jesus. Some saw only a Galilean peasant and turned away. Others saw a prophet and stopped to listen. Some saw the Messiah and worshiped him. Some saw the Lamb of God and looked to him to save them from sins.

There are people today who see in Jesus merely a perfect man, and they get nothing more from him than the example of a perfect life. Others look upon him and see the Lamb of God — the divine chosen Sacrifice and Savior —true God and true man, and they come to him for salvation. When you look to Jesus, what do you see?

— The Expositor

ref. 613-619

† † †

629   Turn your eyes upon Jesus
Look full in his wonderful face;
And the things of earth will grow strangely dim
In the light of his glory and grace.

— Anon

ref. 614

† † †

630 The human and divine natures in Jesus Christ, the God-Man, are distinct, yet inseparable. It was necessary that he be true man that he might serve as man's Substitute by fulfilling the Law for man and by suffering and dying to pay the penalty for man's sins: Ro 8:3; 10:4; Ga 3:13; 4:4-7; He 2:14,15. To do this he had to be a sinless Substitute: 2 Cor 5:21; He 7:26,27. At the same time it was necessary for him to be God that he might be able to endure the full penalty for sin and that his Sacrifice might be an all-sufficient ransom for the sins of all men of all ages: Jn 1:29; Ro 5:11; 1 Cor 15:57; 1 Tm 2:5,6; He 10:14,18; 1 Jn 1:7.

631 The Nicene Creed, confessed by the Christian church throughout the ages, stresses the divine-human nature of Jesus Christ in the words:

... And in one Lord Jesus Christ, the only-begotten Son of God, begotten of his Father before all worlds, God of God, Light of Light, Very God of Very God, begotten, not made, being of one substance with the Father, by whom all things were made; who for us men and for our salvation came down from heaven and was incarnate by the Holy Ghost of the Virgin Mary and was made man; and was crucified also for us under Pontius Pilate. He suffered and was buried; and the third day he rose again according to the Scriptures; and ascended into heaven, and sitteth on the right hand of the Father; and he shall come again with glory to judge both the quick and the dead; whose kingdom shall have no end.

ref. 613-619.

† † †

632 No founder of any other religion dreamed of dying for his followers. Buddha shunned death until he was eighty. Confucius and Zoroaster did not conceive of the idea of sacrificing themselves for the good of others. Mohammed established his religion by killing rather than by being killed. Heathen religions may contain some admirable precepts, but not one of them has a redeemer. Jesus Christ alone gave his life to save a lost world.

— A. C. Dixon

ref. 613,621

† † †

633 The same poverty and humility that marked Christ's coming into the world was evident throughout his life and ministry. He had no fixed dwelling place. When traveling he slept outdoors, or found shelter in the home of friends. For the greater part, the only people who received him and associated with him were those whom the Scriptures refer to as "publicans and sinners," the lowly and the despised, the outcasts of society: Lk 15:1,2; 19:7. When he needed a boat or a beast of burden to ride upon, he had to borrow them: Mk 11:1-6; Lk 5:1-3; 22:7-13. When called upon to pay taxes he had to perform a miracle to obtain the money: Mt 17:24-27. When at his death men took inventory of his belongings they found that he had nothing save the clothes on his body, and when he was buried his body was laid in another man's grave: Mt 27:35,57-60; *ref. 621.*

† † †

634 Christ's humility is set forth in Scriptures as an example for us to follow: Mt 11:29; Jn 13:15; Php 2:5f; 1 Pe 2:21. As his disciples we are to learn from him that the way to greatness and glory lies in the path of humble obedience to the will of God and sacrificial service to our fellowmen.

Unlike the kingdoms of this world, greatness in Christ's kingdom does not consist in being a lord but in being a servant; not in being a master but a slave; not in being served but in serving; not in seeking one's selfish interests but in devoting one's life in service to others: 1 Cor 10:33. In his kingdom those who seek to save their life lose it, while those who lose their life for his sake find it: Mk 8:35. In his kingdom,

> No service in itself is small,
> None great, though earth it fill;
> But that is small that seeks its own,
> And great that does God's will.

635 George Washington Carver, the chemist who derived many products from the peanut, told this story about himself: He implored God, "Tell me the mystery of the universe." God answered, "The knowledge of that mystery is reserved for me alone." Then Dr. Carver asked, "God, tell me the mystery of the peanut." And God said, "Now that is more nearly your size, George, and I will reveal it to you."

636 John Wesley once said; "True humility is a kind of self-denial." "Oh, to be nothing," was the plea of the saints of old. Today men smile at such an idea; they want to be something. So they pump away at their little cistern of selfishness and miss the rivers of living water.

— *The Free Methodist*

637 Humility must always be the portion of any man who receives acclaim earned in the blood of his followers and the sacrifices of his friends.

Conceivably a commander may have been professionally superior. He may have written a chapter that will glow forever in the pages of military history. Still, even such a man if he existed would sadly face the fact that his honor cannot hide in his memories the crosses marking the resting places of the dead.

— General Eisenhower

638 After Christ had stooped to the lowly service of washing his disciples' feet, he said: "I have given you an example, that you should do as I have done to you," Jn 13:15. How sorely they needed that lesson! How often they had argued among themselves as to who among them would be the greatest in the kingdom of God: Mt 18:1f; 20:21f; Lk 22:24.

We, too, need to be reminded that only he is great who is so small that he is nothing and Christ is all in all: see Jn 3:30.

639 Have you ever thought of it, that only the smaller birds sing? You never heard a note from the eagle in all your life, nor from the turkey, nor from the ostrich. But you have heard from the canary, the wren and the lark. The sweetest music comes from those Christians who are small in their own estimation and before the Lord.

— *Watchman-Examiner*

ref. 621

Prophesied and Fulfilled

640 God declared through Moses, "The Lord your God will raise up for you a prophet like me from among your own brothers. You must listen to him.... I will put my words in his mouth, and he will tell them everything I command him. If anyone does not listen to my words that the prophet speaks in my name, I myself will call him to account," Dt 18:15,18,19;

This prophecy found its fulfillment in the prophetic office of Christ in which he revealed himself by word and deed as the Son of God and the heaven-sent Savior of the world: Mt 21:11,46; Mk 6:15; Lk 4:16-21; 7:16; 24:19; Jn 1:21,45; 4:19-26; 6:14; 7:40; 9:17; 12:49; 14:10; 17:8; cp Mt 3:17; 17:5; *ref. 642-644.*

A Prophet "Like Moses," Yet Infinitely Superior to Him

641 Like Moses, Christ was a descendant of the Jewish people according to the flesh: Ro 9:5; but unlike Moses who was of this world, Christ came from heaven: Mt 1:18-21; Lk 1:34,35; Jn 1:18; 3:13;

Although Moses had an intimate relationship with God, he was not allowed to see God's face: Ex 33:11,18-20; Nu 7:89; 12:6-8; but Christ is the very Son of God who is in the bosom of God the Father and who fully shares God's glory: Jn 1:18; 3:13; 10:30; 14:9-11; 17:5; Col 1:15; He 1:2;

Moses performed miracles at God's direction and by God's power: Ex 4:1f; 6:13; Dt 34:11; Christ performed miracles of his own will and by his own power: Mt 8:3,26; Mk 2:10,11; 5:8; Lk 7:14; Jn 2:7f; 3:2; 4:46f; 11:43,44 etc; cp Ac 2:22;

Both Moses and Christ revealed God's will to his people. But while God had first to reveal his will to Moses: Ex 3:2f; 19:3-7; 24:3,12; Christ already knew the will of his Father: Jn 1:18; 3:11-13,31,32; 5:37; 6:38-40; 14:10,24; 17:8;

Moses was sent to deliver the Israelites from the bondage of Egypt: Ex 3:7-10; Christ was sent to deliver the whole world from the curse of the law of God and from the bondage of sin, death, Satan and hell: Lk 1:68-75; Ga 3:13; 4:4,5; Col 1:12-14; He 2:14,15; 1 Jn 3:8;

Both Moses and Christ established a covenant between God and his people: Ex 19:3-7; Mt 26:28; Jn 1:17; He 8:5-13; 12:24; but the covenant established by Christ was the more glorious: 2 Cor 3:6-18;

Moses, like Christ, was a mediator between God and his people: Ex 19:18-25; 20:18-21; Dt 5:23-31; but Christ's work as Mediator continues forever: Lk 22:32; 23:34; Jn 17; Ro 8:32-34; 1 Tm 2:4,5; He 7:25; 1 Jn 2:2;

Moses was mortal and his work came to an end: Dt 34:1-6; Christ is eternal, and his work goes on forever: Mic 5:2; Jn 8:58; 17:5,24; Col 1:17; He 7:22-28; 13:8;

Moses led the people of God to an earthly Canaan: Dt 32:48,52; Christ brings the people of God into the heavenly Canaan: Jn 14:2,3; 10:27-30; He 4:9;

God threatened to punish those who would not listen to Moses: Nu 12:5-9;

16:28f; God threatens an even greater punishment to those who will not listen to Christ: Dt 18:18,19; Mt 3:17; 17:5; Mk 16:16; Jn 3:18,36; 8:24; Ac 3:22,23; He 10:25-31; 2 Pe 2:1;. *ref. 642-644.*

Resources

642
   His wondrous works and ways
    He made by Moses known.
   But sent the world his truth and grace
    By his beloved Son.
— Isaac Watts

643 Although Christ has withdrawn his visible presence from the earth, he continues his prophetic office by supplying his church with pastors and teachers who, through the preaching and teaching of his word, continue to reveal him as the Son of God and the Savior of the world: Lk 10:16; Jn 17:17-20; 20:21; Eph 4:10-12; cp 1 Th 2:13.

644
   While thy ministers proclaim
   Peace and pardon in thy name,
   Through their voice, by faith, may I
   Hear thee speaking from the sky.
— John Montgomery

   ref. 641

(ref.: Redemption 1223-1252; Sacrifices, Blood 1297-1308)

645 The Old Testament prophesied that Jesus Christ would be a priest: Ps 110:4; and his priesthood was typified by the office of the Old Testament high priest: Hebrews chapters 5,7-10.

646 While possessing similarities, there are marked differences between Christ's office as our great High Priest and the office of the high priest in the Old Testament:

The Old Testament high priest was a representative of the people. — Christ was "made like unto his brethren," that he might serve as their representative. To this end he, the eternal Son of God, took upon himself our nature: Ga 4:4-7; He 2:14-18;

Not anyone could be a high priest, but only the person chosen by God. —God appointed Christ for this office: He 3:1,2; 5:4,5; but unlike the Old Testament high priest, who was anointed with oil, God anointed Christ for this office with the Holy Ghost: Ps 45:7; Ac 10:38; He 1:9; Is 61:1;

The Old Testament high priest served only for a time because he was mortal, subject to death. — But Christ is the eternal Son of God, without beginning and without end, whose priesthood continues forever: He 7:11,16,17,22-28;

The Old Testament high priest could only enter a tabernacle made with hands, where there was only a reflection of God's glory. — Christ, our perfect High Priest, entered a more perfect tabernacle not made with hands, into heaven itself, there to appear in the very presence of God for us: He 9:12,24; 10:19-23;

The Old Testament high priest offered the blood of animals for sacrifice. — Christ offered his own blood: He 9:11-14;

The Old Testament high priests were but men and therefore first had to offer a sacrifice for their own sins before they could offer a sacrifice for the sins of the people. And because neither their persons nor the animal which they offered were perfect, these rituals had to be repeated year after year. Christ, the holy Son of God, did not have to offer a sacrifice for himself, for he had no sin and in him was no sin: Is 53:9; Jn 8:46; 2 Cor 5:21; He 9:14; 1 Pe 1:19; 2:22; 1 Jn 3:5. And because Christ was both the Sacrifice and the priest, the offering which he brought was the perfect sacrifice of himself which never has to be repeated: He 7:26,27; 10:1-4,14,18;

The Old Testament high priest sacrificed only for the sins of the people of Israel. Christ sacrificed himself for the sins of all men of all times: Jn 1:29; 2 Cor 5:14,19; 1 Jn 2:2;

The Old Testament sacrifices had only limited cleansing power; they only sanctified the flesh and thus cleansed the people from their bodily defilement: Nu 19:2-9. Christ's sacrifice purifies the conscience from guilt and cleanses from sin: He 9:11-15; 10:22; 1 Jn 1:7; that we might serve God in holiness and righteousness: Ro 6:6; 1 Cor 6:19,20; Tt 2:14; He 12:14; 1 Pe 1:18-22;

The Old Testament high priest was an imperfect mediator between God and the people of Israel. Christ is our perfect Mediator who ever lives to intercede for us: He 7:28; Ro 8:34; 1 Tm 2:5,6; 1 Jn 2:1,2. And in that he himself suffered, having been tried, he is able to help all who are tried: He 2:18; 4:14-16; *ref. 647-649.*

Resources

647 According to the Scriptures, Christ was to have a following, a priesthood of believers, who through faith in him would be his own, have free access to God through him, and who would serve him in holiness and righteousness: Ps 110:3,4; Is 61:6. This prophecy is fulfilled in the New Testament, where believers in Christ constitute a universal priesthood: 1 Pe 2:9; Re 1:5,6; 5:10.

As the Old Testament priesthood foreshadowed Jesus Christ as the perfect High Priest, so it was also a shadow of the universal priesthood of all believers in Christ. Like the Old Testament priests, though in a far superior manner, Christians:

Are called and chosen by God: 2 Tm 1:9; 1 Pe 2:9;

Are consecrated for their calling; they are washed in holy baptism, sanctified in the name of the Lord Jesus and clothed in the garments of his righteousness, and anointed with the Holy Spirit: Is 61:6,10; 1 Cor 1:30; 6:11; 2 Cor 5:21; Ga 3:27; Eph 1:13; Tt 3:5,6; 1 Jn 2:20; Re 7:14;

Have direct access to God through Christ: Ro 5:1,2; Eph 2:18; 3:12; He 10:19-22;

Offer up spiritual sacrifices: by presenting themselves to God as a living sacrifice: Ro 12:1; by offering the sacrifices of praise and thanksgiving: He 13:15; 1 Pe 2:5; and by being active in works of faith and labors of love: Eph 2:10; Php 4:18; He 13:16; 1 Pe 2:9-12; *ref. 645,646.*

† † †

648
    Dear dying Lamb, Thy precious blood
      Shall never lose its power
    Till all the ransomed church of God
      Be saved to sin no more.
                 — William Cowper

649
    Jesus, my great High Priest,
    Offered his blood and died;
    My guilty conscience seeks
    No sacrifice beside.
    His pow'rful blood did once atone,
    And now it pleads before the throne.
                 — Isaac Watts

ref. 646

JESUS CHRIST, KINGLY OFFICE OF 650-663

Jesus Christ as King

650 Scriptures ascribe kingly titles to him:

King: Ps 2:6; Jr 23:5,6; Zch 9:9; Mt 21:5; Jn 18:37;

King of Glory: Ps 24:7-10;

King of the Jews: Zch 9:9; Mt 2:2; 21:5; 27:37; Jn 1:49; 19:14,15,19-22;

King of kings and Lord of lords: 1 Tm 6:15; Re 1:5; 17:14; 19:16;

He spoke of himself as a King: Mt 25:34; Jn 18:37; *ref. 657,658,663.*

His Kingdom of Power

651 This is the kingdom in which he rules over the entire world and exerts his power in the social structure either directly or through his followers: Ps 72:8; Mt 11:27; 28:18; Jn 19:11; 1 Cor 15:24-28; Eph 2:20-22; 1 Pe 3:22; see also Dt 4:39; 1 Chr 29:11,12; 2 Chr 20:6; Ps 47:2; 83:18; 135:6; Is 40:15; Dn 2:20-22; 4:35; Php 2:9-11;*ref. 661.*

His Kingdom of Grace and of Glory

652 His kingdom of Grace is the Christian church on earth in which he rules the hearts of his followers by his Word: Mt 4:17; 16:18; Lk 17:20,21; Jn 18:37; Ro 14:17; 1 Cor 1:2. The church is also spoken of as "Zion" and "Jerusalem": Ps 149:2; Is 37:22; 40:9; 52:1; 62:11; Zch 9:9; Mt 21:5; *ref. 659,660,662.*

653 His Kingdom of Glory is the consummation of the Christian church in heaven: Mt 5:10; 7:21; 8:11; 25:34; Ac 14:22; 2 Th 1:5; 2 Tm 4:18; Jas 2:5; 2 Pe 1:11; *ref. 662,663.*

654 Various expressions used to denote his kingdom:

The kingdom: Mt 13:19,38; 25:34; Jas 2:5; see also Is 9:6; Dn 2:44; 4:3; 7:14;

The kingdom of God: Mk 1:14,15; 9:1; Lk 4:43; 8:1; 9:2,62; 21:31; Ac 1:3; 8:12; 14:22; 20:25; 28:23; Ro 14:17; 1 Cor 4:20; 2 Th 1:5;

The kingdom of heaven: Mt 3:2; 4:17; 5:3,10; 10:7; 13:24,31,33,44,45,47; 20:1; 22:2; 25:1;

His (Christ's or God's) kingdom: Dn 7:14; Is 9:6; Mt 6:10; 16:28; Lk 22:30; 23:42; Jn 18:36; He 1:8; Re 11:15; 17:14; 19:16;

Kingdom of Christ and of God: Eph 5:5.

His Kingdom Differs From the Kingdoms of This World

655 Unlike the kingdoms of this world, it has its origin in heaven and its purpose is to lead men to heaven: Dn 7:14; Mt 25:34; Jn 18:36,37;

It is not visible and physical, but unseen and spiritual: Lk 17:20,21; Jn 18:37; Ro 14:17;

Its goal is not to enslave men, but to free them: Ps 72:1-4,12; Is 9:7; 11:4; 42:1-4; 52:7-10; 61:1-3; Mt 1:21; Mk 10:45; Lk 19:10; 1 Tm 1:15;

It is not marked by pomp and splendor, but by meekness and humility: Mt 8:20; 11:29; 20:25-28; 21:1-9; Lk 2:7; Jn 13:4,5; Php 2:5-8;

Its royal attendants are not men, but angels: Ps 103:19-21; Mt 26:53; Re 5:11-13;

It is not ruled by force, but by love: Ps 72:7; Is 2:4; 9:7; Zch 9:10; Mt 5:43-45; 26:52-54; Jn 18:36; 2 Cor 10:4; Re 12:11;

Its realm is not confined, but embraces the entire universe: Ps 2:7-9; 47:7; 59:13; 72:8; 103;19; Zch 9:10; Mal 1:11; Eph 1:20,21; Php 2:9-11;

Its power is unlimited and extends into the world to come: Is 9:7; Zch 9:10; Mt 11:27; 28:18; Jn 5:22,27; 17:2; Ac 10:42; 1 Cor 15:24-29; Eph 1:20,21; Php 2:9-11; 1 Pe 3:22; Re 1:5; 17:14; 19:6,16;

It is not temporal, but eternal: Ps 2:8; 45:6; 72:8; Is 9:6,7; Dn 4:3,34; 7:14; Mic 5:2; Mt 16:18; 28:20; Lk 1:33; Eph 1:20,21; Php 2:10,11; Col 1:16,17; 1 Tm 1:17; 2 Pe 1:11; Re 5:13; 11:15;

Membership in it is not by birth, but by spiritual rebirth; and entrance into it is by repentance and faith: Mt 3:2; 4:17; Mk 1:14,15; Jn 1:12,13; 3:3,5; Ac 2:39; 2 Cor 5:17; Tt 3:5; 1 Pe 1:23; 1 Jn 5:1;

Those who hold membership in it render willing service out of love to Christ and to their fellowmen: Mt 25:34-40; Mk 10:42-45; Lk 1:74,75; Jn 12:26; Ro 8:18; 1 Cor 7:22; 2 Cor 5:15; Ga 5:13; 6:2,10; Eph 6:6; 1 Jn 4:19-21;

Those who hold membership in his Kingdom of Grace are also heirs of his Kingdom of Glory: Mt 25:34; 26:29; Lk 10:20; 22:30; Jn 14:2,3; 17:24; Ac 14:22; Ro 8:14-18; Php 3:20,21; Col 3:1-4; 2 Tm 2:12; 4:18; 1 Pe 1:3-9; 1 Jn 3:1,2.

The Extent and Purpose of His Office

656 As the King of Kings and the Lord of Lords, he rules with his almighty power over all creatures, governs and protects his church, and finally leads it to glory: Mt 28:18; Jn 18:36,37; Eph 1:20-23; Col 1:16-18; 2 Tm 4:18; *ref. 658-663.*

Resources

657 The Jews considered it an insult when Pilate placed the title "This is the King of the Jews" on Christ's cross. Not only had Christ not turned out to be the kind of king for whom they were looking, that title also branded the Jews as his followers. They therefore demanded that the title be changed. "Do not write, 'The King of the Jews,'" they said, "but that this man claimed to be king of the Jews." Pilate answered, "What I have written, I have written," Jn 19:19-22. The truth is, what Pilate had written, God himself had written long before in prophecy, and that truth could not be changed.

658 The sacred writers tell us that the title on Christ's cross, "This is the King of the Jews," was written in Hebrew, Greek and Latin. Those three languages were representative of the whole ancient world. Hebrew was the Jewish language of religion, Greek that of commerce, and Latin the language of law and government. Christ was declared King of them all. "On his head are many crowns. He is King in the religious sphere, the King of salvation, holiness, and love. He is the King in the realm of culture; the treasures of art, of song, of literature, and of philosophy belong to him. He is the King in the political sphere, King of kings and Lord of lords, entitled to rule in the social relationships, in trade and commerce, in all the activities of men"; *ref. 650-656.*

† † †

659
　　　　　　　He rules the world with truth and grace
　　　　　　　And makes the nations prove
　　　　　　　The glories of his righteousness
　　　　　　　And wonders of his love.
— Isaac Watts

660 When at the end of his conquests Napoleon was banished to a lonely prison on the island of St. Helena, he said, "There is no possible term of comparison between Jesus Christ and every other person in the world. Alexander, Caesar, Charlemagne, and I founded empires. But on what did we found them? Upon force. But Jesus Christ founded his empire upon love; and at this hour millions of men would die for him"; *ref. 651-656.*

† † †

661
　　　　　　　Jesus shall reign where'er the sun
　　　　　　　Does his successive journeys run,
　　　　　　　His kingdom stretch from shore to shore
　　　　　　　Till moons shall wax and wane no more.

　　　　　　　Let every creature rise and bring
　　　　　　　Peculiar honors to our King;
　　　　　　　Angels descend with songs again,
　　　　　　　And earth repeat the loud Amen.
— Isaac Watts

662 The second petition of the Lord's Prayer, "Thy Kingdom come," is a prayer that the Kingdom of Grace may come to all men, and that God may speed the coming of the Kingdom of Glory: Mt 6:10; Lk 11:2; Re 22:20; *ref. 651-656.*

† † †

663 When King George of England heard a rendition of Handel's oratorio *The Messiah* for the first time, he was deeply moved by its grandeur. And when the choir sang the "Hallelujah Chorus" he, the greatest king on earth, arose and stood reverently until the chorus was completed. Millions have stood thus in reverence ever since; *ref. 653-656.*

JESUS CHRIST — HIS SUFFERING AND DEATH 664-671

664 The suffering and death of Christ, followed by his triumphant resurrection, forms the heart and center of all Scriptures: Lk 1:68-75; 2:29-32; 24:25-27, 44-46; Jn 1:41,45; 5:39,46,47; 20:30,31; Ac 3:18; 10:43; 13:26-33; 1 Cor 2:2; 15:1-4; 2 Tm 3:15; 1 Pe 1:10-12;

173

665 In recognition of this, the centrality of the church's preaching and teaching must ever be Jesus Christ and him crucified: Ac 8:5,35; 9:20; 1 Cor 1:23; 2:2; 15:1-4; 2 Cor 4:5; Ga 3:1,8,9; *ref. 666-671.*

Resources

666 Because of the supreme significance it attaches to the suffering, death and resurrection of Jesus Christ, the Christian church has from ancient times designated the six weeks preceding Easter as a season in which to center its attention on Christ's cross in a special way. These weeks are known as the Season of Lent.

The Lenten season begins with Ash Wednesday, a day so named from the ancient custom of worshipers coming to church on this day in sackcloth, with bare feet, and having their foreheads daubed with the ashes of palms which had been blessed the previous Palm Sunday, as a sign of repentance. The last week in Lent, known as Holy Week, begins with Palm Sunday and culminates with Good Friday, the day of Christ's death on the cross; *ref. 664,665.*

† † †

667 The cross of Christ is the center of all things. "Here two eternities meet. The streams of ancient history converge here, and here the river of modern history takes its rise. The eyes of patriarchs and prophets strained forward to Calvary, and now the eyes of all generations and of all races look back to it. This is the end of all roads, . . . the center of all knowledge"

— Stalker

† † †

668
Lord, lead me to Gethsemane!
Engrave upon my memory
Not to forget thine agony,
To render endless thanks to thee.

Lord, lead me on to Calvary!
Enlighten me thy cross to see;
Nor let it e'er forgotten be,
That there thy life was giv'n for me.

Lord, thou hast borne sin's curse for me,
Endured the shame to set me free!
Now may I live my life to thee,
Thine wholly be eternally.

— R. C. R.

ref. 664,665

† † †

174

669 The account of Christ's suffering and death as recorded by the four evangelists is the most gripping narrative that has ever been written. It is God's revelation to man as the only way to salvation: Ac 4:12. It is like an inexhaustible well of water from which men of all ages have drawn and from which men today draw the refreshing Water of Life, which quenches the thirst of sin-parched hearts and souls: Jn 4:14; 6:35. Its very words are spirit and life and the power of God unto salvation to all who believe them: Jn 6:63; Ro 1:16,17.

> For ev'ry thirsty, longing heart
> Here streams of bounty flow
> And life and health and bliss impart
> To banish mortal woe.

> Here springs of sacred pleasure rise
> To ease your ev'ry pain;
> Immortal fountain, full supplies!
> Nor shall you thirst in vain.

> Dear Savior, draw reluctant hearts;
> To thee let sinners fly
> And take the bliss thy love imparts
> And drink and never die.
> — Anne Steele

ref. 664,665

† † †

670 When Gottfried V. Bullion, the leader of a crusade to the Holy Land, victoriously entered the city of Jerusalem he was acclaimed as a great conqueror by the admiring multitude. A kingly crown was offered him, but he replied, "Should I wear a crown of gold where my Savior wore a crown of thorns?"

The season of Lent is a solemn call to follow Christ in spirit to the scenes of his suffering for our salvation. Shall we, then, wear the crown of worldly indifference while our Savior goes forth to suffer and die in our stead?

> Do we pass that cross unheeding,
> Breathing no repentant vow,
> Tho' we see thee wounded, bleeding,
> See thy thorn-encircled brow?

> Yet thy sinless death has bro't us
> Life eternal, peace, and rest;
> Only what thy grace has taught us
> Calms the sinner's stormy breast.

> Jesus, may our hearts be burning
> With more fervent love for thee!
> May our eyes be ever turning
> To thy cross of agony

Till in glory, parted never
From the blessed Savior's side,
Graven in our hearts forever,
Dwell the cross, the Crucified!
— Cirolamo Savonarola
ref. 664,665

† † †

671 It is easy to view the characters of the Passion story objectively and to regard the death of Christ as a mere historical event, instead of seeing ourselves in the place of those who took part in the betrayal, denial, condemnation and crucifixion of Christ, and instead of recognizing that his suffering and death was for the penalty of our sins. — A converted African once said, "When the story of Christ's suffering and death was first read to me, I cursed Pilate and the Jews. But when I understood it, I cursed myself, for I, too, have crucified Jesus Christ."

My burden in thy Passion,
Lord, thou hast borne for me,
For it was my transgression
Which bro't this woe on thee.
— Bernard of Clairvaux
ref. 664,665

JESUS CHRIST — IN GETHSEMANE 672-681

His Agony

672 The nature of his agony and suffering:

The vision of the bitter cup of suffering which was placed before him to drink filled his very soul with fear and trembling. In that cup were mixed all the vials of wrath of a holy and righteous God who hates and punishes sin. While his disciples slept, he trod the winepress of God's wrath alone: Is 63:1-6; Re 14:19; 19:15. As he wrestled with Satan and the forces of hell, the agony of his soul evidenced itself in his bloody sweat: Mt 26:36-46; Mk 14:32-42; Lk 22:39-46; cp Gn 3:15; Jn 12:23,27,28; *ref. 678,679.*

673 Its meaning for us:

Christ's warning to his disciples to "watch and pray" lest they fall into temptation, is repeated in Scriptures for our warning also: Ps 1:1; Ac 20:31; Ro 12:2; 1 Cor 10:12; 2 Cor 6:14-18; Jas 4:7; 1 Pe 5:8; 2 Pe 3:17; 1 Jn 2:15-17;

The agony that Christ suffered should be a constant reminder to us of the dreadfulness of sin and of God's punishment for sin, and it should cause us to flee from sin: Is 13:9; Jr 10:10; Ho 5:10; Ro 1:18; 2:5; 1 Cor 6:18; 10:14; Eph 5:6; 1 Th 1:10; 1 Tm 6:11; Re 16:19;

The sufferings that Christ endured, he endured for us, and the victory he won over Satan was won for us: Is 53:4-6; Jn 1:29; 1 Cor 1:30; 2 Cor 5:21; He 2:14,15; 1 Jn 3:8; *ref. 678,679.*

His Prayer

674 The nature of his prayer:
He prayed that, if it were possible, his heavenly Father might remove the cup of suffering from him. But he added: "Not my will, but yours be done," Lk 22:42; cp Jn 12;23,27,28. Here, as in all of his ministry, he submitted his will to the will of his heavenly Father: Jn 6:38; 14:31; 15:10; Php 2:5-8; He 10:9; *ref. 680,681*;

675 Its meaning for us:
By precept as well as by example, Christ has taught us how we are to pray by submitting our will to the good and gracious will of our heavenly Father: Mt 6:10; Lk 11:2; Jas 4:13-17; 1 Pe 2:21; *ref. 680.*

Resources

676 Gethsemane was a garden, east of Jerusalem, on the slopes of or near the Mount of Olives. Christ often resorted there with his disciples for rest, meditation and prayer. It is still a hallowed spot because it was the scene of our Savior's suffering: Mt 26:30,36; Mk 14:26,32; Lk 22:39; Jn 18:1,2; *ref. 672,673.*

677 It is significant to note that the Savior's Passion should begin in a garden, for it was in such a place as this, in the Garden of Eden, that our first parents Adam and Eve fell into sin. By reason of their fall, sin and all its woes have passed upon the entire human race. Here, now, in another garden, in fulfillment of God's promise of redemption, Christ, the second Adam, who again represented the entire human race, faced the great issue of bearing the penalty for the world's sin so that, as by one man's disobedience all were made sinners, by the obedience of one all might be made righteous; and so that, just as sin reigned unto death through Adam, grace might reign through righteousness unto eternal life through Jesus Christ our Lord: Ro 5:19,21; *ref. 672,673.*

— selected and adapted

† † †

678
Take off thy shoes from off thy feet,
Draw near unto the blest retreat, Gethsemane;
Where angels, bending from the great white throne,
Saw him who trod the winepress all alone.
His face and form and brow were wet
With beads of blood and clammy sweat.
And yet the prayer of God's own Son
Was "Not my will but thine be done!"
O Lord of love, O Fount of grace,
Teach us anew thy steps to trace,
To follow all the mournful way
From Olivet to Calvary;

To count all other things but loss
To gain the blessing of thy wondrous cross.
— Anon
ref. 672,673

† † †

679 The finite mind of man cannot fathom the greatness of Christ's sufferings for our sins. The three disciples who were with him in the Garden saw only a part of it when they observed it and heard him say, "My soul is exceedingly sorrowful, even unto death": Mt 26:37,38; Mk 14:33. The sacred account tells us that he prayed "being in agony," Lk 22:44. Moreover, the depth and extent of his suffering is indicated by the fact that he prayed three times for deliverance from the cup of suffering; it is also shown by the drops of blood he sweat: Lk 22:44; cp Ps 22:14,15.

You who think of sin but lightly
    Nor suppose its evil great
Here may view its nature rightly,
    Here its guilt may estimate.
— Thomas Kelly
ref. 673

† † †

680 Christ's fervent prayer in Gethsemane was that, if there were some other way in which the divine plan of salvation might be accomplished, his heavenly Father might remove this bitter cup of suffering from him. But whatever the cost might be, his only desire was to do the will of his Father.

Go to dark Gethsemane,
    Ye that feel the Tempter's pow'r;
Your Redeemer's conflict see,
    Watch with him one bitter hour;
Turn not from his griefs away,
Learn of Jesus Christ to pray.
— James Montgomery
ref. 674,675

† † †

681

Who is this that comes from Edom,
    All his raiment stained with blood,
To the captives speaking freedom,
    Bringing and bestowing good,
Glorious in the garb he wears,
    Glorious in the spoil he bears?
'Tis the Savior, now victorious,
    Trav'ling onward in his might;
'Tis the Savior; oh, how glorious
    To his people is the sight!

178

Satan conquered and the grave,
    Jesus now is strong to save.

Why that blood his raiment staining?
    'Tis the blood of many slain;
Of his foes there's none remaining,
    None the contest to maintain.
Fall'n they are, no more to rise;
    All their glory prostrate lies.

Mighty Victor, reign forever,
    Wear the crown so dearly won;
Never shall thy people, never,
    Cease to sing what thou hast done.
Thou hast fought thy people's foes;
    Thou hast healed thy people's woes.

                                    — Thomas Kelly
ref. 673

JESUS CHRIST, THE BETRAYAL AND DENIAL OF 682-699

His Betrayal by Judas

682 The act of betrayal and its results for Judas:
Moved by avarice and prompted by Satan, Judas covenanted with the chief priests to deliver Christ to them: Mt 26:14-16; Mk 14:10,11; Lk 22:3-6; Jn 6:70; 13:27;

The shameful act of betrayal in the Garden of Gethsemane: Mt 26:47-50; Mk 14:43-46; Lk 22:47,48; Jn 18:1-5;

Judas' terrible end: Mt 27:3-10; Jn 17:12; Ac 1:16-20; *ref. 686.*

683 An example of warning for Christ's followers
Not to sell their heavenly birthright: cp Gn 25:29-34; He 12:16,17; Mk 8:36-38;

Not to betray Christ or the sacred trust committed to them by forfeiting their Christian principles for the paltry price of enjoying the pleasures of sin for a season: 1 Tm 6:9,10,20; 2 Tm 1:14; He 11:24-26; 1 Jn 2:15-17; Re 3:11; *ref. 687-690,699.*

His Denial by Peter

684 The act of the denial: Mt 26:69-75; Mk 14:66-71; Lk 22:54-62; Jn 18:15-18,25-27.
Causes that contributed to his denial:
His self-reliant boasting and refusal to heed Christ's warnings: Mt 26:31-35; Mk 14:27-31; Lk 22:31-34;

Joining with bad company: Mt 26:58; Lk 22:55; Jn 18:18;
Results of the denial:
He acknowledged his sin and repented: Mt 26:75, Mk 14:72; Lk 22:61,62;

The sincerity of his repentance and faith was attested to by his subsequent conduct and from the witness of his epistles: cp Jn 21:15-17; Ac 2:14f; 4:8f; 5:29f; 1 Pe 1:3f,18,19f; see also Lk 24:34; cp Lk 22:31,32 with 1 Pe 5:1-11; *ref. 691,695.*

An Example for Christ's Followers

685 An Example for Christ's Followers:

To be on guard against temptations: Mt 26:41; Mk 13:22; Eph 6:11,12; 1 Tm 6:9-12; Jas 1:14; 1 Pe 5:8,9; 2 Pe 3:17; *ref. 692;*

To guard against the sin of pride and self-reliance: Pr 3:5; 11:2; 16:18; Lk 18:11,14; Ro 11:20; 1 Co 10:12; 1 Pe 5:5,6;

To avoid evil associations: Ps 1:1; Pr 1:10; 4:14,15; Is 52:11; 1 Cor 5:11; 10:21; 15:33; 2 Cor 6:14-18; Ga 5:9; Eph 5:11; 1 Th 5:22; 2 Th 3:6; Jas 4:4; 1 Jn 2:15-17;

To repent: Ps 32:5; 51:1-9; Lk 15:18-21;

To look to Christ for forgiveness; 1 Jn 1:7; 2:2;

To strive to amend one's sinful life: Ps 51:10-13; Mt 3:8; 1 Pe 2:24,25; *ref. 692-698,1253-1262.*

Resources

686 Judas Ischariot was the son of Simon Ischariot, Jn 6:71, and is distinguished by his surname from another of the twelve disciples who was also named Judas: Lk 6:16; Jn 14:22. He was the treasurer of the group of Christ's disciples and was guilty of stealing money from this fund: Jn 12:5,6. It appears that he was at first a devoted follower of Christ, but as time went on he became more and more estranged. Finally he permitted his avarice to cause him to commit the heinous crime of betraying his Lord. When at the time of the betrayal Christ addressed him as "friend," Mt 26:50, that word should have sunk deep into Judas' heart; it should have reminded him that he was once Christ's friend and that he even now could enjoy that friendship once more if he would but repent of his sin: see Is 1:18; Jn 6:37; Ro 5:20; 1 Jn 1:7; *ref. 682.*

† † †

687
It may not be for silver,
  It may not be for gold,
But still by tens of thousands
  Is this precious Savior sold.
Sold for a godless friendship
  Sold for a selfish aim,
Sold for fleeting trifle,
  Sold for an empty name.
                — William Blane

688 If we search our hearts we shall find that we, too, have been guilty of betraying Christ and the sacred trust he has committed to us, if not directly then indirectly by our failure to confess him as we ought or by forfeiting Christian principles for personal profit. Sooner or later the realization of this horrible guilt will be forced upon us. But when that happens let us not despair, as Judas did, but let us look to our Savior who bore the sins of Christian traitors as well as all other sins. And let us remember that no guilt is too black and no sin too great that it cannot be pardoned by his precious blood.

— selected and adapted.

689　　　　　Lord, let me not with scorning
　　　　　　　View Judas' shocking deed,
　　　　　　　But take from it a warning
　　　　　　　Against deceit and greed.
　　　　　　　　　— Clara Seuel Schreiber

690 History tells us that Lysimachus, King of Thrace, offered his whole kingdom to his enemies if they would but quench his thirst. After his request had been granted he remarked, "O what a miserable wretch I have been, to lose such a kingdom for a momentary gratification of my desire." How much greater would be the folly to forfeit one's right in the kingdom of God for the gratification of sinful lust, to sell one's soul to Satan for the sake of enjoying the pleasures of sin for a season! cp Mk 8:34-38; *ref. 683.*

† † †

691 Simon Peter was the son of John, a native of the town of Bethsaida, Jn 1:44, and later a resident of the city of Capernaum: Mt 8:14; Lk 4:38. His trade was that of a commercial fisherman on the Sea of Galilee: Mt 4:18. His brother Andrew brought him to Christ, and Christ chose him early in his ministry to be one of his twelve disciples: Jn 1:40-42; Mt 4:18,19. Christ named him "Cephas," the rock-man: Jn 1:42; Mt 16:18; and he permitted Peter, together with James and John, to be with him on three important occasions in his ministry: at the raising of Jairus' daughter from the dead, Mk 5:37; on the Mount of Transfiguration, Mt 17:1; and at the time of his Passion in the Garden of Gethsemane, Mt 26:37.

Peter became the spokesman of all the disciples: Mt 16:15,16,21,22; 19:27; Jn 6:67,68. He was eager and impulsive and often spoke and acted without first giving thought to what he was about to say or do: Mt 16:22; 26:33-35; Jn 18:10,11; 21:7.

Following his shameful denial, he became a fearless confessor of Christ and, according to tradition, suffered a martyr's death: cp Jn 21:15-19; Ac 2:14-24; 3:11-21; 4:8-20; 5:17-42. Two of the Epistles of the New Testament are ascribed to him; *ref. 684.*

† † †

692
> In the hour of trial,
>   Jesus, plead for me
> Lest by base denial
>   I depart from thee.
> When thou see'st me waver,
>   With a look recall
> Nor from fear or favor
>   Suffer me to fall.
>
> — James Montgomery

693 Christ is being denied by false prophets who preach another gospel:- Ga 1:7-9; 2 Pe 2:1. He is also being denied by the multitudes who ignore what his death means for them and who pass his cross unheeding: cp Lm 1:12. But the denial of which Peter was guilty, and of which we, too, have been guilty, is a sin that is committed by Christian people, by those who know him and who have accepted him as their Savior. He is denied thus by those who once vowed allegiance to him but who later forsook him because they were overcome again by the love of this world: 2 Tm 4:10; 1 Jn 2:15-17; by those who bear his sacred name but who crucify him anew by unholy living: Ro 6:6; 13:13,14; Ga 5:24; 6:14; He 6:6; and by those who remain silent instead of confessing him when his name is blasphemed and his gospel is ridiculed, because they fear the consequences if their identity as his followers were known: cp Mt 10:32,33; Mk 8:34-38.

694 Confessing Christ is a requirement for Christian discipleship: Mt 10:32,33; Mk 8:38; Ro 10:9; 2 Tm 2:12; 1 Jn 2:22; 4:15. To deny Christ is, therefore, a most grievous and heinous sin. Those who commit and fail to repent of it are eternally lost, because they reject Jesus Christ as the Son of God and Savior through whom alone they can obtain forgiveness: Ac 4:12; 2 Pe 2:21.

695 Tradition tells us that every night after he had denied Christ, whenever he heard a cock crow, Peter would again ask for forgiveness as he fell on his knees and wept bitterly. Whether this be true or not cannot be determined. But the Scriptures do tell us that following his repentance, Peter's all-consuming desire was to serve his wonderful and merciful Savior who had snatched him from the very jaws of hell.

696
> Jesus! and shall it ever be,
>   A mortal man ashamed of thee?
> Ashamed of thee, whom angels praise,
>   Whose glories shine through endless days?
>
> Ashamed of Jesus, that dear Friend
>   On whom my hopes of heav'n depend?
> No; when I blush, be this my shame,
>   That I no more revere his name.
>
> — Joseph Grigg

ref. 685

† † †

697 Examples of sinful pride: Pharaoh: Ex 5:2; Hezekiah: 2 Chr 32:25; Nebuchadnezzar: Dn 4:30; Belshazzar: Dn 5:23; Herod: Ac 12:21-23.

698
> When I survey the wondrous cross
>   On which the Prince of Glory died,
> My richest gain I count but loss
>   And pour contempt on all my pride.
>
> Forbid it, Lord, that I should boast
>   Save in the death of Christ, my God;
> All the vain things that charm me most,
>   I sacrifice them to his blood.
> — Isaac Watts

ref. 685

† † †

699 Sam Davis, Confederate spy, was executed at Pulaske, Tennessee. The Union Army captured him and found on him papers of great value. The officers knew that it was impossible that he was the one responsible for his having those papers. After he had been court-martialed and blindfolded before the firing squad, the officer in charge said: "If you will give us the name of the man who furnished you this information, you may go free," to which Sam Davis replied: "If I had a thousand lives, I would give them all before I would betray a friend." — Are you a friend of Jesus?
— *Florida Baptist Witness*

ref. 683

JESUS CHRIST, THE TRIAL OF 700-714

Before the High Priest Caiaphas and the Jewish Council (Sanhedrin)

700 The trial:

False witnesses accused Christ of many things and testified that he said that he would destroy the Temple and rebuild it in three days: Mt 26:59-61; Mk 14:53-59; cp Jn 2:18-22; Ps 27:12; 35:11;

The servants of the Council mocked Christ and smote him: Mt 26:67,68; Mk 14:65; Lk 22:63-65; cp Ps 22:6-8; Is 50:6;

At the demand of the high priest, Christ testified under oath that he is the Son of God: Mt 26:63-66; Mk 14:60-64; Lk 22:66-71; *ref. 704,705.*

701 Its implications for us:

God's commandment in the Decalog, "Thou shalt not bear false witness against thy neighbor": Ex 20:16; Dt 5:20; Mt 19:18; Ro 13:9; is reinforced in Scriptures by many similar warnings and threats of punishment for disobedience: Lv 19:11; Ps 5:6; 63:11; 101:5; Pr 6:16,19; 12:17,22; 14:5; 19:5,9; 21:6,28; 25:18; Mal 3:5; Re 21:8; *ref. 1494,1495;*

Christ's followers will not escape the hatred and mockery of the unbelieving world: Mt 5:11,12; 10:17,22; 24:9; Jn 15:18-21; 16:2; Ac 7:54f; 2 Tm 3:12; 1 Pe 3:16;

If Christ's testimony under oath in which he declared that he is the Son of God were not true, he would not be the Savior but an impostor guilty of the greatest deception and not worthy of any following. But his witness was true: cp Lk 5:21; Jn 5:17,18; 8:58,59; 10:33; *ref. 614-619.*

Before Pilate and Herod

702 The trial:

The Jews accused Christ of perverting the nation, stirring up the people, refusing to give tribute to Caesar, and saying that he is a king: Lk 23:1,2,5; Jn 19:12; and again they accused Christ for saying that he is the Son of God: Jn 19:7; cp Mt 17:25-27; 22:16-22; Jn 18:33-38;

Finding no fault in Christ, Pilate sent him to Herod, who also pronounced him innocent: Lk 23:7-15;

Pilate's conscience told him to do the right thing, to release Jesus. His wife also warned him not to have anything to do with condemning "this just man," Mt 27:19;

In a desperate attempt to free Christ, Pilate hoped that the Jews would ask for the release of Jesus instead of Barabbas, but to his great disappointment the Jews asked for Barabbas: Mt 27:15-20; Mk 15:6-11; Lk 23:18,19;

Pilate finally yielded to the persistent demands of the Jews and, after telling them that they would bear the guilt for this decision, he had Christ scourged and then sentenced him to be crucified: Mt 27:19-26; Mk 15:6-15; Lk 23:13-25; Jn 19:1,16. Thereupon the soldiers crowned Christ with a wreath of thorns, dressed him in a purple robe and, after mocking him, led him away to be crucified: Mt 27:27-31; Mk 15:16-20; Jn 19:2-16; *ref. 706-709.*

703 Its implications for us:

Pilate and Herod are examples of rulers, government officials, military leaders and others who, entrusted with authority, are often corrupted by the power which they possess. The Bible repeatedly warns judges and rulers not to be partial and to grant people justice: Ex 23:6-8; Dt 16:18-20; 25:1; Pr 21:3; 29:4; 31:4,5; Is 1:23; 3:13-15; 10:1-4; Eze 45:9;

Pilate's question, "What shall I do with Jesus?" Mt 27:22, is one which every person must answer; and the either-or choice between Christ or Barabbas, who represents the world of evil, is one which every person who comes into contact with Christ must make. This choice permits no compromise, and the decision results in eternal consequences: Jn 3:18,36; 2 Cor 6:14-18; Jas 4:4; 1 Jn 2:15-17;

Pilate's flippant question, "What is truth?" Jn 18:38, is being asked by many today who doubt that anything like truth exists. Like Pilate, they refuse to let Christ answer this question for them; *ref. 1553-1566*;

Christ made a good confession before Pilate: 1 Tm 6:13; Re 1:5. As Christ's followers we are to be faithful and fearless witnesses for him: Ac 1:8; 4:20; 5:32; 1 Pe 3:15; 1 Jn 1:1-4; *ref. 1020-1081*;

Like Pilate, even unbelievers have some knowledge of right and wrong, of justice and injustice. The knowledge of God's law is inscribed on their hearts. Though largely obscured because of sin, it has not been entirely lost: Ro 1:19,20; 2:14,15. In his dealings with Christ, Pilate knew what his duty was, and his conscience told him what action he should take. Yet he persistently ignored the promptings of his conscience and repeatedly silenced its voice. — The voice of conscience should be heeded, lest its voice grow dangerously weak or silent; *ref. 210-224,710-714*.

Resources

704 The Jewish Council, or Sanhedrin, was composed of seventy members from the classes of priests, elders, and scribes. Some belonged to the sect of the Pharisees, others to the sect of the Sadducees, and still others to the sect of Herodians: Mt 3:7; 16:1,6; 22:15,23; Mk 8:15; Lk 7:30; Ac 23:6. The seventy-first member was the high priest, who was the official president of the body;

At the time of Christ's trial the office of high priest was held by a cunning and impious man named Caiaphas. It was he who had previously counseled the assembly that it would be expedient for one man to die so the entire nation would not perish: Jn 11:51,52; 18:14;

Another member of the Council at that time was a man by the name of Annas. He was father-in-law to Caiaphas: Jn 18:13. He himself had previously been the high priest. Although the Roman government had deposed him because of his evil deeds, the Jews continued to bestow upon him the honor of this sacred office, which he therefore shared with Caiaphas: Lk 3:2;

It appears from the Gospel records that there were only two just men on the entire council, Joseph of Arimathea and Nicodemus, both of whom afterward assisted in Christ's burial. Apparently these two were not present at the trial of Christ; *ref. 700,763f.*

† † †

705 An oath is a solemn declaration in which a person calls upon God to help him speak the truth and to punish him if he speaks a lie. Oaths of allegiance and oaths for the sake of bearing witness are permitted when demanded by those whom God has placed in authority: Dt 6:13; 1 Kgs 8:31; 2 Kgs 11:4; Jr 12:16; Mt 26:63,64; Jn 19:11; Ro 13:1,2; but every false oath profanes the holy name of God and invokes his wrath and punishment: Ex 20:7; Lv 19:12; Mt 5:34; Ga 6:7; Jas 5:12. The most reckless and devastating of all oaths was that sworn by the Jews when they cried, "Let his blood be on us and on our children," Mt 27:25. Other examples of rash oaths: Jacob and Esau: Gn 25:33; Jephthah: Jdg 11:30,31; Herod: Mk 6:23; the Jews who took an oath to kill Paul: Ac 23:12; *ref. 700,701.*

† † †

706 Pontius Pilate was appointed by emperor Tiberius around the year A.D. 26 as the fifth Roman procurator of Judea. Historians describe him as a merciless ruler who was willing to compromise and set aside justice if the occasion would benefit him: see Jn 11:49,50. He had incurred the disfavor of the Jews on a number of occasions before coming into contact with Christ, for example, by using funds from the Temple treasury for public improvements. Whenever the Jews protested his actions he ordered his soldiers to disperse them with violence: see Lk 13:1,2; *ref. 702.*

† † †

707 Pilate's wife: Tradition has given her the name of Procula. She is supposed to have been a convert to Judaism; the Greek Church has even elevated her to sainthood. During the course of Christ's trial she sent Pilate the message: "Don't have anything to do with that innocent man, for I have suffered a great deal today in a dream because of him," Mt 27:19; *ref. 702.*

† † †

708 Scourging was a painful punishment which the Romans inflicted on desperate criminals. The scourge was made of cords or thongs. Pieces of lead, or small sharp-pointed bones, were attached to the lashes. The victim was stripped to the waist and bound to a whipping-post in a stooping position. Each lash deeply scored the flesh and drew blood. Often the flesh was completely severed from the back and the ribs and bones of the victim were made bare. Roman law demanded that not even a slave should be crucified if he had already been scourged; *ref. 702.*

† † †

709 Herod, the tetrarch, son of Herod the Great, was a weak and frivolous ruler. He was an adulterer, who had estranged Herodias, his brother Philip's wife. For this he had to hear the stern rebuke of John the Baptist. According to the wishes of Herodias, Herod had John beheaded: Mt 14:1-12. Because of Herod's cunning, Christ called him a fox: Lk 13:31,32. When Christ's fame spread abroad, Herod's evil conscience made him fear that Jesus was really John the Baptist risen from the dead: Mt 14:1,2. At the time of Christ's trial, Herod's only interest in Christ was to be entertained by him: Lk 23:8-11; *ref. 702.*

† † †

710 Barabbas should have been crucified and Jesus released, but the order was reversed. The door of the prison swings open, and Barabbas is free. He reaches the surging mob about the cross, stands in the outer circle a moment and then pushes his way to the very inner circle, so near that he can reach out his hand and touch the dying Savior. I can hear him say, "I do not know who you are, but I know you are there in my stead." Until you can give a better theory of the atonement, take Christ, Barabbas' Substitute and yours, dying in your place!

— adapted from John McNeill

711
> Barabbas in his prison cell
>   Gazed on the heavens fair
> And saw the pascal moon ascend
>   In night's empurpled air.
> The hours crept on; with awe and dread
>   He waited for the morn;
> He heard at last the soldier's tread
>   And saw the bolt withdrawn.
>
> "Barabbas," so the soldier spake,
>   "I bring thee news of grace;
> For Christ, the Man of Nazareth,
>   Today shall take thy place.
> Without the gate shall Jesus bear
>   The cross prepared for thee;
> Go thou to the atoning feast!" —
>   The man of crime went free.
>
> Barabbas saw the darkened earth
>   When came the hour of noon
> And slept in peace when Jesus wept
>   Beneath the pascal moon. —
> O man of sin, in thee I see
>   Myself redeemed by grace;
> The blood-stained cross that rose for thee
>   Took every sinner's place.

— Hezekiah Butterworth

712 Barabbas was a notorious criminal who had been convicted of robbery, sedition and murder: Mt 27:16; Mk 15:7; Lk 23:18,19; Jn 18:40. He represents the world of sin. Next to him stands Christ, the Savior from sin. The one represents darkness, the other light; the one death, the other life; the one salvation, the other damnation. These are the two choices that are held up whenever the gospel is preached: see 2 Cor 2:15,16; Jn 3:18,36. Many choose Barabbas because their works are evil and they love darkness rather than light: Jn 3:19; *ref. 703.*

† † †

713 Pilate discovered that one's dealing with Christ permits of no compromise. One cannot choose Christ and still remain popular with the unbelieving world: Mt 6:24; 22:37; Jas 4:4; 1 Jn 2:15-17. One cannot be a partaker of the Lord's table and of the table of devils: 1 Cor 10:21; 2 Cor 6:14-18. Moreover, the choice is one that everyone must make personally. Although Pilate tried to shift this responsibility upon the Jews, he finally discovered that it was a choice that he himself had to make: see Jos 24:15; 1 Kgs 18:21.

714

> Let thoughtless thousands choose the road
> That leads the soul away from God;
> This happiness, dear Lord, be mine,
> To live and die entirely thine.
> — Joseph Hoskins

Pilate's name is remembered in an infamous manner whenever Christian people confess the words of the Apostles' Creed ". . . suffered under Pontius Pilate." Throughout the ages his name is mentioned with contempt as the cowardly and unrighteous judge who, against the voice of conscience and contrary to all rules of justice, condemned the Son of God to the inhuman punishment of scourging and to the yet more gruesome death by crucifixion; *ref. 703.*

On the Way to the Cross

715 The weeping women of Jerusalem: Lk 23:27-31:

As they followed the procession to the cross they expressed their compassion and sympathy for Christ by weeping and lamenting him. But while their eyes were filled with tears, their hearts were not melted by sorrow and repentance for their own sins and for the sins of their rulers and their nation, who had rejected Christ as the Messiah: Jn 1:11. Their sorrow was only the sorrow of this world, which ends in damnation: 2 Cor 7:10. Christ therefore told them not to weep for him, but to weep for themselves and for their children. His words were a prophetic reference to the impending destruction of Jerusalem: see Ho 10:8; Mt 23:37,38; 24:19; Lk 19:41-44; and his exhortation was for them to weep over their sins, which made it necessary for him to suffer and die. He was innocent and holy, like a green tree that flourished with fruit, while they were sinful and false, like a barren tree ready to be cut down and cast into the fire: Mt 3:10; 7:19; Lk 13:7. If God would permit the Romans to execute such terrible punishment on him who was innocent, how could they who were guilty hope to escape an even greater punishment? He 2:3; cp He 10:28,29; 12:25.

Their example points to the need for true repentance. True repentance involves something other than tears because of the pain that one brings upon himself or another through sinning:*ref. 718-719,1253-1262.*

716 Simon of Cyrene: Mt 27:32; Mk 15:21; Lk 23:26:

As the procession was leaving Jerusalem, Simon of Cyrene was on his way to the city. The soldiers seized him and compelled him to bear Christ's cross.

Like Simon of Cyrene, all followers of Christ are called upon to bear the Christian cross: *ref. 262-272,721-723.*

The Crucifixion

717 Jesus was crucified at Golgatha (Calvary), outside the city of Jerusalem: Mt 27:33-35; Mk 15:22-25; Lk 23:33; Jn 19:18; by dying like a criminal who is cursed, he was made a curse for us: Lv 24:14; Dt 17:5; Ga 3:13; He 13:11,12; *ref. 724.*

His cross was placed between the crosses of two malefactors, in fulfillment of prophecy: Is 53:12; Mt 27:38; Lk 23:33. Thus he who knew no sin was made to be sin for us: 2 Cor 5:21; 1 Pe 2:24. Moreover, his cross, standing in the center, divides all mankind into two camps: some, like the penitent malefactor, accept him in faith and find the preaching of the cross to be the power of God unto salvation; others, like the impenitent malefactor, reject him in unbelief and persistently regard the preaching of the cross as foolishness: 1 Cor 1:23,24; 2 Cor 2:15,16; cp Mt 25:31-33f; *ref. 725.*

His suffering on the cross was in our stead and in fulfillment of prophecy: Is 53:4-6,12; Lk 24:25,27,44-46; Ac 3:18; 1 Cor 15:3. Even the minutest details of his suffering were foretold, e.g., that his hands and feet would be pierced: Ps 22:16; Zch 12:10; 13:1; Jn 19:34,37; 20:25-27; Re 1:7; but that no bone would be broken: Ps 34:20; Ex 12:46; Jn 19:33; that he would be ridiculed and insulted: Ps 22:6-8; Mt 27:39-44; Mk 15:29-32; Lk 23:35-39; that the soldiers would cast lots for his coat: Ps 22:18; Mt 27:35; Mk 15:24; Lk 23:34; Jn 19:24; that he would be given wine and vinegar in his thirst: Ps 69:21; Mt 27:34,48; Mk 15:23; Lk 23:36; Jn 19:29,30; *ref. 725*.

He hung upon the cross from 9 o'clock in the morning until 3 o'clock in the afternoon, and he died at the time of the offering up of the evening sacrifice in the Temple: Mt 27:45; Lk 23:44. Thus, as the holy and spotless Lamb of God, he offered the sacrifice of himself: Jn 1:29; Eph 5:2; He 7:26,27; 9:11-14; 10:12-14; 1 Pe 1:18,19; *ref. 753*.

The title placed on his cross, "JESUS OF NAZARETH, THE KING OF THE JEWS," was written in Hebrew, Greek and Latin: Mt 27:37; Mk 15:26; Lk 23:38; Jn 19:19-22. These three languages were representative of the entire ancient world and indicated that the saving message of the cross was to be proclaimed to all nations: Mt 28:18-20; Mk 16:15; Lk 24:46-48; Jn 12:32; cp Gn 49:10; *ref. 650-663,726-730*.

His crucifixion symbolized that his followers are to bear his reproach, that they are to die with him by crucifying their flesh with its sinful affections and desires and thus to have fellowship with him in his death: Ro 6:6; 8:17,36; 2 Cor 1:5; 4:10,11; Ga 2:20; 5:24; 6:14; Php 3:10; Col 3:3-6; 1 Tm 4:10; 2 Tm 2:11,12; 1 Pe 4:1,2,13,14; *ref. 262-272,716,721,723,728*.

Resources

718

> With broken heart and contrite sigh,
> A trembling sinner, Lord, I cry.
> Thy pard'ning grace is rich and free —
> O God, be merciful to me!
>
> I smite upon my troubled breast,
> With deep and conscious guilt opprest;
> Christ and his Cross my only plea —
> O God, be merciful to me!
>
> No alms nor deeds that I have done
> Can for a single sin atone.
> To Calvary alone I flee —
> O God, be merciful to me!
>
> — Cornelius Elven

ref. 715

† † †

719 It is likely that the pious women of Galilee who accompanied Christ on his last journey to Jerusalem and who ministered to him were also in the "great company" that followed him on the way to the cross. Several of them are in fact, referred to later as standing by his cross at Calvary: Jn 19:25.

But the women who here bewailed and lamented him were residents of the city of Jerusalem, for Christ addressed them as "daughters of Jerusalem," Lk 23:27,28.

We do not know how many, if any, of these women heeded Christ's final call to repentance. But we do know from history that the people of Jerusalem as such did not repent, and therefore their city was utterly destroyed. So great and so complete was the destruction that Josephus, a Jewish historian, wrote: "There has never been a race on earth, and there never will be one, whose sufferings can be matched with those of Jerusalem in the days of the siege": see Lk 19:43,44.

By the grace of God we have witnessed Christ's completed work of redemption and what it means for us and for the world. Accordingly, a judgment infinitely worse than that which befell Jerusalem awaits us if we do not repent of our sins which caused Christ's death. For, says the holy writer, "How shall we escape if we neglect so great salvation?" He 2:3; 12:25; Re 6:12-17; ref. 715.

† † †

720 The city of Cyrene was situated on the Mediterranian coast of North Africa, a district which in Christ's day was under Roman rule. Simon, as his name implies, was a Jew. He had made his home in a foreign land, as did many other Jews who did not return to their homeland after their release from the captivity in Babylon. Like other devout Jews, Simon gave evidence of his faith by appearing at the Temple in Jerusalem on the occasion of the annual Jewish festivals, in accordance with the Lord's command: Dt 16:16; cp Ps 122:1-4. In some instances Jews from foreign lands maintained their own synagogues in Jerusalem: see Ac 2:5-11; 6:9; ref. 716.

† † †

721 Our sinful flesh resists the Christian cross as Simon also resisted it. He had to be compelled to bear Christ's cross. But how great must have been the amazement that filled his heart as later he heard the Savior's words from the cross, and as he witnessed the miracles that attended the Savior's death! We can imagine with what eagerness he later told the story to his household. The fact that the names of his two sons, Alexander and Rufus, are mentioned by the Evangelist Mark suggests that they had become well-known disciples of Christ by the time that Mark's Gospel was written; ref. 716.

— selected

† † †

722 With the crucifixion of Christ, the cross, which was once a symbol of shame, has become an emblem of glory. As a tree was the means for introducing the curse of sin into the world, so God ordained that the tree of the cross should be the means for removing that curse. Thus Satan, who once by a tree overcame man, was by a tree overcome through Christ our Lord, who on that tree won salvation for the whole world of mankind: see Gn 3:15-19; Ga 3:13; 1 Jn 3:8; ref. 716.

723

Am I a soldier of the Cross
A foll'wer of the Lamb,
And shall I fear to own his cause
Or blush to speak his name?

Sure I must fight if I would reign;
Increase my courage, Lord!
I'll bear the toil, endure the pain,
Supported by thy Word.

— Isaac Watts

ref. 716

† † †

724 The painful and shameful mode of execution by crucifixion was frequently employed by the Romans. It was a punishment that was reserved for slaves and criminals of the worst type, and no Roman could be subjected to it. The fact that Christ suffered this form of death was shameful enough in itself. But to add to the shame and disgrace, his cross was placed in the center, between the two malefactors who were crucified with him. Thus everyone who passed by would reason that all three were malefactors and that he who hung in the middle was the worst of the three: see Dt 21:23; Is 53:12; Ga 3:13; Php 2:8; *ref. 717.*

† † †

725 The meaning of Calvary's three crosses can be summarized in the three little prepositions: for, in and to. The center cross signifies Jesus Christ who died *for* sin: 1 Cor 15:3; the cross on Jesus' right represents the malefactor who died *to* sin 1 Pe 2:24; and the cross on Jesus' left represents the malefactor who died *in* sin: Jn 8:24; *ref. 717,*

† † †

726 In foretelling his death by crucifixion, Christ declared: "But I, when I am lifted up from the earth, will draw all men to myself," Jn 12:32,33; cp Is 45:22. His lifting up on the cross signified victory and triumph. By his cross he conquered sin, death, Satan and hell, and through his cross he was exalted to the right hand of God's majesty and power: Eph 1:19-23; Php 2:9-11. His cross is the key which unlocks the door to heaven and eternal life for a sinlost world: Re 1:18. Through the preaching of his cross the kingdom of salvation is being extended throughout the world, and many precious souls are being drawn into it as they are delivered from Satan's kingdom of darkness and made partakers of the inheritance of the saints in light: Col 1:12-14. Other prophecies made by Christ concerning his death and resurrection include: Mt 16:21; 17:9,22,23; 20:18,19; 26:2,31,32; Mk 8:31; 9:9-12,31; 10:33,34; 14:8,27,28; Lk 9:22,24; 17:25; 18:31-33; 22:15,37; 24:45,46; Jn 2:19-21; 3:14,15; 7:33; 8:28; 10:11,15-18; 13:21; 14:2,28; 16:5,16-22; *ref. 717.*

† † †

727 Drawn to the Cross, which thou hast blest
With healing gifts for souls distrest,
To find in thee my life, my rest,
   Christ Crucified, I come.
                    — Genevieve M. Irons

ref. 717

† † †

728 While holding the position of British consul at Hong Kong, Sir John Bowring visited Macao on the coast of South China. Here Vasco De Gama, the Portuguese explorer, had built a great cathedral on the crest of a hill, with a splendid approach of stone steps. A violent sea typhoon, however, had destroyed it; but, strange to say, although the cathedral fell, the front wall remained standing, defying wind and storm. On the very top there stood a large bronze cross standing clear cut against the sky, defying rain and lightning and typhoon. It was a striking sight, and beholding it Sir John Bowring was inspired, in 1825, to write the grand hymn which multitudes love to sing:

In the Cross of Christ I glory,
   Tow'ring o'er the wrecks of time.
All the light of sacred story
   Gathers round its Head sublime.

When the woes of life o'ertake me,
   Hopes deceive, and fears annoy,
Never shall the Cross forsake me;
   Lo, it glows with peace and joy.

When the sun of bliss is beaming
   Light and love upon my way,
From the Cross the radiance streaming
   Adds more luster to the day.

Bane and blessing, pain and pleasure,
   By the Cross are sanctified;
Peace is there that knows no measure,
   Joys that thro' all time abide.
                    — selected

ref. 717

† † †

729 Among the various designs of crucifixes is one which depicts a coiled serpent under the feet of the crucified Savior. It illustrates the fulfillment of the first Messianic prophecy in Genesis 3:15. In the act of crushing the serpent's head the Victor is poisoned, showing how it cost Christ his life to free the world from Satan's power: see He 2:9,14,15; *ref. 717.*

† † †

730 Why do we say "X marks the spot?" We designate a particular place on paper with an "x." The idea originated with the early Saxons who placed a cross after all signatures as a symbol of the cross on which Christ was put to death. Those unable to write used the symbol of the "x" to show their good faith; *ref. 717.*

JESUS CHRIST — HIS SEVEN WORDS
FROM THE CROSS 731-752

731 "Father forgive them, for they do not know what they are doing," Luke 23:34
Christ freely forgave his enemies and prayed for them: cp Is 53:12; 1 Pe 2:23;
As his followers we are to learn from him: Mt 11:29; 1 Pe 2:21:
  We are not to seek revenge by repaying evil with evil: Ro 12:19; 1 Th 5:15; 1 Pe 3:9; see examples of Joseph: Gn 50:15-21; Stephen: Ac 7:60;
  We are to love our enemies: Mt 5:44,45; Ro 12:20; and freely to forgive others as God for Christ's sake has forgiven us: Mt 6:12,14,15; 18:21-35; Lk 6:36,37; Eph 4:32; *ref. 902,926-934;*
  We are to rejoice and find comfort in the fact that Christ, as our great High Priest, has entered the holiest sanctuary of heaven, where he lives to intercede for us at the throne of grace: Ro 8:34; 1 Tm 2:6; He 4:14-16; 7:25; *ref. 738,739,751,777,800,814,823,1168.*

732 "I tell you the truth, today you will be with me in Paradise" Luke 23:43: Christ promised to grant eternal life to the malefactor who repented of his sins and confessed him: Lk 23:39-42.
The incident teaches us that
  The way to salvation is found in confession of sin and faith in Christ: Ps 32:5; 51:1-4; Ac 16:31; Ro 10:9; 1 Jn 1:8-10; *ref. 1253-1262;*
  Even the vilest sinner has forgiveness in Christ: Is 1:18; Jn 3:16; 6:37; Ro 5:20; 1 Jn 1:7;
  Salvation is not of works but the free gift of God's grace and mercy in Christ: Ro 3:23-28; 6:23; Eph 2:8,9; 2 Tm 1:9; Tt 3:5-7; see *Grace 461-478; Good Works 416-434;*
  At death the soul of the believer enters heaven at once. There is no purgatory through which the soul must first pass: Lk 16:22; Jn 5:24; Php 1:23; Re 14:13; *ref. 1263f;*
  A penitent sinner can be saved in his dying moments. But the example of the dying thief who was saved is a rarity — the only example of its kind in the Bible. It is just as important to note that the other malefactor was not saved. The lesson in either case is a solemn warning not to delay one's salvation: Is 55:6,7; Lk 19:42; 2 Cor 6:2; He 4:11; *ref. 739,740.*
733 "Dear woman, here is your son! . . . Here is your mother!" John 19:26,27: As our Substitute and Savior, Christ fulfilled all the righteousness of the

Law for us: Mt 3:15; 5:17; Ro 10:4; Ga 3:13; 4:4,5. This included the commandment, "Honor your father and mother," Ex 20:12. Moreover, Christ's compassionate concern for his sorrowing mother and for his grief-stricken followers standing at the foot of his cross portrays his pity, love and compassion for all who weep and mourn: see also Lk 7:11,15; Jn 11:35.

As Christ's followers we should learn

To honor our parents, hold them in love and esteem, and care for them when they are not able to provide for themselves: Eph 6:1-3; Col 3:20; 1 Tm 5:4,8;

To be sympathetic toward the needs of others and offer them help as we are able: Is 58:7,10,11; Mt 5:7,42; Ac 20:35; Ro 12:13,15; Ga 6:1,2,9,10; He 13:16;

To find comfort in the assurance that Christ knows our needs and is able to help us: He 2:18; 4:16; *ref. 741-743.*

734 "My God, my God, why have you forsaken me?" Mt 27:46; see also v. 45:

The meaning of that cry for Christ:

His agonizing cry from the cross reflected the climax of his suffering for our salvation. Forsaken by God, he endured the indescribable punishment of hell in our stead: Is 53:5,6; 2 Cor 5:21;

His cry was preceded by the darkness which covered all the earth, v.45, which symbolized that this was the hour when, for a moment, Satan the prince of darkness triumphed: Lk 22:53;

The meaning of that cry for us:

The indescribable greatness of Christ's suffering should impress upon us not to regard sin lightly or to underestimate its dreadful and damning consequences. Sin separates man from God and causes God to turn his face from the sinner: Dt 31:18; Is 1:15; 59:2; 64:7; Eze 39:23; Mic 3:4. For impenitent sinners that separation extends into all eternity, where thy are separated from God forever in the "outer darkness" of hell: Mt 13:30,49; 25:32; Lk 16:26; 2 Th 1:7-10; Re 14:15;

By suffering the punishment of hell for us, Christ has delivered us from Satan's power of darkness: Ac 26:18; Col 1:12-14. Having failed to frustrate Christ in his work of redemption, Satan and his forces of evil now seek to prevent men from receiving the salvation prepared for them: 2 Cor 4:3,4. As Christ's followers, we are admonished to resist these forces of darkness steadfastly: Eph 6:11-17; 1 Pe 5:8,9; *ref. 744,745.*

735 "I thirst," John 19:28:

For Christ that cry meant

That he suffered for us the agonizing pain of the damned in hell: see Lk 16:23,24;

That this detail of his suffering was in fulfillment of prophecy: cp Ps 22:15,16; 69:21 with Lk 24:25-27,44-46.

The meaning of that cry for us:

He thirsted thus for us so that none of us need suffer the thirst of the damned. Thus he chose to be tormented that our doom might be prevented: Is 53:5; 2 Cor 5:21;

He who thirsted thus for us is himself the living water that can forever quench the thirst of sin-sick souls: Jn 4:14. His life-giving word is the power of God unto salvation to everyone who believes: Jn 6:63; Ro 1:16; it is a gracious invitation: ". . . He who comes to me will never go hungry; and he who believes in me will never be thirsty," Jn 6:35; 7:37; Re 22:17; see also Is 55:1; Lk 14:17. — Having found in Christ the Water of Life, as did the woman of Samaria, let us like her hasten to share this wonderful discovery with others: Jn 4:28,29; cp 2 Kgs 7:9; *ref. 746,747.*

736 "It is finished," John 19:30:

For Christ this triumphant cry signified

That his sufferings had come to an end;

That he had accomplished the wonderful work of redemption for which he came into the world: Mk 10:45; Lk 19:10; Jn 10:11; Ga 4:4-7; 1 Tm 1:15.

Its meaning for us:

It proclaimed that our redemption has been completed and that no further sacrifice for sin is needed: He 9:11,12; 10:14,18;

It is for all believers a cause for endless thanksgiving and praise: Ac 8:5,8,39; 16:30-34; Ro 5:11; Php 4:4; Re 5:11-14; *ref. 748-750.*

737 "Father, into your hands I commit my spirit," Luke 23:46:

The significance of these dying words in relation to Christ:

The fact that he uttered this dying cry with a loud voice recalls that men had not taken his life but that he offered his life willingly in fulfillment of his promise: Mt 20:28; Jn 10:11,17,18;

The life that he offered, he offered without spot to God: He 9:14.

The significance of these words for us:

The Bible declares that the fullness of the Godhead dwelt bodily in Christ: Col 2:9; and that "God was in Christ reconciling the world unto himself," 2 Cor 5:19; and that "we were reconciled to God by the death of his Son," Ro 5:10; our finite minds cannot fathom the mystery of Christ's death: see also Is 55:8,9; Ro 11:33-36;

When the summons of death comes to a believer, he confidently commits his soul to his heavenly Father, as Christ did, knowing that, because of Christ, death is only the gate to eternal life: Lk 2:27-32; Ac 7:59; Ro 8:38,39 *ref. 750,751.*

Resources

738 It was in the power of the forgiving love of God in Christ that thousands of Negro slaves in Jamaica, on the night of their emancipation in 1838, showed their forgiveness toward their cruel masters by digging a grave and making a mahogany coffin into which they placed their handcuffs, branding irons and other relics and remains of their previous bondage and sorrow, and then lowered the coffin into the grave while singing the Doxology.

— selected

ref. 731

† † †

739
> There is a fountain filled with blood
>   Drawn from Immanuel's veins,
> And sinners plunged beneath that flood
>   Lose all their guilty stains.
>
> The dying thief rejoiced to see
>   That fountain in his day;
> And there have I, as vile as he,
>   Washed all my sins away.

— William Cowper

740 On the tombstone of the renowned Copernicus is the following inscription, which he himself penned:

> Not for the grace of Paul I ask,
> Nor for the love once shown to Peter;
> Only the forgiveness bestowed on the thief —
> For this do I humbly petition.

ref. 732

† † †

741 It is assumed that Joseph, the foster-father of Jesus, died early in Jesus' life since no further reference to him is made after the time when Jesus was twelve years of age: Lk 2:41f.

742 One tradition tells us that the Apostle John had a house at the foot of Zion hill in Jerusalem and that Mary lived there for eleven years. According to this tradition, John did not go out to preach the gospel until after her death. Another tradition states that Mary died and was buried in Ephesus where John labored. The last reference to Mary in the Bible is recorded in the Book of Acts, where she is spoken of as being in the company of the women, the eleven disciples and other followers of the Savior: Ac 1:13-15.

743 Christ's purpose in addressing Mary as "woman," rather than "mother," was not to shield her identity from the Roman soldiers. They very likely knew who she was. Rather here, as in Cana, Christ used the word "woman" to impress upon Mary that in his work of redemption there was another relationship which he held to her. He was not a mere human son who was providing for his mother, he was the Son of God, her Lord and Savior, who was now fulfilling the fourth commandment for her and for all mankind, and was now shedding his blood for her sins and the sins of the world: see Jn 2:4; *ref. 733.*

† † †

197

744 Those who place their faith in Christ need not fear that God will ever forsake them. Since Christ has suffered the wrath and punishment of God for them, there is now nothing that can separate them from God's love in Christ: Ro 8:38,39; He 13:5. This comforting assurance is portrayed in the beautiful hymn, "How Firm A Foundation," based on Is 43:1-7. One poet, Keen, paraphrased the Lord's promise to Israel in the words:

> The soul that on Jesus hath leaned for repose
> I will not, I will not, desert to his foes;
> That soul, though all hell should endeavor to shake,
> I'll never, no never, no never, forsake!

745 The story of the Napoleonic campaigns is familiar to all, how in the early wars a man was drafted in France, and being unable to go to the field himself hired a substitute and paid a good price for him, who went to the war, and fell on one of the battlefields. In a subsequent draft the same man was drafted again. He went to the recruiting office and produced his papers, proving he had hired and paid for a substitute, who had died on the field; and entry was accordingly made against his name: "Died in the person of his substitute on the battlefield of Rivoli!"

— A. T. Pierson, D.D.

ref. 734

† † †

746 A wealthy Arabian merchant (named Ibnel Hatib), dying of thirst in the Sahara desert, traded his camel driver a money belt containing $20,000 for the camel driver's last drink of water. They were both found dead, one thousand feet from an oasis. The money, together with a signed statement of the transfer, was found on the body of the driver and was paid to his widow.

— selected

747 In the Battlefield of Fredericksburg, December 13, 1862, the Confederate Army was firmly lodged behind a stone wall. 13,000 Federal troops were either wounded or killed trying to storm the Southern position. The next day, moved beyond endurance by the suffering of the wounded who were trapped in the no-man's-land across the wall, Sgt. Richard Kirkland, 2nd South Carolina volunteers, sought permission to help the fallen enemy. Forbidden to carry a white flag or arms, Kirkland loaded himself down with canteens and hurled the wall. In their astonishment, the Northern soldiers gave him a moment's grace. That was enough. They saw him lift a Union soldier's head, give him a drink and, in the bitter cold, cover the man with his own overcoat. Up from the Union lines went a mighty cheer. For an hour and a half, Kirkland moved back and forth across the wall, carrying water to the wounded, and not a shot was fired. Less than a year later, the brave Kirkland himself fell at Chickamauga.

— A. L. P. B tract No 721

ref. 735

† † †

748 Professor Beare of the Presbyterian College, Montreal, points out that Christ's word from the cross "It is finished" (*tetelestai*) is a word that is repeatedly found in tax receipts in the sense of "paid." The word *"tetelestai"* on a papyrus tax receipt is the exact equivalent on an English rubber stamp, "Received payment." Thus Christ paid our account in full, the price had been paid, the debt has been wiped out.

— adapted from
The Sunday School Times

cp Col 2:13,14

749
      'Tis finished! Let the joyful sound
        Be heard through all the nations round.
      'Tis finished! Let the echo fly
        Through heaven and earth, through earth and sky.

— Anon

750 When the Union Pacific Railway was built, linking the Atlantic and the Pacific Oceans, the tracks were laid from either end. Excitement grew as the line neared completion. Finally the last rail was laid and the link was completed by driving a golden spike. The bolt was connected by electricity with a bell in the Capitol at Washington and with a fire-bell at San Francisco. The hammer that drove it home immediately started both bells ringing. The continent had been crossed, and the bells tolled forth the joy. —What joy there must have been among the angels when Christ completed the great work of redeeming our lost world! see Lk 2:10-14; 15:7,10; *ref. 736.*

† † †

751
      When my last hour is close at hand,
        Lord Jesus Christ, attend me;
      Beside me then, O Savior, stand
        To comfort and defend me.
      Into thy hands I will commend
        My soul at this my earthly end,
        And thou wilt keep it safely.

— Nikolaus Herman

752 Most people today are interested only in learning how to live. It is more important that we know how to die. Of all that we learn from Christ's utterances on Calvary, most important is how to die. Calmly, quietly, the Savior commended his spirit into the hands of his Father. His thoughts soared heavenward. If we believe in Christ, if we live for Christ, on our death-bed we may also pray with Christ, "Father, into thy hands I commend my spirit."

— *A.L.P.B.* tracts

ref. 737

The Effects of His Death

753 Its effects in the realm of nature:

The earth quaked, the rocks rent, and the graves were opened. The very foundations of the earth were shaken. All creation became terrified at the gruesome sight: Mt 27:50-53. This was a testimony to the fact that he who died is the Creator of all things: Jn 1:1-3; Col 1:16,17; He 1:2,3;

Darkness covered the earth: Mt 27:45. This was a testimony that this was "the power of darkness" when, for a time, Satan triumphed because Christ "the Light of the world" was dead: Lk 22:53; Jn 8:12; cp Ac 26:28; 2 Cor 4:3,4; Eph 6:12; Col 1:13; 1 Pe 2:9; *ref. 734;*

The veil in the Temple was torn from top to bottom at the time of the evening sacrifice: Mt 27:51. This was a testimony to the fact that the way into the holiest sanctuary, heaven itself, was now opened and that no more sacrifice for sin was needed: He 9:8-12; 10:1-4,14,18-22;

The graves were opened, and the bodies of the saints arose and came out of the graves after Christ's resurrection: Mt 27:52,53. This was testimony to the fact that Christ by his death had conquered the power of death and brought life and immortality to light: 1 Cor 15:54-57; 2 Tm 1:10; He 2:9,14,15; Re 1:18; and it foreshadowed that all believers will rise from the dead and inherit eternal life: Jn 5:29; 11:25,26; Php 3:20,21; 1 Th 4:14-18; *ref. 756.*

754 Its effects upon the hearts of men:

All the people who came together to that sight and saw what happened there, smote their breasts and returned: Lk 23:48. This was a testimony to the conviction of guilt caused by sin: Ps 32:3; 38:4; 73:21; Lk 18:13; Ac 24:25;

Unlike those who remained impenitent, the centurion and some of the soldiers with him who witnessed Christ's death and the events associated with it, feared greatly and were led to confess Christ as the Son of God: Mt 27:54; Mk 15:39; Lk 23:47,48. This was a testimony to the twofold effect that the preaching of the cross would have on those who hear it: 1 Cor 1:23,24; 2 Cor 2:15,16; *ref. 757-759.*

755 The meaning of his death:

He died to atone for the sins of the world: Jn 10:11; Ro 4:25-5:6,8,11; Ga 1:4; 1 Cor 15:3; 2 Cor 5:15,19; 1 Pe 2;24; 3:18; 1 Jn 2:2; Re 1:5; 5:9;

He died to destroy the power of death and the devil: 1 Cor 15:54-57; 2 Tm 1:10; He 2:9,14,15; 1 Jn 3:8; Re 1:18;

As a consequence of his death, all who believe in him as their Savior have peace with God: Ro 4:25-5:1,10; Col 1:21,22; God has adopted them as his children and they are the heirs of heaven and of eternal life: Jn 1:12,13; Ro 8:15-17; Ga 3:26; 4:4-7; Tt 3:7; 1 Pe 1:3-5; *ref. 759,761,762.*

756

      Well might the sun in darkness hide
        And shut his glories in
      When God, the mighty Maker, died
        For man the creature's sin.

                                 — Isaac Watts

ref. 753

† † †

757 All that we know about the centurion is what is recorded in connection with Christ's crucifixion. Tradition has given him the name of Longinus. It is said that he became a devout follower of Christ and that he later died a martyr's death. It is quite possible that, like the centurion of Capernaum, he may have learned of Christ during the time of Christ's ministry: see Mt 8:5f. During the six hours in which Christ hung on the cross, he noted how Christ bore his suffering in silence. He heard Christ's pardoning words, "Father, forgive them," and realized that this prayer was meant for him also. He heard how Christ addressed God as Father, and how he promised the penitent malefactor that he would be with him in Paradise. He observed the strange darkness that came over the land for three hours. He witnessed how Christ died, crying out with a loud voice, and heard the rumblings of the earthquake. To what extent all this impressed him is not known. In any case, it was a wondrous act of God's mercy and grace that this man acknowledged the Crucified as the Son of God and fearlessly confessed this in the presence of Christ's enemies.

758 It is related of another centurion, by the name of Gordius, who served in the city of Caesarea, that he was brought before the tribunal of Caesar during the time of the great persecution of the church in the year 303. Many attempts were made, by entreaties and threats, to get him to deny Christ and thus to save his life. But he replied, "I think of that first centurion who stood by the Savior's cross and was led by the wonders which he saw to recognize Christ's divine glory and who did not hesitate, in spite of the rage of the Jews, to confess his name, saying, 'Surely this is the Son of God.'" After this, he made the sign of the cross and calmly and joyfully gave himself to die for the confession of Christ; *ref. 754*.

† † †

759 The twofold effect of Christ's cross was illustrated by the opposite results it had on the two malefactors who were crucified with him. The same twofold effect was evidenced when the message of the cross was preached in apostolic times; Ac 2:12,13; 4:1-4; 5:14-18; 13:44-50; 14:1-4; 17:32; 19:8-10.

For many Jews this message was a stumblingblock. In their failure properly to understand the Scriptures of the Old Testament they expected that the Messiah would be an earthly king who would establish a utopia: see Jn 6:15. The fact that Christ had been born in a stable, that his life was marked by deepest poverty and humility, and that he died on an accursed tree as a malefactor was abhorrent to them. Thus, instead of being the Rock of their Salvation, Christ became to them a stone of stumbling over which they fell: Is 8:14,15; Lk 2:34; 1 Cor 1:18,22; 1 Pe 2:4-8.

For many Greeks the preaching of the cross was foolishness. They gloried in the wisdom of the world and would believe only that which could stand the test of reason and be proved by logical arguments. They were aware of the fact that the cross was associated with guilt and crime, and with slavery and shame. To them, as to many in our day, it was the height of foolishness to hold that one could be saved by the death of one who had been crucified: 1 Cor 1:22.

This same twofold effect is evident when the message of the cross is preached today: 2 Cor 2:15,16. But, says the Scripture, to those who are called the preaching of the cross is "the power of God, and the wisdom of God," 1 Cor 1:24. Preaching is God's way of saving sinners, and its power is demonstrated in all who are saved: Ro 1:16; 1 Cor 1:18; 2:1-8; *ref. 755.*

† † †

760 All four evangelists, Matthew, Mark, Luke and John, record the wondrous story of Christ's death. But John is the only one of the four who himself stood and watched on Mt. Calvary when Christ passed through his last great agony: see 1 Jn 1:1-4; *ref. 753,754.*

† † †

761
Come to Calv'ry's holy mountain
　Sinners, ruined by the Fall;
Here a pure and healing fountain
　Flows to you, to me, to all,
In a full, perpetual tide,
　Opened when our Savior died.

Come in sorrow and contrition,
　Wounded, impotent, and blind;
Here the guilty free remission,
　Here the troubled peace, may find.
Health this fountain will restore;
　He that drinks shall thirst no more.
　　　　　　　— James Montgomery

762
Thy death, not mine, O Christ,
　Has paid the ransom due;
Ten thousand deaths like mine
　Would have been all too few.
To whom save thee, who canst alone
For sin atone, Lord, shall I flee?
　　　　　　　— Horatius Bonar
ref. 755

The Act of His Burial

763 His burial was performed by Joseph of Arimathea and Nicodemus, both of whom were members of the Jewish Council. The women who followed Christ from Galilee were also present: Mt 27:55-61; Mk 15:40-47; Lk 23:49-56; Jn 19:38-42;

His body was placed in a new grave that was hewn in a stone, in fulfillment of the prophecy that he would make his grave with the rich in his death: Is 53:9; and in fulfillment of the prophecy that his body would see no corruption: Ps 16:10; Ac 2:27; 13:35-37; *ref. 765-767.*

Its Meaning for Us

764 He hallowed the grave for us and destroyed its power: 1 Cor 15:55-57; 2 Tm 1:10; Re 1:18;

There are times, for example in bereavement, when, like Joseph and Nicodemus, our works of faith and labors of love speak more eloquently than would the words which we might express: see Ga 5:6; Jas 2:17. For the greater part, however, others receive no encouragement or help from us when we keep our faith hidden. There comes a time, as it did in the case of Joseph and Nicodemus, when what we do for Christ is done too late, when those who might have benefited from our witness can no longer be reached: see Mt 5:16; 1 Pe 2:9-12;

The bodies of Christian people, which in life were the dwelling place of the Holy Spirit are deserving of an honorable and dignified Christian burial: see Mt 14:12; 1 Cor 6:19,20; *ref. 768.*

Resources

765 The Gospel writers state that Joseph of Arimathea was a just and honorable person, a rich man, a member of the Jewish Council, and a secret disciple of Christ: Mt 27:57; Lk 23:50; Jn 19:38. Though a member of the Council, he did not approve of their actions in dealing with Christ, yet he remained silent for fear: Lk 23:51; Jn 9:22; 11:57. Now, however, when all the disciples had fled and when it was most dangerous to make his convictions known, he boldly came to Pilate and asked permission to bury the body of Christ: Mk 15:43.

† † †

766 Nicodemus was a member of the Jewish Council. It was he who came to Christ by night, for fear of the Jews, to learn more of Christ's teaching: Jn 3:1f. Following that memorable visit, and after hearing Christ's wonderful instruction, he should have been one of Christ's earliest followers. His influence could have meant much. Instead, like Joseph of Arimathea, he remained a secret disciple. On one occasion, when the question of Christ's work was being discussed in the Council, Nicodemus ventured to ask: "Does our law judge a man before it hear him and know what he does?" But when he was rebuked, he held his peace: Jn 7:50-52.

Now, however, at the death of Christ, he came forth boldly and, encouraged by the example of Joseph, was not afraid to confess his love for Christ. He brought a mixture of spices and assisted Joseph in wrapping Christ's body with the spices in linen clothes to prepare it for burial: Jn 19:39-42.

767 It was not common practice to remove bodies from the cross immediately after death. However, in the case of Christ's death there was urgency because 6 p.m. was the beginning of the Sabbath, in fact the very special Sabbath of the Passover. The ceremonial law considered it unclean for the Jew to touch, or even to look upon, a dead body, and such an act would be all the more abominable if it occurred on the Sabbath: see Lv 5:1-3; Nu 5:1-4; 19:11-22; *ref. 763.*

† † †

768 The act of Christian burial constitutes a confession. No one could doubt the relationship between the Savior and that little group who bestowed such loving care upon him at his burial. So, too, every Christian burial service affords an opportunity to testify to our faith in the Lord Jesus, who through his death abolished death and brought life and immortality to light: 2 Tm 1:10; *ref. 764.*

JESUS CHRIST, THE RESURRECTION OF 769-807

(ref.: Resurrection of the Body 1263-1275)

In Prophecy and Fulfillment

769 Prophecies relating to the resurrection: Ps 16:10; Job 19:25; Is 53:10-12; Mt 12:38-42; 16:21; 20:19; 26:32; Mk 8:31; 9:9; 14:28; Lk 18:33; 24:25-27,44-46; Jn 2:19-21; 10:17,18; Ac 26:22,23; 1 Pe 1:10-12;

770 The Gospel accounts: Mt 28:1-8; Mk 16:1-8; Lk 24:1-6; Jn 20:1-18;

771 It is the central theme of the New Testament: Ac 2:22-24,36; 3:14,15; 4:10-12,33; 5:27-32; 8:5,35; 10:34-43; 13:26-39; 17:2,3,31; 20:21; 24:14,15; 26:15-18,22,23; Ro 1:1-4; 4:25; 8:11,34; 10:9; 1 Cor 1:23; 2:2; 15:1-58; 2 Cor 4:1-6; Ga 1:1-4,8,9; Eph 1:3,20; Col 1:25-29; 3:1-4; 1 Tm 1:11-16; 2 Tm 1:1,8-13; 3:14,15; 4:1,2; Tt 1:1-4; 3:4-8; He 1:1-3; 1 Pe 1:1-5; 1 Jn 1:1-3; *ref. 791,792.*

The Significance of the Resurrection

772 Its meaning in respect to Christ:
Christ's resurrection proves that he is the Son of God, as he claimed to be: Mt 26:63,64; Mk 14:61-64; Lk 22:66-71; Jn 4:25,26; 5:17,18; 8:56-59; 10:17,18,30; 14:9-11; 17:1,3,5; Ro 1:3,4; and that his teaching is the truth: Mt 16:21; 20:19; 26:32; Jn 2:19; 5:36; 7:16,17; 8:31,32; 18:37;

773 By raising Christ from the dead and exalting him as Lord of all, God the Father declared that he had accepted the sacrifice of his Son for the redemption of the world: Ac 10:40-42; 13:32-34,37; 17:31; Ro 6:4; 2 Cor 5:19; Ga 1:1; Eph 1:2-23; 4:10; Php 2:8-11; Col 1:18; 1 Pe 1:21; 3:22; Re 5:9-12; *ref. 793.*

774 Its meaning for us for eternity:
All the enemies of our salvation have been overcome and vanquished and the debt of our sins has been paid: Is 53:5,6; Mt 1:21; Jn 1:29; Ac 13:38,39; Ro 4:25-5:1; 5:8; 8:1,34; 1 Cor 15:3,4; 2 Cor 5:19; Ga 1:4; Eph 5:2; Col 1:14; 2:13-15; 1 Tm 1:15; He 7:27; 9:26; 10:14,18; 1 Pe 1:18,19; 2:24; 3:18; 1 Jn 1:7; 2:2; Re 1:5,6;

We are freed from the curse of the Law: Jn 8:34,36; Ac 13:39; Ro 3:23-28; 10:4; Ga 3:13; 4:4-7; 5:1;

We are at peace with God: Jn 20:19; Ac 10:36; Ro 4:25-5:1; 2 Cor 5:19; Eph 2:14; Col 1:20; Php 4:7;

The power of death has been destroyed: 1 Cor 15:54-57; 2 Tm 1:10; He 2:9,14,15; Re 1:18; 20:14; *ref. 793-797.*

The dominion of the devil has been broken: Jn 12:31; Ac 26:18; Ro 8:33,34; Col 2:15; 1 Pe 3:18,19; 1 Jn 3:8; Re 1:18; 12:10; 20:10; *ref. 793-797.*

775 All believers will rise to eternal life with Christ: Jn 3:16,36; 5:24,28,29; 6:40,47; 10:10,27,28; 11:25,26; 14:1-3,6,19; 17:3; 20:30,31; Ro 6:23; 8:16,17; 1 Cor 6:14; 15:54-57; 2 Cor 4:14; Php 3:10; Col 2:12; 3:1-3; 2 Tm 1:10; 1 Th 4:14-18; Tt 1:2; 1 Pe 1:3-5; 1 Jn 4:9; 5:11,12; *ref. 793,798,799.*

776 Its effects on believers in time (in his Kingdom of grace):
We have peace with God that flows from the certainty of sins forgiven: Is 53:5; Jn 14:27; 16:33; 20:19; Ac 10:36; 13:38,39; Ro 4:25-5:1; 8:1,31-34; Php 4:7; Col 1:12-14; 2:13,14; 1 Jn 1:7; 2:2; *ref. 793.*

777 We have access to the throne of grace: Jn 16:23; Ro 5:2; 8:14-17,34; 1 Tm 2:5,6; He 4:14-16; 10:18-21; 1 Jn 2:1,2; Re 1:5,6; *ref. 800.*

778 We have joy in the assurance that Christ has destroyed the power of death: Mt 28:8; Lk 24:41; Jn 20:20; Ac 13:32,33; Ro 14:17; 1 Cor 15:55-57; Php 4:4-7; 2 Tm 1:10; He 2:9,14,15; Re 1:18; and the certainty of knowing that because he lives we will live with him forever: Gn 3:24; Job 19:25; Jn 3:14-16,36; 5:24; 6:40,47; 10:27,28; 11:25,26; 14:1-3,19; Ro 5:21; 6:23; 1 Cor 15:55-57; Php 3:20,21; 1 Th 4:14-18; 1 Tm 1:10-12; 1 Jn 4:9; 5:11,20; Re 22:14; *ref. 793-797,801-803,805.*

779 We have hope that sustains us in the midst of trials and revives us on our earthly pilgrimage: Ro 5:3-5; 8:18; 2 Cor 4:16-18; 6:10; Php 3:20; Col 1:3-5; Tt 1:2; He 6:19,20; 11:10,16; 1 Pe 1:3-5,13,21; *ref. 799,802;*

780 We have strength to carry on the Lord's work despite obstacles: Ac 4:33; 5:41; 8:1,4; 16:23,25; 20:24; 1 Cor 15:58; Php 3:7-11; 4:13; 1 Tm 1:12; 3:7,8; He 10:34; 1 Pe 1:3-9; 4:12,13;

781 We have power to walk in newness of life: Ro 6; 7:22-25; 1 Cor 6:19,20; 10:31; 2 Cor 5:15,17; Ga 2:20; 5:24,25; Eph 4:22-32; Php 1:21; 3:8-12; Col 3:1-10; Tt 2:11-14; He 13:20,21; 1 Pe 1:15-22; 2:11,12,24; 2 Pe 3:11,12; 1 Jn 3:3; *ref. 787,788,804,805;*

782 We have a compelling desire to share this good news with others: Mt 28:8,19,20; Mk 16:7,14-16; Lk 24:9,33-35,44-46; Jn 20:21-23; Ac 1:8; Php 2:15,16; 1 Pe 2:9; cp Lk 2:17; *ref. 789,806.*

Proofs of the Resurrection

783 *The empty tomb*: The tomb had been sealed and a watch had been set, but on Easter morning the tomb was empty: Mt 27:62-66; Lk 24:3; *ref. 1274;*

784 *The announcement of the angel* to the women that Christ was risen: Mt 28:5-7; Mk 16:5-7; Lk 24:4-7;

785 *The graveclothes*:The spiral strips of cloth, with the spices between the layers of linen, had not been cut or disturbed but were lying wrapped just as they were last seen when Christ was buried, but now the body of Christ was not enclosed. The napkin which had been wound around his head was lying with the linen strips but in a place by itself, neatly wrapped: Jn 20:3-9;

786 *The appearances*: Following his resurrection Christ showed himself alive on numerous occasions: Mt 28:9; Mk 16:19; Lk 24:13-35; 36-42; Jn 20:1-18,19-29; 21:1f; Ac 1:3f; 9:1-9; 10:39-41; 1 Cor 15:1-8; cp. Re 1:9f;

787 *The change that came over his disciples*: They had not expected him to rise from the dead: Mk 16:1; Lk 24:9-11,21,36,37; Jn 20:11-13. When the fact of his resurrection was told to them they did not believe: Mk 16:10,11,13,14; Lk 24:10,11. They demanded the most convincing proof of his resurrection: Lk 24:36-43; Ac 1:3; 1 Jn 1:1-3. Once weak and cowardly followers of Christ, Mt 26:56, they now became bold confessors. They testified fearlessly, in the very face of Christ's enemies, and were willing to lay down their lives rather than to deny the fact of his resurrection: Ac 2:14f; 4:18-20; 5:27-33,41,42; 7:51,52; 8:4;

788 *The conversion of Saul of Tarsus* from a most violent persecutor of Christians to a most fearless confessor of Christ after the risen Savior appeared to him: Ac 9:1-8,20,27-29; 22:1-21; 26:11-18; 1 Cor 1:23; 2:2; 15:1-4,8,9; *ref. 807;*

789 *The spread of the Christian Church throughout the world*: Ac 2:36-41,47; 4:4,33; 5:14; 6:7; 9:31; 11:21,24; 14:1; 16:5; 17:4; 18:8; Ro 10:18; Col 1:6,23. The countless number of Christ's followers who assemble for worship the first day of the week which commemorates his resurrection and who confess: "The third day he rose again from the dead." The influence that the Christian religion has exerted upon the world, e.g., the restoration of human rights, the elevation of womanhood, the compassionate concern for those in need; *ref. 1275;*

790 *The testimony of Holy Scriptures*: The evidence for Christ's resurrection from the dead is supported by a mass of infallible proof: Ac 1:1-3; 1 Jn 1:1-4; yet it is not the historical evidence but only a Spirit-wrought faith in God's unerring Word that convinces, convicts and saves: Lk 24:32; Jn 1:12,13; 5:24; 6:63; 7:17; 20:29-31; Ro 1:16,17; 8:14-17; 10:17; 1 Cor 1:18,23,24; 2:4,5; 15:3,4; Eph 1:13; Php 2:16; 1 Th 1:5; 1 Pe 1:23; 2 Pe 1:16-21; 1 Jn 2:3; 3:24; 4:13; 5:10; miracles do not create saving faith: See Lk 16:31; Jn 11:47; Ac 4:16,17.

791 Shortly after the close of World War II a German pastor by the name of Martin Niemoeller visited our country. He had been imprisoned by the Nazis for six years because of his faith and Christian witness. The newspaper reporters who had rushed to a meeting to hear an account of his wartime experiences left the meeting with undisguised disappointment on their faces. As they walked down the steps of the building, one of them said, "Six years in a Nazi prison camp, and all he's got to talk about is Jesus Christ!"

792 A man stood before the window of an art store, looking at a picture of Jesus on the cross. As he stood there, a boy stopped to look at the picture also. Noticing the boy, the man pointed to the picture and asked, "Do you know who that is?"

"Yes, sir!" replied the boy, "that's our Savior." The look on the boy's face showed that he was surprised that anyone should not know who Jesus is. Anxious to tell the man more, the boy pointed to the picture and said, "Them's the soldiers, mister, the Roman soldiers."

When the man did not answer, the boy added "They killed him, mister, yes, sir, they killed him. "

The man gave no answer, and after glancing at the picture once more he walked away. He had not gone far before he noticed that the boy was running after him. He stopped and turned around to face the boy with a questioning look.

"Mister! Say, Mister!" said the boy, "I wanted to tell you: He rose again! Yes, Mister, He rose again!" *ref. 771.*

† † †

793   E aster
A ssures
S inners
T heir
E ternal
R edemption

† † †

794 When the Battle of Waterloo was being fought all England, waiting in anxiety for the result of that day, was dependent for news upon the signals flashed from station to station by semaphore. One of these stations was on the tower of Winchester Cathedral. Late in the day it received the signal, "Wellington defeated." At that moment a cloud of fog appeared and shut out the light falling upon the land. The news of the disaster quickly circulated in the city. After a little while it reached London, and the whole land was in gloom bordering despair. Then the fog lifted and the message was completed: "Wellington defeated the enemy." And now sorrow was immediately turned into joy, and defeat into victory.

It was so when Christ died on the cross. The only words legible then, before the darkness and gloom of Good Friday set in, were the words: "Christ defeated." With that new hope died in the hearts of men. But on the third day the darkness and gloom of Good Friday was lifted and dispelled by the glorious light of Easter Day, and now the completed sentence read: "Christ defeated death!" Then sorrow was turned into joy, defeat into victory, and death into life.

795

He's risen, He's risen, Christ Jesus, the Lord;
He opened Death's prison, the Incarnate Word.
Break forth, hosts of heaven, in jubilant song,
And, earth, sea, and mountain, the paean prolong.

The Foe was triumphant when on Calvary
The Lord of creation was nailed on the tree.
In Satan's domain did the hosts shout and jeer,
For Jesus was slain, whom the evil ones fear.

But short was their triumph, the Savior arose,
And Death, hell, and Satan he vanquished, his foes;
The conquering Lord lifts his banner on high.
He lives, yea, he lives, and will nevermore die.

— C. F. W. Walther

ref. 774

† † †

796 During Napoleon's Austrian campaign his army advanced to within six miles of Feldkirch. It looked as though the troops would take Feldkirch without a shadow of resistance. But as Napoleon's men advanced by night toward their objective, the Christians of Feldkirch gathered in a little church to pray. It was Easter Eve.

The next morning at sunrise the bells of the village pealed out across the countryside. Napoleon's army, not realizing it was Easter Sunday, thought that the Austrian army had moved into Feldkirch in the night and that the bells were ringing in jubilation. Napoleon ordered a retreat, and the battle of Feldkirch never took place. The Easter bells had caused the enemy to retreat, and peace reigned in the Austrian countryside.

— *Decision*

ref. 774

† † †

797

All hail the pow'r of Jesus' name!
Let angels prostrate fall;
Bring forth the royal diadem
And crown him Lord of all.

Ye seed of Israel's chosen race
Ye ransomed from the Fall,
Hail him who saves you by his grace
And crown him Lord of all.

Oh, that with yonder sacred throng
  We at his feet may fall!
We'll join the everlasting song
  And crown him Lord of all.
                    — Edward Perronet
ref. 774

† † †

798
"Why must I sleep, why early go to bed
While others play?" a little child once said.
  "Your mother thinks it best
  For you to take your rest,
And at your wakening, you shall be refreshed."
"Why must I die so early and so young,"
I sighed, "though others live so long?"
  "Your Father knews 'tis best
  Asleep in Jesus now to rest,
And then awake to be forever blest."
The resurrection morn will clearly prove
God's thoughts and ways
        were thoughts and ways of love.
                    — Arthur T. Bonnet

799 A soldier who had been mortally wounded in battle was able to crawl back to his tent. There he was found dead. Under him was a Bible, and his hand was resting on the page which relates the story of the raising of Lazarus. The print of the words "I am the resurrection and the life," Jn 11:25, had been transferred from the page to his blood-stained hand. He was buried just as he was found, with these words written on his hand.

Happy are they who have these words of the Savior printed on their hearts and who die in the glorious hope of the resurrection to life eternal; *ref. 774.*

† † †

800
He ever lives above
  For me to intercede,
His all-redeeming love,
  His precious blood to plead;
His blood atoned for all our race,
  And sprinkles now the throne of grace.

Five bleeding wounds he bears,
  Received on Calvary;
They pour effectual prayers,
  They strongly speak for me;
Forgive him, O forgive, they cry,
  Nor let that ransomed sinner die!
                    — Charles Wesley
ref. 777

† † †

801 When Martin Luther was especially downcast and cheerless for a number of days, due to the many cares and sorrows that had entered his career, his wife dressed in mourning and came into his study. Startled at her strange appearance, Luther inquired: "Who has died?" "Jesus Christ has died," she replied, "and I am preparing to mourn for him."

"But, surely," said Luther, "Jesus Christ cannot die."

"That's what I always believed," replied his wife, "but when I observed how downcast and cheerless you have been, I concluded that Jesus Christ must have died."

Thanking his wife for the valuable lesson she taught him, and filled with renewed courage, Luther took a piece of chalk and wrote on his desk, "*Vivit!*" the Latin word for "He lives!"

802
> Christ Jesus lay in death's strong bands,
> For our offenses given;
> But now at God's right hand he stands
> And brings us life from heaven;
> Therefore let us joyful be
> And sing to God right thankfully
> Loud songs of hallelujah.
>
> — Martin Luther

ref. 778-780

† † †

803
> If Easter be not true,
> Then all the lilies low must lie;
> The Flanders poppies fade and die;
> The spring must lose her fairest bloom;
> For Christ were still within the tomb,
>   If Easter be not true.
>
> If Easter be not true,
> 'Twere foolishness the cross to bear;
> He died in vain who suffered there:
> What matter though we laugh or cry,
> Be good or evil, live or die,
>   If Easter be not true?
>
> If Easter be not true —
> But it is true, and Christ is risen!
> And mortal spirit from its prison
> Of sin and death with him may rise!
> Worthwhile the struggle, sure the prize,
>   Since Easter, aye, is true.
>
> — Henry H. Barstow

ref. 776-782

† † †

210

805

It is Easter in our churches
    Where white-robed choirs sing.
And in tall church steeples,
    Where Easter anthems ring.

It is Easter at the sunrise,
    When dawn opens up a way,
And life receives new courage
    For the challenge of the day.

Throughout the world it's Easter
    In every single part;
But the most important question,
    Is it Easter in your heart?
                    — Adelaide Blanton
ref. 776-782

† † †

806

Then sing your hosannas and raise your glad voice;
Proclaim the blest tidings that all may rejoice.
Laud, honor, and praise to the Lamb that was slain,
Who sitteth in glory and ever shall reign.
                    — C. F. W. Walther
ref. 782

† † †

807 Two of England's literary stars, Sir Gilbert West and Lord Lyttleton, determined to disprove the Gospel records. The first agreed to write a refutation of the resurrection of Christ, the latter of the conversion of Saul of Tarsus. Both worked independently, and at the conclusion of their work they met by appointment.

Gilbert West asked: "What is the result of your work?" Llord Lyttleton replied, "I have fully investigated the narrative of the conversion of Paul, and I am satisfied that this man, on his journey along the Damascus highway, really saw Jesus of Nazareth and that this resurrected Jesus was the very Christ of God."

Sir Gilbert West then reported, "I have thoroughly investigated the resurrection of Jesus Christ and have come to the conclusion that he who is said to have come forth from the sepulchre in Joseph's garden was, as he claimed to be, the veritable Son of God."
                    — selected
ref. 788

211

Prophetic References

808 Ps 2:6-9; 24:3-10; 47:5-9; 68:18; 110:1,2; Lk 22:69; Jn 6:62; 7:33,34; 14:2,3,28; 16:5,10,16,28; 20:17.

The Account

809 Mt 28:16-20; Mk 16:19,20; Lk 24:5-53; Ac 1:1-11.

Its Meaning

810 For Christ the ascension is

The crowning act of his victory over sin, death, Satan and hell: Eph 4:8-10; Col 2:15; He 10:10-13; 1 Pe 3:22; *ref. 817-822;*

811 His exaltation from poverty, humility, suffering and death to the right hand of God's majesty, power and glory as the omnipotent and eternal King of Kings, Lord of Lords, and Ruler of all things in heaven and earth: Mt 28:18; Mk 16:19; Eph 1:2-23; 4:8-10; Php 2:5-11; Col 1:18; 1 Tm 3:16; He 1:3; 1 Pe 3:22; Re 5:12,13; 17:14; *ref. 817-824.*

812 For us the ascension affords

The certainty that, as our great High Priest, Christ entered the holy of holies of heaven with his own blood, having obtained eternal redemption for us: He 4:14-16; 9:12,14-26; 10:11-13,19-22; *ref. 825;*

813 The confidence that Christ is the omnipotent Ruler of his church: Eph 1:15-23; that he is with us always: Mt 28:20; that there is nothing that can separate us from his love: Ro 8:35-39; that he grants us the presence and power of the Holy Spirit to guide us into all truth: Jn 14:26; 15:26; 16:7; Ac 1:8; that our work in his kingdom cannot fail: Mt 16:18; Mk 16:19,20; Lk 24:50-53; 1 Cor 15:58; *ref. 817;*

814 The assurance that he lives to intercede for us at the throne of grace: Jn 16:23; Ro 8:34; 1 Tm 2:5,6; He 4:14-16; 7:25; 9:24; 1 Jn 2:1,2; *ref. 823;*

815 The comfort of knowing that he has gone into heaven to prepare a place for us, and that he will come again to receive us unto himself when he returns in majesty and glory to judge the living and the dead: Mt 25:32-34; Jn 5:26-29; 14:1-3,19; Ac 1:11; 10:42; 17:31; Col 3:1-4; 1 Th 1:7-10; 2 Tm 4:1; Tt 2:11-14; 1 Pe 1:5-9; Re 1:7; *ref. 824-826;*

816 The joy of knowing that as Christ's human nature was exalted, so our human nature will also be exalted to a place of honor and glory with him and that, as redeemed sinners, our glorified bodies will be restored to communion and fellowship with God and we will reign with Christ forever: Lk 22:28-30; Ro 8:17,23; 1 Cor 15:49,53-57; Php 3:20,21; Col 3:1-4; 1 Jn 3:2; Re 1:5,6; 3:21; 5:10; 22:3-5; *ref. 825,826.*

Resources

817 The Ascension of Christ was a day on which, amid the songs and praises of angels, the gates of heaven were lifted to receive the King of Kings as the Victor over sin, death, Satan and hell: see Ps 24:3-10.

> See, the Conqu'ror mounts in triumph;
>   See the King in royal state,
> Riding on the clouds, his chariot,
>   To his heav'nly palace gate!
> Hark, the choirs of angel voices
>   Joyful alleluias sing,
> And the portals high are lifted,
>   To receive their heav'nly King.

> Who is this that comes in glory
>   With the trump of jubilee?
> Lord of battles, God of armies —
>   He hath gained the victory.
> He who on the cross did suffer,
>   He who from the grave arose,
> He hath vanquished sin and Satan;
>   He by death hath spoiled his foes.
>   — Christopher Wordsworth

818 Colossians 2:15 tells us that, having spoiled principalities and power, Christ made a show of them openly, triumphing over them in it. This suggests the picture of an oriental king who, victorious in battle, leads his captives subdued and bound through an arch of triumph amid waving banners and the acclaim of his people; *ref. 808-811.*

† † †

819 Holy Scriptures use the expression "right hand of God," to denote God's authority and power: Ex 15:6; Ps 21:8,9; 77:15; 89:13; 110:1,2; 118:16; 138:7; 139:10; Is 41:10. Christ's sitting at the right hand of God means that now, also according to his human nature, he fills all things, that he rules with divine power and majesty and, especially, that he governs and protects his church, of which he is the Head, and that he will finally lead it to glory: Dn 7:13,14; Mt 26:64; Mk 16:19; Ac 2:33; 5:31; 7:56; Eph 1:20-23; Php 2:9-11; He 1:3; 2:9; 10:12-14; 12:2; 1 Pe 3:22; Re 5:11-13.

> Crown him the Lord of heaven,
>   Enthroned in worlds above,
> Crown him the King to whom is given
>   The wondrous name of Love.
> Crown him with many crowns
>   As thrones before him fall;
> Crown him, ye kings, with many crowns,
>   For he is King of all.
>   — Matthew Bridges

820 As our glorified Savior, who has been exalted to the right hand of God's majesty and power, Christ continues to exercise his threefold office as our Prophet, Priest and King. Thus he continues to see to the fulfillment of the

213

purpose for which he suffered, died and rose again: Dt 18:15; Ps 110:4; Jr 23:5,6; Lk 1:33; Jn 6:14; He 9:11:

As our Prophet he revealed himself by word and deed as the Son of God and Savior of the world during the course of his earthly ministry. His prophetic office continues through his followers, who preach and teach his Word, through which he reveals to men the treasures of his redemptive work and opens their hearts to receive his blessing: Mt 28:18-20; Mk 16:15,16; Lk 24:44-48; Jn 20:21-23; Ac 1:8; 2:47; 11:21; 16:14; Eph 4:8-12; Col 4:3;

As our perfect High Priest, Christ offered himself for us: He 7:26-28; 9:11-14,26; 10:11-14. His priestly office continues as he intercedes for us at the throne of grace: Ro 8:33,34; 1 Tm 2:5,6; He 4:14-16; 7:25; 9:24; 1 Jn 2:2;

As our glorified and exalted Savior, Christ continues to exercise his office as our King in that he mightily rules over all creation and all of history. He especially governs and protects his church and will finally lead it to glory; *ref. 650f,808-811.*

† † †

821 Julian the Apostate sought to destroy Christianity. In his campaign against the Persians in the year 363 he was mortally wounded. Realizing that his end was near he dipped his hand in the blood of the wound and, throwing it toward heaven, exclaimed, "Thou hast conquered, O Galilean!"

822
Crowns and thrones may perish,
Kingdoms rise and wane,
But the church of Jesus
Constant will remain.
Gates of hell can never
'Gainst that church prevail;
We have Christ's own promise,
And that cannot fail.
Onward, Christian soldiers,
Marching as to war,
With the cross of Jesus
Going on before.
— Sabine Baring-Gould
ref. 808-811

† † †

823 God's dwelling place in heaven is spoken of in Scriptures as the throne of power and glory: Ps 45:6; 103:19; Is 6:1-3; 66:1; Mt 5:34; Re 4:2; 20:11. No sinner dare come near this throne, for God's holiness, righteousness, and justice would consume him: see Is 6:1-5. But in Christ this throne has become a throne of grace, a throne of undeserved love and mercy, where guilty sinners pleading the merits of Christ's blood may boldly approach and receive full and free pardon. It has become so by reason of the new and living way into the holy of holies that Christ prepared for us: Jn 14:6; He 10:19-22.

Approach my soul, the mercy-seat
    Where Jesus answers prayer;
There humbly fall before his feet,
    For none can perish there.
O wondrous love, to bleed and die,
    To bear the cross and shame,
That guilty sinners such as I
    Might plead thy gracious name!
                    — John Newton
ref. 814

† † †

824 Saint Sophia, a stately Christian church in Istanbul was transformed by infidel hands into a Mohammedan mosque. It was one of the most beautiful churches in the world. But now all the Christian inscriptions and symbols have been painted out, and Moslem inscriptions and symbols have been put in their place. — Standing under the great dome and looking up at these paintings an American tourist saw that the figure of the ascending Christ with outstretched hands in blessing, which had been painted out, was coming back through the wearing off of the covering paint. Turning to the man standing next to him, the American said: "He is coming back. You cannot blot him out. Through all the daubs and dust of the centuries he is coming back again. He shall reign. The future belongs to him."
                    — E. Stanley Jones, *Christ at the Round Table*
ref. 815

† † †

825   Our place he is preparing;
    To heav'n we, too, shall rise,
With him his glory sharing,
    Be where our Treasure lies.
Bestir thyself, my soul!
    Where Jesus Christ has entered,
There let thy hope be centered;
    Press onward toward the goal.
                    — Gottfried W. Sacer

826   Thou hast raised our human nature
    On the clouds to God's right hand;
There we sit in heavenly places,
    There with thee in glory stand.
Jesus reigns, adored by angels;
    Man with God is on the throne.
Mighty Lord, in thine ascension
    We by faith behold our own.
                    — Christopher Wordsworth
ref. 815,816

215

JESUS CHRIST — HIS SECOND COMING 827-849

(ref.: World, The End of the 1600-1620)

The Certainty of His Coming

827 Christ's own testimony: Matthew 24-25; Mark 13; Lk 17:22-37; Lk 21; Jn 14:1-3; 21:23;

828 Testimony of the New Testament writers: Ac 1:11; Php 3:20; 2 Th 1:7; Tt 2:13; He 9:28; 1 Pe 1:3-9; 1 Jn 2:28; Jude 14; Re 22:20; *ref. 815.*

The Time of His Coming

829 His coming will be preceded by signs in nature, in the affairs of the world, and conditions in the church: Mt 24:5-9,11,14; Mk 13:24,25; Lk 17:22-37; 21:25; 2 Th 2; 1 Tm 4:1-3; 2 Tm 4:3,4; 2 Pe 3:3,4; 1 Jn 4:1;

830 The day and the hour of his coming are unknown: Mt 24:27; Mk 13:32; Lk 21:34,35; Ac 1:7; 1 Th 5:2; 2 Pe 3:10; *ref. 843.*

The Manner of His Coming

831 He will come visibly: Lk 21:27; Ac 1:11; Re 1:7;

832 He will come with power and glory, accompanied by his holy angels: Mt 24:30; 25:31; Mk 8:38; 1 Th 4:16; 2 Th 1:7; Jude 14.

The Purpose of His Coming

833 To judge the living and the dead: Mt 13:30; 25:31,46; Jn 5:28,29; Ac 10:42; Ro 14:10; 2 Cor 5:10; 2 Th 1:7-10; 2 Tm 4:1; He 9:27; 1 Pe 4:5; 2 Pe 3:7f; Jude 14,15; *ref. 839,840;*

834 To receive all believers into his heavenly kingdom: Lk 21:28; Jn 14:1-3,19; Ro 8:23; Php 3:20,21; 1 Th 4:16-18; 2 Tm 4:18; Tt 2:13,14; 1 Pe 1:3-9; *ref. 839,840.*

Needful Preparations for His Coming

835 Watchfulness and prayer: Mt 25:13; Mk 13:32-37; Lk 12:37; 21:36; *ref. 841;*

836 Godly living: Lk 21:34,35; Ro 13:12-14; 2 Cor 7:1; Php 4:5; 1 Th 5:5,6; Tt 2:11-14; *ref. 842-849;*

837 Diligent use of the means of grace: Ps 84:1-4; 122:1; Lk 11:28; 22:19,20; 1 Cor 11:25,26; He 10:25; 1 Pe 5:8,9; Re 3:11; 16:15; 22:7.

Resources

838 We are told that there is a town in the extreme north of Norway where each year, about January 18th, the people climb a hill to see the sun rise after long months of night. Nothing more than a little ray of sunlight is seen at first; but the people are satisfied, because they know that the days are not far behind when the sun once again will shine with all its strength; *ref. 835.*

† † †

No Millennium

839 The Christian church expresses its belief in the purpose of Christ's second coming in the words of the Apostles' Creed ". . . He ascended into heaven, and sitteth at the right hand of God the Father Almighty; from *thence he shall come to judge* the quick and the dead." This belief is well founded on the Scriptures. Not only is the concept of a millennium denied by the fact that Christ's kingdom is not a kingdom of this world: Jn 18:36,37; Ro 14:17; *ref. 650-663*; but also by the fact that at his coming the world will be destroyed: Mt 13:39; He 1:10-12; 2 Pe 3:10f; *ref. 1600-1620*.

The idea of a millennium had its origin with the Jews who misinterpreted the Messianic prophecies to mean that Christ would set up an earthly kingdom with Jerusalem as its capitol, that the Jews would be his people, and that they would rule with him in power and glory over all the nations of the earth. Even Christ's disciples had similar ideas until they were enlightened by the Holy Spirit on the Day of Pentecost: see Mt 18:1f; 20:20-28; Lk 24:21; Jn 6:15; Ac 1:6; cp Lk 18:34; 24:25; Jn 12:16.

One reason why the Jews rejected Christ was that he did not turn out to be the kind of king they expected. That is also why they objected to the title "The King of the Jews" which Pilate placed on his cross and told him to write instead "He said, I am the King of the Jews" Jn 19:21.

840 The idea of a millennium is supposed to have its basis in Revelation, Chapter 20. However, there is ample evidence to show that there is no basis for such a claim.

The Book of Revelation is a prophetic book which abounds with symbols and pictures. Chapter 20 does not even speak of a return of Jesus Christ to this world, much less of a visible return. To interpret the "thousand years" of verse six literally forces a literal interpretation of the preceding verses, if one is consistent. That would be to say that the angel who came down from heaven had a real, material key dangling from his side; that he carried in his hand a real, material chain made up of a number of huge links; that he found somewhere on earth a live monster, called a dragon; and that he literally bound the dragon with the chain; that there was at hand a large opening in the earth through which he cast the dragon into a bottomless pit; and that he then literally shut it up and set a seal upon it.

Contrary to such a visionary interpretation, the binding of Satan refers, in a symbolical way, to Christ's victory over Satan which is shared by all believers: Jn 12:31; 16:11; Ac 26:18; Eph 1:3f; Col 1:13,14; He 2:14,15; 1 Jn 3:8; 5:4,5; Re 1:6; 5:10. The meaning of Revelation 20 is as follows: The restraint upon Satan will continue "a thousand years," an indefinite period of time; it will then be removed, and Satan will be more active than ever before. But in the end Satan and his legions will be cast into eternal hell. In that final judgment all mankind will stand before the judgment seat of Christ. The believers, who had part in the first resurrection, i.e., from being dead in trespasses and sins, will escape the second death, i.e., eternal damnation: Eph 2:1; Jn 5:24,25,28,29; Col 2:12; 3:1.

841

> Teach us in watchfulness and prayer
> To wait for the appointed hour
> And fit us by thy grace to share
> The triumphs of thy conquering power.
> — William H. Bathhurst
> *ref. 833-835*

† † †

842 Even if I knew that the world would come to an end tomorrow, I would nevertheless plant an apple tree today. Let us live as though Christ were crucified yesterday, risen today, and coming again tomorrow.
— Martin Luther

ref. 835-837

843 Speaking of the uncertainty of the time of Christ's return, St. Augustine said, "This one day God has concealed from us that we might keep a better and closer watch over all the other days of our life"; *ref. 830,835.*

844 The great preacher G. Campbell Morgan once said: "To me the second coming of Christ is the perpetual light on the path which makes the present bearable. I never lay my head on my pillow without thinking that, maybe, before the morning breaks, the final morning may have dawned. I never begin my work without thinking that perhaps he may interrupt my work and begin his own. Until he comes, I am not looking for death, I am looking for him"; *ref. 835-837.*

† † †

845 The Duke of Vincenza, who was in charge of Napoleon's cavalry, tells us that in Napoleon's campaign against the Russians and the disastrous retreat from Moscow (in 1801), the soldiers of the Guard, overcome by cold, fell out of the ranks and lay prostrate in the snow too weak or too numb to stand. Every effort to rouse them proved futile.
— McCartney

ref. 835-837

846 Many Of the victims who died in Hurricane Camille which struck the Gulf States in 1969 might have been saved if they would have heeded the warnings that were given of the approaching storm. Despite four warnings, twenty-three people refused to leave their apartment and instead gathered on the top floor of the apartment for a party: see Lk 17:26-30; *ref. 835-837.*

847 Civil Defense Administrator Val Peterson, who inspected the Louisiana hurricane disaster area, reported to President Eisenhower that an estimated 500 victims perished needlessly. "Not a single life needed to have been lost," he said, "if people had only heeded the warnings of the weather bureau and moved to places of refuge"; *835-837.*

† † †

848 A minister who had preached a sermon on the last judgment was afterward confronted by a skeptic who said: "I attended your church and heard you preach on the last judgment. I believe that there is a dispute between you and me concerning this matter." "What is it?" the pastor asked. "You said that those who remain impenitent will be eternally damned," replied the skeptic, "and I don't think they will." "Well," said the pastor, "If that is all, there is no dispute between you and me. If you will turn to Matthew 25:46, you will find that the dispute is between you and the Lord Jesus Christ and I would urge you to go immediately and settle it with him"; *ref. 835-837.*

849 When General MacArthur was ordered to evacuate the beleaguered fortress on Corregidor and speed to Australia, he said to the hard-pressed defenders: "I shall return!" And the Philippine people hugged it to their hearts as a pledge, a watchword and a battle cry. The future might look dark and the prospects appalling, but he would return, as he promised, and final victory would be theirs. And so through the next maddening years they held on with grim determination, with surpassing courage, and with unbeatable faith. I wish you might have heard them that glorious day when MacArthur stepped ashore with the shock-troops on Leyte and announced to the cheering throng: "I have returned"; see Jn 14:1-3; Php 3:20,21; Lk 21:28; Re 22:20; *ref. 832-834.*

— selected

JUSTIFICATION 850-864

(ref.: Faith 359f; Grace 461f; Redemption 1223f)

Its Meaning

850 It is the central teaching of Holy Scriptures that God declares sinners righteous, not because of their works but solely by grace, for Christ's sake, through faith: Ac 10:43; 13:39; 15:11; Ro 1:16,17; 3:21-28; 4:16,25; 5:1; 6:23; 11:6; 1 Cor 6:11; Ga 2:16; 3:6,10,11,24; Eph 2:4-9; Php 3:9; 2 Tm 1:9; Tt 3:4-7. This teaching is the chief article of the Christian religion because the subject of Christ's atoning work forms the heart and center of all Holy Scriptures. It is this teaching, above all else, that distinguishes the Christian religion from all other religions; *ref. 112,860,862.*

Its Essence

851 God has declared the whole world of sinners justified through the atoning sacrifice of his Son, Jesus Christ (Objective Justification): 2 Cor 5:19; Is 53:6; Jn 1:29; 3:16; Ro 5:18,19; 11:32; 1 Tm 2:4,5; Tt 2:11; 2 Pe 3:9; 1 Jn 2:2; *ref. 861,862.*

852 The salvation that God prepared through Christ is made known and freely offered to everyone through the means of grace (the gospel in word and sacraments): Is 55:1; Mt 11:28; 26:26-28; 28:19; Mk 16:15,16; Lk 14:17; Jn 3:3,5; 5:24; 6:63; 15:3; Ac 2:37,38; 11:14; 22:16; Ro 1:16,17; 10:17; 2 Cor 5:18-20; Ga 3:27; Tt 3:5-7; Jas 1:18,21; 1 Pe 1:10-12,23; 3:21; Re 3:20; 22:17;

853 This salvation becomes man's personal possession when he believes in Jesus Christ as his Savior from sin, death and hell (Subjective Justification): Jn 3:15,16; 5:24; 6:40; Ac 16:31; Ro 3:26; 10:9; Ga 2:16; 3:26; 2 Tm 3:15. Man is justified *through faith, not because of faith* as though faith were his own work. Saving faith is the gift of God, wrought by the Holy Spirit: Jn 4:14; Ro 5:18,19; 6:23; Ga 3:26; Eph 2:8,9; Php 1:6; 2:13; *ref. 860,862.*

Its Results For Believers

854 Their sins are forgiven. Holy Scriptures use many and various expressions to assure them of this. They declare, e.g., that their sins are

Forgiven: Ps 78:38; 85:2; 103:3; Jr 31:34; Mk 2:5; Ac 5:31; 13:38; 26:18; Eph 1:7; Col 2:13;

Atoned for: Ex 29:36; Ro 5:11;

Taken away: 2 Sm 12:13; Jn 1:29

Covered: Ps 32:1; 85:2;

Remitted: Mt 26:28; Lk 24:47; Jn 20:23; Ac 2:38;

Purged: Is 1:25;

Pardoned: Is 55:7; Jr 33:8; Mic 7:18;

Cleansed: Jr 33:8; Eze 36:25; 1 Jn 1:7;

Removed as far as the east is from the west: Ps 103:12;

Washed away: Ac 22:16; 1 Cor 6:11; Re 1:5; 7:14

Nailed to Christ's cross: Col 2:14;

Blotted out as a thick cloud: Is 43:25; 44:22; Col 2:14;

Cast into the depths of the sea: Mic 7:19; Is 38:17;

They are healed of them: Is 53:5; 57:18; Jr 3:22; 17:14; Ho 14:4; Lk 4:18;

They are delivered from them: Ps 56:13; Mt 6:13; Lk 1:74; 2 Cor 1:10; Col 1:13; 1 Th 1:10; 2 Tm 4:18;

They are not charged to their account: Ps 103:10; 2 Cor 5:19;

God does not remember them: Is 43:25; Jr 31:34; He 8:12; *ref. 863,864.*

855 They are at peace with God: Ro 4:25-5:1; God is their Father, they are his children and heirs of heaven and eternal life: Ro 8:14-17; Ga 3:24-27; Col 1:12-14; Eph 1:3-7; Tt 3:5-7; 1 Jn 3:1,2; there is nothing that can separate them from God's love: Ro 8:35-39; *ref. 863.*

856 Christ has set them free. They are no longer slaves of sin and under the bondage of the law, but are under grace: Jn 8:34-36; Ro 6:14; 8:1-13,33,34; 10:4; Ga 3:13; 4:4-7; 5:1; *ref. 863.*

857 Christ is their Lord and King, whom they gladly serve: Lk 1:74,75; Ro 6:6; Ga 2:20; Php 1:21; Col 3:23,24; He 9:13,14. In him they are a new creation, zealous of good works: 2 Cor 5:17; Eph 2:10; 4:14; Col 3:10; Tt 2:11-14;

858 God's love for them through Christ is reflected in their love for their fellowmen: Jn 13:34,35; 1 Jn 2:10; 3:14,16,23; 4:7,8,11,16,19-21; 5:2,3; and God's forgiveness given to them through Christ causes them to forgive those who sin against them: Mt 6:12,14,15; 18:21-35; Mk 11:25; Lk 17:4; Eph 4:32; Col 3:13;

859 Having found Christ (been found by him), they desire to tell others about him: Mk 5:18-20; Lk 2:17,38; Jn 1:41,45; 4:28-30; Ac 26:22,23.

Resources

860 When Luther went to Rome in 1510, being at that time a devout papist, he determined, as was customary among pilgrims to the city, to climb on his knees what were called the Holy Stairs. They were reputed to be the same steps by which Jesus had entered Pilate's house in Jerusalem. Luther climbed on his knees as a form of penance, to obtain forgiveness for his sins.

According to one report, when half-way up he thought he heard a voice saying, "The righteous will live by faith" (Ro 1:17). And he wondered to himself, "How foolish am I to be climbing these steps to obtain forgiveness, when all the time God wants to forgive me. And I am only to believe this." He climbed no farther, but went down to think over what the voice had said to him. *ref. 851-853.*

† † †

861
    Oh, for a thousand tongues to sing
      My great Redeemer's praise,
    The glories of my God and King,
      The triumphs of his grace!

    Look unto him, ye nations; own
      Your God, ye fallen race.
    Look and be saved through faith alone,
      Be justified by grace.

            — Charles Wesley

862 When God forgives through the risen, glorified Jesus, he not only forgives, but he justifies. It is impossible for an earthly judge to both forgive and to justify a man. If a man is justified, he does not need forgiveness. Imagine a man charged with a crime going into court, and, after the evidence is all in, he is pronounced not guilty, and the judge sets him free. Someone says, as he leaves the building, "I want to congratulate you. It was very kind of the judge to forgive you." "Forgive? He did not forgive me; I was justified. There is nothing to forgive." You cannot justify a man if he does a wicked thing, but you can forgive. God not only forgives but he justifies the ungodly, because he links the believer with Christ, and we are made "accepted in the Beloved."

            — H. A. Ironside

863
    Jesus, thy blood and righteousness
      My beauty are, my glorious dress;
    Midst flaming worlds, in these arrayed,
      With joy shall I lift up my head.

Bold shall I stand in that great Day,
　For who aught to my charge shall lay?
Fully thro' these absolved I am
　From sin and fear, from guilt and shame.

Jesus, be endless praise to thee,
　Whose boundless mercy hath for me,
For me, and all thy hands have made,
　An everlasting ransom paid.
　　　　　　　　— Ludwig von Zinzendorf
ref. 850-857

† † †

864 Sin, repentance, and pardon are like the three vernal months of the
year, March, April and May. Sin comes in like March, blustering, stormy,
full of bold violence. Repentance succeeds like April, showering, weeping,
singing, and full of joys and flowers. Our eyes must be full of April, with the
sorrow of repentance; and then our hearts shall be full of May, with the true
joy of forgiveness.

　　　　　　　　— Thomas Adams

ref. 854-857

LAW OF GOD 865-896

(ref.: Ten Commandments 1460-1502)

Ceremonial Laws

865 The ceremonial laws regulated the religious practices of the Jews in the Old Testament and involved such ceremonies as circumcision, sacrifices, the observance of festival days, and the like, e.g., Numbers 28-30; *ref. 893.*

Note: These laws were abolished with the coming of Christ: Col 2:16,17; cp He 9, 10.

Political Laws

866 The political, or civil, laws governed the Jews as a state or nation under Moses, Joshua, and the Kings: see Ex 3:1-22; Nu 27:15-23; Jos 1:1-9; 1 Sm 9:15-17; etc.

Note: While Israel was a theocracy in Old Testament times, civil government, which grew out of household government, was a divine institution which God established for the preservation of order, discipline, and peace in this world of sin. As such, in principle, it applies to all men: Mt 22:21; Jn 19:10,11; Ro 13:1-7; 1 Tm 2:1-3; Tt 3:1; 1 Pe 2:13,14; *ref. Civil Government 435-460.*

The Moral Law

867 The moral law tells all men their duties toward God and their fellow men: Mt 22:36-40; *ref. 894.* The moral law is known to all men:

It was written in the heart of man at the time of creation: Gn 1:27; Ro 1:18-21; 2:14,15; Eph 4:24; *ref. Image of God;*

Work-righteousness, the religion of natural man, is an effort to appease God by living according to this law: Mt 19:20; Lk 18:11,12; *ref. 892.*

868 By reason of sin, this law has become largely obscured in the heart of man. Man still has some knowledge of the letter of the law, e.g., Lk 10:27, but he lacks the full understanding of the spirit of the law, e.g., Lk 10:29; Ro 7:7; 1 Jn 3:15;

869 The moral law was given on Mt Sinai on two tablets of stone: Ex 20:1-17; Dt 5:16-21:

It was written by God himself: Ex 31:18; 32:15,16; 34:1,28; Dt 4:13;

It was given to Moses, who broke the first set of tablets: Ex 32:19. The second set of tablets became a part of the content of the Ark of the Covenant: Dt 10:4,5, which was later placed in the holy of holies in the Temple: 1 Kgs 8:6-9;

It was given to the Jews to know it: Ex 18:16; to observe it: Dt 6:2; to remember it: Mal 4:4; and to teach it to their children: Dt 6:7;

It is meant for all mankind to tell them what God expects of them: Mt 19:17; Lk 10:28; Ro 10:5; and to be observed by them till the end of time: Mt 5:18; Lk 16:17; *ref. 896.*

870 The general division of the moral law:

It is divided into ten words: Ex 34:28; Dt 4:13; 10:4;

The order of enumerating the commandments is not important: Mt 19:18,19; Mk 10:19; Ro 13:9;

The sum of the entire laws is love: Ro 13:10; see also 1 Tm 1:5; Ga 5:14; Jas 2:8;

871 The detailed division of the moral law:

Introduction: "I am the Lord thy God": Ex 20:2;

Commandments 1-3, or the first Table, comprising our duties toward God: Mt 22:37,38;

872 Commandments 4-10, or the Second Table, comprising our duties toward our fellow men: Mt 22:39,40;

Conclusion, with its threats and promises: Ex 20:5,6;

873 God threatens to punish all who transgress these commandments: Ex 20:5; Lv 26:14-39; Dt 27:26; 28:15-68; Ga 3:10; Jas 2:10; *ref. 895,1350;*

874 God promises to bless all who obey these commandments: Ex 20:6; 23:22-23; Dt 28:1-14; 1 Kgs 3:14; Eze 20:11; Lk 10:28; Ro 10:5; Ga 3:12.

875 The threefold use of the law:

It serves as a curb, to maintain outward discipline and decency in the world: Ro 2:15; 1 Tm 1:8-10; *ref. 896.*

876 It serves as a mirror, to bring men to the knowledge of their sins: Ro 3:20; 7:7; to the knowledge of God's wrath and punishment for sin: Ro 1:18; 3:19; 4:15; 6:23; Ga 3:10; Jas 2:10; and to show them their need for a Savior: Ac 2:37-39; Ga 3:23,24; *ref. 892,895,896;*

877 It serves as a rule, to show the regenerate what are truly good works: Ps 40:8; 119:9; Jn 15:10; 1 Th 4:3; 1 Jn 2:3,4; *ref. 895,896.*

878 Christ and the law:

Christ explained the spirit of the law and gave us the full meaning of it by the example of his sinless life: Mt 5-7; 1 Pe 2:22; 1 Jn 3:5;

879 He fulfilled all the righteousness of the law for us: Mt 3:15; 5:17,18; Ga 4:4; Ro 10:4; *ref. 850f,896;*

880 He suffered the punishment for our transgressions of the law: Is 53:5,6; Ga 3:13; 4:5; 2 Cor 5:21; He 9:28; 1 Pe 2:24; *ref. 850-864,896.*

881 Christians and the law:

They are not justified by the law: Ac 13:39; Ro 3:20,28; Ga 2:16; 3:11; Eph 2:8,9; *ref. 461-478,895,896;*

882 They are free from the bondage and curse of the law: Ro 6:14; 7:6; Ga 3:13; 4:5; *ref. 896;*

883 They love the law and delight in it: Ps 1:1-3; 119:77,113; Ro 7:22; *ref. 895,896.*

The Difference Between the Law and the Gospel

884 Law and gospel are alike in that both are God's word and divine doctrines. While both are necessary to salvation, they differ in many ways:

885 The law, which tells us what we are to do and not to do, is written in the heart of man: Gn 1:27; Ro 1:18-21; 2:14,15; the gospel, which tells us what

God has done and still does for us through Christ, is known only by revelation: Ro 16:25,26; 1 Cor 2:6-10;

886 The law shows us our sin: Ro 3:20; the gospel shows us Jesus Christ as our Savior from sin: Jn 1:29: *ref, 896;*

887 The law shows us God's wrath: Ps 7:11; Is 59:2; 64:5; Ro 4:15; the gospel shows us God's grace in Christ: Ro 5:9; *ref. 896;*

888 The law shows us our unworthiness: Ro 3:20; Is 64:6; the gospel shows us Christ's worthiness for us: 2 Cor 5:21; 1 Pe 2:22,24;

889 The law demands complete fulfillment from us: Ga 3:10; Jas 2:10; the gospel shows Christ's complete fulfillment of the law for us: Ga 3:13; 4:4,5; 2 Cor 5:21; *ref. 895;*

890 The law threatens with death and damnation: Eze 18:20; Ro 6:23; Ga 3:10; the gospel offers and gives forgiveness and salvation: Jn 3:16; 6:47; Ac 5:20,31; 16:27-31; Ro 1:16; 6:23; 2 Cor 3:6,7,9; Php 2:16; *ref. 895;*

891 The law must be preached to those who do not realize that they are sinners: e.g., the Pharisee in Lk 18:9-14; the gospel must be preached to those who know they are sinners and who long for forgiveness: e.g., the publican in Lk 18:9-14; *ref. 395.*

Resources

892 How the Moral Law serves as a mirror which reflects our sin is illustrated in a striking way by an incident recorded by the London Bible Society.

In order that a missionary might gain access to the tribes in South Africa, the Society sent some trinkets to trade with the natives, and among them there was a package of little hand-glasses such as the ladies use. The natives had never seen their own faces before, except in the reflections from the waters of some lake or stream, and the news of this wonderful little instrument by which people could see their own features was spread abroad until the missionary was invited by tribe after tribe to visit them with his hand-glass.

In one of the remote tribes there was a princess who had been told that she was the most beautiful woman in the tribe and that her face was the most beautiful on earth. Now, when she heard of this instrument, in which she might see what a beautiful creature she was, she sent for the missionary and bade him bring one of these looking-glasses. The truth, however, was that the princess was the homeliest woman in the whole tribe, but could not find it out.

She got the looking-glass and went into her hut to take one good, long, delicious look at her beauty. When she held up the glass and saw what a hideous creature she was, she lifted her royal fist and dashed the glass to pieces, banished the missionary, and made a law that no looking-glass should ever be brought into the tribe.

— selected

ref. 877,886

† † †

893 The ceremonial laws had a hygenic purpose. They were intended to keep the Israelites physically pure and to keep them from intermingling with their heathen neighbors and becoming contaminated with their pagan practices. These laws were also intended, in part, to be a heavy burden on the Israelites to keep awake in them the desire for the Messiah who would redeem them from the curse of the law. Most important, the many blood sacrifices required by the ceremonial laws were a shadow of the gospel, a prototype of the complete and perfect sacrifice of Christ, the Lamb of God: cp Jn 1:29; He 9-10; 1 Pe 1:18,19; ref. 865.

† † †

894 Various expressions are used in the Scriptures when referring to the law. It is spoken of: as the ark of the testimony because the two tables of the law were placed in the ark: Ex 25:22; 31:7; Nu 1:50; with reference to the Old Testament: Jn 15:25; 1 Cor 14:21; as the entire revelation of God: Ps 1:2; 119:1ff; the law of Moses Lk 24:44; a message which also embraces the gospel; Is 2:3; ref. 867.

† † †

895 The moral law offers eternal life to anyone who can keep it: Lk 10:28; Ro 10:5. However, its demands are so great that no one can meet them, for the demands are perfection in thoughts, desires, words and deeds, and the law condemns everyone who offends even in a single point: Ga 3:10; Jas 2:10,11; compare a tow-chain which fails when a single link is broken. Far from attaining the perfection that the law requires, all mankind is guilty of failing to keep it: Ps 53:3; 130:3; Ec 7:20; Is 64:6; Ro 3:23; 1 Jn 1:8. The purpose of the law is not to save sinners, but to show them that they have need of a Savior through whom they can be justified by faith alone: cp Ga 3:24-26. Once man has become a Christian, the moral law serves as his guide for living a God-pleasing life: Ps 119:9ff; ref. 873,874,876,877,886.

† † †

896
The law of God is good and wise
And sets his will before our eyes,
Shows us the way of righteousness,
And dooms to death when we transgress.

Its light of holiness imparts
The knowledge of our sinful hearts
That we may see our lost estate
And seek deliv'rance ere too late.

226

To those who help in Christ have found
And would in works of love abound
It shows what deeds are his delight
And should be done as good and right.

When men the offered help disdain
And willfully in sin remain,
Its terror in their ear resounds
And keeps their wickedness in bounds.

The law is good; but since the Fall
Its holiness condemns us all;
It dooms us for our sin to die
And has no power to justify.

To Jesus we for refuge flee,
Who from the curse has set us free,
And humbly worship at his throne,
Saved by his grace through faith alone.

— Matthias Loy

ref. 869

LORD'S PRAYER (Mt 6:9-13; Lk 11:2-4) 897-940

(ref.: Prayer 1147-1187)

Our Father Who Art In Heaven

897 As children of God by faith in Christ Jesus, God invites us to come before him with all boldness and confidence as dear children come before their dear father: Mt 7:7-11; Jn 1:12,13; Ro 8:14-17; Ga 3:26; 1 Jn 3:1; 5:14,15; *ref. 907-909;*

We are to say "*Our* Father," because all believers in Christ throughout the world are the children of God, and therefore we are to pray for and with one another: Ro 8:14; Ga 3:26,27; Eph 3:14,15; 4:6; *ref. 908, 915,923,928;*

The words "Who art in heaven," are to remind us that our Father is Lord over all and is therefore able to do far more than we can ask or think: Eph 1:19;3:20;

The words "Who art in heaven," should also remind us that as God's children our home is in heaven and cause us to set our affections on things in heaven: 1 Chr 29:15; Jn 14:1-3; Php 3:20; Col 3:1-3; Tt 2:13; He 11:16.

Hallowed Be Thy Name

898 God's "name" is every revelation that he has given us of himself through his Word: Ex 3:13,14; Dt 28:58; Is 42:8; 43:15; 44:6; 47:4; Jr 23:6; 32:18; Mt 1:21; Ac 4:12;

God's name is hallowed among us when we revere it as holy: Ps 111:9; Is 66:2; when we teach his word in its truth and purity; Is 8:20; Jr 23:28; Jn 8:31,32; 17:17; Re 22:18,19; when we as children of God live a holy life according to it: Mt 5:16,43-48; Php 2:15; 1 Pe 2:9; and use it to proclaim his praise: Ps 30:4; 35:28; 72:17-19; 96:2; 103:1,2; 113:1-3; Mal 1:11; Col 3:16;

God's name is profaned when anyone teaches or lives otherwise than his Word teaches: Ex 20:7; Jr 23:21; Eze 22:26; Ro 2:23,24 *ref. 913.*

Thy Kingdom Come

899 God's kingdom comes to us when the heavenly Father gives us his Holy Spirit, so that by his grace we believe his holy Word and lead a godly life here in time and hereafter in eternity: Jn 3:3,5; Col 1:12-15; 2 Tm 4:18; *ref. 650-663,915;*

In praying "Thy kingdom come," we pray that God would graciously grant us true faith and a godly life: Mk 1:15; Col 2:6; that we may obey his Word, submit to Christ's rule, and serve him in holiness and righteousness: Lk 1:74,75; Jn 8:31; 15:3-7; 1 Cor 6:19; 2 Cor 5:15; Tt 2:11,12;

In praying "Thy kingdom come," we pray that God would extend his kingdom of grace on earth: Mt 9:38; Ac 4:19,30; 2 Th 3:1; *ref. 1020-1081;* and that he would hasten the coming of his kingdom of glory: Lk 12:32; 21:28; Ac 14:22; Ro 8:16-18,22,23; 2 Tm 4:18; Tt 2:13; Re 22:20; *ref. 914,915.*

Thy Will Be Done On Earth As It Is In Heaven

900 God has revealed his will concerning us in his Word:
It is his will that we should believe in his Son Jesus Christ and be saved: Jn 6:38-40;

It is his will that all men should be saved: Jn 3:16; 1 Tm 2:4; 2 Pe 3:9; and that we who have been saved should proclaim the glad tidings of salvation to others: Mt 28:18-20; Mk 16:15; Lk 24:46-48; Jn 20:21; Ac 1:8; *ref. 1020-1081;*

It is his will that all who have been saved should live their lives to his praise and glory; Lk 1:74,75; Mt 5:16; 7:21; Ro 6:4-19; 12:1; 1 Pe 2:9-12.

God's will is done indeed, without our prayers: Ps 115:3; Is 14:27; 46:10,11; Ro 9:19; but we pray that his will may be done among us and by us, because the devil, the world and our own sinful flesh oppose his good and gracious will: Ro 7:18,19; Ga 5:17; Eph 6:12; 1 Pe 5:8; 1 Jn 2:15-17; 5:19; *ref. 1309-1321;*

As redeemed and grateful children we are to seek to do the will of our heavenly Father as revealed in his holy law: Ps 1:2; 19:7-11; 119:9,11,47,72, 92,97,104,105,129; 143:10; Mt 12:50; 1 Jn 2:17. Moreover, we are to submit our will to his will and to do his will gladly: Ps 40:8; Mt 26:39,42,44; Eph 6:6; Jas 4:15; *ref. 916,917;*

Our prayer is that God's will may be done by us on earth just as cheerfully, quickly, and perfectly as angels do his will in heaven: Ps 103:21; 104:4; *ref. 47-68.*

Give Us This Day Our Daily Bread

901 We are to ask God to supply our bodily needs as well as our spiritual needs: Php 4:6; however, by placing this petition in the middle rather than at the beginning of this prayer, Christ teaches us that the physical needs of our body are far less important than the spiritual needs of our immortal soul: Is 55:1-3; Mt 16:25,26; Jn 6:26,27,51; 1 Tm 4:8;

In his goodness, God gives daily bread to all, even to the wicked: Ps 145:9,15,16; Mt 5:45; Ac 17:25,28; but in teaching us to ask for it, God would have us acknowledge that all our gifts come from him and that we are to thank him for them: Ps 24:1; 36:6; 136:1,25; Eph 5:20; Jas 1:17; *ref. 918;*

The words "Give us each day our daily bread," Lk 11:3 teach us to be content with the things we have for the day and not to worry about the future, as do heathen people, since our heavenly Father knows the things we need and will supply them: Ps 23:1; 127:2; Pr 30:7-9; Mt 6:25-34; Lk 12:15f; Ro 8:32; Php 4:19; 1 Tm 6:6-10; He 13:5; 1 Pe 5:7; *ref. 919-924;*

The word "our" teaches us that God wants us to receive our daily bread through honest efforts, and that we are not to be slothful or desirous of anything that would not rightfully be ours, such as that which might be obtained by dishonest means: 2 Th 3:10-12. The word *"our"* also teaches us that we are to pray for our fellowmen who likewise require daily bread, and that we are to share with all who are in need: Is 58:7; Mt 25:35; Ga 6:10; He 13:16; Jas 2:14-17; 1 Jn 3:17; 4:20,21; *ref. 919-924.*

Forgive Us Our Trespasses, As We Forgive
Those Who Trespass Against Us

902 Our sins constitute an incalculable debt which we are unable to pay: Ps 40:12; 49:7,8; 51:1; 90:8; Is 64:6; Jr 2:22. Therefore we ask God in mercy to forgive them: Ps 51:1; 85:7; 130:1-8; Lk 18:13; cp Mt 18:23-25; *ref. 926-928;*

God graciously grants us forgiveness of our sins for the sake of Christ's merits who paid the penalty for our transgressions: Is 53:4-6; Jn 1:29; 2 Cor 5:19,21; Eph 1:7; Col 2:13,14; 1 Jn 1:7; *ref. 461-478;*

In gratitude for our forgiveness we are to forgive our fellow men who sin against us as freely as God forgives us: Mt 5:44-48; 18:21,22; Ro 12:19-21; Eph 4:32; Col 3:13; cp Gn 50:15-21. Unless we are willing to forgive, God does not forgive us: Mt 6:14,15; 18:35; Mk 11:25,26; *ref. 926-934.*

Lead Us Not Into Temptation

903 We pray God to guard and keep us against every temptation: Lk 8:12; 2 Cor 2:11; 11:14; Eph 6:12; 1 Pe 5:8; the sinful world: 2 Tm 4:10; Jas 4:4; 1 Jn 2:15,16; 5:19; and our own sinful flesh: Mt 26:41; Ro 7:18-24; Ga 5:17; Eph 4:22; Jas 1:13-15;

We pray God to grant us grace to avoid temptation: Pr 1:10; 4:14,15; Mt 26:41; Ac 20:29-32; Ro 12:2; 1 Cor 10:11-13; 2 Cor 6:14-18; Eph 5:11; 6:10-17; 1 Tm 6:12; 1 Pe 5:8,9; *ref. 935-939.*

Deliver Us From Evil

904 We pray God to keep every evil from us: 1 Chr 4:10; Ps 19:13; 25:19,20; 31:1,2,15; 32:7; 35:19-23; 40:13,14; 51:14; 64:1,2; 70:1,2; 141:3,4; Jn 17:15;

We pray God to grant us strength to overcome temptation when evil befalls us: Ro 12:21; 1 Cor 10:13; 1 Jn 5:4; and to turn the evil that befalls us into good: Gn 50:20; Ro 8:28; Php 1:12-14;

We pray God finally to deliver us from all evil by a blessed death: Nu 23:10; Lk 2:29,30; Php 3:20; 2 Tm 4:18; *ref. 280,737,750,751.*

For Thine Is The Kingdom And The Power
And The Glory Forever And Ever. Amen.

905 The doxology expresses the reasons for asking all these things of God:

He alone is the *King* from whom we seek help: Dt 4:39; 1 Chr 29:11; Ps 47:2; 83:18; 1 Tm 6:15; Re 19:16;

He alone has the *power* to grant our petitions: 1 Chr 29:11-14; Ps 62:11; 115:3; 135:6; Mt 28:18; Jas 1:17; Re 19:6;

He alone shall have all *glory* and praise for all that he has done for us: 1 Chr 29:11-13; Ps 22:23; 67:3; Is 6:3; Ro 16:27; Re 5:13.

906 The "Amen," which means, "verily it shall be so," expresses our confidence that God will grant our petitions, for he himself has commanded us so to pray, and has promised to hear us: Ps 50:15; 72:19; 91:15,16; 106:48; Is 65:24; Lk 11:9; Jn 15:7; 16:23; 2 Cor 1:20; 1 Jn 3:22.

Resources

907 In his holy Word God not only instructs us to honor him with a life of prayer, but he also teaches us how we are to pray. We have an example in the words of the Lord's Prayer. This prayer is the most comprehensive, the most beautiful, and the most excellent of all prayers. Its words are the very words which Jesus Christ, the Son of God and our Lord and Savior, has taught us to pray. But while it is indeed the most perfect prayer it is also, as Martin Luther called it, the most "martyred" of all prayers because it is often repeated thoughtlessly and carelessly; *ref. 897.*

† † †

908 It is essential that we understand that the Lord's Prayer was given to Christian people. In both instances where the prayer is recorded in the Scriptures Christ taught these words to his disciples, to those who knew him and believed in him. This prayer is intended only for such; only such can pray it rightly; only such can truly address God as their heavenly Father.

While it is true that God is the Father of all mankind in the sense that he is the Creator of the entire human race: Mal 2:10; Ac 17:26; and while it is true that in this sense all men are brothers, still the world's concept that spiritually there is a universal "Fatherhood of God and Brotherhood of Man" is a myth. Because of sin and apart from Christ there is no father-son relationship between God and man. Only in Christ has that relationship been restored: Jn 1:11-13; Ro 8:13,14; Ga 3:26.

Those who reject Jesus Christ are of their father, the devil: Jn 8:44; they are outside of the "kingdom" of which this prayer speaks Jn 3:3,5; it is vain for them to pray "Forgive us our trespasses," for God forgives sins only for the

230

sake of Christ's merits and substitutionary death on the cross: Jn 8:24; 14:6; Ac 4:12; Col 1:12-14; *ref. 897.*

† † †

909 A blind teenage girl had an entirely new world opened to her when her sight was miraculously restored through surgery. The first person she saw when the bandages were removed was her father who was bending over her with a loving smile. Gazing into his kind face she was overcome with awe and joy and exclaimed: "To think that I have always had such a wonderful father, and yet have never seen him!" — What a wonderful God we see in "Our Father in heaven," when the bandages are removed from our spiritually blind eyes and we see him through the eyes of faith as he really is! *ref. 897.*

† † †

910 It is possible for a person to pray and not to be a Christian, but it is impossible for a person to be a Christian and not to pray; *ref. 897.*

† † †

911 The daughter of an atheist once said to a friend: "I was brought up without any religion. I do not believe in God." Then she added a little wistfully, "But the other day in an old German book I came across a prayer, and if the God of that prayer exists I think I could believe in him."
"What was the prayer?" her friend asked. Then she repeated slowly, in German, the Lord's Prayer.

— Macartny

ref. 897

† † †

912   Before our Father's throne
  We pour our ardent prayers;
Our fears, our hopes, our aims are one,
  Our comforts and our cares.

— John Fawcett

ref. 897

† † †

913   It chills my heart to hear the blest Supreme
  Rudely appealed to on each trifling theme.
Maintain your rank, vulgarity despise;
  To swear is neither brave, polite, nor wise.
You would not swear upon the bed of death;
  Reflect! Your Maker now can stop your breath.

— Anon

ref. 898

† † †

231

914
    Oh, for a thousand tongues to sing
      My great Redeemer's praise,
    The glories of my God and King,
      The triumphs of his grace!

    My gracious Master and my God,
      Assist me to proclaim,
    To spread thro' all the earth abroad,
      The honors of thy name.

                     — Charles Wesley

ref. 898,899

† † †

915 There are many people who wrongly believe that when Christ taught us to pray "Thy kingdom come," he was referring to a new social order which should be ushered into the world with the coming of the kingdom of God. This, they hold, is the yearning and expectation of people throughout the world who in one way or another, and in a greater or lesser measure, are being exploited by heartless rulers and dictatorial powers that regiment and suppress their subjects by burdening them with taxes and depriving them of their rights. As they observe the many evils in the present social order and the rivalries and wars among nations, they long for a better world. Thus they pray, "Thy kingdom come!" — Establish thy rule on earth in which all the evils of society will be removed, in which poverty will be a thing of the past, in which wars will be done away, in which men of all races and nationalities will live in harmony and in which there will be a utopian reign of unbroken peace and prosperity for everyone.

Included among the erroneous views of "the kingdom of God" is also the false hope of a millennium (see *Millennium*). But Christ repeatedly disavowed any intention of establishing such an earthly kingdom: see Jn 6:14,15; 18:36,37; *ref. 650-663,897.*

† † †

916 The will of God also includes whatever afflictions and crosses God chooses to send us in order to discipline us, to strengthen our faith, to draw us closer to himself, to conform us more to the image of his Son, etc.: Mt 16:24; Ro 8:28; He 12:5f; 1 Pe 2:21. Even as his Son prayed, "Not my will, but your will be done," when the bitter cup of suffering was placed before him, so it behooves us as his followers to pray:

    Tho' dark my path and sad my lot,
      Let me be still and murmur not
    Or breathe the prayer divinely taught,
      "Thy will be done!"

                     — Charlotte Elliott

917 The beautiful hymn "My Jesus, as Thou Wilt" was written by Benjamin Schmolck. His home town was nearly destroyed by fire. Two of his own children perished in the flames. Later he himself was stricken with paralysis which eventually led to blindness. Yet he could sing:

> My Jesus. as thou wilt!
>   Oh may thy will be mine!
> Into thy hand of love
>   I would my all resign.
> Through sorrow or through joy,
>   Conduct me as thine own,
> And help me still to say,
>   "My Lord, thy will be done."

ref. 900

† † †

918 The word "bread" signifies food in general and refers to everything that belongs to the support and wants of the body, such as "food, drink, clothing, shoes, house, home, land, cattle, money, goods, a pious spouse, pious children, pious servants, pious and faithful rulers, good government, good weather, peace, health, education, honor, faithful friends, good neighbors, and the like" (Luther).

919 A noble heart will disdain to subsist like a drone on the honey gained by others' labor; or, like vermin, to filch food from the public granary; or, like the shark, to prey on lesser fry; but will, one way or another, earn his subsistence, for he that doth not earn can hardly own his bread. When we say "Give us our daily bread," we pray even in that one word, that we may live lives of happy industry and honest aim.

— Barrow

920 Worry is useless. It never changes anything. It contributes nothing to solving a problem. It cannot correct a mistake. It cannot alleviate pain. It cannot improve health. It cannot prolong life. It cannot add a single cent to one's income.

Worry is not only futile, it is also hurtful. It robs us of our energy. It keeps us from thinking straight. It prevents us from doing our best. It affects our health. It generates fear and frustration, despondency and despair, and induces organic disease. It not only harms us but aggravates others around us and makes life unpleasant and miserable for them as well as for us.

Worst of all, worry is sinful because it leaves God out of the picture. It ignores his help by assuming that we are the helpless and hopeless victims of circumstances and that our lives are controlled by blind fate. It doubts that God exists; or, if he exists, that he is interested; or, if he is interested, that he is able to help.

921
> Said the sparrow to the swallow,
>   "I would really like to know
> Why these anxious human beings
>   Rush about and worry so!"

Said the swallow to the sparrow,
"Friend, I think that it must be
That they have no heavenly Father
Such as cares for you and me."

— Anon

cp *Mt 10:29-31*

922 The word "sabotage" is derived from the French word *sabot,* which means a wooden shoe. Sabotage derives its meaning from the fact that disgruntled workers would sometimes throw a wooden shoe into a machine and thus stop the wheels of industry. Worry is a wooden shoe that Satan hurls into the life of Christian people to cause them to question God's loving care and providential concern for them.

923 The only sure cure for worry is to know God as our kind, merciful, loving and forgiving heavenly Father. And the only way to know God thus is to know him through faith in Jesus Christ, his Son, our Savior: Jn 14:6; 17:3; Ga 3:26. To know God thus is to be able to cast all our cares on him, knowing that he cares for us and that he will supply our every need Php 4:6,19; 1 Pe 5:7.

924 God ordinarily provides our daily bread by granting us wisdom, health, and the ability to work. But when necessity demands it, he is able to provide the necessities of life in a supernatural manner: e.g., Israel in the wilderness: Ex 16:4f; the prophet Elijah and the widow of Zarephath: 1 Kgs 17:3f; the feeding of the four thousand and the five thousand: Mt 14:15f; 15:32f; *ref. 901.*

† † †

925 The account in Matthew's Gospel reads: "Forgive us our debts, as we forgive our debtors." The account in Luke's Gospel reads: "Forgive us our sins; for we also forgive everyone that is indebted to us." — The words sin, debt and trespasses are synonymous. Our debts are sins, and our sins are transgressions of God's holy Law 1 Jn 3:4. Each word expresses the thought of an account of guilt that is charged against us.

926 God does not forgive our sins as a reward, as though we earned it by forgiving those who sin against us. The phrase ". . . as we forgive those who sin against us," does not belong to justification but to sanctification; it is a fruit of faith. Only one who is already a Christian can pray it; only one who has experienced God's mercy to him in Christ can be merciful and forgiving: Eph 2:8,9.

927 It is said that while Leonardo da Vinci, the great artist, was painting his great masterpiece of "The Last Supper," he had a quarrel with one of his companions. He had already finished a number of the portraits of the disciples and now, in revenge for wrong received, he painted his companion's portrait as Judas in the great picture. His work was duly completed, except for the face of Christ. It was his ambition to paint the noblest and most perfect portrait of Christ that had been put on canvass, but try as he would he could not succeed. In the meantime his conscience had been working on him, so at last he took his brush, painted out his companion's portrait and forgave him his wrong. That night in his dream he saw a wonderful vision of Christ. The next day he took his brushes and painted such a wonderful picture of Christ that thousands have gazed at it in wonder ever since.

928 When a debt was settled it was an oriental custom that the creditor took the cancelled bond and nailed it over the door of the debtor so that all who passed by could see that the debt was paid. So God has cancelled our debt of sins through the atoning death of Christ, as it is written: "God made you alive with Christ. He forgave us all our sins, having canceled the written code, with its regulations, that was against us and stood opposed to us; he took it away, nailing it to the cross," Col 2:13,14; see also Is 43:25; 2 Cor 5:19.

† † †

929 It is recorded of a certain Chinese emperor that, upon learning that his enemies had started an insurrection in a distant province, he said to his officers: "Come, follow me, and we shall quickly destroy them." On his arrival the rebels submitted to him, and all expected that he would take signal revenge. Instead of this, the captives were treated with the utmost humanity.

"How!" cried his minister of state. "Is this the manner in which your promise is fulfilled? Your royal word was given that your enemies should be destroyed, and you, you have pardoned them all, and even some of them have been caressed."

"I promised," said the emperor, generously, "To destroy my enemies. I have fulfilled my word, for, they are enemies no longer. I have made them into my friends."

930 The Tuscan Captain Venustianus had both hands of Bishop Sabinus cut off. Not long after this his eyes became sore, and many thought that he would become blind. When Sabinus heard of it he prayed: "O Lord, behold, I forgive my debtor all his debts: O heavenly Father, forgive me also all my debts and sins; hear my prayer and help my enemy Venustianus that he may not become blind."

God heard the prayer of Bishop Sabinus. When Venustianus got well and heard of it, he became a Christian.

931 No really great man ever nurses a grudge. Douglas insulted Lincoln; but Lincoln gave him a place of honor at his inaugural. Wendell Phillips called Lincoln "the slave hound of Illinois"; but Lincoln publicly thanked Phillips for his work of abolition. Edwin Stanton humiliated and deeply grieved Lincoln in the McCormick reaper suit, yet Lincoln forgave and forgot and made Stanton Secretary of War. Chase pelted Lincoln with oratorical stones and tried to wrest the nomination from him in 1864; still Lincoln made Chase Chief Justice of the United States. Chase wrote a friend: "I cannot understand the man." A second-rate scrub cannot understand such sentiments. The manly act of self-defense is magnanimity. Would you completely win your fight? — forgive!

— *The Upper Room Bulletin*

932 You can never get ahead by getting even.

933 A retentive memory may be a good thing, but the ability to forget is the true token of greatness.

— E. Hubbard

934 Guilt not only affects and injures a person's state of mind, but his whole life. Healing cannot be produced by lifting repressed feelings into the conscious mind through psycho-therapy. Guilt is eliminated only in our readiness to forgive the trespasses. And this assurance is found only in Jesus Christ.

> Jesus only can impart
>   Balm to heal the smitten heart;
>   Peace that flows from sin forgiv'n,
>   Joy that lifts the soul to heav'n.

— William McComb

ref. 902

† † †

935 The word "tempt" is also used in Holy Scriptures in a good sense, and it is thus used of God. While God never tempts anyone to evil in order to bring him harm: Jas 1:13; he is said to tempt man in the sense of "*testing,* in order to accept," or of "*proving,* in order to approve."

Thus, for example, God "tempted" Abraham by asking him to offer his son Isaac for a burnt-offering on Mt. Moriah. The purpose was to see whether Abraham loved God more than he loved his son, and whether Abraham's faith was strong enough to do whatever God would command him to do: Gn 22:1ff. Similarly, Christ tested the faith of Philip: Jn 6:5,6; and the faith of the Syrophenician woman: Mt 15:21-28. The trials that God permits Christian people to endure have similar purposes: see Jas 1:2,3,12; 1 Pe 1:6,7; 4:12,13.

Such "temptations" are not intended to satisfy God, as though he did not already know. Rather, they are for the benefit of the person who is being tempted; *ref. 1-36,903.*

936 A man once asked a king how he might avoid temptation. The king replied, "Take a vessel full of oil and carry it through the streets of the city without spilling it. If you spill so much as one drop I shall have you killed." Then the king ordered his executioners to walk behind the man with drawn sword. The man walked through the city and, needless to say, was extremely careful not to spill a single drop of the oil. When he returned the king asked: "What did you see in the city?" "Nothing," replied the man, "I was thinking only of the oil." "Very well," said the king, "you have learned your lesson. To avoid temptation fix your mind on God and his commandments and think of nothing else."

937 Bernard of Clairvaux asked himself three questions every time he was tempted: 1) Is it lawful — i.e., may I do it and not sin? 2) Is it becoming for me as a Christian — i.e., may I do it and not wrong my profession? 3) Is it expedient — i.e., may I do it, and not offend my weak brother?

938 Martin of Tours was once meditating in his cell, when a radiant form appeared to him, with a jeweled crown on his head, a countenance resplendent with glory, and with a manner so impressive that it seemed to demand homage and love. The heavenly vision said to Martin: "I am Christ; worship me!" and the legend goes on to say that the saint looked upon this glorious form in silence, then gazed upon the hands, and asked, "Where is the print of the nails?" Forthwith the vision vanished, and Martin knew that it was the crafty tempter.

— selected

ref. 903

939

My soul be on thy guard,
   Ten thousand foes arise;
And hosts of sin are pressing hard
   To draw thee from the skies.

O watch, and fight, and pray,
   The battle ne'er give o'er;
Renew it boldly every day,
   And help divine implore.

Ne'er think the vict'ry won
   Nor lay thine armor down;
Thine arduous work will not be done
   Till thou obtain thy crown.

Fight on, my soul, till death
   Shall bring thee to thy God;
He'll take thee at thy parting breath
   To his divine abode.

— George Heath

ref. 903,904

† † †

940

Thou art coming to a King,
Large petitions with thee bring;
For his grace and pow'r are such
None can ever ask too much.

— John Newton

ref. 905

LORD'S SUPPER 941-962

(ref.: Baptism 69-90)

Origin

941 It was instituted by Christ, following the Passover-meal on the night he was betrayed by Judas Ischariot: Mt 26:17-29; Mk 14:12-25; Lk 22:7-20; 1 Cor 11:23-25; *ref. 948,949.*

Meaning

942 It is a holy sacrament which, by virtue of Christ's words, "given and shed for you for the remission of sins," offers and conveys all the blessings of Christ's redemptive work by giving Christ's body and blood in, with, and under the consecrated bread and wine as a seal and pledge. — While the remission of sins is offered to all who partake of the sacrament, it is received only by those who believe Christ's words: 1 Cor 11:27-29; *ref. 948-951.*

943 It is a holy communion which unites believers in fellowship with Christ, and a bond of union which binds all believers as members in the body of the Christian Church, of which Christ is the Head: 1 Cor 10:16,17; Eph 1:22,23; 4:15; 5:23; Col 1:18; 2:19; *ref. 950,957.*

944 It is a memorial of Christ's matchless love for us: Lk 22:19; 1 Cor 11:24,25; *ref. 952-956.*

945 It is a witness to one another and a public testimony to the world that we have been redeemed by the atoning death of Christ: 1 Cor 11:26; cp 1 Cor 15:56,57; 2 Tm 1:10; He 2:9,14,15; *ref. 956.*

946 It is a sign and foretaste of the heavenly feast in the kingdom of glory: Mt 26:29; Mk 14:25; Lk 22:16; *ref. 958,959.*

Proper Preparation

947 We are to approach this Supper after careful self-examination: 1 Cor 11:27-29; see also 1 Cor 10:20,21; 11:20-22; *ref. 960,961.*

Resources

948 This sacrament is named the Lord's *Supper,* because it was instituted at night, the night on which Christ celebrated the Passover-supper with his disciples. It is called Holy *Communion* (Greek: *koinonia*), because it is a communion, or participation, of believers with Christ and with one another. It is sometimes spoken of as the *"breaking of bread,"* from the reference in Ac 2:42. At times it is also spoken of as the "Sacrament of the Altar," because it is celebrated at the altar in the church; *ref. 941.*

949 The four accounts differ in wording, but they agree in all essentials and supplement each other in detail. All quote Christ's words, "This is my body." With reference to the cup, Matthew and Mark emphasize the contents, the blood of the New Testament; Luke and Paul stress the blessing given with the cup, the forgiveness of the new covenant, procured by the blood of Christ, which is offered and given to the communicants in the sacrament; *ref. 941.*

950 The words "This is my body" are further explained in 1 Cor 10:16 where the apostle tells us that the bread is the communion or participation of the body and the cup is the communion or participation of the blood of Christ. All four elements, bread and wine and body and blood, are again spoken of in 1 Cor 11:27 (see also v. 29).

While the earthly elements of bread and wine are received in a natural manner, the heavenly elements of Christ's body and blood are received in an incomprehensible, supernatural manner which reason cannot understand.

> An awful mystery is here
> To challenge faith and waken fear:
> The Savior comes as food divine,
> Concealed in earthly bread and wine.
>
> In consecrated wine and bread
> No eye perceives the myst'ry dread;
> But Jesus' words are strong and clear:
> "My body and my blood are here."
> — Matthias Loy

ref. 941-946

951 The Lord's Supper and the preaching of the gospel are both means of grace. However, there is also a difference: preaching is addressed to all hearers, believers and unbelievers, but in the Lord's Supper the blessings of forgiveness of sins, life, and salvation are offered and conveyed *individually* to each communicant under the pledge of Christ's body and blood received under the form of the consecrated bread and wine. Thus the Lord's Supper serves in a special way to assure, to comfort and to promote sanctification. It strengthens a person's faith, increases his love to God and fellow men, deepens his union with Christ and his mystical body, the Church, and confirms his hope of eternal life; *ref. 941-946.*

952 As a memorial the Lord's Supper is a constant reminder of Christ's matchless love for us in that he sacrificed himself for our deliverance from the slavery of Satan, the servitude of sin, and the bondage and dominion of death and damnation that we might forever be his own and live under him in his kingdom and serve him: Lk 1:74,75; 2 Cor 5:15.

953 God's people of old were instructed to commemorate the Passover as an everlasting memorial of God's delivering them from the bondage of Egypt: Ex 12:14; so Christ instructs us to celebrate his Holy Supper in remembrance of the infinitely greater redemption that he wrought for us. "This do in remembrance of me," he says. It is his will, his inmost heart's desire, that we should celebrate this holy sacrament again and again so that the fact and the memory of his sacrifice may ever be before us and that we may never forget the matchless price at which he purchased our redemption; cp 1 Cor 5:7; 1 Pe 1:18,19.

954
   Gethsemane, can I forget,
    Or there thy conflict see,
   Thine agony and bloody sweat,
    And not remember thee?

   When to the cross I turn my eyes
    And rest on Calvary;
   O Lamb of God, my Sacrifice,
    I must remember thee.

           — Anon

955 In bidding us, "Do this in remembrance of me," Christ would not only have us recall again and again the perfect love which prompted him to give his life for us, he would also have us remember his entire ministry on earth, his work, his teaching, and his example, so that as his disciples we might strive in an ever-increasing measure to follow in his steps by loving one another as he loved us, and by losing our life in humble, sacrificial service to others: Mk 10:43-45; Jn 13:15,35; Ac 10:38; 1 Pe 2:21.

956 While the biographies of great men celebrate the things they accomplished during their life, Holy Scriptures give special attention to Christ's *death,* because the greatest thing that Christ did is that he died for us. All other men reach the climax of their career in life, but Christ reached the climax of his earthly career in death. In the case of all other men death marks the close of their greatness; but in the case of Christ death was only the beginning of his greatness. Far from being an end or a defeat, the death of Christ was a glorious victory.

           — selected

ref. 944

† † †

957
   One bread, one cup, one body, we,
   United by our life in thee,
   Thy love proclaim till thou shalt come
   To bring thy scattered loved ones home.
         — Henry E. Jacobs

ref. 943

† † †

958 Christ's reference to the fact that he would drink this cup anew with his disciples in his Father's kingdom was not a mere reference to his meeting with them again after his resurrection, but a direct promise that he would meet with them again in the kingdom of heaven: Jn 14:1-3; there, in his eternal kingdom of glory, they and his disciples of every generation will meet with him to eat of the eternal manna and drink of the river of his pleasures forever: Ps 16:11; Re 19:7,9.

Thus this holy sacrament not only points us to the past but also directs us forward to our heavenly home. As the Israelites ate the Passover-lamb which strengthened them for their journey to the promised land of Canaan, so the Lord's Supper, in which Christ, our Passover-Lamb, feeds us with his body and gives us to drink of his blood, strengthens us for our journey to our heavenly home: 1 Cor 5:7.

959   Lord Jesus Christ, we humbly pray
                              To keep us steadfast to that day
                              That each may be thy welcomed guest
                              When thou shalt spread thy heavenly feast.
                                            — Henry E. Jacobs

ref. 946

† † †

960 Fasting and bodily preparation are indeed a fine outward training; but he is truly worthy and well prepared who has faith in these words, "Given and shed for you for the remission of sins." But he that does not believe these words, or doubts, is unworthy and unprepared; for the words "for you" require all hearts to believe.

                                          — Martin Luther

961   Grant that we worthily receive
                                  Thy Supper, Lord, our Savior,
                              And, truly grieving o'er our sins,
                                  May prove by our behavior
                            That we are thankful for thy grace
                            And day by day may run our race,
                                  In holiness increasing.
                                  — Samuel Kinner, 1638

Prayer Before Communion

962 O Lord Jesus Christ, I desire to receive thy Holy Sacrament, as thou didst command me in the night of thy precious death.

O Lord, I am not worthy to come to thee, because I have done many things that displease thee; but thou canst make me worthy, O Lord Jesus, and thou canst take away my sins. Help me to struggle against them. O Lamb of God, that takest away the sin of the world, take away mine; have mercy upon me.

O Jesus, give me faith, that I may believe that thou art present in this Holy Sacrament and wilt give thyself to me. Help me to forgive all who have wronged or vexed me. Take away from my heart all unkind thoughts, and all feelings of bitterness; and help me to be loving to every one. For thy name's sake. Amen.

                                      — *My Church*

ref. 947

LOVE 963-1002

(ref.: Grace 461-478; Service 1322-1342)

The Nature of God's Love

963 It is a part of God's essence: 1 Jn 4:8,16; *ref. 976-978;*

964 It is constant and unchanging: Gn 9:16; Is 54:10; Jr 31:3; Mal 3:6; Jn 13:1; Ro 8:38,39; He 13:5,8,20; Jas 1:17; *ref. 977,979.*

The Manifestation of God's Love

965 In the creation and preservation of the world: Gn 1:31; 8:22; Ps 104:24; 139:14; 145:9,15-20; Mt 5:45; Ac 14:17; 17:25; 1 Tm 6:17; He 1:3;

966 In the person and redemptive work of Jesus Christ: Jn 1:14,18; 3:16; 14:9-11; 17:8; Ro 5:8; 8:32; Tt 3:4-7; 1 Pe 1:18,19; 1 Jn 1:7; 4:9,10,14; *ref. 978-983.*

The Nature of Christian Love

967 It is derived from God's love for us: 1 Jn 4:7,16;

968 We become partakers of it through regeneration: Jn 3:3,5; 2 Cor 5:17; Ga 5:22; Eph 2:1-10; 1 Jn 5:1;

969 It flows from Christ's love for us: 2 Cor 5:14,17; Ga 2:20; 1 Jn 4:19;

970 It is a proof of saving faith: Jn 13:35; Ga 5:6,14; Jas 2:17,18; 1 Jn 3:14.

The Manifestation of Christian Love

971 In relation to God:

In giving God the first place in our life and striving to glorify him in all that we think and say and do: Mt 22:37,38; 1 Cor 6:19,20; 10:31; Ga 2:20; Php 1:21; *ref. 981,982;*

972 In doing Christ's commandments: Jn 14:15,21,23 and following his example: Mk 10:42-45; Jn 13:15; Eph 5:1,2; 1 Pe 2:21; *ref. 981,982,1002;*

973 In love for God's Word and God's house: Ps 26:8; 84:1,2; 122:1; 119:72,97,103,162.

974 In relation to our fellow men:

In seeking their salvation by bringing them the gospel: Mt 9:38; 28:18-20; Mk 5:19,20; 16:15; Lk 2:10,11; 16:15; 24:46-48; Jn 1:40-42,45; Ac 1:8; Ro 10:1; 1 Cor 9:22; *ref. 984,992,995,1001;*

975 In showing Christ-like love to all men, especially to those in need: Mt 5:44; 22:39; 25:35-40; Jn 13:34,35; Ac 10:38; Ro 13:8,10; 1 Cor 13:4-7; Ga 6:10; Eph 4:32-5:2; He 13:16; 1 Jn 4:20,21; *ref. 984-1002.*

Resources

976
Could we with ink the ocean fill,
Were every blade of grass a quill,
Were all the world of parchment made,
And every man a scribe by trade,

To write the love
Of God above
Would drain that ocean dry;
Nor would the scroll
Contain the whole,
Though stretched from sky to sky!
— Nehorai Meir Ben Isaac, 1050

ref. 963

† † †

977 Mr. Spurgeon was riding in the country, and on a farmer's barn he saw a weather wane. On its arrow were inscribed the words; "God is Love." He turned in at the gate and asked the farmer, "What do you mean by that? Do you think God's love is changeable; that it veers about as that arrow turns in the wind?" "Oh no," said the farmer, "I mean that whichever way the wind blows, God is still Love;" *ref. 964.*

† † †

978 Years ago, when Mr. La Guardia, the famous late mayor of New York, was presiding at a police court, there was brought before him a trembling old man, charged with stealing a loaf of bread. He said his family was starving. "Well, I must punish you," Mr. La Guardia said, "the law makes no exception, and I must sentence you to a fine of ten dollars." Then he reached into his pocket and added: "And here are the ten dollars to pay your fine. And now I remit the fine." Then he tossed the ten dollars into his outsized hat and said: "Furthermore, I am going to fine everybody in this courtroom fifty cents for living in a town where a man has to steal bread to eat. Mr. Bailiff, collect the fines and give them to the defendant." The hat was passed, and the surprised old man, with the light of joy in his eyes, left the courtroom with forty-seven dollars and fifty cents. But God's love is far greater, "For he hath made him to be sin for us who knew no sin, that we might be made the righteousness of God in him."

— *The Methodist Recorder*

ref. 963,966

† † †

979   Oh, the height of Jesus' love!
Higher than the heav'ns above,
Deeper than the depths of sea,
Lasting as eternity,
Love that found me, — wondrous tho't —
Found me when I sought him not.
— William McComb

980 A prayer was being offered for a sick pastor in which the petitioner made mention, among other things, of the pastor's tender watchfulness in feeding the lambs of the flock, and used this expression: "Lord, thou knowest how he loved thee." When the sick pastor heard this, he said: "Do not pray thus! When Mary and Martha went to Jesus, their message was not, 'Lord, he who loveth thee is sick,' but 'he whom thou lovest!' It is not my imperfect love for him that gives me comfort, but his perfect love for me"; *ref. 964,966.*

† † †

981 When Gustave Dore, the great artist, had about completed one of his famous faces of Jesus, as he was in the act of putting on the last delicate touches, a lady stepped quietly into his studio. She stood for a moment admiring the wonderful production of his genius.

Presently he became aware of her presence and, with his usual politeness, said: "Pardon, madam, I did not know you were here." She said, "Monsieur Dore, you must love him very much to be able to paint him so." — "Love him, Madam," he replied, "I think I do love him, but if I loved him more I would paint him better."

This is also true of our whole Christian stewardship life. When we love Jesus more, we will serve him better. The love of Christ constrains us to love him because he first loved us.

— selected

982
Jesus, thy boundless love to me
  No thought can reach, no tongue declare;
Unite my thankful heart to thee
  And reign without a rival there.
To thee alone, dear Lord, I live;
  Myself to thee, dear Lord, I give.

Oh, grant that nothing in my soul
  May dwell but thy pure love alone!
Oh, may thy love possess me whole,
  My Joy, my Treasure, and my Crown!
All coldness from my heart remove;
  My ev'ry act, word, thought, be love.

— Paul Gerhardt

ref. 966,971,972

† † †

983 A little boy was told that he must give some blood to save his sister's life. He went about saying good-bye to everybody and kissed his father and mother with deep emotion. Then it was discovered that the boy was under the impression that in giving his blood for his sister he would have to give his life. He was asked, "Would you actually be willing to die for your sister?" "Why, of course," he answered, "she's my sister, isn't she?"

984
Do you know the world is dying
  For a little bit of love?
Everywhere we hear them sighing
  For a little bit of love;

244

For a love that rights a wrong,
  Fills the heart with hope and song,
They have waited, oh, so long,
  For a little bit of love.

While the souls of men are dying
  For a little bit of love;
While the children, too, are crying
  For a little bit of love;
Stand no longer idly by,
  You can help them, if you try;
Go, then, saying, "Here am I,
  With a little bit of love."

                           — Anon

985 I expect to pass through this world but once; any good thing therefore that I can do, or any kindness that I can show to any fellow creature, let me do it now: let me not defer or neglect it — for I shall not pass this way again.

                           — Anon

986 William Tyndale, who translated the Bible into English, had many enemies who hated him bitterly and plotted his death. One day he said to one of his enemies: "Sir, you may take away my house, you can rob me of everything I have, you may slander me and deprive me of my good name, but as long as I have Jesus in my heart, I shall keep on loving you"; *ref. 974,975.*

† † †

987 A church member complained bitterly to his pastor, saying: "I have been a member of your church for thirty years, but when I was sick only one or two people came to visit me." "Tell me," said the pastor, "how many sick people have you yourself visited during those thirty years?" "Oh," said the member, "I never looked at it that way. I never thought of my relation to others, but only of their relation to me."

988
    Lord help me to live from day to day
    In such a self-forgetful way,
    That even when I kneel to pray,
    My prayer shall be for — OTHERS.

    Help me in all the work I do
    To ever be sincere and true
    And know that all I'd do for You
    Must needs be done for — OTHERS.

    Let 'self' be crucified and slain
    And buried deep; and all in vain
    My efforts be to rise again,
    Unless to live for — OTHERS.

    And when my work on earth is done
    And my new work in heaven's begun,
    May I forget the crown I've won,
    While thinking still of — OTHERS.

Others, Lord, yes, others,
Let this my motto be,
Help me to live for others,
That I may live for thee.
— Charles D. Meigs

989
Because I have been given much,
  I, too, shall give;
Because of thy great bounty, Lord,
  Each day I live.
I shall divide my gifts from thee
  With every brother that I see
Who has the need of help from me.
— Grace Noll Crowell

990 A very sick woman who had devoted many years of her life to the care of her motherless brothers and sisters asked her minister: "How shall Jesus recognize me when I meet him?" The minister replied: "Show him your hands."

991
If any little word of mine
  May make a life the brighter;
If any little song of mine
  May make a heart the lighter,
God help me speak the little word
  And take my bit of singing,
And drop it in some lonely vale
  To set the echoes ringing.

If any little love of mine
  May make a life the sweeter;
If any little care of mine
  May make a friend's the fleeter;
If any lift of mine may ease
  The burden of another,
God give me love, and care, and strength,
  To help my toiling brother.
— Anon

ref. 975

† † †

992 Lo, my God, without any merit on my part, of his pure and free mercy, has given to me, an unworthy, condemned, and contemptible creature, all the riches of justification and salvation in Christ, so that I am no longer in want of anything, except of faith that this is so. Having such a Father, then, who has overwhelmed me with these inestimable riches of his, why should I not freely, and with my whole heart, and from voluntary zeal, do for him all that I know will be pleasing to him and acceptable in his sight? I will therefore give myself, as a sort of Christ, to my neighbor, even as Christ has given himself to me; and I will do nothing in this life except what I see will be needful, advantageous, and wholesome for my neighbor, since by faith I abound in all things in Christ!

— Martin Luther

ref. 974,975

993 An ancient painter was requested to paint the picture of Alexander the Great. The request put the painter in a quandry, for Alexander had a bad scar on his forehead, which disfigured him. The artist mused: "If I paint the scar, I'll offend my admirer; and if I don't, I will not be able to portray a true image of the king." Then a happy thought came to him. He painted the renowned king with his head resting on his hand, so that the hand covered the scar.

Thus with the hand of love we should cover the scars and the blemishes and the frailties of our fellow men, explaining in their favor as much as truth will permit.

— Ed A. Krause

994 Once the sun and the north wind saw a traveler wearing a fine new robe. They made an agreement to see who would be the first to get the robe off the owner. The north wind swept down with fury and tried its level best to strip off the robe. But when chilled to the bone the man drew the robe closer to his body. Next the sun tried. The sun sent out warm and friendly rays and kept on shining until the man was so warm that he opened the clasps and took off the robe and carried it. Gentleness and patience accomplish much more than unkind and rough behavior or impatience.

— selected

995 "All men will know that you are my disciples," said Christ, "if you love one another," John 13:35.

Love and concern for our fellow men is not only the test of our Christian discipleship, it is also our only effective witness for Christ to others. People are not drawn to Christ by costly church buildings furnished with cushioned pews, cathedral windows, marble altars, and mammoth organs, but by hearing the gospel of peace and forgiveness from the lips of those whose lives reflect Christ's redeeming love; see 2 Cor 3:2,3.

Thus our Christian witness resolves itself not only in the proclamation of the gospel but also in our ministry of mercy in the name of Christ and in his stead as we go into the crowded streets and into the highways and byways of life "mid the homes of want and woe, where the shadows deepest lie," reaching out healing hands to the sin-burdened and sorrowing, to the terrified and troubled, to the weary and worn, to the outcast and forlorn, seeking the lost, reclaiming the erring, restoring the fallen, and speaking hope to the dying. To this end Christ has placed us next to our sin-sick and suffering fellow men in the world, so that their needs might be the channels through which we can bring them the gospel of forgiveness and peace.

> Yes, the sorrow and the sufferings
> Which on every hand we see
> Channels are for gifts and offerings
> Due by solemn right to thee;

Right of which we may not rob thee,
　Debt we may not choose but pay,
Lest that face of love and pity
　Turn from us another day.
— Eliza S. Alderson

ref. 974,975

† † †

996

Lord, lead the way the Savior went,
　By lane and cell obscure,
And let love's treasures still be spent,
　Like his, upon the poor.

Like him, thro' scenes of deep distress,
　Who bore the world's sad weight,
We in their crowded loneliness
　Would seek the desolate.

For thou hast placed us side by side
　In this wide world of ill;
And that thy foll'wers may be tried,
　The poor are with us still.

Mean are all off'rings we can make;
　But thou hast taught us, Lord,
If given for the Savior's sake,
　They lose not their reward.
— William Crosswell

ref.974,975

† † †

997 There is a legend which relates that on a cold, stormy night, Martha was busy in her home preparing for a visit by Christ. While in her preparations, she heard a knock at the door. Opening the door she saw a ragged beggar standing there in the cold rain. "I have no time for beggars," she said, "I am expecting Jesus tonight." Then she closed the door. Soon after she heard another knock and, opening the door, she saw a frail and sickly child. "I have no time to give you," she said, "I am expecting Jesus tonight." But before she could close the door, the form changed and she saw Jesus stand before her.

998 One evening in John Falls's Orphan House, in Weimar, one of the boys said the prayer, "Come, Lord Jesus, be our guest, and let these gifts to us be blessed." Following the prayer another boy asked: "Why does the Lord Jesus never come? We ask him every day to sit with us, and he never comes."

"Dear child," said Mr. Falls, "only believe, and you may be sure he will come; for he does not despise our invitation."

"I shall set him a seat," said the little fellow; and just then there was a knock at the door. A poor frozen apprentice entered, begging a night's lodging. He was made welcome and was given the empty chair. Every child offered his

248

plate, and every one was ready to give up his bed. The little one had been thinking hard all the time. "Jesus could not come, and so he sent this poor one in his place — is that it?" said the child.

"Yes, dear child, that is just it," answered Falls. "Every piece of bread and every drink of water we give to the poor, or the sick, or to the prisoner for Jesus' sake, we give to him. "Whatever you did for one of the least of these brothers of mine," he says, "you did for me," Mt 25:40.

999 The Christian Queen of Sweden turned her jewels into cash to give her people hospitals and orphanages. On a visit to a convalescent home that her gift had provided, tears of gratitude from one of the patients fell on her hand. Looking down at those tears with awe and wonder, the Queen exclaimed: "God has sent me back my jewels"; *ref. 975.*

† † †

1000

> The fairest rose in the garden of life is
>   the fellowship of friends;
> Time but glorifies its beauty with a
>   fragrance that never ends.
> No cloud can shade its loveliness,
> No storm its petals part,
> For the flower of friendship dwells fore'er
>   in the shrine of the human heart.
>
> — Anon

1001 A little girl, observing a beautifully colored church window radiant with light, asked her mother: "Who do the figures in the window represent?" Her mother replied: "Those are the saints!" "Oh," said the child, "now I know what saints are. They are people who let the light shine through." Yes, saints are the redeemed people of God who let the light of Christ's gospel shine through them, people who in their homes, and in all their associations with their fellow men, by word and deed show forth the praises of him who called them out of darkness into his marvelous light; 1 Pe 2:9.

1002 Tradition reports that when the Apostle John had grown old and feeble he had to be carried by his followers into the meeting place of the congregation at Ephesus. Since he was no longer able to address his congregation at length it was his custom to stretch forth his arms to them and say, "Little children, love one another." At length, when his hearers grew weary of hearing him repeat the same words, one of them reverently asked, "Why do you always speak thus?" John's reply was, "It is the Lord's command, and if only this be done, it is enough"; *ref. 972,974,975.*

249

MARRIAGE 1003-1019

(ref.: Children 142-158; Home 534-556; Women 1567-1583)

Origin

1003 Instituted by God at the time of creation: Gn 2:21-24; *ref. 1009,1017.*

Definition and Purpose

1004 A life-long union of one man and one woman as one flesh: Mt 19:4-6; Ro 7:2; 1 Cor 7:39; entered by mutual consent freely given: cp Gn 24:57,58; for the purpose of:

Companionship and mutual help: Gn 2:20; Eph 5:21-25; Col 3:19; 1 Pe 3:7; *ref. 1010-1013*;

The procreation of children: Gn 1:28; 9:1;

Legitimate sexual intercourse: Gn 2:18-24; 1 Cor 7:2; He 13:4.

Mutual Responsibilities

1005 Duties of husbands: Eph 5:25-29; Col 3:19; 1 Pe 3:7; *ref. 1011,1014, 1016,1019*;

Duties of wives: Eph 5:22-24; Col 3:18; 1 Pe 3:1-6; *ref. 1011-1013,1015, 1016,1019*;

1006 Mutual duties to remain faithful to each other and to avoid impurity: Mt 5:27,28,31,32; 15:19; 19:9; Ro 7:3; 1 Cor 6:9,18-20; 10:8; Eph 5:3-12; Col 3:5; 1 Th 4:3-7; 1 Tm 5:22; 1 Pe 2:11;

Duties of husbands and wives as parents: *ref. Education, Christian 321-324,339-347,535,540-545,548-555.*

Rewards

1007 Joy: Is 62:5; Jr 33:11; Jn 3:29; see also Pr 31:10-31; Re 19:7;

Blessings of God: Ps 127:3-5; 128:1-6; Pr 18:22.

Symbolism

1008 Figurative of God's union with his people in Old Testament times: Is 54:5; 62:5; Jr 3:14; Ho 2:19,20;

Figurative of Christ's union with the church: Mt 9:15; 22:2; 25:1; Jn 3:29; 2 Cor 11:2; Eph 5:23,24,32; Re 19:7; 21:2; 22:17.

Resources

1009 Sometime ago the Supreme Court of the U.S. declared that "marriage is an institution in the maintenance of which, in its purity, the public is deeply interested, for it is the foundation of the family and of society, without which there would be neither civilization nor progress.... Any trend or system that attacks the home condemns itself as hostile to public and personal welfare."

— *Decision,* Feb. 1971

ref. 1003

1010 Christ explained that Moses allowed divorce because the Jews were hard of heart, and then added: "from the beginning it was not so," Mt 19:8. He declared that the only permissible cause for putting away one's husband or wife was fornication, Mt 19:9. . . . Malicious desertion severs the marriage relationship and thereby forces separation: 1 Cor 7:15. *ref. 1004.*

1011 The Greek language has three different words to desribe love. The first word, *eros*, means merely the love of sexual attraction. The second word, *philia,* goes beyond this and refers to the kind of love one has for a brother (cp the word Philadelphia — the "city of brotherly love"). The third and most important is the Greek word *agape,* which means a self-giving, self-sacrificing love that desires only the welfare of another. This third word is the one that the Bible uses when it speaks of God's love, or Christ's love, for us, e.g., Jn 3:16; Ga 2:20; 1 Jn 3:1,16; 4:8-11. This is also the word that the Bible uses when it speaks of the love that husbands and wives are to have for each other in their marriage relationship: Eph 5:22-29; *ref. 1004.*

1012 Mrs. Isadore Strauss was one of the few women who were not rescued when the *Titanic* was sunk in 1912. She had been offered safety, but because her husband could find no room in the lifeboat, she said: "We have been together through a great many years. We are old now. Where he goes, I will go"; *ref. 1004.*

1013 In one of his wars, Cyrus took captive an Armenian princess. She was condemned to death. Hearing of this, her husband came into the camp of his conqueror and offered his life in her stead. Cyrus was so touched with the devotion of the prince that he pardoned them both. Officers and soldiers stood there, talking over the magnanimity of their great leader. The princess was near by, her eyes filled with tears. Someone turned to her with the question: "What do you think of Cyrus?" "I was not thinking of Cyrus," she answered. "Of whom, then, were you thinking?" Looking up into the face of her husband, her eyes luminous with love, she answered: "I was thinking of the one who would willingly have died for me."

— selected

ref. 1006

1014
Lord, may there be no moments in her life
When she regrets that she became my wife,
And keep her dear eyes just a trifle blind
To my defects, and to my failings kind.

Help me to do the utmost that I can
To prove myself her measure of a man;
But, if I often fail as mortals may,
Grant that she never sees my feet of clay!

And let her make allowance — now and then —
That we are only grown-up boys, we men,
So, loving all our children, she will see,
Sometimes, a remnant of the child in me!

Since years must bring to all their load of care,
Let us together every burden bear,
And when Death beckons one its path along,
May not the two of us be parted long!

— Mazie V. Caruthers

ref. 1005

† † †

1015 What quality is most essential in a wife? That question has been asked and answered thousands of times; yet I make bold to give my opinion. Some say, Give me the thrifty wife; others say, Give me the common-sense wife, while still others cry out, Give me the broadminded and forgiving wife. Well, my friends, after forty years of experience with a wife who possesses all these qualities and more, let me tell you a secret. No one wants a perfect wife or husband. They are impossible. But here is my secret, mark it well. Do you want an ideal wife? Get a real Christian woman, and you act the part of a real Christian man, and you will have solved the problem of being happy though married; see Pr 31:10-31.

— "Voice of the People," *Chicago Tribune*

1016
O perfect Love, all human tho't transcending,
Lowly we kneel in prayer before thy throne
That theirs may be the love which knows no ending,
Whom thou forevermore dost join in one.

O perfect Life, be thou their full assurance
Of tender charity and steadfast faith,
Of patient hope and quiet, brave endurance,
With childlike trust that fears nor pain nor death.

Grant them the joy which brightens earthly sorrow;
Grant them the peace which calms all earthly strife
And to life's day the glorious unknown morrow
That dawns upon eternal love and life.

— Dorothy F. Gurney

1017 The best advice that can be given to young people contemplating marriage is to invite Jesus to their wedding, as did the young people in Cana, of Galilee, of whom we read in Jn 2:1-11. Not only did Jesus hallow their wedding by his presence, he also proved to be a Friend in need when he came to their aid by wondrously changing water into wine. Today, as then, he comes into the hearts and homes of all who worship him as their Savior: Re

3:20. Today, as then, he is the almighty Helper to whom they can turn in their every time of need: He 2:18; 4:15,16; *ref. 1003,1005,1006.*

† † †

1018   GOLDEN WEDDING ANNIVERSARY

They walked along life's pathway hand in hand,
Thy blessings, Lord, as countless as the sand,
Through fifty years of wedded bliss and love,
Were daily sent them from thy throne above.

They lived in thy commands and walked thy ways,
Thy wondrous peace and blessing crowned their days,
Long life thou gavest them to see
Their children's children also serving thee.

They shared alike their poverty and wealth,
Their joys and tears, their sicknesses and health,
In common faith their hearts were joined as one
In mystic sweet communion with thy Son.

When through great trials of fire their path did lie,
Thy grace, sufficient, was their full supply;
Behind each frowning providence they traced,
Through clouds of gloom, thy kind and smiling face.

Their wants and fears to thee were always known,
Their sorrows, griefs, and tears were all thine own,
In dangers thou didst guard them from alarms
By stretching forth thine everlasting arms.

They poured their prayers before thy throne on high,
And thou didst hear and grant their humble cry,
Lord, hear them now, as toward thy throne they bend,
And bless them with thy love e'en to the end.

At eventide, let thy light guide them still,
Supply their needs, and their desires fulfill;
Renew their strength, and hear their soul's complaint,
Be ever near to comfort them when faint!

Oh, may they still thy love and goodness see,
Thy tender kindness ever full and free.
And, in thy boundless grace and love so blest,
Bring them at last to thine eternal rest!
— R.C.R.

ref. 1005,1006

† † †

1019 In Ephesians 5:22-24, and in 1 Peter 3:1, wives are instructed to submit themselves to their husbands. On the surface this directive sounds harsh. However, Holy Scriptures make it very clear that the obedience that the wife owes to her husband is not like that of a slave to his master. Rather, it is the loving obedience of a helpmate and companion to him whom God has placed as the head of the house. The Bible refers to this as the order which God established in the creation. Adam was first formed, and then Eve.

But the relation of Christian husbands and wives is also much deeper than the order of creation. It includes the order of redemption. Nowhere is this order set forth more beautifully than in the Letter to the Ephesians where the holy writer declares: "Wives, submit to your husbands as to the Lord. For the husband is the head of the wife as Christ is the head of the church, his body, of which he is the Savior. Now as the church submits to Christ, so also wives should submit to their husbands in everything. Husbands, love your wives, just as Christ loved the church and gave himself up for her," Eph 5:22-25.

As the church renders willing obedience to Christ, her Head, because of his great love for her, even so the Christian wife renders willing obedience to her Christian husband because of his great love which, patterned after the love of Christ, is so great that he is willing to lay down his life for her. As redeemed children of God both husband and wife are one in Christ. As such both are heirs of eternal life, and as such both are to submit themselves to one another in the fear of God: Ga 3:26-28; Eph 5:21; 1 Pe 3:7; *ref. 1005,1006*.

MISSION WORK 1020-1081

(ref.: Discipleship 300-314)

Definition

1020 Seeking to bring others to the knowledge of Jesus Christ as Savior and Lord: *ref. 1028-1030,1080*:

By teaching and preaching the gospel: Mt 28:18; Mk 16:15; Lk 24:47,48; *ref. 1037*;

By publishing the good news of salvation through personal witness: Ac 1:8; and joint mission work with fellow-Christians in the church: Ac 8:1,5,14,15; 11:22-26; 13:1-3; 14:26,27; 15:3; Ro 1:8; 1 Th 1:8; *ref. 1031,1038-1040*;

Through the testimony of a Christian life: Mt 5:16; 2 Cor 3:3; Php 2:15,16; 1 Tm 4:12; 1 Pe 2:9-12; 3:15,16; *ref. 1033,1034,1041-1044*.

The Need for Mission Work

1021 All mankind is lost in sin: Is 59:2; Ro 3:23; 5:12; Ga 3:22; Eph 2:1; 1 Jn 5:19; and no one can save himself: Ps 49:7,8; Is 64:6; Jr 2:22; Ro 3:20; 10:14; *ref. 1035,1036*;

God earnestly desires the salvation of everyone: Eze 33:11; 1 Tm 2:4; 2 Pe 3:9. He has prepared salvation for all through Christ: Jn 3:16; Ac 10:35; 2 Cor 5:15,19; 1 Tm 2:5,6; Tt 2:11; and there is no other way in which anyone can be saved: Mk 16:16; Jn 3:18,36; Ac 4:12; 1 Jn 5:11,12; *ref. 1053,1057*;

Christ has commanded his followers to bring the good news of salvation to all mankind: Mt 28:18-20; Mk 16:15; Lk 24:47,48; Jn 20:21; Ac 1:8; *ref. 1037,1045-1047,1051,1058.*

The Urgency of Mission Work

1022 The fields are white unto the harvest, and the need for workers is great: Mt 9:36-39; Lk 10:1,2; Jn 4:35; *ref. 1047,1049,1069,1070;*

Death limits the time allotted to us and to those to whom we are to witness: 1 Chr 29:15; Ps 90:9,10; 95:7,8; 102:1; Is 55:6,7; Lk 19:42; 2 Cor 6:2; Jas 4:14; *ref. 1048,1050,1055;*

The end of the day of grace for the world will end all opportunity to witness for Christ: Mt 25:10-13; Lk 12:40; 13:25; Jn 9:4; 2 Pe 3:10-12; *ref. 1051, 1055,1081.*

Opportunities for Mission Work

1023 In the church: Ac 5:20,21,22; cp Mt 21:15,16;

At home: Mk 5:18-20; Ac 5:42; Col 3:16; *ref. 1052;*

In the community: Mt 5:16; 2 Cor 3:3; Php 2:15,16; 1 Tm 4:12; 1 Pe 2:9-12; 3:15,16;

In every village and city: Mt 9:35; Lk 10:1; Ac 5:28; *ref. 1031,1077;*

In all the world: Mt 24:14; 28:19; Mk 13:10; 16:15; Lk 24:47; Ac 1:8; 8:1; Ro 10:18; Col 1:23; Re 14:6; *ref. 1035,1036.*

Examples of Personal Mission Work

1024 Christ's example in dealing with the Syrophenician woman: Mk 7:24ff; Nicodemus: Jn 3:1f; the woman of Samaria: Jn 4:7f; the nobleman of Capernaum: Jn 4:46f; the man born blind: Jn 9:1f; Zacchaeus: Lk 19:1f; the malefactor on the cross: Lk 23:39-43;

Other examples: the Hebrew maid in Naaman's household: 2 Kgs 5:1f; the shepherds: Lk 2:17; Anna: Lk 2:38; Andrew: Jn 1:40-42; Philip: Jn 1:45; the healed demoniac: Mk 5:19,20; the woman of Samaria: Jn 4:28,29; the early Christians: Ac 8:4; Paul: 1 Cor 9:19-23; *ref. 1031,1054,1056,1057,1059-1069, 1071.*

Requirements for Mission Work

1025 A deep Christian conviction and dedication: Ps 66:16; 71:15; 119:46; 145:1,2; 146:2; Jn 6:68,69; 11:27; Ac 4:20; 26:22,23; 1 Cor 9:16; 2 Cor 4:13; Ga 2:20; Php 1:21; 2 Tm 1:12; 4:1,2; *ref. 1069-1075;*

Christlike compassion for souls: Mt 9:36; 18:14; Lk 19:10; 15:7,10; Ro 9:3; 10:1; 1 Cor 9:19-23; *ref. 1069,1072;*

Christlike prayer: Mt 9:38; Lk 22:32; Jn 17:20; Ac 13:3; Eph 6:18-20; Php 4:6; Col 4:2,3; *ref. 1069,1071,1074,1076.*

Rewards of Mission Work

1026 Joy in witnessing the salvation of others: Lk 10:17; 15:7,10; Ac 11:22,23; 15:3; 1 Th 2:19,20; He 12:2; Jas 5:19,20; *ref. 1078,1079;*

Inheritance in heaven: Dn 12:3; Mt 10:32; 19:27-29; 25:21,23,34; Jn 4:36; 2 Tm 4:7,8; 1 Pe 5:4; Re 2:10; *ref. 1079.*

Resources

1027 Mission work is not some incidental phase of the church's work, but the very heart and center of her work.

1028 A church can be busy pouring out its energies into things that are little if any of her concerns and meanwhile give little attention to that which is her real business. — One of the strangest battles of the Revolutionary War was that of an all-night "fight" between a French battleship and a barren, defenseless island in the West Indies. The island, which is called "Sail Rock," is strikingly similar in appearance to a full rigged sailing ship. That rock was sighted one night by the French battleship. Mistaking the rock for an enemy ship, the captain of the French battleship hailed it. When he received no reply, he decided that it was an English warship and immediately ordered a broadside to be fired. The tumult of the firing and the splashing of the shells and bits of rock led the captain to believe that the fire had been returned. So he ordered more firing. All night the French crew poured out a deadly hail of shot into the island rock which they had mistaken for a ship.

1029 The church that talks about evangelism, but is not evangelistic in action, is no longer evangelical in teaching. To insist on pure doctrine, but to do nothing towards sharing it with the unchurched in the community is hypocrisy. The entire program of the congregation must be evangelistic in outlook and endeavor.

— Australian Lutheran

1030
          Give us a watchword for the hour,
          A thrilling word, a word of power;
          A battle-cry, a flaming breath —
          That calls to conquest or to death;
          A word to rouse the church from rest,
          To heed her Master's high behest.

          The call is given: Ye hosts arise!
            Our watchword is: Evangelize!

          The glad evangel now proclaim
          Through all the earth in Jesus' Name;
          This word is ringing through the skies:
            Evangelize! Evangelize!
          To dying men, a fallen race,
          Make known the gift of gospel grace.

          The world that now in darkness lies —
            Evangelize! Evangelize!

— Anon

ref. 1020

            † † †

1031 Aunt Sophie, a converted washerwoman, was always eager to share the gospel of Christ. One day she was seen talking about Christ to a wooden

Indian figure outside a tobacco store. Someone ridiculed her for this, but she replied: "Some people say they saw me talking to a wooden Indian outside a cigar store about Jesus. That may be so. I do not know. My sight's not so good as it used to be. But that ain't nearly so bad as being a wooden Christian and talking to nobody about Jesus."

— selected

1032 "Does Jesus Christ live here?" The question was asked by the new pastor as he visited one of his parishioners. The housewife had answered the door. That evening when her husband returned from work she told him of the pastor's visit, and then added: "He asked a very strange question. He asked, does Jesus Christ live here?" The husband was somewhat startled too, and said: "Didn't you tell him that we are respectable people, that we read the Bible occasionally, that we pray, and that we usually go to church every Sunday?" "He didn't ask those questions," said the wife, "he only asked: Does Jesus Christ live here?" *ref. 1020,1023.*

† † †

1033
You are writing a gospel, a chapter a day,
By the deeds that you do and the things that you say.
Men read your record, whether faithless, or true —
Pray tell, what is the gospel according to you?

— Anon

1034
Thee may our tongues forever bless,
    Thee may we love alone,
And ever in our lives express
    The image of thine own.

— Anon

1035
The great world's heart is aching,
Fiercely aching in the night,
And God alone can heal it,
And God alone can give it light;
And the men who bear the message
And who speak the living Word
Are you and I, my brothers,
And the millions who have heard.

— Frederick G. Scott

1036 "Tell me," said an African chief to David Livingstone, "since it is true that all who die with their sins unforgiven are lost forever, why did your people not come and tell us about Jesus long ago?" *ref. 1020,1021.*

† † †

1037 There is a legend which tells that when Jesus ascended into heaven following the completion of his great work of redemption, he was asked by an angel, "How do you propose to make known to the world the fact that you have died for the sins of all?" In reply, the Savior said: "I have my followers on earth, and I have commanded them to go into all the world and preach the

257

gospel to men everywhere." "But," said the angel, "What if they should fail?" "If they fail," concluded the Savior, "I have no other plan."

1038 In a bombed-out city in Germany there stood the remains of a church building. Only a bit of the walls stood here and there, the sky serving as the only roof. But the bombs had left the altar untouched and also the statue of Christ over the altar — untouched except for one thing: the hands of the statue had been blown off. After the war had ended the members of the church considered plans for rebuilding. When the question as to what to do with the statue arose, there were differences of opinion. Some felt that a new statue should be purchased. Others wanted to hire a sculptor who could replace the hands. But the counsel of a third group prevailed. They said: "Let us leave the statue as it is. It will be a reminder to us of God's grace even during the war. Besides, the handless statue is a message to us from God. He is telling us that Jesus has no hands but our hands to do his work."

1039

We do not well to hold our peace,
While men beleagured need release;
Sin's siege is broken; let us sound
The tidings all the world around.
We do not well ourselves to feast,
Till famine of the Word has ceased,
Our souls from leanness shall be cursed,
Though all our barns with plenty burst.
O, fellow-heirs of God's rich grace,
No longer tarry, but apace
Tell all the household of the King
The joyful tidings angels sing.
For he who is the Gift of gifts
The curtain of the future lifts,
And shows us in a vision fair,
That they alone do well who share.
— C. S. Hoyt

ref. 1020

† † †

1040 A doctor moved into town. One of the first patients to come to him was a man with a dreadful skin disease. The doctor cured him. The man told his neighbor about the doctor. The neighbor told his wife. His wife told the grocer. The grocer told the truck driver. The truck driver told the men at the warehouse. Before long the whole town knew about the wonderful ability of the new doctor, and his office was always crowded. — What would happen if every church member would tell his neighbor about the great Physician? How quickly would the glad tidings of salvation pass from lip to lip throughout the world without the cost of a single penny?

1041 It is said that the North American Indians refused Christian baptism because of the wicked examples that they observed in the lives of the Spaniards who were supposed to be Christians. They said, "He must be a wicked God who has such wicked servants!"

1042 A Chinaman, of whom it was known that he had never heard the gospel, came to the mission compound and expressed the desire to join the Christian congregation. When he was asked why he wished to take this step without first learning the teachings of Christianity, he replied: "But I have *seen* the gospel!" The Christian missionaries whom he had observed were "living letters" of Christ, 2 Cor 3:3. By their exemplary lives and self-sacrificing service they had so impressed this man with the power of the Christian religion that he wanted to investigate and embrace it.

1043 Tertulian, who later became one of the great fathers in the early Christian church, confessed that he and most of the converts to Christianity in his day were won for Christ, not by sermons which they had heard preached, not by books which they had read, but by the living examples which they observed in the lives of those who were Christ's followers.

1044   You are the only Bible the careless world will read.
      You are the sinner's gospel, you are the scoffer's creed.
      You are the Lord's last message, given in deed or word —
      What if the type is crooked? What if the print is blurred?
                                          — Anon

ref. 1020

† † †

1045 An ocean liner was wrecked on a dangerous reef off the New England coast. When the captain of the Coast Guard gave a command to attempt a rescue, one of the young seamen turned to him and said: "Sir, the wind is offshore; the tide is running out. We can go out, but we can never come back." But the captain replied: "Launch the boat. We have to go out. We don't have to come back." — Our Lord says "Go!" He says nothing about coming back.

1046 Christ says to every lost sinner "Come!" and to every converted sinner "Go!"

1047 The following words were spoken by a missionary to India just before returning to his field following a furlough:

"I do not mind the burning sun of the country, nor the separation from my loved ones here in America, for I know they want me to go, nor the isolation, nor the hardships. I can face all of them with courage. But what takes the life out of me, and what goes with me like a chain about my feet into the scattered villages that have never heard or seen the name of Christ, is the indifference of many Christians in my own homeland. It is sometimes hard for me to shake this chain off. I know some are praying, some are giving, and some are going. I thank God for them. But how few they are, how few they are!"

1048 John and Henry were good friends. For twenty years they had been as brothers. John belonged to church. Henry did not. Henry took sick, and as the days passed it became certain that his sickbed would be his deathbed. One day as John sat at his friend's bedside, he told him about Jesus, the Savior. The only answer which he received was, "John, I've waited twenty years for you to tell me about things like that, but now it's too late." The same night Henry died. — Is there someone in your home who does not believe in Jesus? Do you have an unbelieving friend or acquaintance? Will you try to gain such a person for Christ — before it is too late?

1049 In 1901, Dr. John R. Mott wrote, "If in the next few years we can send 10,000 missionaries to Japan, we may win that land for Jesus Christ. But if not, forty years from now we shall have to send 100,000 bayonets." — The only error in that prophecy was that Dr. Mott far underestimated the number of soldiers that we would have to send. The forty years he wrote of in 1901 passed, and we sent not 100,000 men but more than a million to defeat Japan.

— The Chaplain

1050 In the battle to gain possession of New Orleans in the War of 1812, the British lost 2,600 men in twenty-five minutes. A sad fact that became known later was that this battle was fought after the treaty of peace had been agreed upon at Ghent [Dec. 24, 1814]. Thus the tragic truth that this terrible loss of life was unnecessary.

But what about the multitudes who are unnecessarily dying without Christ? Why are they not being told of the peace that Christ purchased for them through his death on the cross? *ref. 1020,1022.*

1051 A missionary in England once asked a soldier, "If the Queen were to write something very important, and print it, and then give it into the hands of the army, telling the soldiers, 'Go into all the world and tell everybody,' how long would it take?" In reply the soldier said, "We could manage that in about eighteen months." — That was at a time when ships were slow and there were no automobiles, airplanes and radios. What a pity that the Christian church has not accomplished in all these years what the British army could have accomplished in eighteen months when, in addition, the church has access to all modern means of communication and travel and when it has a message infinitely more important to proclaim! *ref. 1020,1022.*

† † †

1052 So often the mention of mission work conjures up in the minds of many only the vision of heathen people in foreign lands. In reality, however, mission work begins at home. And only to the extent that it is effective there will it be effective elsewhere. The light that shines the farthest is the one that burns the brightest at its base. Our concern for the salvation of people in other lands is measured by our concern for the salvation of the souls of those who are near and dear to us; *ref. 1023.*

† † †

1053 While the Gospels call attention to the fact that Christ preached and taught large audiences: Mt 5:1; Mk 8:8,9; Jn 6:10-12; they also portray many touching scenes in which he spent much time with individuals. Nor can we overlook the fact that he did not wait for men to come to him. He went out to them. In fact, he spent his entire ministry in seeking and saving the lost. Some of his best-remembered sayings are those that he spoke to individuals: e.g., Jn 3:16; 4:14; Mt 9:6; Lk 19:10. In his parables of the Lost Sheep, the Lost Coin, and the Lost Son, he portrayed his own compassionate concern for the one who was lost: Lk 19:10-14; Lk 15:3-14. Moreover, he contrasted the value of a single soul with the combined wealth of the world and said, "What shall it profit a man, if he shall gain the whole world and lose his own soul? Or what shall a man give in exchange for his soul?" Mk 8:36,37; *ref. 1021.*

† † †

1054 There's not enough darkness in the whole world to put out the light of a single candle. Witness for Christ!

1055 W. W. Martin tells of putting these words over the clock in a certain mission church: "83 a minute." At last a deputation came to him and said: "Will you kindly take that down? It haunts us." They knew that it meant eighty-three souls a minute were passing into eternity — into the dark. Most of them had never heard about Jesus Christ.

— selected

1056 A publisher of business books has published the results of a survey on salesmanship. It show that 80% of all sales are made *after* the fifth call. 48% of all salesmen make one call and quit; 25% make two calls and quit; 12% make three calls and quit. Only 15% keep on calling, and these make 80% of the sales. — Have you given up too quickly in making mission calls? *ref. 1022,1024.*

† † †

1057 Many years ago, as an aged Scottish minister came to his church before the service was to begin, he was met by one of his deacons who criticized his preaching which during the whole year had won only one new member, a boy. With a grieved and heavy heart the old pastor went to the pulpit that Sunday, preaching as impressively as he could. No one remained to speak to him an encouraging word about his sermon and work — no one but that boy. "Do you think," asked the lad, "that if I study hard, I might become a minister, perhaps a missionary?" The minister laid his hand on the boy's head. "Robert," he said, "with God nothing is impossible. Pray and study hard, and leave the rest to God." Many years later, when the aged minister had long ago passed to his eternal reward, that young lad returned to his home town, now himself an aged man. His name was spoken with reverence everywhere. When he addressed a Christian assembly, no one dared utter a word. Deep silence, the effect of deep interest in his mission enterprise, held everybody spellbound. Princes stood uncovered before him. Nobles invited him to their homes. Robert Moffat had brought Christ to the most savage of African chiefs, had given to strange tribes the Bible in their own language, had enriched with valuable knowledge the Royal Geographical Society, and had brought honor to his humble place of birth. The aged minister had won only a boy, but oh, what that boy meant to the Church!

— *Canadian Lutheran*

1058
You sent the money across the sea
That bought a Bible for young Sing Lee,
And young Sing Lee, when he'd read therein,
Proceeded to turn his back on sin.
Then he rested neither night nor day
Till his brother walked in the narrow way;
And his brother worked till he had won
Away from their gods his wife and son.
The woman told of her new-found joy,
And Christ was preached by the happy boy.
Some of the folks who heard them speak
Decided the one true God to seek.
It wasn't long until half the town
Had left its idols of wood and stone.
And the work's not ended yet, my friend,
You started something that ne'er should end
When you sent the money across the sea
That bought a Bible for young Sing Lee.

      — Amelia Price Ayers, in
      The Sunday School Times
ref. 1020,1021

† † †

1059 I will go anywhere provided it is forward.

      — Livingston

1060 As he knelt on India's coral strand, Henry Martyn prayed, "Now let me burn out for God."

1061 If men will perish, at least let them perish with our arms about their knees begging them to be turned and saved. And if men will plunge into hell, at least let them plunge over our prostrate bodies begging them to be turned and saved.

      — Spurgeon

1062 Expect great things from God. Attempt great things for God.

      — William Carey

1063 I have one passion, and that is Christ — he only.

      — Count Zinzendorf
ref. 1024

† † †

1064 Thomas Bridges ... as an infant, unwanted in this life, Bridges had been left beside a bridge in the city of London. Workmen found him wrapped in newspaper. They saved his life and he was placed in an orphanage. They found him on St. Thomas Day, so they called his first name Thomas. They found him near a bridge, so they called his last name Bridges.

Thomas Bridges was converted as a young man and later went to the cannibal land of Tierra del Fuego as a foreign missionary. Charles Darwin had earlier visited Tierra del Fuego and had come away saying that there was no hope for those people. Through the work of Thomas Bridges, God effected a transformation. Darwin later paid tribute to Christian work in that part of the world and became a financial contributor to the South American Missionary Society.

— selected

1065 A mother who was dying in Germany called her son to her bedside and said, "I am leaving you a treasure, a very great treasure." It was a Bible. Her son was Bartholomew Ziegenbalg. The treasure became more and more precious to him, and his desire to share it with others became more and more fervent, until he made an agreement with another student, Henry Pluetschau, "never to seek anything but the glory of God, the spread of his kingdom, and the salvation of mankind."

Almost a century before Carey sailed from England, both of them sailed for India and there established the first Protestant Mission.

— selected

1066 David Brainerd, missionary to the North American Indians 1718-1747, declared, "Lord, to thee I dedicate myself. Oh, accept me, and let me be thine forever. Lord, I desire nothing else; I desire nothing more."

1067 Dwight L. Moody implored, "Use me, then, my Savior, for whatever purpose and in whatever way thou mayest require. Here is my poor heart, an empty vessel; fill it with thy grace."

1068 Hudson Taylor declared, "I feel as if I could not live if something is not done for China"; *ref. 1024.*

† † †

1069

Stir us, oh, stir us, Lord, we care not how,
But stir our hearts in passion for the world,
Stir us to give, to go, but most to pray;
Stir till the blood-red banner be unfurled
O'er lands that still in heathen darkness lie,
O'er deserts where no cross is lifted high.

— Anon

1070

Is it nothing to you as you hear from abroad
    How millions of heathen today
Are waiting to hear of the only true God
    Who taketh transgressions away?
If you have rejoiced in the gift of God's love
    And gladly his bidding would do,
Can you turn a deaf ear to the call from above?
    Dear friend, is it nothing to you?

— Anon

1071

Lord, lay some soul upon my heart,
    And love that soul through me;

And let me gladly do my part,
To win that soul for thee.

— Anon

ref. 1022,1025

† † †

1072 The longer one studies the sacred Gospel accounts, the more clearly it appears that the most striking trait in Christ, the one that best characterizes his person, describes his work and portrays his soul, is that of his compassionate love. This wonderful quality revealed itself on the one hand, in his many miracles of mercy. Without limitations his merciful heart was filled with pity and love for all men in their many and varied needs, and it extended itself to Jews and Gentiles alike, to the rich and to the poor, to the maimed and to the blind, to the grief-stricken and sorrowing, to the demon-possessed and to others afflicted with countless maladies. Without discrimination and exception, we read, that he healed them all: Mt 4:24; 15:32; 20:34; Mk 1:41; Lk 7:13 etc.

But infinitely greater than his concern for the temporary bodily welfare of men was his compassion and compelling concern for the needs of their immortal souls. Nothing moved him more, or caused his bitter tears to flow, than the realization of the helplessness of men under the fearful power of sin, or the tragic fact that some refused to accept his offer of salvation: Mt 23:37; Lk 19:41,42; Jn 11:33-35.

His compassionate love as revealed in his all-consuming desire to seek and to save the lost was the crowning characteristic of his entire life and work. And it was for the joy of saving sinners that he endured the cross despising its shame: He 12:2.

1073

Oh, give me Lord, thy love for souls,
For lost and wandering sheep,
That I may see the multitudes
And weep as thou did'st weep.
From off the altar of thy heart
Take thou some flaming coals,
Then touch my life, and give me, Lord,
A heart that burns for souls.

— Anon

ref. 1025

† † †

1074 In asking his disciples to pray for laborers, Christ did not ask them to do something that he did not do himself. The Gospel records tell us that before calling his disciples and inducting them into their office, Christ spent the entire night in prayer: Lk 6:12,13. He instructed them, and us, to pray the Lord of the harvest that he would send forth laborers into his harvest. The work of gathering souls into the garner of heaven is his work, not ours.

He is the Lord of the Harvest. The harvest belongs to him, and it is entirely his work to supply the laborers. They cannot be furnished in any other way.

> Saints of God, the dawn is bright'ning,
>   Token of our coming Lord;
> O'er the earth the field is whit'ning;
>   Louder rings the Master's word:
> Pray for reapers, pray for reapers,
>   In the harvest of the Lord!
> — Mary H. Maxwell

1075 A young lady said to her friend, "I cannot get interested in missions." "No," replied her friend, "you can hardly expect to. It is just like getting interest in a bank. You have to put something in before you can get interest. And the more you put in — time, money, prayer — the more the interest grows."

1076 When closing a missionary meeting, a minister said to those present: "Let me ask you to spend fifteen minutes each day praying for Christian missions. But let me also warn you that it will be a costly experiment." The congregation asked the minister to explain his remarks, and he answered: "When the great missionary Carey began to pray for the evangelization of the heathen, it cost him himself. When David Brainerd, the well-known missionary among the Stockbridge Indians, prayed for the conversion of the American natives, it cost him his life after only two years of blessed service among them. When two students in Moody's summer school began to ask the Lord to send forth more laborers into his harvest, it cost our country five thousand young people, who in the course of time dedicated themselves to missionary work. If you pray for missions, it will cost you either money or labor or even your life. As you pray, you soon will pay."
— *The Sunday School Times*

ref. 1025

† † †

1077 Do we assume that the unchurched know what the Christian church teaches and that they will come of their own accord if they are interested? The truth is that they do not know, and they will never become interested unless they are confronted. And if they are to be confronted, we must bring the gospel to them: cp Ro 10:14; 1 Cor 2:14; Eph 2:1.

This was demonstrated many years ago by a rather unique incident. When fire threatened to destory a church in one of our large cities, much of the church furniture was hurriedly carried out to the street. Included was a life-size statue of Christ which had stood above the altar. Passers-by stood and gazed with wonder at the statue, and many eagerly inquired who the statue represented. For years Christ had been in the church, but many outside of the church never heard of him and consequently did not know him. Is this true of many in our community? Surely, it is important that Christ be in our church, that he form the center of all of our preaching and teaching, and that he be the object of our worship. But until we bring him to the people outside of the church by telling them of him, he will remain a stranger to them. And if ever we become content only with keeping him in the church, we ourselves will lose him. For the mission of the Christian church is mission work, and once a congregation has lost sight of its mission, it has forfeited the right for its existence; *ref. 1023.*

† † †

1078

O happy the harvester reaping the grain,
The tall rows of green-ribboned, succulent cane!
He has no regrets for the sweat on his brow,
For the strength he put forth when guiding the plow,
The prick of the thorn whilst uprooting the weeds,
The stress of the day when he planted the seeds.

His eyes light with joy as he views his fair lands,
For God has rewarded the work of his hands.
His soul is at peace, in his heart there is song
As he turns toward home when the shadows grow long.
He gives not a thought to past labors and pain,
But thanks the good Lord as he garners the grain.

So likewise the worker in God's mission-field
Regards not the toil, but the harvest's rich yield.
He tills, and he sows whilst his Lord is away;
With faith he looks forward to harvesting-day.
Oh, great is his joy, all his longings are stilled,
When his Lord does return and the mansions are filled.

— Clare Breacher Wichman

ref. 1026

† † †

1079

When I enter the beautiful city,
    Far, far removed from earth's sorrow and care,
I want to hear somebody tell me,
    It was you who invited me here.

When at home in those mansions above,
    And the redeemed all around me appear,
I want to hear somebody tell me
    It was you who invited me here.

To our Savior alone be the praise
    Who through his Spirit the witness did bear,
Yet to this joy I might not have come,
    Had you not invited me here.

— Anon

1080 A famous preacher once said that the most beautiful painting he had ever seen was that of the Rock of Ages which showed a shipwrecked woman

266

clinging with both hands to the Rock of the Cross. Later he changed his mind and regarded as the most beautiful painting one which was similar, but which showed the same woman clinging to the Rock of the Cross with one hand and rescuing a victim with the other hand; *ref 1020,1026*

† † †

1081   Work for the night is coming,
            Under the sunset skies;
            While still their bright rays are glowing
            Work, for the daylight flies;
            Work till the last beam fadeth,
            Fadeth to shine no more;
            Work while the night is dark'ning,
            Before man's work is o'er.

— Anon

ref. 1022

MOTHERS 1082-1098
(ref.: Home 534-556; Women 1567-1583)

God Requires That Mothers Should Be Honored

1082 See Ex 20:12; Lv 19:3; Dt 27:16; Pr 1:8,9; 6:20; 23:22; 30:17; Mt 19:19; Eph 6:2; Col 3:20; good examples: David, 1 Sm 22:3; Solomon, 1 Kgs 2:19; Jesus, Lk 2:51; Jn 19:25,26; *ref. 1086-1090,1092,1094,1096,1098.*

Duties of Mothers

1083 To love and care for their children: Gn 21:16; Ex 2:3; 1 Sm 2:19; 2 Sm 21:9,10; 1 Kgs 3:26; 2 Kgs 4:20; Is 49:15; Mt 15:22; see IV; *ref. 321f,1088, 1091,1093,1095,1097.*

A Portrait of a Pious Mother
According to Proverbs 31:10-31

1084 A faithful helpmate for her husband: v.11,12; cp Gn 2:18;
An example of piety, virtue, and charity: v.10,20,25,26,30,31; cp 1 Pe 3:1-6;
A diligent and loving provider for her family: v.13-22,24,27;
A worthy member of society: v.23,26.

Examples of Pious Mothers

1085 Sarah: Gn 11:29; 17:15,16; 21:1-7; He 11:11; 1 Pe 3:6;
Hannah: 1 Sm 1:10,11, 19-28; 2:1-10,19;
Elizabeth: Lk 1:5,6,24,25,39-45,57-60;
Mary: Mt 1:18-25; Lk 1:26-38,46-55; 2:1f; Jn 19:25;
Eunice: Ac 16:1; 2 Tm 1:5; 3:15; *ref. 1098.*

1086 The observance of Mother's Day originated with Miss Anna Jarvis, of Philadelphia, Pennsylvania, in 1908. Her mother died in 1906 on the second Sunday in May. A year later Miss Jarvis, with some friends, was at her home in remembrance of the anniversary of her mother's death. She discussed with her friends her desire to dedicate a day to all mothers. Within a year she had interested many local groups and organizations in the observance.

The first Mother's Day was celebrated in Philadelphia, May 10, 1908. But that celebration was only the beginning of Miss Jarvis' plan. She sought the attention of state organizaitons and national figures in all walks of life. In 1912 the Governor of Texas observed the day by pardoning a number of prisoners for the sake of their mothers. State after State adopted the plan. Rapidly it spread to other countries where the movement was taken up with equal enthusiasm.

— selected

ref. 1082

† † †

1087 Behind every great man there has been a great mother. President Garfield said: "I owe everything I have and am to my mother." Just before taking the oath as president he walked over to where his proud mother sat, and taking her in his arms, tenderly kissed her.

When the painter West showed his mother his first little sketch she kissed him and he afterwards said that kiss made him a painter.

John Newton was one of the wildest and openly most rebellious men who ever walked the earth, but he said that, while pacing the deck of a vessel on the wild seas, he seemed to feel the pressure of his mother's gentle hand upon his head again; that, he said, by God's grace pressed him back into the kingdom of heaven.

John Adams said: "As a child I enjoyed the greatest blessings that can be bestowed upon men — that of a mother who was anxious and capable to form the character of her children rightly."

Abraham Lincoln said: "I remember my mother's prayers, and they have always followed me. They have clung to me throughout my life."

John Wanamaker wrote: "My first love was my mother, and my first home was on her breast. My first bed was upon her bosom. Leaning my arms upon her knees, I learned my first prayers. A bright lamp she lit in my soul, that never dies down nor goes out, though the winds and waves of fourscore years have swept over me."

1088 Among the mothers of history of whose lives we know, a high place is forever assured to Monica, the mother of Augustine, one of the great teachers of the Christian Church. In his early manhood Augustine was a brilliant, but dissolute, teacher of rhetoric. His mother was an earnest Christian and grieved over her son's sinful ways. But she never ceased to pray for him, and she always hoped for the day when he would eventually become a Christian. Her prayers were answered. Augustine not only became a Christian but also one of the most influential men the Christian church has ever known.

In his religious classic, *The Confessions of St. Augustine,* he not only recorded his own inner life, but also expressed his noble appreciation for the faithfulness of his mother. At the time of his conversion, he said: "If I am thy child, O God, it is because thou didst give me such a mother."

1089 As a young man George Washington was about to go to sea as a midshipman. Everything was in readiness; his trunk had been taken on board the boat. As he went to bid his mother farewell, he saw tears in her eyes. Realizing that his plans were against his mother's will, he said to his servant, "Go and tell them to bring my trunk back. I will not go away and break my mother's heart."

His mother was very much impressed with her son's decision and said: "George, God has promised to bless the children that honor their parents; and I believe he will bless you"; *ref. 1082.*

† † †

1090
> To mothers weary and distrest
> Send comfort; to the toil-worn rest.
> The mother sick restore to health,
> Give needy mothers of thy wealth.
> Pity the mother children shun,
> And visit the forsaken one.
> Keep motherhood from sin and shame,
> Worthy of its exalted name.
> God bless the kind and busy hands
> Of faithful mothers in all lands.
> Keep thou the lips pure, undefiled,
> That form the language of a child.
> — Anon

ref. 1082

† † †

1091 The true beauty of women is not something external, but something within the heart, "a meek and quiet spirit, which is in the sight of God of great price" 1 Pe 3:4, the life of a regenerate soul, the life that is renewed in the image of Christ, the life that is hidden with Christ in God, the life which the Holy Spirit produces through the heart-changing and soul-saving Word of God: Ps 45:13; 2 Cor 5:17.

This beauty is not something corruptible, like perishable ornaments of gold or silver which may be seen, but an inward beauty of the soul unseen by men but precious in the eyes of God. But though invisible, its presence may be known by the fruits it produces, fruits of the Spirit, such as "love, joy, peace, longsuffering, gentleness, goodness, faith, meekness, and temperance," Ga 5:23,24.

Betsey Patterson, of Baltimore, was regarded as the most beautiful woman in America in the early years of the 19th century, and the charm of her beauty was acknowledged in the highest circles of Europe. Fortune smiled on her. She was wealthy, and, in the words of the TV commercial, she had everything. However, already in middle age she wrote to a friend: "I am dying with boredom. The Princess Galitizin tries to keep me up to the toil of dressing by telling me I am a beauty. I am tired of life, and tired of having lived." Such was the melancholy confession of a woman who had great beauty of body. But it adds up to nothing when compared to the inner beauty of the soul; *ref. 1083.*

† † †

1092
Thanks God for mothers, young and old,
Who live today within Christ's fold;
Who pattern, as in days of yore,
The godly mothers, gone before,
Whose hands repose — complete their task.
Thank God for these! Then Lord, we ask,
Bless mothers who for us still pray.
Thank God for them this Mother's Day.
— Anon

ref. 1082

† † †

1093 A teenager who was the idol of her mother became involved in a car accident with a boy friend. Brought to the hospital in a critical condition she was placed in intensive care. After the doctor had examined her condition, she regained consciousness and overheard him speaking to her mother. Then, calling to her mother, she said: "Mother, you have taught me how to primp, how to dance, how to sip my cocktail, and how to hold my cigarette, but you have not taught me how to die!" *ref. 1083.*
— Watchman Examiner, adapted

† † †

1094 J. Sterling Morton, founder of Arbor Day and one of Nebraska's two famous sons in Statuary Hall, took his motherless sons to visit his wife's grave. He asked the boys to read the inscription on the newly erected tombstone which mentioned her name, that she was the wife of J. Sterling Morton and mother of the three sons whose names were chiseled in full. The father told the boys that if any of them ever disgraced his mother, he had arranged with a stonecutter to chisel off his name.

Often the sons, who rose to places of eminence, recalled with admiration the warning of their father, but they attributed the real preventive against disgracing their mother to her Christian training and example. Love rather than fear kept their names there; *ref. 1082.*
— The Chaplain, adapted

† † †

1095
A careful mother I must be,
A little daughter follows me,
I do not dare to go astray,
For fear she'll go the selfsame way.

She's only just a bit past three,
But I see in her a smaller me.
Like me she says she's going to be,
This precious babe who follows me.

She likes to help me cook and sew,
She follows me where'er I go.
Not once can I escape her eyes,
Whate'er I do she always tries.

She acts like I'm almost divine,
Believes in every word of mine.
The base in me she must not see,
This trusting child who follows me.

Lord! make me conscious as I go,
Through summer sun and winter snow,
That I am building for the years to be,
A future mother who follows me.
— Martha E. Lambert, in
Christian Parent
ref. 1083

† † †

1096
GIVE THEM THE FLOWERS NOW

Closed eyes cannot see the white roses,
Cold hands cannot hold them, you know;
Breath that is stilled cannot gather
The odors that sweet from them blow.
Death, with a peace beyond dreaming,
Its children of earth does endow;
Life is the time we can help them,
SO GIVE THEM THE FLOWERS NOW.

Just a kind word or a greeting,
Just a warm grasp or a smile —
These are the flowers that lighten
The burdens of many a mile.
After the journey is over,
After tired hands drop the plow,
What is the use of them, tell me?
SO GIVE THEM THE FLOWERS NOW!
— Anon
ref. 1082

† † †

271

1097 God has designated woman's place in the world and defined her relationship to her husband, and the history of the human race testifies to the wisdom of God's design. Let there be no desire on the part of woman to be different from what God wants her to be. Let there be no attempt to withdraw from the sphere in which God has placed her. Let her not be envious of man's place in life, as though it were more important than the place God has given her. Let her, rather, thank God for the noble position she occupies, for the many wonderful privileges and advantages she enjoys, and for the tremendous influence she exerts.

— selected

ref. 1082

† † †

1098 Anna Jarvis, who first suggested that one day each year be set aside and observed as Mother's Day, once wrote:

"The man who does not esteem some good woman as a mother is to be pitied, not only because he has missed life's crowning joy, the inspiration of a mother's love, but because his manhood has lost a gentleness and a sympathy and a reverence that ennobles in a way nothing else does. A man without mother-love in his heart is next in isolation to a man without a country"; *ref. 1082*.

(ref.: Education 315-358; Teachers 1434-1459)

The Office of Pastor

1099 To be a pastor one must be called by God: Ac 20:28; 1 Cor 4:1; 12:28,29; Eph 4:11,12;

The pastoral office is a continuation of the ministerial office of the apostles: Mt 28:18-20; Jn 20:21-23; 2 Cor 5:19,20; Php 2:25; Col 4:7; 2 Tm 2:2; Tt 1:5; 1 Pe 5:1; *ref. 643,644,1104.*

Alternate Titles

1100 Pastors are also referred to as:

Angels of the Church: Re 1:20;
Ambassadors for Christ: 2 Cor 5:20;
Elders: 1 Tm 5:17;
Fishers of men: Mt 4:19;
Laborers together with God: 1 Cor 3:9;
Ministers of Christ: 1 Cor 3:5; 4:1;
Pastors: Jr 3:15; Eph 4:11;
Preachers: Ro 10:14; 2 Pe 2:5;
Servants of Christ: Php 1:1;
Servants of the church: 2 Cor 4:5;
Servants of God: 2 Tm 2:24; Tt 1:1;
Shepherds: Jr 23:4; Eze 34:10; Jn 21:15-17; Ac 20:28;
Soldiers of Christ: Php 2:25; 2 Tm 2:3,4;
Stewards of the mysteries of God: 1 Cor 4:1; Tt 1:7; 1 Pe 4:10;
Teachers: Is 30:20; 1 Tm 3:2; 4:11;
Watchmen: Is 62:6; Eze 3:17; He 13:17; *ref. 1109.*

Qualifications

1101 They are required to be:

Faithful: Jr 23:28; 1 Cor 4:2; 1 Pe 4:11; *ref. 1109,1118;*

Able to teach: 1 Tm 3:2; 2 Tm 2:2,25,26;

Well indoctrinated, able rightly to divide the "word of truth" (law and gospel): 2 Tm 2:15;

Humble: Mt 23:8,10; Mk 10:42-45; Lk 22:26; Ro 12:3,10; Php 2:5f; 1 Pe 5:5; *ref. 1110,1122;*

Patient: 1 Tm 3:3;

Able to endure hardness: 1 Tm 6:12; 2 Tm 1:8; 2:3,4; 3:9-14;

Of good reputation: 1 Tm 3:2-7,15; 2 Tm 2:22; Tt 1:6-9; 2:7,8; *ref. 1107,1110,1120,1121,1123.*

Duties of the Pastoral Office

1102 They are called to:

Preach the Gospel of Christ: Mk 16:15; Lk 24:47,48; Ac 5:42; 10:36; Ro 16:25; 1 Cor 1:23; 2:2; 9:16; 2 Cor 4:5; 5:19,20; Ga 1:8,9; 2 Tm 4:2; *ref. 162,168,1104,1108,1111-1115,1119;*

Teach all things that Christ has commanded: Mt 28:18-20; 2 Tm 2:2; 3:14-17; and declare all the counsel of God: Ac 20:27;

Present the truths of God's Word clearly and intelligently: 1 Cor 2:4,5,13; 14:8; *ref. 1111,1124,1133;*

Feed and guard the flock entrusted to their care: Jn 21:15-17; Ac 20:28; He 13:17; 1 Pe 5:2; *ref. 1109;*

Give heed to doctrine: 1 Tm 1:3,4; 4:16; 2 Tm 1:13,14; 4:2,3; Tt 2:1,7; 1 Pe 4:11; study the Scriptures: 1 Tm 4:13;

Admonish, reprove, rebuke, exhort and comfort: Ac 20:21; Ro 15:4; 2 Cor 1:3,4; 1 Th 4:18; 5:11,14; 1 Tm 5:20; 2 Tm 3:16,17; 4:2; Tt 2:15; 3:10; *ref. 1109,1112,1114,1123,1126;*

Be impartial in their dealings with members: 1 Tm 5:21;

Be an example to their flock: 1 Cor 4:16; Php 4:9; 1 Tm 4:12; 5:22; 6:11,12; Tt 2:7; 1 Pe 5:3; *ref. 422;*

Pray for the members of their flock: Ro 1:9; Eph 1:15f; 3:14f; Php 1:4; Col 1:3f; 4:12; 1 Th 1:2f;

Be active in mission work: 2 Tm 4:5. Cp Mt 9:35-38; Jn 10:16; Ac 1:8; *ref. 1125.*

The Duties of Members to Their Pastor

1103 The members of their flock are to:

Regard them as Christ's ministers: 1 Cor 4:1; 2 Cor 5:20; *ref 1103,1105;*

Receive their proclamation of God's word as God's message: Lk 10:16; 1 Th 2:13; while at the same time being on guard against false doctrine: Mt 7:15; Ac 17:11; 20:29-31; Ro 16:17; 2 Cor 11:13; Eph 4:14; Col 2:8; 1 Tm 4:1-3; 2 Tm 3:13; He 13:9; 2 Pe 2:1-3; 2 Jn 7; Jude 3; *ref. 1116,1117,1131;*

Honor them because of their office: 1Th 5:12,13;

Follow their instruction: He 13:17;

Follow their example: 2 Th 3:9; 1 Tm 4:12; Tt 2:7; He 13:7;

Pray for them: Eph 6:18,19; 1 Th 5:25; 2 Th 3:1; *ref. 1127-1130;*

Provide for their needs: Lk 10:7; Ga 6:6,7; 1 Cor 9:14; 1 Tm 5:18; *ref. 1132.*

Resources

1104 The Scriptures distinguish between the office of the ministry and the priesthood of all believers. All true believers in Christ are made kings and priests who bring spiritual sacrifices: Ro 12:1; He 10:19-22; 13:15; 1 Pe 2:9; and into their charge Christ has given all the rights and powers of his kingdom: Mt 18:18-20; 1 Cor 3:21-23. But God has also established Christian congregations and groups of congregations and has instituted the office of the holy ministry for the purpose of publicly preaching his word, administering the sacraments, and ministering to the needs of the members.

When Christ called the twelve apostles: Mt 10:1f; Lk 9:1f; and later the seventy, Lk 10:1f; he made provision that the New Testament church, beginning with the Day of Pentecost, might perform its work in the world through congregations: Ac 2:41,42,47; 4:4; each having its own servant of the Word, Ac 20:28. These ministers were given duties which paralleled those of the apostles, and the apostles regarded them as fellow-servants of the Lord: 1 Cor 3:5,22; Col 1:7; 2 Tm 2:2; He 13:17; 1 Pe 5:1,2; *ref. 1099.*

† † †

1105 I consider the Christian ministry the highest calling in the world and most intimately related to the most exalted life and service here and the destiny beyond. I consider it my greatest joy and glory to hold up Christ as the Hope and Savior of the world.

— Theodore Roosevelt

ref. 1103

† † †

1106
Fishers of men, what a calling sublime,
Fishing for men in the ocean of time,
Casting the net of the gospel abroad,
Drawing in souls for the kingdom of God!

Fishers of men, though you struggle and strain,
Facing great odds, often toiling in vain;
Jesus, your Master, who bids you to do,
Blessings abundant has promised you!

Toil on in patience, proclaim to the end
Jesus, the Savior, the sinner's great Friend!
Labor and pray till the victory is won,
Till you receive his approving "Well done!"

— W. G. Polack

ref. 1100

† † †

1107 A Texas paper commented as follows: "The preacher has a great time. If his hair is gray, he is old. If he is a young man, he hasn't had experience. If he has ten children, he has too many; if he has none, he isn't setting a good example. If his wife sings in the choir, she is presuming; if she doesn't, she isn't interested in her husband's work. If a preacher reads from notes, he is a bore; if he speaks extemporaneously, he isn't deep enough. If he stays at home in his study, he doesn't mix enough with the people; if he is seen around the streets, he ought to be at home getting up a good sermon. If he calls on some poor family, he is playing to the grandstand; if he calls at the home of the wealthy, he is an aristocrat. Whatever he does, someone could have told him to do better." *ref. 1101.*

† † †

1108
　　Sow thou the seed, in every clime
　　　And by all waters sow,
　　In God's own way, in God's own time,
　　　Thy far-flung seed shall grow.

　　　　　　　　　　　　　　　　— Anon
　　ref. 1102

† † †

1109 When Pompeii was destroyed there were many persons buried in the ruins who were afterward found in very different positions. They found some in vaults, as if they had gone there for security. There were some found in lofty chambers. But where did they find the Roman sentinel? They found him standing at the city gate, where he had been placed by the captain, with his hands still grasping the weapon. There, while the earth shook beneath him; there, while the floods of ashes and cinders overwhelmed him, he had stood at his post; and there, after a thousand years he was found. So let Christians stand by their duty and the post at which their Captain places them.

　　　　　　　　　　　　　　　　— *Gospel Trumpet*
ref. 1102

† † †

1110
　　I do not ask
　　　That crowds may throng the temple,
　　That standing room be priced;
　　　I only ask that, as I voice the message,
　　They may see Christ!

　　I do not ask
　　　For churchly pomp or pageant,
　　Or music such as wealth alone can buy;
　　　I only ask that, as I voice the message,
　　He may be nigh!

　　I do not ask
　　　That men may sound my praises,
　　Or headlines spread my name abroad;
　　　I only ask that, as I voice the message,
　　Hearts may find God!

　　I do not ask
　　　For temporal place or laural,
　　Or of the world's distinction any part;
　　　I only ask, when I have voiced the message,
　　My Savior's Heart!

　　　　　　　　　　　　　　　　— Anon
　　ref. 1101

† † †

1111 A pastor, whose congregation had become much dissatisfied with his preaching, on entering his pulpit one Sunday morning found a slip of paper with the words of John 12:21 written on it: "Sir, we would see Jesus." After much thought and self-examination he resolved, with the help of God, to preach Christ more clearly. The next Sunday he took for his text John 20:20, "Then the disciples were overjoyed when they saw the Lord."

— selected

1112 A modernist minister preached to a vacant congregation. He tried to show the people that there was no punishment after death and so also no hell. "The doctrine of hell," he said, "is a cruel invention of man's imagination and contrary to the love of God." When he had completed his talk he told the congregation that he could preach for them again in four weeks and asked whether they wanted to hear him again. Finally, one of the most respected merchants of the town arose and said: "Sir, if your doctrine is true we do not need you; if it is false, we do not want you. So you need not come again."

— *Bible Expositor and Illuminator*

ref. 1102

1113 The only thing that will do men permanent good is the preaching of the gospel, that gospel which men, as a rule, do not like to have preached "at them." Preaching without the grand, rugged truths of the cross of Christ is a mere wind pleasing, or unpleasing, according to the endowments of the preacher, ruffling for a moment the surface places, but leaving the greater depths untouched and undisturbed. On the great bell of St. Paul's Cathedral in London is graven the text from St. Paul: "Woe is me if I preach not the gospel!" Would that that motto might speak in all our church bells and be blazed over every pulpit in our land! Woe is me, not if I lack the gifts of imagination and poesy, not if my logic falters, not if I lack the silvery tongue of Apollo, but woe is me if when the sermon is ended and the last hymn has been sung and the benediction has been pronounced and the congregation dispersed, never again to meet together in the same units — then woe is me if I have not preached to them the gospel, if I have not told them of the wages of sin and pointed them to that Savior in whom implicitly resting and trusting we have mercy and forgiveness of all of our sins.

— Rev. C. E. Macartney

1114   I preach as never sure to preach again,
                  And as a dying man to dying men.

— Richard Baxter

1115 Everybody knows that large flocks of pigeons assemble at the stroke of the great clock in the square of St. Mark, Venice. Believe me, it is not the music of the bell that attracts them; they can hear that every hour. They come, Mr. Preacher, for food, and no mere sound will long collect them. This is a hint for filling your meeting house; it must be done not merely by that fine bell-like voice of yours, but by all the neighborhood's being assured that spiritual food is to be had when you open your mouth. Barley for pigeons, good sir, and the gospel for men and women. Try it in earnest and you cannot fail; you will soon be saying: "Who are they that fly as a cloud and as doves to their windows?"

— C. H. Spurgeon

ref. 1102

† † †

1116 "Know ye not that a little leaven leaveneth the whole lump?" That is why the church should be very careful that no false prophet gets into her pulpits. A man full of modern theories might do more harm in a single sermon than could be counteracted in a month of Sundays. The leaven never changes. It is a condition of decay and decay is incipient death. The only thing to do with the leaven of false doctrine is to purge it out and keep it out. The gateway of your heart should have a guard set before it. The true guard of the heart is the knowledge of the truth with a deep conviction as to its eternal value and effect. Your spirit should be as sensitive to false doctrine as your flesh is sensitive to fire; it should shrink from it as a consuming curse.

— Parson

1117 A liberal young minister, full of "higher critical theories," came to a congregation and began to expound his theories to the members. Two years later he was called to one of the leading members who was very ill. "Shall I read to you from the Bible and pray with you?" he asked. "Yes," answered the man and beckoned to his wife to bring the minister his Bible. As he opened it, he saw a strange sight. Some books were taken out of it altogether; some pages were torn out; some chapters were gone; some verses were cut out; in short, the whole Bible was shamefully mutilated. "Have you no better Bible than this?" the minister asked. "No," said the sick man, "when you came, I had a whole Bible. But as soon as you told us that one book was fiction, I tore it out; and that one chapter was not true, I removed it; and that some of the stories were just fables, I cut them out. If you stay here for another year, I am afraid I shall have only the two covers and nothing else."

— *Moody Monthly*

ref. 1103

† † †

1118 John Shepherd, a famous preacher, declared: "The secret of my success as a preacher is in these three things: 1) The studying of my sermons very frequently cost me tears. 2) Before I preach a sermon to others, I derived good from it myself. 3) I have always gone into the pulpit as if I were immediately after to render an account to my Master;" *ref. 1101*.

† † †

1119 God's Word has been my sole study and concern, the sole subject of my preaching and writing. Other than this I have done nothing in the matter. This same Word has, while I slept or made merry, accomplished this great thing.

— Martin Luther

ref. 1102

1120   An eloquent word for the Master,
       Yet half for the speaker, too;
   For he sought as his gain the praises of men
       And not the good he might do.

   So the angels sadly left it,
       And for all of its lofty sound
   Men tossed it a while to and fro with a smile
       And then let it fall to the ground.

   A stammering word for the Master —
       Blundering, timid, and slow;
   But the best he could do, for his purpose was true,
       But his heart was a-thumping so.

   Yet the angels seized it and bore it
       On pinions happy and strong
   And made it a sword in the war of the Lord,
       The struggle of right against wrong.

   For the battle is not to the giant,
       The race is not to the fleet,
   And an armor of might for the bitterest fight
       Is found at the Savior's feet.
                    — Anon

ref. 1101

† † †

1121 The elders of a vacant congregation once approached their bishop to suggest to them a pastor to fill the vacancy. "How big a man do you want for your church?" they were asked. One of the elders immediately answered: "We don't care so much about his size, but we want him to be tall enough to reach heaven when he is on his knees;" *ref. 1103.*

† † †

1122   Any little corner, Lord
   In thy vineyard wide,
   Where thou bidst me work for thee,
   There will I abide;
   Miracle of saving grace
   That thou gavest me a place
   ANYWHERE.

   Where we pitch our nightly tent
   Surely matters not;
   If the day for thee be spent
   Blessed is the spot.
   Quickly we the tent may fold,
   Cheerful march through storm and cold
   ANYWHERE.

All along the wilderness
Let us keep our sight
On the moving pillar fixed,
Constant day and night;
Then the heart will make its home
Willing led by thee to roam
ANYWHERE!

— Anon

ref. 1101

† † †

1123 It is said of a famous preacher that he always preached "as a dying man to dying men." Such preaching is always effective. — A minister visiting a penitentiary one Saturday was invited by the Christian warden to speak to the inmates the next day. That evening the minister felt impressed to go to the penitentiary and learn the details regarding the service. Noting two chairs draped in black in the main assembly room, he inquired as to the reason. Said the warden: "Those two chairs are draped for death. Your sermon will be the last which these men, to be executed, will hear." You can understand that Browning and Emerson figured very little in that sermon. In most audiences there are chairs invisibly draped for death.

— adapted

ref. 1102

† † †

1124 A minister preached on 1 Corinthians 13:1. The reporter of the daily newspaper got it right, but the linotype operator, in setting the word "charity," made the mistake of using an "l" instead of an "h," and the proofreader overlooked it. So the minister was reported in the morning paper as having preached from the following text: "Though I speak with the tongues of men and of angels, and have not *clarity*, I am become as sounding brass, or a tinkling cymbal." Commenting on the story the editor says: "As it appears in print it was not New Testament truth, but it was truth, nevertheless. The people want the preacher to be luminous rather than voluminous, and the preacher who is without clarity will soon be without a congregation."

— *Moody Monthly*

ref. 1102

† † †

1125 Two ministers' wives were sitting on the veranda of a parsonage, chatting with each other as they mended their husbands' trousers. "I can't understand," said one of them, "why your congregation is growing so fast and becoming so prosperous while ours is not." "Well," said the other wife, "if you were an observant person, you would have noticed that I am patching my husband's trousers at the knees, whereas you are putting patches on the seat!"

— selected

ref. 1101,1102

1126 A minister, serving a new church, was highly complimented on his first sermon. Many members told him that it was just what the congregation needed. The next Sunday the congregation was greatly puzzled because he preached the same sermon as before. The third Sunday, when the same sermon was preached again, the elders asked the pastor for an explanation. He said: "You told me the first Sunday how much you needed just that sermon, and I watched day after day for some change in your life. But there was none, and so I preached the same sermon over and over."

— Moody Monthly

ref. 1102

† † †

1127 An aged pastor was once asked: "What is the first thing you would do if you were a layman in the church?" After a moment's reflection he replied: "The first thing I would do is to fire the minister." "You mean you would fire him out?" "No," said the pastor, "I mean I would fire him up."

1128 When the children of Israel came to the wilderness of Rephidim, they were attacked by the Amalekites. Whereupon we read, "Moses said to Joshua, 'Choose some of our men and go out to fight the Amalekites. Tomorrow I will stand on top of the hill with the staff of God in my hands.' So Joshua fought the Amalekites as Moses had ordered, and Moses, Aaron and Hur went to the top of the hill. As long as Moses held up his hands, the Israelites were winning, but whenever he lowered his hands, the Amalekites were winning. When Moses' hands grew tired, they took a stone and put it under him and he sat on it. Aaron and Hur held his hands up — one on one side, one on the other — so that his hands remained steady till sunset. So Joshua overcame the Amalekite army with the sword," Ex 17:9ff. — Symbolically the scene portrays the support which the members of the congregation are to give their pastor in the church's battle against the spiritual powers of darkness. Only when church members uphold the hands of their pastor can the cause of the church prevail.

1129
> The servants thou hast called
>   And to thy church art giving
> Preserve in doctrine pure
>   And holiness of living.
> Thy Spirit fill their hearts,
>   Endue their tongues with power;
> What they should boldly speak,
>   Oh, give them in that hour!

— Eberhard L. Fischer

1130
> Lord of the Church, we humbly pray
> For those who guide us in thy way
>   And speak thy holy Word.
> With love divine their hearts inspire
> And touch their lips with hallowed fire
>   The needful strength afford.

Help them to preach the Truth of God,
Redemption thro' the Savior's blood,
    Nor let the Spirit cease
On all the church his gifts to show'r —
To them a messenger of pow'r;
    To us, of life and peace.

So may they live to thee alone,
Then hear the welcome word "Well done,"
    And take their crown above;
Enter into their Master's joy
And all eternity employ
    In praise and bliss and love.

— Edward Osler

1131 A good way to get behind the Pastor is to be in front of him every Sunday.

1132 A farmer objected to his pastor getting $40 per week for preaching two sermons. He argued: "That's $20 per hour." The next week the farmer brought a load of wheat to the mill. The minister happened to be there and watched him unload, then go into the office and get a check for $250 for the wheat. "See here," said the minister, "you objected to me getting $20 per hour and you are making ten times that." "Oh, no," said the farmer, "I just come to the mill to unload." The minister replied: "And so do I just go to the pulpit to unload." "I see the point," said the farmer, "and I am going to pay more toward your salary; but, hereafter, pastor, please don't take so long to unload"; *ref. 1103.*

† † †

1133 David Garrick, the great English actor, was once asked why actors were so much more effective than preachers in moving the audience. This was his answer: "Actors present fiction as though it were fact; too many preachers present fact as though it were fiction."

— *Sunday School Times*
ref. 1102

1134 Peace with God which man originally enjoyed in Paradise was broken by sin: Gn 3:1-24; Is 48:22; Jr 8:14,15; As a consequence,

Man became an enemy of God: Is 48:18,22; 65:2; Jr 7:23,24; Ro 8:7; Eph 2:2; 1 Pe 4:3;

Hatred, racial strife and warfare resulted among mankind: Ps 120:7; 140:2; Jr 17:9; Mt 15:19; Lk 9:53; 21:10; Jn 4:9; Ac 10:28; 11:3; 19:34; Ga 2:12; 5:19-21; Jas 4:1; *ref. 1138-1140.*

1135 God re-established peace between sinful man and himself through Christ:

This reconciliation was effected through the atoning death of Jesus Christ, the Prince of Peace: Is 9:6; 53:5; Jn 14:27; 16:33; 20:19,21; Ro 4:25-5:1; 2 Cor 5:19; Col 1:20-22; *ref. 1138-1144,1146;*

It is proclaimed and offered to all mankind freely, by grace, through faith: Lk 2:10,11,14; Ac 10:36; Ro 5:1; 10:15; Eph 2:13,14,17; *ref. 1146;*

It is a gift of the Holy Spirit to all believers: Eph 2:8,9; Ga 1:3; 5:22; 2 Th 3:16; Tt 3:4-7; He 13:20,21.

1136 Peace with God produces blessed results:

It brings inner peace: Ps 4:8; 29:11; 119:165; 125:5; 147:14; Is 26:3; Lk 2:28-32; Jn 14:27; 16:33; Ro 5:1f; 14:17; Php 4:7; 1 Pe 1:2; *ref. 1141-1144,1146;*

It creates peace between man and his fellowmen: Pr 16:7; Eph 2:13-22; Col 1:20; 1 Pe 5:14; *ref. 1141-1144.*

1137 Christians are exhorted to strive for peace:

In their relations with their fellowmen: Ps 34:14; Jr 29:7; Mt 5:9; Ro 12:18; 1 Tm 2:1,2; 2 Tm 2:22; He 12:14; Jas 3:18; 1 Pe 3:8-11; *ref. 1139,1140,1145,1146;*

In the church: Ps 122:6-9; Ro 14:19; 15:6; 1 Cor 1:10; 14:33; 2 Cor 13:11,12; Eph 4:1-3; Php 1:27; Col 3:15; 1 Th 5:13.

Resources

1138

Were half the power that fills the world with terror,
Were half the wealth bestowed on camps and courts,
Given to redeem the human mind from error
There were no need of arsenals or forts!

The warrior's name would be a name abhorred!
And every nation, that would lift again
Its hand against a brother, on its forehead
Would wear forevermore the curse of Cain!

Down the dark future, through long generations,
The echoing sounds grow fainter then cease;
And like a bell, with solemn, sweet vibrations,
I hear once more the voice of Christ say, "Peace!"

Peace! and no longer from its brazen portals
　　The blast of war's great organ shakes the skies!
But beautiful as songs of the immortals,
　　The holy melodies of love arise.
　　　　　　　　　　　　— Henry W. Longfellow
　　　　ref. 1134,1135

1139 The night before Franklin D. Roosevelt died, he wrote: "We seek peace — enduring peace. More than an end to war, we want an end to the beginnings of all wars — yes, an end to this brutal, inhuman, and thoroughly impractical method of settling differences between governments. The mere conquest of our enemies is not enough. We must go on to do all in our power to conquer the doubts and fears, the ignorance and the greed which made this horror possible. Today we are faced with the pre-eminent fact that, if civilization is to survive, we must cultivate the science of human relationships — the ability of all peoples, of all kinds, to live together and work together, in the same world, at peace. Today as we move against the terrible scourge of war — as we go forward toward the greatest contribution that any generation of human beings can make in this world — the contribution of lasting peace, I ask you to keep up your faith ... The only limit to our realization of tomorrow will be our doubts of today. Let us move forward with strong and active faith."

1140 When Japan surrendered, General McArthur said: "We have had our last chance. If we do not now devise some greater and more equitable system, Armageddon will be at our door. The problem basically is theological and involves a spiritual recrudescence and improvement in human character. . . It must be of the spirit if we are to save the flesh"; *ref. 1134,1137.*

† † †

1141 Where in all the world could we find one eloquent enough adequately to describe the great benefits of peace and the awful harm and detriment wrought by war? In days of peace we enjoy all those good things which God is pleased to give us, and he prevents the numerous evils that may harm us from touching us. Where peace reigns, there half of heaven on earth may be said to be.
　　　　　　　　　　　　— Martin Luther
ref. 1136

† † †

1142　　　　The world can neither give nor take,
　　　　　　　　Nor can they comprehend,
　　　　　　　The peace of God which Christ has brought —
　　　　　　　　The peace which knows no end.
　　　　　　　　　　　　　　— Anon

1143　　　　Jesus only can impart
　　　　　　　　Balm to heal the smitten heart;

Peace that flows from sin forgiv'n,
Joy that lifts the soul to heav'n.
— William McComb

† † †

1144 Around the year 1907 there was fear of war over the boundary line between Argentina and Chile. Both nations had bought cannon and were preparing for war when the two countries settled the matter by arbitration. They took the bronze which was bought for the cannon and from it the statue of the *Christ of the Andes* was made. It stands on the new boundary line. In one hand of the Christ there is a cross, and the other hand is held out as in a blessing. On one side of the tablet below the figure is written, "He is our Peace, who hath made both one"; and on the other side, "Sooner shall the mountains crumble into dust than the people of Argentina and Chile break the faith which they have pledged at the feet of Christ the Redeemer"; *ref. 1135,1136.*

† † †

1145   Lord make me the instrument of your peace;
Where there is hatred may I bring love;
Where there is malice, pardon;
Where there is discord, harmony;
Where there is error, truth;
Where there is doubt, faith;
Where there is despair, hope;
Where there is darkness, your light;
Where there is sadness may I bring joy.
O Master, may I seek not so much
To be comforted as to comfort,
To be understood as to understand,
To be loved as to love,
For it is in giving that we receive,
It is in losing our lives that we shall find them,
It is in forgiving that we shall be forgiven,
It is in dying that we shall rise up to eternal life.
— Francis of Assisi

ref. 1137

† † †

1146 "Peace be with you!" Jn 20:19. These were the first words with which the resurrected Christ greeted his terrified disciples. These words assured them that he still loved them despite the fact that they had so shamefully forsaken him in his hour of greatest need. But these words had far greater meaning. They were words of benediction which conferred on them all the blessings of his death and resurrection.

This same blessing is bestowed upon us as the resurrected Christ comes to us through his life-giving word, which "tells of benediction, of pardon, grace,

285

and peace, of joy that has no ending, of love which cannot cease." Faith is the hand that reaches out and takes what Christ freely offers. It does not rely on visible evidence, as did doubting Thomas, but simply believes Christ's words and trusts in his promises: Jn 20:24-29.

Having experienced the blessings of Christ's peace in our own lives we will recognize our solemn obligation and blessed privilege to bring this peace to others: Ro 10:15. This is the great unfinished task that Christ entrusted to his disciples and to us when he said: "As the Father has sent me, I am sending you." And today, as then, he enables us to perform this task by granting us the presence and power of his Holy Spirit: Jn 20:21-23; Ac 1:8; *ref. 1135.*

PRAYER 1147-1187

(ref.: Lord's Prayer 897-940; Thanksgiving 1503-1531)

Definition

1147 Prayer is an act of worship in which we commune with God to:

Adore and praise him: 1 Chr 29:10-13; Ps 8:1; 51:15; 95:1-6; 96:1-13; 103:1-5; 107:21; 137:1; 139:14; *ref. 1160,1175;*

Confess our sins and unworthiness and implore his mercy, grace and forgiveness: Gn 32:10; Ps 32:5-6; 51:1-12; 86:3; Lk 15:18,19; 18:13; *ref. 1160.*

Ask for help in time of need: 2 Kgs 19:14-19; Ps 54; 56; 69; 102; 140; Jon 2:1-9; *ref. 1151, 1154-1157.*

Intercede for others: 1 Tm 2:1; Jas 5:16; *ref. 1156,1160,1185;*

Thank God for his goodness: Ps 16:7; 100:1-5; 136:1, Lk 17:15,16; Eph 5:20; Php 4:6; Col 3:17; 1 Th 5:18; *ref. 1158-1160.*

Why We Are To Pray

1148 Prayer is commanded by God: 1 Chr 16:1; Ps 27:8; 50:15; Mt 7:7; Php 4:6; and God promises to hear our prayers: Ps 50:15; 65:2; 91:15; 145:18; Is 65:24; Mt 6:6; 7:7,8; Jn 16:23; Eph 3:20; He 10:23; *ref. 1161,1172,1187;*

We are to pray because of our needs and the needs of others: Ps 122:6; Jr 29:7; Mt 5:44; 6:9-13; 26:41; Eph 6:19; 1 Th 5:25; 1 Tm 2:1,2; Jas 5:13,16; *ref. 1163,1167,1176,1180.*

To Whom We Are To Pray

1149 Our prayers are to be addressed only to the Triune God, Son and Holy Ghost, for to him alone such honor is due, and he alone is able and willing to hear and to grant our prayers: Ps 65:2; 96:4,5; 115:3-8; Is 42:8; Mt 4:10; Jn 5:23; 14:13; 16:23; Ro 8:26; 1 Cor 8:5; Eph 2:18; He 10:19-22; *ref. 1169,1175,1180.*

How We Are To Pray

1150 In Christ's name, with faith in him as our Redeemer: Jn 14:13; 15:7,26; 16:23; Eph 5:20; 1 Tm 2:5; He 4:14-16; *ref. 1168,1172, 1186,1187;*

With firm trust that God will grant our prayer for the sake of Christ's merit: Mt 21:22; Mk 11:24; Jn 16:23; He 11:6; Jas 1:6; 1 Jn 5:14; *ref. 1161,1164,1169,1181;*

Persistently: Gn 18:32; 32:26; Mt 15:27; Lk 11:5-10; 18:1-7; Ac 12:5; but not with vain repetition: Mt 6:7; *ref. 1170.*

For What We Should Pray

1151 We are to pray for all things: Mt 6:11; Mk 11:24; Eph 5:20; Php 4:6; Col 3:17; 1 Th 5:17,18; 1 Tm 2:1; Jas 1:5; 5:13,14,18; 1 Pe 5:7;

Our prayers for spiritual blessings should be made unconditionally, for it is the Lord's will that we should have them, e.g., Lk 11:2,13; 17:5;

Our prayers for temporal blessings should be made conditionally, asking God to grant them if it is his will: Mt 6:10; 8:2; Lk 22:42; 1 Jn 5:14; cp Mt 20:20-23; 2 Cor 12:7-9; *ref. 1161,1162,1164,1165,1179.*

For Whom We Are To Pray

1152 For ourselves: Mt 26:41; Lk 21:36;

For our fellow men: Gn 18:23-32; Mt 8:5-9; 15:21-25; Eph 6:18; Jas 5:16;

For all men: 1 Tm 2:1; including our enemies: Mt 5:44; Lk 23:34; but not for the dead: He 9:27; *ref. 1174;*

For all who are in trouble: Lk 22:31,32; Ac 12:5; Jas 5:14; *ref. 1186;*

For the ministers of the Word and for the Christian Church: Jn 17:20; Ro 1:9; 2 Cor 1:11; Eph 1 :15,16; 3:14-19; 6:18,19; Php 1:4; Col 1:3; 4:12; 1 Th 1:2; 5:25;

For the conversion of others: Mt 9:37,38; Jn 17:20;

For all who are in authority: 1 Tm 2:2; *ref. 1182,1184,1185.*

Where We Are To Pray

1153 In private: 2 Kgs 4:33; Mt 6:6; and in the family circle: Jos 24:15; Mt 18:19,20; Lk 5:15,16; 6:12; Ac 10:1,2; *ref. 1173,1176;*

In the house of worship: Ps 26:12; 134:1,2; Lk 2:37; 19:46; Ac 1:14; 12:12; *ref. 1183;*

Everywhere: Mal 1:11; Jn 4:20-24; 1 Tm 2:8.

When We Are To Pray

1154 At all times: Ps 55:17; Lk 2:36; 18:1; 21:36; Ro 12:12; Eph 5:20; 6:18; Php 4:4; Col 3:17; 4:2; 1 Th 5:17; *ref. 1171;*

Especially in time of trouble: Ps 34:17,18; 50:15; 91:15; 102:2,17; Is 26:16; Jas 5:13. Examples: Israel in Egyptian bondage: Ex 2:23-25; the disciples in the storm at sea: Mt 8:23-27; Paul and Silas in prison at Philippi: Ac 16:25; *ref. 1176.*

Examples Of People Who Prayed

1155 Christ's example:

He prayed in private: Mk 1:35; 6:46,47; Lk 5:15,16; 6:12; 9:18; 22:41,42;

He prayed in public: Mt 11:25; Lk 3:21; Jn 11:41; 12:27,28;

He prayed for his disciples: Lk 22:31,32; Jn 14:16; 17:1f; cp He 7:25;

He prayed for his enemies: Lk 23:24;

He taught us to pray: Mt 6:5-15; Lk 11:1-13; *ref. 1177.*

1156 Examples of people who offered intercessory prayers:

Abraham prayed for the inhabitants of Sodom: Gn 18:23-33;

Moses prayed for the Israelites: Ex 32:31,32; Nu 14:19; Dt 9:26-29; cp the prayers of Samuel: 1 Sm 7:5f; of Daniel: Dn 9:3-19; and of Ezra: Ezr 9:5-15;

David prayed for his son Solomon: 1 Chr 29:19;

The Syrophenician woman prayed for her daughter: Mt 15:22f;

Stephen prayed for his enemies: Ac 7:60;

Paul prayed for his converts: Eph 1:16f; 3:14f; Col 1:9f; *ref. 1178, 1184,1186.*

1157 Other notable prayers:

The patriarch Jacob's prayer at Peniel: Gn 32:24-30;

King David's prayer of thanksgiving: 1 Chr 29:10-19;

King Solomon's prayer at the dedication of the temple: 1 Kgs 8:22-53; 20:1-11;

King Hezekiah's prayer for deliverance: 2 Kgs 19:14-19; 20:1-11;

The prayer of the prophet Jonah; Jon 2:1-9; *ref. 1184,1185.*

Resources

1158
> Prayer is the soul's sincere desire
> Unuttered or expressed,
> The motion of a hidden fire
> That trembles in the breast.
>
> Prayer is the Christian's vital breath,
> The Christian's native air,
> His watchword at the gates of death —
> He enters heaven with prayer.
>
> O Thou by whom we come to God,
> The Life, the Truth, the Way,
> The path of prayer thyself hast trod —
> Lord, teach us how to pray.
> — James Montgomery

1159 Remember, God respecteth not the arithmetic of our prayers, how many they are, nor the rhetoric of our prayers, how long they are, nor the music of our prayers, how methodical they are, but the divinity of our prayers, how heartsprung they are. Not gifts, but graces, prevail in prayer.
> — Trapp

1160 The various forms of prayers are summarized in the letters that form the word "Acts":

A doration
C onfession
T hanksgiving
S upplication
ref. 1147

† † †

1161 The fact that God has promised to hear and to answer prayer does not mean that he always grants the request for which we ask. Like the answer of a loving parent to the foolish and hurtful request of a child, God answers "No!" when in his wisdom and love he knows that the granting of our request would not serve for our good; cp Ex 33:20; Mt 20:21,22.

Again, God does not answer the prayers of those whose hands are defiled with blood and whose lips speak lies: Is 59:1-3f. On the contrary, the assurance of God's answer to prayer is contingent upon our repentance: 2 Chr 7:14; Lk 18:9-14; upon our sincerity: Ps 145:18,19; Jr 29:12,13; and upon our faith: Mt 21:22; Jn 15:7; 16:23; Jas 1:6,7; *ref. 1148.*

† † †

1162 A mother once had a deathly sick child. She insisted that God must heal him. The pastor who visited her counseled her not to dictate to God but to pray, "Not my will, but thine, be done." But she refused to pray thus and demanded that God hear and answer her prayer. Her request was granted. But after her son had grown to manhood he caused her much grief and was finally hanged on the gallows as a murderer; *ref. 1151.*

† † †

1163 Dr. Hyslop, one time superintendent of Bethlehem Royal Hospital, at an annual meeting of the British Medical Association, said: "As an alienist and one whose whole life has been concerned with the sufferings of the mind, I would state that of all hygienic measures to counteract disturbed, sleep-distressed spirits, and all the miserable sequels of a distressed mind, I would undoubtedly give the first place to the simple habit of prayer"; *ref. 1148.*

† † †

1164

> I know not by what methods rare,
> But this I know . . . God answers prayer.
> I know that he has given his word,
> Which tells me prayer is always heard,
> And will be answered, soon or late,
> And so I pray and calmly wait.
>
> I know not if the blessing sought
> Will come in just the way I thought,
> But leave my prayers with him alone,
> Whose will is wiser than my own . . .

Assured that he will grant my quest
Or send some answer far more blest.

— Anon

ref. 1151

† † †

1165 Prayer is not a blank check which the petitioner fills in indiscriminately and then presents to the Throne of Grace. In that event man would rule the world, and the result would be conflict, chaos, and disorder. Thoughtful parents have a plan for their children, one that is designed for their welfare. Within the scope of this plan the wishes and requests of the children are granted. So, too, our heavenly Father has a plan of wisdom and love for us, and it is within that plan that our prayers are answered. "This is the assurance we have in approaching God: that if we ask anything according to his will, he hears us," 1 Jn 5:14; *ref. 1151.*

† † †

1166 Martin Luther stated that at times he was so busy with his work that he required three hours of prayer in a day. No wonder that a historian speaks of the Reformation as having been born and sustained in Luther's prayer-closet.

Never find the time too short or the business too rushing to offer a prayer for the Lord's guidance and blessing; *ref. 1148.*

† † †

1167 One day when a student entered the laboratory of Pasteur, he found the scientist bending over his microscope. Not wishing to disturb him the student was about to leave. When Pasteur looked up, the student said: "I thought you were praying." "I was," said Pasteur, as he turned again to his microscope; *ref. 1148.*

† † †

1168   From every stormy wind that blows,
From every swelling tide that flows,
There is a calm, a sure retreat;
'Tis found beneath the mercy-seat.

Ah, whither could we flee for aid,
When tempted, desolate, dismayed;
Or how the hosts of hell defeat,
Had suffering saints no mercy-seat?

— Anon

ref. 1150

† † †

1169 In a little country telegraph office a visitor sat by the stove while the operator prepared to send out a message he had just received. The visitor happened to get a glimpse of the destination of the message. "That's one of those little places up in the Northwest, isn't it?" he asked. When the operator nodded in the affirmative, the visitor continued: "Well, according to the papers, they have been having a terrible snowstorm up there lately — roads all blocked and everything. More than likely, the message will never get into the hands of the man it's intended for even after you sent it." The operator listened with growing impatience, and then replied: "I'm not running both ends of the line. I'm only responsible for this one. Probably there is someone at the other end who understands his business without me trying to carry his worries for him."

— selected
ref. 1149

† † †

1170 Prayer pulls the rope below and the great bell rings above in the ears of God. But some scarcely stir the bell, for they pray languidly. Others give an occasional pluck at the rope. Those, however, who win the victory are the Christians who grab the rope boldly and pull continuously with all their might.

— Spurgeon
ref. 1150

† † †

1171
The camel, at the close of day,
Kneels down upon the sandy plain
To have his burden lifted off
   And rest again!

Then thou, too, O traveler, to thy knee,
When daylight draweth to a close,
And let the master lift the load
   And grant repose!

The camel kneels at break of day
To have his guide replace the load,
Then rises up anew to take
   The desert road.

So, pilgrim, kneel at morning's dawn,
That God may give thee daily care,
Assured that he no load too great
   Will make thee bear.

— Anon
ref. 1154

† † †

1172
The Savior can lift every burden,
   The heavy as well as the light;
His strength is made perfect in weakness,
   In him there is power and might.

291

The Savior can strengthen the weary,
   His grace is sufficient for all,
He knows every step of the pathway,
   And listens to hear when we call.

                          — Anon

ref. 1150

† † †

1173 When we consider the manifold weakness of the strongest devotions in time of prayer, it is a sad consideration. I throw myself down in my chamber, and I call in and invite God and his angels thither, and when they are there I neglect God and his angels for the noise of a fly, for the rattling of a coach, for the whining of a door; I talk on . . . knees bowed down as though I prayed to God, and if God and his angels should ask me, when I thought of God last in that prayer, I could not tell.

                          — John Donne

ref. 1150,1153

† † †

1174
I knelt to pray when day was done
And prayed, "O Lord, bless every one,
Lift from each saddened heart the pain,
And let the sick be well again."
And then I woke another day
And carelessly went on my way.
The whole day long I did not try
To wipe a tear from any eye;
I did not try to share the load
Of any brother on my road;
I did not even go to see
The sick man just next door to me.
Yet once again when day was done
I prayed, "O Lord, bless every one."
But as I prayed, into my ear
There came a voice that whispered clear:
"Pause, hypocrite, before you pray;
Whom have you tried to bless today?
God's sweetest blessings always go
By hands that serve him here below."
And then I hid my face and cried,
"Forgive me, God, for I have lied;
Let me but see another day,
That I may live the way I pray."

                          — Anon

ref. 1152

1175   O Triune God, who can thy glory tell,
    Or find him words to give thee fitting praise!
    In vain creation's hosts their voices raise.
Nor men nor angels' anthems laud thee well.
Too great thou art! Too feeble, all who dwell
    Beneath the shadow of thy wings. They gaze
    With wondering rapture at they marvelous ways,
And, then, too full with love, the heart is still.
And yet I know that thou dost not despise
My humble prayers of gratitude that rise,
    Born on the wings of faith, thee to extol,
And bless thy saving grace, which made me whole.
    Firm in this trust I waft them to the skies,
    And they return with blessings for my soul.
                         — J. T. Mueller

ref. 1147

† † †

1176 I have been driven to my knees many times by the conviction that I had nowhere else to go. My own wisdom and that of all about me seemed insufficient for the day.

                         — Abraham Lincoln

ref. 1148

† † †

1177 A missionary's wife had living with her a little Hindu orphan. She taught him about Jesus. One night, when the little orphan was six years old, she said to him: "Now pray a little prayer of your own."

After a moment's thought, the child prayed: "Dear Jesus make me like you were when you were six years old"; *ref. 1155.*

† † †

1178 The Bible records numerous instances of the wonders wrought by prayer:

Abraham's servant prayed, and Rebekah appeared. — Jacob prayed and prevailed with Christ; Esau's mind was wonderfully turned from the revengeful purpose he had harbored for twenty years. — Moses cried to God, and the sea was divided. — Joshua prayed, and Achan was discovered. —Hannah prayed, and Samuel was born. — David prayed, and Ahithophel hanged himself. — Asa prayed, and a victory was gained. — Jehoshaphat cried to God, and God turned his foes. — Isaiah and Hezekiah prayed, and 185,000 Assyrians were slain in twelve hours. — Daniel prayed, and God revealed his dream. — Daniel prayed, and the lions were muzzled. — Daniel prayed, and the seventy weeks were revealed. — Mordecai and Esther prayed, and Haman was hanged on the gallows. — Ezra prayed at Ahava, and God answered. — Nehemiah prayed, and the king's heart was softened.

— Elijah prayed, and a drought succeeded; he prayed again, and rains descended apace. — Elisha prayed, and the Jordan was divided. He prayed another time, and a child's soul came back, for prayer reaches eternity. —The church prayed, and Peter was delivered from prison by an angel.

— Rev. J. Ryland

ref. 1156

† † †

1179 God grant me the serenity to accept the things I cannot change; courage to change the things I can, and wisdom to know the difference.

— Prayer of Alcoholics Anonymous

† † †

1180 Most of us worry twice as much as we pray. We read twice as much as we pray, we talk twice as much as we pray. We run around all day long like frantic ants trying to keep life right side up, when what we really should do, is run around less and pray more. Millions of people would bear me out when I say that if we put into prayer for peace one-tenth the energy, the concentration, the self-sacrifice, the study that we put into waging war, we might begin to see emerging the better world for which we all long.

— Helen S. Shoemaker

ref. 1148

† † †

1181
Some tell us that prayer is all in the mind,
That the only result is the solace we find;
That God does not answer, nor hear when we call;
We comune with our own hearts in prayer; that is all!
But we who have knelt with our burden and care,
And have made all of our problems a matter of prayer,
Have seen God reach down from his heaven above,
Move mountains, touch hearts, in his infinite love;
We know that God works in a wonderful way
On behalf of his children who trust him and pray.

— Barbara Corner Ryberg,
in *NOW*

ref. 1150

† † †

1182 At the opening session of the Federal Constitutional Convention on June 28, 1787, Benjamin Franklin arose and said: "Mr. President, in the beginning of the contest with Great Britain, when we were sensible of danger, we had daily prayer in this room for divine protection. Our prayers were heard and answered. I have lived long, sir, a long time, and the longer I live the convincing proofs I see of the truth that God governs in the affairs of men. I therefore beg leave to move that henceforth prayers, imploring the assistance of heaven, be held in this assembly every morning." The motion was carried; *ref. 1152.*

† † †

1183 A crowded gathering of distinguished scientists had been listening, spellbound, to the masterly expositions of Michael Faraday. For an hour he held his brilliant audience enthralled as he demonstrated the nature and the properties of the magnet. He brought his lecture to a close with an experiment so novel, so bewildering, and so triumphant that, for some time after he had resumed his seat, the house rocked with enthusiastic applause.

Then the Prince of Wales, afterward King Edward the Seventh, rose to propose a motion of congratulations. The resolution, having been seconded, was carried with renewed thunders of applause. But the uproar was succeeded by a strange silence. The assembly waited for Faraday's reply; but the lecturer had vanished! What had become of him? Only two or three of his most intimate friends were in on the secret. They knew that the great chemist was something more than a great chemist; he was an elder of a little church that never boasted more than twenty members. The hour at which Faraday concluded his lecture was the hour of the midweek prayer meeting. That meeting he never neglected. And under cover of the cheering applause the lecturer had slipped out of the crowded hall and hurried off to the little meeting-house.

— selected

ref. 1153

† † †

1184 The following prayer is from the pen of Thomas Jefferson:

"Almighty God, who hast given us this good land for our heritage; we humbly beseech thee that we may always prove ourselves a people mindful of thy favor and glad to do thy will. Bless our land with honorable industry, sound learning, and pure manners.

Save us from violence, discord, and confusion; from pride and arrogance, and from every evil way. Defend our liberties, and fashion into one united people the multitudes brought hither out of many kindreds and tongues.

Endow with the spirit of wisdom those whom in thy Name we entrust the authority of government, that there may be justice and peace at home, and that through obedience to thy law, we may show forth thy praise among the nations of the earth.

In time of prosperity, fill our hearts with thankfulness, and in the day of trouble, suffer not our trust in thee to fail; all of which we ask through Jesus Christ our Lord. Amen"; *ref. 1152.*

† † †

1185 Chief Justice Ryan of the Supreme Court of Wisconsin used the following prayer each day:

"O God of all truth, knowledge, and judgment, without whom nothing is true, or wise, or just: Look down with mercy upon thy servants whom thou sufferest to sit in earthly seats of judgment to administer thy justice to thy people. Enlighten their ignorance and inspire them with thy judgments. Grant them grace truly and impartially to administer thy justice to thy people. Enlighten their ignorance and inspire them with thy judgments. Grant them grace truly and impartially to administer thy justice and to maintain thy truth to the glory of thy name.

"And of thy mercy so direct and dispose my heart that I may this day fulfill my duty in thy fear and fall into no error of judgment. Give me grace to hear patiently, to consider diligently, to understand rightly, and to decide justly. Grant me due sense of humility, that I may not be misled by my willfulness, vanity, or egotism. Of myself I humbly acknowledge my own unfitness and unworthiness in thy sight, and without thy gracious guidance I can do nothing right. Have mercy on me, a weak, frail sinner, groping in the dark; and give me grace to judge others now that I may not myself be judged when thou comest to judge the world with thy truth. Grant my prayer, I beseech thee, for the love of thy Son, my Savior, Jesus Christ. Amen"; *ref. 1152.*

† † †

1186 When Aeschylus was condemned to death by an Athenian court, his brother, Amyntas, a brave warrior, came into the court-room. Amyntas had lost his hand during a battle in which the Athenians had gained a glorious victory. Entering the court-room he did not say a word, but merely held up the stump of his arm in the sight of all. When the judges saw this mark of his suffering, they remembered what he had done and, for his sake, pardoned the guilty brother.

> Christ ever lives above
> For me to intercede,
> His all redeming love,
> His precious blood to plead.
>
> Five bleeding wounds he bears,
> Received on Calvary;
> They pour effectual prayers,
> They strongly speak for me.
>
> The Father hears him pray,
> His dear Anointed One;
> He cannot turn away,
> Cannot refuse his Son.
>
> My God is reconciled,
> His pardoning voice I hear;
> He owns me for his child,
> I can no longer fear.
> — Charles Wesley (adapted)

ref. 1150,1152

1187 Many years ago a ragged Indian, at the point of starvation, straggled into a western settlement begging food. He wore a bright-colored ribbon about his neck from which hung a small, dirty pouch. When asked what the pouch contained, he said that it was a charm that had been given him in his younger days. He opened the pouch and took from it a crumbled piece of paper which he handed to the person speaking to him. The paper proved to be a regular discharge from the Federal Army which entitled him to a pension for life. It was signed by the Commander-in-Chief, George Washington.

Here was a man with a promise duly signed, which if presented in the right place would have secured for him ample provision for life. Yet he was wandering about homeless, hungry, helpless and forlorn, begging bread to keep from starving.

As redeemed children of God by faith in Jesus Christ we have a credit card, signed with the holy, precious blood of Christ, which entitles us to all the riches and treasures that the inexhaustible storehouse of heaven offers for this life and for the eternal life to come. What a pity, what a tragedy, if we should fail to make use of it! *ref. 1148.*

PREDESTINATION 1188-1194

Predestination Is Taught in Holy Scriptures

1188 Christ spoke of it repeatedly: Mt 20:16; 22:14; 24:22,24,31; Lk 18:7; Jn 13:18; 15:16,19;

The writers of the New Testament refer to it again and again: Ac 13:48; Ro 8:28-33; 9:11; 11:5; Eph 1:3-6; 3:11; Col 3:12; 1 Th 1:4; 2 Th 2:13,14; Jas 2:5; 1 Pe 1:2; 2:9;

It is a part of the counsel of God which is to be taught: Mt 28:20; Ac 20:27; 2 Tm 3:16,17; 4:1,2.

Predestination Defined

1189 It is God's decree from eternity in connection with Christ's work of redemption: Ro 8:28-30; Eph 1:3-7; 2 Th 2:13; 2 Tm 1:9; cp Mt 25:34; *ref. 1193,1194;*

It is carried out through the operation of the Holy Spirit in the Word, by which he calls, converts, justifies and sanctifies believers and keeps them in true faith to the end: Jn 10:27-29; 15:3; Ro 8:28-30; 2 Th 2:13,14; Php 1:6; 1 Pe 1:2-5; *ref. 1194;*

It is a decree of grace which is effected according to the good pleasure of God's will, and not because of any worthiness in man: Eph 1:5,6; 2:4-9; 2 Tm 1:9; Tt 3:5-7; 1 Jn 4:10; *ref. 1193.*

There Is No Predestination to Damnation

1190 God's love in Christ extends over the whole world of sinlost mankind: Lk 2:10,11; Jn 1:29; 3:16,17; 2 Cor 5:14,19; Tt 2:11; 1 Jn 4:14;

God earnestly desires the salvation of all mankind: Eze 33:11; Ac 10:34,35; 1 Tm 2:4; 2 Pe 3:9.

Predestination Involves God's Unsearchable Ways

1191 Human reason cannot understand why some are saved while others are lost, since:

All are in like condemnation: Ro 3:22,23; Eph 2:1,2. There is, therefore, no lesser guilt, lesser resistance, or greater willingness on the part of some;

Those who are saved are saved by grace alone; their faith is a gift of God: Ro 3:24-28; Eph 1:5-7; 2:8,9; 2 Tm 1:9; Tt 3:5; 1 Jn 4:10; and those who perish in unbelief are lost because of their own fault: Ho 13:9; Mt 23:37;

Human reason is not capable of searching out this mystery, which is hidden with God: Is 40:28; 55:8,9; Ro 11:33-36; 1 Cor 2:16; 2 Cor 10:5.

How Believers Are To View This Doctrine

1192 For their comfort: The very fact that they are believers in Christ assures them that they are the children of God and heirs of heaven: Ro 8:14-17; Ga 3:26-29. This should cause them to praise and to thank God: Eph 1:3-6; 1 Pe 1:3-5, and should comfort them in every time of trial and trouble:- Ro 8:18,28-39; 1 Pe 1:6-9;

For their admonition: They should always be mindful of the fact that God has chosen them that they "should be holy and without blame before him in love": Eph 1:4; 1 Pe 1:15,16. This should cause them to be zealous to do good works: Mt 5:16; Eph 2:10; Tt 2:14; 1 Pe 2:9-12; to give diligence to make their calling and election sure: Php 2:12; 3:12-14; 2 Pe 1:10; and to proclaim the gospel to others; *ref. Mission Work 1020-1081.*

Resources

1193
> Now I have found a firm foundation
> Which holds mine anchor ever sure;
> 'Twas laid before the world's creation
> In Christ my Savior's wounds secure;
> Foundation which unmoved shall stay
> When heav'n and earth will pass away.
> — Johann A. Rothe

1194
> From eternity, O God,
> In thy Son thou didst elect me;
> Therefore, Father, on life's road
> Graciously to heav'n direct me;
> Send to me thy Holy Spirit
> That his gifts I may inherit.
>
> Faith and hope and charity
> Graciously, O Father, give me;

Be my Guardian constantly
  That the devil may not grieve me;
Grant me humbleness and gladness,
  Peace and patience in my sadness.

Help me speak what's right and good
  And keep silence on occasion;
Help me pray, Lord, as I should,
  Help me bear my tribulation;
Help me die and let my spirit
  Everlasting life inherit.
— Caspar Neumann

ref. 237,1189,1192

PROVIDENCE, DIVINE 1195-1221

(ref.: Creation 242-261)

Its Meaning and Extent

1195 It is the activity of God whereby he uninterruptedly upholds, governs, and directs the world which he has made: Ps 47:7; 104:1-33; Mt 4:4; Ac 17:25-28; Col 1:16,17; He 1:3; *ref. 1201,1203,1205,1207,1210.*

It provides for the continued existence of all creatures and created things, directs their actions, and controls their destinies. It extends over

All the lifeless creation: Job 9:5-10; 28:25,26; Ps 89:8,9; 145:9; 148:8; *ref. 1207,1208;*

All plants, birds and animals: Job 38:41; Ps 104:10-25; 145:15,16; Mt 6:26-30; Lk 12:6,7; *ref. 1202,1204,1206;*

The world of mankind and each individual: Ps 31:15; 89:10; 91:1-16; 121:1-8; 139:1-18; 145:14-21; Pr 20:24; 21:1; Jr 1:5; 10:23; Mt 5:45; 6:26-30; 18:14; Lk 12:6,7; Ac 17:26; *ref. 1203,1207.*

The Manner in Which Divine Providence Operates

1196 It normally expresses itself in definite laws which God has formulated, and is exercised through secondary causes or means through which God operates (Laws of Nature): Gn 1:14-18; 8:22; Ps 19:1-6; 65:6-13; Is 55:10; Ac 14:17; see also Job 38:1-41; Is 40:12-31; *ref. 1208,1210,1215-1217.*

1197 At times God acts above or beyond these laws (miracles). Examples: God performed miracles in sustaining Israel in the wilderness: Ex 16:4-18; 17:5,6; Dt 8:3,4; in sustaining the prophet Elijah and the widow of Zarephath: 1 Kgs 17: 2-16; see also the feeding of the five thousand and the four thousand: Mt 14:15-21; 15:32-38; *ref. 1208,1209,1211-1215,1217.*

1198 Divine providence neither deprives men of their liberty nor of their responsibility; it neither reduces men to automata nor makes God responsible for their sin: Ps 50:16-21; Ro 1-19-32; 2 Th 3:10-12; *ref. 1216.*

From the Viewpoint of God

1199 All is predetermined and immutably fixed: Job 14:5; Is 14:27; Jr 51:29; Ac 4:27,28; He 6:17. Yet from the human viewpoint all things happen contingently; events can be modified and depend on circumstances and decisions which men can make and for which they are responsible. Examples: Is 38:1-5; Mt 10:23; 23:37; Ac 9:23-25; Jas 5:14,15; *ref. 1219.*

The Ultimate Goals of Divine Providence

1200 The temporal and eternal welfare of men, especially the salvation of the elect: 2 Chr 16:9; 20:29; Ps 2:1-5; 34:7; 125:2; Ro 8:28-39; Eph 1:3-9; 3:11. Examples: Gn 50:20; Ex 14:20; Nu 22:12f; 2 Kgs 6:17; 7:6,7; 19:35; Dn 6:22; *ref. 1211,1213-1221.*

The preaching of the gospel. See e.g., Ac 5:17-21; 12:1-11; 16:6; 27:20-25; cp Mt 2:13-16;

The promotion of the glory of God: Ps 19:1; 27:6; 65:13; 69:34; 98:8; 145:1-13; 148:1-14; 150:1-6; Is 12:4-6; 25:1; *ref. 1221.*

— adapted from an essay by
Paul F. Bente in *The Abiding Word,* Vol 2.

Resources

1201 God is not like a builder who leaves the house he has completed without any further concern for it. He who created the world is also the cause for its continued existence and growth. He who fills heaven and earth is not far from everyone, "for in him we live and move, and have our being": Ac 17:27,28; Jr 23:24; Ro 11:36. To say that God does not know the world's needs and our own, or that he does not care, or that he is not able to govern and to provide, is to deny God's omnipresence, omniscience and omnipotence. It is to close one's eyes to the wisdom, power and love of God, which is clearly evident in the universe in which we live: Ps 19:1; Ec 3:11; Ac 15:18; Ro 1:20; *ref. 1195-1197.*

† † †

1202
God sees the little sparrow fall,
   It meets his tender view;
If God so loves the little birds,
   I know he loves me too;

He paints the lily of the field,
   Perfumes each lily bell;
If he so loves the little flowers,
   I know he loves me well.

God made the little birds and flowers,
   And all things large and small;
He'll not forget his little ones,
   I know he loves them all.

— Maria Straub

1203 Were God to withdraw himself from the world, the world would disappear without a trace. Were God to withdraw himself from a part of the world, that part in the world would cease to exist.

1204

Behold the lilies of the field
In stately beauty grow,
They toil not, neither do they spin,
Nor do they reap or sow.
Yet Solomon in glory great
With pomp and fine display,
Though robed in costly silk and gems,
Was not arrayed as they.

Ah, then, if God so clothe the grass
That withers and decays,
Will he not give to you who ask
Sufficient for your days?
Oh, take no thought for raiment, then,
Nor what the morrow brings,
But trust the Father, for he knows
Your need for all these things.

And if his care is over all
His creatures great and small,
Will he not give much more to you,
Is, then, your faith so small?

Consider, then, the lilies fair,
The lessons they have taught;
Ask all, and all receive, and say
"Behold, what God hath wrought."
— Odelia R. Butenschoen

1205

Around, within, below, above,
His providence extends;
He everywhere displays his love,
And power with mercy blends.
— James Cowden Wallace

1206 Both spring and fall witness one of the mysteries of nature, the migration of birds. Every fall the Pacific golden plover leaves Alaska for New Zealand, 7,800 miles away, stopping over on small coral islands in the South Pacific which they find after flights of up to 2,400 miles over open water, a feat which no highly trained airplane could equal without thousands of dollars worth of equipment in the plane and many thousands more on the islands. The Arctic tern flies 12,000 miles. Many of those terns cross trackless wastes of the North and South Atlantic, to summer in Antarctica. Thousands of other species perform lesser miracles of navigaiton. The question science has never been able to answer is: How do they find their way? William Cullen Bryant, in *To A Waterfowl*, suggests the answer:

He who, from zone to zone,
Guides through the boundless sky
    thy certain flight,
In the long way that I must tread alone,
Will lead my steps aright.
— Christian Economics

1207
Who measureth the waters,
    The dust of all the land,
And holds them in the hollow
    Of his unfailing hand?

Who meteth out the heavens,
    The hillsides, and the dales
And weighs the mighty mountains
    In his unerring scales?

Who counteth all the nations,
    Each prince and underling,
Together with the islands
    A very little thing?

Who bringeth out by number
    The stars, forgetting none,
And in their ordered courses
    Doth name them one by one?

Have ye not heard nor known him,
    The Strength of all his saints,
The Lord and great Creator,
    Who wearies not nor faints?

Unto the faint he giveth
    The courage of a knight
And strength to strength increasing
    To them that have no might.

And they that wait upon him
    Shall soar without constraint,
Shall run and not be weary,
    And walk and never faint.
— W. M. Czamanske

1208 William Jennings Bryan once said: "I was eating a piece of watermelon several years ago and was struck with its beauty. I took some of the seeds and dried them and weighed them. I found that it would require 5,000 seeds to weigh a pound. And then I applied mathematics to that forty-pound melon. One of these seeds, put into the ground, then warmed by the sun and moistened by the rain, takes off its coat and goes to work. It gathers from somewhere 200,000 times its own weight and, forcing this raw material through the tiny stem, constructs a watermelon. It ornaments the outside with a covering of green; inside the green it puts a layer of white and within the white a red core; and through the red it scatters seeds, in some varieties black, in others dark brown, each one capable of reproduction. What architect drew this plan? Whence does the little seed get its tremendous strength? Where does it find its coloring matter? How does it collect its flavoring extract? How does it build a watermelon? Until you can explain a watermelon, do not be too sure that you can limit the ability of the Almighty to say just what he would do or how he could do it. Everything that lives, in like manner, mocks by its mystery, beauty and power the proud intellect of presumptuous man"; ref. 1195.

† † †

1209 Strictly speaking, all divine providence is miraculous (e.g., the miracle of life, the seemingly infinite varieties of plants and animals each with an individual and unique power of reproduction, the complexity and power of an atom, the marvelous mechanism of the universe of outer space, gravity, electricity, etc.). When speaking of "miracles," therefore, we merely adopt a human expression to speak of deviations from that which in itself is miraculous; ref. 1197.

† † †

1210 God does not constantly change his mind but has established design, order, and unity in governing and preserving the universe he made. To be sure, the present world, corrupted by sin and under the rule of Satan, is not the original and perfect world in which everything was "very good," but a world cursed by sin in which the whole creation groans and travails in pain, Ro 8:19-22. Nevertheless, even catastrophies like tidal waves, volcanic eruptions, earthquakes, eclipses and other unusual phenomena of nature obey and follow definite laws of cause and effect.

Father Lynch, world famous seismologist of Fordham University, New York, when asked how he could find satisfaction in studying great and small vibrations that happen in the earth, replied: "The laws of nature are deep in the folds and faults of the earth. By encouraging men to learn those laws one can lead them further to a knowledge of the Author of all laws": *Life*, Apr. 15,1946; ref. 1196.

† † †

1211 "How can you believe that stuff?" exclaimed a college student coming upon his classmate reading the Bible. "Don't you have difficulty with such a miracle as the dividing of the Red Sea?"

"Yes, I have some difficulty with the Red Sea," was the reply, "but my difficulty is not how it was divided but how it was made. For surely he who made it could also divide it."

1212 Eddie Rickenbacker tells how he and his companions, adrift on the Pacific praying for rain, saw a shower pass by a short distance away and, as they kept on praying, turn against the wind and overtake them providing the water they needed to preserve their lives. No less miraculous was the strange appearance of the seagull that settled on their raft and provided them food.

1213 It is strange that we have wrestled an empire from these people [the Spaniards] with the loss of only a few men. I am a Christian man, believing firmly in Christ and the Book, and I say most assuredly it was the hand of God. I remember when we engaged the fleet seeing shells fired directly at us, and I do not understand under heaven why we escaped, unless it be through divine superintendence so forcibly expressed in these familiar lines:

> God moves in a mysterious way
> His wonders to perform;
> He plants his footsteps in the sea,
> And rides upon the storm.

— Admiral George Dewey

1214 When in World War II the first convoys with our troops came near to the North African shores, two conflicting storms approached. Each one of these could have brought disaster. Now who neutralized those hurricanes, so that the sea before Casablanca was smoother than observers had recorded in sixty-eight years? Officers in charge of the North African armies have answered in the Congressional Record and called this a miracle of God. When later our troops, advancing toward Europe, pushed on to Sicily, who made the Mediterranean, in the words of the late Ernie Pyle, "as smooth as the top of a billiard table?" — The Almighty repeatedly regulated wind and weather to help our cause.

— selected

1215 Among the secondary causes which God employs to govern the world are also men — good men and evil men. The proud king of Assyria is an axe in the hand of the Most High: Is 10:12-15. King Herod becomes the agent by whom God fulfills his prophecy regarding Jesus "Out of Egypt I called my son": Mt 2:15. When Jezebel persecuted the prophets of the Lord, pious Obadiah became the agent by whom the Lord saved the lives of a hundred prophets: 1 Kgs 18:4. Ebed-Melech, the Ethiopian, was the instrument of God by whom the prophet Jeremiah was rescued from the cistern: Jr 38:4-13.

Men become the causes through which God works. Balaam may accept the bribe of Balak to curse Israel, but as Balaam later explained to Balak: "But can I say just anything? I must speak only what God puts in my mouth . . . Even if Balak gave me his palace filled with silver and gold, I could not do anything of my own accord, good or bad, to go beyond the command of the Lord — and I must say only what the Lord says?" Nu 22:38; 24:13.

— Paul F. Bente

ref. 1196,1197,1200

† † †

1216 Men are responsible for their actions. But their corrupt nature seeks out a way which opposes whatever is good and pleasing to God. Though they know the truth, they suppress it by their disobedience and wickness: Ro 1:19,21,28; Eph 4:18,19.

Sin does not originate with God, but with Satan and from within man's corrupt nature: Gn 3:1f; Mt 15:19; Jn 8:44; Jas 1:13,14. Nevertheless, God directs wickedness in such a course that it is made to serve God's plan of world government, God's honor, and at times the welfare of the sinner himself. When man sins, God supplies only the capability of action; God does not work along in determining the direction the action takes. In other words, God is not to be judged as morally responsible; cp 2 Sm 24:1-4 with 1 Chr 21:1-4; *ref. 1196,1198.*

† † †

1217 To assume, from the human viewpoint, that the course of all events is unalterably fixed, that we can do nothing about it, that things must happen as they do so that no variation is possible, is to deny the possibility of miracles and to believe in fatalism. But the truth is that events can often be altered or modified. Thus, for example, prayer can change things: Is 38:1-5; Jas 5:14,15. God expects us to exercise discretion and to use the means which he has placed at our disposal: see Mt 10:23; Ac 9:24. We are not to resign ourselves to "blind destiny," but to life in hope: Ps 16:7-9; 39:7; 42:11; 71:1-5; 119:114; 130:5; 146:5; Jr 17:5-8; Lm 3:26; Ro 4:18-25; 5:2; 12:12; *ref. 1197,1199.*

† † †

1218 In a state of hypochondria, William Cowper resolved to take his own life. He rode to the river Thames, but there he found a man seated on some goods at the very point from which he expected to spring. He rode back to his house that night and tried to stab himself with a knife. But the blade broke. Then he tried to hang himself, but the rope parted. When God mercifully delivered him from that awful dementia he wrote the memorable hymn: "God Moves in a Mysterious Way His Wonders To Perform"; *ref. 1200.*

† † †

1219 "All things work together for good" to those who love God, who are the called according to his purpose. The ultimate goal of divine providence is their eternal welfare. As God's adopted children by faith in Christ, an eternal inheritance awaits us in heaven: Jn 10:27-29; Ro 8:14,17,28-32; 1 Pe 1:3-9.

1220

Commit whatever grieves thee
  Into the gracious hands
Of him who never leaves thee,
  Who heav'n and earth commands,
Who points the clouds their courses,
  Whom winds and waves obey,
He will direct thy footsteps
  And find for thee a way.

Though all the powers of evil
  The will of God oppose,
His purpose will not falter,
  His pleasure onward goes.

Whate'er God's will resolveth,
   Whatever he intends,
Will always be accomplished
   True to his aims and ends.

Arise, my soul, and banish
   Thy anguish and thy care,
Away with thoughts that sadden
   And heart and mind ensnare!
Thou art not lord and master
   Of thine own destiny;
Enthroned in highest heaven,
   God rules in equity.

Leave all to his direction;
   In wisdom he doth reign,
And in a way most wondrous
   His course he will maintain.
Soon he, his promise keeping,
   With wonder-working skill
Shall put away the sorrows
   That now thy spirit fill.

                              — Paul Gerhardt

ref. 1200

† † †

1221 One of Rabbi Ben Jochai's scholars once asked: "Why did not the Lord furnish enough manna to Israel for a year, all at one time?"

The great teacher said: "I will answer you with a parable. . . . Once there was a king who had a son whom he gave a yearly allowance. It soon happened that the day on which the allowance was due was the only day in the year when the father saw the son. So the king changed his plan and gave his son day by day that which sufficed for the day. Now the son visited the father every morning, realizing his continual need for his father's love, companionship, wisdom, and giving."

So God deals with his children. he gives them a daily supply in order that supplication, communion and thanksgiving might continue.

                              — selected

ref. 1200

306

1222 "Am I my brother's keeper?" Gn 4:9.

"How long will you waver between two opinions?" 1 Kgs 18:21

"Why are you downcast, O my soul: Why so disturbed within?" Ps 42:11

"Whom shall I send? And who will go for us?" Is 6:8

"Can anyone hide in secret places so that I cannot see him? Do not I fill heaven and earth? declares the Lord." Jr 23:24

"Will a man rob God?" Mal 3:8

"If you, then, though you are evil, know how to give good gifts to your children, how much more will your Father in heaven give good gifts to those who ask him!" Mt 7:11

"You of little faith, why are you so afraid?" Mt 8:26

"Who is the greatest in the kingdom of heaven?" Mt 18:1

"What do you think about the Christ? Whose son is he?" Mt 22:42

"Could you men not keep watch with me for one hour?" Mt 26:40

"What shall I do, then, with Jesus who is called Christ?" Mt 27:22

"What good is it for a man to gain the whole world, yet forfeit his soul:Or what can a man give in exchange for his soul?" Mk 8:36,37

"However, when the Son of Man comes, will he find faith on the earth?" Lk 18:8

"Suppose one of you wants to build a tower. Will he not first sit down and estimate the cost to see if he has enough money to complete it?"   Lk 14:28

"What shall I do, Lord?" Ac 22:10; cp 9:6

"Sirs, what must I do to be saved?" Ac 16:30

"We died to sin; how can we live in it any longer?" Ro 6:2

"If God is for us, who can be against us?" Ro 8:31; see also v. 36-39

"How can they hear without someone preaching to them?" Ro 10:14

"What is truth?" Jn 18:38

"Do you not know that your body is a temple of the Holy Spirit, who is in you, whom you have received from God? You are not your own; you were bought at a price." 1 Cor 6:19

"If the trumpet does not sound a clear call, who will get ready for battle?" 1 Cor 14:8

"How shall we escape if we ignore such a great salvation?" He 2:3; cp He 10:28,29

"For anyone who does not love his brother, whom he has seen, cannot love God, whom he has not seen." 1 Jn 4:20; cp 1 Jn 3:17

(ref.: Justification 850-864)

Definition

1223 The word "redeem" means to buy back, or to set free. In Holy Scriptures it refers to the saving work of Jesus Christ in which he, through his sinless life, innocent suffering and death, and shedding of his holy blood redeemed mankind from the bondage of the law, sin, death, Satan and hell: Lk 1:68; 2:38; Ro 3:24; 1 Cor 1:30; Ga 3:10,13; 4:4-7; Eph 1:7; Col 1:14; Tt 2:14; He 9:12; 1 Pe 1:18,19; Re 5:9. Christ, the Redeemer: Job 19:25; Is 44:6; 54:5; 59:20 *ref. 1238,1239.*

The Need For Redemption

1224 All mankind by nature are transgressors of God's law, subject to divine wrath, and condemned to eternal death: Gn 8:21; Ps 7:11; 14:1-3; 40:12; 51:5; 53:3; 90:8; 130:3; Ec 7:20; Is 53:6; 59:2; Eze 18:4; Ro 1:21f; 3:19,23; 11:32; Ga 3:10,22; Eph 2:1f; Jas 2:10; 1 Jn 1:8; *ref. 1244;*

None can save himself or another: Ps 49:7,8; Is 64:6; Jr 2:22; Ro 3:20; 1 Tm 1:9; Tt 3:5; *ref. 1240,1244,1246.*

The Manner in Which God Prepared Redemption

1225 God's justice demanded punishment for sin, but his love provided a way in which his justice could be satisfied and man could be saved:

1226 Christ, the eternal Son of God, took man's nature upon himself and placed himself under the law, that so he might fulfill all the righteousness of the law for us: Mt 3:15; Ro 10:4; Ga 3:13; 4:4-7; 1 Cor 1:30; Php 3:9; 1 Tm 1:14-16; He 5:9 cp Is 59:16; Jr 23:6; 33:16;

1227 Christ took upon himself the sins of all mankind and suffered their punishment in man's stead: Is 53:4-6; Jn 1:29; Ro. 3-24,25; 4:25, 2 Cor 5:19-21; Ga 1:4; Col 1:14; 1 Tm 2:6; Tt 2:14; He 9:12; 10:14; 1 Pe 1:18,19; 2:24; 3:18; 1 Jn 1:7; 2:2; 3:5; Re 1:5,6. The Holy Scriptures use various expressions to describe Christ's redeeming work to assure us that our salvation is complete. The words "for us" occur repeatedly and mean "in our stead," or "in our behalf," e.g.:

He was pierced for our transgressions, he was crushed for our iniquities: Is 53:5;

Jesus Christ laid down his life for us: 1 Jn 3:16; cp Jn 10:11;

He gave himself for us: Tt 2:14;

He gave himself for our sins: Ga 1:4; 2:20; Eph 5:25,26;

He gave his life as a ransom for many: Mk 10:45; 1 Tm 2:6;

He sacrificed himself for us: 1 Cor 5:7; Eph 5:2; He 7:26,27; 10:12;

He was made a curse for us: Ga 3:13; 4:4-7;

God made him who had no sin to be sin for us: 2 Cor 5:21;

He suffered for our sins: 1 Pe 2:21,24; 3:18; cp Is 53:4,5;

Christ died for our sins: Ro 5:6,8; 8:32; 1 Cor 15:3;

Christ died for the ungoldly: Ro 5:6;

He died for us: 1 Th 5:10;

He died for all: 2 Cor 5:15;

He tasted death for everyone: He 2:9,14,15;

He is the atoning sacrifice for our sins, and not only for ours but also for the sins of the whole world: 1 Jn 2:2; Jn 1:29;

He was delivered over to death for our sins and was raised to life for our justification: Ro 4:25; 8:32.

Additional Expressions

1228 The Son of Man came to seek and to save what was lost: Lk 19:10;

Christ Jesus came into the world to save sinners: 1 Tm 1:15;

The Son of God appeared to destroy the devil's work: 1 Jn 3:8; Jn 12:31; Col 2:15;

Having canceled the written code, with its regulations, that was against us and that stood opposed to us; he took it away, nailing it to the cross: Col 2:14

We were reconciled to him through the death of his Son: Ro 5:8-10; 2 Cor 5:19;

He himself bore our sins in his body on the tree: 1 Pe 2:24;

Through him we have now received reconciliation: Ro 5:11; cp Ex 29:36; 30:10,15; 32:30; Lv 16:34; 17:11; 23:27,28; 25:9; 1 Chr 6:49;

He gave himself for us to redeem us from all wickedness: Tt 2:14;

Christ redeemed us from the curse of the law: Ga 3:13; 4:4-7;

He was slain, and with his blood purchased men for God: Re 5:9;

We were redeemed with the precious blood of Christ: 1 Pe 1:18,19; cp Eph 1:14;

The blood of Jesus, his Son, purifies us from all sin: 1 Jn 1:7;

To him who loves us and has freed us from our sins by his blood: Re 1:5; *ref. 1238,1239.*

1229 This wondrous plan of redemption for lost mankind, whose fall into sin he had foreseen but not decreed, was conceived in the loving heart of God from eternity: Ac 2:23; 4:27,28; 1 Cor 2:7; Eph 1:4-6; 2 Tm 1:9; Tt 1:2; 1 Pe 1:18-20; Re 13:8.

1230 This wondrous plan of redemption was foretold in Old Testament times in prophecy and has been proclaimed through the gospel with the coming of Christ: Mt 1:21f; 3:2,3; 4:17; Mk 1:1-3; Lk 2:10,11; 24:25-27,45,46; Jn 1:14,45; 5:39; Ac 10:43; 13:32,33; Ro 16:25; 1 Cor 2:7-13; Eph 1:9; 3:4,5,8,11; 6:19; Col 4:3; 1 Tm 1:15; 2 Tm 3:15; Tt 2:11; 1 Pe 1:10-12; 1 Jn 1:1-3; 4:14.

The Redemption Wrought by Christ Is Complete and Effectual for All Time

1231 It is for all mankind: Lk 2:10,11; Jn 1:29; 3:16; 1 Tm 2:4-6; Tt 2:11; He 7:26,27; 9:12,28; 10:14,18; 1 Jn 1:7; 2:2; 4:14;

1232 There is no other way in which anyone can be saved: Mk 16:15,16; Jn 3:18,36; 8:24; 14:6; Ac 4:12; 13:39; 1 Cor 3:11; Ga 1:3-9; 1 Jn 5:11,12; 2 Jn 9; *ref. 1240-1242,1245,1246.*

1233 Redemption becomes man's personal possession when he believes in Jesus Christ as his Savior: *ref. 359-383.*

The Purpose for Which We Have Been Redeemed

1234 Christ has redeemed us that we might be his own and live under him in his kingdom and serve him: Lk 1:74,75; Jn 12:26; Ro 6:4f; 12:1;1 Cor 6:15; 7:22,23; 2 Cor 5:15; Ga 2:20; 5:24; Eph 2:10; Php 1:21; 2:15; Col 3:1-10; Tt 2:11-14; He 9:12-14; 12:28; 1 Pe 2:9-12,24; *ref. 1243,1247-1252.*

1235 He has redeemed us that we might be his witnesses in proclaiming the gospel of redemption to all the world: Mt 24:14; Lk 24:46-48; Ac 1:8; *ref. 1020-1081,1247.*

1236 Our redemption will be consummated when Christ returns in glory to receive us into his heavenly kingdom: Mt 25:31-34; Lk 21:28; Jn 14:2,3; Ro 8:16-18,22,23; Php 3:20,21; Col 3:1-4; 1 Th 4:16,17; 2 Tm 4:18; Tt 2:13; He 9:28; 13:14; 1 Pe 1:3-9; *ref. 1241.*

Resources

1237 A father was walking down the street with his son by his side. They passed a window where hung a star. "What does that star in the window of this house mean, Daddy?" asked the inquisitive lad. "That means that a son has gone out from the house to serve his country," said the father. They passed many homes until they came to one where a gold star hung in the window. "Look, that is a gold star!" exclaimed the child. "Yes," said the father, "that gold star means that that son died for his country."

As they walked on, the evening star appeared in the heavens. "Look, look!" cried the child to his father, "God has a star in his window. His Son died, too, for his country!"

— selected

ref. 1226,1227

† † †

1238 On the roof of Keble College, Oxford, there is a dragon with its mouth wide open. Standing over the dragon is an angel about to thrust a sword in the shape of a cross down its throat. The thought conveyed to the onlooker's mind is that the cross of our Lord Jesus Christ is the secret of victory over the awful thing, sin.

— selected

ref. 1223,1226-1228

† † †

1239 At the request of President Eisenhower, the Red Cross assured a twelve-year-old girl that an ample supply of a rare type of blood would be available when she underwent a major heart operation.

The girl had written to the President telling him that surgeons would close "a hole in my heart." "Please," she said in a postscript, "if you know anyone who has B-negative blood, tell them to call my mother . . . it is very important."

In reply to the girl's request, an assistant to the President wrote: "Because the President did not know of anyone who had B-negative blood, he asked me to send your letter to the Red Cross. The President hopes the doctors at Walter Reed Hospital will be good to you and that you may make a quick recovery."

Red Cross officials assured the girl's parents that twenty pints of the required blood would be available.

A very special type of blood, the blood of God's own Son was required for our redemption from sin and its dreadful, deadly, and damning power, and One infinitely greater than the President not only helped to secure it, but actually provided it.

— Adapted from *NOW*

ref. 1223,1227,1228

† † †

1240 Having no other way to explain that his salvation was a merciful act of God, a heathen convert built a circle with twigs, then put a worm in the center and set fire to the twigs. As the helpless worm, finding no other way to escape, was about to be consumed, he snatched it from the consuming fire and set it free; *ref. 1224,1225.*

† † †

1241 A little boy had wandered far from home and lost his way. As he was sobbing his heart out, a kind policeman asked where he lived. All the little fellow could say was: "Just bring me to the white cross on a hill and I'll find my home!"

Only when we have been brought in faith to the Cross, once placed on a faraway hill, can we find our way to our heavenly home; *ref. 1236.*

1242
    Seek where you may to find a way
        That leads to your salvation;
    My heart is stilled, on Christ I build,
        He is the one Foundation.
    His Word is sure, his works endure;
        He doth o'erthrow my ev'ry foe;
    Thro' him I more than conquer.

    Seek him alone, who did atone,
        Who did your souls deliver;

Yea , seek him first, all you who thirst
For grace that faileth never.
In ev'ry need seek him indeed;
To ev'ry heart he will impart
His blessings without measure.
— George Weissel
ref. 1228,1232,1236

† † †

1243 When the body of Abraham Lincoln lay in state at Cleveland on the sad journey to Springfield, a poor Negro woman held her little child up to see his face, saying, "Take a long, long look, honey. That man died for you."
— Charles L. Wallis
ref. 1234

† † †

1244 There is an ancient legend concerning the Roman Governor, Pontius Pilate, which relates that, after a number of years of unjust administration, Pilate was summoned before the emperor Tiberius, the Terrible. The emperor, having heard of the abuses of the governor, was minded to pass severe punishment upon him. Pilate appears, but strangely, Tiberius' conduct toward him is most courteous and affable; not a word of reproach does he utter against the accused. But no sooner is Pontius Pilate out of his presence then his anger waxes all the hotter, and he upbraids himself for having dealt with him so leniently. Then, with fixed determination to punish him, he summoned him back. But the first reception is enacted over again; the emperor is courteous and obliging as before. At last by intrigue the secret is discovered. Pilate wore under his tunic a strange coat — none other than the coat of our Savior which he had purchased from the soldier who had won it by casting lots. The coat was removed, and now Tiberius, all the more because of the deception, let his fury loose upon his faulty official.

It is only a legend, but the thought underlying it is deep and precious. There is a garment, the garment of Christ's righteousness, which, if we have it on, assures us faulty and miserable offenders against the wrath of the eternal and terrible Judge.

— selected
ref. 1225,1227,1228

† † †

1245 There are some who ask Christian ministers to be broadminded and to accuse those of narrow-mindedness who preach Christ crucified as the only way to salvation. But all of life is narrow, and success is found only in passing through the narrow gate.

There is no room for broadmindedness in the chemical laboratory. Water is composed of two parts of hydrogen and one part oxygen. The slightest deviation from that formula fails.

There is no room for broadmindedness in music. The skilled director will not permit the first violin to play even so much as half a note off the written score.

There is no room for broadmindedness in mathematics. Neither geometry nor trigonometry allows any variation from accuracy.

There is no room for broadmindedness in the garage. The mechanic there says that the piston rings must fit the cylinder walls within one-thousandth part of an inch.

Why, then, should broadmindness rule in the realm of Christ's divine religion where he is the only Way, Truth, and Life?

> — *The Church Herald*

ref. 1232

† † †

1246 A Welsh minister, beginning his sermon, leaned over the pulpit and said with a solemn air: "Friends, I have a question to ask. I cannot answer it. You cannot answer it. If an angel from heaven were here, he could not answer it. If a devil from hell were here, he could not answer it."

Every eye was fixed on the speaker, who proceeded: "The question is this, 'How shall we excape if we ignore such a great salvation?' " He 2:3;

> — *Free Methodist*

ref. 1232

† † †

1247 In his summary of the Second Article of the Apostles' Creed, which treats of Jesus Christ and his great redeeming work, Martin Luther has given us a beautiful confession of Christian faith in the words:

"I believe that Jesus Christ, true God, begotten of the Father from eternity, and also true man, born of the Virgin Mary, is my Lord. He has redeemed me, a lost and condemned creature, purchased and won me from all sins, from death and from the power of the devil, not with gold or silver, but with his holy, precious blood and with his innocent suffering and death; that I should be his own, and live under him in his kingdom, and serve him in everlasting righteousness, innocence and blessedness, just as he has risen from death and lives and rules eternally. This is most certainly true"; *ref. 1234.*

† † †

1248
> Laid on thine altar, O my Lord divine,
> Accept this gift today, for Jesus' sake;
> I have no jewels to adorn thy shrine,
> No far-famed sacrifice to make;
> But here within my trembling hand I bring
> This will of mine — a thing that seemeth small

But thou alone, O Lord, canst understand
How when I yield thee this, I yield mine all.

— Anon

1249 When President Garfield was shot, he was taken to an isolated farm-house where he could have absolute quiet and rest in his fight for life. A special railway was constructed to facilitate the bringing of doctors, nurses, and loved ones to his bedside. The engineers laid out the line to cross a farmer's front yard, but he refused to grant the right of way until they explained to him that it was for the President, when he exclaimed, "That is different. If that railroad is for the President, you can run it right through my house."

Who has the right of way in your life?

1250 Martin Luther once said: "If someone would rap at the door of my heart and ask: 'Who lives here?' I would answer: Martin Luther once lived here, but he moved out and Jesus Christ moved in."

1251   Lord, in the strength of grace,
With a glad heart and free,
Myself, my residue of days,
I consecrate to thee.

Thy ransomed servant, I
Restore to thee thy own;
And, from this moment, live or die
To serve my God alone.

— C. Wesley

1252 A Roman servant, knowing that his master was being sought by his enemies who would put him to death, dressed in his master's clothes that he might be taken for him. He was taken and put to death in his master's stead. In memory of this event the master caused a statue of brass to be erected in gratitude for the servant's loyalty and faithfulness. — What monument have you erected to Jesus Christ, who died for you that you might have forgiveness of sins, life and salvation? *ref. 1234.*

—————

REPENTANCE 1253-1262

(ref.: Confession 205-209; Faith 359-383)

The Nature of Repentance — What It Includes

1253 Heartfelt sorrow for sin produced by the Law of God, that is, terror smiting the conscience through the knowledge that because of sin one has merited God's wrath, temporal and eternal punishment; *ref. 1258,1259,1261;*

Faith, born of the gospel, which believes that sins are forgiven for the sake of the redemption that Christ won for us: Mt 9:2; Mk 1:15; Lk 24:47; Ac 16:31; *ref. 1258,1259;*

Fruits of repentance, evidenced in a changed life: 2 Chr 7:14; Is 55:7; Eze 18:21; Mt 26:75; Lk 3:8-14; 19:8; Ac 16:33,34; 26:20; 2 Cor 5:17; Ga 5:22,23; *ref. 1258,1260,1262.*

The Results Of Repentance

1254 Forgiveness of sins: 2 Chr 7:14; Ps 32:5; Is 55:7; Lk 15:17-24; 18:13,14; Ac 2:38; 3:19; 5:31; 1 Jn 1:7-9;

Restoration into God's fellowship: Ps 34:18; 51:7,8; Ro 5:1;

Desire to walk in newness of life: Ps 37:30,31; 40:8; Jn 15:8; Ro 6:4; 7:22; 2 Cor 5:17; Ga 2:20; 5:22-26; *ref. 1260.*

Calls to Repentance

1255 See 2 Kgs 17:13; 2 Chr 30:6; Eze 14:6; 18:30,31; 33:11; Dn 4:27; Jl 2:12,13; Mal 3:7; Mt 3:2; 4:17; 9:13; Mk 1:15; Lk 3:3; 13:1-5; 24:47; Ac 2:37,38; 3:19; 8:22; 17:30; 26:20; Re 2:15,16; 3:3,19.

Examples of Repentance

1256 Job: Job 42:1,6; David: Ps 32:3-5; 40:12; 51:3,4; Jl 2:12,13; the Ninevites: Jon 3:1-9; Peter: Mt 26:75; the Prodigal Son: Lk 15:21; the Publican: Lk 18:13; the Jews: Ac 2:36,37; see also 2 Cor 7:10.

Resources

1257 The mission of John the Baptist was to prepare the way for the coming of Christ: Is 40:1-5; Mt 3:1-3. John's message to the people was, "Repent, for the kingdom of heaven is near," Mt 3:2. This was also Christ's message when he began his public ministry, according to Mt 4:17. It is also the only proper way to prepare for Christ's coming today; *ref. 1252,1255.*

† † †

1258 The word "repent" is one of the most important words in Scriptures. Next to the word "believe," and embracing within it the concept of faith, the word "repentance" describes all that is necessary for salvation from sin and its punishments.

Repentance involves a total change of heart and life. It embraces not merely a breaking of evil habits, but a change of mind, change of heart: Jl

2:12-14. It requires sorrow for sin, reliance on God's mercy and forgiveness through the merits of Christ, an earnest resolve with the help of the Holy Spirit to amend one's sinful life, and the fruits of repentance in a new life; Mt 3:8; Lk 3:8; *ref. 1253.*

† † †

1259 Both contrition and faith are necessary in repentance. Contrition, which is really something done *to* a person, plows the hard soil of the heart so that the seed of the gospel can be sown into it and bear the fruit of faith. The former is accomplished by the preaching of the law, the latter by the preaching of the gospel: see Jr 23:29; Mt 3:2; 4:17; Mk 1:4; Ac 2:37,38; 3:19; 30:21; *ref. 1253.*

† † †

1260 No one can have eternal life without repentance: Lk 13:3,5; 15:7; Jn 3:3,5; Ac 2:38; 17:30; 2 Pe 3:9. It is God's work when man's heart is changed: Jr 31:18,19; Ac 5:31; 26:16-18; and once man has become converted his entire life becomes a constant and unending life of repentance: Ps 13:2; 61:8; 72:15; 86:3; 88:9; Lk 9:23.

In the first of his *Ninety-five Theses* nailed on the door of the Castle Church in Wittenberg, Martin Luther wrote: "When our Lord and Master Jesus Christ said, Repent ye! He makes clear that the whole life of his believers is to be a constant or unending repentance ... He does not want us to think alone of inner repentance. Yea, inner repentance is nothing and not repentance unless it outwardly effects all manner of crucifixion of the flesh"; *ref. 75,86-89,1253.*

† † †

1261 Missionaries who worked in China tell us of the pitiful attempts of the Chinese people to appease the wrath of their idol-gods by pretending to give them money, when in reality it is only paper-money that they lay at the altar. In the case of the Chinese such a deception is all the more foolish since the idols whom they worship are only man-made gods of wood and stone. How very much more foolish it is to imagine that one can deceive the all-wise and all-knowing God who says: "I the Lord search the heart and examine the mind, to reward a man according to his conduct, according to what his deeds deserve"; Jr 17:10; see also Jr 23:24; *ref. 1253.*

† † †

1262 It is related of emperor Theodosius that, about the year 400, he commanded a great massacre in the rebellious city of Thessalonica. In three hours 7,000 people were mercilessly slain. No regard was shown to sex or age. When Ambrose, bishop of Milan, heard of this inhuman deed he forbade the emperor to enter the church. Theodosius tried to excuse himself by referring to David and his blood-guiltiness. But Ambrose answered: "If you are guilty of David's sin, bring forth David's repentance"; cp Ps 51; Jl 2:12,13; *ref. 1253.*

RESURRECTION OF THE BODY 1263-1275
(ref.: Jesus Christ, Resurrection of 769-807)

The Fact of the Resurrection

1263 Though denied and ridiculed by unbelievers: Mt 22:23; Ac 17:18,32; 23:8; 26:22-24; the resurrection of the body is a doctrine that is clearly revealed in Holy Scriptures: Job 19:25,26; Ps 17:15; 16:9-11; 49:15; 71:20; 73:24; Dn 12:2; Is 26:19; Eze 37:1-14; Ho 13:14; Mt 22:31,32; Jn 5:28,29; 6:40; 11:25,26; Ac 24:15; Ro 8:11; 14:8-10; 1 Cor 15:12-22,35-38; 2 Cor 4:14; 5:8,10; Php 1:23; 1 Th 4:14-18; Re 6:9-11; 20:12,13; *ref. 1267-1275.*

Examples Recorded in Scriptures

1264 Son of the widow of Zarephath: 1 Kgs 17:22; son of the Shunamite: 2 Kgs 4:35; the dead man who arose when buried in the grave of Elisha: 2 Kgs 13:21; the daughter of Jairus: Mt 9:25; the widow's son of Nain: Lk 7:15; Lazarus of Bethany: Jn 11:44; the bodies of the saints who arose and appeared to many in Jerusalem at the time of Christ's resurrection: Mt 27:52,53; Dorcas: Ac 9:40; *ref. 1271.*

The Nature of the Resurrection

1265 The soul of the believer, separated from the body at death: Ec 12:7; Lk 16:22; 23:42,43,46; Ac 7:59; Php 1:23; 2 Pe 1:14; Re 14:13; will be reunited with the same body in which it previously dwelt: Jn 19:25-27; just as Christ rose with the same body that died on the cross: Lk 24:39; Jn 20:27. However, the body will now be transformed into a glorified state, like the bodies of Moses and Elijah on the Mount of Transfiguration: Mt 17:1-3; it will be fashioned like Christ's glorious body and will no longer be subject to hunger, thirst, pain or death: Lk 20:35,36; 1 Cor 15:42-57; Php 3:20,21; Col 3:4; 1 Jn 3:1,2; Re 7:13-17; 21:3,4; cp Gn 5:24; He 11:5; 2 Kgs 2:11; *ref. 1267,1269,1270,1275.*

Differences in the Resurrection

1266 All the dead will be raised. But while the believers in Christ will be raised to everlasting life, the unbelievers will be raised to eternal damnation: Dn 12:2; Mt 25:46; Jn 5:28,29; Ac 24:15; 2 Th 1:7-10; 1 Jn 5:11,12; Re 20:12-15; *ref. 1271,1273.*

Resources

1267 Nothing in the world is annihilated in the sense that it no longer exists. Certain substances may disappear in the sense that they pass out of view, but they do not cease to exist. They are merely assimilated by other substances and reappear in another form.

In the laboratory of the scientist Faraday a highly prized silver goblet was once dropped carelessly by a workman into a vat of acid. Immediately the fierce acid attacked the silver, eating it atom by atom until the whole goblet disappeared in the liquid. The workman was in despair, but the great chemist, assuring him that all would be well, set about to recover the treasure. By pouring the right chemicals into the solution the silver quickly precipitated. Then it was gathered together and sent to a silversmith with the proper design. In a few days the goblet was back in its place, none the worse for its strange experience.

1268 The story is told of a woman in Germany who did not believe in immortality. In keeping with her unbelief, she caused herself to be buried in a sepulcher of heavy masonry covered with a heavy stone slab on which was inscribed her declaration that for her this was the end. But in some way a seed found lodgement in the mortar and, feeding upon her dead body, grew to be a tree that burst asunder the stone coffin.

— Macartnay's Illustrations

ref. 1263

1269 The resurrection of the body is a truth that cannot be known or understood by reason, 1 Cor 2:14. At the same time, it is a truth that cannot be denied or disproven by reason.

When after his trial before Felix the Apostle Paul was brought to trial before king Agrippa, he again explained why the Jews had accused him, and then he asked the king: "Why should any of you consider it incredible that God raises the dead?" Ac 26:8. The question is still pertinent today. Until one can explain how a seed dies and disintegrates in the earth and then produces a new life, or how a caterpillar emerges from a cocoon in the form of a beautiful butterfly, why should one think it incredible that God should raise the dead? See Jn 12:24.

However, Christian faith does not rest on arguments deduced from reason, but only on the revelation that the Holy Spirit gives through the eternal and changeless Word of God, the truth of which has been vindicated through the centuries and most gloriously demonstrated by the resurrection of Jesus Christ from the dead; see Lk 24:32, *ref. 1263*.

† † †

1270 It is said that, to give evidence of their belief in the resurrection, the early Christians taught their children to place their hand over their heart and to confess: "I believe that *this* body will rise again," *ref. 1263,1265*.

† † †

1271 Robert Ingersoll, the infidel, told this story: "I was never nonplused but once. One night I was lecturing and took occasion to show that the resurrection of Lazarus was probably a planned affair to bolster the waning fortunes of Jesus. Lazarus was to take sick and die. The girls were to bury him and send for Jesus. Lazarus was to feign death until Jesus should come and say, "Lazarus, come forth!" To emphasize the situation, I said: "Can anyone tell me why Jesus said, 'Lazarus, come forth?' " Down by the door a pale-faced man rose and with a shrill voice said: "Yes, I can tell you. If my Lord had not said, 'Lazarus,' he would have had the whole graveyard of Bethany coming out to him"; *ref. 1266*.

† † †

1272 I am standing upon the seashore. A ship at my side spreads her sails and starts for the blue ocean. She is an object of beauty and strength, and I stand and watch her until at length she is only a ribbon of white cloud just where the sea and sky come to mingle with each other.

Then someone at my side says, "There! She's gone!" Gone where? Gone from the sight — that is all . . . and just at the moment when someone at my side says, "There! She is gone!" there are other voices glad to take up the shout, "There! She comes!"

— O. O. McIntyre

ref. 1263

† † †

1273 Today, as in the days of the Apostle Paul, some will ridicule the doctrine of the resurrection and will go on living their vain philosophy of "let us eat and drink, for tomorrow we die": 1 Cor 15:32; Ac 17:32; but such unbelief always collapses, and such scoffing often turns into screaming when the hour of death approaches; *ref. 298,1266.*

† † †

1274 All religions have tombs, or sacred shrines, which their faithful followers venerate. But Christianity is the only religion that has an *empty* tomb; *ref. 783.*

† † †

1275 The editor of a religious journal was walking along the cliffs near the sea one Easter morning. In his walk he encountered an old fisherman, and during their conversation the editor was struck by the old man's simple faith in his risen Savior. "How do you know that Christ is risen?" he asked.

"Sir," came the reply, "do you see those cottages near the cliffs? Well, sir, sometimes when I'm far out at sea I know the sun is risen by the light that is reflected from the cottage windows. How do I know that Christ is risen? Why, sir, do I not see his light reflected from the faces of some of my fellow men every day, and do I not feel the light of his glory in my own life? You might as soon tell me that the sun is not risen, although I see its reflected light, as to tell me that my Lord is not risen when I see his reflected glory"; *ref. 1265.*

RICHES 1276-1296

(ref.: Trust 1532-1552)

The Source of Riches

1276 Earthly wealth is a gift from God: Dt 8:18; 1 Chr 29:12; Ps 24:1; 50:10-12; Ec 5:19; Hg 2:8; 1 Tm 6:17.

1277 Riches are not sinful in themselves. Examples of rich people who were pious: Abraham: Gn 13:1,5,6; Isaac: Gn 26:13,14; Jacob: Gn 32:5,10; 36:7; Joseph: Gn 45:8,13; David: 1 Chr 29:28; Solomon: 2 Chr 1:11,12; Job: Job 1:3; Joseph of Arimathea: Mt 27:57.

The Abuse of Riches

1278 They may draw the heart away from God and cause self-reliance: Dt 8:13,14; Ps 52:7; Jr 9:23,24; Eze 28:5; Mt 19:22,23; Lk 12:19; 1 Tm 6:17-19;

They may be used for selfish, sinful purposes: Lk 16:19; 1 Tm 6:9,10; Jas 5:1-6;

The love of money is the root of all evil: 1 Tm 6:10; *ref. 1282,1284*.

1279 They are vain, fleeting and uncertain: Pr 23:4,5; 27:24; *ref. 1288*;

They are deceitful: Ps 49:10-14; Ec 6:2; Hg 1:6; Mt 13:22; *ref. 1282-1284*;

They cause anxiety and trouble: Pr 15:27; Ec 5:12; *ref. 1282-1284*;

They cannot save: Ps 49:6-9; Pr 11:4; 23:5; 27:24; Jr 17:11; Zph 1:18; Mk 8:36,37; Lk 12:21; 1 Pe 1:18,19; *ref. 1288-1291*.

1280 The Bible warns against coveting them: Ex 20:17; Ps 62:10; Pr 15:27; 28:20; Is 5:8; Lk 12:15; 1 Tm 6:6f; He 13:5. Examples of coveting: Achan, Jos 6-7; Ahab, 1 Kgs 21:1f; Gehazi, 1 Kgs 5:21f; Judas, Mt 26:15,16; *ref. 1282-1292*.

A Right Attitude Toward Riches

1281 God's Word exhorts us to seek the true riches that are found in Christ: Mt 6:19,20,33; 19:21; Jn 6:27; Eph 1:3,18; 2:7; 3:8; Php 3:8; 4:19; Col 2:3; 1 Tm 6:17; He 11:26; Jas 2:5; 1 Pe 1:4,5; Re 3:18; and to use them in service to God and our fellow men: 1 Chr 29:3,14; Mt 19:21; 1 Tm 6:17-19; 1 Jn 3:17; *ref. 1285,1293-1296*.

Resources

1282 "The love of money is a root of all kinds of evil," 1 Tm 6:10. Covetousness, the craving for riches, the desire for wealth, is the source and fountainhead from which all evil flows. It draws the heart away from the love and service of God and makes man a selfish creature who shows no love and concern for his fellow men.

Moreover, when given free reign, greed leads to the grossest forms of transgressions against every commandment of God. To what depths of degradation will not men stoop to satisfy their craving for earthly riches! Think of Judas Ischariot who betrayed his Savior for a small amount of money, thirty pieces of silver. Think of those who sell their country for a sum of gold, of racketeers and gunmen who will not hesitate to commit murder in their desire to be rich, or of unscrupulous politicians who betray their trust and sell their honor and good name because of their love for money! Think of the countless acts of deceit and fraud perpetrated by those who operate black-markets and who are prompted by greed!

1283 Greek mythology tells of a Phrygian king, named Midas, whose one and constant desire was gold. To fulfill his desire he was granted the power to change everything he touched into gold. But now even his food, and his own daughter, turned into gold when touched, and he anxiously begged that the power might be taken from him.

1284 A Greek wrestler, Jussuf by name, who coveted wealth, was accustomed to carry his earnings in gold in a belt fastened around his waist. He had finished a match in America and was returning victoriously to his homeland. In the belt around his waist was $90,000 in gold. When the ship was but a short distance from land it was wrecked and quickly sank. Without a moment's hesitation the strong wrestler cast himself into the sea, confident that he could easily swim to the shore close by. But he had forgotten about the heavy weight of gold in the belt around his waist. The weight of the gold swiftly carried him to a watery grave.

1285 A penny will hide the biggest star if you hold it close enough to your eye; *ref. 1279,1285.*

† † †

1286 Speaking of riches in his commentary on Genesis 13:2, Matthew Henry wrote: "There is a burden of care in getting them, fear in keeping them, temptation in using them, guilt in abusing them, sorrow in losing them, and a burden of account, at last, to be given up concerning them"; *ref. 1279.*

† † †

1287 Mr. J. Paul Getty is reputed to be "the richest man in the world." He is 71 and is called "The Solitary Millionaire." He lives alone in a magnificent mansion a Sutton Place, in Surrey, England.

He owns oil wells, refineries, tankers and pipelines; also hotels, a life insurance company, a finance company and aircraft companies.

He has surrounded his 700 acre estate with bodyguards, vicious dogs, steel bars, searchlights, bells and sirens. In addition to being afraid of planes and ships and crackpots, he fears disease, old age, helplessness and death. He is lonely and gloomy. He admits that money cannot buy happiness.

— LeTorneau, *NOW*

1288 Time was running out on Corregidor. The fortress with its vaults contained one hundred million dollars which could not be taken off the island nor left for the enemy. The only thing to do was to burn it. Silent soldiers watched dollar bills go up in smoke. One of them picked up a $100 bill, lit his cigarette with it, and said "I always wanted to do that!" — For once, money didn't mean a thing; *ref. 1279.*

† † †

1289 The almighty dollar bequeathed to children is an almighty curse. No man has the right to handicap his son with such a burden as great wealth.
— Andrew Carnegie

1290 On his deathbed Alexander the Great expressed the wish that his hands might be left bare and open at his burial, not wrapped in cloth as was customary, that all might see that he was taking nothing out of the world. He had conquered all of the then known world. If he could take nothing out of the world, how vain and foolish is it not that people today spend their lifetime in amassing earthly wealth and fortune?

1291 Years ago, when men went to Alaska to look for gold, some penetrated far into the interior. There they came upon a miner's hut which seemed as quiet as a grave. Entering in, they found the skeletons of two men and a large quantity of gold on a rough table. There was also a letter which told of their successful hunt for gold. They were so eager to secure gold that they ignored the early coming of winter in that faraway northland. The more they mined, the more gold they found. Suddenly one day a fierce snowstorm was upon them. The snow became deeper and deeper, and at last there was no way to escape. Gradually their food gave out, and they lay down to die surrounded by gold.

There are many people like those two foolish miners. They covet wealth, houses and lands. Suddenly the icy hand of death is upon them, and they perish eternally. "What is a man profited if he shall gain the whole world and lose his own soul?"
— The Sunday School Times

ref. 1279

† † †

1292 "Do not wear yourself out to get rich," says the holy writer, "for they will surely sprout wings and fly off to the sky like an eagle," Pr 23:4,5. How many have learned this painful lesson when their possessions were lost through bad investments, through dishonest dealings, through theft, through fire or flood, or through confiscation!

Often the benefits that people hope to derive from their possessions are never realized. Many spend their health to gain wealth, only to find that they must spend their wealth to regain health; *ref. 1279.*

† † †

1293 Christ said, "Where your treasure is, there your heart will be also," Mt 6:21. He whose heart is bound to this world looks upon the things of the world as his treasure. His thoughts, affections, ideals and hopes are centered in the things this world has to offer. These are his God. His heart is so attached to these that he cannot and will not give them up. Such was the

322

case with the rich young ruler of whom we read that, when confronted with the decision to give up his riches and follow Christ, "he went away sad, because he had great wealth," Mt 19:21,22.

1294 The true and lasting treasures for which we are to strive are those which are found in Jesus Christ: Col 2:3,9. They are the priceless treasures of forgiveness of sins, peace with God, and the assurance of heaven and eternal life: Jn 17:3. These are the pearls of matchless price that we are to seek, and for the possession of which we should be ready to suffer the loss of all things: Mt 13:44-46; Php 3:8.

> Jesus, priceless Treasure
> Source of purest pleasure
>   Truest friend to me!
> Long my heart hath panted,
> Till it well-nigh fainted,
>   Thirsting after thee!
> Thine I am, O spotless Lamb!
> I will suffer naught to hide thee,
>   Ask for naught beside thee.
>   — Johann Franck

1295
> What is the world to me,
>   And all its vaunted pleasure,
> When thou, and thou alone,
>   Lord Jesus, art my Treasure!
> Thou only, deareast Lord,
>   My soul's Delight shalt be;
> Thou art my Peace, my Rest —
>   What is the world to me!
>   — Georg M. Pfefferkorn

1296 Using the riches God has entrusted to us for the purpose of helping others is one way in which we prove that we are the children of God. In so doing we are laying up for ourselves treasures in heaven and making investments in God's bank that will repay us with the dividend of eternal life. Our works of faith and labors of love, and our gifts to the poor and needy not only benefit them during our lifetime, but even after we are gone they go on to help others and on the last day they will testify to our living faith in Christ: Mt 25:34-36; Re 14:13.

> We lose what on ourselves we spend;
> We have as treasure without end
> Whatever, Lord, to thee we lend,
>   Who givest all;
> To thee, from whom we all derive
> Our life, our gifts, our power to give,
> Oh, may we ever with thee live,
>   Who givest all!
>   — Christopher Wordsworth

ref. 1281

SACRIFICES, BLOOD 1297-1308

(ref.: Redemption 1223-1252)

1297 In Old Testament times the Israelites had to bring many sacrifices and offerings to the Lord for various purposes, see *1299f*. But all offerings for sin had to be made by blood sacrifices: Lv 1:1-7; 3:1-17; 4:1-35. In prescribing these sacrifices the Lord said: "For the life of a creature is in the blood, and I have given it to you to make atonement for yourselves on the altar; it is the blood that makes atonement for one's life," Lv 17:11; cp He 9:22; *ref. 1299,1300,1302-1306.*

1298 The Old Testament blood sacrifices were types that pointed forward to Christ's complete sacrifice:

The animal for sacrifice had to be without blemish: Lv 1:3,10; 3:1,6; 4:3. —So Christ, our Sacrifice for sin, was the Lamb of God without spot: Jn 1:29; 1 Cor 5:7; 1 Pe 1:18,19; Re 13:8;

The sins of the worshipers were transferred to the animal by the laying on of hands, and the life of the innocent animal for sacrifice became a substitute for the life of the worshiper which had been forfeited through sin. — So God laid our sins upon his sinless Son who sacrificed himself for us as our substitue: Is 53:4-6,12; Jn 10:11,17,18; 2 Cor 5:21;

The shed blood of the sacrificial animal represented the blood of Christ. And because the blood that Christ shed is the very blood of the Son of God, his blood has the power to cleanse the sins of all men of all ages: Ac 20:28; 1 Jn 1:7; 2:2;

The blood sacrifices were an atonement for sin only by virtue of Christ's redeeming sacrifice which they typified. Moreover, those sacrifices only sanctified and purified the flesh of the worshipers; they could only make the people outwardly and ceremonially clean from their bodily defilement, and therefore they had to be repeated again and again. — But Christ's perfect sacrifice accomplished infinitely more, for it purifies the conscience and cleanses the heart from sin: He 9:9-14; 10:1-4; cp Nu 19:2-10. And because Christ's sacrifice was perfect and complete, no more sacrifices for sins are needed: He 7:26,27; 10:14,18;

While the Old Testament blood sacrifices had no power of their own to atone for sin, God intended them as a constant, daily reminder to the Israelites that sin is something so terrible, so heinous, so dreadful, deadly, and damning that is can be atoned for only by the matchless sacrifice which Christ would bring. And he alone would atone for the sins of the whole world by the shedding of his blood on the altar of Calvary's cross. Without the shedding of the holy blood of his Son there could be no remission of sins: Ex 29:38,39; Lv 17:11; Ro 5:9,10; Col 1:14,20; He 9:22; Re 7:14;

While the Old Testament sacrifices were offered, the prayers of the worshipers ascended heavenward. God showed his pleasure by accepting the smoke that rose from these sacrifices as a savor that was sweet to him: Ex

29:41; Ps 141:2; cp Gn 8:21. — So also God showed his pleasure in accepting Christ's sacrifice by raising him from the dead: Mt 3:17; 17:5; Ac 2:24; 3:15; 10:40; Eph 5:2;

As the Israelites dedicated their life to God in gratitude for the life that had been sacrificed for them, so we are to dedicate our life to Christ in never-ending thanks for having sacrificed himself for us that we might have eternal life: Lk 1:74,75; Ro 6:4,19; 12:1; 1 Cor 5:7; 6:20; 2 Cor 5:15; Php 1:21; Tt 2:14; He 9:14; 13:15; 1 Pe 1:18-22; 2:5; Re 5:9-12; 7:9-12; *ref. 1299,1300, 1302-1308.*

Resources

Sacrifices in Israel

1299 All sacrifices in Israel were acts of worship. The word "sacrifice" as used in the Old Testament means a gift, or presentation to God. These presentations were made to the Lord, either by individuals or in behalf of the nation, as thank-offerings or as an atonement for sin. Sacrifices made without the shedding of blood were presentations only. However, the offering always consisted of some product of labor and as such represented self-sacrifice. But animal sacrifices that involved the shedding of blood were more than a presentation to the Lord. In addition to being a gift that cost the offerer something, the blood testified of a life that had been substituted for the life of the worshiper and as such was a means of atonement.

Many references are made in the Book of Leviticus and elsewhere to burnt offerings: Lv 1-7. All burnt offerings involved the shedding of blood. In connection with every burnt offering there was also a meat and drink offering, which was an offering of devotion and which consisted of grain, or of meal, of bread, of cakes, or of fruits, of wine or olive oil.

The combination of the meat and drink offering with the burnt offering was intended as a constant reminder to the Israelites that even as they were indebted to God for redeeming their life from destruction by the atonement of blood, so they were also indebted to God for their daily food and all earthly sustenance: Ex 29:38-46; Nu ch. 28 and 29; *ref. 1297.*

1300 Every morning and every evening a lamb without blemish was offered in the Temple as a daily sacrifice for sin: Ex 29:38-46; Nu 28:3-8; and on Sabbath days that number was doubled: Nu 28:9,10. Besides these *Morning and Evening Sacrifices,* additional offerings were made on the occasion of the *New Moon*: Nu 28:11-15; the *Day of Atonement*: Lv 16; *ref. 1306;* and on *National Festival Days*: Dt 16:16,17; *ref. 1301.*

In addition to these sacrifices which were made in behalf of the entire nation there were offerings which were made by individuals either because the Lord had commanded them, or freewill offerings which individuals brought in gratitude for blessings received: Lv 22:17-25; Nu 7; 15:1-16; Dt 12:6; 16:10; cp 1 Kgs 8:62,63; Ezr 3:5; 7:16; 8:28; *ref. 1297.*

Festivals in Israel

1301 The *Passover,* also known as the *Feast of Unleavened Bread,* was the first of three annual festivals at which all male members among the Israelites had to appear before the Lord in the sanctuary: Ex 23:14-17; 34:18; Dt 16:16; Mk 14:12. It commemorated their redemption at the time of the slaying of the firstborn in Egypt: Ex 12; and was a time for renewing the covenant that God made with them when he adopted them as a peculiar treasure, a kingdom of priests and a holy nation: Ex 19:5,6; cp 1 Pe 2:9,10.

The second annual festival was the *Feast of Weeks*: Ex 34:22,23. It was so named because it was held seven complete weeks after the Passover, when the harvest season was consecrated by offering a sheaf of the first ripe barley: Lv 23:15,16; Dt 16:9,10. It also bore the name *Day of First Fruits,* because the first fruits of the wheat harvest were then presented: Ex 23:16; 34:22. In later time it was also known as *Pentecost,* meaning the fiftieth, because it was celebrated on the fiftieth day after the Passover: Ac 2:1; 20:16; 1 Cor 16:8.

The third annual festival was known as the *Festival of the Tabernacles,* or *Ingatherings,* which occurred in the fall of the year at the time of the final harvest: Lv 23:34-44; Dt 16:16; 2 Chr 8:12,13. During the observance of this festival, which lasted one week, the children of Israel lived in booths to remind them of their journey from Egypt through the wilderness: Lv 23:43; Ho 12:9.

There are a number of references in the New Testament which indicate that Christ attended these festivals in fulfillment of all righteousness: Mt 26:17; Mk 14:12f; Lk 22:8; Jn 2:23; 7:2-37; 13:1; see also Lk 2:21-24.

1302 In 1 Corinthians 5:7 the inspired apostle wrote: "Christ, our Passover Lamb, has been sacrificed." The unmistakable reference is to the Old Testament Passover-festival which offers both a striking comparison and a striking contrast: Ex 12:1-30:

The Israelites could not free themselves from the bondage of Egypt: Ex 1:11,13; 5:4-9. — So no one could free himself from the bondage of sin: Jr 2:22; Ro 3:20; *ref. Justification 850-864*;

The passover-lamb had to be without blemish: Ex 12:5. — Thus it was a symbol of Christ, the sinless Lamb of God: Jn 1:29; 1 Pe 1:18,19;

No bone of the passover-lamb was broken: Nu 9:12. — So, too, no bone was broken in Christ, our Passover-Lamb, when he sacrificed himself for us: Jn 19:36; 1 Cor 5:7;

The Israelites were instructed to place the blood of the passover-lamb on the doorposts of their homes as a sign for the Angel of Death to pass over; only they were spared who followed this instruction. Ex 12:7,13,23,27. —Those who do not believe in Christ as their Savior, whose hearts have not been sprinkled with his atoning blood, will not escape the final judgment of God: Jn 3:18,36; Ac 4:12; 2 Th 1:9,10; He 2:3; 10:28-31; *ref. Redemption 1223-1252*;

The Israelites ate the passover-lamb and thus were strengthened for their journey to the promised land: Ex 12:8. — Christ strengthens us through his life-giving Word and through the holy sacrament of his Supper as we journey to our heavenly home: Mt 26:26-28; Jn 6:35,63;

The passover was eaten with bitter herbs to remind the Israelites of the bitterness of their former bondage: Ex 12:8. — As we taste the bitterness of sin which caused our spiritual bondage we are reminded of the matchless price that Christ paid for our redemption, and this should lead us to repentance: see 1 Cor 5:8.

Israel's redemption from the bondage of Egypt was a time for great rejoicing: Ex 12:42; 15:1-21; cp Ps 14:7; 126:1. — Our redemption through Christ is an infinitely greater cause for rejoicing: Lk 1:46,47,67,68; 2:10,11; Ac 8:5,8; 8:38; 16:34; Ro 5:2; Php 4:4; 1 Pe 1:8.

1303 The story is told that on the night of the first Passover a boy, the firstborn in the family, lay in bed sick. He called to his father and asked whether he had placed the blood of the lamb on the door of their home. "Yes," said the father, "I told the servant to take care of it." But as the hour of midnight drew near the boy became very restless. Anxiously calling to his father again he asked: "Father, are you sure that the blood of the lamb is on the door?" This time the father went to look for himself and, to his great surprise, he saw that there was no blood on the door. Hurriedly he had his servant prepare the passover lamb and then sprinkled the blood on the door just a few moments before the hour of midnight arrived.

Has indeed the blood of Christ, the Lamb of God, been sprinkled on the door of your heart?

1304
Not all the blood of beasts
   On Jewish altars slain
Could give the guilty conscience peace
   Or wash away the stain.

But Christ, the heav'nly Lamb,
   Takes all our sins away;
A sacrifice of nobler name
   And richer blood than they.

Believing, we rejoice
   To see the curse remove;
We bless the Lamb with cheerful voice
   And sing his bleeding love.
                    — Isaac Watts

1305
Pascal Lamb, by God appointed,
   All our sins on thee were laid;
By almighty love anointed,
   Thou hast full atonement made.
Ev'ry sin may be forgiven
   Thro' the virtue of thy blood;

Open is the gate of heaven,
Peace is made 'twixt man and God.

— Anon

1297-1300

The Day of Atonement

Leviticus 16:7-34

1306 On the Day of Atonement, which occurred once a year, the Jewish high priest entered the holy of holies, which was but an earthly sanctuary made with hands. — Christ, our great High Priest, entered the sanctuary of heaven, there to appear in the presence of God for us: He 9:11,12,24;

The Jewish high priest entered the holy of holies with the blood of sacrifices for his own sins and for the sins of the people. — Christ's sacrifice was wholly in our behalf; he needed no sacrifice for himself for he was without sin: He 7:26,27; *ref. 613,623,626,629,632.*

The sacrifice which the Jewish high priest brought was the blood of an animal. And because both the priest and the sacrifice were imperfect the ritual had to be repeated year after year. — The sacrifice which Christ offered was his own blood, and because it was perfect it is effectual forever: He 9:11-14,25,26; 10:11-14;

When the Jewish high priest entered the holy of holies he sprinkled the blood of the sacrifice on the mercy-seat and there interceded for the people. The mercy-seat was the golden lid that covered the Ark of the Covenant: He 9:3-5. There God's glory was manifested as he communed with his people through the high priest: Ex 25:17-22; 30:6; Nu 7:89; Lv 16:2,13-17. The Ark of the Covenant contained the two tables of the law. The law with its demands and threats condemned the people, but the sprinkling of the blood of the sacrifice on the mercy-seat symbolized that the sins of the people had been covered. — Symbolically, the mercy-seat represents the "throne of grace" in heaven where Christ entered with his own blood, which redeems us from the curse of the law and cleanses us from our sins, and where he ever lives to intercede for us: He 4:16; 9:7-12,24; 10:19-22; Ga 3:13; 1 Pe 1:18; 1 Jn 1:7; cp Ro 3:24,25; 8:34; 1 Jn 2:2;

On the Day of Atonement the high priest cast lots upon two goats, the one to be slain for a sacrifice and the other to be "presented alive before the Lord, to make an atonement with him, and to let him go for a scapegoat into the wilderness." After the rituals pertaining to the first goat were completed the high priest laid both of his hands upon the head of the live goat and confessed over it all the sins of the people. This scapegoat was then sent away by the hand of a fit man into the wilderness where it was lost: Lv 16:7-10,20-22. — So God the Father laid upon Christ the iniquities of us all, and Christ bore our sins and their punishments in our stead, and now they are lost forever: Is 44:22; 53:4-6,12; Jr 31:34; Jn 1:29; Ac 3:19; Ro 5:11; 2 Cor 5:21; Col 2:14; He 8:12; 10:17; 1 Pe 2:24; 1 Jn 2:2; 3:5.

1307
From morn till eve my theme shall be
  Thy mercy's wondrous measure;
To sacrifice myself for thee
  Shall be my aim and pleasure.
My stream of life shall ever be
  A current flowing ceaselessly,
  Thy constant praise outpouring.
I'll treasure in my memory
O Lord, all thou hast done for me,
  Thy gracious love adoring.

— Paul Gerhardt

1308
Were the whole realm of nature mine,
  That were a tribute far too small;
Love so amazing, so divine,
  Demands my soul, my life, my all.

— Isaac Watts

ref. 1298

SATAN AND THE EVIL ANGELS 1309-1321

(ref.: The Good Angels 47-68)

Their Origin

1309 Though originally created by God as good angels: Gn 1:31; they sinned and fell from their first estate: 2 Pe 2:4; Jd 6. As a consequence of this God sentenced them to the eternal fires of hell: Mt 25:41; Re 20:10; and therefore they tremble at the very mention of God's name: Mt 8:29; Jas 2:19;

Their leader is Satan, and their kingdom is spoken of as the kingdom of darkness: Mt 12:24,26; Lk 11:18; Ac 26:18; Eph 6:12; Col 1:12-14; *ref. 1315.*

Their Names

1310 Satan: Mt 4:10; Lk 10:18; 2 Cor 11:14. The word "Satan" (Greek: *Satanas*) occurs 51 times in the Bible. It is a proper noun and is always used in the singular. The word "devil" (Greek: *Diabolos*) occurs 35 times. It, too, is always used in the singular and is the Greek equivalent for Satan. The Greek word *daimonion*, which also means "devil," is used both in the singular and plural and occurs 56 times. Satan is also called:

Adversary: 1 Pe 5:8;
Beast: Re 19:19;
Beelzebub: Mt 12:24;
Belial: 2 Cor 6:15;
Deceiver: Re 12:9;
Devil: Mt 4:1; Jn 8:44;
Dragon: Re 12:9;
Father of lies: Jn 8:44;
God of this world: Jn 12:31; 2 Cor 4:4;

Murderer: Jn 8:44;
Prince of this world: Jn 12:31; 14:30; 16:11; Eph 2:2;
Serpent: 2 Cor 11:3; Re 12:9; 20:2;
Tempter: Mt 4:3;
Wicked one: Mt 13:38; *ref. 1315.*

The evil angels, who are also called
Devils: Mt 8:28; Lk 10:17;
Evil spirits: Lk 7:21;
Unclean spirits: Mt 10:1; Mk 5:2;
Rulers of the darkness of this world: Eph 6:12; *ref. 1315,1321.*

General Considerations

1311 The Bible relates that there are different ranks, such as thrones, dominions, principalities, and powers among the evil angels as well as among the good angels: Ro 8:38; Eph 1:21; 3:10; Col 1:16; 2:15;

They are the rulers of the darkness of this world: Jn 14:30; 2 Cor 4:4; Eph 6:12; 1 Jn 5:19;

They are of great number: Mk 5:9; 16:9; Lk 8:30;

They possess great power and extraordinary wisdom: Mk 5:2-4,13; Lk 11:21; Eph 6:12; 1 Pe 5:8; Re 13:2; but their power is limited by God: Job 1:12; 2:5,6; Lk 10:19; 22:32; Ro 16:20;

They are full of cunning, lies, and deceit: Jn 8:44; 2 Cor 2:11; 4:4; 11:3,14; Eph 6:11; 2 Th 2:9,10; Re 2;24; 12:9; 20:8.

Their Work

1312 They are intent upon destroying God's works: Job 1:12f; 2:7; cp Mt 8:30-32; and at times take possession of man's faculties: Mt 8:28-34; 9:32; 12:22; 15:22; Mk 1:23; Lk 8:2; 11:14; 13:16; Ac 5:16; 10:38;

Having failed in their attempt to frustrate Christ's work of redemption: Mt 4:1-11; Lk 4:1-13; Jn 13:2; they are intent upon frustrating the work of Christ's church: Mt 13:24-30,38,39; Ac 5:3; 2 Cor 2:11; 1 Th 2:18; 2 Th 2:8-10; Re 2:10. To this end:

They constantly seek to seduce man into sin: Gn 3:1-5; Lk 22:31; Ac 5:3; 2 Cor 11:3; Eph 2:2; 6:11; 2 Tm 2:26; 1 Pe 5:8; 1 Jn 2:13;

They seek to prevent man from hearing the saving message of the gospel: Mk 4:15; Lk 8:12; or to blind his heart so that he cannot understand the Word: 2 Cor 4:4; Eph 2:2; 2 Tm 2:26;

They are assisted in their work by the unbelieving world, which lies in their power: 1 Jn 2:15-17; 5:19; cp Jn 15:18-21; 17:14; 2 Cor 6:14-18; Eph 5:11; *ref. 1316,1318,1321.*

Christ's Victory Over Them

1313 Christ has overcome the power of Satan for us: Mt 12:22; Lk 10:18; Jn 12:31; 14:30; Ac 10:38; Col 2:15; 2 Tm 1:10; He 2:14,15; 1 Jn 3:8; Re 20:10;

Christ's victory becomes our victory through faith: Lk 10:19; 22:31,32; Jn 16:33; Ro 8:33-37; 16:20; 1 Cor 15:55-57; He 2:18; 1 Pe 5:8,9; 1 Jn 5:4; Re 15:2, *ref. 673,681,755,774.*

Our Spiritual Warfare Against Them

1314 Holy Scriptures admonish us:

To resist the devil by watchfulness and prayer, lest we fall into temptation: Mt 26:41; Eph 4:27; Jas 4:7; 1 Pe 5:8;

To avoid evil and evil associations: Ps 1:1; Pr 4:14; 1 Cor 5:11; 15:33; 2 Cor 6:14-18; Eph 5:3-12; 1 Jn 2:15-17;

To arm ourselves with the Word of God: Ps 1:1-3; Mt 4:4,7,10; 2 Cor 10:4; Eph 6:11-17; 1 Th 5:8; Re 12:11; *ref. 1317-1320.*

Resources

1315 One night Thomas Carlyle took Ralph Waldo Emerson through the dark streets of London's worst section and then asked: "Do you believe in the devil now?" *ref. 1309,1310.*

— selected

ref. 1309,1310

† † †

1316 Men don't believe in a devil now as their fathers used to do;
    They've forced the door of the broadest creed to let his majesty
        through.
    There isn't a print of his cloven hoof or a fiery dart from his bow
    To be found in earth or air today, for the "wise" have voted so.

But who is mixing the fatal draught that palsies heart and brain,
And leads the bier of each passing year with ten hundred thousand slain?
Who blights the bloom of our youth today with the fiery breath of hell?
If the devil isn't and never was? Won't some of these people tell?

Who dogs the steps of the toiling saints and digs the pit for his feet?
Who sows the tares in the field of time wherever God sows wheat?
The devil is voted not to be, and of course the thing is true!
But who is doing the kind of work the devil alone can do?

Won't somebody step to the front forthwith and make his bow and show
How the frauds and crimes of a single day spring up? We want to know.
The devil was fairly voted out, and of course "the devil's gone"!
But simple people would like to know *who carries his business on.*

— Anon

ref. 1309-1312

† † †

1317   Rise, my soul, to watch and pray,
                From thy sleep awaken; Be not by the evil day
                Unawares o'ertaken.

For the Foe,
Well we know,
Oft his harvest reapeth
While the Christian sleepeth.

Watch against the devil's snares
    Lest asleep he find thee;
For indeed no pains he spares
    To deceive and blind thee.
Satan's prey
Oft are they
Who secure are sleeping
And no watch are keeping.

Watch! Let not the wicked world
    With its pow'r defeat thee.
Watch lest with her pomp unfurled
    She betray and cheat thee.
Watch and see
Lest there be
Faithless friends to charm thee,
Who but seek to harm thee.

— Johann B. Freystein

ref. 1314

† † †

1318 Speaking of Satan's cunning and craft, St. Paul wrote, "Satan himself masquerades as an angel of light," 2 Cor 11:14.

There is a strange legend about Martin Luther which tells that one day, as he sat engaged in his sacred studies, there was a knock at the door and a stranger appeared of lordly look and in princely attire.

"Who are you?" asked Martin.

"I am Christ," was the answer.

The confident bearing and the commanding tone of the visitor would have overawed a man less wise. But Martin simply gave his visitor one deep, searching glance and then quickly asked: "Where is the print of the nails?" He had noticed that this one indubitable mark of Christ's person was wanting. There were no nail-scars upon those jeweled hands. And the kingly mien and the brilliant dress of the pretender were not enough to prove his claim while the print of the nails was wanting.

Confused by this searching question and his base deception exposed, the Prince of Evil — for it was he — quickly fled.

— selected

ref. 1312

† † †

1319   A mighty Fortress is our God,
                A trusty Shield and Weapon;

He helps us free from ev'ry need
  That hath us now o'ertaken.
The old evil Foe
Now means deadly woe;
Deep guile and great might
Are his dread arms in fight;
  On earth is not his equal.

Tho' devils all the world should fill,
  All eager to devour us,
We tremble not, we fear no ill,
  They shall not overpower us.
This world's prince may still
Scowl fierce as he will,
He can harm us none,
He's judged; the deed is done;
  One little word can fell him.
                    — Martin Luther

1320   Lord Jesus, who dost love me,
O spread thy wings above me,
And shield me from alarm!
Though Satan would devour me;
Let angel guards sing o'er me;
"This child of God shall meet no harm!"
                    — H. Isaac

ref. 1314

† † †

1321 In a symbolic way the Bible associates light with God: Ps 27:1; 1 Jn 1:5. Christ is spoken of as the Light of the world: Jn 1:4,5,8,9; 8:12; Is 60:1; and as the Sun of Righteousness: Mal 4:2; see also Lk 1:78. Christ's followers are spoken of as the sons of light and the children of light who are to walk in the light: Mt 5:14-16; Jn 12:36; Eph 5:8; 1 Th 5:5; 1 Pe 2:9. God's Word is spoken of as a Lamp unto our feet and a Light unto our path: Ps 119:105,130; 2 Pe 1:19.

Conversely, the Bible associates darkness with evil, with judgment and with the outer darkness of hell: Is 5:30; 13:9,10; Jl 2:31; 3:14,15; Mt 8:12; 22:13; 2 Pe 2:17; Jd 6. Satan and his evil angels are called "the rulers of the darkness of this world": Eph 6:12; see also Ac 26:18; 2 Cor 4:3,4. The works of sin are spoken of as the works of darkness: Ro 13:12, and those who live in sin are spoken of as those who love the works of darkness: Jn 3:19,20; cp 2 Cor 6:14-18; *ref. 1310.*

(ref.: Discipleship 300f; Good Works 416f; Talents 1368)

Exhortations To Serve the Lord

1322 See Dt 10:12; Jos 24:14,15; Ps 2:11; 100:2; Mt 5:16; Jn 15:4-8; Ro 6:4,12,13; 12:1,9; 1 Cor 6:19,20; Ga 6:9,10; He 13:16; 1 Pe 2:9-12; *ref. 1342.*

The Nature of Christian Service

1323 It is rendered to God and Christ: Mt 22:37,38; 26:10; Lk 1:74,75; Jn 12:26; 15:8; 1 Cor 7:22; 2 Cor 5:15; Ga 2:20; Eph 6:6,7; Php 1:21; Col 3:24; 1 Pe 4:11; *ref. 1327-1333,1338,1339,1341;*

It involves the service of praise and of Christian life: Mt 5:16; Jn 15:1-8; Ro 6:4,12,13; 12:1; 1 Cor 6:19,20; He 9:13,14; 1 Pe 2:9-12; *ref. 1336;*

It involves service to our fellow men: Is 58:7; Mic 6:8; Mt 22:39; Ga 5:13; 6:9,10; He 13:16; 1 Jn 3:14-18; *ref. 1326,1330,1332,1336-1338;*

It involves service to the church: Ps 100:2f; Is 6:8; Mt 20:1f; 25:14f; Mk 13:34; Ac 9:6; 1 Cor 14:12; 15:58; *ref. 1330,1331,1336,1341,1342;*

It involves service according to ability: Mt 25:14-30; Mk 13:34; Lk 12:48; Ro 12:6-8; 1 Cor 12:6,7; 1 Pe 4:10,11; *ref. 1334,1339,1342.*

Characteristics of Christian Service

1324 It is rendered willingly: Jdg 5:2; 8:25; Ne 11:2; Ps 110:3; 2 Cor 8:3; *ref. 1327,1330,1338,1341,1342;*

It is done joyfully: Ne 8:10; 12:43; Ps 100:2; 126:5,6; Lk 10:17; Jn 4:36; Ac 11:23; *ref. 1336,1342;*

It is done humbly: Mic 6:8; Mk 10:43-45; Ac 20:19; Php 2:5-8; *ref. 1332;*

It is performed wholeheartedly: 2 Chr 15:15; Mt 4:10; 6:24; 22:37; *ref. 1334;*

It is offered without a thought of reward: Mt 25:37-39; Lk 17:7-10; *ref. 1335,1337,1340.*

Christ Our Example

1325 He rendered his service in a spirit of humility: Mt 11:29; Mk 10:45; Lk 22:27; Jn 13:4-17; Ro 15:5; 2 Cor 10:1; Php 2:5-8; *ref. 1332,1341;*

He rendered his service willingly: Jn 10:11,17,18; He 10:7; *ref. 1332,1341;*

He rendered his service joyfully: Jn 15:11; 17:13; He 12:2; *ref. 1331, 1332,1341;*

He rendered his service completely: Jn 4:34; 5:36; 9:4; 17:4; 19:30; *ref. 1332,1336,1341.*

Resources

1326   Lord, what wilt thou that I should do? What is my task?
This question, leaping from my heart, I kneel to ask.
What place of duty can I fill? Where can I go?
To lighten, in thy holy Name, another's woe?

So many hearts are torn today, so many weep,
So many souls are passing now through water's deep;
So many bear their loads alone without thy grace,
So many have not found in thee a resting place.

In such a world, with needs so vast, what can I do?
Fill thou my heart with love like thine, with pity too.
Here are my hands, my feet, my all; lead thou the way,
Where I may do thy work unceasingly while it is day.

— Anon

ref. 1323

† † †

1327 In the days of slavery a sensational preacher in the city of Brooklyn one Sunday brought a number of slaves into his church and called upon his members to purchase their freedom by paying a price for them. All were redeemed. One slave, for whose freedom the purchaser had paid a considerable price, said to his benefactor: "Massa, let me go with you and serve you." "But you are free," replied his benefactor, "you do not have to serve anyone." But the slave persisted, saying, "Massa, you paid a big price for me, I belong to you. Let me serve you till I die, not because I have to, but because I love you, for you bought me"; cp 1 Cor 6:19,20.

— selected

ref. 1324

† † †

1328 Not long before he died, Ty Cobb, the famous baseball player, learned to know Jesus Christ as his Savior. His pastor, Dr. John Richardson, noted that on his death-bed Ty Cobb did not once mention his years of ball playing. Instead, his entire conversation dwelt on the subject of his Savior; *ref. 1323*.

† † †

1329 There is a legend which tells how some years after the event, St. Thomas was again troubled with agonizing doubts as to our Lord's resurrection. He sought the apostles, and began to pour out his soul's troubles into their ears. But first one, and then the other, looked at him in astonishment, and told the unhappy doubter that he was sorry for him, but really he had so much to do he had no time to listen to his tale. Then Thomas would fain have imparted his woes to some of the women. But they, as busy as Dorcas, and in like employment, soon made him understand that they had no leisure for such thoughts as these.

At last it dawned upon Thomas that perhaps it was because they were so busy that they were free from the doubts which tortured him. He took the hint; he went to Parthia, occupied himself with preaching Christ's gospel, and was never troubled with doubts any more; *ref. 1323*.

— W. G. Polack

335

† † †

1330
Three things the Master hath to do —
And we who serve him here below
And long to see his kingdom come,
May pray or give or go!
He needs them all — the open hand,
The willing feet, the asking heart —
To work together and to weave
The threefold cord which shall not part.
— A. F. Johnson
ref. 1323

† † †

1331 I have seen the Great Salt Lake out in the West, whose waters are so brackish and dense with salt that even a fish cannot live therein. It is a veritable Dead Sea. One beautiful moonlight night last summer I stood on the deck of a lake steamer plowing its way from Cleveland to Buffalo through the sparkling waters of the beautiful Lake Erie, so fresh and sweet that cities along its shores get from it their drinking water. The thought came to me that both Lake Erie and Great Salt Lake get their supply from the same reservoir of the skies, and yet what a difference!

The next day I stood on the brink of old Niagara and saw that mighty torrent take its awful plunge, then swirl on through rapids, and on down through the St. Lawrence, kissing into smiling beauty the Thousand Islands, and at last finding a home in the bosom of the ocean.

I had discovered the secret of the difference. Great Salt Lake has no outlet. It keeps all it gets, except what the blazing sun draws out by evaporation. Scientists say that it is actually drying up. But the Great Lakes, by continually emptying themselves, keep forever fresh and sweet. There is a lesson for us here: As God fills us with goodness and grace sent down from heaven, let us not try to keep these blessings for ourselves, and thus become stagnant and bitter, and finally dry up; but let us find an outlet in service and in giving, and in God's great plan for the evangelization of the world. Then will our lives become channels of blessing — rivers of living water, bringing life and beauty and refreshment along the way, until at last we find a home with God in the ocean of his eternity.
— *Choice Morsels*
ref. 1323

† † †

1332 A visitor in a hospital, as she observed a nurse who was engaged in a very lowly service to a suffering patient, said: "I wouldn't do that for a million dollars." The nurse replied, "Neither would I."

Love for Christ and for his matchless sacrifice for us makes the most painful service for him a pleasure. This was the great motivating power in the life of the Apostle Paul, who said: "For Christ's love compels us," 2 Cor 5:14. Motivated by the Savior's wondrous love for him, Paul was ready to "become all things to all men so that by all possible means he might save some," 1 Cor 9:22; *ref. 1323.*

† † †

1333 Far up on the Alpine passes the Romans built their roads that travelers might pass from Italy to northern Europe. But in winter snow would cover the roads and travelers would be lost. A man by the name of Bernard devoted himself to dwelling at the highest pass to rescue those who were lost in storms. They called him St. Bernard. People never forgot his service, and long years afterward when those friendly huge dogs were trained to rescue Alpine travelers, the only name that fit them was the name of the man who had dedicated his life to this work years before.

— Russell J. Clinchy

ref. 1323

† † †

1334 John Wesley had the following as his rule for life:

> Do all the good you can,
> By all the means you can,
> In all the ways you can,
> In all the places you can,
> At all the times you can,
> To all the people you can,
> As long as ever you can.
>
> *ref. 1324*

† † †

1335
> Think not the good,
> The gentle deeds of mercy thou hast done,
> Shall die forgotten all; the poor, the prisoner,
> The fatherless, the friendless, and the widow,
> Who daily own the bounty of thy hand,
> Shall cry to heaven, and pull a blessing on thee.

— Nicholas Rowe

> *ref. 1324*

† † †

1336
> O Master, let me walk with thee
> In lowly paths of service free;
> Tell me the secret; help me bear
> The strain of toil, the fret of care.
>
> Help me the slow of heart to move
> By some clear, winning word of love;
> Teach me the wayward feet to stay,
> And guide them in the homeward way.

Teach me thy patience; still with thee
In closer, dearer company.
In work that keeps faith sweet and strong,
In trust that triumphs over wrong.

In hope that sends a shining ray
Far down the future's broadening way;
In peace that only thou can'st give,
With thee, O Master, let me live.
— Washington Gladden
ref. 1323,1324

† † †

1337 A doctor hesitated when a call for help came on a particularly inclement night, but his love of humanity was strong, and he went through a drenching rain to the home of a poor laborer. His services saved the life of a small child. Years later the doctor said: "I never dreamed that in saving the life of that child on the farm hearth I was saving the life of the leader of England." That child was Lloyd George, onetime British prime minister.
— Robert Scott Wallis

1338 Four hundred years ago there were two brothers in Germany, Franz and Albrecht Duerer. Although very poor in this world's goods, they both wanted to become artists. So Albrecht, the younger, suggested: "Franz, I'll work as a laborer and pay for your training. And when you are finished you can do the same for me."

"Fine," said Franz, "but we'll do it my way. I want you to go and study first, and I'll work." Franz recognized his brother's talent for painting was far greater than his own. So it was that for many years Albrecht studied painting under the finest painters of his day, while Franz toiled to pay the cost.

At last Albrecht returned, joyfully greeted Franz, and cried: "Now you'll be able to go."

Silently Franz held up his hands. For now they were no longer the hands of an artist, but the hands of a workman, so gnarled with years of hard labor that they were not able to hold a pencil, much less an artist's brush.

Stunned at the sight of the calloused hands, Albrecht put his arms around his brother's shoulder. Tearfully he sobbed, "Franz, I can repay you in only one way. I will paint a picture that will speak to men's hearts, a picture of those hands of sacrifice and love."

Today, Albrecht Duerer's world famous painting "The Praying Hands" immortalizes his brother's tribute.

As we look upon Christ's nail-pierced and bleeding hands and recall the matchless sacrifice he brought for us, must not our grateful heart respond:
Thou gavest thyself for me,
I give myself to thee!
ref. 1323,1324

1339 Otto Baganz, rated among the top concert harpists, practiced three hours daily. When asked why he needed so much practice, he replied: "I am working for the Lord. My best is the least I can give him. Every man has a gift. Every man owes it to the Lord to use it for him in the best way possible"; *ref. 1323.*

† † †

1340 "Where does your great river go?" David Livingstone asked the natives on the banks of the mighty Congo. "It is lost in the sands," they said. They did not know of the mightier sea, but only of the sands about them. But the Congo flowed steadily onward to the vast ocean. It was not lost.

Nor are our labors for Christ lost. They bring blessings to our own life, they enrich the lives of others, and they flow on and on into the endless ocean of eternal life with Christ in heaven: cp Re 14:13; *ref. 1324.*

† † †

1341 Speaking of the services he rendered for Christ, David Livingstone said: "People talk of the sacrifice I have made in spending so much of my life in Africa. Can that be called a sacrifice which is simply paid back as a small part of a great debt owing to our God, which we can never repay? . . . Say rather it is a privilege. Anxiety, sickness, suffering, or danger now and then with a foregoing of the common conveniences and charities of this life, may make us pause, and cause the spirit to waver and the soul to sink, but let this only be for a moment. All these are nothing when compared with the glory which shall hereafter be revealed in and for us. I never made a sacrifice. . . . We remember the great sacrifice which he made who left his Father's throne on high to give himself for us"; *ref. 1323-1325.*

† † †

1342
> Hark! the voice of Jesus crying,
>   "Who will go and work today?
> Fields are white and harvests waiting,
>   Who will bear the sheaves away?"
> Loud and long the Master calleth,
>   Rich rewards he offers thee;
> Who will answer, gladly saying,
>   "Here am I, send me, send me?"
>
> If you cannot speak like angels,
>   If you cannot preach like Paul,
> You can tell the love of Jesus,
>   You can say he died for all.
> If you cannot rouse the wicked
>   With the Judgment's dread alarms,
> You can lead the little children
>   To the Savior's waiting arms.

If you cannot be a watchman,
  Standing high on Zion's wall,
Pointing out the path to heaven,
  Off'ring life and peace to all,
With you prayers and with your bounties
  You can do what God demands;
You can be like faithful Aaron,
  Holding up the prophet's hands.

Let none hear you idly saying,
  "There is nothing I can do,"
While the souls of men are dying
  And the Master calls for you.
Take the task he gives you gladly,
  Let his work your pleasure be;
Answer quickly when he calleth,
  "Here am I, send me, send me."
                — St. 1,2,4 Daniel March
                   St. 3, author unknown
  ref. 1323,1324

SIN 1343-1364

(ref.: Law of God 865-896; Ten Commandments 1460-1502)

Definition

1343 Sin is every transgression of God's law: 1 Jn 3:4, whether it be in thought: Ex 20:17; Mt 5:22,28; Ro 7:7; 1 Jn 3:15; or in word: Ex 20:16; Mt 12:36; Jas 3:2; or in deed: Ex 20:13-15; Ga 5:19-21; Eph 5:3-5;

1344 Other names for sin: iniquity: Ex 34:7; debts; Mt 6:12; faults: Mt 18:15; disobedience: Ro 5:19; unrighteousness: Ro 6:13; trespass: 2 Cor 5:19; wrong: Col 3:25.

How Sin Entered the World

1345 Through Satan, who was once a holy angel but fell from God: Jn 8:44; 2 Cor 11:3; 1 Jn 3:8; *ref. 1309-1321;*

1346 Through our first parents, Adam and Eve, who of their own free will yielded to the temptation of the devil: Gn 3:1-7; Ro 5:12,18,19.

Kinds of Sin

1347 Original sin: The sin and guilt which all mankind inherited from Adam and Eve and which results in the total corruption of man's human nature. As a consequence of it:

The image of God in which God originally created man and which consisted of perfect knowledge, of righteousness and holiness, has been lost: Gn 1:26; cp Gn 5:3; Eph 4:22-24; Col 3:9,10;

All mankind are conceived and born in sin: Ps 51:5; Jn 3:6; all are without righteousness and are guilty before God: Ro 3:10,19,23; 5:18,19. Their carnal mind is enmity against God: Ro 8:7; 1 Cor 2:14; Eph 4:18; they are inclined only to that which is evil in God's sight: Gn 8:21; Ro 7:18,19; and are spiritually dead in trespasses and sins: Eph 2:1,5; Col 2:13.

1348 Actual sins: These involve all manner of transgression against God and fellow men and are a result of original sin: Ps 53:3; Mt 7:17; 15:19; Ro 7:18; Jas 4:1; 1 Jn 3:4. They include doing the evil that God has forbidden (sins of commission): Ga 5:19-21; e.g. Lk 10:30; or neglecting to do the good God has commanded (sins of omission): Mt 23:23; 25:41-45; Lk 10:31,32; 12:47; Jas 2:15,16; 4:17. While every sin merits God's wrath: Ga 3:10; Jas 2:10; there is a difference in degrees of punishment for voluntary and involuntary sins: Lk 12:47,48; Jn 19:11; Mt 11:20-24; 12:41,42:

Voluntary sins are premeditated sins, e.g., Absalom's rebellion: 2 Sm 15:1-6f; Judas' betrayal: Mt 26:14-16;

Involuntary sins, or sins of weakness, are sins committed due to lack of knowledge, or caused by momentary passions such as fear, or wrath, e.g., the two hundred men that went out of Jerusalem with Absalom not knowing of his wicked intentions: 2 Sm 15:11; Peter who denied Christ and his fellow disciples out of fear: Lk 22:54-62; Ga 2:12f; *ref. 1352-1355,1358.*

1349 The sin against the Holy Ghost (the unpardonable sin): This sin consists in "a knowing, conscious, stubborn, and malicious opposition to divine truth once recognized as such, and in blasphemous hostility against it." It is unpardonable, not because God's grace is insufficient: Ro 5:20; but because the sinner willfully hardens his heart: Mt 12:22-32; Mk 3:22-30; Lk 12:10; Ac 7:51f; He 6:4-6; 10:29; 1 Jn 5:16; *ref. 1356.*

Punishment for Sin

1350 God's wrath and displeasure against sin is revealed: Ex 20:5; 2 Kgs 22:13; Ps 7:11; Is 59:2; Ro 1:18; 2:8; Ga 3:10-12; Eph 2:3; 5:6; e.g., in the Flood: Gn 7; in the destruction of Sodom and Gomorrah: Gn 19;

"The wages of sin is death," Ro 6:23; "death," which means "separation," has two meanings:

Temporal death: Gn 2:17; Ro 5:12; 6:23; Cor 15:56; Jas 1:15;

Eternal death (damnation, or, the second death): Eze 18:20; Mt 23:33; 25:46; Lk 3:9; Ga 3:10; 2 Th 1:9; He 10:28-31; *ref. 1357-1359.*

Freedom from the Curse of Sin

1351 No one can obtain this freedom through his own efforts: Ps 49:7,8; 130:3; Is 64:6; Jr 2:22; Ro 3:10; *ref. 850-864,1354-1362;*

Christ has won this freedom for all mankind: Jn 1:29; 8:34-36; 1 Cor 15:3; 2 Cor 5:15; Ga 1:4; 2:16; 3:13; Eph 2:8,9; Col 2:14; 2 Tm 1:9; Tt 3:5; 1 Pe 2:24; 1 Jn 2:2; Re 1:5; *ref. 461f,1223f,1359,1361,1362;*

This freedom becomes the personal possession of all who confess their sins and repent of them: Ps 32:5; Pr 28:13; Lk 15:21; 1 Jn 1:9; and who acknowledge Christ as their Savior: Ac 16:31; Ro 3:23-29; Ga 2:16; 1 Jn 1:7; *ref. 1253-1262,1363;*

All who have been released from the bondage of sin have been freed that they might now serve God in holiness and righteousness: Lk 1:74,75; Ro 6:16-18; Ga 5:22,23, Tt 2:14; *ref. 1364.*

Resources

1352 A ship was wrecked on the Irish coast. The captain was a careful man. Nor had the weather been so severe as to explain the wide distance to which the vessel had swerved from her proper course. The ship went down, but so inexplicable was the disaster that a diver was sent down after her. Among other portions of the vessel that were examined was the ship's compass, and inside the compass box was detected a bit of steel, which appeared to be the small point of a pocket-knife blade.

When the rescued sailors were questioned, it was learned that the day before the wreck a sailor had been sent to clean the compass. He had used his pocket-knife and had, unwittingly, broken off the point and left it in the box. The bit of the knife-blade had exerted its influence on the compass to a degree that deflected the needle from its proper bent and rendered it wholly useless as a guide for the helmsman. That piece of knife-blade wrecked the vessel.

Thus one trifling sin, no matter how small, is able to rob your conscience of peace and happiness and to wreck the ship of your life. Beware of sin!

— selected

1353 Sin poses as being something that is quite innocent and desirable. But, too late, those who are overcome by its charm discover its dreadful and deadly nature.

History records the striking story of the Trojan Horse. In their march of conquest the Greeks, a hundred thousand strong, crossed the Aegean Sea in a thousand ships and encircled the ancient city of Troy. They planted their catapults and then battered the city. But the Trojans laughed them to scorn because they rested secure behind, what they considered, an impregnable defense. Daunted in their attempts to storm the city, the Greeks resorted to strategy; they built a huge wooden horse and left. The horse, they said, was a peace offering to the gods of Troy. In jubilant glee the Trojans broke down their wall, hauled the horse into the city and celebrated their victory. But in the night the horse opened, a band of Greek warriors came out, and opened all the gates to their returning comrades. And so Troy fell.

— selected

1354 Sin gives the impression of being something quite harmless which one can shake off quickly and with little effort whenever he likes. But once it has made its entry, there is nothing one can do to free himself from its power.

The incident is told of a soaring eagle that spied the dead body of a lamb floating down the Niagara River. Relying on its strength, the eagle swooped down and sent its sharp claws into the carcass of the sheep. But when the eagle now tried to rise it found that its prey was too heavy to carry, nor could it free its claws which were imbedded deep into the carcass. Soon the eagle was carried by its prey to a certain death over the falls; cp 1 Tm 6:9,10; *ref. 1348.*

† † †

1355 While every sin provokes God's wrath, there are some particular sins that cry to heaven for vengeance. Included among these are: Murder: Gn 4:10; especially the murder of Christ's followers: Re 6:9,10; oppressing those who cannot help themselves, such as widows, orphans, the poor and slaves:- Ex 22:21-24; 23:6-9; Is 3:14,15; withholding a laborer's due wages: Jas 5:4; *ref. 1348.*

† † †

1356 The sin against the Holy Ghost does not refer to the following:

To unbelievers in general, for we are to pray for them: 1 Tm 2:1,4;

To persons who have been excommunicated from the congregation, for we are to pray for such: 1 Cor 5:5; 2 Cor 2:6-11;

To lingering unbelief, for some are saved in their dying moments, e.g., Lk 23:39-43;

To every kind of resistance to the work of the Holy Spirit, for all men by nature regard the gospel as foolishness and resist it: 1 Cor 2:14;

To those who blaspheme the truth out of spiritual ignorance: 1 Tm 1:13;

To those who deny the truth out of fear: Lk 22:61,62;

To those who worry about having committed it, for the very fact that they are concerned about receiving forgiveness indicates that the Holy Spirit has not forsaken them; *ref. 1349.*

† † †

1357 "Be sure your sin will find you out," Nu 32:23

A man broke into the church intending to steal the silver communion vessels. Hearing a noise, he rushed to the end of the building, seeking for a way to escape. He saw a rope hanging there, and supposed by climbing it he would find an outlet. The rope was fastened to the church-bell, and no sooner had he seized it than the bell began to ring. Of course, this attracted people. The church was opened, and the would-be thief was arrested.

— selected

ref. 1350

† † †

1358 After a minister had spoken strongly against sin, he was confronted by one of his members who said, "We don't want you to talk as plainly as you do about sin because if our boys and girls hear you talking so much about sin they will more easily become sinners. Call it a mistake, if you will, but do not speak so plainly about sin."

The minister went to the medicine shelf and brought back a small bottle of

343

strychnine marked "Poison." He said: "I see what you want me to do. You want me to change the label. Suppose I take off this label 'Poison' and put on some mild label, such as 'Essence of Peppermint.' Can't you see what would happen? The milder you make the label, the more dangerous you make the poison."

— J. Wilbur Chapman

ref. 1348,1350

† † †

1359   Enslaved by sin and bound in chains,
        Beneath its dreadful tyrant sway,
And doomed to everlasting pains,
        We wretched, guilty captives lay.

Nor gold nor gems could buy our peace,
        Nor all the world's collected store
Suffice to purchase our release;
        A thousand worlds were all too poor.

Jesus, the Lord, the mighty God,
        An all-sufficient ransom paid.
O matchless price! His precious blood
        For vile, rebellious traitors shed.

— Anne Steele

1360 During the Middle Ages there lived a smith who boasted that he could break any chain, except those forged by himself. He committed some act which displeased the noble whom he served, and he was punished by being condemned to the dungeon. On the way to the dungeon he boasted that he would soon be out again as he was sure he could break any chain put upon him. When he was chained, he immediately started to look for the flaw in the links which would set him free, but he found his own mark on the links, and knew he was hopelessly bound by his own handiwork. He could not escape because his chains were his own.

So many sins start so small and so innocently, and we are certain we can break these self-forged chains at will, but they grow strong until we cannot break them, and it is we ourselves who have made our chains, for all evil comes from within, existing first in the mind.

— adapted from the *Gospel Herald*

ref. 1351

† † †

1361 *Aqua Regio,* royal water, is the name of the acid that will dissolve gold. It is called "royal water" because it is the master of the king of metals. Gold will resist almost everything else that can be poured upon it, but it is helpless before this acid. So, too, there is nothing but the blood of Christ that can cleanse us from our sins: 1 Jn 1:7. "You know," says the holy writer, "that it was not with perishable things such as silver or gold that you were redeemed. . . . but with the precious blood of Christ, a lamb without blemish or defect," 1 Pe 1:18,19.

1362
        Not the labors of my hands
          Can fulfill thy law's demands;
        Could my zeal no respite know,
        Could my tears forever flow,
        All for sin could not atone;
          Thou must save, and thou alone.
                    — Augustus M. Toplady

ref. 1351

† † †

1363 It was a rule in England that children should ask to join the church. A little girl who had experienced a change of heart applied for membership. "Were you a sinner," she was asked, "before this change of which you speak?" "Yes, sir," she replied. "Well, are you a sinner now?" "Yes, sir; I am a greater sinner than ever." "Then what change is there in you?" she was asked. "I don't quite know how to explain it," she said; "but I used to be a sinner running after sin, and now I am a sinner running away from sin." She was received into the church.

                        — selected

1364 Chrysostom at one time incurred the displeasure of the Emperor Arcadius by reproving him for his sins. His offended majesty was unable to find any punishment that seemed adequate. One of his counselors said, "Exile him!"

But the Emperor replied, "What good will that do? He looks upon the whole world as his fatherland."

"Confiscate his property," said another.

"Whom will that harm?" asked his majesty. "Not Chrysostom, but only the poor, to whom he gives all he has."

"Cast him into prison," said a third.

"What would be the use? He would glory in his chains."

"Well, then kill him," the courtiers said.

"How would that help? It would only open the gates of heaven to him."

Finally, one, wiser than the rest, proposed: "We must try to make him sin. Chrysostom is afraid of nothing but sin."

                        — W. G. Polack

ref. 1351

STEWARDSHIP 1365-1433

(ref.: Discipleship 300-314; Service 1322-1342)

Definition

1365 Christian stewardship is the acknowledgment and fulfillment of one's personal privilege and responsibility as a redeemed and grateful child of God to live one's life to the praise and glory of his Maker and Redeemer:

By using all material, mental, physical and spiritual endowments of life according to the will of God and in the best interests of his kingdom: Ro 14:7,8; 1 Cor 10:31; 2 Cor 5:14,15; Ga 2:20; Php 1:21; 1 Pe 2:9-12; 4:11; *ref. 1372;*

In recognition of the fact that God is the Owner of all that we are and have: 1 Chr 29:14; Ps 24:1; 50:12; 100:3; 1 Cor 4:7; 6:19,20; *ref. 1372, 1410,1412;*

And mindful of the fact that we shall have to give an account of our stewardship of his possessions: Mt 25:19; Lk 16:1,2; 19:15; Ro 14:12; 2 Cor 5:10; *ref. 1372.*

Stewardship of Body and Mind

1366 Body and mind with their wonderful faculties are precious gifts entrusted to us by God who created them: Ps 8:4-8; 139:14; Ec 3:11; they are to be safeguarded:

By avoiding defilement through sin: Ro 13:13,14; 1 Cor 6:11,15; 2 Cor 6:14-18; Eph 5:3-18; Php 4:8; 1 Tm 5:22; 2 Pe 1:3-9; *ref. 1373,1374;*

By daily crucifying our sinful flesh with its affections and lusts: 1 Cor 9:27; Ga 5:24; Tt 2:11,12.

They are to be used to the praise of our Maker and Redeemer:

By nourishing and developing their faculties through wholesome use and through study of God's Word: Ro 12:1-8; 2 Cor 10:5; Eph 4:15; Php 4:8; 1 Pe 2:2; 2 Pe 3:18; *ref. 1375;*

By loving service to God and fellow men: Pr 23:26; Mt 22:37-39; Ro 12:10-21; *ref. 1375;*

By daily presenting ourselves to God as a living sacrifice: Ro 6:3-6,12,13; 12:1; 1 Cor 6:19,20; 10:31.

Stewardship of Time

1367 Time is a precious gift of God:

We are to be conscious of its rapid flight: Job 14:1,2; Ps 90:5,6; 103:15,16; *ref. 1376-1379;*

We are not to waste it in meaningless pursuits: Ac 17:21; *ref. 1376, 1377,1388;*

We are to recognize that the time allotted to each person is limited: Ps 31:15; 90:10,12; 103:15,16; 1 Cor 7:29-31; Jas 4:14; *ref. 1376,1380-1382.*

Time is a sacred trust which, like all other gifts, has been entrusted to us as stewards to be used wisely and properly to fulfill our life's purpose to the glory of God:

We are to make full use of our time: Ps 90:12; Jn 9:4; 1 Cor 7:29-31; Eph 5:15-17; Col 4:5,6;

There is a time for every purpose: Ec 3:1-8;

All of our time is to be sanctified for holy purposes: 1 Cor 10:31; Eph 5:15,16; Col 4:5; 1 Pe 4:11; *ref. 1383-1387.*

The greatest of all tragedies is when people delay the things that belong to their peace with God: Pr 27:1; Ex 12:1; Is 55:6,7; Mt 23:37,38; Lk 12:19,20; 19:41,42; Ac 24:25; 2 Cor 6:2; He 3:14,15; *ref. 1389-1394.*

Stewardship of Talents

1368 Natural talents as well as spiritual talents are gifts from God: Jn 3:27; 1 Cor 4:7; 1 Tm 6:7; Jas 1:17; *ref. 1395,1396*:

Natural talents: Ex 28:3; 31:3-6; 1 Kgs 7:14; 2 Chr 26:15;

Spiritual talents: Lk 11:13; Ro 6:23; 12:3-8; 1 Cor 12:4-30; Eph 2:8; 4:8,11-13.

God distributes talents as he wills: Mt 25:15; Ro 12:6-8; 1 Cor 7:7; 12:11; Eph 4:11.

Talents are a sacred trust. They are not to be used for selfish and sinful purposes, but for God's praise and glory and for our own and our neighbor's temporal and eternal welfare: Mt 25:16-18; Lk 19:12-26; 1 Cor 10:31; 12:7f; 1 Pe 4:10,11; *ref. 1377,1397-1409.*

All mankind will have to give an account of the use of the talents given them: Mt 25:19-30; Lk 19:15-26; Ro 14:10-12; 1 Cor 4:1-5; 2 Cor 5:10; *ref. 1408,1427.*

Stewardship of Treasure

1369 Money and all earthly treasure belong to God: Lv 25:23; Ps 24:1; 50:10-12; Hg 2:8; Ac 17:25; 1 Tm 6:7; Jas 1:17; *ref. 1411-1413,1424.*

While God has entrusted us with money and earthly treasure for our sustenance and enjoyment: 1 Tm 6:17; he warns us to beware of covetousness: Pr 15:27; Lk 12:15; Eph 5:3; Col 3:5; 1 Tm 6:8-10; He 13:5; *ref. 1276-1296,1414, 1416,1421.*

God expects us to give a worthy portion of our income:

For the work of the church, which ministers to us with word and sacraments: 1 Cor 9:14; Ga 6:6; 1 Tm 5:18; *ref. 1417,1421-1426;*

For the work of extending Christ's kingdom throughout the world: Mt 28:18,19; Mk 16:15; Lk 24:47,48; Ac 1:8; *ref. 1426,1430;*

For worthy causes of charity: Ps 41:1; Is 58:7; Ac 20:35; Ro 12:13; Ga 6:10; 1 Tm 6:18; He 13:16; cp Mt 25:34-40; *ref. 1415,1419.*

Biblical guidlines for giving:

We are to recognize that when we give, we give what already belongs to God: 1 Chr 29:14; Mt 10:8; *ref. 1372,1410,1418;*

We are to give the firstfruits of all our income: Pr 3:9,10; cp Mt 6:33;

We are to give in proportion to our income: Lk 12:48; Ac 11:29; 1 Cor 16:2; 2 Cor 8:12; cp Dt 16:17;

We are to give willingly and joyfully: Ex 25:2; 1 Chr 29:9; Mt 10:8; 2 Cor 8:12; 9:7; *ref. 1430;*

We are to give as an act of worship: Gn 4:3,4; 8:20,21; 1 Chr 29:9-22; Ps 96:8; Mt 2:11; 2 Cor 8:5; *ref. 1426.*

Stewardship of the Gospel

1370 Christ has committed the gospel to us as Christian stewards: Mk 16:15; Lk 24:46-48; cp The Parable of the Pounds, Lk 19:1-26;

It is our obligation as Christian stewards:

To guard the gospel by diligently preserving it in its purity and by zealously contending for its truth against all who from within the church seek to corrupt it, and against all who from without the church seek to destroy it: Mt 7:15; Ac 13:8-10; 20:29-31; Ro 16:17,18; 1 Cor 16:9; Php 3:18,19; 2 Tm 4:2-5; 2 Pe 2:1,2; Jd 3; *ref. 1431;*

To share its saving truth with all who do not as yet know Jesus Christ as their Savior from sin: Mt 28:18,19; Mk 5:19,20; 16:15; Lk 24:46-48; Ac 1:8; Ro 10:14; 1 Cor 9:16; 2 Cor 5:19-21; *ref. 1020-1081,1432;*

To reflect the truths of the gospel by a Christian life: Mt 5:13,16; Jn 13:35; 2 Cor 3:3; Php 2:15-16; 1 Pe 2:9-12; *ref. 1020-1081,1433.*

Rewards of Christian Stewardship

1371 See "Rewards"; *ref. 1420,1428.*

Resources

1372 The word "steward" as used in the language of the Bible refers to a servant in whose care the master has entrusted his goods for proper management. Thus, for example, we read that when Joseph was brought to Egypt as a slave, the Lord prospered him and Potiphar made him steward, or the overseer of his household, and put all that he had in Joseph's hand: Gn 39:1-4.

Christian stewardship refers to the proper management and use of all the gifts God has entrusted to us as his servants. It involves "the practice of systematic and proportionate giving of time, abilities and material possessions based on the conviction that these are a trust from God to be used in his service for the benefit of all mankind in grateful acknowledgement of Christ's redeeming love"; *ref. 1365.*

† † †

1373 Sins of impurity are not the only sins that impair and destroy the body. Overwork, lack of sleep, and improper diet also militate against the proper stewardship of the body. In the words of William Hodges, "One of the strange spectacles to be seen everywhere every day is that of men operating their bodies at a loss in order to operate their business as a profit."

1374 Body and mind are interrelated and interdependent. What affects the one affects the other also. "Not a thought or feeling arises in our consciousness but it quickens or slows the heartbeat, vibrates the muscles and otherwise reverberates through the physical organism. On the other hand, there is scarcely a bodily change, save the most automatic, like breathing, but registers itself either consciously or unconsciously" (Dr. Maurice Allan).

1375 The body finally reaches a stage where it no longer grows. But not so the mind. It is capable of constant growth and development. If we are faithful in our stewardship of mind, it should be true of us that with each passing day we "see Christ more clearly, love him more dearly, follow him more nearly and serve him more sincerely"; *ref. 1366.*

† † †

1376 Assuming that your life would continue for seventy years, that would be a total of 25,500 days. When you deduct from this amount your childhood years, your time for eating, sleeping, illness, bodily exercise and other necessities, you will find that you do not have so much as twelve solid years left for work.

> "How soon life's day is past and gone
> And evening shades appear!
> Lord, help us ever keep in mind
> The night of death draws near!"

1377 One day a visitor came to the city of Sparta with the purpose of displaying what he regarded as a remarkable achievement. Choosing a place where many people passed by, he stood for a long time on one leg. But the Spartans were not greatly impressed by his performance, and their indifference vexed and annoyed him. Finally, challenging a passer-by, he said, "I do not believe you can do as much." "True," said the Greek, "but every goose can." — Let us not waste our time and our talents on things that are not worthwhile; see Ac 17:21; 1 Cor 14:12; 1 Tm 4:8; *ref. 1368.*

1378 Thomas Edison said: "Time is the most valuable thing in the world."

The learned Grotius had for his motto: *"Hora ruit,"* — the hour rushes.

John Bedford said: "I count that hour lost in which I have done no good by my pen or tongue." Martin Luther said the same.

Queen Charlotte said, "I am always quarreling with time; it is so short to do something and so long to do nothing."

Henry Martyn, the missionary, won the honorable title, "The man that never wasted an hour."

George Washington once told his secretary, who had come late because his watch was slow, "You will have to get another watch or I another secretary."

Napoleon used to say to his marshals: "You may ask anything of me but time."

1379
> The time is short!
> If thou wouldst work for God, the time is now;
> If thou wouldst win a garland for thy brow,
> Redeem the time!

Shake off earth's sloth!
Go forth with staff in hand while yet 'tis day;
Set out with girded loins upon the way;
Up! Linger not!

— Bonar

1380   Swift to its close ebbs out life's little day;
Earth's joys grow dim, its glories pass away.

— Henry F. Lyte

1381 It is said that on her death-bed Elizabeth, the gifted and ambitious Queen of England, cried, "Millions of money for an inch of time!" — With a kingdom on which "the sun never sets" at her feet, all was of no value now as she shrieked for "an inch of time."

1382   The clock of time is wound but once,
And no one has the power
To tell just when the hands will stop,
At late or early hour.

Now is the only time you own,
Live, love, toil with a will,
Place no faith in "tomorrow,"
The clock may then be still.

— Anon

1383 The time we spend at work is time spent in a holy purpose providing our work is a God-pleasing occupation. The same is true of time devoted to sleep, eating and recreation, for the stewardship of body and mind requires that we preserve and protect these wonderful faculties so that they may be of the highest possible service to God and our fellow men. And not the least of these requirements is that we take time to give our body and mind proper food, rest and relaxation; *ref. 1367.*

† † †

1384 Whether or not one's daily occupation serves a holy purpose depends upon his attitude toward his work. — Three workmen performing the same task were asked what they were doing. One said, "I am earning ten dollars a day." The second said, "I am cutting stone." The third said, "I am helping to build a cathedral." If we merely work to make money to spend on ourselves, God is not pleased with our occupation. But if we work in order to supply not only our own needs but also for the purpose of contributing toward the welfare of our family and of our church, and for the purpose of helping others, God is well pleased. The time we spend in such labor is time dedicated to God.

1385   Only one life, it will soon be past;
Only what's done for Christ will last.

1386 When Dwight Moody, the evangelist, was once asked how many he had converted on a certain evening in his preaching mission, his answer was: "Two and a half — two children and one adult. The children," he said, "are giving their full lives to Christ, but the adult has but half of his left"; cp Ec 12:1.

1387
        Take my life and let it be
          Consecrated, Lord, to thee;
        Take my moments and my days,
          Let them flow in ceaseless praise.
              — Frances R. Havergal
      ref. 1367,1368

† † †

1388 A tragedy: Lost yesterday, somewhere between sunrise and sunset, two golden hours, each set with sixty diamond minutes. No reward is offered, for they are lost forever.

              — Horace Mann

1389 An irreligious young man was asked by his companion to give serious thought to his spiritual welfare. But he ignored his friend's plea, saying, "I've still got a lot of time for religion. Remember the thief on the cross?"

"Which one?" asked his companion.

Yes, which one? Remember, there were *two* thieves crucified with Christ, and for one the eleventh hour was too late.

1390
        He was going to be all that a mortal could be
          Tomorrow.
        No one should be kinder or braver than he
          Tomorrow.
        A friend who was troubled and weary, he knew,
        Who'd be glad of a lift and who needed it, too;
        On him he would call and see what he could do
          Tomorrow.

        Each morning he stacked up the letters he'd write
          Tomorrow;
        And he thought of the folks he would fill with delight
          Tomorrow;
        It was too bad indeed, he was busy today,
        And hadn't a minute to stop on his way;
        "More time I'll have to give others," he'd say,
          Tomorrow.

        The greatest of workers this man would have been
          Tomorrow.
        The world would have known him had he ever seen
          Tomorrow.
        But the sad fact is he died, and he faded from view,
        And all that he left when living was through
        Was a mountain of things he intended to do
          Tomorrow.
              — Edgar Guest

1391

Never mind about tomorrow —
  It always is today;
Yesterday has vanished —
  It has no more to say.
Each minute must be guarded —
  Made worth the while somehow;
There are no other moments;
  It always is: JUST NOW.

Just now's the hour that's golden,
  The moment to defend.
Just now's without beginning;
  Just now can never end.
Then never mind tomorrow —
  It's today you must endow
With all that's true and noble,
  And the time for this is — NOW.

                                           — Anon

1392

Defer not till tomorrow to be wise;
Tomorrow's sun for thee may never rise.

                                           — Anon

1393 There is an old legend which says that once upon a time a conference was called in hell. The devil himself acted as chairman. The purpose of the conference was to lay plans for successfully keeping men from believing in Christ as their Savior. Several evil spirits arose, in turn, to offer suggestions. The first said: "I will tell the people that the Bible is not true." But Satan rejected this suggestion at once stating that the Bible shines in the light of its own glory, and that many saved sinners can be referred to as undeniable proof for the divine authority of the Book.

Then another evil spirit arose and suggested, "I will tell the people that Christ is not divine." But again Satan ruled out this suggestion as not being worthy of further consideration because the prophecies foretelling the coming and work of Christ had been most minutely fulfilled and because Christ had repeatedly proven that he was indeed and in truth the very Son of God.

Then a third spirit suggested: "I will tell the people to do their best and leave the rest to God because he is always merciful." But once more Saten rejected this suggestion, saying that men know only too well that their best efforts are not sufficient to appease the anger and wrath of a holy and righteous God who hates and punishes sin.

Finally a fourth evil spirit arose, and said: "I will go and tell the people that the Bible is true, that Christ is divine, that the only way to be saved is by faith in the crucified and risen Lord as their Savior. But, I will tell them to wait and think the matter over and to look forward to a more convenient season." — This suggestion was at once received by Satan and unanimously approved by the other evil spirits, and they have been busy ever since in carrying out this hellish mission.

                                         — selected

1394   Delay not, delay not, O sinner, draw near,
              The waters of life are now flowing for thee.
        No price is demanded; the Savior is here;
              Redemption is purchased, salvation is free.

        Delay not, delay not, O sinner, to come,
              For mercy still lingers and calls thee today.
        Her voice is not heard in the vale of the tomb;
              Her message, unheeded, will soon pass away.

        Delay not, delay not! The Spirit of Grace,
              Long grieved and resisted, may take his sad flight
        And leave thee in darkness to finish thy race,
              To sink in the gloom of eternity's night.

        Delay not, delay not! The hour is at hand;
              The earth shall dissolve, and the heavens shall
                fade.
        The dead, small and great, in the Judgment shall
                stand;
              What pow'r, then, O sinner, shall lend thee its aid?

        Delay not, delay not! Why longer abuse
              The love and compassion of Jesus, thy God?
        A fountain is opened; how canst thou refuse
              To wash and be cleansed in his pardoning blood?
                       — Thomas Hastings

ref. 1367

† † †

1395 Even the smallest talent is important. — Once when Sir Michael Costa was having rehearsal with a vast array of performers and hundreds of voices, some man who played the piccolo far away up in some corner, said within himself, "In all this din it matters not what I do," and so he stopped playing. Suddenly the great conductor stopped, flung up his hands and shouted: "Where is the piccolo?" The quick ear of the master missed it, and all was spoiled because the tiny piccolo had failed to take its part.
                                          — selected

1396 Both great and small gifts are needed in the work of the church. We cannot get along without rivers and lakes, just because the ocean is so much larger. We cannot do without the stars, just because the sun and moon shine so much brighter. We cannot do without the grass and flowers, just because the oak is so much taller. In the army not all men can be officers and generals, for what use would the general be without the rank and file of the soldiers?
                                        — selected

1397 I thank thee, my Creator and Lord, that thou hast held me worthy of all the joy and ecstasy which the study of thy creation and the works of thy hand have offered me. I have explained unto man the glory of thy works, as far as my human mind was able to grasp and understand thy divine works.

If I have said anything not worthy of thee or coveted mine own glory, graciously forgive me, O Lord!

— Johannes Kepler

1398 As to all the blessings and talents wherewith thou hast entrusted me, I have looked to thee with a thankful heart as the only Author and Giver of them. I have looked upon myself as unworthy of them. I have looked upon them as committed to my trust and stewardship to manage them for the ends that they were given — the honor of my Lord and Master. I have therefore been watchful and sober in the use and exercise of them lest I should be unfaithful in them. If I have at any time, through weakness, or inadvertence, or temptation, misemployed them, I have been restless till I have in some measure rectified my miscarriage by repentance and amendment.

— George Washington

1399 Shortly after the First World War, the main feature of a concert in London was the violin performance of the great Fritz Kreisler. A newspaper published this item the morning of the performance: "The crowd tonight will not be there to honor a man who fought under the Austrian flag. It will attend only to hear the remarkable Guarnerious violin that will be played."

The thunderous applause had hardly died down, after Mr. Kreisler's first number, when he shocked the audience into silence by breaking the violin over his knee. "I bought this thing at a department store this morning for two pounds, six pence," he explained. "Now I shall play the rest of the program on my Guarnerious." Then he went on to thrill the audience with the fact that the wonderful music was not in the instrument, but in the master who held the instrument.

Sometimes the world gives acclaim to a Christian who has done great things for the Kingdom of God when actually it is not the instrument which is to be marveled at — but the Master who knows how to use the instrument for his own matchless glory.

— selected

† † †

1400 "If only I had five talents!" — One guess as to why the one-talent man didn't make use of his talent is that he felt it was too small to bother with. In every church there are those who, because they can't do big things, are unwilling to do lesser things. There are those who would gladly go around the world for Christ if they had the opportunity, yet are unwilling to go around the corner to serve him.

"It's not what you'd do with a million,
If riches should e'er be your lot;
But what you are doing at present
With the dollar and a quarter you've got."

1401 The greatest loss to the human race has not been caused by floods or by fire, not by epidemics which have spread disease over vast areas and with the sickle of death mowed down millions, nor by earthquakes and tropical storms, neither by record-breaking crashes on Wall Street . . . the great loss has been in the buried talents of God's people.

— Arthur Brisbane

1402 Use the talent you possess. Many a woods would be silent if no birds sang except those that sing best.

1403 Do the best you can with what you've got where you are.

1404
> Fret not because thy place is small;
> Thy service need not be;
> For thou canst make it all there is
> Of joy and ministry.
>
> The dewdrops, as the boundless sea,
> In God's great plan have part;
> And this is all HE asks of thee:
> Be *faithful* where thou art!

— Anon

1405
> I am only one, but I am one;
> I can't do everything, but I can do something.
> And what I can do, that I ought to do;
> And what I ought to do, by the grace of God,
> I shall do.

— Edward Everett Hale

1406 When Aunt Sarah, a church member, was asked about the bandage on her wrist, she explained that it was a bad sprain. And then she added, "When the pastor visited me he first spoke words of comfort, and then he said: 'You know now how the church feels in not having the use of all of its members.' He didn't mean that just as a joke either. I had sense enough, too, to feel I deserved to have him say it to me. A word like that comes pretty straight when one of your members is useless and worse. . . . There are lots of things I need to do, but I can't use this useless wrist to do them. That's the way the pastor has felt about me, I guess. I have been a useless member of Christ's church for thirty years — that's the long and short of it. I am ashamed of myself, I truly am, and things are going to be different from now on."

1407
> The Lord had a job for me,
> But I had too much to do,
> I said, "You get somebody else,
> Or wait till I get through."
>
> I don't know how the Lord came out,
> But he seemed to get along.
> But I felt a'sneaking-like,
> Knew I'd done God wrong.
>
> One day I needed the Lord,
> Needed him myself right away,
> And he never answered me at all,
> But I could hear him say.

Down in my accusing heart:
  "I've got too much to do;
You get somebody else,
  Or wait till I get through."
Now whenever the Lord has a job for me,
  I never try to shirk;
I drop what I have on hand
  And do the good Lord's work.
And my affairs can run along,
  Or wait till I get through.
Nobody else can do the job
  That God's marked out for you.
— Paul Lawrence Dunbar

ref. 1268

† † †

1408 A tourist who visited a beautiful garden on the grounds of a castle in Northern Italy was met at the gate by a friendly gardener who was the only inhabitant of the castle.

"How long have you been here?" asked the tourist.

"Twenty-four years," replied the gardener.

"When was your master here the last time?" inquired the tourist.

"Twelve years ago," said the gardener.

"But," said the tourist, "you keep this garden in such fine condition and take such excellent care of all the plants as though you expected your master to come tomorrow."

"Not tomorrow," said the gardener, "but today, sir, today!"

1409 Doctor Horatius Bonar was constantly mindful of the Lord's return. Before retiring at night his last action before lying down to sleep was to draw aside the curtain and to look up into the starry heavens. Then he would say: "Perhaps tonight, Lord?" In the morning, as he arose, his first action was to raise the blind and, looking out upon the gray dawn, he would say: "Perhaps today, Lord?" *ref. 1367,1368.*

† † †

1410 Two men who were quarreling over the ownership of a certain piece of land came to a rabbi and asked him to settle the dispute. The rabbi said, "I will ask the land to which of you it belongs." He put his ear to the ground for a moment, and then said: "The land says it belongs to neither of you, but that both of you belong to it. Dust thou art, and to dust shalt thou return."

1411
      The wealth of earth, of sky, of sea,
      The gold, the silver, sparkling gem,
      The waving corn, the bending tree,
      Are thine; to us thou lendest them.
— Edward A. Dayman

1412

We give thee but thine own,
Whate'er the gift may be;
All that we have is thine alone,
A trust, O Lord, from thee.

May we thy bounties thus
As stewards true receive
And gladly, as thou blessest us,
To thee our firstfruits give!

— William Walsham How

1413 When Henry Thornton, who was known as a liberal giver, was asked on a certain occasion to give something for missions, he made out a check for five pounds. While he was writing the check he received a telegram. As he opened it he turned pale. Turning to his visitor he said: "I have received terrible news. I have lost hundreds of pounds. Give me back the check!" The visitor returned the check. But instead of voiding it out, Mr. Thornton took the check and changed the amount from five pounds to fifty pounds, saying, "God has just taught me that I may not much longer possess my property and that I must use it well;" *ref. 1365,1369.*

† † †

1414 Martin Luther once said: "A man needs three conversions: first of the heart, then of the head, then, lastly, of the purse."

1415

Because I have been given much,
I, too, shall give;
Because of thy great bounty, Lord,
Each day I live.
I shall divide my gifts from thee
With every brother that I see
Who has the need of help from me.

— Grace Noll Crowell

1416 A wealthy lady, who had lived in luxury while on earth, died. Entering heaven she met an angel and asked him to direct her to her abode. The angel pointed to a small shack in the distance. "Do you mean to tell me that that is to be my abode? Nothing better than that?" "That is right," said the angel, "we can only build them with the materials we receive."

1417 A father bitterly complained to a friend that his growing son was "costing" him so much. There seemed to be no end to buying clothes, more books, more things for school, etc. The friend replied, "My boy does not cost me a cent any more. But I wish we could spend something on him." "Why?" inquired his friend. "We buried him last month," was the answer.

1418 One day a little girl told me that she was going to give her father a pair of slippers on his birthday. "Where will you get your money?" I asked. She opened her eyes like saucers and said, "My father will give me the money!"

For half a minute I was silent, as I thought that the dear man would buy his own birthday present. The father loved his little girl for her gift, although he had to pay for it. She had not anything in the world that he had not given her. Nor do you have anything of your own to give to God. You can give him back only what belongs to him, and of which he has made you a steward for a short time.

— *The Sunday School Times*

1419
For we must share,
If we would keep,
Those blessings from above.
Ceasing to give,
We cease to have,
Such is the law of love.

— Anon

1420 This thing of giving I do not understand any more than you do, but there is something about it that blesses us. Those who give most have most left. I believe that everyone who dries a tear will be spared the shedding of a thousand tears. I believe that every sacrifice we make will so enrich us in the future that our regret will be that we did not sacrifice more. Give, and somewhere, from out of the clouds, or from the sacred depth of human hearts, a melody divine will reach your ears and gladden all your days upon the earth.

— George F. Burba

1421 The church member who growls because the LORD insists on proper proportionate giving and says he cannot now make ends meet, will never be able to make ends meet because his own hands hold both ends. If he will let GOD have HIS end, they should easily come together.

— selected

1422 "A giving church is a living church."

1423 The heathen people of the New Hebrides at their feasts cut off the tails of the pigs they are about to eat and throw them into the bush as an offering to their gods while they enjoy the delicious meat. They could easily spare the left-over tails.

Such "pigtail giving" is also found in the church. There are those who give only the leavings to the Lord. They first supply all of their personal needs and satisfy their own luxurious tastes. Then, if anything is left they give it to the church.

1424 When we die we leave behind us all that we have and take with us all that we are.

1425 Average is the worst of the best and best of the worst.

1426 Fritz Kreisler, the famous violinist, said, "It is public money. It is only a fund entrusted to my care for proper disbursements." Dr. William Mayo, of the famous clinic in Rochester, Minnesota, came closer to the truth when he called it "holy money," saying, "That holy money, as we call it, must go back into the service of that humanity which paid it to us." David Livingstone, the great missionary to Africa, expressed the full truth when he said: "I will place no value on anything I have or may possess except in the relation to the kingdom of God. Anything I have will be given or kept according as giving or keeping it I shall promote the kingdom of my Savior."

1427 Some years ago a newspaper in Cincinnati told about a shabbily dressed woman who went to Dr. George Herman, asking him to make an x-ray examination of her heart free of cost. She said she was very poor and couldn't pay. The doctor consented to do the work. But when he turned his machine a little below the heart, he saw a concealed pocket in which was a purse with twenty-dollar gold pieces. "Your heart is very bad," he said; "you have lied when you said you were poor." — God's law is an x-ray which penetrates the darkest recesses of our heart and reveals the evil thoughts and desires that are lurking there.

— selected

1428
>We lose what on ourselves we spend,
>We have, as treasure without end,
>Whatever, Lord, to thee we lend,
>>Who givest all.
>
>Whatever, Lord, we lend to thee,
>Repaid a thousandfold will be;
>Then gladly will we give to thee,
>>Who givest all.

— C. Wordsworth

ref. 1365,1369

† † †

1429 Horace Greeley once received a letter from a woman seeking advice in the distressing financial condition of her church. She said they had tried everything they could think of, fairs, strawberry festivals, oyster suppers, a donkey party, turkey banquet, Japanese weddings, poverty socials, mock marriages, grab bags, necktie socials, and asked Mr. Greeley if he would be so kind as to suggest a new device to keep the struggling church from disbanding. The great editor replied: "Try religion!"

1430
>Lord of glory, who hast bought us
>>With thy life-blood as the price,
>Never grudging for the lost ones
>>That tremendous sacrifice,
>
>Give us faith to trust thee boldly,
>>Hope, to stay our souls on thee;
>But, oh! best of all thy graces,
>>Give us thine own charity.

— Eliza S. Alderson

ref. 1369

1431 There was a very definite reason why the Lord inspired Jude, the brother of James, to exhort his Christian readers thus: "Earnestly contend for the faith which was once delivered unto the saints," v.3,4. For already at that time false prophets in sheep's clothing were attempting to corrupt the truth of the gospel, as the Letters of the New Testament show. Some of the opposition to the gospel came from within the church, from Judaizing teachers who sought to confuse the truth by mixing law and gospel and saying that men are saved by their works and not by the sacrifice of Christ alone.

Opposition to the gospel also came from without the church, for the Christian church was being vehemently assailed by pagan authorities who controlled the power of the state and who regarded Christianity, which pledged its allegiance to Christ as Lord and King, as a dangerous organization whose purpose was to overthrow the Roman Empire. The history of the first few centuries are stained with the blood of countless martyrs who were ready to lay down their lives in contending for the faith.

There was also a definite need earnestly to contend for the faith during Luther's time, when papal Rome perverted and corrupted the truth of the gospel. A few hundred years later, when the spirit of rationalism swept over Europe, many faithful confessors again contended for the faith, often at a great sacrifice.

Today, too, faithful stewardship requires that we guard the gospel against similar attacks from without, and that we preserve its purity in the face of attempted corruption by the spirit of liberalism and other evils from within; *ref. 1370.*

1432 There is a striking story in the Old Testament which tells about a group of lepers outside the city gate of Samaria. When the Syrian army fled and the siege of the city of Samaria was broken the lepers, discovered an abundance of food for the starving multitude. They did not keep this good news to themselves, but said one to another: "We're not doing right. This is a day of good news and we are keeping it to ourselves. If we wait until daylight, punishment will overtake us. Let's go at once and report this to the royal palace," 2 Kgs 7:9.

In a far greater measure it is our responsibility to share the good tidings of the gospel by telling others that Christ has broken Satan's siege of sin and by directing them to the Word of God, that heavenly food which sustains a life which will embrace all eternity.

1433 Some Christians were trying to persuade a Jew to accept Christ, but the Jew replied, "Why do you boast and exalt yourselves? Your performance is not worthy of imitation. You drink to excess, make light of adultery, despise father and mother, take advantage of the other fellow in your business deals. You curse one another in the name of God and by the suffering of your Christ, and still you confess to be redeemed by such suffering. Why do you lead such ungodly lives? Who will believe that you are God's people?" *ref. 1370.*

TEACHERS AND TEACHING 1434-1459

(ref.: Education 315-358; Pastors-Preaching 1099-1133)

Teachers Are God's Gifts to His Church

1434 In Old Testament times they were: Moses, the Levitical prists, and the prophets through whom God communicated his will to his people: Ex 4:12,13; Lv 10:11; Dt 24:8; 33:10; 2 Kgs 17:13,14; 2 Chr 35:3; Ne 8:9;

In New Testament times they are the apostles, evangelists and others whom God endowed with special gifts to teach: Ac 5:42; 11:26; 13:1; 15:35; 18:11,25; 28:31; 1 Cor 12:28; Eph 4:11.

The Privileged Position of Teachers

1435 They are laborers together with God: Mt 9:37,38; 1 Cor 3:5-9; 1 Cor 4:1; 2 Cor 6:1; *ref. 1450,1457*;

They are deserving of special honor: Ac 28:10; 1 Cor 4:1; Ga 6:6; Php 2:29; 1 Th 5:12,13; 1 Tm 5:17; He 13:7; cp Ex 33:8; *ref. 1443,1444,1451,1459*.

The Responsibilities of Teachers

1436 They are to teach the Word (law) of God and make known his wonderful works: Mt 5:19; Ac 14:21; 15:35; 18:11; Col 1:28; 2 Th 3:4; 1 Tm 4:11; cp Ex 24:12; Dt 4:1,5,10,14; 6:1; 11:19; 33:10; 2 Chr 17:9; Ez 7:10; Ps 78:6; Is 58:1; and especially to proclaim the gospel of Christ: Mt 28:20; Ac 4:2; 5:20,42; 20:20,21; Eph 4:21; Col 2:6,7; 1 Tm 6:3-5; 2 Tm 4:1-5; *ref. 1445,1448,1452,1453*;

1437 They are to guard against falsifying the Word of God: Jos 1:7; Is 8:20; Jr 23:28,31; Eze 13:1,2; Ac 20:28-31; 1 Tm 6:3-5; 2 Tm 4:3-5; Re 22:18,19; cp Dt 12:32; Mt 7:15; Mk 13:22; 2 Pe 2:1; *ref. 1370,1431*;

1438 They are to care for the members of the flock entrusted to them: Jn 21:15-17; Ac 20:28; 1 Pe 5:2; cp Jr 3:15; 23:14; to be an example to them: 2 Th 3:9; 1 Tm 4:12; Tt 2:7; 1 Pe 5:3; and to pray for them: Eph 1:16f; 3:14f; Php 1:3-11; Col 1:9f; 4:12; 1 Th 1:2f; 2 Th 1:3; 2 Tm 1:3; *ref. 1446,1449*;

1439 They are to improve their teaching ability through study of God's Word: Jos 1:8; Mt 13:52; Ac 18:24-26; Ro 12:6,7; Col 4:17; 1 Tm 4:13-16; 2 Tm 2:15; He 5:12-14; 1 Pe 2:2; 2 Pe 3:18; *ref. 1449,1458*.

The Teacher's Source of Strength

1440 Their strength does not lie in their own power but in the power that God supplies through his Holy Spirit: Zch 4:6; Mk 16:20; Jn 3:27; 14:26; 15:5; 1 Cor 3:5-9; 2 Cor 3:5; 4:7; 6:1; Php 2:13; 4:13; cp Ex 4:12-15; *ref. 1448, 1450,1452,1457*.

The Teacher's Reward

1441 The joy of sharing the message of salvation with others: Lk 2:17, 18,38; 10:17; He 12:2; cp Lk 15:7,10; Ac 8:5,8,39;

The confidence that their labor is never in vain: Ps 126:5,6; Is 55:10,11; Ro 1:16; 1 Cor 15:58; 1 Th 2:13; He 4:12;

The satisfaciton that they build not only for time but also for eternity: Jn 4:35,36; 5:24; 15:16; 17:3; 1 Cor 3:9-14; Eph 2:19-22; 1 Tm 4:8; Jas 5:19,20;

The assurance of an eternal reward: Dn 12:3; Mt 10:32; 25:23; 2 Tm 4:7,8,18; He 6:10; 1 Pe 5:4; *ref. 1442-1445,1451-1456.*

Resources

1442 If I had to give up preaching and my other duties, there is no office I would rather have than that of schoolteacher. For I know that next to the ministry it is the most useful, greatest, and best; and I am not so sure which of the two is to be preferred. . . . Therefore let it be considered one of the highest virtues on earth faithfully to train the children of others, which duty but very few parents attend to themselves. *ref. 1435,1441.*

— Martin Luther

1443 I sing the praise of the unknown teacher. Famous educators plan new systems of pedagogy, but it is the unknown teacher who delivers and guides the young. He lives in obscurity and contends with hardship. He keeps watch along the borders of darkness and makes the attack on the trenches of ignorance and folly. Patient in his daily duty, he strives to conquer the evil powers which are the enemies of youth. He awakens sleeping spirits. He quickens the indolent, encourages the eager, and steadies the unstable. He communicates his own joy in learning and shares with boys and girls the best treasures of his mind. He lights many candles which, in later years, will shine back to cheer him. This is his reward. Knowledge may be gained from books; but the love of knowledge is transmitted only by personal contact. No one has deserved better of the republic than the unknown teacher.

— Henry Van Dyke

1444 The teacher is like a candle which lights others in consuming itself.

— Ruffini

ref. 1425,1441

† † †

1445

Let children hear the mighty deeds
  Which God performed of old,
Which in our younger years we saw,
  And which our fathers told.

Make unto them his glories known,
  His works of pow'r and grace;
And we'll convey his wonders down
  Thro' ev'ry rising race.

Oh, teach them with all diligence
  The truths of God's own Word,
To place in him their confidence,
  To fear and trust their Lord.

To learn that in our God alone
Their hope securely stands,
That they may ne'er forget his works,
But walk in his commands.

— Isaac Watts
ref. 1436

† † †

1446 Teaching methods, curriculum, discipline . . . none of these are relatively important. What the teacher *is* matters more than what he does. What the teacher is, and what motivates him in teaching, is far more important than what or how he teaches.

— Karl A. Menninger

1447 The teacher himself is the most important "visual aid."

1448

Holy Father, Lord above,
Give me patience, courage, love;
Make me firm, yet kind and true;
Touch my heart and make it new.

In my work from day to day
Help me mold the living clay
In the image of thy Son;
Perfect what I have begun.

Let me seek not paths of ease
Where doth blow the balmy breeze,
But in heat of summer day
Help me labor, help me pray.

Like the Master Teacher, Lord,
For my work seek no reward,
Though unpraised by men I'll be,
May I hear "Well done" from thee.

When my work shall finished be,
May I then present to thee
Lives which thou to me hast given,
Fit for earth, prepared for heaven.

— Anon
ref. 1438,1440,1441

† † †

1449 Mistakes to avoid:

Postponing lesson preparation until Saturday night.

Plunging into the lesson before getting the interest of the class.

Answering all questions instead of making the class feel that it is their responsibility to answer.

Speaking in such a low tone that you give the impression that what you have to say is not important.

Allowing yourself to be distracted by questions which have nothing to do with the lesson.

Using words and language which the class does not understand.

Asking questions so vaguely that the members of the class are not able to answer.

Indulging in mannerisms which attract attention to yourself.

Showing that you are nervous, jumpy, uncertain, and making the class feel the same way.

Letting class discussion become a dialog between yourself and one class member.

Using sarcasm, finding fault, never smiling.

Asking a second question before the first one has been answered satisfactorily.

Trying to crowd too much into a lesson.

Talking too much about yourself.

Keeping your spiritual experiences in the background.

— adapted

ref. 1436,1438,1439.

† † †

1450
Thou biddest me, Lord, thy lambs to feed,
But I have none of the skills I need.
I lack in the virtues it takes to share
Thy Bread with the small ones. Hear my prayer.
Shepherd and Master, I would know
Thy precepts better that I might grow
To greater stature in word and deed.
Teach me to follow before I lead.
Make me a constant learner, Lord,
Able to rightly teach thy Word.
Help me to wear it outwardly,
Stamped on my life for the world to see.
Open my lips that I may speak
With zealous fervor. When I am weak,
Strengthen my soul. Dismiss my doubt,
And banish the love that would crowd thee out.
A sense of duty and willingness
To serve are needed. I ask no less.
I have but little thy task demands,
But here am I and my outstretched hands.

— Lucille M. Klosowsky

ref. 1440

† † †

1451 An aged teacher, replying to a letter she received from a former pupil, wrote: "I cannot tell you how much your note has meant to me. I am now in my eighties, living alone in a small room, cooking my own meals, lonely, and like the last leaf of fall, lingering behind. You will be interested to know that I had taught school for fifty years, and that yours is the first note of appreciation that I ever received. It came on a blue, cold morning and cheered me as nothing has done in years."

— selected

ref. 1435,1441

† † †

1452
Dear Lord I do not ask
That thou shouldst give me some high work of thine,
Some noble calling, or some wondrous task;
Give me a little hand to hold in mine;
Give me a little child to point the way
Over the strange, sweet path that leads to thee;
Give me a little voice to teach to pray;
Give me two shining eyes thy face to see.
The only crown I ask, dear Lord, to wear
Is this: That I may lead a little child.
I do not ask that I may ever stand
Among the wise, the worthy, or the great;
I only ask that softly, hand in hand,
A child and I may enter at the gate.

— Anon

ref. 1440

† † †

1453 If we work on marble, it will perish. If we work on brass, time will efface it. If we rear temples, they will crumble into dust. But if we work upon men's immortal souls, if we imbue them with high principles, with the just fear of God and love of their fellow men, we engrave on those tablets something which no time can efface, and which will brighten and brighten to all eternity.

— Daniel Webster

ref. 1441

† † †

1454
I took a piece of plastic clay
And idly fashioned it one day,
And as my fingers pressed it still,
It bent and yielded to my will.

I came again when days were past,
The bit of clay was hard at last.
The form I gave it still it bore,
But I could change that form no more.

365

I took a piece of living clay
And gently formed it day by day,
And molded it with power and art —
A young child's soft and yielding heart.

I came again when years were gone,
He was a man I looked upon.
The early imprint still he bore,
But I could change him then no more.

— Anon

ref. 1436-1439

1455
Where teachers are building temples
   With loving and infinite care,
Planning each arch with patience,
   Laying each stone with prayer,
The temple the teacher is building
   Will last while the ages roll;
For the beautiful unseen temple
   Is the child's immortal soul.

— Anon

1456
A builder builded a temple,
   He wrought it with grace and skill;
Pillars and groins and arches
   All fashioned to work his will.
Men said as they saw its beauty,
   "It shall never know decay.
Great is thy skill, O builder;
   Thy fame shall endure for aye."

A mother builded a temple
   With loving and infinite care,
Planning each arch with patience,
   Laying each stone with prayer.
None praised her unceasing efforts,
   None knew of her wondrous plan;
For the temple the mother builded
   Was unseen by the eyes of man.

Gone is the builder's temple,
   Crumbled into the dust;
Low lies each stately pillar,
   Food for consuming rust.
But the temple the mother builded
   Will last while the ages roll,
For that beautiful unseen temple
   Is a child's immortal soul.

— Hattie Vose Hall

ref. 1441,1455

† † †

1457   I heard the Father say, "Go teach,"
        And marveled at his call.
        "I cannot others teach," said I,
        "For I am least of all."

        "Though thou be least," the Father said,
        "Yet I have need of thee;
        Where thou art weak, I am full strong,
        Thou canst do all through Me."

        And since I've yielded to his call,
        Whene'er his help I've sought,
        His Spirit fills my every need
        And, teaching, I am taught.

                             — Hazel M. Lindsey

ref. 1435,1440

† † †

1458 Those who teach must take time to learn; *ref. 1439.*

† † †

1459 To be a teacher is next to being a king. Do you count it mean employment to imbue the minds of your fellow-citizens in their earliest years with the best literature and with the love of Christ, and to return them to their country honest and virtuous men? In the opinion of fools it is a humble task, but in fact it is the noblest of occupations.

                             — Erasmus

ref. 1435

† † †

THE TEN COMMANDMENTS 1460-1502

(ref.: Law of God 865-896)

The First Commandment

"You shall have no other gods before me," Ex 20:3-5

1460 *Forbids* every form of worship outside and apart from the worship of the Triune God, as well as any worship in addition to the worship of him alone: Is 42:8; 45:22; Mt 4:10; 6:24; 1 Cor 8:4-6; *ref. 1479-1482*. Examples:

Idol worship: Ex 32:1-6; Jdg 16:23,24; 1 Kgs 18:18-29;

Worship of material things: Mt 19:22; Mk 10:24; Lk 16:19; Eph 5:5; Php 3:19; 1 Tm 6:9,10; 1 Jn 2:15-17;

Christless worship: Mt 11:27; Jn 3:16,18,36; 5:23; 8:24; 14:6; 15:23; 17:3; Ac 4:12; 1 Tm 2:5; 1 Jn 2:23; 5:11,12,20; 2 Jn 9; *ref. 1482*.

1461 *Requires* that we fear, love, and trust in God above all things: Pr 3:5; 8:13; Mt 10:28,37; 22:37; *ref. 1480*. Examples:

Abraham: Gn 22:11,12; Joseph: Gn 39:9; Job: Job 13:15; David: 1 Sm 17:37,45-47; Daniel and his three companions: Dn 3:16-18; 6:10-17.

The Second Commandment

"You shall not misuse the name of the Lord your God," Ex 20:7

1462 *Forbids* the misuse of God's name:

By cursing: Lv 24:15; Jas 3:9,10. Examples:

Goliath: 1 Sm 17:43; Rabshakeh: 2 Kgs 19:21,22; Peter: Mt 26:74; *ref. 1483*;

By swearing: Lv 19:12; Mt 5:33-37. Examples:

Herod: Mt 14:6-9; certain Jews: Ac 23:12; *ref. 1483*;

By using witchcraft: Lv 19:31; Dt 18:10-12. Examples:

The Egyptian sorcerers: Ex 7-8; the witch of Endor: 1 Sm 28; Simon, the sorcerer: Ac 8:9-11;

By lying and deceiving by God's name: Jr 23:31; Mt 7:15,21; 15:8,9. Examples:

False prophets: 1 Kgs 13:11-19; scribes and Pharisees: Mt 23:13-33; Ananias and Sapphira: Ac 5:1-11.

1463 *Requires* the proper use of God's name:

By calling upon him in every trouble: Ps 50:15; Mt 7:7. Examples:

The ten lepers: Lk 17:11-13; the blind beggar: Lk 18:35-37;

By praising and thanking him: Ps 100:1-5; 103:1,2; 1 Th 5:18. Examples:

Hannah: 1 Sm 1:26-2:10; the demoniac whom Christ healed: Mk 5:18-20; the grateful Samaritan: Lk 17:15-18; *ref. 1484*.

The Third Commandment

"Remember the Sabbath day by keeping it holy," Ex 20:8-11

1464 *Forbids* us to despise preaching and God's Word: Ec 5:1; Lk 10:16; Jn 8:47; He 10:25-31. Examples:

The scribes and Pharisees: Lk 7:30; the Jews: Ac 13:45,46; *ref. 1485-1487*.

1465 *Requires* that we hold the Word of God sacred and gladly hear and learn it: Ps 1:2; 26:8; 84:1,2; 122:1; Lk 11:28; Ac 2:42; Col 3:16; 1 Th 2:13. Examples:

The psalmist: Ps 119:97; Mary, the mother of Jesus: Lk 2:19; Mary of Bethany: Lk 10:39; the Bereans: Ac 17:11.

Also requires us to support the ministry of the Word: Mk 16:15; Lk 10:7; 1 Cor 9:14; Ga 6:6; 1 Tm 5:18; He 13:17; *ref. 1020-1081,1485-1487*.

The Fourth Commandment

"Honor your father and your mother, so that you may live long in the land the Lord your God is giving you," Ex 20:12

1466 *Forbids* us to despise parents and masters, or to provoke them to anger: Pr 23:22; 30:17; Ro 13:1-7; Tt 3:1; 1 Pe 2:13,14,18. Examples:

The sons of Eli: 1 Sm 2:12,22-25; Absalom: 2 Sm 15:1f;

1467 *Requires* that we give them honor, serve and obey them, and hold them in love and esteem: Lv 19:32; Eph 6:1-9; Col 3:20; 1 Tm 2:1-3; 5:4. Examples:

Joseph: Gn 46:29; 47:11,12; Solomon: 1 Kgs 2:19; Elisha: 2 Kgs 2:12; *ref. 1488*.

The Fifth Commandment
"You shall not murder," Ex 20:13

1468 *Forbids* us to take our own life or the life of another person, or to hurt and harm another in his body, or to bear anger and hatred against him: Gn 9:6; Mt 5:22; 15:19; 26:52; Ro 12:19; Eph 4:26; 1 Jn 3:15. Examples:

Cain, Gn 4:5-8; Joseph's brothers: Gn 37:23-35; David: 2 Sm 11:15; Judas: Mt 27:5; the Jewish rulers: Ac 7:54; *ref. 1489,1490*.

1469 *Requires* us to be kind, merciful and forgiving, and to help and befriend our neighbor in every bodily need: Mt 5:5,7,9,25; 6:15; Ro 12:20; Eph 4:32. Examples:

Abraham: Gn 14:12-16; Joseph: Gn 45:1-6; David: 1 Sm 26:1-12; the centurion: Mt 8:5-13; the Good Samaritan: Lk 10:33-35; *ref. 1490*.

The Sixth Commandment
"You shall not commit adultery," Ex 20:14

1470 *Forbids* breaking the marriage vow, as well as all unchaste and unclean thoughts, desires, words, and deeds: Mt 5:28; 15:19; 19:6,9; 1 Cor 6:9; Eph 5:3,4,12; He 13:4. Examples:

Potiphar's wife: Gn 39:7-12; Samson: Jdg 16:1; David: 2 Sm 11:2f; Herod: Mk 6:18; *ref. 1491,1492*.

1471 *Requires* that in the fear of God we fight to overcome all impure thoughts and desires with God's Word and prayer, work, and temperance, and that we lead a chaste and decent life: Gn 39:9; Ps 51:10; Pr 1:10; 23:31-33; Mt 26:41; Ro 13:13,14; 1 Cor 6:18-20; Eph 4:29; Php 4:8; Col 3:5; 1 Th 4:3-7; 2

Tm 2:22; 1 Pe 2:11; 5:8,9. Example:
Joseph: Gn 39:7-12.

Also requires that husband and wife each love and honor the other: Eph 5:22-29; Col 3:18,19; 1 Pe 3:6,7; Example:
Jacob, Gn 29:20; *ref. 1003-1019.*

The Seventh Commandment
"You shall not steal," Ex 20:15

1472 *Forbids* robbery, theft and fraud, as well as longing for anything that belongs to our neighbor: Lv 19:35; Jr 22:13; Mt 15:19; Eph 4:28; 2 Th 3:10. Examples:

Achan: Jos 7:20-22; Gehazi: 2 Kgs 5:20-24; the robbers: Lk 10:30; Judas: Jn 12:6; *ref. 1493,1494.*

1473 *Requires* that we help our neighbor to improve and protect his property and business, assist him in time of need, and rejoice when we see him prosper: Ex 23:4; Pr 19:17; Is 58:7; Mt 5:42; 7:12; 22:39; 1 Cor 10:33; 13:4,5; Ga 6:10; Php 2:4; He 13:16. Examples:

Abraham: Gn 13:9; 14:12-16; Joseph: Gn 50:21; Jonathan: 1 Sm 18:4.

The Eighth Commandment
"You shall not give false testimony against your neighbor," Ex 20:16

1474 *Forbids* us to tell lies about, betray slander or defame our neighbor: Ps 50:19-22; Pr 11:13; 19:5; 22:1; Ec 7:1; Zch 8:17; Mt 18:15; Lk 6:37; Eph 4:25; Jas 4:11. Examples:

Doeg: 1 Sm 22:6-19; Absalom: 2 Sm 15:1-6; Gehazi: 2 Kgs 5:22,25; false witnesses against Naboth: 1 Kgs 21:13; Judas: Mt 26:14-16; false witnesses against Jesus: Mt 26:59-61; false witnesses against Stephen: Ac 6:11-14; false witnesses against Paul: Ac 25:7; *ref. 1495-1499.*

1475 *Requires* that we defend our neighbor, speak well of him, and put the best construction on everything: Pr 22:1; 31:8,9; 1 Cor 13:7; 1 Pe 4:8. Examples:

Jonathan: 1 Sm 19:4; the people of Capernaum; Lk 7:4,5; Paul: Ro 16:3,4; *ref. 1495-1499.*

The Ninth and Tenth Commandments
"You shall not covet your neighbor's house. You shall not covet your neighbor's wife, or his manservant or maidservant, his ox or donkey, or anything that belongs to your neighbor." Ex 20:17

1476 *Forbids* having a sinful desire for anything that belongs to our neighbor (i.e., anything that does not rightfully belong to us): Ps 10:3; Pr 6:24,25; Hab 2:9; Mt 5:28; 15:19; Lk 12:15; Ro 7:7; 1 Th 4:5; 1 Tm 6:8-10; 2 Tm 2:22; Jas 1;14,15; 2 Pe 2:14; 1 Jn 2:15,16. Examples:

Achan: Jos 7:21; David: 2 Sm 11:2-4; Absalom: 2 Sm 15:1-6; Ahab: 1 Kgs 21:1-16; *ref. 1500-1502.*

1477 *Requires* that our hearts be filled with holy desires, which move us to help our neighbor in keeping what is his: Lv 19:2; Ps 37:4; Mt 5:48.

370

Example:
Paul returned a slave who had run away: Letter to Philemon; *ref. 1500-1502.*

Resources

1478 On April 9, 1918, a bronze tablet was unveiled in a hall of justice in Pittsburg. The tablet contained the fundamental principle of all righteous laws — the Ten Commandments.

1479 Idolatry may take on various forms. People who do not know the one true God make their own gods by carving images in wood or stone. Thus some have pictured their god as a hideous and terrifying monster. Others worship the sun, or the moon, or a mountain, or some other object as God and in various ways give expression to their belief by engaging in mysterious forms of worship, which may even involve human sacrifice.

Others, like the children of Israel, who know the true God, deliberately leave him and worship idols: 2 Kgs 17:9,18.

Still others attempt the impossible — to worship the true God and to serve other gods at the same time: 2 Kgs 17:33; cp Is 48:11; Mt 4:10; 6:24.

A further form of idolatry is that of revering a picture, a statue, or some other object as a visible reminder of God and giving it the honor that belongs to God alone; Ex 20:4,5; 1 Kgs 12:28-30.

Since the only true God is the Triune God revealed in Holy Scriptures, every form of worship which rejects or ignores Jesus Christ is false and must be regarded as one of the worst forms of idolatry.

1480
Too weak to stand
Too weak to even grasp thy hand —
Wearied and faint I lie
Upon thy breast.
O thou eternal Refuge!
Wounded and spent am I
And sore distressed;
But O, what comfort 'tis to know
Thy love will never let me go,
And never can I fall below
The everlasting Arms.

— Anon

1481 St. Augustine tells of a heathen who came and showed him his gods. Pointing to one idol after another, the man repeated. "This is my god; where is yours?" Says St. Augustine, "I showed him not my God, not because I had not one to show him, but because he had not eyes to see"; *ref. 1460,1461.*

† † †

1482 "I'll give you five dollars," said a man to one who was in the habit of cursing, "if you will go into the village graveyard at twelve o'clock tonight and there, when you are alone with God, repeat the same curse you just uttered.

"I agree," said the man, "it's an easy way to make five dollars."

"Come back to me tomorrow," said the first, "and say you have done it, and you shall have the money."

Midnight came. It was a night of great darkness. As the man entered the cemetery not a sound was heard; all was still as death. The other man's words came to his mind, "Alone with God!" rang in his ears. He did not dare to utter a curse, but fled from the place, crying, "God be merciful to me a sinner!"

1483 George Washington issued the following order to the Continental Army on August 3, 1776: "The General is sorry to be informed that the foolish and wicked practice of profane cursing and swearing, a vice heretofore little known in the American Army, is growing into fashion; he hopes the officers will by example as well as by influence endeavor to check it; and that both they and the men will reflect that we can have little hope of the blessing of Heaven on our arms if we insult it by impiety and folly; added to this, it is a vice so mean and low, without any temptation, that every man of sense and character detests and despises it."

1484. The word "thank" comes from "think." In order to thank one must think. Many persons fail to give thanks because they do not think; *ref. 1462, 1463.*

† † †

1485 The third commandment is broken by people who do not go to church at all, by those who go only now and then, by those who go and listen to God's word but do not believe it, and by those who go and listen and believe God's word but then fail to do it.

1486 In this actual world, a churchless community, a community where men have abandoned and scoffed at or ignored religious needs, is a community on the rapid down grade.

Church work and church attendance mean the cultivation of the habit of feeling some responsibility for others.

There are enough holidays in the year for most of us. Sundays differ from other holidays in the fact that there are fifty-two of them every year —therefore on Sundays go to church.

Yes, I know all the excuses. I know that one can worship the Creator in a grove of trees, or by a running brook, or in a man's own house just as well as in church. But I also know that as a matter of fact the average man does not so worship.

He may not hear a good sermon at church. He will hear a sermon by a good man, who, with his good wife, is engaged all the week in making hard lives a little easier.

He will listen to and take part in reading some beautiful passages from the Bible. And if he is not familiar with the Bible he has suffered a loss.

He will take part in singing good hymns.

He will meet and nod or speak to good, quiet neighbors. He will come away feeling a little more charitable toward all the world, even towards those excessively foolish young men who regard church-going as a soft performance.

I advocate a man's joining in church work for the sake of showing his faith by his works.

— Theodore Roosevelt

1487 Going to church does not make a person a Christian, but if a person is a Christian he will go to church; *ref. 1464,1465.*

† † †

1488 An old anecdote of the great Napoleon records that, while walking along a country road attended by some of his officers, he encountered a peasant, an old man, laden with fagots of fuel. The old man was about to be jostled aside, as a matter of course, by his social superiors, when the Emperor, laying his hand on the arm of the foremost member of his escort, arrested the whole party, and gave the laboring man the use of the road, with the remark, "Messieurs, respect the burden"; see Lv 19:32; *ref.1466,1467.*

† † †

1489 The Fifth Commandment reads: "You shall not murder." Capital punishment, executed by lawful government on condemned criminals, is not murder but the exercise of a God-given right and duty. The same is true when the government is engaged in a just war and is compelled to kill the enemies who threaten the safety of its citizens: Ro 13:1-4.

1490 The command, "You shall not murder," also means that we are not to hurt or to harm our neighbor in his body: see 1 Jn 3:15. That, among other things, means that we do not jeopardize our own life or the lives of others by reckless driving of a car. The warning is just as necessary for the highway as it is for the home, the factory, or the playground.

> Grant me a steady hand and watchful eye
> That no man shall be hurt when I pass by.
> Thou gavest life, and I pray no act of mine
> May take away or mar that gift of thine.
> Shelter those, dear Lord, who bear me company
> From disastrous evils and calamities.
> Teach me to use my car for others' need,
> Nor miss through frantic love of speed
> The beauties of thy world, that thus I may
> With joy and courtesy go on my way.
> — *London Church Times*

ref. 1468,1469

1491 To adulterate means to mix a pure substance with an impure one. When mixed thus an article is no longer pure. This is also true of sexual impurity, against which the Scriptures warn; see 1 Cor 6:15-20.

1492 Idleness is the devil's workshop; *ref. 1470,1471.*

1493 The smallness of the object which one steals does not justify the act. It is a sin to steal a pin.

1494 Time is a precious gift of God. It can be stolen by wasting it or by devoting it to selfish and sinful pursuits; *ref. 1472,1473.*

1495

If you are tempted to reveal
　A tale to you someone had told
About another, make it pass,
　Before you speak, three gates of gold;
These narrow gates: First, "Is it true?"
　Then, "Is it needful?" In your mind
Give truthful answer. And the next
　Is last and narrowest, "Is it kind?"
And if to reach your lips at last
　It passes through these gateways three,
Then you may tell the tale, nor fear
　What the result of speech may be.
　　　　　— Beth Day

1496 The gossiping tongue of a member can do more harm to a church than the most vehement attack of an infidel.

1497

"The boneless tongue, so small and weak,
Can crush and kill," declared the Greek.
"The tongue destroys a greater horde,"
The Turk asserts, "Than does the sword."
The Persian proverb wisely saith,
"A lengthy tongue, an early death,"
Or sometimes takes this form instead:
"Don't let your tongue cut off your head."
"The tongue can speak a word whose speed,"
Says the Chinese, "outstrips the steed,"
While Arab sage does this impart:
"The tongue's great storehouse is the heart."
From Hebrew hath the maxim sprung,
"Though feet should slip, ne'er let the tongue."
The sacred writer crowns the whole,
"Who keeps his tongue doth keep his soul."
　　　　　— Anon

1498 There is a legend which tells of a king who sent an ox to a wise man in his realm, requesting that he kill the ox and return the best and the worst piece. To his great surprise the wise man returned the tongue. In his opinion the tongue — he, of course, was referring to the human tongue — is capable of doing the greatest good as well as the greatest evil. And he was right. With the tongue bless we God, even the Father, and with it also proclaim the saving gospel of Jesus Christ to poor sinners. Greater than this there is nothing. On the other hand, we may with our tongue lead men to eternal damnation by preaching false doctrines. Besides this, unspeakable damage can be done to other people's character by lying, slandering, and defaming. No power on earth can recall such evil words. The damage is done and is irretrievable. Let us guard our tongue and use it only for noble purposes; see James 3.

— selected

1499
A careless word
　May kindle strife;
A cruel word
　May wreck a life;
A bitter word
　May hate instill;
A brutal word
　May smite and kill;
A gracious word
　May smooth the way;
A joyous word
　May light the day;
A timely word
　May lessen stress;
A loving word
　May heal and bless.

— Anon

ref. 1474,1475

† † †

1500 To covet means to lust, to have a strong wish or desire to have something that rightfully belongs to another. By repeating the command "Do not covet," God would impress upon us that it is a sin even to have a sinful wish or desire; see Ro 7:7.

Lust has its origin in the sinful heart: Mt 15:19; Jas 1:14,15; and once conceived it leads to other sins, as it did in the case of Aachan who confessed: "I coveted them and took them," Jos 7:21; *ref. 1476.*

Conversely, these two commandments require that our hearts be filled only with holy desires and that we covet only that which pleases God; see 1 Cor 12:31.

1501 A story is told of a young man who picked up a golden coin lying on the road. Ever after, as he walked along, he kept his eyes fastened on the ground in hope of finding another. In the course of a long life he picked up a good deal of gold and silver, but in all these years he never saw the lovely flowers by the wayside or the grassy dell, or mountain peak and silver stream. He caught no glimpse of the blue heaven above, or snowy clouds, like angel pillows, telling of purity and glory beyond. God's stars came out and shone like gems of everlasting hope, but he kept his eyes upon the mud and filth in which he sought the treasure; and when he died, a rich old man, he knew this lovely earth only as a dirty road in which to pick up money as he walked along.

— selected

1502 A Quaker once advertised that he would give forty acres of rich farm land to anyone who was perfectly satisfied with that which he had. One seeker came to the Quaker.

"Are you perfectly satisfied with what you have?"

"Yes," answered the hopeful guest.

"Then why do you want this land?" was the Quaker's significant reply.

— *Gospel Herald*

ref. 1476,1477

THANKSGIVING 1503-1531

Exhortations To Give Thanks

1503 See Dt 8:10-14; Ps 50:14; 95:1,2; 100:4,5; 103:1-5; 105:1; 107:1; 118:1; 136:1; 148-150: Eph 5:20; Php 4:6; Col 3:15,17; 1 Th 5:18; *ref. 1509-1514.*

Directions For Giving Thanks

1504 *For what* we are to give thanks:

Temporal blessings: Gn 8:22; Ps 68:19; 103:5; 145:9-19; Dn 2:23; Mt 5:45; 6:28-32; 14:19; 15:36; Ac 14:17; 17:25; 27:25; 1 Tm 6:17; *ref. 1513-1522,1524-1526;*

Spiritual blessings:

For our redemption through Christ and all of its blessings: Ro 3:24,25; 4:25-5:2,8; 7:23-25; 8:1,32-39; 1 Cor 1:30; 15:55-57; 2 Cor 9:15; Eph 1:5-8; Col 1:12-14; Tt 3:5-7; 1 Pe 1:3-5; Re 5:9; *ref. 1516;*

For God's goodness, mercy and truth: Ps 100:4,5; 103:10-17; 118:1; 136:1; *ref. 1526;*

At the remembrance of God's holiness: Ps 30:4; 97:12; 119:62; 145:17;

For the power of the gospel in our lives and in the lives of others: Ro 1:8; 6:17; 2 Cor 2:14; 1 Th 2:13; 2 Th 1:3.

In short, for everything: 1 Chr 29:10-14; Ac 17:25; 2 Cor 9:11; Eph 5:20; 1 Th 5:18; Jas 1:17; *ref.1521.*

1505 *When* we are to give thanks:

At all times: Ps 145:1,2; Eph 1:16; 5:20; 1 Th 1:2;

"All times" includes times of want and trouble: Hab 3:17-19; Mt

5:11,12; Ac 16:23-25; Ro 5:3; 8:28; 12:12; 2 Cor 6:10; He 12:6-11.

1506 *Where* we are to give thanks:

In private worship: Ps 103:1-5; 119:62; Dn 6:10;

In public worship: Ps 22:25; 26:6,7; 35:18; 100:1f; 116:12-14; 135:1,2; 149:1-3; 150:1.

1507 *How* we are to give thanks:

By acknowledging our unworthiness of the Lord's blessings: Gn 32:10; Ps 103:10; and with the prayer that the Lord's goodness will lead us to repentance: Ro 2:4;

In the name of Christ, in whom and through whom we live our lives as grateful children of God: Ro 1:8; Eph 5:20; Col 3:17; He 13:15;

By singing God's praises, bringing him our offerings, telling of his wonderful works: Ps 13:6; 68:19; 72:17,18; 95:1-7; 96:1-10; 98:1-4; 100:1-5; 105:1-5; 107:22; 113:1-4; 145:1-5; 148-150; He 13:15; and by proclaiming his salvation to others that they too might rejoice and thank God: Ps 96:2,3; Mk 5:19; 2 Cor 9:12-15; 1 Pe 2:9-12; *ref. 1020-1081,1522,1523, 1526,1527.*

By translating our thanksgiving into thanks-living, in striving to keep his commandments, to serve him with gladness and to glorify him in all that we think and say and do: Ps 100:1,2; 1 Cor 6:19,20; 10:31; 1 Jn 5:3; *ref. 1514.*

By sharing our bounties with those in need: Is 58:7; Mt 25:35,36,40; Ac 20:35; Ga 2:10; 6:9,10; 1 Tm 6:17,18; He 13:15,16; Jas 1:27; 1 Jn 3:17,18; *ref. 1527-1531.*

1508 Examples of thanksgiving:

Christ: Mt 11:25; 26:26,27; Jn 6:11; 11:41; 17:1f;

Believers:
  Noah: Gn 8:20;
  Hannah: 1 Sm 2:1f;
  David: 1 Chr 29:10f;
  Levites: 2 Chr 5:12,13; Ezra 3:11;
  Hezekiah: 2 Chr 29:3f;
  Daniel: Dn 2:23;
  Jonah: Jon 2:9;
  Simeon: Lk 2:28f;
  Anna: Lk 2:38;
  The thankful Samaritan: Lk 17:15,16;
  Paul and Silas: Ac 16:23-25.

The heavenly host: Re 4:9; 7:11,12; 11:16,17; *ref. 1521,1522,1524,1530.*

Resources

1509 Gratitude is not an inborn trait. Little children are not thankful by birth and nature. They must be taught to say "Thank you," and they must be reminded again and again to do so. Nor are grownups any different. Tragically, this is also true of many who call themselves Christians. Like the ungrateful lepers who were mercifully healed by the Savior, they fail to return to give thanks to God: Lk 17:11-19. The Lord himself declared that the irrational beasts put his people Israel to shame in the matter of ingratitude when he said: "The ox knows his master, the donkey his owner's manger, but Israel does not know, my people do not understand," Is 1:3.

1510 According to an old legend, two angels leave heaven each morning with bags over their shoulders. One collects the praises, the other the petitions in human prayers. During the course of the day the petition-collector makes several trips back and forth, emptying his bag each time. But the angel who collects the praises is barely able to cover the bottom of his bag by nightfall.

— His

1511 An employee of the Dead Letter Office in Washington, D.C., reported that annually hundreds of thousands of requesting letters to Santa Claus are received. Only one child, however, has ever sent a "thank you" letter.

1512
Blow, blow, thou winter wind,
Thou art not so unkind
As man's ingratitude;
Thy tooth is not so keen,
Because thou art not seen,
Although thy breath be rude.

— Shakespeare, As You Like It

1513 We have been the recipients of the choicest bounties of heaven. We have grown in numbers, wealth, and power as no other nation has grown. But we have forgotten God. We have forgotten the gracious hand which preserved us in peace and multiplied and enriched and strengthened us; and we have vainly imagined, in the deceitfulness of our hearts, that all these blessings were produced by some superior wisdom and virtue of our own. Intoxicated with unbroken success, we have become too self-sufficient to feel the necessity of redeeming and preserving grace; too proud to pray to the God that made us.

— Abraham Lincoln's "Thanksgiving Proclamation"
ref. 1503,1504

† † †

1514
Oh, may we ne'er with thankless heart
Forget from whom our blessings flow!
Still, Lord, thy heav'nly grace impart;
Still teach us what to thee we owe.
Lord, may our lives with fruit divine
Return thy care and prove us thine.

— Anon

378

1515 Like Israel of old, God has permitted us to live in a good land, a land of brooks, rivers, lakes and oceans, of mountains and prairies, of forest and fruitful plains; a land abounding in natural resources, a land in which freedom and justice prevail, a land in which religion, education, science, industry and commerce can be pursued without undue restraint, a land so blessed that it excels every land on the face of the earth; see Dt 8:7-20.

1516
We thank thee, O Father, for all that is bright —
The gleam of the day and the stars of the night,
The flowers of our youth and the fruits of our prime,
And the blessings that march down the pathway of time.

We thank thee, O Father, for all that is drear —
The sob of the tempest, the flow of the tear;
For never in blindness, and never in vain,
Thy mercy permitted a sorrow or pain.

We thank thee, O Father, for the power
Of aiding each other in life's darkest hour;
The generous heart and the bountiful hand
And all the soul-help that sad souls understand.

We thank thee, O Father, for days yet to be;
For faith that our Savior has called us to thee.
Let all our eternity form, through thy love,
Our Thanksgiving Day in the mansions above.
— Will Carleton

1517 "Have you given thanks to God today for the use of your reason?" asked one stranger of another stranger as they met on the street. Startled for a moment by the unusual question the stranger paused, and then said: "No! I have not!" "Go, then," said the maniac, "and do so at once, for I have lost mine."

1518 Matthew Henry, the Bible commentator, was once robbed of his purse. In his diary he wrote: "Let me be thankful: first, because I have never been robbed before; second, because although they took my purse, they did not take my life; third, because although they took my all, it was not much; and fourth, because it was I who was robbed, not I who robbed."

1519
We plow the fields, and scatter
   The good seed on the land,
But it is fed and watered
   By God's almighty hand;
He sends the snow in winter,
   The warmth to swell the grain,
The breezes and the sunshine,
   The soft, refreshing rain.

He only is the Maker
   Of all things near and far;
He paints the wayside flower;
   He lights the evening star;

379

The winds and waves obey him,
  By him the birds are fed;
Much more to us, his children,
  He gives our daily bread.

We thank thee, then, O Father,
  For all things bright and good,
The seedtime and the harvest,
  Our life, our health, our food;
No gift have we to offer
  For all thy love imparts,
But that which thou desirest,
  Our humble, thankful hearts.

              — Matthias Claudius

1520 "Have you so very much to be thankful for?" said a rich innkeeper to his neighbor, a poor weaver. "Why do you sing every morning, 'Now Thank We All Our God'? Your occupation yields you little profit, and as a large family is dependent upon your support, you must find it hard to make both ends meet."

"The last is true, neighbor," said the weaver; "but as to thanking God, it is this way: We thank God for what we have, because what he has given us is for our benefit; and we thank him for what we have not, because we do not need it."

Contentment with the ways of God and a cheerful heart are worth more than all earth's riches; and he who by God's grace can call the Lord of heaven and earth his dear Father in Christ may indeed go his way comforted and even rejoicing though the sun does not always brighten his path: see Pr 30:7-9; 1 Tm 6:6-8f; He 13:5.

              — *Die Abendschule*

1521 "God be praised for everything!" was the motto of Chrysostom, Bishop of Constantinople. When in his old age he was removed from office, banished from his country, thrust into misery and abused, made to flee and suffer hunger and pestilence, his dying words were, "God be praised for everything!"

1522 Secular history as well as biblical history testifies that the people who have taught us to really thank and praise God were people who were acquainted with grief and sorrow. A striking example is that of the Rev. John Mentzer. After having suffered manifold reverses, privations, and hardships, he finally lost all of his possessions and escaped only with his life from his burning home. But in the depth of that sorrow his grateful heart still triumphed, and he exclaimed: "The devil shall not say that he filled me with sorrow or discouragement!" Whereupon he sat down and penned the immortal lines of the beautiful paean of praise:

O that I had a thousand voices!
  A mouth to speak with thousand tongues!
My heart which in the Lord rejoices,
  Would then proclaim in grateful songs,

> To all, wherever I might be,
> What great things God hath done for me.
> — selected

1523 There is an old Jewish legend which says that after God had created the world and mankind he asked the angels what they thought of his creation. "One thing is lacking," said the angels, "it is the sound of praise to the Creator." So, the legend continues, "God created music in the voice of the birds, the whisper in the winds, the murmur in the oceans, and planted melody in the hearts of men." It is, of course, only a legend, but it expresses the truth that all creation, and especially man, has been created for the praise of his Maker.

1524 During the early days of our nation's history the colonists endured many privations and hardships. As a result, their hearts and minds were filled with gloom bordering on despair, and many were disposed to return to their fatherland with all of its persecutions. When they met to decide on a day for fasting and prayer an old man who attended the meeting arose to address the assembly. He said that he thought that they had brooded long enough over their misfortune and that it seemed high time that they should consider their blessings instead. The colony was growing strong, he said. The harvests were becoming more plentiful, the rivers were full of fish and the woods with game, the air was sweet and the climate was pleasant. Above all, he reminded them that they now possessed what they had come for, full civil and religious liberty. Accordingly he recommended that they appoint a day for thanksgiving rather than a day for fasting. His advice was followed, and from that time forward Thanksgiving Day has been regarded as a day of joy.

— selected

1525
> When you are discouraged, thinking all is lost,
> Count your blessings!
> Name them one by one,
> And it will surprise you what the Lord has done.
> — Anon

1526
> When all thy mercies, O my God,
> My rising soul surveys,
> Transported with the view, I'm lost
> In wonder, love, and praise.
>
> Through all eternity to thee
> A joyful song I'll raise;
> But, oh! eternity's too short
> To utter all thy praise.
> — Joseph Addison

1527
> As thy prospering hand hath blest,
> May we give thee of our best
> And by deeds of kindly love
> For thy mercies grateful prove

381

Singing thus through all our days
Praise to God, immortal praise.

— Anna L. Barbauld

1528 King Agud of Persia decreed that in his empire a rich man had to die for every poor man that starved to death. — Christ will hold us accountable for the least among our brethren who had to suffer while we might have helped him: Mt 25:41-44.

1529 In Africa there is a fruit called tasteberry. When it is eaten, it changes a person's taste, so that everything that is eaten becomes sweet and pleasant. Sour fruit, even if eaten several hours after the tasteberry, tastes sweet and delicious. — Gratitude to God is the tasteberry of human life. The thankful spirit in the heart sweetens the whole life. Every sorrow is sweetened by gratitude. Every burden is made lighter by praise. Every loneliness may be dispelled by making others grateful. Even sickness may strengthen the soul if there is a spirit in the heart that thanks God for loving us enough to chasten us.

— selected

1530 If someone should give me a dish of sand and tell me there were particles of iron in it, I might look for them with my eyes, and search for them with my clumsy fingers, and be unable to find them; but let me take a magnet and sweep over the sand, and it would draw to itself the most invisible particles of iron by the power of attraction. The unthankful heart, like my finger in the sand, discovers no mercies, but let the thankful heart sweep through the day and, as the magnet finds the iron, so it will find in every hour some heavenly blessings; only the iron in God's sand is gold.

— Oliver Wendell Holmes

1531
Not what we give, but what we share,
For the gift without the giver is bare;
Who gives himself with his alms feeds three,
Himself, his hungering neighbor and Me.

— James Russell Lowell

ref. 1504,1507

TRUST 1532-1552

(ref.: Faith 359-383; Hope 557-564; Riches 1276-1296)

1532 Exhortations to trust in the Lord: Ps 4:5; 37:3,5; 62:7,8; 115:11; Pr 3:5; Is 26:4; 50:10; *ref. 1537-1552.*

1533 Promises to those who trust in the Lord: Ps 2:12; 31:19; 32:10; 33:18; 34:8,22; 37:5,39,40; 91:1-16; 125:1,2; Pr 28:25; 29:25; Is 26:3; Jr 17:7; Na 1:7;

1534 Examples of trusting in the Lord: Moses: Ex 15:2; Job: Job 13:15; David: 1 Sm 17:45; 2 Sm 22:33; Ps 4:8; 23:4; 27:1; cp Ps 42:11; 44:4-8; 46:1-3; 71:5; Hezekiah: 2 Kgs 18:5; Jehoshaphat: 2 Chr 20:12; Daniel's companions: Dn 3: 16-18; Paul: 2 Cor 3:4,5; 10:4; 2 Tm 1:12;

1535 Warnings against placing trust in man or in earthly things: Ps 49:6,7; 146:3,4; Pr 11:28; 28:26; Is 31:1; 47:10,11; Jr 17:5; Am 6:1; Mk 10:24; 1 Tm 6:17;

1536 Examples of false trust: Goliath: 1 Sm 17:43-45; Benhadad: 1 Kgs 20:10; Sennacherib: 2 Chr 32:8f; the rich fool: Lk 12:16-21.

Resources

1537 A large ocean liner on its way to New York was crowded with passengers. During the early morning hours a violent storm overtook the ship. It seemed as though the ship could never reach port. Passengers and crew were learning again to pray. While all were filled with fear, a little girl played about. Suddenly she began to sing, apparently unaware of all danger. A surprised passenger asked her: "How can you sing while we are in this storm. Are you not afraid?"

The child answered: "Afraid? Why, no! My father's at the wheel steering the ship. He will bring us home safely."

1538 A father took his little son with him for his first fishing trip. After the boat was pushed from the shore, the lad nervously asked, "Daddy, is the water over my head?" "Yes," said the father. Then the boy asked, "Is it over your head?" And again the father answered, "Yes, son, it is." After another moment the boy asked, "Daddy, is it over God's head?" "No, my boy," answered the father. And from that moment the child's anxiety ceased.

1539
Take thou my hands and lead me, thou gracious Lord
Till at my end I see thee, drawn by thy Word.
Alone, I can but falter and lose my way;
But thou my life canst alter — be thou my Stay.

In mercy without measure enfold my heart
And make me calm in pleasure or sorrow's smart.
Let thy poor child lean gently upon thy breast
And close its eyes intently to find sweet rest.

If never thou revealest thy wondrous might,
Yet to the goal thou leadest me e'en through night.

Then take my hands and lead me till life is o'er,
And I shall thank and praise thee forevermore.
— B. H. Schrein

1540 Just before a battle between the French and the Spanish, General Cloigny, the French commander, received a note from the Spaniards which read: "Surrender! We have you outnumbered!" Fastened to an arrow he shot back this note into the Spanish camp: "Surrender? Never! We have a king with us."

1541
So dark the clouds around my way
    I cannot see,
But through the darkness I believe
    God leadeth me.
I gladly place my hand in his
    When all is dim,
And, closing then my weary eyes,
    Lean close to him.

Through thorny paths though he may lead
    My tired feet,
Through hours of grief when teardrops flow,
    But it is sweet
To know that he is close to me,
    My Friend and Guide;
So while he leads me I will walk
    Quite satisfied.

To my blind eyes he may reveal
    No light at all,
But while I lean on his strong arm
    I cannot fall;
So, trusting him, I trudge along
    Life's weary way,
Content to think that soon will dawn
    A brighter day.
— Grant Colfax Tullar

1542 During an earthquake the people living in an affected village were very much frightened. At the same time they marvelled at the calm and peace of an aged woman whom they all knew. "Are you not afraid, Mother?" someone asked. "No," said the old lady, "I rejoice to know that I have a God who can shake the world."

1543
Wait, my soul, and tarry,
Tarry with God;
He will help thee carry
Ev'ry grievous load.
Why fret or fear
When the morn is near?
With the passing winter,
Spring will reappear.

384

When storms distress thee,
In ev'ry ill,
God will surely bless thee;
My soul, be still!

Wait, my soul, and tarry,
Tarry with God!
He will help thee carry
Ev'ry grievous load.
When all things fail,
God will still prevail;
He can safely lead thee
Through the darkest vale,
Lord God eternal,
Lead to the goal!
Christ, forever faithful,
Save thou my soul!

— Anon

1544 We do not know what the future holds, but we do know who holds the future.

1545 The oriental shepherd was always ahead of his sheep. He was out in front leading them. Any attempt upon them had to take him into account. Our God is always that way. He is down in front leading his flock. He is always in the tomorrow. It is always tomorrow that fills men with fear. But God is there already. How often we forget that! And all our tomorrows of life have to pass him before they get to us.

— F. B. Meyer

1546   God liveth ever!
Wherefore, soul, despair thou never!
What though thou tread with bleeding feet
    A thorny path of grief and gloom,
Thy God will choose the way most meet
To lead thee heavenward, to lead thee home;
    For this life's long night of sadness
    He will give thee peace and gladness,
        Soul, forget not in thy pains,
        God o'er all forever reigns.

— Anon

1547 A vessel was wrecked one stormy night, cast upon the rocks off the coast of Cornwall, England. All of the crew perished except one Irish lad who was hurled by the waves high upon the jagged slopes of a great, towering ledge of rock, where he managed to find a place of refuge. In the morning he was discovered by a searching party. Almost dead from cold and exposure, he was lifted tenderly into the rescue ship and brought to shore. After he had recuperated sufficiently he was asked, "Didn't you tremble out there on the rock in all that storm?"

385

"Tremble? Sure I trembled. But do you know, the rock to which I held never trembled once all night."

Christ Jesus is the steadfast and immovable Rock of our salvation. "On him, the solid Rock, we stand; all other ground is sinking sand." He is our Light in darkness, our Comfort in sorrow, our Companion on the way, our ever present Help in time of need. With our faith rooted and grounded in him, we need never fear.

— selected

1548
Here we have a firm Foundation;
    Here the Refuge for the lost;
Christ, the Rock of our salvation,
    His the name of which we boast;
Lamb of God, for sinners wounded!
    Sacrifice to cancel guilt!
None shall ever be confounded
    Who on him their hope have built.

— Thomas Kelly

1549 In 1861, when America was trembling in the crisis of the War between the States, the Secretary of the Treasury wrote to the director of the mint at Philadelphia, saying, "No nation can be strong except in the strength of God, or safe except in his defense. I recommend that the trust of our people in God be declared on our coins. Prepare a motto to express national recognition of and trust in God."

The first motto prepared was: "God, our Trust." This was soon changed to: "In God we trust."

1550 Back in the days of sailing ships, a young inexperienced seaman was sent aloft in a storm to distangle a broken rigging from the mainmast.

Despite the raging winds, the youngster climbed up swiftly and did the job. But as he started to descend he looked down and became dizzy and frightened when he saw the vessel tossing and rolling in the angry sea. Soon he felt his grip weakening and cried to the first mate on the deck far below: "I'm falling!"

"Don't look down, boy! Look up!", the mate shouted back. Following this advice he soon regained his calm and made his way safely back to the deck.

— selected

1551 Trust in yourself, and you are doomed to disappointment; trust in your friends, and they will die and leave you; trust in money, and you may have it taken from you; trust in reputation, and some slanderous tongue may blast it; but trust in God, and you are never to be confounded in time or eternity.

— Dwight L. Moody

1552
How firm a foundation, ye saints of the Lord,
    Is laid for your faith in his excellent Word!

What more can he say than to you he hath said
Who unto the Savior for refuge have fled?
— G. Keith (?)
ref. 1532,1535

TRUTH 1553-1566

Truth Exists and Can Be Found

1553 It exists in God who is the essence of truth: Ex 34:6; Dt 32:4; Ps 31:5; 33:4; 119:160; 146:6; Ro 3:4; 2 Cor 1:18; Tt 1:2; He 6:18; Re 3:7; 16:7; *ref. 1562*;

1554 It has been revealed and is conveyed to us:

In the Bible — God's Word is Truth: Ps 119:142; Jn 8:31,32; 17:17; Eph 1:13; Col 1:5; Jas 1:18; Re 19:9; 21:5; 22:6; *ref. 1562,1563,1566*;

In Jesus Christ, the incarnation of truth: Jn 1:1f,14,17; 8:31,32; 14:6; 18:37; Eph 4:21; Col 2:3; 1 Jn 5:20; *ref. 1565*;

In the work of the Holy Spirit, who works through the Word of Truth, the Bible: Jn 14:17; 15:26; 16:13; Eph 5:9; 1 Jn 5:6.

1555 Like God, who is its source, it is unchangeable and eternal: Ps 100:5; 117:2; 119:89,152; Is 40:8; Mal 3:6; Mt 5:18; 24:35; 1 Pe 1:22,23; *ref. 1562,1564*.

God's Word Has Divine Power

1556 It frees man from sin and its power, produces faith in Christ, and sanctifies: Jn 6:63; 8:31,32; 15:3; 17:17,19; Ro 1:16; 10:17; Jas 1:18,21; 1 Pe 1:23; cp Jr 23:29; He 4:12,13; *ref. 1565*;

1557 It serves as the Christian's defense against error: Is 8:20; 1 Tm 6:3-5; 1 Jn 4:6; and against the temptations of Satan: Mt 4:4,7,10,11; 2 Cor 6:7; Eph 6:17; Re 12:11; *ref. 1562*.

God's Word Makes Demands

1558 It is to be heard: Jr 22:29; Mic 1:2; Lk 11:28; Jn 18:37; Ro 10:14-17; 1 Jn 4:6; *ref. 1562*;

1559 It is to be believed and obeyed: Ro 2:8,9; Ga 3:1; 2 Th 2:10-15; He 4:2; *ref. 1565*;

1560 It is to be lived: Ps 26:3; 86:11; Pr 12:19; Zch 8:16; Eph 4:15; 6:14;Jas 1:18-22; 2 Jn 4; 3 Jn 3; *ref. 1566*;

1561 It is to be shared: Ps 119:172; 1 Tm 2:4; *1020-1081,1566*.

Resources

1562 Pilate's question, "What is truth?" Jn 18:38, is still being asked by millions of people today. They have followed the vain philosophies of would-be intellectual leaders. They have bowed to the idols of science. They have paid homage at the shrine of knowledge. They have worshiped at the altar of pleasure. Failing to find a satisfactory answer to their questions there, they have turned to outer space, hoping to find an answer in the stars or in a landing on the moon. But in each instance they have come up bankrupt, disappointed, disgusted and disillusioned, and have repeated the cry "What is truth?"

For many it is not a question which implies a search for the truth, but a cynical question which implies that there is no such a reality as the truth. But truth does exist, as it always existed in the past also. Failure to find it lies with sinful, corrupt man, who looks for it everywhere else but in the place where it can be found.

The only place where truth can be found is in the Bible, which claims to be, has proven itself to be, the revealed Word of God: 1 Cor 1:20-25. Truth has its origin with God, who is the Source and the Essence of Truth. Truth is of God. It is eternal. It cannot die, because it was never born. "It may be obscured," as it often is, "by the clouds of falsehood or buried by the debris of sinful ignorance, but it can never be destroyed — as little as God can be destroyed, from whom all truth eminates"; *ref. 1553,1554.*

† † †

1563

> We search the world for truth. We cull
> The good, the pure, the beautiful,
> From graven stone and written scroll,
> From all old flower-fields of the soul;
> And, weary seekers of the best,
> We come back laden from the quest,
> To find that all the sages said
> Is in the Book our mothers read.
> — Whittier

ref. 1554

† † †

1564

> Wide as the world is thy command,
> Vast as eternity thy love;
> Firm as a rock thy truth must stand
> When rolling years shall cease to move.
> — Isaac Watts

ref. 1555

† † †

1565 Christ's reply to Pilate was a challenge to put his claim to a test by hearing and heeding his voice: Jn 18:37; see also Jn 7:17. Today, as then, he says, "If you hold to my teaching, you are really my disciples. Then you will know the truth, and the truth will set you free," Jn 8:31,32.

> Thou are the Way, the Truth, the Life;
> Grant us that Way to know,
> That Truth to keep, that Life to win,
> Whose joys eternal flow.
> — George W. Doane

1566
Oh, make thy Church, dear Savior
A lamp of burnished gold
To bear before the nations
Thy true light as of old!
Oh, teach thy wand'ring pilgrims
By this their path to trace
Till, clouds and darkness ended,
They see thee face to face!
— William H. How
ref. 1554,1561

WOMEN 1567-1583
(ref.: Children 142-158; Home 534-556; Marriage 1003-1019)

The Place of Women in Society

1567 Woman was created by God and taken from man to be a suitable helper for man: Gn 1:27; 2:18-23; *ref. 1577,1580,1581;*

1568 She was the first to fall into sin, then led her husband to disobey God, and brought God's curse upon herself and upon her husband: Gn 3:1-20; 2 Cor 11:3; 1 Tm 2:14;

1569 She, as well as her husband, has been redeemed by Christ; all believers in Christ, men and women, are heirs together of eternal life: Gn 3:15; Ga 3:26-28; 1 Pe 3:7; *ref. 1577;*

1570 Her subjection to her husband is not that of a slave to his master, but an honorable place in God's order of creation: Gn 3:16; 1 Cor 11:11,12; Eph 5:22,28; 1 Pe 3:1-7; *ref. 1577-1581.*

The Work of Women

1571 In the home: Pr 31:13-27; Tt 2:3-5;

1572 In the church:
In specific: Ex 15:20,21; Jdg 4:4f; 2 Kgs 22:14f; Lk 2:36-38; Ac 21:9;
In general: Ex 35:25,26; Ac 18:26; Ro 16:1-6,12; Php 4:3;
In ministering to Christ: Mt 27:55,56; Lk 7:37,38; 8:1-3; 10:38; Jn 12:1-8; *ref. 1582,1583.*

Special Distinction Given to Women in the New Testament

1573 They were:
The last to remain at the cross of Christ: Mk 15:47;
The first to arive at the empty tomb: Mt 28:1-6; Jn 20:1;
The first to proclaim Christ's resurrection: Mt 28:8; Jn 20:18;
The first to greet the Christian missionaries in Europe: Ac 16:13-15.

Women As Examples

1574 Examples of pious women:
Sarah: Gn 17:15,16; He 11:11; 1 Pe 3:5,6;

Ruth: Ruth 1:16; 3:11;
Hannah: 1 Sm 1:11,24-28; 2:19;
Elizabeth: Lk 1:5,6;
Mary, the mother of Jesus: Lk 1:26-38;
Mary and Martha of Bethany: Mt 26:6-13; Lk 10:38-42;
Dorcas: Ac 9:36;
Lydia: Acts 16:14,15;
Lois and Eunice: 2 Tm 1:5.

1575 Examples of evil women:

Delilah: Jdg 16:4f;
Jezebel: 1 Kgs 18:4; 19:2; 21:7-15,25;
Athaliah: 2 Kgs 11:1;
Maachah: 2 Chr 15:16;
Zeresh: Est 5:14;
Job's wife: Job 2:9,10;
Herodias: Mt 14:6-10.

1576 Example of a pious wife and mother: Pr 31:10-31.

Resources

1577 Christ's work of redemption has removed every distinction between Jews and Gentiles, between slaves and freemen, between males and females. By faith in Christ all are the children of God and heirs of heaven: Ga 3:26-28. However, this does not alter their status in God's order of creation where there is a difference between men and women, children, rulers and subjects in their respective duties to one another: Ro 13:1-7; Eph 6:1-9; Col 3:18-4:1; cp, 1 Cor 15:28. This subordination in nature has been placed there by God not to indicate that someone is more worthy than another, but for the sake of orderly function and for the welfare of all.

Redemption does not change the nature of man and woman; they are still male and female. The fact that they are different is a gift of God. It is a result of God's will that they have different functions both in the home and in the church. God would have both men and women look upon the position for which woman was created as a high and glorious one.

The true relationship between husband and wife is best described in the relationship between Christ and his bride, the church: Eph 5:22-30; *ref. 1569.*

† † †

1578 There can be no denial of the fact that Christianity has elevated woman, that it has given her a high, honorable, and noble position in life. Among heathen nations and heathen religions woman counts for little. The Moslem woman is regarded as the personal property of her husband; she merely exists for the purpose of bearing him children. If she becomes incapable of this through ill health or other causes, he may cast her aside, neglect her, leave her to die, divorce her, or, at best, allow her a miserable existence in the household presided over by another wife. Hinduism teaches that woman is such a low creature tht she does not even have a soul. The "sacred cow" means much more to the Hindu than does his wife. For the Buddhist woman there are eighteen special hells. The national religion of Japan permits a father to compel his daughter to lead a sinful life to help him pay his debts. In India the birth of a baby boy causes joy, that of a baby girl, however, sorrow; indeed it is looked upon as a punishment upon the mother for her sins. Confucianism, the national religion of China, considers woman a necessary evil; she may be bought and sold for domestic service, for the stage, or for immoral purposes; and the killing of baby girls is not considered a crime. In short, the servitude and indignities which heathen women must suffer beggar description.

— selected

1579 "Surely your Bible was written by a woman," said a Hindu woman to the Christian missionary. "What prompts you to say that?" inquired the missionary. "Because," she replied, "it says so many kind things about women. Our religious leaders never refer to us but in reproach."

1580 Why did God create the woman? In order to be the helpmate of man. Surely no creature can aspire to greater honor and glory than to fulfill the destiny for which it was created. It is in the realization of this fundamental truth that the greatest women in history have found their greatness. There is no finer virtue for a woman than true womanliness.

— W. G. Polack

1581 Woman was not taken from man's head, as though she should rule over him, nor from his feet, as though she should be his slave, but from his side, in order that she might be his equal and his bosom companion.

— St. Augustine

ref. 1570

† † †

1582 Looking back in the history of the church we find that women formed an integral part of the earliest Christian community. . . . In general, woman's service was along womanly lines, such as showing hospitality, caring for the poor, the sick, the prisoners, the orphans, taking oversight and instructing women and children.

Special offices for women came into existence at a very early time. Official widows serving the church appeared at the close of the apostolic age: 1 Tm 5:3-10. They were to continue in prayer and fasting. Their work was to care for other widows and for the poor in general, especially for orphans and for those who were in prison for conscience' sake.

In the 4th century, which marks the zenith of woman's activity in the early church, the development of hospitals and hospices displaced the early activities of Christian women. Helena, the mother of emperor Constantine, under whose reign Christianity became firmly established in the heathen world, built the first hospice for strangers and pilgrims. A group of noble matrons followed suit and did much to promote Christianity by founding hospitals and fostering education.

— selected

1583 St. Luke... gives us the psalms of Elizabeth and Mary;... gives us the names of Joanna and Susanna, who ministered to Christ of their substance; ... gives us that Galilaean idyl in which the nameless "woman" bathes Jesus' feet with tears;... speaks of the widow Zarephath, who welcomed and saved a prophet men were seeking to slay;... tells of the widow of Nain, of the woman bent with infirmity, and of the woman grieving over the lost piece of silver. And as St. Luke opens his Gospel with woman's tribute of song, so in the last chapter he paints for us that group of women, constant amid man's inconstancies, coming ere the break of day to wrap around the body of the dead Christ the precious and fragrant offering of devotion. But ever first and foremost among the women of the Gospels we must place the mother of Jesus.

— Burton

ref. 1571,1572

WORK 1584-1599

1584 By placing man in the Garden of Eden "to dress and keep it" God indicated that it is his will that man should work: Gn 2:15;

1585 Despite the fact that sin turned the joy of work into a burden and drudgery: Gn 3:17-19; it is still God's will that man should work: Ex 20:9; and that he should obtain his livelihood by the labors of his own hands and not by stealing from another: Ex 20:13; Pr 13:11; 16:8; 22:16; Eph 4:28; 1 Th 4:11; 2 Th 3:11,12. God's will that man should work is indicated:

By God's own example in the work of creating and preserving the world: Ex 20:11; Col 1:17; He 1:3; 4:10;

By Christ's work: Jn 4:34; 5:17; 9:4; 17:4;

By the example of creatures: Pr 6:6-10;

By the work of the holy angels: Ps 103:20;

By God's promises to bless man's labors: Ps 128:1,2; Pr 10:4; 13:4; 14:23; 22:29; *ref. 1588-1590,1596,1598.*

1586 All work should be done to the glory of God: 1 Cor 10:31; 1 Pe 4:10,11; and with a sense of love toward one's family and fellow men: Mt 22:39; Ga 5:13; 1 Tm 5:8; 1 Jn 4:20,21; *ref. 1591-1595,1597.*

1587 God's Word commands a mutual regard and respect between capital and labor:

Employers are to be considerate of the welfare of their employees, avoid threats and oppression, and pay them a just wage: Dt. 24:14,15; Eph 6:9; Col 4:1; 1 Tm 5:18; Jas 5:1-6; *ref. 1599;*

Employees are to be obedient to their employers and are to work diligently for their wages: 1 Cor 7:22; Eph 6:5-8; Col 3:22-25; 1 Tm 6:1; Tt 2:9; 1 Pe 2:18; *ref. 1599.*

Resources

1588 God wants no idleness. It is his will that man should work, and man's body is so constituted that it cannot remain healthy and strong unless it is engaged in some activity.

There were members in the church at Thessalonica who refused to work because they falsely assumed that the Lord's return was imminent. Besides being idlers they busied themselves in other peoples' business by trying to unsettle the stable members of the church with their false notions: cp Ac 17:21. As a messenger of Christ, the Apostle Paul commanded them to cease imposing themselves on others, to get back to work and to earn their own livelihood: 2 Th 3:10-12.

1589 The result of idleness and loafing breeds crime and vice. Instead of being busily engaged in the work of their calling and devoting their energy to the production of something good and useful, idlers become busybodies and officious meddlers. The simple truth is that man must have some activity to engage his mind. If he does not attend to his own affairs he will busy himself interfering with someone else's business. Without work, life soon becomes drab and dreary, full of restlessness and dissatisfaction. It has been correctly said that "idleness is the devil's workshop." It is the parent of many crimes and produces all manner of misery.

1590 God cannot use idlers. When he wants workers he goes to people who are already busy:

Moses was busy with his flock at Mt. Horeb when the Lord called him.

Gideon was busy threshing wheat.

Saul was busy searching for his father's lost sheep.

Elijah was busy plowing.

Nehemiah was busy bearing the king's wine-cup.

Amos was busy following the flock.

Peter and Andrew were busy casting a net into the sea.

James and John were busy mending their nets.

Matthew was busy collecting taxes.

— selected

ref. 1584,1585

† † †

1591   Whether you're working in office or shop,
And however far you may be from the top,
And though you may think you're just treading the mill,
Don't ever belittle the job that you fill;
For however little your job may appear,
You're just as important as some little gear
That meshes with others in some big machine,

393

That helps keep it going though never is seen.
They could do without you, we'll have to admit,
But business keeps on, when the big fellows quit!
And always remember, my lad, if you can,
The job's more important — oh, yes — than the man!
So if it's your hope to stay off the shelf,
Think more of your job than you do of yourself.
Your job is important; don't think it is not,
So try hard to give it the best that you've got!
And don't think ever you're of little account,
Remember, you're part of the total amount.
If they didn't need you, you wouldn't be there,
So always, my lad, keep your chin in the air.
A digger of ditches, mechanic, or clerk —
Think well of your company, yourself, and your work!

— Anon

1592 When we build let us think that we build forever. Let it not be for present delight, nor for the present use alone, let it be such work as our descendants will thank us for, and let us think, as we lay stone on stone, that a time is to come when those stones will be held sacred because our hands have touched them, and that men will say as they look upon our labor and the wrought substance of them, "See! this our fathers did for us!"

— John Ruskin

1593
Let us do our work well,
  Both the unseen and the seen,
Make the house where God may dwell
  Beautiful, entire and clean.

— Anon

ref. 1586

† † †

1594 A worker who does only what he has to do is somebody's slave. Only he who is willing to do more than is required of him is truly a free man.

1595 I would rather fail in a cause that will ultimately succeed than succeed in a cause that will ultimately fail.

— Woodrow Wilson

ref. 1586

† † †

1596
With the Lord begin thy task,
  Jesus will direct it;
For his aid and counsel ask,
  Jesus will perfect it.
Ev'ry morn with Jesus rise,
  And when day is ended,

394

In his name then close thine eyes;
Be to him commended.
                    — German author unknown
ref. 1585

† † †

1597 It should go without saying that Christian people who strive to do the will of God will never be engaged in a work which is sinful. Mindful that they are serving the Lord, they will not work for selfish reasons but for the glory of their Maker and Redeemer, whether it be the work of the husband in the shop, or the work of the housewife in the home, or the work of children who attend school, peddle papers, or run errands. With such a God-pleasing attitude toward work, the Christian maid glorifies God as she sweeps the room, the Christian farmer sings as he plows and sows his field, the Christian man in the factory takes pride in his product, the Christian secretary smiles as she carries out her assignments, Christian children willingly and cheerfully run their errands. And so it is with every task, be it ever so humble. "Whether you eat or drink or whatever you do," writes the Apostle, "do it all for the glory of God," 1 Cor 10:31. Christian people know that God has created them for work, and that by their work they are observing the will of their Maker. They know that in their work they have a part in God's ongoing work of creation, and that gives divine dignity to their labors.
                    — selected and adapted
ref. 1586

† † †

1598 There were fainthearted prophets who predicted the doom of society because of lack of work at the time of the Industrial Revolution and at the time the oxcart was supplanted by the railroad and automobile. But there were also those who saw in these developments a new era of progress and a new day of blessing that would prove to be of priceless benefit to mankind.

The revolutionary changes that are now taking place in our machine age will prove no less a blessing. God who created man for work still guides the future and the affairs of men and nations of men. As old jobs are discontinued, new jobs will be created. Nor will there be a problem of increased leisure time. The fact is that there are so many unfinished tasks, especially in the work of the church, that no amount of leisure time will wholly suffice to accomplish them. Instead of asking what people may do with their leisure time, let us thank God for the prospect of finding more time for worship and Christian fellowship, for Christian education, for personal mission work and Christian service, for paying more attention to the aged and underprivileged, for visiting the sick and shutins, for spending more time with our children and youth, for recreation, for culture and art, and for many more worthy causes for which we now plead lack of time.
                    — selected and adapted
ref. 1585

† † †

1599 From a sermon preached in Flint, Michigan on Labor Day, 1937, in the wake of the Fisher Body strike:

Seated in my study I can hear through the open window the whistles of two of the leading factories that have made our city famous. As I close my eyes I see men wipe their sweated brow, lay down their tools, pick up their lunch-baskets, and hurry to their homes. With few exceptions they are all red-blooded Americans, either by birth or in spirit and ideals. They are a peace-loving group, men who take no pleasure in causing dissention and strife between employers and employees, men who are not given to strikes and riots, men who do not walk around with a chip on their shoulder, men who do not believe that might makes right, men who do not believe in having paid agitators from Russia destroy their jobs, their homes, their church, their government — but honest, upright, God-fearing, law-abiding citizens who ask only that they be given a fair deal for themselves and for others in this our beloved land of abundance and opportunity.

I see many others coming from offices and shops, from places of business, and from farms, thousands upon thousands of them, hurrying at the close of the day to their homes and families where they will sit down to eat their own bread in peace and quietness.

There, in that great army of loyal, law-abiding, and God-fearing workers, I see the spirit of America in the fulness of its strength and beauty. May God preserve this noble heritage unto us and unto our children!

— R. C. R.

ref. 1587

WORLD, THE END OF THE 1600-1620

(ref.: Christ's Second Coming 827-849)

Holy Scriptures Teach That This World Will End

1600 See Ps 102:25-27; Is 34:4; 51:6; Mt 5:18; 13:39,49; 24:14,35; 28:20; Mk 13:31; Lk 21:33-36; 1 Cor 7:31; 2 Cor 4:18; He 1:10-12; Jas 5:7,8; 2 Pe 3:7,10; 1 Jn 2:17; Re 6:13-17; 21:1; *ref. 1605-1610,1612.*

When and How The End Will Come

1601 The exact time of the end is not known: Mt 24:36,42; 25:13; Mk 13:32,33. It will come suddenly and unexpectedly: Mt 24:27,43,44; Mk 13:35-37; Lk 12:40; 21:34-36; 1 Th 5:2,3; Re 16:15; and the world will be destroyed: 2 Pe 3:7,10; *ref. 1611,1616,1617.*

1602 There will be signs that precede the end:

In the realm of nature — signs in the sun, moon and stars: Jl 2:30,31; Mt 24:29,30; Mk 13:24-26; Lk 21:25-27; *ref. 1605,1609;*

In the history of the world — wars and rumors of wars, famines, pestilence and earthquakes in diverse places: Mt 24:6-8; Mk 13:7,8; Lk 21:9-11; Re 6:4-8;

In society — increasing iniquity, worldliness and carelessness: Mt 24:12,37-41,48-51; 25:6-10; Lk 17:26-30; 21:34,35; 1 Th 5:1-3; 2 Tm 3:1-5; 2 Pe 3:3,4; Jd 17-19;

In the church — a growing number of false prophets: Mt 24:11,24-27; Ac 20:29,30; 2 Th 2:3-11; 1 Tm 4:1-3; 2 Pe 2:1-3; 3:1-4; a lack of love and a falling away from the truth: Mt 24:12; 2 Tm 3:5; 4:3,4; *ref. 1611;*

In the extension of Christ's kingdom — his gospel will be preached in all the world: Mt 24:14; Mk 13:10; and his church will prevail against all the forces of evil: Mt 16:18; Lk 1:32,33; Php 2:9-11; Re 11:15; cp Is 9:7; Dn 2:44; 7:13,14.

Events That Will Occur When the End Comes

1603 Christ will return visibly in the clouds of heaven in majesty and glory, accompanied by all the holy angels: Mt 24:30; 25:31; 26:64; Mk 13:26; Lk 9:26; 21:27; Ac 1:11; Php 2:9-11; Re 1:7; *ref. 1614;*

All the dead will be called from their graves: Jn 5:28,29; 1 Th 4:16,17; Re 20:11-15; and the bodies of the believers will be transformed: 1 Cor 15:49-53; Php 3:20,21; Col 3:4;

The living and the dead will be judged: Mt 16:27; 25:31-33; Ac 17:31; 24:15; 1 Cor 4:5; 2 Cor 5:10; 2 Tm 4:1; He 9:27; 2 Pe 2:9; 3:7; 1 Jn 4:17; Jd 14,15; Re 20:11-15; *ref. 1613,1615,1619;*

The present world will be destroyed: *ref. 1600;*

God will create a new heaven and a new earth: Is 65:17; 66:22; 2 Pe 3:13; Re 21:1-7; *ref. 1615.*

Necessary Preparations for the End

1604 On the part of unbelievers — a need to recognize their time of grace, to repent and accept God's offer of salvation through Christ: Is 55:6,7; Lk

19:41; Ro 2:3,4; 13:11-14; 2 Cor 6:2; *ref. 1616,1617,1620.*

On the part of believers, a need:

To be watchful and ready for Christ's return: Mt 24:44; Lk 21:28,33-36; Php 3:20,21;

To live soberly and righteously: Php 1:10; Col 3:1-5; Tt 2:11-14; 1 Th 5:5,6; Jas 1:27; 1 Pe 1:17; 2:11,12; 4:7; 2 Pe 3:11-14; 1 Jn 2:15-17,28; see also Mt 6:19,20;

To be active in mission work: Jn 9:4; Php 2:15; *ref. 1020-1081.*

Resources

1605 In the June 1947 issue of the "Bulletin of the Atomic Scientists" the cover page pictured a clock, the hands of which pointed to the hour 11:52. The picture was reproduced on the cover page with each new issue, with only slight changes in the position of the hands on the clock. By September, 1953 the clock hands were pointing to 11:58.

1606 Already at the beginning of the atomic age, Professor Einstein declared, "We are drifting toward a catastrophe beyond comparison. We shall require a substantially new manner of thinking if mankind is to survive." In the years that followed scientists have penetrated more mysteries of nature and broken more barriers than men dreamed of during the rest of recorded history.

1607 At the opening of the first session of the UN Commission on Atomic Energy, Bernard Baruch said, "Let us not deceive ourselves; we must elect world peace or world destruction." — The frightening fact is that our world of today is kept at peace only by a "balance of power." In the arsenal of weapons today, a single bomb contains power to destroy more than all the destruction wrought by all the weapons of World War II.

1608 Astronomers testify that through their telescope they repeatedly see stars, far greater than our globe, melt in fervent heat. Geologists testify that the core of this earth is a molten fiery mass above which are vast supplies of highly inflammible gas, thus making the whole globe itself a potential bomb which can explode and melt with fervent heat. Chemists testify that the very air we breathe is composed of oxygen, nitrogen, and hydrogen, an imbalance of which can cause an explosion beyond description. Even the mighty oceans will not put out that fire; for water is not only made up of the same combustible hydrogen and oxygen, in many cases it is also saturated with elements that burn easily.

— selected

1609 "All mankind is at the edge of the valley of death."

— Dr. Harrison Brown,
atomic energy scientist

1610 Whether God will allow sinful men to destroy the universe by making a wrong move or pressing the wrong button, or whether he himself who by his own Word called the world into being will simply by the same Word call it out of existence, as Scripture seems to indicate, this much is certain: the heaven and the earth now are kept in store, reserved for the fires of Judgment Day — and the perdition of ungodly men; 2 Pe 3:5-7.

1611 Despite the fact that Scriptures repeatedly state that no one can know the exact time of the Lord's return, there have been false prophets in every age who presumed to know this mystery and who predicted the date for this event. During the last century, for example, a man by the name of William Miller (1782-1849), an uneduated farmer, predicted that Christ would return within a year after March 21, 1843. He traveled over the country proclaiming his message, and by 1843 his followers numbered fifty thousand. As the appointed time of his prophecy drew near there was great excitement among his followers, who sold or gave away their possessions and, arrayed in white apparel, went forth to the hilltops there to await Christ's coming. Needless to say, nothing unusual happened. Yet out of that man's preaching there originated the sect known as the "Adventists," the "Church of God," and a number of other organizations. — Similarly, the Russelites, the present-day Jehovah's Witnesses, announced that Christ would visibly return in the year 1914 to set up a kingdom of peace on earth. Instead, however, 1914 was the year in which World War I began. This same sect later announced that all who would live to the year 1925 would never die. — Other examples could be mentioned; *ref. 1602.*

† † †

1612 The expression "day of the Lord" is used in Scriptures with reference to the Lord's return at the end of the world: Mal 4:5; 1 Cor 5:5; 2 Cor 1:14; 1 Th 5:2; 2 Pe 3:10; *ref. 1600.*

† † †

1613 A man who was on trial for a criminal offense stood trembling before the judge. "Don't be afraid," he was told, "you'll get justice." "I know, Judge," replied the offender, "but that's just what I don't want!" — Is that not our exact position before God? We do not want justice; we want mercy. If we received only justice, we would be condemned. Only God's mercy can save us. So we pray with Habakkuk, "O Lord . . . in wrath remember mercy," Hab 3:2.

— selected

1614
> Though the mills of God grind slowly,
> Yet they grind exceeding small;
> Though with patience he stands waiting
> With exactness grinds he all.

— Anon

1615 An irreligious farmer, in one of the western States, gloried in his irreligion. He wrote a letter to the local newspaper in which he stated: "Sir, I have been trying an experiment with a field of mine. I plowed it on Sunday. I planted it on Sunday. I dressed it only on Sunday. I reaped it on Sunday. I carted the crop home on Sunday to my barn. And now, Mr. Editor, what is the result? I have more bushels to the acre in that field than any of my neighbors have had this October."

In an early edition of the paper this farmer found his letter printed in full, and without any comment except this significant sentence that appeared below it: "God does not always settle his accounts in October"; *ref. 1603.*

† † †

1616 In the year 1888 a number of engineers came to Johnston, Pennsylvania, to examine the dam that controlled the waters flowing down the valley. They pronounced the dam unsafe and issued the warning that the people in the valley were in constant danger. But nobody paid attention to the warning. That same fall the engineers returned, re-examined the dam, and again issued the warning. Yet nothing was done about it. The following spring the engineers warned the people for a third time, but the warning was not heeded even then. Fifteen days later the dam broke, and in a short time the swirling waters inundated the city of Johnstown. More than thirty-seven hundred people were swept away, and the city was completely ruined. — Our blessed Savior also uttered a warning which millions fail to heed: "You refuse to come to me to have life," Jn 5:40. His loving heart longs to save souls from hell. That is why he wept over impenitent Jerusalem. "How often I have longed to gather your children together . . . but you were not willing," Mt 23:37.

— *The Prairie Overcomer*

1617 In Frank, Alberta, a small mining town in the Canadian Rockies, the year 1902 brought sudden disaster. In the middle of the night ninety million tons of limestone broke away from a high mountain and sent an avalanche 250 feet deep and 3,000 feet wide roaring into the narrow canyon. It took just 100 seconds and the roar subsided, but seventy lives were snuffed out. —Thus will the end of the world come, suddenly, unexpectedly, with the roar of a thousand avalanches thundering into the valleys of the world. Now is the time to pray the Holy Spirit to use us more and more as witnesses to Christ and Calvary, that a few more souls will escape the final tragedy of hell.

— selected

ref. 1604

† † †

1618 Whether the new heaven and the new earth will be a reproduction of the old in a far more glorious form, through the agency of refining fire, or an absolutely new creation, cannot be definitely determined. But this much is known, the new heaven and the new earth of which Scriptures speak is nothing else than the place of future bliss that the Bible so frequently speaks of as heaven, and of which we so frequently speak as the world to come, or the world without end; *ref. 1603.*

† † †

400

1619 On May 19th, 1780, a strange darkness overspread New England. It is known in history as the Dark Day. Though the sun was visible, it was shorn of all its power of illumination. Witnesses and accounts describe the darkness as supernatural and unaccountable. — The legislature of Connecticut was in session and many of the members were seized with a panic, thinking, as did thousands of others, that Judgment Day was at hand. When a motion was made to adjourn, the president of the assembly rose and said: "Gentlemen, if this is not the Great Day we are foolish and alarmed, and if it is, I wish to be found by my Maker doing my duty. I ask, therefore, that candles be lighted and brought in, and that we proceed with the work at hand"; *ref. 1600,1602.*

† † †

1620 On Sunday night, October 8, 1871, D. L. Moody preached to the largest congregation that he had yet addressed in Chicago. His text was, "What shall I do, then, with Jesus who is called Christ?" Mt 27:22. At the close of the sermon he said, "I wish you would take this text home with you and turn it over in your minds during the week, and next Sabbath we will come to Calvary and the Cross, and we will decide what to do with Jesus of Nazareth."

Then came the roar of fire engines on the streets outside, and before morning Chicago lay in ashes. Moody to his dying day was full of regret that he had told that congregation to come next Sabbath and decide what to do with Jesus. "I have never since dared," he said, "to give an audience a week to think of their salvation. If they were lost they might rise up in judgment against me. I have never seen that congregation since. I would rather have that right hand cut off than to give an audience a week now to decide what to do with Jesus."

— selected

ref. 1604

YEAR, OLD AND NEW 1621-1667

(ref.: Time, Stewardship of 1367; Trust 1532-1552)

The Close of the Old Year

1621 A time for reflection:

On the rapid flight of time and the transitory nature of all earthly things: 1 Chr 29:15; Job 14:1,2; Ps 31:15; 90:3,4; 102:11; 103:15,16; He 1:10-12; 1 Pe 1:24; Jas 4:14; *ref. 1625-1628;*

On God's goodness and mercy and our own unworthiness: Gn 32:10; Ps 68:19; 90:8; 103:8-14; 145:8,9,15-20; Is 64:6; Lm 3:22; Mt 5:45; Ac 14:17; Ro 3:23; *ref. 1626,1628-1630,1632,1635;*

On our need to repent of our sins and ask for forgiveness: Ps 51:1-4; 130:1-4; 143:2; Pr 28:13; Is 55:7; Eze 18:31; Jl 2:12,13; Lk 13:1-5; 15:21; 18:13; 1 Jn 1:7-10; 2:1,2; and to thank the Lord for his goodness: Ps 68:19; 103:1-5; 136:1; Eph 5:20; 1 Th 5:18; *ref. 1632.*

1622 A time for earnest resolve:

To amend our sinful life: Dt 10:12; Ps 19:12; 27:11; 51:10-13; 79:9; Mt 3:8; Eph 4:22-24; Col 1:10; cp Lk 13:6-9; *ref. 1632;*

To be more diligent in the use of our time in serving God and our fellowmen: Ps 90:12; Jn 4:35; 9:4; 1 Cor 7:29-31; Eph 5:14-17; Col 4:5,6; ref. 1633.

The Beginning of the New Year

1623 A time to trust in:

God's everlasting mercy: Dt 33:27; Ps 27:1,5; 46:1,2,7; 91:1-16; 145:18,19; 121:1-8; Pr 18:10; Is 26:4; Jr 31:3; Mt 6:31,32; 10:29-31; Ro 5:8-10; 8:31-34; *ref. 1639-1641;*

God's steadfast love to us in Christ: Ro 8:35-39; Ga 2:20; He 7:25-27; 13:8; 1 Jn 4:9,10,16; *ref. 1636,1637;*

God's never-failing promises: Ps 50:15; Is 41:10; 43:1,2; 54:10; Mt 11:28; 28:20; Lk 11:13; Jn 6:37; 14:1-3,19; 2 Cor 1:20; Php 4:6,7,19; 2 Tm 1:12; He 10:23; 13:5,6; 1 Pe 4:19; 5:6,7; cp Jos 23:14; 1 Kgs 8:56; Lk 1:68-75; *ref. 1638,1639,1642,1644,1647,1648.*

1624 A time to live

As Christian pilgrims: 1 Chr 29:15; Ps 39:12; 119:19; Mt 5:16; Ro 6:6f; 12:1,2; 1 Cor 7:31; Eph 5:1-11,15,16; Php 1:27; 2:15,16; 3:20,21; Col 3:1-10; Tt 2:11; He 11:13; 13:14; 1 Pe 1:13-17; 2:11,12; Jd 20:21; *ref. 1628;*

In joyful service to God and fellow men: Ne 12:43; Ps 43:3,4; 100:2; 126:5,6; Lk 10:17; Jn 4:35,36; Ac 2:46; 20:24; 1 Cor 15:58; *ref. 1631-1634,1643-1646;*

In constant readiness for the Lord's return: Mt 24:42-44; 25:13; Mk 13:32-37; Lk 12:35-40; 21:28,34-36; 2 Pe 3:10-12; *ref. 1604.*

Resources

1625 The world and all that it contains is constantly changing and growing older. Rivers change their course. Earthquakes change geographical locations. Tornadoes, cyclones, fires and floods wipe out cities and hamlets. Towering trees of the forest yield to the axe and saw of the lumberman. Railroads change the map of the country. New highways, new homes, new cities and villages change the wasteland. Wherever you go and wherever you look, the world and all things in it change.

And what is said of the world and all that it contains must also be said of man. In his physical sphere man changes constantly. Not a minute passes but man, too, grows older. With every passing second he takes another step toward his grave.

This constant change will continue until, at length, time will end. Then, at the last, the world and all that it contains will pass away and man's final judgment will be at hand: He 9:27; 1 Jn 2:15-17.

But in the midst of this constant change, God in his boundless love and Christ in his saving grace remain unchanged: Mal 3:6; He 13:8.

> Change and decay in all around I see,
> O thou, who changest not, abide with me.
> — Henry F. Lyte

1626 We preach a changeless Christ for a changing world.

1627
> Life is changing, changing ever
>   As the seasons come and go;
> Friends we loved no longer with us,
>   Thus 'tis ever, ever so;
> But our Savior changeth never
>   Nothing from his love can sever.
>
> All around is swiftly fading,
>   Fading as an autumn leaf;
> Earthly fame and earthly honor,
>   All below is very brief.
> But our Savior changeth never
>   He abides the same as ever.
>
> Yes! below there naught remaineth,
>   All is frail and fleeting here;
> But his Word our soul sustaineth,
>   This our path doth cheer;
> That our Savior changeth never
>   Nothing from his love can sever.
>   — Anon

1628
> While with ceaseless course the sun
>   Hasted thro' the former year,
> Many souls their race have run,
>   Nevermore to meet us here;

Fixed in an eternal state,
  They have done with all below,
We a little longer wait,
  But how little, none can know.

As the winged arrow flies
  Speedily the mark to find;
As the lightning from the skies
  Darts and leaves no trace behind,
Swiftly thus our fleeting days
  Bear us down life's rapid stream.
Upward, Lord, our spirits raise;
  All below is but a dream.

Thanks for mercies past received;
  Pardon of our sins renew;
Teach us henceforth how to live
  With eternity in view.
Bless thy Word to young and old,
  Fill us with a Savior's love;
And when life's short tale is told,
  May we dwell with thee above.

           — John Newton

1629

We gather up in this brief hour
  The mem'ry of thy mercies;
Thy wondrous goodness, love, and pow'r
  Our grateful song rehearses.

           — James Hamilton

1630

The Lord hath helped me hitherto
  By his surpassing favor;
His mercies ev'ry morn were new,
  His kindness did not waver.
God hitherto hath been my Guide,
  Hath pleasures hitherto supplied,
  And hitherto hath helped me.

I praise and thank thee, Lord, my God,
  For thine abundant blessing
Which heretofore thou hast bestowed
  And I am still possessing.
Inscribe this on my memory;
  The Lord hath done great things for me
  And graciously hath helped me.

Help me henceforth, O God of grace,
  Help me on each occasion,
Help me in each and ev'ry place,
  Help me thro' Jesus' Passion;

Help me in life and death, O God,
　Help me thro' Jesus' dying blood;
　Help me as thou hast helped me.
— Amilie Juliane

ref. 1621, 1623

1631　　The old year, with its record,
　　　　　　Is gone forevermore;
　　　　　The new year, full of promise,
　　　　　　Stands waiting at the door.

　　　　　With high resolve and holy,
　　　　　　With purpose firm and true,
　　　　　Let us go forth with meekness
　　　　　　God's will and work to do.

— Anon

1632　　He came to my desk with a quivering lip,
　　　　　　The lesson was done.
　　　　　"Have you a new leaf for me, dear Teacher?
　　　　　　I have spoiled this one!"
　　　　　I took his leaf, all soiled and blotted
　　　　　And gave him a new one, all unspotted.
　　　　　　Then into his tired heart I smiled:
　　　　　　"Do better now, my Child!"

　　　　　I went to the throne, with trembling heart.
　　　　　　The year was done.
　　　　　"Have you a New Year for me, dear Master?
　　　　　　I have spoiled this one!"
　　　　　He took my year, all soiled and blotted
　　　　　And gave me a new one, all unspotted,
　　　　　　Then, into my tired heart he smiled:
　　　　　　"Do better now, my Child!"

— Anon

1633 "It's going to be a beautiful year," said a girl as she tacked up a new wall calendar. When her friend who was standing at her side asked, "How do you know that it is going to be a beautiful year? A year is a long time," she replied: "A year is a long time, but a day is not a long time. And I'm going to take a day at a time and see to it that each day has something beautiful in it. Then it will be a beautiful year."

1634　　In the midnight pealing
　　　　　Through the darkness stealing,
　　　　　The chapel bells now chime:
　　　　　　Loudly knelling,
　　　　　　Calmly telling,
　　　　　　Sweetly ringing,
　　　　　　Message bringing,
　　　　　Loud and strong, and far and near,
　　　　　Of the coming of the year.

In the chamber striking,
Through the stillness citing,
The mantel clock marks time.
  Hands are joining,
  New year coining,
  All fears quelling,
  Truly spelling,
Long and slow, and soft and clear,
At the advent of the year.

In the bosom beating,
Through the soul repeating,
The thankful heart sublime —
  Rhythmic pounding,
  Joy resounding,
  Vows revolving,
  And resolving
Faith, hope, charity, and cheer
All throughout the coming year.

— R. C. R.

ref. 1622-1624

† † †

1635

Though great our sins and sore our woes,
  His grace much more aboundeth;
His helping love no limit knows,
  Our utmost need it soundeth.

— Martin Luther

ref. 1621

† † †

1636

Wait, my soul, and tarry,
Tarry with God!
He will help thee carry
Ev'ry grievous load.
Why fret or fear
When the morn is near?
With the passing winter,
Spring will reappear.
When storms distress thee,
In ev'ry ill,
God will surely bless thee;
My soul, be still!

Wait, my soul, and tarry,
Tarry with God!
He will help thee carry
Ev'ry grievous load.

406

When all things fail,
God will still prevail;
He can safely lead thee
Through the darkest vale,
Lord God eternal,
Lead to the goal!
Christ, forever faithful,
Save thou my soul.

— Anon

1637 In his autobiography Martin Luther wrote, "I have one preacher that I love better than any other on earth; it is my little tame robin, who preaches to me daily. I put crumbs upon my window sill, especially at night. He hops onto the window sill when he wants his supply, and takes as much as he desires to satisfy his need. From thence he always hops to a little tree close by and lifts up his voice to God and sings his carols of praise and gratitude, tucks his little head under his wings and goes fast to sleep, and leaves tomorrow to look after itself. He is the best preacher that I have on earth"; *ref. 1623.*

† † †

1638 God does not want lazy, gormandizing bellies, who shun both care and work and act as though they should just sit around and wait until God lets a roasted goose fly into their mouths. But he commands us to go into action and to labor honestly. Then he will be present with his blessing and give us what we need.

— Martin Luther

† † †

1639
O fathomless mercy! O infinite grace!
With humble thanksgiving the road I retrace.
Thou never hast failed me, my Strength and my Stay!
To whom should I turn for the rest of the way?

Through dangers, through darkness, by day and by
night,
Thou ever hast guided, and guided aright;
In thee have I trusted, and peacefully lay
My hand in thy hand for the rest of the way.

Thy cross all my refuge, thy blood all my plea,
None other I need, blessed Jesus, but Thee!
I fear not the shadows at close of life's day,
For thou wilt go with me the rest of the way.

— Anon

1640
I cannot bear the cross alone
Which thou dost place on all thine own;
Nor can I see thy face that shines
Beyond affliction's darkened lines.

Take thou my hand, Lord, be my Guide
And keep me ever near thy side.

I cannot walk a single day
The paths that mark life's rugged way;
Nor can I rest secure from fear
Unless I feel thy presence near.
Uphold me with thine outstretched arm
And shield me ever from alarm.

I cannot walk the way alone
That leads to my celestial home;
Nor can I face my dying hour
Unless supported by thy power.
Grant me thy strength, Lord, through this strife
And bring me to eternal life.

— R. C. R.

1641 When on November 30, 1938, the Russians bombed Luther Church in Finland, the entire building collapsed in ruin. But on the altar stood a glowing cross and above it a painting of Christ, his arms outstretched in blessing. "In this," said Bishop Lehtonen, "we saw a gripping testimony of the truth, mercy and compassion of God in forgiving our sins for Christ's sake. . . . Only in this assurance are we able to endure. With the conviction that nothing can separate us from the love of God, we have peace in our hearts in the midst of the storm. God suddenly becomes living and real when all the supports to which we have been accustomed crumble to pieces and God alone becomes our Refuge and Strength."

1642
God hath not promised
　　Skies always blue,
Flower-strewn pathways
　　All our lives through;
God hath not promised
　　Sun without rain,
Joy without sorrow,
　　Peace without pain.

But God hath promised
　　Strength for the day,
Rest from the labor,
　　Light for the way,
Grace for the trials,
　　Help from above,
Unfailing sympathy,
　　Undying love.

— Anon

ref. 1623

† † †

408

1643   Another year is dawning!
    Dear Master let it be,
In working or in waiting
    Another year with thee.

Another year is dawning!
    Dear Master let it be
On earth, or else in heaven
    Another year for thee.
             — Frances Ridley Havergal

1644 Today is ours. The book of yesterday is closed. Tomorrow's page has not been opened. Over yesterday God has placed the cloak of his forgiving mercy. Over tomorrow he has written words of gracious promise. Yesterday's mercy and tomorrow's promise should inspire today's trust and confidence. Write, then, the story of today. Dip your pen in the blue of God's heavenly love, and write in the gold of his shining promises.
             — selected

1645   To be a greater service, Lord.
A closer student of thy Word;
To help to bear a brother's load
And cheer him on the heavenly road;
To tell the lost of Jesus' love,
And how to reach the home above;
To trust in God whate'er befall,
Be ready at the Master's call
For any task that he may give
For him who gave himself for me
And taught me that my life should be
A life unselfish, not self-willed,
But with the Holy Spirit filled.
             — selected

1646   Father, let me dedicate
    All this year to thee,
In whatever earthly state
    Thou wilt have me be.
Not from sorrow, pain, or care
    Freedom dare I claim;
This alone shall be my prayer;
    Glorify thy name.
             — Lawrence Tuttiett
ref. 1624

† † †

1647   Our God, our Help in ages past,
    Our hope for years to come,
Be thou our Guard while troubles last
    And our eternal Home!
             — Isaac Watts

1648 Mountains symbolize greatness and stability, and they link the past with the present. But they are inadequate to portray the eternal love and the almighty protecting care of our God who existed before the earth was formed and before the mountains were brought forth: Ps 90:2; 121:1,2. Secure as mountains appear to be at a given moment, they are in a continual process of disintegration and change caused by rain, snow, glaciers, avalanches and, at times, by volcanic eruptions. In contrast to them the psalmist says of Mt. Zion, where God dwells, that it cannot be removed: Ps 125:1,2; cp Ps 148:1-4; Mt 16:18. It is this eternal, almighty and unchanging God who assures us: " 'Though the mountains be shaken and the hills be removed, yet my unfailing love for you will not be shaken nor my covenant of peace be removed,' says the Lord, who has compassion on you," Is 54:10; see also Mt 28:20; Ro 8:31-39. With that confidence we can say with the psalmist: "God is our refuge and strength, an ever present help in trouble. Therefore we will not fear, though the earth give way and the mountains fall into the heart of the sea, though its waters roar and foam and the mountains quake with their surging. . . . The Lord Almighty is with us; the God of Jacob is our fortress"; Ps 46:1-3,7; *ref. 1623.*

YOUNG PEOPLE 1649-1668

(ref.: Children 142-158; Education 315-358)

Special Instructions to Young People

1649 They are to:

Rejoice in their youth: Ec 11:9,10; see also Pr 20:29.

Remember the Lord and serve him: Ec 12:1; Pr 23:26; Is 55:6,7; Ro 12:1,2; 1 Cor 6:19,10; 2 Cor 5:15; 1 Tm 4:12; *ref. 1652-1654,1656,1662;*

Guard against sins besetting youth: Ps 25:7; Pr 1:10; Ec 11:9,10; 1 Cor 7:31; 1 Tm 5:22; 2 Tm 2:22; 1 Jn 2:12-17; He 11:24-26; 12:1,2; *ref. 1655,1657-1659;*

Be soberminded: Tt 2:6; 1 Pe 5:8,9; *ref. 1661;*

Obey parents: Ex 20:12; Mt 15:4; Eph 6:1-3; Col 3:20;

Honor their elders: Lv 19:32; Pr 23:22; 1 Pe 5:5, *ref. 1659;*

Receive correction: Pr 3:11,12; Lm 3:27; He 12:5-11;

Make God's Word their guide for life: Ps 1:1-6; 119:9,105,130; Eph 6:10-17; cp Mt 7:24-27; *ref. 1660;*

Grow in grace and in the knowledge of Christ: 1 Cor 13:11; Eph 4:14,15; 1 Pe 2:2; 2 Pe 3:18; *ref. 1663-1669.*

Examples

1650 Examples of pious youth:

Joseph: Gn 39:7-9;
Jephthah's daughter: Jdg 11:36-40;
Ruth: Ru 1:16;
Esther: Est 4:16;

Samuel: 1 Sm 2:26; 3:1;
David: 1 Sm 17:33-37;
Joash: 2 Chr 24:1,2;
Josiah: 2 Kgs 22:1,2f; 23:1f;
Timothy: 2 Tm 1:5; 3:15; *ref. 1664.*

1651 Examples of wicked young people:
Cain: Gn 4:8; 1 Jn 3:12;
Esau: Gn 25:31-34; He 12:16,17;
Sons of Eli: 1 Sm 2:12;
Sons of Samuel: 1 Sm 8:1-3;
Absalom: 2 Sm 15:1-6;
Rehoboam: 1 Kgs 12:8-15;
Jeroboam: 1 Kgs 12:26-33;
Children of Bethel: 2 Kgs 2:23;
Manasseh: 2 Kgs 21:1,2

Resources

1652 O my young people, God wants our whole life. He desires not the dregs of our old age only, but also the beading wine of our youth. He would have us place upon his altar not only the sear and withered leaves of the autumn of our lives, but also the swelling buds and the fragrant blossoms of the smiling springtime of life. He asks us to be his, not when we are become bent and broken, unable to enjoy the pleasures of this life any longer, but when we come to the parting of the ways where sin caressingly invites us to enjoy her charms — even then he would have us renounce sin, place our hand in his, and pledge him our hearts, saying, "Thou, O Lord, shalt be the Master of my young life also. Thee will I love, thee will I serve, unto thee shall my heart beat, and thou shalt possess it altogether."

— C. F. W. Walther

† † †

1653

Remember thy Creator
  In youth's bright early days,
And give to him thy service,
  Thy heart's sincerest praise.
Remember thy Creator,
  Thy God will remember thee;
O love and serve him ever
  In sweet sincerity.

Remember thy Creator
  He will thy labours bless,
And crown thy toils and trials
  With life's supreme success.

411

Remember thy Creator
In all thy earthly strife,
To trust his grace and guidance,
And gain eternal life.
— *Canadian Hymnbook,* No. 441

1654

Just as I am, thine own to be,
Friend of the young, who lovest me,
To consecrate myself to thee,
O Jesus Christ, I come.

In the glad morning of my day,
My life to give, my vow to pay,
With no reserve, and no delay,
With all my heart I come.

I would live ever in the light,
I would work ever for the right,
I would serve thee with all my might,
Therefore to thee I come.

Just as I am, young, strong, and free,
To be the best that I can be,
For truth, and righteousness, and thee,
Lord of my life, I come.

For thy dear sake to win renown,
And then to take my victor's crown,
And at thy feet to cast it down,
O Master, Lord, I come.
— *Canadian Hymnbook*, No. 279

1655 "Is the young man Absalom safe?" When King David asked this question, Cushi, a messenger, had to inform him that Absalom was anything but safe. Absalom had met with a tragic end. At the very moment his father asked this question, Absalom's body was lying in disgrace under a heap of stones, a warning example that God will not allow his holy commands to be violated without punishment.

Are our children and young people safe? As for their physical needs, the answer may well be, "It is well with them," for there is little if anything that they lack. But what of their spiritual welfare, the needs of their immortal souls? Here the answer must be, "No, it is not well with them, it is not well at all!" It is not well with them from the very moment of their birth, for they are conceived and born in sin, and the imagination of the heart is evil from youth: Gn 8:21; Ps 51:5; Jr 17:9; Mt 15:19. They are sinful flesh born of sinful flesh, and unless they are spiritually reborn they face eternal ruin: Jn 3:3-6; Ro 8:7,13; Ga 5:19-21.

Moreover, even after they are spiritually reborn, their sinful flesh still cleaves to them so that living their new life in Chrit is a constant struggle: Mt 26:41; Ro 7:18-25; Ga 5:17; Eph 4:22-24. In addition, young people, in many cases even more so than adults, are exposed to the allurements of the sinful world: Lk 15:13; 2 Tm 4:10; Jas 4:4; 1 Jn 2:15-17; 5:19; and to the wiles and temptations of Satan; Lk 22:31; 2 Cor 2:11; 11:3; Eph 6:12; 1 Pe 5:8; *ref. 1649.*

† † †

1656
Tomorrow, he promised his conscience,
   Tomorrow I mean to believe,
Tomorrow, I will think as I ought to,
   Tomorrow my Savior receive;
Tomorrow, I will conquer the habits
   That hold me from heaven away,
But ever his conscience repeated
   One word and one only — "Today!"

Tomorrow, tomorrow, tomorrow,
   Thus day after day it went on,
Tomorrow, tomorrow, tomorrow,
   Till youth like a vision was gone;
Till age and his passions had written
   The message of fate on his brow —
And forth from the shadows came death
   With the pitiless syllable — "Now!"
                         — Anon

† † †

1657 Our age in its glorification of crime, in its adoration of immorality, and in its general disregard for God, is swift to minimize the greatness of sin and to close its eyes to the terrible consequences and the dreadful punishment for sin. But the conscience of every person testifies within him that fleshly lust is in itself a sin. Or otherwise, why do those who want to stoop to unchastity try to keep it a secret? Why do they seek to throw a mantle of darkness over the fact? Is it not because the holy and chaste God has written in the heart of every person that he loathes and hates every form of uncleanness? Dt 5:18; Mt 5:28; Eph 5:3-5,12; Col 3:5; 1 Th 4:3-5; 1 Pe 4:1-5.

1658 The sin of sensual pleasure is deadly and damning poison, to the body, to the mind, and to the soul. The youth who yields to it, be it only in thoughts and desires, but especially in deeds, will discover that this sin will gnaw, like an evil worm, at the very root of his life. It will deprive him of the joy of youth. It will weaken his mind. It will pollute every drop of his blood. It will slink, like a venomous serpent through his veins. It will consume the marrow of his strength. It will erase the lustre from his cheeks. It will extinguish the fire of youth in his eyes. It will transform the body into a tree that will begin to wither when in reality it ought first to blossom; it will make of youth an old man who is ripe for the grave, when in reality he should first begin to live. The living proof for these statements is to be found in the persons of many men and women inmates of our hospitals and institutions.
                              — selected

1659 Our youths now love luxury. They have bad manners, contempt for authority, disrespect for older people. Children nowadays are tyrants. They no longer rise when their elders enter the room. They contradict their parents, chatter before company, gobble their food, and tyrannize their teachers.

— Socrates

† † †

1660
How shall the young secure their hearts
  And guard their lives from sin?
Thy Word the choicest rules impart
  To keep the conscience clean.

Thy Word is everlasting truth;
  How pure is every page!
That holy Book shall guide our youth
  And well support our age.

— Isaac Watts

† † †

1661 When Walpole in the House of Commons accused William Pitt with the atrocious crime of being young, Pitt rejoined by wishing that he might "be one of those whose follies cease with their youth, and not one of those who continue ignorant in spite of age and experience."

— selected

ref. 1649

† † †

1662
O God of youth whose spirit in our hearts is stirring,
Hope and desire for noble lives and true,
Keep us, we pray thee, steadfast and unerring,
With light and love divine our souls imbue.

Fill thou our hearts with zeal in ev'ry brave endeavor
To right the wrongs that shame this mortal life.
Give us the valiant spirit that shall never,
Falter or fail however long the strife.

Teach us to know the way of Jesus Christ our Master,
Give us a clear-eyed faith, a fearless heart.
And through life's darkness, danger, and disaster,
O may we never from his side depart.

May we be true to him, the Giver of salvation,
Bearing his cross in service glad and free,
Winning the world to that last consummation,
When all God's children shall his kingdom be.

— Anon

1663 O Lord Jesus Christ, Master of men, whom to see is to love, and whom to know is eternal life: in thy life we see all things which we fain would be.

May the influence of thy gracious Spirit be with us enabling us to surrender ourselves to thy love and service. May the vision not fade, and our loyalty not slacken. May we grow daily into the likeness of thy Spirit. And to thee, together with the Father and the Holy Spirit, be glory and praise, now and evermore. Amen.

— selected

ref. 1649

† † †

Achievements of Young People

1664 Joseph was only 17 when he was made the steward of Potiphar's house in Egypt. By the age of 30 he was made the head of the Department of State in Egypt.

David was only a boy when, with the help of God, he wrought a great victory in Israel.

Josiah was only 8 years old when he became king in Judah. By the age of 20 he effected a great reformation.

Alexander the Great ascended the throne at 20 and conquered the known world by 33.

At the age of 14, Chopin composed his Rondo in C Minor.

At 26, Hannibal had subdued Spain.

At 16, Elbert Hubbard, a famous writer and publicist was a successful salesman, earning a man's salary.

Charles Dickens published his first book at 24.

Galileo, inventor of the telescope, discovered the principle of the pendulum at age 19.

George Washington was appointed adjutant general at 19. At age 21 he was sent as an ambassador to France. He was age 22 when he won his first battle as a colonel.

Gladstone was in the British Parliament before he was 22, and at the age of 24 he was Lord of the Treasury.

† † †

1665

My youth, O gracious Lord, secure
    From every lurking foe;
Teach me to flee each tempting lure
    That seeks my overthrow.

For, ah! what floods of lust and pride
    Unite their subtle force
To court and draw my heart aside;
    But thou canst stay their course.

Direct my inexperienced feet
    That they shall stray no more;
Thou know'st their proneness to repeat
    The steps they trod before.

Lord, send thy Spirit from above
    To shed his rays benign
That I decidedly may prove
    Myself a child of thine.

Help me to let my neighbors see
    That Jesus is my Friend;
My Savior and my Refuge, he,
    On whom my hopes depend.

I'll sing the glories of thy grace,
    The meltings of thy love,
And mine affections will I place
    On thee and thine above.

Yea, earth shall sink beneath my feet
    If thou but speak the word;
And my quick ardent pulse shall beat
    But to exalt my Lord.

— Anon

ref. 1649

† † †

1666 A beautiful young girl delayed becoming a Christian because she felt that by so doing she might lose some of the pleasures of her youth. She said again and again that when she was older she would consider looking into it more. One day, as her mother lay sick in a hospital, she came with a bouquet of beautiful fresh carnations. The nurse commented on their loveliness and then said: "We will not take them up to your mother now. They are too fresh and beautiful. We will wait a few days."

The young girl looked at her in surprise and indignation, and said: "How dare you do that! If you wait a few days, these flowers will lose all their freshness and beauty."

"But," said the nurse, "is not this what you are doing to your heavenly Father? Are you not by your conduct reserving for yourself the beauty and freshness of your life and waiting to offer him the faded blossoms from which all the lovely beauty and freshness have departed?"

1667 Judge Gilliam of Denver Juvenile Court had some interesting advice which he issued in the form of an open letter to a teenager. Here is a part of what he wrote:

Always we hear the plaintive cry of the teenagers: What can we do? Where can we go? The answer is; go home. Hang the storm windows, paint the woodwork, rake the leaves, mow the lawn, shovel the walk, wash the car, learn to cook, scrub some of the floors, repair the sink, get a job, study your lessons, read a good book.

Your parents do not owe you entertainment. Your village does not owe you recreation facilities. The world does not owe you a living. You owe the world something. You owe it your time and energy and your talents so that no one will be at war or in poverty or sick or lonely again.

In plain words, "Grow up!" Quit being a cry-baby, get out of your dream world, develop a backbone not a wishbone, and start acting like a man or a lady. I'm a parent. I'm tired of nursing, protecting, helping, appealing, begging, excusing, tolerating, denying myself needed comforts for every whim and fancy just because your selfish ego instead of common sense dominates your personality.

The above was published by the *Daily Kennebec Journal*.

———————

GENERAL INDEX
(Main outlined topics are in captial letters)

Advent: *see* Jesus Christ, 578f, 827f

AFFLICTION, 1-36 (*see also* Cross, Christian , 262-272): source of, 1, 13, 935; not always same as Christian cross, 2, 262, 263; false views regarding, 3 4, 5; God's purpose in it for unbelievers, 6; for believers, 7, 14-26, 916, 917, 1161; purpose not always evident, 25-31, 798, 802; Christian attitude toward, 9-12, 32-36, 153, 1541, 1543, 1546

AGE, OLD, 37-46 (*see also* Young People, 1649-1668): a time of physical infirmity, 37, 42, 297; to be regarded with respect and honor, 38, 43; God's special promises to the aged, 39, 44; Christ, the living hope of the aged, 45, 46; examples of honoring and dishonoring, 41, 1089, 1488

Altar, Family (*see also* Christian Education, 321-324): importance for home and nation, 540-545, 548-555

Amen, meaning of, 909

America (*see also* Government, 435-460): our good land, 1513, 1515, 1524; spirit of in its workmen, 1599

ANGELS, THE GOOD, 47-68 (*see also* Satan and the Evil Angels, 1309-1371): origin of, 47, 61; nature of, 48, 56, 61; heaven the abode of, 481; names and ranks of 49, 50, 54, 57; angel of the Lord, 60; worship God and do his commands, 51, 52, 63, 64, 900; serve God's people, 53, 56, 62-64, 67; rejoice at spread of gospel, 55; serve as our example, 58, 68; ministered to Christ, 54; will assist in the final judgment, 57, 832, 1603

Apostles: writers of the New Testament, 93, 95, 96, 100; church built on their teachings, 160

ASCENSION OF CHRIST, 808-826: prophetic references to, 808; the account of, 809; its meaning for Christ, 810, 811, 817-822; its meaning for us, 812-816, 824-826; to the right hand of God, 819, 820; to the throne of grace, 731, 777, 800, 814, 823, 1186

Atheism (*see also* Creation, 242-261; God, 395f): evolution impossible, 245-251; reality of hell cannot be ignored, 501, 1268; not worthy of counterfeiting, 576

Atonement, Day of, 1306 (*see also* Sacrifices, 1297f)

Augustine, St: conversion and confession of, 233; in praise of his mother Monica, 1088

BAPTISM, SACRAMENT OF, 69-90 (*see also* Lord's Supper, 941-962): definition of a sacrament, 68, 69, 76-78, 85; meaning of word "baptize," 79; children to be baptized, 70, 80-83, 90; sponsor's prayer, 83; power of, received from Word of God, 73, 84; benefit of, 74; its relation to Christian life, 75, 86-89; compared with sacrament of Lord's Supper, 78, 88, 951

Barabbas, 710-712

BETRAYAL OF CHRIST, 682-699: its meaning for us 682, 683, 686-690, 699

BIBLE, THE HOLY, 91-141 (*see also* Law and Gospel, 884-891, 895, 896): names and descriptions, 91, 92; written by men, 93, 94; written by inspiration of Holy Spirit, 94, 104-109, 112, 114, 115, 524; witness of Old Testament by Old Testament writers 95; Christ's witness of Old Testament, 95; witness of New Testament writers to Old Testament, 95; Christ's witness to New Testament, 96; witness of New Testament writers to New Testament, 96; witness of the Holy Spirit, 97, 524; unity of, 98, 114, 115; prophecies fulfilled, 98, 582-585; triumph over enemies, 98, 116-120, 141, 821; transforming power of, 98, 121, 134; makeup of, 110, 111; purpose is to lead to Christ, 101, 103, 112, 399, 771, 850, 860, 862, and to guide in Christian life, 101, 113, 138, 1563, 1649, 1660, 1663, completeness of, 102; to be regarded with reverence, 103, 122-125, 1117, 1464, 1465; to be taught to children, 103; its message to be spread, 103, 139, 1033, 1044, 1058, 1566; compared with other so-called holy books, 112; seeming discrepancies in, 106-109; the best translations of, 138, 1033, 1044; opinions of famous men regarding, 112, 115, 118, 119, 123-125, 127-137

BIRTH OF CHRIST: *see* Jesus Christ, 578-607

Blood of Christ (*see also* Sacrifices, 1297-1308): fountain filled with, 739, 761, 863; saving power of 648, 649, 850, 851, 860, 862, 863, 1228, 1239, 1297-1306, 1361; blood on the door, 1303

Books of the Bible, 99, 100, 110

Bunyan, John, conversion of, 235
Burial, Christian (*see also* Burial, Christ's, 763-768): Christ hallowed the Christian's grave, 764; constitutes a confession, 768
BURIAL OF CHRIST, 763-768: the act of, 763, 765-767; its meaning for us, 764, 768
Capital and Labor (*see also* Work, 1584-1599): obligations of employers and employees, 1587; example, regarding a strike in Flint, Michigan, 1597
Centurion: conversion of at the cross, 754-756; conversion of Gordius, 757
Ceremonial laws (*see also* Law of God, 856-896), have been abrogated, 865
CHILDREN 142-158 (*see also* Education, 315-358; Home, 534-556; Young People, 1649-1667): a gift of God, 142, 146; bring joy to parents, 142; each one precious to God, 142; can believe, 143, 149, 1363; can be effective missionaries, 142, 155, 181, 222; learn by example as well as by precept, 143, 150, 151; present at worship services, 143, 153, 157, 158, 322; harm in neglecting them, 343-450; commanded to honor and serve parents, 143, 147, 148, 151, 1098, 1466, 1467, 1488, 1649, 1659; to serve God in early youth, 143, 321-324, 338, 349, 1649, 1652-1654, 1656, 1662; Christ's regard for, 144, 154, 157; duties of parents toward, 321-324; are to be baptized, 70, 80-83, 91; examples of pious and wicked, 143, 145, 1650, 1651
Christian life (*see also* Discipleship, 300-314; Service, 1322-1342): obligations of, 301; rewards of (*see* Rewards), 303; power to live, 700, 793-797, 801-803, 805
Christianity: differs from all other religions, 112,; has elevated womanhood, 1578; triumphs of, 98, 116-120, 141
CHRISTMAS, 578-611: prophecies relating to, 578, 582-588; account of, 579; opportune time for, 586; events associated with, 579, 589-591; visit of Wise Men, 579, 590, 591; purpose of, 580, 588, 592-600; meaning of, 592, 593; for all the world, 580, 597-600; joy of, 595-598; preparing for, 581, 601-611; in the human heart, 581, 601-611; a Christmas legend, 587
CHURCH, 159-200 (*see also* Discipleship, 300-314): various names for, 159, 164; divine institution, 160, 165; one church, 160, 167; marks of, 161; eternality of, 160, 166; work of, to preach and teach, 162, 168, 169, 325, 326, 328, 1020, 1027-1030; mission work and works of love, 163, 168, 169, 1020-1081; membership in, 163; duties of members, 163, 170-200, 301, 302, 306, 307, 312-314, 907, 1103, 1152, 1322-1325, 1464, 1465, 1485-1487; church attendance, 163, 171-184, 186, 187; fellowship in, 176, 186, 188, 189; prayer before attending, 173, 174; need for, 182; workers in, 163, 183, 186, 190-200; church and state, 201-204
CHURCH AND STATE, 201-204: respective spheres of, 201; different functions of, 202; mutual respect and support, 203; examples of cooperation and interference, 204
Citizenship: *see* Government, Civil, 435-460
Commandments: *see* Ten Commandments, 1460-1502
Compassion: for souls of men, 1025; Christ's, 620, 1025, 1069, 1072
Confessing Christ, a requirement for Christian discipleship, 156, 693-696 (*see also* Discipleship, 300-314)
CONFESSION 205-209 (*see also* Faith, 359-383; Repentance, 1253-1262): need for, 205; nature of, 206, 1147; examples of, 207, 208; those who confess their sins are forgiven, 208, 209
CONSCIENCE, 210-224 (*see also* Law of God 865-896): meaning of the word, 212, 213; examples of, at work, 210, 221-223; a good and enlightened, 212, 214, 216, 218, 219; an accusing and evil, 212; an erring, 212, 223; a weak, 212; a seared or dead, 212; a gift of God, 213; the voice of, 213; prayer for a clear, 215, 224; as a guide, 213, 216; unsafe to act against, 220, 223; impossible to flee from, 221, 223; conscientious objector, 223; Christian, can err, 223; Lincoln and, 219; Luther and, 220, 223; testifies to God's existence, 396
Consecration, in gratitude for redemption, 1013, 1307, 1308 (*see also* Discipleship 300-314; Service, 1322-1342)
CONVERSION, 225-241 (*see also* Holy Spirit 506-533; Faith, 359-383): meaning of, in narrow sense, 225; meaning of, in wider sense, 225; other words for, 225; why necessary, 226, 230, 231, 318, 319; when it takes place, 227, 232-236; knowing the time of, not essential, 232; manner of, a mystery, 239;

how it is accomplished, 228 237, 239, 241, 513, 514, 517, 519; work of Holy Spirit without man's efforts, 228, 231, 237, 241, 512, 513, 517-519, 523-528; results of, 229, 241; of Saul of Tarsus, 470, 788, 807; of Augustine, 233; of Martin Luther, 234, 523, 860; of John Bunyan, 235; of John Newton, 475; expect conversions when preaching the Word, 238

Council, Jewish: see Jewish Council

Covenant: God established, in baptism, 75; in Lord's Supper, 940-946

Coveting: see Ninth and Tenth Commandments, 1476, 1477, 1500-1502

CREATION, 242-261 (see also Providence, 1195-1221): God existed before, 242; God created all things by his word, 242, 245-251; of angels, 47, 50; of man and woman, 243, 1567, 1580, 1581; God created man in his own image, 243, 484, 867, 1347; reveals God's goodness, wisdom, and power, 242, 252-257, 259, 261, 899; purpose of, for glory of God and welfare of man, 244, 252, 254, 256, 258-261, 1523; scientists' views regarding, 246-248; evolution impossible, 245-251; Luther's summary regarding, 253; wonders of, 249, 252, 254-257, 259, 261

CROSS, THE CHRISTIAN, 262-272 (see also Affliction, 1-36): not always same as affliction, 1, 262, 263; false views regarding, 262; correct views regarding, 263-273, 1640; Christ's cross alone atones for sin, 263, 268; every Christian has his own cross, 264; Luther's view regarding, 265; Christ's example in bearing, 263, 266; a mark of Christian discipleship, 263, 269, 716, 721-723; the great cost of bearing, 267, 268, 271; the great rewards for bearing, 269; 271, 272, 289; panel on door in shape of, 270; no cheap cross, 268

Crown of life, for bearing Christian cross, 263, 269, 271, 272

CRUCIFIXION OF CHRIST, 715-730: on the way to the cross, the weeping women, 715, 718, 779; Simon of Cyrene, 716, 720-723; the event and its significance, 717, 724-730; the place of, 717; with malefactors, 717, 725; symbolical significance of, 717, 721-723, 725, 729, 730; title on the cross, 717, 726-730; saving power of his cross, 648, 649, 726-730, 739, 761, 863, 1227, 1228, 1239, 1297-1306

Cursing (see also Lord's Prayer, First Petition, 898, 913; Second Commandment 1462, 1463, 1483): forbidden, 1462, 1463; reflect before, 913; General Washington's order against, 1483

Darkness (see also Light): hell, the place of outer, 496; covered the earth at time of Christ's death, 753, 756; Satan and evil angels rulers of, 1310, 1321; sin and hell associated with, 1721

Day of the Lord, 1613

DEATH, 273-299 (see also Resurrection of the Body, 1263-1275): a consequence of sin, 273, 1350; Christ conquered, 274, 774, 793-797; Christ's victory and our victory by faith, 30, 275; preparing for, 276, 280, 1093; recognize that life is short and uncertain, 277, 278, 1022; set affections on things above, 279; pray for blessed end, 280, 737, 750, 751, 904

DEATH OF CHRIST, 753-762: its effects in the realm of nature, 753, 756; its effects upon the hearts of men, 754, 757-759; meaning of, for us, 755, 759, 761, 762, 1313; Lord's Supper commemorates, 984, 996

Dedication: see Service, 1322-1342

Delay: danger in delaying with respect to the gospel, 1022, 1047-1051, 1055, 1081, 1242, 1246, 1367, 1382, 1389-1394, 1615-1617, 1656, 1666, 1668; exhortations not to, 1604-1609, 1662, 1666

DENIAL OF CHRIST by Peter, 682-699: its meaning for us, 684, 685, 691-698 (see also Discipleship, 1322-1342)

Denial of self: see Cross, Christian, 262-272; Lent, 664-671

DISCIPLESHIP, 300-314 (see also Service, 1322-1342): what it means to be a disciple of Christ, 300-305; obligation of denying oneself, 301, 607; bearing the Christian cross, 263, 264, 269, 301, 304, 307, 716, 721-723, 728; leading a Christian life, 460, 1032-1034, 1041-1044, 1234, 1243, 1247-1252, 1307, 1308, 1364, 1472; witnessing for Christ, 302, 310 , 312-314, 1020-1024, 1031, 1109 (see also Mission Work, 1020-1081); Polycarp's witness, 314; witness of martyrs, 310; example of early Christians, 240, 260; support of Christ's kingdom, 302; being active in works of love, 302, 312, 313, 1307, 1308; rewards of, 303, 310, 423, 424, 433, 434; priesthood of believers, 647

Discipline of children, 344
Divorce, cause for, 1010 (*see also* Marriage, 1003-1019)
Door panel in shape of cross, 370
Doubt (*see also* Trust, 1532-1552): doubting conscience, 212; hopelessness in, 378, 383, 1329

EDUCATION, CHRISTIAN, 315-358 (*see also* Children, 142-158; Home, 534-556; Pastors and Preaching, 1099-1133; Young People, 1649-1667): its essence, 315, 330-339; its object, 316, 330-339, 1436, 1445; its means, 317, 320, 330-339, 358; need for, 318, 319, 330, 332-334, 358; growth in, 163, 1649, 1663; duties of home to teach and train children, 321-324, 339-347, 535, 540-545, 548-555; duties of church in, 325, 326, 350; blessings of, for home, 327, 548-552, for church, 328, for nation, 329, 356, 555; examples of godly and ungodly parents, 321, 538
Election, Eternal: *see* Predestination, 1188-1194
End: *see* World, End of, 1600-1620
Epiphany: festival of, 579, 590, 591; Epiphany star, 591
Evangelism: *see* Mission Work, 1020-1081
Evolution an impossibility, 242-244 (*see also* Creation, 242-261)
Exaltation, Christ's State of, 622; 808
Example: parental, 148, 150, 340-343, 346, 1095; teacher as, 1438, 1446-1449; pastor as, 422, 1102; of pious women, 1574, 1576; of evil women, 1575; of children, pious and wicked, 143, 145, 1650, 1651; of Christ's compassion, 1025, 1069, 1072; of Christ's prayer life, 1074, 1155, 1158; of Christ's humility, 634, 638
Expediency: *see* Hypocrisy, 565-577

FAITH, 358-383 (*see also* Trust, 1532-1552): definition of, 359, 368, 370-372, 762, 853; other expressions for, 360, 368, 372; what it involves, 361-363, 369, 375, 379, 853, 1548, 1552; results in spiritual rebirth, 364, 762, 1260; results in love to God and fellowmen, 364, 970-975; a work of God, 359, 853; believers walk by, and not by sight, 365, 371, 374, 376, 380; believers are to grow in, 365; guarding against unbelief, 365, 378, 383; fruits of faith are to be evident, 365, 373, 857-859, 970-975, 984-1002; exhortations to fight the good fight of, 365, 377, 381; contend

for, 365, 382; preserve unity of, 365; testify to the, 365; power of, 275, 364, 370, 373, 377; necessary to salvation, 485, 497, 762; prayer for a strong, 367; examples of strong and weak, 295, 366, 1542, 1547; fruits of unbelief, 378, 383; love a proof of, 970; repentance and, 1253, 1258, 1259
Family: *see* Duties of Parents, 321-324, 340, 341; Home, 534-556
Fathers: *see* Family
Festivals in Israel: Passover, 1301-1305; Feast of Weeks (Day of Firstfruits, Pentecost), 1301; Tabernacle (Ingatherings), 1301
Flag, 450 (*see also* Government, Civil, 435-460)
Forgiveness (*see also* Lord's Prayer, 902, 926-934; Redemption, 1223-1252): through Christ, 854-856, 863, 864, 1623, 1626, 1635, 1644; forgiving others 902, 926-934; Christ's example of forgiving, 731, 732, 738, 739
Formalism (*see also* hypocrisy, 565-577): in religion, 566, 574; ceremonial laws, 865
FREEDOM, CHRISTIAN, 384-394 (*see also* Liberty): its privileges, 384, 386, 387, 391-394, 1594; its responsibilities, 385, 386-390; conscientious objection, 223
Friends (*see also* Love, Christian, 974, 975): fellowship of, 699, 1000; "What a Friend" in Jesus, 36
Gethsemane, Garden, of, 672-681: compared with Garden of Eden, 677; Christ's suffering and prayer in, 672-681, 954, 1313
Gifts, spiritual, 517, 520, 528, 533, (*see also* Holy Spirit, 506-523)
Giving (*see also* Stewardship, Christian, 1369, 1411-1430): as we receive, 1331, 1531; rules for, 1369, 1426, 1430; a test, 200; no substitute for love, 345
Glory; degrees of, in heaven, 484; humility the path to, 635-639
GOD, 395-415 (*see also* Holy Spirit, 506-533; Jesus Christ, 612-639): cannot be perceived by reason, 395, 407; heaven the abode of, 480; existence of world testifies to existence of, 395, 867; so does man's conscience, 396; revealed in Holy Scriptures, 398, 409; revealed in person and work of Christ, 399, 409, 908; God is one (monotheism), 400, 1460, 1461; God is Triune (Trinity), 402 403, 411, 412, 509, 1149; meaning

of idolatry, 401, 408, 1460, 1461, 1479, 1481; eternal and unchangeable, 1621, 1625-1627, 1636, 1641, 1648; other attributes, 404, 413, 977-980, 1175, 1538, 1542, 1547, 1562, 1564; names ascribed to God, 405, 406, 415, 575; Jesus Christ is true God, 614-619; the Holy Spirit is true God, 509-512; misuse of God's name, 898, 913, 1462, 1463, 1482, 1483; God as Father, 897, 907-909; prayer to be addressed to Triune God, 1149, 1175; the essence of love, 963, 976; the essence of truth, 1553, 1562; law of God, 865f

GOOD WORKS, 416-434 (*see also* Grace, 461-478; Justification, 850-864): afflictions prompt, 32; are fruits of a living faith, 365, 417, 428, 429, 432, 905-909, 912-936; do not obtain justification, 234, 416, 427-430, 860, 876, 881, 892, 895, 896, 1224-1227, 1351, 1359-1362; are wrought by the Holy Spirit, 418, 514, 515, 520-522; performed to the glory of God, 419; performed for welfare of neighbor, 420, 432; Christians exhorted to do, 421, 432; Christian pastors to be an example of, 422; of unbelievers, rewarded in this life, 423, 433, 434; believers rewarded for doing, 424, 433, 434; Christ an example of doing, 425; example of believers performing 426, 432; essential to keep this teaching pure, 416-418, 431

Gospel: work of church to preach, 162, 1102, 1106, 1113-1119, 1602; in conversion, 227, 513, 514, 517, 519; difference between law and, 527, 884-891; difference between preaching, and administering Lord's Supper as means of grace, 951; stewardship of, 1370, 1431-1433

Gossip, (*see also* Eighth Commandment, 1474, 1475) 1495-1499

GOVERNMENT, CIVIL, 435-460 (*see also* Lincoln; Washington): a divine institution, 435, 440, 441, 866; an outgrowth of family government, 441, 548, 550, 866; duties of, to citizens, 436, 439, 441, 442, 449, 451, 457, 458; duties of citizens to, 437-460, 1182, 1184, 1185; Christians are citizens of two kingdoms, 438, 448, 460; Christians are ideal citizens, 329, 438, 445, 448, 449, 452, 454, 460, 1599; what constitutes a good, 442, 443, 448, 449, 452, 1549; George Washington's prayer for the U.S., 444; Lincoln's reply to those who

criticize, 446; Luther's praise of good, 445, 454; our national flag, 450; inscription on Statue of Liberty, 451; inscription on Plymouth Rock Monument, 392; America, our good land, 1513, 1515, 1524; prayer for servicemen, 459; Israel as a theocracy, 866; sins of nations punished, 1, 23; blessings through Christian education, 329, 351-356; conscientious objectors, 223

GRACE, 461-478 (*see also* Throne of Grace; Justification, 850-864): God's attitude of kindness toward all creatures, 461; God's loving and forgiving attitude toward sinners, 462, 469-475, 478; enabling grace, 463, 470, 475, 1251, 1440, 1448, 1450, 1452, 1457; through Christ, intended for all, 462, 464, 469-475; offered in gospel in word and sacraments, 462, 465, 471, 478, 1189; received by faith in Christ, 462, 466, 469, 478, 1189; can be resisted and rejected, 467, 476; backsliders can be restored to, 468; "Amazing Grace," 475; not justice, but grace, is needed, 472; excludes works on man's part, 427, 429-432, 462, 469, 471, 473, 478; is all-sufficient and boundless, 469, 470; rewards of, 424, 433, 434

Greatness, humility a mark of, 635-639

Greed: *see* Coveting, 1476, 1477, 1500-1502

Growth, Christian: necessary, 163, 316, 1649, 1660, 1662, 1663; in faith, 365

Happiness (*see also* Peace, 1134-1146): not found in things of this world, 1282, 1287; found only in Christ, 1135, 1136, 1142, 1143, 1146, 1294, 1295

HEAVEN, 479-492 (*see also* Hell, 493-505): created by God, 479, 487-489; the abode of God, of angels, and of the saints in glory, 480-482, 487-489, 897; descriptive nature of, 483, 490-492, 534, 542, 544, 545, 547, 552, 556; future state of believers, 484, 488, 490, 492, 562; faith in Christ needed to enter, 485, 492; object of Christian's hope and striving, 486, 490, 492, 562, 1624, 1628; nature of known only by revelation, 487; natural man's longing for, 488; various expressions for, 489; wrong side and right side of, 491; promised to repentant malefactor, 732, 739, 740; present heaven and earth will be destroyed, 1600, 1603, 1610; promise of new heaven and new earth, 1618

HELL, 493-505 (*see also* Heaven, 479-492; Satan and Evil Angels, 1309-1321): existence of, taught in Bible, 493-495, 503, 1112; prepared for devil and evil angels, 494, 503; destiny of all unbelievers, 495, 503, 1350; place of eternal punishment, 496, 530; degrees of punishment, 496, 499; repentance and faith in Christ needed to escape, 497, 498, 504, 505; names for, used in Scripture, 499; location of, 500; futile to deny or ignore reality of, 501-505, 1112, 1268, 1273; liberal preachers deny existence of, 1112; not inconsistent with love of God, 503; too late to prepare to avoid when day of grace ends, 504

Herod the Tetrarch, Christ's trial before, 702, 709

Holy of holies: veil of, rent at time of Christ's death, 753; Christ entered by a new and living way, 646, 649, 1306

HOLY SPIRIT 506-533 (*see also* God 400f; Jesus Christ 612f): general references to, 506, 524; prophetic references to, in connection with Christ's work, 507, 524; prophetic references to Pentecost, 508, 524, 528, 1301; is true God with Father and Son, 509; divine names ascribed to, 510; divine attributes ascribed to, 511; divine honor and glory ascribed to, 513; participated in creation of world, 512; inspired holy men to write the Scripture, 94, 104-109, 112, 114, 115, 512; instrumental in conception and birth of Christ, 512; anointed Christ and inaugurated him into his ministry, 512; regenerates man, 512, 514-519, 523-528, 530, 968; dispenses spiritual gifts to church, 512, 514-517, 520-522, 528-530, 532, 533; sanctification (in narrow sense), 228, 513, 517-519; sanctification (in wide sense), 228, 514, 520-523, 531-533; makes hearts of men his temple, 514, 521-523; unites believers in Christ, 514, 523; teaches believers, 514; glorifies Christ in believers, 514; enables believers to witness for Christ, 514, 520, 532; keeps believers in the saving faith, 514, 523, 531; fruits of the Spirit, 515, 525, 533; believers exhorted to walk in, 516, 521-523, 525, 530, 533; performs his work through the means of grace, 517; his work is mysterious, 519, 527; Luther's explanation of work of, 523; sin against the Holy Ghost, 1349, 1356

HOME, 534-556 (*see also* Children, 142-158; Education, 315-358; Young People, 1649-1667): a divine institution whose sanctity is to be respected, 534; a place to provide for family needs, 534, 542, 547; to be governed by Christ's teachings, 534, 540-545; a reflection of heaven, 534, 556; the origin of civil government, 542, 543, 546, 548-555; a school for Christian instruction and training, 534, 535, 540-545; virtues that build and strengthen home life, 536, 547-552, 555, 556; evils that disrupt and destroy home life, 537, 539, 546, 548, 553-555; examples of pious homes, 538; examples of unhappy homes, 539; importance of family altar, 541, 544, 545, 548, 549, 551, 552, 555; prayer for God's blessing on, 556; cooperating with the church, 326, 357; blessed through Christian education, 327

Honesty, 569, 570 (*see also* Hypocrisy, 565-577)

HOPE, 557-564 (*see also* Faith, 359-383; Trust, 1532-1552): nature of, 557, 561; a fruit of faith, 364; examples of, 558, 562; basis of, 559, 779; rests on God's promises, 39, 44, 558, 559; provides anchor for soul, 560, 563, 564; causes joy, 560, 561; inspires to Christian living, 560, 562, 779;

Humility (*see also* Pride): Christ's our example of, 621, 634, 638; a trait of Christ's followers, 635-639; Christ's state of humiliation, 621; a humble prayer, 740

Husbands: see Marriage, 1003-1019

HYPOCRISY, 565-577 (*see also* Formalism): warnings against, 565, 569, 570, 1462; various forms of, 566, 572-574, 1174; punishment for, 567, 575; hypocrisy of Jewish Council, 572, 573, 704, and other examples, 568, 571-574; expediency another form of, 573; formalism a form of, 574, 1173, 1174; counterfeit, a form of, 575, 576; honesty the "best policy," 569, 570; prayer to avoid, 577, 1174

Idleness (*see also* Work, 1584-1599), God wants no, 1584-1586, 1588-1590

Idolatry (*see also* God, 395-415): definition of, 401, 1461, 1479, 1481; examples of modern, 408, 1482

Image of God: man created in, 243, 1347; was lost, but will be restored in heaven, 484; Law of God written in man's heart, 267

Ingratitude: *see* Thanksgiving, 1503f

Inspiration of Bible, 93-98, 104-109, 112, 114, 115

JESUS CHRIST, 578f (*see also* God, 395-415; Holy Spirit, 506-533):

— His birth, 578-611: prophecies relating to, 578, 581-585; events associated with, 579, 587, 590, 591, 603; opportune time for, 586; significance of appearance of Wise Men, 590, 591; purpose of his coming, 580, 588, 596-600, 878-880, 1298, 1302, 1306, 1307; his birth in the human heart, 581, 601-603, 607-611;

— Christmas, 581-611: meaning of, 592-595, 604-606; preparing for, 581, 601-611; for all the world, 590, 597-600; joy of, 591, 595-598, 600; greetings, in foreign languages, 589;

— His Person, 612-639: differs from all other men, 613, 623-629, 632; is the incarnation of truth, 1554, 1565; seven outstanding traits of, 620, 1025, 1069, 1072;

— His two natures (God-Man), 612f: his human nature, 612, 816, 826; his sinlessness, 613, 623-626, 629, 632; his divine nature, 590, 614, 627, 628, 641, 701, 772, 790; his divine attributes, works, and glory, 615-618, 815, 824; the mysterious union of the two natures, 619, 627, 630, 631;

— His two states, 621f: state of humiliation, 621, 633, 634, 638; his humility an example for us, 634, 638; state of exaltation, 622, 722-725; the meaning of his exaltation for us, 263, 272, 794-797, 816, 825, 826;

— His prophetic office, 640-649: a greater prophet than Moses, 640, 641; prophecy of Moses fulfilled in him, 640, 641, 820;

— His priestly office, 645-649, 812, 820: greater than O.T. priests, 646, 1298, 1306; a continuing office, 648, 649, 820, 1186, 1306; priesthood of believers, 647, 1104;

— His kingly office, 650-663, 813, 820: he is King, 650, 657, 658, 717; his kingdom of power, 651, 660, 661; his kingdom of grace, 652, 659, 660, 662; his kingdom of glory, 653, 662, 663; various expressions to denote his kingdom, 654; his kingdom differs from earthly kingdoms, 655, 839, 840, 899, 914, 915; membership in his kingdom, 655;

— His passion, 664-768: an introduction to, 664-671; agony and prayer in Gethsemane, 672-681; betrayal and denial, 682-699; trial, 700-714; crucifixion, 715-730; seven words from the cross, 731-752, 1389; death, 753-762; burial, 763-768;

— His resurrection, 769-807: *see* Resurrection of Christ;

— His ascension, 808-826: *see* Ascension of Christ;

— His second coming, 827-849: *see* Second Coming of Christ

Jewish Council (Sanhedrin): make up of, 704; example of hypocrisy, 572, 573; Christ's trial before, 700, 704

John, Apostle, at the cross, 733, 742, 759

Joseph, foster father of Christ, 741

Joseph of Arimathea, 763, 765

Joy (*see also* Peace, 1134-1146): in salvation, 595-598, 600, 778; in saving souls, 1026, 1078, 1079, 1441; in Christian service, 1324, 1336, 1341, 1342

Judas Iscariot: betrayed Christ, 682, 686; his terrible end, 682

Judgment Day: *see* World, End of, 1600-1620

Justice of God in respect to his love, 503

JUSTIFICATION, 850-864 (*see also* Faith, 359-383; Good Works, 416-434; Grace, 461-478; Redemption, 1223, 1252): its meaning, 850, 860, 862, 1144, 1351, 1359-1362; central teaching of Scriptures, 431, 850, 860, 862; objective justification (the whole world has been redeemed), 851, 861, 862; subjective justification (salvation becomes a personal possession by faith), 853, 860, 862, 1351; made known and offered in the gospel, 852; its results in lives of believers, 854-859, 863, 864

Killing (*see also* Fifth Commandment, 1470, 1471), 1468, 1469, 1490, 1491

King, Kingdom (*see also* Jesus Christ — His kingly office): Christ is King, 650, 657, 658; kingdom of power, grace and glory, 651-655, 659, 663

Knowledge, *see* Education, 315-358

Labor and Capital (*see also* Work, 1584-1599), obligations of employers and employees, 1587, 1599

LAW OF GOD, 865-896 (*see also* Ten Commandments, 1460-1502): ceremonial laws, 865, 893; political laws, 866;
— Moral law: written in man's heart, 210-217, 867, 868; given on Mt. Sinai, 869; meant for all mankind, 869, 896; division of, 870-874, 894; Ten Commandments, 869, 870, 1460-1502; punishment for breaking, 873, 895; blessings for keeping, 874, 895; its place in conversion, 513-519; its use as a curb, 210-217, 875, 896; its use as a mirror, 227, 876, 892, 895, 896, 1427; its use as a rule, 877, 895, 896, 1436, 1445;
— Christ, and the law: explained the spirit of, 878; fulfilled all righteousness of, for us, 856, 863, 879, 896, 1226-1228; suffered the punishment for our transgressions, 890, 896, 1226-1228;
— Christians and the law: not justified by the deeds of, 881, 895, 896, 1224-1228, 1244; freed from bondage of, 882, 896; delight to do, 883, 895, 896; difference between law and gospel, 517, 884-891, 895, 896

Lent, 664-671 (*see also* Suffering of Christ, 399)

Liberty (*see also* Freedom, Christian, 384-394): John Adams on, 391; Patrick Henry on, 393; Thomas Jefferson on, 394; Martin Luther on, 386; Plymouth Brethren and, 392; Statue of, inscription, 451

Life, Christian (*see also* Discipleship, 300-314): Bible a guide to, 101, 103, 113, 138; results from conversion, 229; early Christians led, 240; obligations involved in, 338, 898, 1032-1034, 1041-1044, 1243, 1247-1252

Life, origin of, 245-256

Light (*see also* Darkness): associated with God and Christ, 1321; Christians are the children of, 1001, 1321; God's Word is, 1321

Lincoln, Abraham: views on Bible, 124; on conscience, 219; on God's rule in nations, 443; on running the government, 446; on prayer, 1176; on thanksgiving, 1513

LORD'S PRAYER, 897-940 (*see also* Prayer, 1147-1187): intended for Chris-

tian people only, 897, 907, 908, 915, 926; most used and abused prayer, 907; Our Father . . . 897, 907, 909, 915, 923, 928; Hallowed be . . . 898, 913, 1462, 1463, 1483; Thy kingdom come . . . 899, 914, 915; Thy will be . . . 900, 916, 917 (*see also* 674, 675, 678, 680); Give us this day . . . 901, 914-924, 1151, 1221; Forgive us . . . 902, 926-934; Lead us not . . . 903, 935-939, 1314, 1317-1320, 1657, 1658; Deliver us . . . 904 (*see also* 280, 737, 750, 751); Thine is the kingdom . . . 905, 940 (*see also* 650-663, 813, 820); Amen, 906

LORD'S SUPPER, 941-962 (*see also* Baptism, 69-90): a holy sacrament instituted by Christ, 941, 942, 948-951; a holy communion, 943, 950, 957; a memorial, 944, 952-956; a witness, 945, 956; a heavenly sign, 946, 958, 959; proper preparation for, 947, 960, 961; a means of grace, 942, 951; prayer before communion, 962; frequent attendance at, 163

LOVE, 963-1002 (*see also* Grace, 461-477; Christian Service, 1322-1342):
— God's love: a part of his essence, 963, 976-978, 1564; is unchanging, 964, 977, 979; manifested in creation and preservation of world, 965, 1195, 1201-1210; manifested in redemptive work of Christ, 966, 978-980, 982, 1226, 1227, 1237; manifested in all God does, 7, 9, 12, 18, 24-27, 35-41; justice, 503;
— Christian love: derived from God's love, 967; fruit of regeneration, 858, 859, 968; flows from Christ's love for us, 969, 981, 982, 1013, 1325, 1327, 1332, 1336, 1341; proof of saving faith, 163, 970, 1001; gives God and Christ first place, 971-973, 981, 982; does what Christ commands, 972, 982, 1002, 1342; revealed in love for God's word, 973; seeks salvation of fellow men, 747, 974, 984, 992, 995, 1001; revealed in love for fellow men, 975, 984-1002, 1296, 1325, 1326, 1330-1332, 1336-1338, 1341, 1342, 1469, 1473, 1475, 1477; meaning of, in marriage, 1011; does not give offense, 385, 386, 389, 390

Lust (a synonym for covet), 1476, 1477, 1500-1502

Luther, Martin, on: affliction, 28; baptism, 89; books, 127; conscience, 220, 223; converison (his own), 234, 523,

860; creation, 253; cross of Christians, 265; education, 343, 350; faith 373, 376; freedom, 386; good works, 373, 432, 860; government, 445, 454; Holy Spirit's work, 523; judgment day, 842; God's love, 992; peace, 1141; prayer, 1166; preaching and teaching, 1119, 1442; redemption, Christ's work of, 1247; trust in God, 1638, 1639

Lying: see Second Commandment, 1462, 1463, 1474

Man: and woman created in God's image, 243, 1347; created as a free moral agent, 1198, 1199, 1216, 1217, 1346

MARRIAGE, 1003-1019 (see also Children, 142-158; Home, 534-556): origin of, 1003, 1009; definition and purpose of, 1004, 1009; duties of husbands, 1005, 1011, 1014, 1019, 1470, 1476, 1477; duties of wives, 1006, 1011, 1015, 1019, 1097, 1470, 1471, 1477, 1567, 1580, 1581; rewards in, 1007, 1016; virtues that build and strengthen, 536; evils that disrupt and destroy, 537; symbolizes God's union with his people, 1008, 1011, 1577; divorce, 1010, 1470, 1471; love in, 1011-1012, 1016; advice to young people, 1017; golden wedding anniversary poem, 1018

Martyrs, Christian, 310

Means of grace: gospel in word and sacrament constitute, 852; in Christian education, 317, 320; in conversion, 227

Mercy-Seat, 649, 1168, 1306

Millennium: a false dream, 833, 834, 839, 840; Revelation Twenty, 840, 915

Mind, stewardship of, 1366, 1373-1375

Miracles: of Christ, 590, 617; a part of God's providential care, 924, 1197, 1208, 1209, 1211-1215, 1217

MISSION WORK, 1020-1081 (see also Discipleship, 300-314): meaning of, 302, 858, 861, 1020, 1028-1030, 1080; through preaching and teaching 238, 1020, 1022, 1037, 1370, 1431-1433; through personal witness, 302, 856, 861, 1020, 1023, 1024, 1031, 1038-1040, 1054, 1056, 1057, 1059-1069, 1432; through a Christian life, 312, 313, 460, 1001, 1020, 1032-1034, 1041-1044, 1433; need for, 1021, 1035-1039, 1045-1047, 1051, 1053, 1057, 1058; urgency for, 1022, 1047-1051, 1055, 1070, 1081, 1432, 1604-1609, 1616, 1617, 1620; absence of, sign of decaying church, 200; opportunities for, 1023, 1035, 1036, 1052,

1077; examples of personal, 310, 314, 1024, 1031, 1054, 1056, 1057, 1059, 1069, 1071; children as missionaries, 142; requires a deep conviction, 1025, 1069, 1072; requires Christ-like prayer, 1025, 1069, 1071, 1074, 1076; rewards for, 55, 1026, 1078, 1079

Money (see also Riches, 1276-1296): giving, no substitute for love, 345; stewardship of, 1369, 1411-1430

Morality: see Moral Law, 365f

MOTHERS, 1082-1098 (see also Home, 534-556): to be honored, 1082, 1086-1090, 1092, 1094, 1096, 1098, 1467; duties of, 1083, 1088, 1091, 1093, 1095, 1097, 1456; portrait of a pious wife and mother, 1084; examples of pious mothers, 1085, 1098; Christ's regard for his mother, 733, 741-743

Mountains, reflect majesty and strength of God, 1648

Murder (see also Fifth Commandment, 1468, 1469): 1490, 1491

Naaman, cleansing of, an analogy of baptism, 84

Nation: see Government, 435-460

Nature: laws of, in providence, 1196, 1208, 1210, 1215-1217; mystery of, 1206, 1208, 1269; and resurrection, 1208, 1209

New Birth: see Conversion, 225-241

New Testament: see Bible, 91-141

Newton, John, 236, 1087

New Year: see Year, 1621-1648

Nicodemus: a member of the Jewish Council, 766; questioned Christ concerning the new birth, 239; assisted with burial of Christ, 763, 764, 766

Oaths, false and true, 705, 1462

Offense, need to recognize rights of others, 366-390

Office of Keys, church exercises, 162

Old age: see Age, Old, 37-46

Old Testament (see also Bible, 91-141): sacrifices in, 1297-1302, 1306; teachers, in, 1434

Old Year: see Year, 1621-1698

Parables of lost sheep and lost coin, 209

Paradise: see Heaven, 479-492

Parents (see also Home, 534-556): correction of children, 7, 14-17; duties toward children, 153, 157, 158, 321-324; parental example, 321, 340-342, 1095; see also Education, 315-358

Passion, Christ's: see Lent, 148f

Passover: Jewish festival of, 1301-1305; blood on door, 1303

PASTORS AND PREACHING, 1099-1133 (see also Teachers, 1434-1459): called by God, 1099, 1104; continuation of office of apostles, 643, 644, 1099, 1104; titles of, 1100, 1106, 1109; qualifications necessary for, 1101, 1107, 1109, 1110, 1118-1123; duties of, 162, 168, 1102, 1104, 1108, 1111-1115, 1119, 1620; to be an example to the flock, 422, 1102; to preach and teach the gospel clearly, 1102, 1111, 1124, 1133, 1358; God's providence in promoting the gospel, 1200, 1602; preaching and teaching compared, 1442; duties of members to pastors, 163, 170-184, 193, 197, 1103, 1116, 1117, 1127-1132, 1464, 1468

Patience in suffering, 21, 41

Patriotism: see Government, Civil, 435-460

Paul, Apostle, conversion of, 788, 807

PEACE, 1134-1146: with God broken through sin, 1134, 1138-1140; re-established through Christ, 774, 776, 795, 855, 863, 1135, 1138-1144, 1146; a gift of the Holy Spirit, 1135; with God, brings inner peace, 45, 1136, 1141-1144, 1146; with God, brings peace between man and fellow men, 973, 1137, 1139, 1140, 1145, 1146; with God, brings peace in the church, 1137; with God, the way to end war, 1138-1140, 1144

Pentecost: prophecies relating to, 508; festival of Holy Spirit, 528; festival of firstfruits, 528, 1301; birthday of Christian church, 528

Persecution, 263, 269, 301, 310

Peter, Simon, denied Christ, 684, 691

Pilate, Pontius: Christ's trial before, 702, 703, 706, 708, 713, 714; legend of Pilate wearing Jesus' coat, 1244; his wife, 707

PRAYER, 1147-1187 (see also Lord's Prayer, 897-940; Thanksgiving, 1503-1531): defined as adoration, confession, intercession, petitions, thanksgiving, 1147, 1156, 1158-1160, 1175, 1180-1181, 1186; God's command and promise, 1148, 1161, 1172, 1187; needs drive one to, 12, 22, 35, 46, 1148, 1163, 1166, 1167 1176, 1180, 1317; to be directed to Triune God, 1149, 1169, 1175, 1180; to be offered in Christ's name, 1150, 1168, 1172, 1186, 1187; to be of-fered in faith, 365f, 1150, 1161, 1164, 1169, 1181; need to persist in, 1140, 1170; difference in asking for spiritual and temporal blessings, 901, 918-924, 1151, 1161, 1162, 1164, 1165, 1179; to be offered for all men, 1152, 1174, 1182, 1184-1186; for pastors and missions, 163, 173, 1025, 1067, 1071, 1074, 1076, 1103 1128-1130; for power of Holy Spirit, 514, 518, 525, 530; for government, 437, 444, 447, 450, 453, 459, 1152; for servicemen, 459; where we are to pray, 1153, 1173, 1176, 1183; when we are to pray, 1154, 1171, 1176; Christ's example of praying, 674, 675, 680, 1155, 1177; Christ's intercession for us, 731, 777, 800, 814, 820, 823; examples of intercessory prayers, 1156, 1178, 1184, 1186; notable prayers, 1157

PREDESTINATION, 1188-1194; as taught in Scriptures, 1188; a part of the counsel of God which is to be taught, 1188; God's decree from eternity in connection with Christ, 1189, 1193, 1194; carried out through work of Holy Spirit, 1189; a decree of God's grace, 1189; involves God's unsearchable ways, 1191; for the comfort and admonition of believers, 1192, 1193, 1194; there is no predestination to damnation, 1190 predestination and providence, 1200

Pride (see also Humility): led to Peter's denial of Christ, 684; need to guard against, 685, 694; examples of, 687

Priest: Christ our great High Priest, 645-649; priesthood of believers, 647, 1104

Procrastination: see Delay

Promises, relying on God's, 1623, 1637, 1639, 1642, 1648

Prophecies of Bible fulfilled, 98, 578, 581-585, 769-771, 808-811

Prophets: writers of Old Testament, 93, 95; church build on teachings of, 160; prophetic office of Christ, 640-644; guard against false, 1437, 1602, 1611; many false, at end of world, 1602, 1622

PROVIDENCE, DIVINE, 1195-1221 (see also Creation 242-261): its meaning and extent, 901, 965, 1195, 1201, 1210, 1519, 1638, 1639; normally expresses itself in laws of nature, 1196, 1208, 1210, 1215-1217; miracles in providence, 53, 924, 1197, 1208, 1209, 1211-1215, 1217, 1519; man can disrupt, 1198, 1199, 1216, 1217; events can be modified, 1199, 1217; intended for

428

man's temporal and eternal welfare, 7, 36, 40, 1200, 1211, 1213, 1218-1221; serve for spread of the gospel, 1200; promotes glory of God, 1200, 1221; no need to worry, 920-923, 941, 960-964, 1195, 1202, 1204, 1534, 1538

Punishment (see also Sin, 1343-1364): sin the source of all evil, 1; God hates and punishes sin, 6, 135

QUESTIONS for earnest reflection, 1222

Reason: and the Bible, 103, 122-125; cannot perceive God, 395

Rebirth: see Conversion, 225-241

REDEMPTION, 1223-1252 (see also Justification 850-864): meaning of, 1223, 1227, 1228, 1238, 1239, 1327; need for, 1021, 1035, 1036, 1224, 1240, 1244, 1246; Christ redeemed us from the curse of the Law, 1226; Christ redeemed us from sin and its punishment, 8, 880, 1224-1228, 1238, 1239, 1351, 1359, 1361, 1362; various synonyms for, 1227, 1228, 1238, 1239; decreed by God from eternity, 1229; central theme of Scriptures, 850, 860, 862, 1230; complete and effectual for all time, 736, 748-750, 1231; intended for all mankind, 590, 597-600, 1232; no other way to salvation, 1232, 1240-1242, 1245, 1246; becomes ours through faith, 853, 1233, 1242; saved to serve, 1234, 1235, 1243, 1247-1252, 1327; final, at Christ's coming, 1236, 1241

Regeneration see Conversion, 225-241

REPENTANCE, 1253-1262 (see also Confession, 205-209; Faith, 359-383): meaning of, 1258; nature of, 1253, 1258-1262; necessity for, 497, 715; chastening leads to, 6, 7; results of, 1254, 1260; calls to, 603, 607-611, 670, 671, 715, 864, 1255, 1257, 1604, 1621; examples of 732, 739, 740, 1256

RESURRECTION OF CHRIST, 797-807: prophetic references to, 769; Gospel accounts of, 770; Central theme of N.T., 771, 791; 792; proves his deity, 772; proves God the Father accepted his sacrifice, 773, 793; proves that all enemies of our salvation are vanquished, 774, 793-797; proves that all believers will rise to eternal life, 775, 793, 798, 799, 1265; gives peace with God, 776, 793; gives access to throne of grace, 777, 800; gives joy, 778, 793-797,

801-803, 805; gives hope, 779, 799, 802, 803; gives strength to carry on Lord's work, 780, 793-797, 801-803, 805; gives power to walk in newness of life; 781, 787, 788, 804, 805; creates desire to share the good news, 782, 789, 806;

— proofs include: the empty tomb, 783, 1274; announcement of angels, 784; graveclothes, 785; appearances, 786; change wrought in disciples, 787; conversion of Saul of Tarsus, 788, 807; spread of Christianity, 789, 1275; testimony of Scriptures, 790.

RESURRECTION OF THE BODY, 1263-1275 (see also Death, 273-299; Resurrection of Christ, 797-807): denied by unbelievers but taught in Scriptures, 1263, 1267-1275, 1603; nature of, 1265, 1267, 1269, 1270, 1275; nature teaches, 1269, 1272, 1275; nothing is annihilated, 1267; Christ destroyed the power of death, 274, 753, 768, 774; early Christians believed in, 1270; examples of, recorded in Scriptures, 1264, 1271; difference in, of believers and unbelievers, 1266, 1273; bodies of believers glorified, 484; hopelessness of unbelief, 1266, 1273

Revelation (see also Bible, 91-141), the only source of knowledge regarding future life, 487, 488

Revenge, 731, 942, 967, 969-973, 1468, 1469

Rewards: of Christian discipleship, 269, 271, 272, 303, 1026, 1078, 1079, 1420, 1428; for good works of unbelievers, 423; for good works of believers, 424; service without thought of, 1324, 1335, 1337, 1340; of teachers, 1441-1445, 1451, 1456

RICHES, 1276-1296 (see also Trust, 1532-1552): a gift from God, 1276; not sinful in themselves, 1277; danger in possessing, 1278, 1282, 1284, 1287, 1501; are fleeting, uncertain, and deceitful, 1279, 1282-1284, 1288; cannot save, 1288-1291, 1482; love of, root of all evil, 1278, 1282, 1284, 1501; warnings against, 1280, 1282-1292; exhortations to seek true, 1281, 1285, 1293-1296; giving of, no substitute for love, 345

Right hand of God, 811, 819, 820

Sabbath: Sabbath law, 204; Sabbath sacrifices, 1300; bodies on cross to be removed on Sabbath Day, 767

State (*see also* Government, Civil, 435-460), spheres of church and, 201-204

Stealing, 222, 1472, 1473, 1493, 1494 (*see also* Seventh Commandment, 1462, 1473)

STEWARDSHIP: 1365-1433 (*see also* Discipleship, 300-314; Service, 1332-1342): meaning of word "steward," 1372; definition of, 1365; God's ownership, 1365, 1368, 1372, 1410-1414, 1418, 1424;
— of body and mind: gifts of God, 1366; to be safeguarded, 1366, 1374; to be used properly, 1248, 1249, 1366, 1375;
— of time: a gift of God, 1367; rapid flight of, 1621, 1625, 1628; not to be wasted, 1367, 1376-1382, 1388, 1588, 1589; to be used properly, 1369, 1383-1387; tragedy caused by delay, 1367, 1389-1394, 1604-1609, 1615, 1617;
— of talents: gifts of God, 1339, 1368, 1395, 1396; to be used properly, 193, 198, 639, 1368, 1377, 1397-1409, 1591, 1597; accounting for use of will be required, 1368, 1408, 1427;
— of treasure: God is the Owner, 1369, 1411-1413, 1418, 1424; proper use of, 1331, 1369, 1414-1417, 1421-1426, 1430, 1531; rules for giving, 1369, 1426, 1430, 1531;
— of the gospel: duties to defend, share, and live according to, 1370, 1431-1433
— rewards of, 1420, 1428: *see* Rewards

Strikes, labor (*see also* Work, 1584-1599)

Suffering (*see also* Affliction, 1-36; Cross of Christians, 262-272): the why of, 1, 13; patience in, 11, 41

SUFFERING OF CHRIST, 664-671: observed during Lent, 664-671; heart of Scriptures, 664; center of preaching and teaching, 315, 316, 665; the Passion history, 669; personal involvement, in, 668, 670, 671

Talents: *see* Stewardship of, 1368f

TEACHERS AND TEACHING, 1434-1459 (*see also* Education, Christian, 315-358; Pastors and Preaching, 1099-1133): God's gift to his church, 1434; laborers together with God, 1435, 1450, 1457; worthy of special honor, 1435, 1443, 1444, 1451, 1459; to teach law and gospel, 103, 162, 325, 326, 1436, 1445, 1448, 1452, 1453; to guard against falsifying God's word, 1437; to care and pray for the flock, 1438; to be an example to the flock, 1438, 1446-1449; to improve through study of God's Word, 1439, 1449, 1457, 1458; source of strength for, 1440, 1448, 1450, 1452, 1457; reward for, 1441, 1442-1445, 1451-1456; Luther's comparison between preaching and teaching, 1442; praise to an unknown teacher, 1443, 1451; teacher's prayer, 1448, 1450, 1452, 1457; mistakes to avoid, 1449; to build for eternity, 1441, 1453-1456

Temple: *see* Holy of Holies

Temptation: God does not lead into, 903, 935; Satan's work, 1312, 1316, 1318, 1321; warnings to guard against, 903, 936-939, 1314, 1317-1320

TEN COMMANDMENTS, 1460-1502 (*see also* law of God, 865-896): foundation of all righteous laws, 217, 1478; inscribed on hearts of man, 867, 868; given on Mt. Sinai, 869; conscience and, 210-217; First Commandment (idolatry), 408, 1460, 1461, 1479-1482; Second Commandment (use and misuse of God's name), 898, 913, 1462, 1463, 1482-1484; Third Commandment (worship) 179, 1464, 1465, 1485-1487; Fourth Commandment (duties to parents and superiors), 437, 438, 441, 733, 741-743, 1089, 1094, 1466, 1467, 1488, 1649, 1659; Fifth Commandment (murder), 210, 223, 1468, 1469, 1489, 1490; Sixth Commandment (adultery), 210, 1470, 1471, 1491, 1492, 1589, 1657, 1658 (*see also* Marriage, 1003-1019); Seventh Commandment (stealing), 217, 222, 1472, 1473, 1493, 1494, 1585, 1597; Eighth Commandment (sins of the tongue), 701, 975, 993, 1474, 1475, 1495-1499; Ninth and Tenth Commandment (coveting), 1476, 1477, 1500-1502

Testaments, Old and New: *see* Bible, 91-141

THANKSGIVING, 1503-1531 (*see also* Prayer, 1447-1187): a form of prayer, 1147, 1158-1160; exhortations to, 1503, 1509-1514; for temporal blessings, 1175, 1504, 1513-1522, 1524-1526, 1638; for spiritual blessings, 1504, 1516, 1526, 1621, 1628; at all times, 1505, 1521; in private and public worship, 1506; in the name of Christ, 1507; acknowledging our unworthiness, 1507;

singing God's praises and proclaiming his goodness and mercy, 1507; showing, by thanks-living, 1507, 1514; showing, by sharing, 1507, 1527-1531; think-thanks, 1484; examples of, 1508; sin of ingratitude, 1509-1513

Throne of grace, Christ's intercession for us at the, 731, 777, 800, 814, 823, 1168, 1306

Time: see Stewardship of, 1367, 1376, 1394

Tongue (see also Eighth Commandment, 1474, 1475), sins of the, 1474, 1495-1499

TRIAL OF CHRIST, 700-714: by the Jewish Council, 700, 701, 704, 705, 1474, 1475; by Pilate and Herod, 702, 703, 705-714; Barabbas set free, 710-712

Trinity, Holy (see also God, 395-415): three persons, but one God, 402, 412; Augustine's efforts to understand, 411

TRUST, 1532-1552 (see also Faith, 359-383; Providence, 1195-1221): exhortations to, 1532, 1537-1552, 1623, 1636, 1641, 1648; relying of God's promises, 10, 35, 1195, 1204, 1220, 1480; promises to those who, 39, 44, 1533; examples of, 1534; warnings against false, 1535, 1551; false, 1279, 1283, 1287, 1536; waiting upon the Lord, 22, 23, 46, 1483, 1543; God is in the future, 1544, 1545; founded on Christ and his Word, 1548, 1552, 1639; expressed in prayer, 1150

TRUTH, 1553-1566: exists in God who is essence of, 1553, 1562; revealed in God's Word, 102, 1554, 1562, 1563, 1566; Jesus Christ the incarnation of, 1554, 1565; unchangeable and eternal, 1555, 1562, 1564; frees from sin and produces faith, 1556, 1565; the Christian's defense against error and temptation, 1557, 1562; to be heard, believed, lived, and shared, 1558-1562, 1565, 1566

Unbelief (see also Faith, 359-383; Trust, 1532-1551): hopelessness of, 378, 383; guard against, 365; God's purpose in afflicting unbelievers, 6,7

War (see also Peace, 1134-1146): result of sin, 1, 1134, 1138, 1140; cost of, compared to cost of education, 350, 1138; peace possible only through Christ, 1142-1144, 1146; conscientious objector, 223; prayer for servicemen, 459

Warfare, spiritual: guard against unbelief, 365; fight the good fight of faith, 365, 531-533

Washington, George; his prayer for United States, 444; honored his mother, 1089; ordered army to abstain from cursing, 1483

Ways of God in affliction, 8, 18, 38

Will of God: revealed in his Word, 940; desires salvation of all, 851, 861, 862, 1028

Wisdom (see also Education, Christian, 315-358), true, found only in Christ, 315-320, 330-339, 1554, 1562, 1565

Wise Men from the East, 590, 591

Witnessing: see Mission Work, 1020-1081

WOMEN, 1567-1583 (see also Children, 142-158; Home, 534-556; Marriage, 1003-1019; Mothers, 1082-1098): created by God, 1567, 1580, 1581; first to sin, 1568; redeemed by Christ, 1569, 1577; honorable place in society, 1570, 1577-1581; heathen concept of their place, 1578; true beauty of, 1091; their work in the home, 1571; their work in the church, 1572, 1582; special distinction given them in the New Testament, 1573, 1579, 1583; examples of pious women, 1574; examples of pious mothers, 1085, 1098; examples of evil women, 1575; portrait of a pious wife and mother, 1576

Word of God (see also Bible, 91-141): is eternal truth, 102, 1554, 1562, 1564-1566; as means for Christian education, 317, 320

WORK, 1584-1599 (see also Capital and Labor): it is God's will that man should work, 1584, 1585, 1588-1590, 1598; man is not to live by begging, 901, 918-920; idleness breeds crime, 1588-1590; sin has turned the joy of work into drudgery, 1585; to be done to the glory of God and the welfare of neighbor, 1586, 1596, 1597; small jobs important also, 1591; to be done well, 1591-1595; never engage in sinful, 1597; use of leisure time, 1598; for women, 1571, 1572, 1582, 1583; duties of employers and employees, 1587; Christian workers and strikes, 1599

WORLD, END OF, 1600-1620 (see also Second Coming): foretold in Scriptures, 1600, 1612; scientists, recognize signs, 1605-1610; when and how it will occur, 1601, 1611, 1616, 1617; signs that will precede, 1602, 1605-1609,

1611; events that will occur at, 1603, 1613-1619; the door is shut at, 504; necessary preparation for, 505, 1604, 1616, 1617, 1620, 1624; angels will assist in final judgment, 57

Worry: no cause for, 920-924, 1180, 1195, 1202, 1204, 1534, 1538; no subsitute for prayer, 1180

Worship (see also Third Commandment, 1164, 1165): angels worship God, 51; idolatry in, 1460, 1479; church attendance, 1463, 1464, 1485-1487; thanksgiving, 1506, 1507; see also 1503-1531

Wrath of God, 1350

YEAR, OLD AND NEW, 1621-1648 (see also Stewardship of Time, 1367f; Trust, 1532-1552):
— Old Year: a time to reflect on the rapid flight of time, 1621, 1625-1628, and the end of all things, 281, 1600-1620; a time to reflect on God's goodness and mercy, 1621, 1626, 1628-1630, 1632, 1633; a time to reflect on our sins and to repent and give thanks, 1621, 1622, 1632; a time to make amends and resolutions, 1622, 1632, 1633; a time to rely on God's promises for the future, 39, 44, 1544, 1545, 1548, 1552, 1648;

— New Year: a time to trust in God's love and mercy, 1623, 1638-1641; a time to trust in God's promises, 1623, 1638, 1639, 1642, 1644, 1647, 1648; a time to live as Christian pilgrims, 1624, 1628; a time to serve, 1624, 1631-1634, 1643-1646; a time to be ready for Christ's return, 1624; see also Second Coming

YOUNG PEOPLE, 1649-1667 (see also Children, 142-158; Education, Christian, 315-358; Old Age, 37-46):
— Exhortations: rejoice in youth, 1649, 1654; serve God in youth, 1649, 1652-1654, 1656, 1662, 1666, 1667; guard against special sins, 1649, 1655, 1657-1659; obey and honor parents, 1649, 1659; make God's word the guide, 1649, 1660, 1662; marriage advice, 1015, 1017; need to know how to die, 1093; need to know how to grow in grace, 1649, 1663, 1667; evil results when parents neglect duties toward, 344-348, 542, 543, 546, 548, 549, 553;
— Examples: examples of pious young people, 1650; examples of wicked young people, 1651; achievements of, 1664; prayers of, 1662, 1663, 1665

INDEX FOR THE CHURCH YEAR

435